Full IFRS and IFRS for SMEs Adoption by Private Firms

MÜNSTERANER SCHRIFTEN ZUR INTERNATIONALEN UNTERNEHMENSRECHNUNG

Herausgegeben von Peter Kajüter

Band 12

Zu Qualitätssicherung und Peer Review der vorliegenden Publikation

Die Qualität der in dieser Reihe erscheinenden Arbeiten wird vor der Publikation durch den Herausgeber der Reihe geprüft.

Notes on the quality assurance and peer review of this publication

Prior to publication, the quality of the work published in this series is reviewed by the editor of the series.

Maximilian Saucke

Full IFRS and IFRS for SMEs Adoption by Private Firms

Empirical Evidence on Country Level

PL ACADEMIC RESEARCH

Bibliographic Information published by the Deutsche Nationalbibliothek
The Deutsche Nationalbibliothek lists this publication in the Deutsche Nationalbibliografie; detailed bibliographic data is available in the internet at http://dnb.d-nb.de.

Zugl.: Münster (Westfalen), Univ., Diss., 2014

Library of Congress Cataloging-in-Publication Data
Saucke, Maximilian, 1985-
Full IFRS and IFRS for SMEs adoption by private firms : empirical evidence on country level / Maximilian Saucke.
pages cm. – (Münsteraner Schriften zur Internationalen Unternehmensrechnung ; Band 12)
Includes bibliographical references and index.
ISBN 978-3-631-66298-4
1. International business enterprises–Accounting–Standards. 2. Accounting–Standards–International cooperation. 3. Small business–Accounting–Standards. I. Title.
HF5686.I56S266 2015
657'.960218–dc23 2015007836

D 6
ISSN 1868-7687
ISBN 978-3-631-66298-4 (Print)
ISBN 978-3-653-05531-3 (E-Book)
DOI 10.3726/ 978-3-653-05531-3

PL Academic Research is an Imprint of Peter Lang GmbH.
Peter Lang – Frankfurt am Main · Bern · Bruxelles · New York · Oxford · Warszawa · Wien

This publication has been peer reviewed.

www.peterlang.com

Preface

Since the foundation of the IASB in 2001, International Financial Reporting Standards (IFRS) have been adopted by listed companies in more than 130 countries worldwide. During the same period of time, many countries have also expanded the scope of IFRS adoption to the field of private firms. Since the issuance of the IFRS for SMEs in July 2009, the situation has become a lot more complex. The worldwide process towards international accounting harmonization cannot be summarized by simply adding up the number of Full IFRS adopters anymore. Separate analyses are needed for the field of listed and private firms as well as for Full IFRS and IFRS for SMEs adoption. Besides, countries continue to modify IFRS for local purposes instead of adopting IFRS 'as published by the IASB'. They often restrict the mandatory or voluntary use of these standards to the individual or consolidated financial statements of local entities with a certain size or legal form. For this reason, more attention has to be given to the 'how' of IFRS adoption.

While most countries from Africa, Central America and the Caribbean seem to adopt IASB standards without any modification, EU-IFRS clearly differ from IASB-IFRS regarding the accounting for macro hedges (IAS 39 carve-out) and due to postponed EU endorsement. Similarly, it is disputed whether Australia has adopted IFRS and in how far convergence has already been achieved between Full IFRS and US GAAP. The same is true for the adoption of local versions of the IFRS for SMEs within the European Union. Although the United Kingdom, Ireland, Sweden and Estonia have based their national accounting standards on the IFRS for SMEs, several differences remain. Hence, the frequent and inconsiderate use of the word 'adopt' may lead to a deceptive picture of the current state of international accounting harmonization.

Though being of high relevance for standard-setters and practitioners, the characteristics and determinants of worldwide Full IFRS and IFRS for SMEs adoption are largely unexplored in the field of private firms. This research gap is addressed by the work of Maximilian Saucke. His study analyzes the process of international accounting harmonization in the field of private firms in 110 countries between 2002 and 2014. It finds empirical evidence for the vanishing role of Local GAAPs, the continued existence of local versions of IFRS and the worldwide emergence of a 'two standard system'. Due to GAAP complementation, countries tend to face more intra-national GAAP diversity after they have adopted IFRS. Moreover, the empirical results suggest that modifications to IFRS combined with ambiguous IFRS definitions represent a major challenge to financial statement users worldwide. The findings also show that parallel adoption of Full IFRS and IFRS for SMEs has led to an increasing differentiation of local financial reporting regulation for private firms, in particular on the basis of firm size.

By integrating two theoretic concepts (economic theory of networks and institutional theory of isomorphism) into one comprehensive conceptual framework, Maximilian Saucke identifies net economic benefits, network effects, and political pressures as important determinants of Full IFRS and IFRS for SMEs adoption in the field of private firms by 2008 and by 2014. His work thereby provides an insight into the interdependencies between Full IFRS and IFRS for SMEs adoption on country level. He expects that the IFRS for SMEs may become more diffused than Full IFRS in the field of private firms as it can bring considerable net economic benefits compared to the adoption of local standards or Full IFRS.

The empirical results of the study contribute greatly to both accounting theory and practice by providing the IASB and national standard-setters with new insights into the characteristics and determinants of international accounting harmonization in the field of private firms. Considering the valuable scientific contribution and the practical relevance of Maximilian Saucke's work, I wish that this thesis will gain a lot of attention in academia and practice.

Münster, December 2014 Prof. Dr. Peter Kajüter

Acknowledgement

This study was conducted during my time as a PhD student at the Chair of International Accounting at the University of Münster. The thesis was accepted as a dissertation by the Münster School of Business and Economics in November 2014.

In this acknowledgement I wish to thank everyone who supported me during the four-year process of working on my thesis and those who made my time in Münster so enriching and enjoyable. First, I would like to thank my supervisor, boss, and teacher Prof. Dr. Peter Kajüter who accepted me as a PhD student and provided me with great support during my time at his chair. He contributed greatly to the success of this research project by keeping me on the straight and narrow and giving me a lot of guidance regarding the research's focus, design and structure. I would also like to thank Prof. Dr. Hans-Jürgen Kirsch who reviewed and evaluated my thesis as a second referee. My sincere thanks are further given to Prof. Dr. Ulrich van Suntum for being the third referee at my disputation. Furthermore, I like to thank Prof. em. Dr. Jochen Sigloch and StB Prof. Dr. Rolf Uwe Fülbier from the University of Bayreuth who sparked my interest in the field of Accounting and International Financial Reporting in particular.

The empirical results of this thesis would not have been achieved without the support of my research partners Dr. Gernot Hebestreit (Grant Thornton, London) and Prof. Dr. Mathias Schellhorn (PricewaterhouseCoopers, Hannover). By providing access to their international network of auditors, an e-mail based survey could be sent to 238 offices in 138 countries. I thank all participating managing partners of Grant Thornton and PricewaterhouseCoopers for their kind cooperation in the process of data collection and Gernot Hebestreit and Mathias Schellhorn for many valuable discussions, which provided me with new ideas and insights into the field of international accounting harmonization from an auditor's perspective.

I would certainly not have accomplished this thesis without the support and encouragement of my dear colleagues and friends at the Chair of International Accounting. I have many great memories from our time together, which I will not forget – not least thanks to the great design of my graduation cap. In particular, I would like to thank my former roommate and secret (little) brother Moritz Schröder for being a great counselor in accounting, but even more as a friend. I will miss our evening sessions at Nordstern, where his eyes were sometimes bigger than his belly. Special thanks go further to Gregor Hagemann, alias King George, who accompanied me at various special locations and events such as nightly excursions to foreign ships, epic mixed doubles, and unfortunate football games between Eintracht Frankfurt and Werder Bremen.

I am very thankful for having shared my flat with my colleagues Stephanie Eckerth and Friedrich Kalden. I enjoyed the night talks and dinners in our kitchen and appreciate their understanding and endurance during the lengthy and unbearable construction works. My time at IUR would have certainly been a lot less thrilling without my dear fellow Marcel Baki, who was always ready to spring a surprise you would never expect. Many thanks also go to Martin Nienhaus for all his advice concerning my research design and the use of statistical methods. Moreover, I would like to thank Julius Hannemann, Daniel Blaesing, Thomas Poplat, Stefan Hannen, Florian Klassmann, Matthias Nienaber, and Alexander

Schulz for – among many other things – enthusiastic football matches and Christina Voets, Leila Prousch, Ashly Bills, Daniela Peters, Christian Reisloh, Kristian Bachert, and Martin Vogelpohl for being a great team I am very glad to have been a part of. Last but not least, I would like to thank our student research assistants for their indispensable work at IUR and in particular Max Meinhövel who supported me with literature research and assisted me during data collection.

Besides the support and encouragement I received from the IUR team, I am very thankful for the friendship of Christoph Glins and Sebastian Borgsmüller who picked me as their flatmate when I moved to Münster in August 2010. Both of them made my start in Münster so easy and introduced me to the culinary richness of Münster City and surroundings. May 'Leve partus' persist until we are old and feeble! My thesis would certainly not be of similar quality without the dedicated work of my friend Julia Alexandra Weber who spent hours and hours correcting the proofs. Special thanks go further to David Haas who lent me a sympathetic ear whenever necessary and who is the best friend you can ever imagine.

Finally, but foremost, I am sure that I would not have been able to accomplish this thesis without the love and devotion I received from my girlfriend Josephine Mücke, my sister Theresa, and my beloved parents. Dear Josie, you always showed great enthusiasm for my ideas and thoughts and gave me the love that made me overcome the great valleys of the past four years. It is such a gift that you are in my life and I look forward to the future, wherever it will take us.

Zuletzt möchte ich noch ein paar wenige Worte in meiner Muttersprache verlieren, um den beiden Menschen zu danken, denen diese Arbeit gewidmet ist, meinem Vater Hans-Jürgen und meiner Mutter Cordula. Eure Liebe und Unterstützung begleitet mich schon mein ganzes Leben. Ob in Bremen, Stonyhurst, Bayreuth, Nizza oder Münster, ihr habt mich stets liebevoll auf meinem Weg begleitet und mich dabei aufopferungsvoll unterstützt. Dafür danke ich euch sehr herzlich.

Münster, December 2014 Maximilian Saucke

Contents summary

Contents

Index of figures

Index of tables

Index of formulas

Index of abbreviations

AAS	Australian Accounting Standards
AASB	Australian Accounting Standards Board
AASC	Accounting and Auditing Standards Committee
Acc.	Accounting
AcSB	Accounting Standards Board of Canada
AFRS	Accounting Financial Reporting Standards
AG	Aktiengesellschaft
AICPA	American Institute of Certified Public Accountants
AISG	Accountants' International Study Group
ALL	Adoption for all domestic private firms
ANY	Adoption of any kind and within any scope
APB	Accounting Practices Board
ASB	Accounting Standards Board
ASBJ	Accounting Standards Board of Japan
ASC	Accounting Standards Committee
ASCG	Accounting Standards Committee of Germany
ASEAN	Association of Southeast Asian Nations
BB	Betriebs-Berater (Journal)
BC	Basis for Conclusions
BFN	Bokföringsnämnden
BilMoG	Bilanzrechtsmodernisierungsgesetz
BRP	Blue-Ribbon Panel
CAC	Central American and Caribbean
Cf.	Confer
CFA	Chartered Financial Analyst
CL	Comment Letter
Col.	Column
CONS	Adoption in the consolidated financial statements
CPA	Certified Public Accountant
CPC	Comité de Pronunciamentos Contábeis
DIFF	Framework for Differential Reporting
DP	Discussion Paper
DPR	Deutsche Prüfstelle für Rechnungslegung
DRSC	Deutsches Rechnungslegungs Standards Committee
DStR	Deutsches Steuerrecht (Journal)
EC	European Commission
ED	Exposure Draft
Ed.	Editor

Eds.	Editors
EEA	European Economic Area
EEC	European Economic Community
EFRAG	European Financial Reporting Advisory Group
E.g.	Exempli gratia
esp.	especially
Et al.	Et alii
Etc.	Et cetera
EU	European Union
f.	Following (page)
FAF	Financial Accounting Foundation
FAS	Fiji Accounting Standards
FASB	Financial Accounting Standards Board
FEE	Federation of European Accountants (Fédération des Experts comptables Européens)
ff.	Following (pages)
FIA	Fiji Institute of Accountants
FREP	Financial Reporting Enforcement Panel
FRF for SMEs	Financial Reporting Framework for Small and Medium-sized Entities
FRS	Financial Reporting Standard
FULL	Full IFRS
GAAP	Generally Accepted Accounting Principles
GAS	German Accounting Standards
GCSE	General Certificate of Secondary Education
GDP	Gross Domestic Product
GT	Grant Thornton
H	Hypothesis
HGB	Handelsgesetzbuch
HKFRS	Hong Kong Financial Reporting Standard
HKICPA	Hong Kong Institute of Certified Public Accountants
HRK	Croatian Kuna
Hyp.	Hypothesis
IAHR	International Accounting Harmonization Research
IAS	International Accounting Standard(s)
IASB	International Accounting Standards Board
IASC	International Accounting Standards Committee
IASCF	International Accounting Standards Committee Foundation
ICAEW	Institute of Chartered Accountants in England and Wales
ICAI	Institute of Chartered Accountants of India

ICFAR	International Comparative Financial Accounting Research
I.e.	Id est
IFAC	International Federation of Accountants
ifM	Institut für Mittelstandsforschung
IFRIC	International Financial Reporting Interpretations Committee
IFRS	International Financial Reporting Standard(s)
IFRS for SMEs	International Financial Reporting Standard for Small and Medium-sized Entities
IMF	International Monetary Fund
IND	Adoption in the individual financial statements
Ind AS	Indian Accounting Standards
IOSCO	International Organization of Securities Commissions
IRZ	Zeitschrift für Internationale Rechnungslegung (Journal)
ISAs	International Standards on Auditing
ISK	Iceland Krona
KoR	Zeitschrift für internationale und kapitalmarktorientierte Rechnungslegung (Journal)
KPMG	Klynfeld, Peat, Marwick, Goerdeler
LR	Likelihood ratio
MAND	Mandatory adoption
MASB	Malaysian Accounting Standards Board
MPERS	Malaysian Private Entities Reporting Standard
MSEs	Medium-Sized Entities
MTS	Metical
N/A	Not applicable
NACA	National Accounting Council of Albania
NIFA	New International Financial Architecture
NIS	New Institutional Sociology
No.	Number
NPAEs	Non-publicly accountable entities
NZ	New Zealand
OCBOA	Other Comprehensive Basis of Accounting
OECD	Organisation for Economic Co-operation and Development
OHADA	Organisation pour l'Harmonisation en Afrique du Droit des Affaires
OLS	Ordinary least squares

P	Proposition
PCC	Private Company Council
PPP	Purchasing-power-parity
PW	Price Waterhouse
PwC	PricewaterhouseCoopers
PWI	Price Waterhouse International
RDR	Reduced Disclosure Requirements
ROCE	Return on capital employed
ROSC	Report on the Observance of Standards and Codes
ROE	Return on Equity
ROI	Return on Investment
RTJ	Raamatupidamise Toimkonna Juhendid
SACCS	Similar and Contrasting Countries Studies
SAICA	South African Institute of Chartered Accountants
SEC	Securities and Exchange Commission
SME	IFRS for SMEs
SME-FRF&FRS	Small and Medium-sized Entity Financial Reporting Framework and Financial Reporting Standard
SOCPA	Saudi Organization for Certified Accountants
SOME	Adoption for some domestic private firms
SSEs	Small-Sized Entities
SYSCOA	Système Comptable Ouest Africain
TAS	Turkish Accounting Standards
TASB	Turkish Accounting Standards Board
TShs	Tanzanian Shilling
UAS	Uniform Accounting System
UCLA	University of California, Los Angeles
UK	United Kingdom
UN	United Nations
US	United States
USAN	Union of South American Nations
USD	United States Dollar
VIF	Variance Inflation Factor
Vs.	Versus
VOL	Voluntary adoption
WEF	World Economic Forum
WGI	Worldwide Governance Indicators

Index of symbols

β	Regression coefficient
Chi^2	Chi-square
$	Dollar
€	Euro
*	Indicator of significance
ε	Error term
F	Full IFRS
FL1	'Local' Full IFRS Level 1
FL2	'Local' Full IFRS Level 2
FL3	'Local' Full IFRS Level 3
k	number of independent variables
L	Local GAAP
n	Number of countries
p	Probability (significance level)
%	Percent
R^2	Regression coefficient of determination
Σ	Sum
S	IFRS for SMEs (category)
SL1	'Local' IFRS for SMEs Level 1 (category)
SL2	'Local' IFRS for SMEs Level 2 (category)
SL3	'Local' IFRS for SMEs Level 3 (category)
x	independent variable
Y	dependent variable

1 Foundation

1.1 Introduction

1.1.1 Motivation

*Which countries have **actually adopted** Full IFRS and IFRS for SMEs in the field of private firms and **why** have they done so?*

At a first glance, this question does not sound very challenging since the IFRS.org website presents adoption profiles for 130 jurisdictions worldwide. Moreover, the answer to the second part of the question could be given by simply applying common sense. Countries adopt IFRS[1] because today's economic transactions recorded in financial statements have increasingly become international. Raising capital or making business across national borders broadens the group of preparers and users of financial statements across the world. Hence, **adopting international accounting standards appears logical**. This phenomenon should generally affect all kinds of operations regardless of their legal form or size. However, as in some parts of the world local companies might be, to a certain extent, more globalized than elsewhere, the demand for internationally converged and comparable financial reporting standards is likely to vary among firms and countries alike.

For this reason, **not every country in the world has yet adopted IFRS**. Even if the majority of domestic companies strive for IFRS adoption, the countries in which they operate might hesitate to give up legislative power to a supranational organization if the expected outcome is unfavorable. Other countries may only abide by such a decision because they have been put under certain pressures.

The largest and most homogeneous demand for global financial accounting[2] rules certainly exists for companies that seek funds from global capital markets. Apart from their business partners, their owners and/or creditors are spread over the entire world. In such a setting, globally converged accounting standards become indispensable. Unsurprisingly, the harmonization of financial reporting began with exactly those entities. Since the early beginnings of the IASC in the 1970s, the International Accounting Standards (IAS), and from year 2002 onwards the 'Full' International Financial Reporting Standards (**Full IFRS**), have become the predominant accounting language for **listed companies** in more than 130 countries and jurisdictions by 2014 (*Deloitte Touche Tohmatsu* (2014c)).

Although accepting the wide diffusion of Full IFRS as a matter of fact, *Nobes* (2013) specifies the above phrase as follows: *"The consolidated statements of the majority of listed companies in about 90 countries are either required to comply with IASB-IFRS, or choose to do so"* (*Nobes* (2013), p. 103). In fact, the definition of 'IFRS adoption' is not as simple as it seems. It can actually mean many different things. When *Nobes* points out his caveats to statements such as *"IFRS have spread to over 100 countries"*, he wants to draw attention to the **'how' of IFRS adoption**. In order to assess correctly to which extent a country has adopted IFRS or not, it is important to consider which version of IFRS has been adopted

[1] The term 'IFRS' is used as a hypernym for 'Full IFRS' and 'IFRS for SMEs'.

[2] The terms 'financial accounting' and 'financial reporting' will be used synonymously in the following.

and if it has been modified or complemented by local requirements (e.g. EU-IFRS and Australian IFRS). Furthermore, IFRS adoption does not describe the same local conditions if in one country IFRS have become the only mandatory accounting framework for all domestic companies whereas in another IFRS are just one of several different sets of accounting rules local firms are allowed to choose from. It can also be differentiated between countries that have adopted IFRS for all domestic companies or only for a certain type of entities (e.g. listed companies). Finally, IFRS adoption might be restricted to consolidated accounts, because individual financial statements are still heavily influenced by local company or tax law.

As globalization proceeds, the demand for globally converged accounting standards increases for companies acting within and beyond capital markets. As a result, Full IFRS have also been adopted by **private firms** in nearly 100 countries worldwide (*Deloitte Touche Tohmatsu* (2014c)). One could argue that by offering one set of International Financial Reporting Standards (i.e. Full IFRS) to both listed and private companies, the IFRS Foundation had already fully served its purpose. However, in July 2009, something remarkable happened: the International Financial Reporting Standard for Small and Medium-sized Entities (**IFRS for SMEs**) was issued.

Considering the difficulty in precisely defining IFRS adoption, an additional version of IASB-IFRS undeniably adds complexity to this topic. Furthermore, different versions of IFRS are regarded as one reason for the survival of international differences under IFRS (*Nobes* (2006), p. 236). By developing a second set of IFRS, which is meant to be exclusively adopted by companies without public accountability, the IFRS Foundation might violate its principal objective to *"develop a single set of high quality, understandable, enforceable and globally accepted international financial reporting standards (IFRSs) through its standard-setting body, the IASB"* (*IFRS Foundation* (2014g)). Although the *IASB* denies this contradiction by pointing out that 'single set' only refers to entities in similar circumstances (*International Accounting Standards Board* (2013), BC42), the *IASB* members faced a true **dilemma** when putting the IFRS for SMEs on their agenda:

> *"On the one hand, it believed that the same concepts of financial reporting are appropriate for all entities regardless of public accountability. [...] This suggested that a single set of accounting standards should be suitable for all entities. [...] On the other hand, the Board acknowledged that differences in the types and needs of users of SMEs' financial statements, as well as limitations in, and the cost of, the accounting expertise available to SMEs, suggested that a separate standard for SMEs is appropriate. [...] On balance, the Board concluded that the latter approach (separate standard) was appropriate."*
>
> (*International Accounting Standards Board* (2013), BC47)

Despite the fundamental doubts about the reasonableness and the net economic benefits of an IFRS for SMEs, which caused considerable controversies about the new standard,[3] the **global impact of IFRS for SMEs** on the financial reporting of private firms is **re-**

[3] Cf. *International Accounting Standards Board* (2013), DO1-DO6, for the dissenting opinion of James J. Leisenring.

markable. Only a few weeks after its publication in 2009, the IFRS for SMEs was already expected to have *"the potential to revolutionise and harmonise financial reporting by private companies across the world"* (*Grant Thornton* (2009), p. 1). Within fewer than three years, IFRS for SMEs was expected to be adopted in over 80 countries (*IFRS Foundation* (2012a), p. 1). According to former *IASB* member *Paul Pacter*, millions of small companies were already using the IFRS for SMEs by 2012 (*IFRS Foundation* (2011), p. 2). Regardless of the reliability of this number, there is no doubt that since 2009 millions of private firms have at least been given the possibility of adopting the IFRS for SMEs.

While countries such as South Africa, Singapore, or the United States adopted the IFRS for SMEs shortly after (or even before)[4] its issuance, the European Union has not approved IFRS for SMEs as a legitimate accounting framework for European private firms by 2014. Some EU member states have still begun to align their **Local GAAPs** with IFRS for SMEs to an extent that it does not conflict with EU law (e.g. Estonia, Sweden). In spite of that, many national GAAPs of European, African or Asian countries had already been more or less converged with IAS and/or Full IFRS during the past four decades (*Pacter* (2009b), p. 29).

Without a doubt, the **IFRS for SMEs** has mixed up the bipolar financial accounting landscape between Local GAAPs and Full IFRS by adding a **third dimension** to international GAAP choice. As a result, standard-setters and parliaments all over the world are urged to rethink their previous Full IFRS convergence strategies by incorporating IFRS for SMEs into their local financial accounting framework. As pointed out above, there are several alternative ways to adopt Full IFRS and/or IFRS for SMEs in a country's local financial accounting environment. Even though the *IASB* favors complete adoption (*Pacter* (2012), p. 20), it cannot deny that both Full IFRS and IFRS for SMEs have been adjusted to local needs in various jurisdictions (*Pacter* (2014), p. 9), which makes inter-country IFRS comparisons a challenging task. *Hans Hoogervorst*, Chairman of the IASB, often uses the phrase, *"we must speak the same accounting language"* (*Hoogervorst/Teitler-Feinberg* (2012), p. 322). Given the local modifications, carve-outs, and supplements, it seems that IFRS have already become a language with strong dialects. The rise of IFRS for SMEs creates additional **diversity** and **complexity** in the field of private firms.

In contrast to the extensive firm level research that has been conducted so far on the adoption of Full IFRS in the context of listed companies, **little attention** has yet been given to **country level research** on the adoption of Full IFRS and IFRS for SMEs in the field of private firms. Instead, prior research was mostly dedicated to the firm- and country-specific determinants and the economic consequences of Full IFRS adoption by listed companies (e.g. *Gassen/Sellhorn* (2006); *Barth et al.* (2008); *Daske et al.* (2008)). Furthermore, studies on the firm- and country-specific determinants of differences in accounting practice under Full IFRS have become an increasingly important research area (*Jaafar/McLeay* (2007); *Kvaal/Nobes* (2012); *Wehrfritz et al.* (2012)). As far as IFRS for SMEs adoption is concerned, the majority of the empirical, mostly survey-based research has so far focused on firm level analyses covering the due process (*Kajüter et al.* (2008)) and the hypothetical implications of IFRS for SMEs adoption (*European Commission*

4 South Africa adopted the ED-IFRS for SMEs in 2007.

(2010); *Fülbier/Gassen* (2010); *Litjens et al.* (2012)). Country level studies on the de facto determinants of IFRS for SMEs adoption are still rare (*Kaya/Koch* (2013)). This study therefore contributes to the **scarce empirical, cross-country research** that has so far provided evidence on the country-specific characteristics (e.g. *Deloitte Touche Tohmatsu* (2014c)) and determinants (e.g. *Hope et al.* (2006); *Judge et al.* (2010); *Ramanna/Sletten* (2013)) of Full IFRS and IFRS for SMEs adoption in the field of private firms.

1.1.2 Research questions

This study addresses the following two main research questions:

(1) How are accounting systems shaped in the field of private firms?

(2) Why do countries adopt Full IFRS or IFRS for SMEs in the field of private firms?

The **first research question** shall be answered by applying two different empirical research strategies: *time series analysis* and *cross-sectional analysis*. For a sample of 110 countries, the study first displays the *process* of worldwide Full IFRS and IFRS for SMEs adoption in the field of private firms since 2002 and thereby identifies different types of accounting systems for private firms. The time series analysis classifies accounting systems for private firms according to their overall degree of compliance with Full IFRS and IFRS for SMEs and thus identifies to which extent these accounting systems have been converged with Full IFRS or IFRS for SMEs since 2002. For the same 110 countries, the cross-sectional analysis provides insight into the *status quo* of local Full IFRS and IFRS for SMEs implementation in 2014 and presents a detailed overview on the similarities and differences regarding the local implementation of Full IFRS and IFRS for SMEs across the globe.

The **second research question** shall be answered by conducting *three cross-sectional analyses* that reveal which factors have determined a country's decision to adopt Full IFRS and IFRS for SMEs in the field of private firms at two different points in time (2008 and 2014). The cut-off date of the first analysis is 2008, as this was the last year before the IFRS for SMEs was issued. Hence, this study tests the explanatory power of various factors that determined the probability of Full IFRS adoption in the field of private firms at a time where Full IFRS were the only IASB standards in place. The second cross-sectional analysis then examines how the previously identified determinants of Full IFRS adoption change if the years 2009 to 2014 are included in the analysis. The study hereby takes into account the time after the IFRS for SMEs has been issued and aims at analyzing the interdependencies between the two IASB standards. Finally, it is examined which factors have determined the probability of IFRS for SMEs adoption between 2009 and 2014.

The **research fields**, which are addressed within the two sub-studies, and the regarding research approaches are summarized in Figure 1-1.

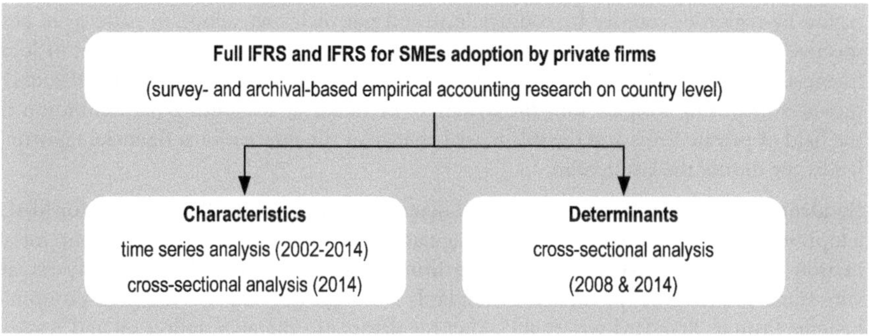

Figure 1-1: Research fields of the study

The study's **contribution** to accounting research, regulation, and practice is manifold. While extensive research was conducted on the determinants and consequences of Full IFRS adoption by listed companies – both on firm and on country level – cross-country accounting research dealing with Full IFRS and IFRS for SMEs adoption by private firms is still at an early stage (*Nobes* (2010), p. 217; 222). Hence, this study closes a current research gap in the area of international accounting harmonization (IAH) research by providing an insight into the country level characteristics and determinants of Full IFRS and IFRS for SMEs adoption by private firms. It is the first study that analyzes in detail the *process* towards Full IFRS and IFRS for SMEs adoption in the context of private firms since 2002 by applying a unique classification methodology. Furthermore, the study provides the most detailed information available on the *status quo* of the two IASB standards' local implementation in 110 countries. Thirdly, it adds to the scarce empirical research that has yet been conducted on the determinants of Full IFRS and IFRS for SMEs adoption in the field of private firms.

The empirical results of the descriptive and explanatory research can help the **IASB** to develop a clearer picture of the shape and the driving factors of worldwide Full IFRS and IFRS for SMEs adoption in the field of private firms. They may thus enable a better understanding of the remaining constraints and difficulties in the global adoption process. Such an understanding is vital to predict any future steps by national regulators in the field of global harmonization of financial reporting, especially regarding private firms.

By describing the characteristics of Full IFRS and IFRS for SMEs adoption on country level, the first sub-study raises the awareness of **IFRS for SMEs' growing impact** on the financial reporting of private firms worldwide. It addresses both countries that have already adopted the standard (e.g. Brazil, Singapore, and South Africa) and those that have yet been rather critical of IFRS for SMEs adoption (e.g. Germany and France). Furthermore, the findings are relevant for all jurisdictions, where IFRS for SMEs has already been formally adopted, but de facto adoption has not gotten under way yet (e.g. United States).

The empirical results allow for various benchmark analyses and highlight which countries are ahead of their peers and which jurisdictions lag behind in terms of international financial accounting harmonization. **National standard-setters** can make comparisons on a region-by-region or country-by-country level and put their own adoption patterns in perspective to the adoption process in other jurisdictions. With regard to the extent of local financial accounting systems' convergence with Full IFRS and IFRS for SMEs, the study provides surprising insights into the dynamics of financial accounting harmonization in the field of private firms and the substantial change of the international financial reporting landscape during the last decade.

By identifying economic and institutional determinants of Full IFRS and IFRS for SMEs adoption, the study provides national regulators and policy-makers with recent information on the **key drivers of their adoption decisions**. In particular, the study reveals why some countries adopt the IASB standards although they expect only little economic benefits from it. Standard-setters and other regulators can therefore reflect on and reassess their own adoption decision and discuss whether Full IFRS or IFRS for SMEs is (or would be) the most favorable accounting system for their jurisdiction.

The empirical results may also be of interest for private firms' **corporate managers** who are responsible for their company's financial reporting or for the internationalization of their business. Local financial reporting requirements are one of the most important confounding factors when it comes to the internationalization of small and medium-sized businesses. Knowing about the current developments in the regulatory environment of the targeted jurisdictions can be crucial for the success of private firms' internationalization strategy. For this reason, the study is not only relevant for macro-level policy makers but also for decision makers in private companies.

Before elaborating on the scientific research strategy and the conceptualization of the conducted research, the following section summarizes the further outline of the study.

1.1.3 Outline

Based on the above comments on the study's motivation, its research questions and contribution, **chapter one** continues with a description of the scientific research strategy and the conceptualization of the conducted research. This step is necessary to explain the reasons why a certain research methodology has been chosen in this study. Subsequently, chapter one provides the conceptual grounding of the study. In a first step, an introduction in the financial reporting of private firms is given. Secondly, the process of international accounting harmonization is examined and the two relevant international accounting systems (i.e. Full IFRS and IFRS for SMEs) are depicted. The study continues with a presentation of the research field and a review of prior research.

Starting from the *economic theory of networks* and the *institutional theory of isomorphism*, **chapter two** develops hypotheses on why countries choose to adopt Full IFRS and IFRS for SMEs in the field of private firms. The two theories underline the theoretical association between the adoption of international accounting standards (Full IFRS and IFRS for SMEs) by countries and the economic benefits, network effects, and institutional pressures these countries are subject to.

Chapter three presents the research design and the empirical results of the first sub-study. The first section describes the conceptual methodology and the data used to fully **charac-**

terize Full IFRS and IFRS for SMEs adoption in the field of private firms. The second section includes the empirical results, which are presented separately for the following nine geographic regions:

North America	European Union	Middle East
Central America & Caribbean	Southeast Europe	Asia
South America	Africa	Australia & Oceania

The chapter ends with a discussion, which integrates the main findings.

Chapter four comprises the research design and the empirical results of the second sub-study, whose focus is on the **determinants of Full IFRS and IFRS for SMEs adoption** in the field of private firms. Having presented the assumptions and variables used in the statistical analyses, the chapter provides descriptive statistics, bivariate, and multivariate findings for three distinct cross-sectional analyses (Full IFRS adoption by 2008 and by 2014 and IFRS for SMEs adoption by 2014). The chapter ends with a discussion of the empirical results, in which interrelationships between the three analyses are established.

The empirical results presented in chapter three and four are briefly summarized at the beginning of **chapter five**. Implications are derived for the IASB and national standard-setters, global policy-makers, corporate managers, and preparers of private firms' financial statements. Moreover, the section highlights the limitations of the study and presents suggestions for future research. Finally, chapter five provides an outlook on future developments in international accounting harmonization in the field of private firms.

The entire outline of the study is displayed in Figure 1-2.

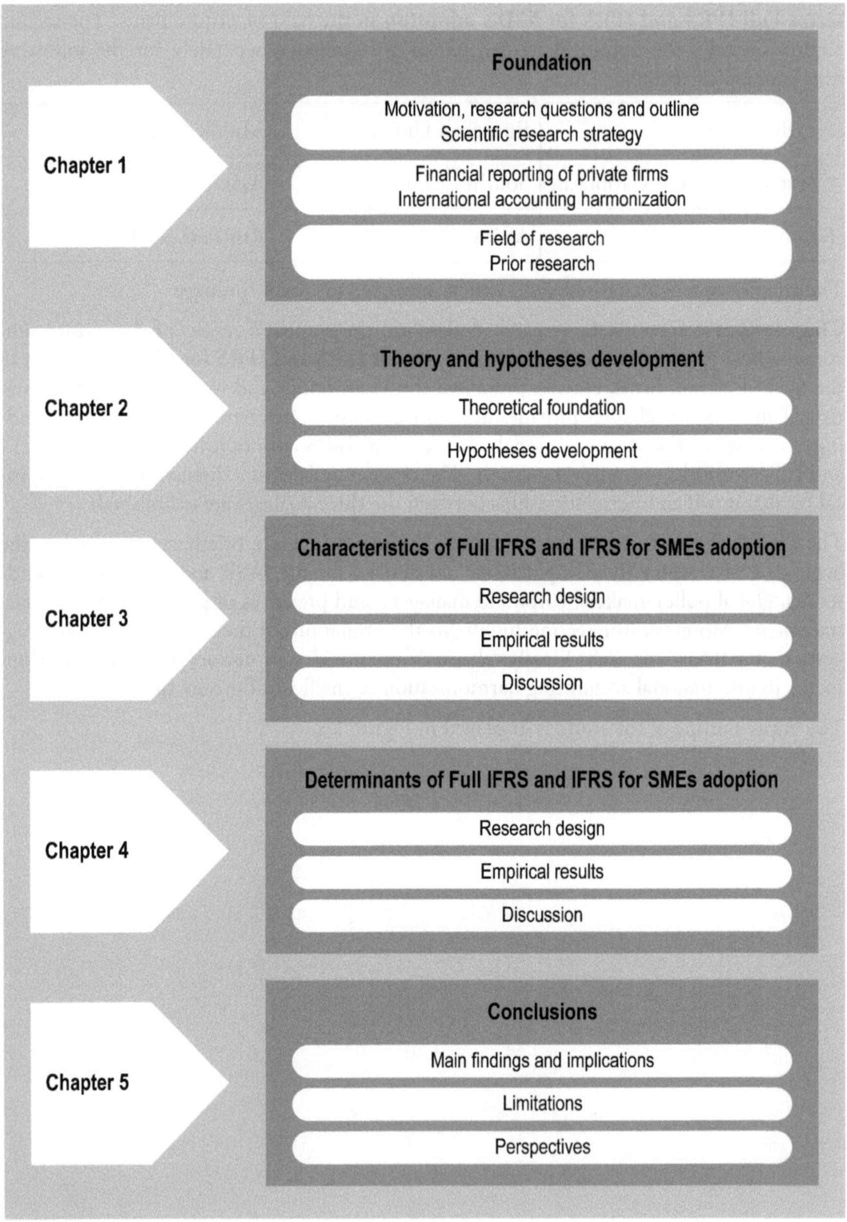

Figure 1-2: Outline of the study

1.2 Scientific research strategy

1.2.1 Science and philosophy of science

As long as people ask questions about truth and search for justifications for their individually, culturally, or religiously influenced beliefs, they will continue to gather knowledge, which is by definition of *Plato* nothing else than 'true, justified beliefs' (*Platon* (1974)). *Raffée* defines **science** in three different ways: firstly, science is described as the process, which aims at the systematic collection of cognition (*Raffée* (1974), p. 13). Secondly, *Raffée* defines science as the institution or organization, in which the process of cognition takes place. Finally, the outcome of this process is also defined as 'science' (*Raffée* (1974), p. 13).

Kosiol differentiates further between the following four general **scientific objectives** (*Kosiol* (1964), p. 745): descriptive research defines real phenomena and describes them with respect to their empirical validity. Based on this scientific objective, theoretical research aims at explaining observations and their characteristics (explanandum) considering certain constraints (explanans). If the hereby gained knowledge is used for practical decision-making, the research follows a pragmatic scientific objective. Besides the questions *"What is A and why does A lead to B?"* science can also deal with philosophical questions asking for *"How should B look like?"*. This type of science strives after normative objectives.

Science can further be differentiated according to the specific **subject area.** While formal sciences (e.g. philosophy, mathematics) do not have any relation to reality and can only be verified by their logical truth, empirical sciences (e.g. physics, economics) try to describe, explain, and shape empirically noticeable reality excerpts (*Ulrich/Hill* (1976a), p. 305). In practice, empirical sciences often use formal sciences as 'auxiliary sciences' by borrowing certain scientific instruments from them in order to gain knowledge over their specific area of study (*Bartel* (1990), p. 54). In addition, empirical sciences can be categorized into 'purely' theoretical sciences (e.g. natural sciences) and applied sciences (e.g. social sciences). While theoretical sciences only focus on the explanation of reality excerpts, applied sciences analyze alternatives for actions in order to shape social and technological systems (*Ulrich/Hill* (1976a), p. 305).

Forming part of the international accounting harmonization (IAH) research stream, this study belongs to the field of modern business and macro-economics. Whether business economics represent a (purely) theoretical or rather an applied science is still controversially discussed (*Kornmeier* (2007), p. 22f.). The primary purpose of modern business economics is to describe, explain, and predict economic reality and thereby present operationally and strategically beneficial and sustainable solutions for economic actors with scarcity problems (*Fülbier* (2004), p. 267). For this reason, this study rather belongs to the field of **applied sciences** than to theoretical sciences.

Philosophy of science can also be regarded as a science – a 'science of science', which addresses the terms, categorizations, principles of cognition, languages, objectives as well as the applicable research methodology (*Fülbier* (2004), p. 266). According to *Frank*, philosophy of science is simply the *"self-evident reflection on what science is and could be"* (*Frank* (2003), p. 289). As a 'meta-scientific discipline' (*Kornmeier* (2007), p. 6) philosophy of science is part of a cognitive science and analyzes a science's purpose and provides the starting point for every scientific research project (*Poser* (2001), p. 16).

1.2.2 Scientific positioning of the study

In order to achieve a general scientific research objective (definition, description, explanation, or prescription) the researcher has to decide which research strategy shall be applied and according to which theoretical concept the research shall be conducted. For the scientific discipline of business economics, *Grochla* distinguishes between the following three basic research strategies (*Grochla* (1978), p. 71ff.):

- the normative-conceptual strategy,
- the empirical strategy, and
- the formal-analytical strategy.

By following the **normative-conceptual strategy**, the researcher simulates reality through theoretical thinking and aims at making the hidden relationships transparent. The scientific objective is to derive recommendations for actions, which are based upon plausibility and speculation. As these conceptually derived statements are neither quantified nor empirically verified and therefore never brought face to face with reality, they remain definitional or logical-analytical sentences. The strategy's success depends highly on the analytical abilities of the researcher (*Grochla* (1978), p. 72f.).

On the contrary, the **empirical strategy's** primary goal is to confront statements with reality in order to give reasons for their validity or proof for their lack of validity. The researcher's focus is on a systematic process of gaining experience by using a sophisticated set of empirical methodologies, which generally require great attention for details and good statistical skills. The hereby derived statements can either describe the investigated area of reality or reveal its causal-analytical context, which may then be analyzed further to predict future developments (*Grochla* (1978), p. 78f.).

In contrast to the normative-conceptual and the empirical strategy, the **formal-analytical strategy** largely simplifies and abstracts from reality for the purpose of solving a specific real-life problem, which is the starting point for every formal-analytical research. Its focus is on the appropriate application of a complex set of decision-logical methods and mathematical models that are able to quantify the researcher's decision problem. The degree of simplification and specification of the investigated problem largely depends on the characteristics and limitations of the applied mathematical functions and the available problem-solving algorithms. This approach leads to a substantial deviation between the applied models and reality. For this reason, the outcome of formal-analytical research is rather a description of problem structures than a precise illustration of reality (*Grochla* (1978), p. 85–87).

The scientific objective of this study is to precisely **describe and explain** the country-adoption of Full IFRS and IFRS for SMEs in the field of private firms by drawing on a comprehensive set of cross-national data. Hence, this study follows an empirical research strategy.

The question which **theoretical methodology** should be applied when doing science has been discussed since antiquity and its philosophical pioneers such as *Socrates*, *Plato*, or *Aristotle*. The two classical theoretical research programs are 'pure deduction' (classical rationalism) and 'pure induction' (classical empiricism). According to the former concept, primarily represented by *Descartes*, *Hobbes*, and *Leibniz*, human rationality is the only source of cognition. Representatives of the latter concept (e.g. *Bacon*, *Locke*, and *Hume*) declare that observation is the original source of all truth (*Raffée/Abel* (1979), p. 12–15). Although these classical concepts still persist in modern science, they have been widely substituted by two more moderate theoretical concepts: critical rationalism and constructivism.

According to *Karl R. Popper*, the creation of knowledge does neither start with perceptions nor with the collection of data or facts, but with problems (*Popper/Keuth* (2005), p. 69). *Popper's* **critical rationalism** is built on four main ideas: most important is the conclusion that all human knowledge is fallible (**fallibilism**). This implies that science can never achieve ultimate truth, as all knowledge can turn out to be wrong at the next moment. The possibility of verifying hypotheses, which are defined as statements that postulate an association between two or more phenomena, is thereby neglected (*Popper/Keuth* (2005), p. 17). According to *Popper*, this is no reason for frustration. On the contrary, this means that researchers can learn from their mistakes and are able to gradually approach the truth. A necessary requirement for the success of this incremental research process is that if a mistake occurs, suitable steps have to be taken in order to correct the mistake (**methodological rationalism**). New statements do not only have to be 'logically true' and consistent, but also 'factually true', which means that they can be subject to intersubjective empirical testing (*Ulrich/Hill* (1976b), p. 345). Reality hereby becomes the touchstone for all new hypotheses, which implies that reality must exist – at least in theory – objectively and independently from the observer (**critical realism**). This can be considered as a non-provable and non-disprovable metaphysic assumption of critical rationalism (*Lingnau* (1995), p. 125).

The wing of **constructivism**, which is associated with *Paul Lorenzen* and the 'Erlanger School',[5] also holds the opinion that human rationality is in principle fallible and therefore shows some similarity with critical rationalism. However, constructivists believe that it is possible to derive 'methodologically correct' decisions from deductive argumentation. In this regard constructivists only believe in fallibilism to a limited extent (*Raffée/Abel* (1979), p. 6). Instead of *Popper's* approach of confronting hypotheses with reality through iterative empirical testing, in constructivism cognition is aimed to be achieved by a broad consensus of argumentative statements, which ideally is the outcome of a comprehensive discussion by different experts (*Fülbier* (2004), p. 269). Following a purely deductive methodology, constructivism is significantly closer to classical rationalism than *Popper's* scientific concept of critical rationalism.

Another key difference between the two research programs is the respective **concept of truth**. While critical rationalists necessarily accept the idea of objective reality (critical

---

[5] Cf. *Schnell et al.* (2008), p. 109ff., for the constructivism of the 'critical psychology', the 'radical constructivism', and other variations of 'social constructivism'.

realism) as an axiomatic premise for the application of their empirical research methodology, constructivists support a pragmatic model of truth, in which truth is defined and decided on through a qualified consensus of experts (*Raffée/Abel* (1979), p. 6). For them, the world is not objectively given, but it is rather a construct developed by human beings through cognitive thinking (*Frank* (2007), p. 2012).

This study uses the research methodology of *Popper's* **critical rationalism**. Hence, the study follows a three step scheme for the purpose of gaining knowledge. Beginning with an observable problem in reality, hypotheses are drafted for the purpose of solving the problem. These hypotheses are then empirically tested and hereby (partly) eliminated. The hypotheses in this study are developed by drawing on **two main theories** (*economic theory of networks* and *institutional theory of isomorphism*) and they are operationalized through deductive argumentation. This process leads to the study's comprehensive conceptual framework. According to *Popper*, the hereby derived 'nomological' hypotheses should be general, falsifiable sentences without a time or space constraint (*Popper/Keuth* (2005), p. 39f.). As nomological hypotheses are extremely rare in business economics (*Raffée* (1989), p. 21), the aim of this study is to strive after hypotheses, which might have certain time or space restraints and therefore lead to so-called 'quasi-theories' with **limited universality** (*Ulrich/Hill* (1976b), p. 346).

Popper's criterion of falsification states that *"a hypothesis is scientific if and only if it has the potential to be refused by some possible observation. To be scientific, a hypothesis has to take a risk, has to stick its neck out"* (*Godfrey-Smith* (2003), p. 58). According to this criterion, a hypothesis is more valuable the easier it can fail in an empirical test (*Lingnau* (1995), p. 124). At *Popper's* time, this opinion was highly contradictory to the prevailing psychoanalytical and Marxist concepts, which tended to build on non-falsifiable statements. This apparent strength turned out to be the biggest weakness according to *Popper's* theoretical program (*Albert* (2000), p. 3). The hypotheses developed in this study shall not only predict the results of different empirical tests, but shall also explain the reasons for the revealed relationships. In accordance with *Popper's* critical rationalism, this study develops **falsifiable hypotheses** that have the potential to be refused through empirical testing (*Godfrey-Smith* (2003), p. 58).

Hypothesis testing procedures compare a conjecture about a population to the information contained in a sample of data (*Hill et al.* (2008), p. 54). In the course of empirical testing, a pair of hypotheses, consisting of the null hypothesis and the alternative hypothesis, is compared to each other (*Siegel* (2012), p. 250). The null hypothesis expresses the idea that an observed difference is due to chance (*Freedman et al.* (1998), p. 479). Hence, it assumes that there is no significant association between the examined variables. In contrast, the alternative hypothesis says that the difference is real (*Freedman et al.* (1998), p. 479). The alternative hypothesis is equivalent to the research hypothesis, which draws on specific theories to suggest that the analyzed variables are associated with each other. If the research hypothesis includes a statement about the direction of the variables' assumed relationship, it is a 'directed' hypothesis. On the contrary, 'undirected' hypotheses postulate an association between variables without stating its direction.

In this study, hypothesis testing procedures are only applied in chapter 4 (Determinants of Full IFRS and IFRS for SMEs adoption). For this reason, this study does not define any falsifiable hypotheses regarding the descriptive analysis in chapter 3 (Characteristics of Full IFRS and IFRS for SMEs adoption). Instead, **research propositions** are developed on the basis of prior research and this study's conceptual framework to unveil the researcher's general expectations regarding the empirical results of the descriptive analysis.

Following the generally non-prescriptive character of critical rationalism (*Frank* (2007), p. 2013) and (neo-) positive accounting research (*Godfrey* (2006), p. 55), this study does not explicitly provide value judgements on the country-specific suitability and advantageousness of Full IFRS and IFRS for SMEs adoption. It does, however, provide valuable prospects on the most likely future developments in international accounting harmonization in the field of private firms.

Having explained the study's scientific research strategy, the next two sections provide the foundations of the two subject areas: the financial reporting of private firms and international accounting harmonization.

1.3 Financial reporting of private firms

1.3.1 Defining private firms

When accountants, managers, or researchers discuss the financial reporting of listed companies, there is almost no risk of misinterpreting the term 'listed'. The unambiguous criterion of stock market quotation clearly defines the relevant item – both nationally and globally. The opposite is the case for **private firms.** In the context of US or IFRS regulations, the expression 'private firms' generally means unlisted entities, although it might also exclude companies, which are non-listed but which take deposits from the public (e.g. banks, insurance companies). In the UK, it might rather be referred to the legal form of 'private limited companies' that are contrasted to 'public limited companies', which themselves might be listed or not (*Nobes/Parker* (2012), p. 298). In economies, where the government often remains a predominant shareholder in the country's largest companies (e.g. China, Russia), the term 'private' might rather be interpreted as 'privately owned', thus describing a company, which is not owned by the state (*International Accounting Standards Board* (2013), BC79(b)).

Given these possible sources of confusion, it is not surprising that even the IASB members had been repeatedly undecided when defining the name of the IFRS for SMEs during its ten-year-long standard-setting process. When the project was duly appropriated in 2003, the IASB referred to it by using the term 'small and medium-sized entities' (SMEs). The intention was to develop simplified IFRS for small and medium-sized companies, whose scope should initially be defined by **quantitative criteria.** Later on, it was decided that the scope's key distinguishing feature should not be size but whether or not a company's securities are listed (i.e. **qualitative criteria**). However, in the following discussion paper (2004) and exposure draft (2007), it was still referred to SMEs, although they were really designed for non-publicly accountable entities (NPAEs). These are basically non-listed entities, except for financial institutions (*Nobes* (2010), p. 215). During 2008, project leader *Paul Pacter* admitted that *"using the term SME to describe non-publicly accountable entities is potentially confusing"* (*Pacter* (2012), p. 7). For this reason, the title was temporarily changed into 'IFRS for private firms' and shortly later into 'IFRS for NPAEs'. Finally, the term 'NPAEs' was again abolished due to its *"ungainliness"* (*Nobes/Parker* (2012), p. 304) and the title was reconverted into IFRS for SMEs.

As unlisted companies form a more heterogeneous group than listed companies, finding appropriate definitions for the purpose of developing a most suitable differential reporting regime is not easy, especially not if the reporting framework is applied globally. The following two sections present some examples of both quantitative and qualitative definitions that have been in use to define SMEs, NPAES, private firms, and small businesses across the globe. Finally, this study's working definition of private firms is displayed in section 1.3.1.3.

1.3.1.1 Quantitative definitions

The distinction of entities by means of quantitative criteria is carried out by drawing on the characteristic 'firm size', which itself is a relative measure that can only be operationalized by the use of auxiliary measures (*Kaminski* (2008), p. 18). These benchmarks either capture firm specific input (e.g. number of employees, capital employed) or output factors (e.g. quantity of sales, net turnover) (*Busse von Colbe* (1964), p. 35ff.). In order to build a set of quantitative criteria, both the appropriate measures have to be selected and the respective thresholds have to be defined. In practice, classifications of entities based on quantitative definitions normally revert to a combination of two or more measures.

In the **European Union**, the first recommendation that established a common SME definition was adopted in 1996 (*European Commission* (2012)). In 2003, the European Commission (EC) adopted a new recommendation concerning the definition of micro, small, and medium-sized enterprises (*European Commission* (2003)). The use of the definition is voluntary, but the European Commission invites all member states to apply it as widely as possible (*European Commission* (2005), p. 6). The corresponding thresholds are displayed in Table 1-1.

Enterprise category[6]	Number of employees	Net turnover	Balance sheet total
Micro	< 10	≤ € 2 million	≤ € 2 million
Small	< 50	≤ € 10 million	≤ € 10 million
Medium-sized	< 250	≤ € 50 million	≤ € 43 million

Table 1-1: SME definition of the European Commission (2003)[7]

6 While it is compulsory to respect the number of employees, an SME may choose to meet either the turnover or balance sheet ceiling. It does not need to satisfy both and may exceed one of them without losing its status as SME (*European Commission* (2005), p. 13).

Besides the recommendation of the European Commission, the EU accounting directive (2013/34/EU) formally defines the categories of undertakings and groups, which are relevant for the differential reporting regime of unlisted limited companies in all 27 EU member states (*European Commission* (2013), p. 28). The European Parliament thereby chooses notably more restrictive thresholds than the European Commission. The categorization of individual limited companies is displayed in Table 1-2.

Enterprise category[8]	Number of employees	Net turnover	Balance sheet total
Micro	≤ 10	≤ € 0.7 million	≤ € 0.35 million
Small	≤ 50	≤ € 8 million	≤ € 4 million
Medium-sized	≤ 250	≤ € 40 million	≤ € 20 million

Table 1-2: SME definition in the EU accounting directive (2013)

In fact, the accounting directive only defines minimum thresholds, which are allowed to be augmented within a certain range[9] by single EU member states. While the United Kingdom and the Republic of Ireland have roughly adopted the above shown quantitative criteria for defining those enterprises, which are eligible for the small companies' regime (*Financial Reporting Council* (2013), Appendix I) and can thereby opt to use the Financial Reporting Standard for Smaller Entities (FRSSE), Germany still defines small limited companies within slightly broader and medium-sized limited companies within slightly narrower limits (§ 267 HGB):[10]

7 In addition to the above listed quantitative criteria, the European Commission sets one qualitative criterion. SMEs are thereafter defined as 'autonomous enterprises' if they are either totally independent, i.e. have no participation in other enterprises and no enterprise has a participation in the SME, or if they have a holding of less than 25% of the capital, or voting rights in one or more other enterprises, and/or outsiders do not have a stake of 25% or more of the capital or voting rights in the SME (*European Commission* (2003), Article 3).

8 In order to be classified in a specific category, companies must not exceed the limits of at least two of the three criteria during two consecutive years (*European Commission* (2013), p. 28).

9 For example, the thresholds for small undertakings shall not exceed € 12 million for net turnover and € 6 million for balance sheet total (*European Commission* (2013), p. 28).

10 In the course of the implementation of the new EU accounting directive, Germany plans to augment the thresholds of small and medium-sized companies. While the criteria for small companies remain within broader limits than in the EU accounting directive (net turnover ≤ € 12 million and balance sheet total ≤ € 6 million), the thresholds for medium-sized companies will be aligned with the EU accounting directive (net turnover ≤ € 40 million and balance sheet total ≤ € 20 million) (*Deutsches Bundesministerium der Justiz und für Verbraucherschutz* (2014), p. 7).

Enterprise category[11]	Number of employees	Net turnover	Balance sheet total
Small	≤ 50	≤ € 9.68 million	≤ € 4.84 million
Medium-sized	≤ 250	≤ € 38.5 million	≤ € 19.25 million

Table 1-3: SME definition in German commercial law (2014)

In Germany, where SMEs (so-called 'Mittelstand') play a very strong role in the national economy, the 'Institut für Mittelstandsforschung' (ifM) in Bonn publishes an alternative SME-definition, which is based on the number of employees and the annual net turnover (*Institut für Mittelstandsforschung* (2014)).[12] The particular thresholds are shown in Table 1-4.

Enterprise category	Number of employees	Net turnover
Small	< 10	< € 1 million
Medium-sized	< 500	< € 50 million

Table 1-4: SME definition by the ifM (Bonn, Germany)

Quantitative definitions arguably create clarity for regulators (*Jarvis/Collis* (2003), p. 6) and appear to be objective and transparent (*Curran/Blackburn* (2001), p. 10). They are also regarded as more practicable and reliable than complex sets of qualitative criteria (*Haller* (2003), p. 419). However, there is no numerical definition, which is not at least semi-arbitrary and the emphasis on size leads to other criteria being neglected (*Curran/Blackburn* (2001), p. 9, 16). The key **disadvantage** of applying a common **quantitative definition** is that what is considered a small business in one country may not necessarily be considered small in another one (*Jarvis/Collis* (2003), p. 6). This clearly impairs the distinction's cross-sector and cross-national transferability.

1.3.1.2 Qualitative definitions

In German literature, several researchers have repeatedly undertaken attempts to describe private firms, respectively SMEs (Mittelstand), in the most comprehensive way. In 1962, *Gantzel* already presents 190 qualitative definitions, which characterize SMEs in general and German individual commercial SMEs in particular (*Gantzel* (1962), p. 136ff.). Both on national and international level, a consistent qualitative definition of SMEs cannot be

11 In order to be classified in a specific category, companies must not exceed the limits of at least two of the three criteria during two consecutive years (§ 267 HGB).

12 The quantitative definition is also supplemented by a qualitative definition.

found. This is mainly due to the wide diversity of businesses (*UK Department of Trade & Industry* (2006)).

The *Bolton Report* (1971) represents one of the most acknowledged approaches to define **'small business'** based on qualitative criteria[13] in the United Kingdom. The overall goal of the report is to capture the distinctive characteristics of the small firm compared with larger enterprises, which is done by constructing an ideal type with three key elements (*Curran/Blackburn* (2001), p. 12):

- First, in economic terms, a small firm is one that has a relatively small share of its market (**small market share**).
- Secondly, an essential characteristic of a small firm is that it is managed by its owners or part-owners in a personalized way, and not through the medium of a formalized management structure (**no separation of ownership and control**).
- Thirdly, it is also independent in the sense that it does not form part of a larger enterprise (**legal independence**) and that the owner-managers should be free from outside control in taking their principal decisions (**economic independence**) (*Bolton* (1971), p. 1).

The topic of legal independence was later revisited by *Curran/Blackburn* (1994), who criticize that small establishments and small independent enterprises are treated as equivalents. They point out that contrary to independently owned single-outlet enterprises, branches of larger firms have their operational procedures dictated by the head office and might be able to access capital, supplies, financial, and other resources from it (*Curran/Blackburn* (2001), p. 16).

In a large-scale cross-country study on the accounting requirements for SMEs in the European Union, *CNA Interpreta* divides SMEs inter alia[14] into three different categories (Type A, B, C) using their **legal form** as criterion for demarcation (*CNA Interpreta s.r.l.* (2011), p. 6).

- Type A: Private joint-stock companies with limited liability for those owning shares (e.g. public limited company (PLC), Aktiengesellschaft (AG)).
- Type B: Personally owned limited and unlimited partnerships – also including other legal forms such as co-operatives (e.g. limited partnership (LP), Kommanditgesellschaft (KG)).
- Type C: Personally owned enterprises with no limit to personal liability, such as sole proprietorships (e.g. sole trader, Einzelunternehmer (EU)).

As legal forms combine several different qualitative factors (e.g. liability of owners, owner-structure, and separation of ownership and control), the classification of SMEs by reference to the legal form-criterion does usually not lead to unambiguous results (*Eierle* (2004), p. 43). In companies with **limited liability of ownership**, credit risk is generally

[13] The qualitative approach was later converted into a quantitative one as its qualitative definition was not easy to operationalize (*Curran/Blackburn* (2001), p. 13).

[14] Further subdivision has been made by size class (i.e. medium- and small-sized, micros 1 and 2).

higher than in unlimited partnerships where the liability of owners leads to the alignment of both parties' interests. In practice, for the protection of creditors (esp. banks) companies with limited liability of ownership often abide by stricter financial reporting rules than unlimited companies (*Eierle* (2004), p. 45).

According to *Page* (1984), the concentration of ownership and the extent of the interest of non-director shareholders is an important issue when assessing the appropriateness of reporting requirements for private firms. He shows that the control of small companies in the United Kingdom is highly concentrated and mainly in the hands of directors (*Page* (1984), p. 274). The **separation of ownership and control** can be assessed by criteria, such as ownership share held by management, transferability of shares, and number of shareholders (*Bollen* (1996), p. 53). The key issue of using this criterion for the differentiation of financial reporting requirements is that, in comparison to firms with outside managers and anonymous shareholders (i.e. public companies), different relationships exist among the stakeholders (such as managers, owners, and banks) of firms with owner-managers and a small number of shareholders (i.e. private companies). Therefore, the role of accounting information differs between these two types of companies, which could hence result in different financial reporting requirements (*Bollen* (1996), p. 51).

Following the general reasoning applied on the abovementioned criterion, companies can also be classified by means of their **public accountability**. The possibility of anonymous participation in a company through publicly acquirable equity or debt instruments thereby serves as the differentiator between publicly accountable and non-publicly accountable entities (NPAEs). Following the Canadian model (*Haller/Eierle* (2004a), p. 1840), the *IASB* defines the scope of the IFRS for SMEs according to the criterion of public accountability. IFRS for SMEs Paragraph 1.2 defines the eligible companies (SMEs) as entities that:

(a) do not have public accountability, and

(b) publish general purpose financial statements for external users. Examples of external users include owners who are not involved in managing the business, existing and potential creditors, and credit rating agencies.

According to IFRS for SMEs Paragraph 1.3, an entity has public accountability if:

(a) its debt or equity instruments are traded in a public market or it is in the process of issuing such instruments for trading in a public market (a domestic or foreign stock exchange or an over-the-counter market, including local and regional markets), or

(b) it holds assets in a fiduciary capacity for a broad group of outsiders as one of its primary businesses. This is typically the case for banks, credit unions, insurance companies, securities brokers/dealers, mutual funds, and investment banks.[15]

[15] After the completion of the Comprehensive Review of the IFRS for SMEs (2012-2014), the second sentence in Par. 1.3 (b) will be rephrased as follows: Most banks, credit unions, insurance companies, securities brokers/dealers, mutual funds, and investment banks will meet this second criterion.

Anonymous debt and equity investors are neither involved in managing the entity nor do they have the power to demand specific financial information for their investment decision-making. The same holds true for clients, customers, or members of companies, which act in a public fiduciary capacity (e.g. banks). For this reason, the users of publicly accountable entities' financial statements have different information needs as those of NPAEs (*International Accounting Standards Board* (2013), BC58).[16]

1.3.1.3 Definition used in this study

As presented in the two previous sections, the available catalogue of quantitative and qualitative criteria for defining and describing small and medium-sized, unlisted, private, and/or non-publicly accountable entities in order to distinguish them from (larger) listed and/or publicly-accountable entities is rich in examples. This study aims at defining the relevant entities in the most precise, non-arbitrary, and workable way. Due to the study's global perspective, the term's cross-national transferability and comprehensiveness are of equally high importance. For these reasons, the term **'private firms'** is chosen. Although this term may be confused with privately-owned enterprises in some jurisdictions, it can be regarded as the most comprehensible term in a global context. The definition of private firms that is used in this study is displayed in Figure 1-3.

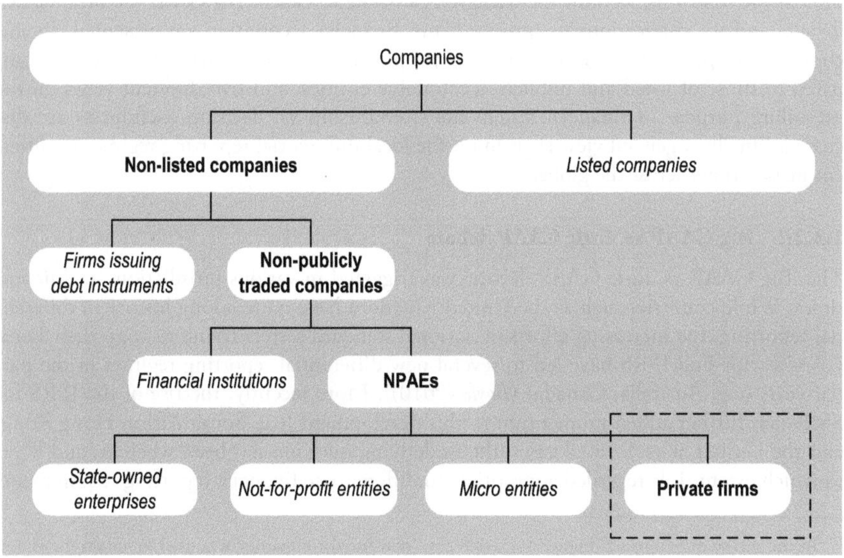

Figure 1-3: Definition of private firms in this study

Following the Canadian, US-American, and IFRS definition, this study defines private firms as entities that publish general purpose financial statements for external users except those entities with **public accountability** (listed companies and firms issuing debt in-

[16] Cf. for the different users' needs *International Accounting Standards Board* (2013), BC45.

struments (i.e. publicly traded companies), as well as financial institutions). Due to the study's specific research focus, three additional criteria are applied to further narrow down the private firms' definition. Owing to the incomparability of financial reporting requirements for state-owned enterprises and for not-for-profit entities, these two types of companies are excluded from the analyses in this study. Neither does this study aim at deriving statements on the accounting requirements of micro entities (e.g. sole proprietorships, sole traders), which are generally exempted from specific financial reporting provisions and generally do not publish general purpose financial statements for external users. Hence, the empirical results of this study do not apply to micro entities.[17] As quantitative financial reporting exemptions differ between countries, this study does not define any size-dependent thresholds to exclude micro entities from the scope of this study. Instead, micro entities are excluded from the scope of this study on the basis of country-specific financial reporting exemptions (if applicable).[18]

1.3.2 Differential reporting

The differentiation of financial reporting requirements for private firms has been discussed by various national standard-setters since several decades (*Haller/Eierle* (2004a), p. 1839) and has increased worldwide in the last twenty years (*Cordery/Baskerville* (2006), p. 22). In the following sections the background of the so-called 'Big GAAP vs. little GAAP debate' and its implications for private firms' financial accounting are presented. In this context, the specific users and users' needs of private firms' financial statements are compared to those of listed and publicly accountable entities, and two different views on the prevailing purpose of financial statements (stewardship vs. decision usefulness) are discussed. Finally, a general view is given on the local differential reporting regimes in different jurisdictions across the globe.

1.3.2.1 Big GAAP vs. little GAAP debate

The 'Big GAAP vs. little GAAP debate' was triggered in various jurisdictions at different times. While countries such as the United Kingdom have quite a long history of differential reporting, the increasing efforts of national standard-setters trying to align their Local GAAPs with Full IFRS have led to several new differential reporting regimes in the past ten years (e.g. Australia, Canada) (*Boyle* (2010)). More recently, the rise of the IFRS for SMEs has further added momentum to this development (e.g. South Africa, Hong Kong, and the United States). In all cases, the underlying question has been whether, and if yes to which extent, it is regarded appropriate to differentiate financial reporting requirements

---

[17] In the survey questions (cf. Figure A-1), the term 'non-listed companies' was used to obtain the widest possible response spectrum. In a second step, all information on the domestic financial reporting requirements of firms issuing debt instruments, financial institutions, state-owned enterprises, not-for-profit entities, and micro entities was eliminated from the answers.

[18] In Germany, for example, sole traders are exempted from all legal obligations to keep records if turnover does not exceed € 500,000 and net profit is not higher than € 50,000 in two consecutive years (§ 241a HGB). In the UK, all businesses are required to keep accounting records for taxation purposes but specific financial reporting measurement and disclosure requirements only apply to companies, not to sole traders or unlimited partnerships (*Nobes/Parker* (2012), p. 342).

between private and listed firms or small, medium-sized, and large companies, respectively.

The **proponents** of differential reporting claim that the users and users' needs of private firms' financial statements differ significantly from those of listed companies, which should therefore be reflected in different accounting purposes and different sets of accounting standards (*American Institute of Certified Public Accountants* (2013), p. 6). Furthermore, they criticize the inadequate level of accounting burdens imposed on small businesses and draw their conclusions from an analysis of the cost-benefit trade-off (*Consultative Committee of Accountancy Bodies* (1994)). The two main **arguments against** differential reporting are the lack of comparability and the conceptual inconsistencies, which arise from the differentiation of financial reporting regulation (*Carsberg et al.* (1985), p. 91–94).[19] In jurisdictions such as the United Kingdom, where the preparation of all financial statements must follow a general principle such as to present *a true and fair view* of the underlying economic transactions, it is hard to explain how this objective can be equally achieved by applying different sets of accounting standards (*Evans et al.* (2005), p. 36). In order to avoid this problem, a substantial differentiation in financial reporting normally goes along with a differentiation of the underlying accounting principles, which can thereafter justify the differences in accounting regulation.

By addressing the question of differential reporting, one can differentiate between the following three alternative models (*Maingot/Zeghal* (2006), p. 514):

- single set of GAAP without exclusions,
- single set of GAAP with exclusions from standards and/or disclosures for certain entities, and
- two sets of GAAP (big GAAP and little GAAP).

The extent of differential reporting can thus vary from minor simplifications and disclosure exemptions (e.g. UK FRSSE vs. UK GAAP) to fundamental differences in recognition and measurement criteria (e.g. IFRS for SMEs vs. Full IFRS).

One key question, which largely determines all country-specific discussions on differential reporting, is which starting point should be chosen for the local companies' financial reporting regulation. While in Germany accounting rules are generally designed for all businessmen alike (§ 238 ff. HGB) and further sophisticated only for corporate enterprises with limited liability of ownership (§ 264 ff. HGB),[20] the US model follows a top-down approach where generally accepted accounting principles (GAAP) are primarily tailored for listed companies.

---

[19] Cf. *Evans et al.* (2005), p. 32–34, and *Janssen/Gronewold* (2010) for an analysis of the conceptual inconsistencies in the IFRS for SMEs.

[20] Cf. *Eierle* (2005) for more details on differential reporting in Germany.

1.3.2.2 Different users and users' needs

> *"Financial statements should be helpful to the intended users in making decisions. Choices about accounting standards should be based on the information needs of those users."*
>
> (*Abdel-Khalik/Collins* (1983), p. 1)

Although the above quoted statement is self-evident, the realization of such thoughts in national or international financial reporting regulation is tougher than it seems. Firstly, it is necessary to **identify the primary users** of the respective firms' financial statements. Thereafter, their specific information needs have to be analyzed. Unfortunately, comprehensive research on the users and users' needs of private firms' financial statements is still fragmentary (*Evans et al.* (2005), p. 29), and as most prior research only looked at single user groups in separate jurisdictions at different points in time, little information is available on the common information needs of various external user groups worldwide (*Schiebel* (2007), p. 11). Furthermore, the conclusions, which have been drawn from prior research, are mixed and sometimes contradictory.[21]

In an early US study from *Mosso* (1981), financial statement users are of the opinion that users' needs are the same for small and large companies whereas Certified Public Accountants (CPAs) hold the opposite opinion (*Mosso* (1981)). Disregarding these inconsistencies, it has been fairly well documented that **bank lenders** can be regarded as the primary user group of (small) private firms (*Nair/Rittenberg* (1983), p. 10). Apart from the purpose of borrowing, financial statements of private firms are prepared mainly for management information (*Collis/Jarvis* (2000), p. vi; *Abdel-Khalik/Collins* (1983), p. 1) and taxation purposes (*Sian/Roberts* (2009)).

While listed companies particularly provide financial information to a large number of anonymous equity and debt investors, which are generally not able to demand specially tailored reports and have to rely on publicly available GAAP information, some of the primary users of private firms' financial statements are in a more influential position. This leads to the argument that GAAP for private firms might be less important for external users than GAAP for listed companies. Nevertheless, *Jarvis* (1996) points out that the lack of observable market prices for small and medium-sized companies means that their external parties have to rely even more on GAAP information than those of listed companies who can use actual market data (*Jarvis* (1996), p. 27). He thus stresses the importance of private firms' financial reporting information to **external users** and cautions against its oversimplification.

Compared to the above listed researchers, the *IASB* defines the primary external users of the **IFRS for SMEs** in a broader way and names the following **five user groups** (*International Accounting Standards Board* (2013), BC80):

- *"banks that make loans to SMEs,*
- *vendors that sell to SMEs and use SMEs' financial statements to make credit and pricing decisions,*

---

[21] Cf. *Stainbank* (2010) and *Göbel/Kornmeier* (2007) for a comprehensive literature review.

- *credit rating agencies and others that use SMEs' financial statements to rate SMEs,*
- *customers of SMEs that use SMEs' financial statements to decide whether to do business,*
- *SMEs' shareholders that are not also managers of their SMEs."*

Although *Cole et al.* show in a study from 2009 that, apart from investors and analysts, suppliers, competitors, customers and consultants are also important user groups of non-publicly traded companies (*Cole et al.* (2009), p. 1), as a rule, **business partners** do not frequently look at private firms' financial statements. In a UK study on the use of financial statements of small companies conducted by *Page* in 1984, only 9% of the respondents would use the financial statements of a new business contact to assess creditworthiness and only 24% had referred to the financial statements of a business contact within the last year (*Page* (1984), p. 279). Regarding employees, more attention is generally given to specially tailored reports (*Jarvis* (1996), p. 21).

As shareholders of small and medium-sized private firms are likely to dispose of other information channels besides financial reporting and as external equity financing is generally more prevalent in larger companies, *Kirsch/Meth* (2007) suggest that the information needs of bank lenders are most relevant for SMEs (*Kirsch/Meth* (2007), p. 9).[22] This view is confirmed by the findings of several **empirical studies.**[23] According to a large-scale executive survey[24] in the Berlin area in 2007, shareholders, tax authorities, as well as bank lenders are by far the most important user groups of the individual financial statements of German medium-sized companies (*Kajüter et al.* (2007), p. 1880). Similarly, Swiss SMEs[25] consider shareholders and bank lenders as significantly more important user groups than other creditors, business partners, employees, and customers (*Stiftung für Fachempfehlungen zur Rechnungslegung/Institut für Rechnungswesen und Controlling der Universität Zürich* (2009), p. 27). In line, a survey[26] among more than 20,000 European SMEs in six countries, 80% of the respondents stated that banks belong to the three main users of their company's financial statements, followed by tax authorities (71%), shareholders (52%), and management (44%) (*Mazars* (2008), p. 9).

Having identified **bank lenders** as one of the primary user groups of private firms' financial statements, the question is whether their specific **information needs** significantly differ from those of equity and debt investors that use listed firms' financial information. The *American Accounting Association's Financial Accounting Standards Committee* doubt

[22] Cf. for more details *Meth* (2007), p. 37ff.

[23] Cf. *ASCG et al.* (2008), p. 2, and *Evans et al.* (2005), p. 28ff., for an overview of these studies.

[24] The basic population of the survey included 934 companies located in the metropolitan area of Berlin, Germany, which met both of the following two criteria in 2006: turnover of more than € 5 mill. and number of employees between 50 and 500. In total, 107 surveys were completed (11.4%). Cf. *Kajüter et al.* (2007), p. 1878.

[25] SMEs are defined as companies with a number of employees between 20 and 500.

[26] The basic population of the survey included 20,225 not publicly accountable companies (no subsidiary companies) located in Germany, the United Kingdom, France, Italy, Spain and the Netherlands, which had an average number of employees between 20 and 499. In total, 1,593 companies completed the survey (7.9%). Cf. *Kajüter et al.* (2008), p. 594f.

that external users of small businesses' financial statements perceive their needs to be substantially different from decision makers who deal with larger companies and refer to the lack of empirical evidence in this field of research (*American Accounting Association's Financial Accounting Standards Committee* (2006), p. 180). As opposed to this, the *Private Company Financial Reporting Task Force* of the *American Institute of Certified Public Accountants* (AICPA) identifies distinctly different needs of US unlisted entities' constituents, including external users and concludes that US GAAP does not adequately meet the specific users' needs of private firms (*American Institute of Certified Public Accountants* (2013), p. 6)

Following the latter thoughts, the *IASB* justifies the development of the IFRS for SMEs with the different information needs of private firms' primary users and provides the following **examples** (*International Accounting Standards Board* (2013), BC45):

"users of financial statements of SMEs may have greater interest in

- *short-term cash flows,*
- *liquidity,*
- *balance sheet strength,*
- *in the historical trends of profit or loss, and*
- *in interest coverage*

than they do in

- *information that is intended to assist in making forecasts of an entity's long-term cash flows, profit or loss and value."*

The wording (*"may have"*) indicates that the assumed differences between the primary users' needs of private and listed firms' financial statements (i.e. between IFRS for SMEs and Full IFRS) have not been sufficiently studied yet. For this reason, the IASB was criticized for not preparing serious worldwide empirical research on that specific topic before issuing the IFRS for SMEs (*Schiebel* (2007), p. 2).

Besides the potentially different users and users' needs of private firms' financial statements, the IASB also considered differences in the level of financial resources and accounting expertise when developing the IFRS for SMEs. Knowing that small entities have fewer financial resources and less accounting expertise than large corporations, **cost-benefit-considerations** can be regarded as the second pillar of the Board's judgement on the nature and the degree of differences between Full IFRS and IFRS for SMEs (*International Accounting Standards Board* (2013), BC46).

Studies on the non-compliance with GAAP have shown that departures from GAAP can also indicate the lack of relevance of certain financial reporting standards for the users of private firms' financial statements and may identify inappropriate accounting burdens imposed on small businesses (*Nair/Rittenberg* (1983), p. 14). *Campbell* (1984) finds that loan officers do not utilize information on earnings per share or deferred taxes (*Campbell* (1984), p. 338), which suggests that these accounting standards in public company GAAP may be less relevant to external users of private company financial statements under certain conditions (*American Accounting Association's Financial Accounting Standards Committee* (2006), p. 187).

1.3.2.3 Stewardship vs. decision-usefulness

If the primary users of private and listed firms' financial statements are not the same, and if their specific information needs differ, too, as a consequence, different purposes for the preparation of private and listed firms' financial statements must exist. In financial accounting research, two main theoretical constructs have been identified as prevalent purposes of financial reporting: stewardship and decision-usefulness.

The stewardship (also accountability) purpose of financial reporting is closely linked to the **relationship between principal and agent.**[27] According to *Coase* (1937), a corporation can be regarded as a 'nexus of contracts' designed to minimize contracting costs. Following the idea of a company as an 'alliance of various economic agents', *Jensen/Meckling* (1976) define an agency relationship as *"a contract under which one or more persons (the principal(s)) engage another person (the agent) to perform some service on their behalf which involves delegating some decision making authority to the agent"* (*Jensen/Meckling* (1976), p. 308).

Over the course of this contracting relationship, the problem of information asymmetry arises. This means that the agent acquires, either before (i.e. 'adverse selection')[28] or during his service (i.e. 'moral hazard')[29], an information advantage, of which the principal does not necessarily take any notice. If both parties are utility maximizers, the agent will probably use this information advantage to increase his own benefits and will thereby not always act in the best interest of the principal (*Jensen/Meckling* (1976), p. 308). Especially if assuming incomplete contracts (*Fama/Jensen* (1983b), p. 304) and bounded rationality (*Simon* (1976), p. 61ff.), the agent is likely to exploit the principal (so-called 'hold up') (*Williamson* (1975), p. 20ff.). The resulting efficiency losses are labeled 'agency costs'[30] and consist of monitoring and bonding costs and the residual loss (*Jensen/Meckling* (1976), p. 308).

Financial reporting can be regarded as one instrument to control and minimize agency costs and thereby serves a so-called stewardship purpose. *Gjesdal* (1981) illustrates that a principal's incentive to monitor management's actions with respect to the control and use of firm resources creates a **stewardship demand for information** (*American Accounting Association's Financial Accounting Standards Committee* (2006), p. 184f.). In fact, due to its universal applicability, stewardship has long been seen as the *"social and organizational backbone of accounting"* (*Ijiri* (1975), p. 32).[31]

From the 1960s onwards, a second theoretical concept significantly grew in importance (*Maingot/Zeghal* (2006), p. 517) and can by now be considered as the prevailing account-

---

[27] Cf. for the basic Principal-Agent-Model *Rees* (1985).
[28] Cf. *Akerlof* (1970).
[29] Cf. *Ng* (1978).
[30] Cf. *Fama/Jensen* (1983a).
[31] Cf. for a historical analysis of the stewardship purpose in the United States *Zeff* (2013), p. 264–276.

ing purpose in financial reporting: the idea of **decision-useful information** (also valuation-useful information) (*Zeff* (2013), p. 276).[32] By focusing on the needs of investors, financial statements should thereafter *"provide financial information about the reporting entity that is useful to existing and potential investors, lenders and other creditors in making decisions about providing resources to the entity."* (*IFRS Foundation* (2010), OB2). While the decision-usefulness purpose particularly requires **forward-looking information** (i.e. the estimation of future cash flows and fair value accounting), which can improve a report's relevance for the subjective evaluation of a firm's performance (*Shivakumar* (2013), p. 379), it necessarily lacks reliability and trustworthiness. In comparison, the stewardship purpose is best served when financial statements provide **'hard' information**, which is created in a way that *"it is difficult for people to disagree"* (*Ijiri* (1975), p. 36).

When it comes to the 'Big GAAP vs. little GAAP debate' and the topic of differential reporting for private firms, one question that emerges is whether the relative importance of the stewardship and the decision-usefulness purpose varies between the preparation of private and listed firms' financial statements (*American Accounting Association's Financial Accounting Standards Committee* (2006), p. 184). According to the *UK Accounting Standards Board* (2004),[33]

> *"for most **smaller entities**, it may be appropriate for greater emphasis to be given to the need for financial statements to show the results of the **stewardship** or accountability of management. There is no active market in smaller entities' shares and thus members and users are not making day by day economic decisions to buy, sell or hold the shares. They tend rather to use the information as an annual check. Therefore the IASB should give more emphasis to stewardship when developing standards which are designed to fit the needs of users of SME financial statements."*
>
> (*UK Accounting Standards Board* (2004), p. 3)

Contrary to this opinion, the *American Accounting Association's Financial Accounting Standards Committee* (2006), p. 186, claims that the stewardship objective is not the key distinguishing factor for private companies' financial statement users and does therefore not support the idea of separate GAAP for private firms.

From an **agency-theoretic perspective**, there is a stewardship demand for information from users of both private and listed firms' financial statements. However, the respective agency-relationships differ in importance. The prevailing agency-relationship in the context of listed firms is between shareholders and managers. In private firms the number of owners is normally much smaller (*Bollen* (1996), p. 53) and the separation of ownership and control may be considerably less relevant, since major shareholders often belong to the management board of the company (*Keasey/Watson* (1993), p. 40).

In conclusion, in most private firms there is no owner-related agency conflict (*Fülbier/Gassen* (2010), p. 23). Instead, the information asymmetry problem mostly arises between the owner(-manager) and the creditor. Especially in case of limited liability companies, the owner(-manager) has incentives to engage in opportunistic activities at the

[32] On the contrary, the stewardship purpose has rather receded into background. Cf. *Zeff* (2013), p. 313.

[33] Cf. for a similar rationale *Fearnley/Hines* (2007), p. 404.

expense of other factor suppliers such as bank lenders (*Bollen* (1996), p. 54). In order to control and minimize the resulting agency costs, financial reporting can play an important role in debt contracting (*Shivakumar* (2013), p. 368–372). As bank lenders have been identified as the most important user group of private firms' financial statements, the **stewardship demand** for information in **private firms** mainly results from the **information needs of creditors.**

Considering the fact that both financial statement users of private and listed companies give rise to a stewardship demand for information in general, there is little evidence that this purpose might be more important for one group's financial reporting than for the other. Nonetheless, there might be a significantly higher demand for decision-useful information among the users of listed companies' financial statements than it is the case for private firms. While capital market investors require forward-looking information for the purpose of buying, selling, and holding shares in listed companies on a daily basis, bank lenders of private firms do not put so much emphasis on valuation issues, but focus more on the solvency and interest-coverage of their clients. This is due to their limited participation in the debtor's firm value growth.[34] This leads to the conclusion that creditors' relatively smaller demand for decision-useful information might result in a relatively higher importance of the stewardship purpose in private firms' financial statements.

1.3.2.4 Examples of differential reporting

Several decades before the IFRS for SMEs was issued in 2009, differential reporting had already been widely applied by various jurisdictions on a local level (*Haller/Eierle* (2004a), p. 1839). In 2003, the IASB surveyed a group of 40 national standard-setters on the topic 'GAAP for SMEs'. From 28 responding countries, ten answered that they had a separate set of national GAAP for SMEs, and another five countries stated that they were in the process of developing separate 'SME GAAP' (*Pacter* (2004), p. 119).

In the **United Kingdom**, prior to the Companies Act 1981, all companies were governed by identical financial reporting requirements, regardless of size, industry, or public interest. Small companies only benefited from disclosure exemptions in isolated cases (*Eierle* (2004), p. 258).[35] The Companies Act 1981 can thus be regarded as the first step in the development of little GAAP in the UK (*Jarvis/Collis* (2003), p. 7). Although the issue of differential reporting had been repeatedly discussed in the 1980s (*Carsberg et al.* (1985)), it took the UK Accounting Standards Board (ASB) until the year 1997 to develop the first separate financial reporting framework for small businesses (Financial Reporting Standard for Smaller Entities (FRSSE)).[36] Five years before, the *Consultative Committee of Accounting Bodies* had been asked to analyze the applicability and relevance of UK accounting standards for smaller entities and was thereafter charged with the development of appropriate differentiation criteria. The committee concluded that the current form of financial reporting did not best serve the needs of certain users and thus recommended a general

[34] Cf. *Basu* (1997) for the asymmetric loss function of creditors.

[35] Cf. *Eierle* (2004), p. 233ff., for a comprehensive review of the history of financial reporting regulation in the United Kingdom.

[36] Cf. *Financial Reporting Council* (2013) for the most recent version of the FRSSE.

exemption from UK accounting standards (except certain 'core standards') for smaller companies (*Consultative Committee of Accountancy Bodies* (1994), Section 10.3).

After several redeliberations, the **FRSSE** was derived from UK accounting standards by using the same or simplified measurement bases. Its primary goal therefore was to reduce disclosure requirements (*Jarvis/Collis* (2003), p. 9). The definitions and accounting treatments remained consistent with the requirements of UK company legislation and the applied recognition and measurement criteria did not significantly differ from UK accounting standards. According to a survey carried out by *Collis* in 2008, 69% of the eligible small companies[37] use the FRSSE (*Collis* (2008), p. 37).

When the **IFRS for SMEs** was developed in the mid-2000s, the countries of the European Union intensely debated whether harmonization of global financial reporting standards for SMEs would be reasonable or not. While French and German SMEs opposed the new standard vehemently, 80 per cent of the British SMEs had no or only little difficulty in the reconciliation of their financial statements from UK accounting standards or FRSSE to ED-IFRS for SMEs (*Association of Chartered Certified Accountants* (2008), p. 8). Since the European Commission has not recognized IFRS for SMEs as an eligible accounting framework for European private firms yet, the ASB had to go its own way regarding the adoption of IFRS for SMEs in the United Kingdom.

Options available	FRSSE	FRS 102 (based on IFRS for SMEs)	EU-IFRS
Entities eligible for small companies regime	✓	✓	✓
Entities not small and not required to apply EU-IFRS		✓	✓
Entities required to apply EU-IFRS			✓

Table 1-5: Three-tier financial reporting system in the United Kingdom (from 2015)[38]

In 2010, the Accounting Standards Boards of the United Kingdom and the Republic of Ireland agreed on a comprehensive reform of their common financial reporting system. According to the initial draft,[39] the UK accounting standards should have been withdrawn completely and replaced by IFRS for SMEs (*Boyle* (2010), p. 58). Due to the IFRS for SMEs' non-compliance with EU law and the massive criticism received by UK preparers and users, the new UK GAAP (**FRS 102**) is still based on IFRS for SMEs but differs from

[37] The definition of a small company is contained in sections 382 and 383 of the Companies Act 2006. The qualifying conditions are met by a company in a year in which it does not exceed two or more of the following criteria: turnover of £6,500,000, balance sheet total of £3,260,000 and average number of employees of 50 (*Financial Reporting Council* (2013), Appendix I).

[38] Cf. *Institute of Chartered Accountants in England and Wales* (2013), p. 2.

[39] Cf. *UK Accounting Standards Board* (2010).

the IASB standard in some significant respects (e.g. revaluation of tangible and intangible fixed assets, capitalization of borrowing costs) (*Institute of Chartered Accountants in England and Wales* (2013), p. 3). The new three-tier accounting system, which is applicable in the United Kingdom and the Republic of Ireland from 1 January 2015, is displayed in Table 1-5.

All in all, there is a strong case for differential reporting between small companies, larger unlisted, and quoted companies on the basis of their different users in the United Kingdom (*Jarvis* (2003), p. 80).

In **Australia**, a form of differential reporting has been incorporated in Accounting Standards since the early 1990s (*Australian Accounting Standards Board* (2010), BC2). At the core of this differential reporting regime is the **reporting entity concept**, which defines reporting entities as:

> *"entit[ies] in respect of which it is reasonable to expect the existence of users who rely on the entity's general purpose financial statement for information that will be useful to them for making and evaluating decisions about the allocation of resources. A reporting entity can be a single entity or a group comprising a parent and all of its subsidiaries."*
>
> (*Australian Accounting Standards Board* (2012), p. 55)

Reporting requirements thereafter differ between reporting entities, which prepare general purpose financial statements, and non-reporting entities that prepare special purpose financial statements. In July 2010, the Australian Accounting Standards Board (AASB) released *AASB 1053 Application of Tiers of Australian Accounting Standards* to implement 'Stage 1' of its revised differential reporting regime (*Deloitte Touche Tohmatsu* (2014a), p. 1). For the first time, a second tier of **Australian Accounting Standards (AAS)** was introduced for reporting entities without public accountability. Previously, all reporting entities, regardless of public or private, had to comply with 'Full' Australian Accounting Standards (AAS), which have been largely converged with Full IFRS since 2005. While it first appeared that the AASB was moving towards full implementation of IFRS for SMEs (*Deloitte Touche Tohmatsu* (2014a), p. 1), the second tier eventually includes all AAS' measurement bases and only differs from AAS due to **reduced disclosure requirements (RDR)**, which are highly similar to those granted by the IFRS for SMEs (*Australian Accounting Standards Board* (2010), p. 6).

By introducing a two-tier financial reporting system, the Board's primary goal was to reduce the burden of financial reporting for those non-publicly accountable entities, which had previously been obliged to apply 'Full' AAS in the preparation of general purpose financial statements (*Australian Accounting Standards Board* (2010), BC19). The adoption of IFRS for SMEs was seen as a retrograde step, as Australia had already adopted Full IFRS (*Australian Accounting Standards Board* (2010), BC73(g)). Although the AASB continues to monitor further changes in the IFRS for SMEs and still considers the possibility of adopting IFRS for SMEs in the future, the AASB has determined that the IFRS for SMEs is yet not suitable as a second tier of financial reporting requirements in the Australian context (*Meade* (2012), p. 3).

The starting signal for differential reporting in **Canada** was in 1999, when the Canadian Institute of Chartered Accountants (CICA) proposed a single set of Canadian GAAP with exclusions from certain standards for small business enterprises (SBEs) (*Canadian Institute of Chartered Accountants* (1999)). Since 2002, all non-publicly accountable entities, which obtain the unanimous consent of their owners, have been exempted from the application of certain accounting rules that do not meet their needs (*Maingot/Zeghal* (2006), p. 515). In the Canadian setting, the pace of **harmonization with US GAAP** had been an important contributing factor to the development of differential reporting. While in the US bylaw standards are only applicable for public companies, in Canada federal and provincial statutory regulations require all companies to prepare financial statements in accordance with Canadian GAAP (*Mersereau* (2002), p. 1). The Canadian differential reporting model thus uses the cost-benefit-constraint in the conceptual framework to justify differences in accounting treatments (*Accounting Standards Board of Canada* (2007), p. 7).

Regardless of the partial relief given to private firms in terms of accounting exemptions, many representatives of the Accounting Standards Board of Canada (AcSB) argued that Canadian GAAP did not sufficiently meet the needs of private enterprises (*Accounting Standards Board of Canada* (2007), A16). For this reason, the AcSB began consultations on the future direction of the Canadian accounting standard-setting process in 2004 and reconsidered its previous harmonization strategy with US GAAP (*Accounting Standards Board of Canada* (2014)). The survey of *Maingot/Zeghal* (2006) illustrates that the **Canadian standards** were regarded as **too complex** and **too costly**, and that certain accounting topics were of little relevance for the users of private firms' financial statements. The AcSB thus approved its new strategic plan and noted that *"one size does not fit all"*, and decided to develop separate financial reporting strategies for publicly accountable enterprises, private companies, and not-for-profit organizations (*Accounting Standards Board of Canada* (2006), p. 1). The Canadian public accountability criterion later served as a role model for the SME-definition in the IFRS for SMEs (*Haller/Eierle* (2004a), p. 1840).

Since 2011, Canadian private firms have been provided a two-tier financial reporting system. Either they choose to apply Full IFRS or they apply a set of made-in-Canada financial reporting standards (i.e. the **Accounting Standards for Private Enterprises** (**ASPE**)). Although the ASPE might not differ materially from IFRS for SMEs in some aspects, the adoption of IFRS for SMEs without alteration was eventually denied. All in all, international comparability was regarded as an issue of minor importance for the vast majority of Canadian private enterprises as the external users of their financial statements (esp. bank lenders) are primarily domestic (*Accounting Standards Board of Canada* (2007), p. 72).

South Africa can be considered as a special case for differential reporting, particularly regarding its **role model** function for the African continent and the early adoption of IFRS for SMEs. The development of differential reporting in Africa began in 2000, when the South African Institute of Chartered Accountants (SAICA) issued a discussion paper, which included proposals for simplified disclosure requirements for companies that are closely held and controlled by owners and whose financial statements are only available to a limited number of users (*Stainbank* (2010), p. 64).

Despite this initial impulse to develop differential reporting requirements, South African private companies were obliged to comply with a single set of South African GAAP that had been almost fully converged with Full IFRS by 2003 until 2007.[40] After the SAICA had already taken the IASB's DP *Preliminary Views on Accounting Standards for Small and Medium-sized Entities* as a template for its own exposure draft (ED 181) in 2004, South Africa adopted the IASB's **ED of an IFRS for SMEs** as a temporarily eligible financial reporting option[41] for private firms in 2007 (*Stainbank* (2010), p. 65). South Africa can therefore be regarded as the first country in the world that adopted IFRS for SMEs for local private firms. The main reason for this unusual development was the intended relief from the burden of Full IFRS (*Stainbank* (2010), p. 66) given the lack of local financial reporting standards for private firms. Shortly after the issuance of IFRS for SMEs in 2009, the ED-IFRS for SMEs was superseded by the final IASB standard, which was then approved by the South African Accounting Practices Board (APB) as the *Statement of GAAP for SMEs.*

Similar to the South African case, differential reporting in **Hong Kong** has also been triggered by the convergence of Local GAAP with Full IFRS. In 2001, the Hong Kong Institute of Certified Public Accountants (HKICPA) adopted the policy of achieving convergence of its standards with Full IFRS within five years. As a result, Hong Kong adopted Hong Kong Financial Reporting Standards (**HKFRS**) in 2005, which are almost identical[42] to Full IFRS (*Financial Standards Foundation* (2010), p. 1). In setting this convergence strategy, the HKICPA was aware of the fact that HKFRS would be more sophisticated than necessary for many smaller companies (*Hong Kong Institute of Certified Public Accountants* (2006), p. 4). Accordingly, a new simplified standard, the Small and Medium-sized Entity Financial Reporting Framework and Financial Reporting Standard (**SME-FRF&FRS**), mainly based on historical cost accounting, was adopted in the same year for certain smaller, non-publicly accountable entities[43] (*Financial Standards Foundation* (2010), p. 2).

One year after the issuance of IFRS for SMEs, the HKICPA introduced a slightly modified[44] version of IFRS for SMEs named Hong Kong Financial Reporting Standard for Private Entities (**HKFRS for Private Entities**) as a reporting option for larger non-

40 South African GAAP ceased to exist in 2012 and was superseded by Full IFRS as issued by the IASB.

41 South African private firms can choose to comply either with Full IFRS or with IFRS for SMEs since 2007. Between 2007 and 2009, the ED IFRS for SMEs had been adopted until the final standard was released.

42 The HKFRS is a continuity of the Hong Kong Statements of Standard Accounting Practice (Local GAAP). In 2005, the Local GAAP was converged to IFRS word by word and renamed as HKFRS (i.e. equivalent to then IFRS). While HKFRS have been converged with IFRS, differences remain primarily in respect of transitional provisions.

43 HK SME-FRF&FRS is applicable for entities without public accountability that meet the following criteria: Hong Kong companies satisfy the criteria under Section 141D of the Companies Ordinance or do not exceed any two of the following thresholds: total annual revenue of Hong Kong $ 50 million, total assets of Hong Kong $ 50 million, 50 employees.

44 Apart from the replacement of the term 'SMEs' by 'Private Entities', the HKFRS for Private Entities has been modified in the area of tax and deferred tax accounting (*Hong Kong Institute of Certified Public Accountants* (2010b), p. 3).

publicly accountable entities (*Hong Kong Institute of Certified Public Accountants* (2010a), p. 4). Since 2010, private firms that meet certain criteria[45] can therefore choose between three different sets of accounting rules for the purpose of financial reporting (HKFRS, SME-FRF&FRS and HKFRS for Private Entities).

Over the past four decades, the 'Big GAAP vs. little GAAP debate' might have been nowhere as intensive as in the **United States of America**. Despite the general consensus that this issue – as such – is of great importance, there are **fundamental disagreements** about how the differentiation of financial reporting regulation should be shaped (*Henry/Holzmann* (2012), p. 87). While the American Institute of Certified Public Accountants (AICPA) recommended in 1976 that the same measurement principles should be applied to the general-purpose financial statements of all entities (*American Accounting Association Committee on International Accounting Operations and Education 1976-1978* (1978), p. 8), only a few years later the same organization considered certain US accounting standards as particularly burdensome for small non-public businesses (*American Institute of Certified Public Accountants* (1983), p. 2). The Financial Accounting Standards Board (FASB) was therefore recommended to strive for simplicity in accounting standards setting and to analyze in which cases differential disclosures and measurements are appropriate (*Knutson/Wichmann* (1985), p. 387f.).

Even though **US GAAP** had been repeatedly criticized for being too sophisticated and burdensome in the context of unlisted firms, no steps were taken to develop a specific 'little GAAP' until 2005. This is mainly due to the fact that US unlisted firms are not obliged to comply with any statutory regulations when preparing financial statements for external users. In case of voluntary disclosure, unlisted firms can choose to apply the Other Comprehensive Basis of Accounting (**OCBOA**), which is a cash-based, non-GAAP accounting option.[46] While OCBOA is a purely US-American accounting system, US GAAP has been increasingly influenced by IFRS since 2002. At their joint meeting in Norwalk, USA, the FASB and the IASB declared:

> *"to use their best efforts to (a) make their existing financial reporting standards fully compatible as soon as is practicable and (b) to coordinate their future work programs to ensure that once achieved, compatibility is maintained."*
>
> (*Financial Accounting Standards Board/International Accounting Standards Board* (2002), p. 1)

Although in recent years the convergence process between US GAAP and IFRS has slowed down, there are numerous accordances between both accounting systems. In 2008, the AICPA governing Council recognized the IASB as an accounting standard-setting body and hence provided US private firms the additional option to prepare generally accepted financial statements in conformity with either **Full IFRS** or **IFRS for SMEs** (*Fitzpatrick/Frank* (2009), p. 51).

---

45 Companies incorporated under Hong Kong Companies Ordinance are required to prepare financial statements using HKFRS unless they satisfy the criteria under Section 141D (i.e. non-public accountability and size test) for using HKFRS for Private Entities or SME-FRF&SME-FRS.

46 Cf. *Ratcliffe* (2003) for more details on OCBOA.

Despite these two additional accounting options, US private firms use IFRS-based standards only in very rare circumstances (*American Institute of Certified Public Accountants* (2011), p. 25). The discussion on **'US GAAP for Private Companies'** has therefore been reinflamed when a working group of the AICPA published a report in 2005, in which it called for fundamental changes in the current US GAAP standard-setting process and proposed the development of separate GAAP for private enterprises based on concepts that are appropriate for the distinctly different needs of their financial statements' preparers and users (*American Institute of Certified Public Accountants* (2005), p. 6). The **Blue-Ribbon Panel** (BRP) thereafter specified these fundamental changes and advised the trustees of the Financial Accounting Foundation (FAF) to establish a separate standard-setting body for the purpose of appropriate private firms' financial reporting requirements (*Blue-Ribbon Panel on Standard Setting for Private Companies* (2011), p. 2). These recommendations led to an increasingly controversial debate among US standard-setters (i.e. FASB), certified public accountants (i.e. AICPA), and practitioners, in which some parties supported the idea of an independent private company accounting standards board (*Kamnikar et al.* (2012)), whereas others did still not see the need for differential reporting at all (*American Accounting Association's Financial Accounting Standards Committee* (2006)).

By 2014, a final solution to this issue has not been found and the opposing parties have not reached an agreement. While the FASB advocates the model of **modified US GAAP**, derived by the Private Company Council (PCC), the AICPA released a new *non-GAAP* set of accounting standards called 'Financial Reporting Framework for Small and Medium-sized Entities' (**FRF for SMEs**) in 2013 (*Pounder* (2013), p. 16). In view of the fact that IFRS for SMEs is an international financial reporting framework especially tailored for the needs of private firms (available for US private companies since 2009), external observers might be surprised by the rigid efforts of FASB and AICPA to develop further sets of local financial reporting standards for US private firms. The AICPA justifies the issuance of FRF for SMEs by stating that the framework will be more understandable and more useful than the IFRS for SMEs, because it is specially written for US entities and will be more in line with US tax law (*American Institute of Certified Public Accountants* (2013), 19).

The recent history of worldwide differential reporting regimes illustrates that national standard-setters in various local financial reporting environments have developed an increased **awareness of the differential financial reporting needs** of private firms and their financial statements' users. Especially the growing diffusion of Full IFRS and IFRS for SMEs has contributed to an ongoing discussion on differential reporting worldwide. The above described examples of differential reporting are summarized in Table 1-6.

Country	Differential financial reporting standard(s)	Established since
Australia	Australian Accounting Standards – Reduced Disclosure Requirements (RDR)	2010
Canada	Accounting Standards for Private Enterprises (ASPE)	2011
Hong Kong	Small and Medium-sized Entity Financial Reporting Framework and Financial Reporting Standard (SME-FRF & FRS)	2005
	Hong Kong Financial Reporting Standard for Private Entities (HKFRS for Private Entities)	2010
South Africa	IFRS for SMEs *(ED IFRS for SMEs)*	2009 *(2007-2009)*
United Kingdom	Financial Reporting Standard for Smaller Entities (FRSSE)	1997
	Financial Reporting Standard 102 (FRS102)	2015
United States	Other Comprehensive Basis of Accounting (OCBOA)	1970s
	IFRS for SMEs	2009
	Financial Reporting Framework for Small and Medium-sized Entities (FRF for SMEs)	2013
	(Modified US GAAP)	*(planned)*

Table 1-6: Examples of differential reporting

The next section displays different views on international accounting harmonization and presents an overview on the history of financial reporting's international harmonization, particularly focusing on the development of Full IFRS and IFRS for SMEs.

1.4 International accounting harmonization

1.4.1 Definitions and fundamentals

Before discussing the different arguments in favor and against international accounting harmonization, it is important to define the necessary vocabulary in a precise manner. Even though the terms 'harmonization', 'standardization', and 'convergence' are often used interchangeably, there are slight differences between them. *Tay/Parker* (1990) define harmonization as a movement away from total diversity and standardization as a movement towards uniformity. Harmony can thus be any point on the continuum between the two states of total diversity and uniformity (*Tay/Parker* (1990), p. 73). As this in-between state is hard to determine, it is practical to use the terms **'harmonization'** and **'standardization'** synonymously in this study. **'Convergence'** is a term that has particularly come into use in the context of narrowing the gap between a set of national accounting rules and IFRS (*Ball* (2006), p. 9). More recently, the term 'convergence' has especially been used when describing the process of approximation between US GAAP and IFRS. Consequently, convergence with IFRS describes the process of domestic accounting standards' (gradual) harmonization with IFRS. In contrast, IFRS adoption means that countries permit or require domestic companies to use accounting standards that are in full compliance with IFRS.

Before applying the term 'harmonization' in the context of international financial accounting research, it is necessary to further distinguish between the harmonization of accounting rules (**formal** (*de jure*) **harmonization**) and the harmonization of accounting practice (**material** (*de facto*) **harmonization**) (*van der Tas* (1988), p. 158; *Tay/Parker* (1990), p. 74). This is due to the fact that even in a state of total de jure harmony (i.e. single set of international GAAP), de facto harmony might not be achieved due the existence of overt or covert accounting options or due to non-compliance (*Nobes* (2006), p. 237). By contrast, de facto harmony can be achieved without de jure harmony when market forces persuade preparers from different countries to produce comparable English-language financial reports by applying common recognition and measurement practices (*Nobes/Parker* (2012), p. 81). The overall goal of institutions promoting international harmonization of financial reporting is to achieve de facto harmony through de jure harmony accompanied by effective enforcement mechanisms.

Even though the advantages of accounting practices' international harmonization might be as self-evident as the universal use of the English language or a single currency, **opponents** to international accounting harmonization argue that harmonization efforts are unnecessary as they do not believe that a state of harmony can ever be achieved in the field of financial reporting. According to *Goeltz* (1991):

> *"consistent worldwide accounting standards are virtually certain to remain an elusive goal" because "the record of domestic standard setting bodies [...] does not offer much hope that the infinitely more difficult task of gaining international agreement can be achieved in any reasonable time period".*
>
> (*Goeltz* (1991), p. 85)

Although the record of the International Accounting Standards Committee (IASC) and its successor organization IASB has proved that a certain level of de jure harmony can be achieved on a global level by international agreements between various national parties, its net benefits are still questioned by researchers and national standard-setters alike.

In general agreement with the *"French resistance to IFRS adoption"* (*Godfrey/Chalmers* (2007), p. 5), *Hoarau* criticizes international accounting harmonization for the **predominance of the Anglo-Saxon accounting model** and the indifference to the economic, social, and cultural environment of national accounting systems (*Hoarau* (1995), p. 217).[47] *Fülbier/Gassen* provide empirical evidence on the fact that the financial accounting outcome of private firms (measured by the degree of income smoothness) differs significantly across the countries of the European Union (*Fülbier/Gassen* (2010)). They suggest that this difference is caused by **different accounting objectives** of the respective firms, which are again the result of different country-level governance infrastructures (esp. taxation, income distribution, and debt contracting) that shape the incentives of the firms' major contractual partners. The authors draw the conclusion that the necessary preconditions

[47] Cf. for similar critique *Briston* (1978) and *Samuels/Oliga* (1982).

for private firms' accounting harmonization are not yet met in the European Union (*Fülbier/Gassen* (2010), p. 6).

The **advantages** of international accounting harmonization are quite clear for listed firms, which provide their financial statements primarily to global equity and debt investors, from which they obtain most of their financial funding. Enhanced quality and international comparability of financial statements can thereby prevent investors to direct their investments to less efficient and productive companies just because they have problems to understand the financial statements of other companies in different jurisdictions and generally regard them as more risky (*Saudagaran* (2001), p. 32). Against this, the need for international financial reporting standards is less intuitive in the context of private firms. As they are primarily financed by domestic banks and do not necessarily have international recipients of their financial reports, the importance of a globally harmonized accounting system might be relatively low for private firms, as it influences only a small part of the overall national accounting function (*Briston* (1978), p. 120).

As globalization proceeds, however, the expanding **international trade and investment** flows brought about by multinational enterprises foster the demand for international accounting harmonization (*Choi/Mueller* (1978), p. 153) – both for listed and private firms. According to the *Summary Report* (2010) of the responses received to the European Commission's consultation on the IFRS for SMEs, the potential benefits of an international financial reporting system for private firms are (among others): expanded cross-border trade, increased international growth of companies, more foreign merger and acquisition activity, a lowering cost of capital, and a broadened capital base (all resulting from an enhanced international comparability of financial statements). On the other hand, duplicated reporting requirements, high setup costs, and the potential impairment of financial accounts' within-country comparability are seen as the most important impediments for international accounting harmonization in the context of EU private firms (*European Commission* (2010), p. 2).

In the end, the question is which types of private firms do really need internationally comparable financial statements and whether the predicted benefits do actually overcompensate the costs of harmonization, which may arise from the necessary adaptation of local governance infrastructures such as taxation, income distribution, and debt contracting. The debate on international accounting harmonization has meanwhile turned from whether there should be international accounting standards to what is the best way to achieve them (*Gernon et al.* (2001), p. 41).

1.4.2 Early attempts of harmonization

The pros and cons of international accounting harmonization have been discussed since the late 1950s (*Doupnik* (1987), p. 47). In a key note at the Seventh International Congress of Accountants in 1957, *Jacob Kraayenhof* was one of the first who formulated the need for international accounting harmonization and thereafter proposed the establishment of multinational accounting standard-setting committees (*Kraayenhof* (1960), p. 37). *Kraayenhof* supported the idea of eliminating some of the differences in accounting practice, but he did not advocate rigid uniformity. It took until 1966 to establish the first international institution that conducted cross-country research on accounting principles (*Choi/Bavishi* (1982), p. 161). The **Accountants' International Study Group** (AISG) was an association of accountancy bodies from Canada, the United Kingdom, and the United States, whose purpose was to study and report on accounting practices in the three countries. In the following eleven years, 20 studies were issued, mainly on financial reporting matters (*Nobes/Parker* (2012), p. 95).

The agreement of six European countries (Belgium, France, Germany, Italy, Luxembourg, and the Netherlands) to establish one common market in the 1957 Treaty of Rome marked the starting point for the growing European influence on international accounting harmonization in the following decades. In fact, the foundation of the London-based International Accounting Standards Committee (**IASC**) in 1973, the year the United Kingdom joined the European Community, can be regarded as an Anglo-Saxon counter-reaction to the Continental European accounting harmonization process that led to the two EU Accounting Directives in 1978 and 1983 (*Benston et al.* (2006), p. 229). Authorities in the United States, the United Kingdom, Canada, and Australia believed that their domestic standards were superior to those of Continental European countries and therefore wanted to take the lead in the international harmonization process (*Zeff* (2003), p. 2).

Other international organizations such as the **United Nations** and the Organization for Economic Cooperation and Development (**OECD**), which set up a permanent Working Group on Accounting Standards in 1979, also promoted the development of a common set of international financial reporting standards, but operated rather in a review and advisory capacity than to establish formal standards (*Doupnik* (1987), p. 48). The major milestones of early international accounting harmonization are displayed in Figure 1-4.

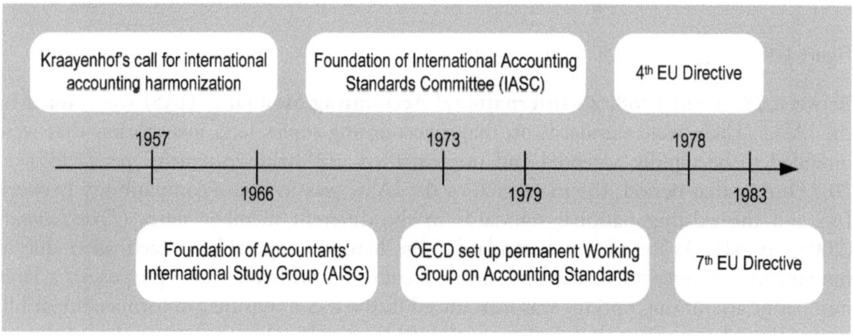

Figure 1-4: Milestones of early international accounting harmonization

1.4.3 Development of Full IFRS

At the 10th World Congress of Accountants in Sydney in 1972 the professional accountancy bodies of nine countries (United States, United Kingdom (jointly with the Republic of Ireland), Canada, Mexico, the Netherlands, France, Germany, Japan, and Australia) committed to use their best efforts to bring about adoption of International Accounting Standards (IAS) as their generally accepted national accounting principles (*Pacter* (2005),

p. 67). At that time, the purposes of the nine countries' national accounting systems differed rigorously from each other. On the one hand, the accounting standards from the United States, United Kingdom, Canada, the Netherlands, and Australia were primarily shaped for the information needs of investors. In the other countries (France, Germany, Japan, and Mexico) the national accounting systems were mainly driven by income tax law (*Zeff* (2003), p. 1). In view of this fact, it is not surprising that until the IASC was succeeded by the IASB in April 2001, every one of the nine countries still had its own national GAAP (*Pacter* (2005), p. 67).

Besides the continuing **persistence of local accounting systems** during its four decades long history, the IASC (later IASB) has proven to be the world's most important global standard-setter. While striving after a common set of internationally harmonized accounting standards, the IASC went through four phases from its foundation in 1973 to the present, which are displayed in Figure 1-5.

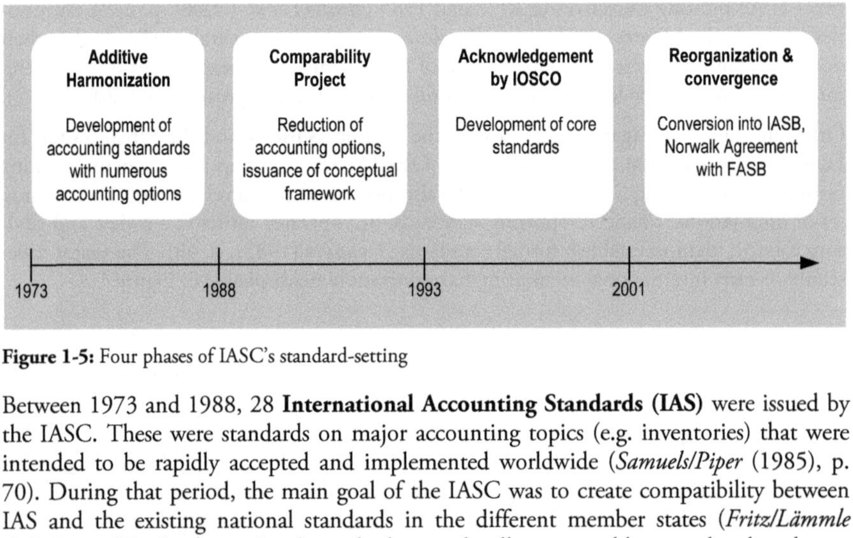

Figure 1-5: Four phases of IASC's standard-setting

Between 1973 and 1988, 28 **International Accounting Standards (IAS)** were issued by the IASC. These were standards on major accounting topics (e.g. inventories) that were intended to be rapidly accepted and implemented worldwide (*Samuels/Piper* (1985), p. 70). During that period, the main goal of the IASC was to create compatibility between IAS and the existing national standards in the different member states (*Fritz/Lämmle* (2003), p. 41). As the national standards were hardly comparable to each other due to fundamental differences in the underlying accounting principles (and purposes), a large number of accounting options was introduced in the IAS to ensure pro forma compatibility (additive harmonization) (*Pellens et al.* (2011), p. 88). Due to the parallel validity of different accounting measures, the Anglo-Saxon and the Continental European accounting philosophies were allowed to persist. The level of harmonization can albeit be regarded as low during that time.

By the end of the 1980s it had become evident that the large number of accounting options was an obstacle to the future enhancement of IAS and the IASC's status as the global standard-setter in financial reporting (*Nobes/Parker* (2012), p. 88). Especially the International Organization of Securities Commissions (**IOSCO**) and its most influential member, the United States Securities and Exchange Commission (**SEC**), were interested in promoting greater comparability of financial statements around the world and put pressure on the IASC to remove most of the options and specify in more detail how each standard is to be interpreted (*Zeff* (2003), p. 4). Following this advice, the IASC released ED 32 *Comparability of Financial Statements* in 1989 proposing an improved set of international accounting standards (*Purvis et al.* (1991), p. 25).

The **Comparability Project**, which was triggered two years before by the setup of a Steering Committee, led to the creation of the Framework (1989), which became the conceptual basis for all previous and future IAS. By means of the Framework's qualitative characteristics and underlying principles, all remaining inconsistencies between different IAS and the Framework were to be resolved (*Pellens et al.* (2011), p. 88). The major challenge was that for the first time all member countries had to be willing to cooperate with the IASC rather than promote their national interests. The success of the Comparability Project was highly dependent on the level of willingness to compromise, which was regarded as the most critical concern (*Purvis et al.* (1991), p. 39). Apart from the Framework, three more IAS were released between 1989 and 1993.

After several years of discussions over the removal of accounting options, ten revised standards (e.g. IAS 2, elimination of the LIFO method) were agreed on in 1993 to come into force in 1995 (*Nobes/Parker* (2012), p. 88). The IOSCO welcomed the revisions but called for further changes and for new IAS, which should then constitute a set of **core standards** that could be accepted for the financial reporting of companies with cross-border listings in all global capital markets (*Nobes/Parker* (2012), p. 89). In addition, IOSCO defined two more preconditions, which the IASC had to comply with: high quality standards that result in comparability, transparency and full disclosure, and rigorous interpretation and application of the standards (*Zeff* (2003), p. 5). In 2000, IOSCO finally accepted all IAS and recommended them to its members. Due to the strong interference by IOSCO and the SEC, the IAS had been tailor-made for the needs of global capital market investors, whereas the interests of private firms were not specifically considered in the standard-setting process.

The **acknowledgement by the IOSCO** gave worldwide IAS adoption enormous impetus. Furthermore, the IASC's efforts were boosted by the fact that the European Union had abandoned its goal of developing unique European accounting standards (*Epstein/Mirza* (2001), p. 21). In March 2000, the European Commission proposed a regulation that requires all parent companies that issue stocks or bonds on a regulated market in the European Union to prepare their consolidated financial statements in accordance with IAS by 2005. The 'IAS-Regulation' 1606/2002 was finally released in 2002.[48] Similarly, the IASC was optimistic that the SEC would allow IAS financial statements for cross-border listings on US stock exchanges sooner or later. However, a necessary precondition for such an IAS-friendly decision was that the IASC had to become a full-time, independent body whose members are chosen on the basis of their technical expertise, and which is supervised by a board of trustees composed of individuals representing the public interest (*Zeff* (2003), p. 7). Again, the SEC had essentially influenced the history of the IASC and brought about its reorganization and professionalization in 2001.

[48] Cf. for the Regulation (EC) No 1606/2002 *European Commission* (2002).

The IASC was restructured into the **International Accounting Standards Board (IASB)**, which is composed of twelve full-time and two part-time members, and subject to the oversight of the International Accounting Standards Committee Foundation (IASCF). The IASCF was a nineteen-member board of trustees that was renamed into IFRS Foundation in 2010. As a further manifestation of its reorientation the IASB decided to label all future standards as **International Financial Reporting Standards (IFRS)**. There is evidence to suggest that IAS were culturally different from IFRS as the IASC's standards were primarily shaped by Anglo-American countries, whereas IFRS have increasingly been influenced by Pan-European accounting traditions (*Ramanna/Sletten* (2009), p. 8).

According to former IASB member *Paul Pacter*, the mission of the standard-setter also changed importantly to one of convergence of global accounting standards (*Pacter* (2005), p. 71). In preparation of the SEC acceptance of IFRS for cross-border listings, the IASB and the US-American FASB agreed in 2002 to work closely together in order to eliminate most of the remaining inconsistencies between US GAAP and IFRS until 2005 (*Financial Accounting Standards Board/International Accounting Standards Board* (2002)). Nevertheless, it took the SEC until 2007 to accept IFRS for foreign registrants (*Nobes/Parker* (2012), p. 101) and the convergence process has retarded after the global financial crisis in 2009. In summary, the recent history of IFRS standard-setting has been strongly shaped by the United States and by the specific accounting requirements demanded by the international capital markets.

Furthermore, the financial reporting needs of emerging economies and small and medium-sized entities (SMEs) gradually came into view of the IFRS Foundation in the late 2000s, when these two issues were added to its mission statement (*IFRS Foundation* (2014a)). Since the issuance of IFRS for SMEs in 2009, IFRS have been newly referred to as **'Full IFRS'**. This is due to the fact that the IFRS for SMEs, even though it can be considered as a stand-alone document, forms part of IFRS in a wider sense. Consequently, in this study the term 'Full IFRS' is used for describing all IAS and IFRS except for the IFRS for SMEs.

1.4.4 Development of IFRS for SMEs

Even though IAS and IFRS were primarily designed for listed companies, and focus on the information needs of global capital market investors, in the early 2000s more and more countries adopted Full IFRS also in the context of private firms (e.g. Albania, Croatia, Botswana, Mongolia, and Nicaragua). In the European Union, by the time when listed parent companies were obliged to comply with Full IFRS in 2005, many of the national accounting standard-setters also indicated that they intend to base their national standards applicable to non-listed companies on Full IFRS (*Pacter* (2005), p. 76). Although there was no statutory duty to adopt **Full IFRS for private firms**, the majority of EU countries decided to make Full IFRS applicable for all local companies either for mandatory or for voluntary use (*European Commission* (2012)).

The question whether a single accounting system can be suitable for all companies within a certain country had been discussed long before IAS or IFRS were issued. However, this debate has been provoked once again in the context of continuing international accounting harmonization on the basis of Full IFRS, especially regarding developing countries. *Fortin et al.* (2010) describe it as **'paradoxical'** that the countries with **relatively small securities markets adopted the most ambitious standards** (i.e. Full IFRS) and required them for the broadest range of companies, including SMEs (*Fortin et al.* (2010), p. 80). While the domination of global accounting harmonization efforts by developed Western countries (esp. by the UK and by the US) is rather accepted on the global capital markets, it has been increasingly criticized in the area of private firms (*Saudagaran/Meek* (1997), p. 138).

Contrary to the opinion that Full IFRS are suitable for all types of companies in all countries and that Full IFRS adoption will support poorer countries' economic development, opponents argue that **developing countries have special needs** and circumstances that should be allowed for (*Singh/Newberry* (2008), p. 490). It is further argued that what is considered to be an important accounting issue in a Western country is not necessarily important in a developing country, which would therefore justify the application of different standards (*Samuels/Oliga* (1982), p. 82). The lack of financial and educational resources has been regarded as one of the main impediments to IAS/IFRS adoption by developing countries since the 1970s (*American Accounting Association Committee on Accounting in Developing Countries* (1976), p. 211). In addition, local enforcement bodies do often not exist or are unable to cope with the volume of work required, which leads to non-compliance that undermines de facto adoption (*Fortin et al.* (2010), p. 78).

In a **World Bank** publication on the lessons learned from the Accounting and Auditing Reports on the Observance of Standards and Codes (ROSC), Full IFRS are declared to be inappropriate for the use by all reporting entities. Furthermore, the authors conclude that separate standards should apply to entities without public interest (*Hegarty et al.* (2004), p. 7).

> *"Many countries have traditionally applied a single set of accounting requirements to all companies [...], irrespective of size. However, the use of IAS/IFRS as that single set of requirements has frequently led to unintended negative consequences, hindering successful implementation, as full IAS/IFRS are not appropriate for small- and medium-sized entities."*
>
> (*Hegarty et al.* (2004), p. 8)

In summary, the worldwide adoption of Full IFRS by developing countries in the field of private firms has been increasingly criticized by national standard-setters and supranational organizations since the early 2000s, and can therefore be regarded as one of the principal reasons for the development of IFRS for SMEs. According to former IASB member *Paul Pacter*, many SMEs were concerned that Full IFRS or national GAAPs based on Full IFRS are burdensome, costly, and unnecessary, and that the users of their financial statements are more interested in information about short-term cash flows, liquidity, and solvency than in firm valuation (*Pacter* (2009b), p. 29). The overall **objective** of the **IFRS for SMEs-project** can therefore be summarized as the attempt to design an internationally harmonized, self-contained accounting standard of limited size but high quality, which is tailored for the special needs and capabilities of SMEs around the world. According to *Pacter*, the principal benefit of an IFRS for SMEs compared to local standards is the improved access to capital. In his opinion, IFRS for SMEs brings about improved comparability of financial statements, enhanced quality of reporting (as compared to many existing national GAAPs) and reduced burden for entities in jurisdictions where Full IFRS are required (*Pacter* (2012), p. 464).

When the IASB took over the SME-project from its predecessor IASC in July 2003, the **European accounting harmonization process** was an important influencing factor on the subsequent steps towards IFRS for SMEs. At that time, one of the project's main purposes was to align the national accounting systems in the European Union (*Pacter* (2004), p. 75). As stated above, EU member states adopted Full IFRS also in the context of private firms after the IAS-Regulation had mandated Full IFRS adoption in the group financial statements of European publicly traded companies. However, many of them allowed the continuous use of their national GAAPs, which were more or less converged with Full IFRS and already included accounting exemptions and simplifications for SMEs. The IASB feared that there could be two dozen or more sets of national standards that pretend to be adaptations of IFRSs suitable for SMEs within the European Union. A similar scenario was assumed to occur on a global level (*Pacter* (2004), p. 75).

Until the final standard was issued in July 2009, the previously released draft papers (i.e. the DP (2004) and the ED (2007)) had been criticized in several ways. One of the most important aspects was the IFRS for SMEs' status as a **stand-alone document**. In the comment letters received to the Discussion Paper *Preliminary Views on Accounting Standards for Small and Medium-sized Entities* (2004) more than 60 per cent of the respondents denied cross references to Full IFRS (*Pacter* (2009a), p. 15). In the DP (2004), the IASB had proposed a **mandatory fallback** to Full IFRS for any particular accounting or measurement issue, which was not addressed in the IFRS for SMEs. This approach was heavily criticized for impairing the comparability of SMEs' financial reporting due to the vast number of accounting combinations resulting from an arbitrary mixture of IFRS for SMEs and Full IFRS (*Sharp* (2004), p. 76).[49] In the final standard the mandatory fallback was eliminated. Nevertheless, Full IFRS can still be relevant for preparers of IFRS for SMEs financial statements. Paragraphs 10.4 and 10.6 of the IFRS for SMEs allow the use of Full IFRS principles in the absence of specific guidance in the IFRS for SMEs, provided that Full IFRS requirements do neither conflict with the requirements in the IFRS for SMEs nor with the IFRS for SMEs' concepts and pervasive principles laid down in IFRS for SMEs Section 2 (*International Accounting Standards Board* (2012), p. 1).

The IFRS for SMEs has also been criticized for its disproportionate **complexity** (*Mackintosh* (2008), p. 83). Although the Exposure Daft *International Financial Reporting Standard for Small and Medium-sized Entities* (2007) did not have more than 255 pages, it was criticized for containing too many accounting options and burdensome disclosures stemming from Full IFRS (e.g. revaluation of property, plant, and equipment by reference to IAS 16).[50] **Opponents to the SME-project** argued that if the IFRS for SMEs was not simplified to a larger extent, the remaining differences to Full IFRS would not suffice to

---

[49] Cf. the dissenting opinion of *James J. Leisenring* (*International Accounting Standards Board* (2013), DO1-6).

[50] Cf. for a summary of Full IFRS accounting options included in the ED *Pacter* (2009a), p. 12.

justify a second IFRS accounting system. During the last phase of the due process most of the complex options were eliminated and additional guidance was developed on the remaining ones (*International Accounting Standards Board* (2013), BC34 (b)).

Apart from the issuance of the DP (2004) and the ED (2007), the project team took further preparatory steps in order to involve as many parties in the due process as possible (e.g. via public round-table discussions and cross-border field tests on the Exposure Draft). The most important milestones of the IFRS for SMEs' due process are displayed in Table 1-7.

1999	Project is put on IASC agenda
July 2003	IASB takes over the project and begins with deliberations
June 2004	Discussion Paper *Preliminary Views on Accounting Standards for Small and Medium-sized Entities* (112 comment letters received)
April 2005	Recognition and measurement questionnaire
October 2005	Public round-table discussions on recognition and measurement simplifications
February 2007	Exposure Draft *International Financial Reporting Standard for Small and Medium-sized Entities* (162 comment letters received)
June 2007	Field tests in 20 countries: 116 companies prepare trial financial statements according to the Exposure Draft *IFRS for SMEs*
July 2009	Final Standard: *International Financial Reporting Standard for Small and Medium-sized Entities (IFRS for SMEs)*
June 2012	*Request for Information* introducing the first comprehensive review of the IFRS for SMEs (87 comment letters received)
October 2013	Exposure Draft *Proposed amendments to the IFRS for SMEs* (51 comment letters received)
First half of 2015	Final revisions to the IFRS for SMEs (effective date: 1 January 2016)

Table 1-7: Milestones of the IFRS for SMEs' due process

One major point of criticism, which still prevails after the publication of IFRS for SMEs in 2009, refers to the **conceptual inconsistencies** of the standard. By developing a second stand-alone accounting system for a certain group of entities, the IASB acknowledges the different accounting capabilities of listed and private firms and – more importantly – realizes that there are substantial differences between the information needs of both entities' primary financial statement users. In view of this fact, it was considered to be a reasonable and necessary step to account for these differences by developing a separate set of accounting purposes and qualitative characteristics for the financial reporting of SMEs (*Janssen/Gronewold* (2010), p. 78). However, this has not been the case for the IFRS for SMEs. Instead, the **IASB rejected a 'fresh start' approach** on the grounds that there would be sufficient convergence of users' needs relative to the general purpose financial statements of entities with and without public accountability. Although the IASB realized the inconsistency of the aforesaid, it considers the alternative approach as costly, time-consuming and ultimately futile (*International Accounting Standards Board* (2013), BC97).

Schiebel criticizes the IASB for not having sufficiently examined the common information needs of SMEs' financial statements external users and concludes that there is **no solid empirical foundation for the IFRS for SMEs** (*Schiebel* (2007), p. 18).[51] This lack of empirical research might have contributed to the non-adjustment of the Full IFRS Conceptual Framework, which was inserted into the IFRS for SMEs without modification. As a consequence, the differences in standard-setting between Full IFRS and IFRS for SMEs cannot be based on the conceptual differences between the accounting purposes of listed and private firms' financial reporting – which would then have resulted in different pervasive principles laid down in Section 2 of the IFRS for SMEs – but can only be grounded on cost-benefit considerations regarding the limited accounting capabilities of private firms.

In June 2012, the IASB began with the first **Comprehensive Review** of the IFRS for SMEs. By publishing a request for information, the public was invited to make recommendations on possible amendments to the IFRS for SMEs. In an Exposure Draft that was issued in October 2013, the IASB proposed minor changes to the IFRS for SMEs (mainly regarding the accounting for income tax, useful lives of goodwill and other intangibles and the definition of related parties).[52] The final revisions to the IFRS for SMEs are expected to be released in the first half of 2015.

Having displayed the background of Full IFRS and IFRS for SMEs by outlining the accounting needs of private firms and the international accounting harmonization process, the following section provides an insight into the field of research this study forms part of and thereby forms the basis of the subsequent selection and review of prior research.

1.5 Field of research

By characterizing IFRS-related accounting systems for private firms and presenting reasons for and against Full IFRS and IFRS for SMEs adoption by countries, this study can generally be assigned to the field of **international accounting research**. According to *Samuels/Piper* (1985), literature identifies four areas of international accounting:

i) "the historical dimension; the spread of accounting ideas from country to country,

ii) Universal Accounting: this includes attempts at harmonization, at achieving similar levels of disclosure and similar methods of measurement from one country to another,

iii) Comparative accounting: one reason for describing and comparing the different accounting practices that exist around the world is to enable the accountant to understand the differences and so be able to assess their effects on financial reports. [...]

---

[51] *Schiebel's* critique was directed at the Exposure Draft (2007).

[52] Cf. for all proposed changes *International Accounting Standards Board* (2013), p. 6–12.

iv) *the technical problems of parent-foreign subsidiary accounting, foreign currency translation, segmented accounts, and primary and secondary statements."*

(*Samuels/Piper* (1985), p. 3f.)

Although parent-foreign subsidiary relationships are one important reason for international accounting harmonization and the adoption of IFRS-related accounting rules in the field of private firms, technical problems of international accounting practice are of no relevance for this research. Instead, various aspects from the other three areas of international accounting are dealt with in this study.

First, the time series analysis of domestic accounting systems' gradual convergence with Full IFRS and IFRS for SMEs elaborates on the transnational spread of international accounting ideas over time (*historical dimension*). Moreover, cross-country comparisons are drawn between different categories of less and more strongly internationalized accounting systems for private firms (*comparative accounting*). Another focus of the study is on the determinants of international accounting harmonization in the area of private firms, which relates to the area of *universal accounting*.

As this study only deals with financial accounting issues, the research area can further be narrowed down to **international financial accounting research.** For the purpose of a detailed review of those areas of international financial accounting research, which are most relevant for this study, the research area of this study is further specified in the following two sections. The first section includes comparative studies by drawing on the international comparative financial accounting research (ICFAR) framework created by *Wallace/Gernon* in 1991. The second section presents a series of studies from the field of international accounting harmonization (IAH) research as defined by *Baker/Barbu* in 2007.

1.5.1 International comparative financial accounting research

"Comparative research undertakes to identify, explain and interpret similarities and differences between phenomena in different locations or cultures."

(*Carnegie/Napier* (2002), p. 694)

In accordance with the above definition of comparative research, there are two basic approaches to reflect on similarities and differences of accounting phenomena: a culture free and a culturally grounded approach. In this study, both the descriptive and the explanatory research are conducted from a **culture free perspective.** Comparisons are drawn between 110 different countries and jurisdictions, respectively. Each of the 110 countries' development towards Full IFRS and IFRS for SMEs adoption is analyzed in view of economic factors, network effects, and political pressures. Cultural influences are not considered in the analysis.

According to *Carnegie/Napier* (2002), p. 695f., the mode of comparisons in accounting research can take three different forms:

- 'Synchronic' comparisons of accounting across several countries that use a particular moment of time in the past as the reference point,

- 'Parallel' studies of accounting that take a given period of time and study accounting phenomena of that particular period at different locations, and
- 'Diffusion' studies that focus on the *"spread of accounting ideas from country to country"* (*Samuels/Piper* (1985), p. 3).

In fact, the three above stated forms of comparisons in accounting are not mutually exclusive and can overlap each other. While the descriptive part of this study can rather be characterized as a **'parallel' comparison** of accounting systems over a total period of 13 years (2002-2014), in the explanatory analysis two different moments in time (2008 and 2014) are used as reference points. That part of the study can therefore rather be classified as a **'synchronic' comparison** of accounting phenomena.

The comparative approach in international financial accounting research is either applied to study accounting regulation (e.g. *de jure* harmonization of accounting) or accounting practice (e.g. *de facto* harmonization of accounting). This can be seen from the fact that *Gray* and *Wallace/Gernon* have different views on the purpose of comparative accounting research:

> *"Comparative international accounting is defined to include the description and analysis of* ***accounting systems*** *at the national level, including their historical evolution; comparative analyses of national systems of accounting and financial reporting; and the classification of accounting systems according to patterns of development."*
>
> (*Gray* (1983), p. 19)
>
> *"Comparative accounting is the study of* ***accounting practices*** *in various countries and socioeconomic systems for the purpose of providing explanations for the similarities and differences identified and developing and testing universal accounting theories."*
>
> (*Wallace/Gernon* (1991), p. 210)

This study clearly focuses on the analysis of **accounting systems**, especially on the degree of their compliance with Full IFRS and IFRS for SMEs (*de jure* harmonization of accounting). For this reason, studies on the harmonization of accounting practice (*de facto* harmonization of accounting) are not further discussed in the analysis of prior research. Disregarding this fact, selected research papers on the similarities and differences in national accounting practice are included in the following summary of the international comparative financial accounting research (ICFAR) framework.

Wallace/Gernon (1991) examine the scientific literature on international comparative financial accounting and criticize the lack of research on coherent explanations for the similarities and differences between various national accounting systems. Their review calls for a more rigorous and theoretical evaluation on the different types of accounting and motivates researchers to put more emphasis on typologies and problems of cross-national comparisons (*Wallace/Gernon* (1991), p. 209). The authors classify comparative accounting studies into four different types of research, which can be seen as a progression from nation as object studies to transnational studies (*Wallace/Gernon* (1991), p. 246). Their international comparative financial accounting research (ICFAR) framework is displayed in Figure 1-6.

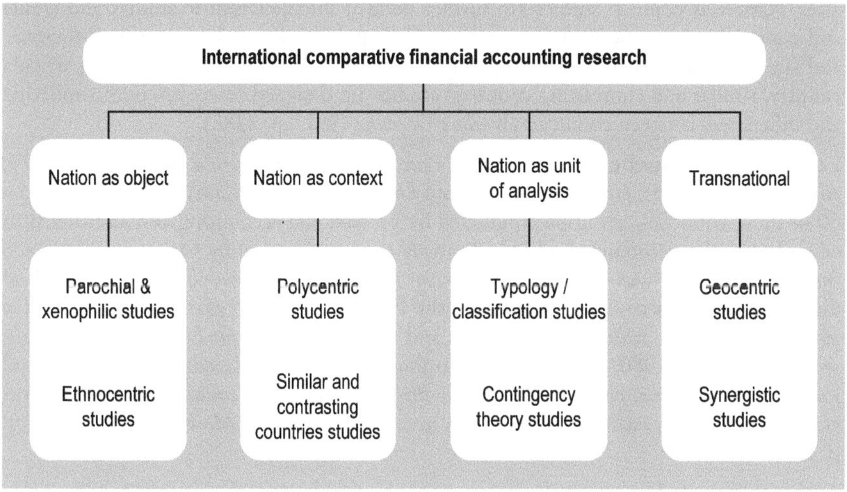

Figure 1-6: ICFAR framework[53]

Single-country studies are generally categorized as **'nation as object' studies.** They include all types of studies that are designed to find unique national accounting phenomena, whose appropriateness is evaluated and compared to the accounting in other countries. Depending on whether the researcher stems from that particular country or not, 'nation as object' studies are further differentiated into parochial and xenophilic studies (*Wallace/Gernon* (1991), p. 223). As an example of the latter, *Briston* (1978) studies the accounting systems of Indonesia, Nigeria, and Tanzania and finds that each country has its own political, social, economic, and cultural characteristics. He concludes that the global process of accounting standardization creates a system that is inappropriate for satisfying local information needs (*Briston* (1978), p. 120). Replications of domestic accounting studies in foreign countries, which analyze whether theories that are applicable in one country can be extended to another country, are summarized as ethnocentric studies (*Wallace/Gernon* (1991), p. 237).

Although this study covers more than 100 countries in total, and hence takes a rather superordinate research perspective, input from single-country studies are valuable if local accounting phenomena are representative for an entire group of countries within a geographic region. For example, *Lainez et al.* (1999) show that the degree of consensus of the Spanish accounting system with IFRS is only moderate (*Lainez et al.* (1999), p. 104). This holds true for the financial reporting systems of several other Continental European countries prior to the year 2005.

[53] Adopted from *Wallace/Gernon* (1991), p. 224.

Wallace/Gernon classify cross-country studies into the field of **'nation as context' studies** if countries are used as 'vehicles' for investigating the context in which accounting operates. 'Nation as context' studies are further divided into polycentric studies and similar and contrasting countries (SACC) studies. While polycentric studies are rather *descriptive* and stress the individuality and uniqueness of accounting phenomena within a particular country, similar and contrasting countries studies are designed to *explain* both similarities and differences between countries (*Wallace/Gernon* (1991), p. 238f.).

Large **descriptive studies** like those from *Price Waterhouse/Fitzgerald* (1973, 1976, 1979), *AICPA* (1964, 1975), *Gray et al.* (1984) and *Ordelheide/KPMG* (2001), which cover up to 60 or more countries, are often conducted by professional accounting and auditing firms or professional accountancy bodies and mostly consist of nation-by-nation descriptions of financial reporting rules or practices in text or tabular form (*Reisloh* (2011), p. 72). In addition, the 'world accounting' surveys by the Financial Times (*Lafferty et al.* (1979), *Lafferty/Cairns* (1980), *Stilling et al.* (1984)), and the *Organisation for Economic Co-operation and Development* (1980) also contribute to the large field of polycentric accounting studies. Some of the research (e.g. those from *Price Waterhouse International*) has been criticized for confusing accounting rules with accounting practice (*Meek/Saudagaran* (1990), p. 147).

As this study only focuses on the international harmonization of accounting rules, a clear differentiation between accounting rules and accounting practice is crucial for its correct positioning in the field of international comparative financial accounting research. Especially in the context of international accounting harmonization and compliance with IFRS, most of the recent studies rather discuss differences in accounting practice under IFRS (e.g. *Kvaal/Nobes* (2012); *Wehrfritz et al.* (2012); *Nobes* (2013); *Voets* (2013)) than differences between accounting systems. In summary, **polycentric studies** on national accounting systems represent the **starting point** for all analyses on international accounting harmonization and can therefore be regarded as a necessary precursor of the descriptive research part in this study.

While polycentric studies deny universality, similar and contrasting countries (SACC) studies explain observed similarities (universality) and differences (country specifics) by drawing on country-specific factors (**explanatory studies**). This type of research tries to define similar country patterns that emerge from all nations that are examined (*Adler* (1983), p. 35). Countries are often selected on the basis of specific features such as size, geographic proximity, political systems or historical heritage. As the primary objective of SACC studies is rather to learn than to formulate or test a theory (*Wallace/Gernon* (1991), p. 239f.), this branch of research is of minor relevance for this study.

The goal of **'nation as unit of analysis' studies** is to reduce variety into different categories and find general relationships that can explain the differences in accounting between these categories (*Wallace/Gernon* (1991), p. 241). The classification of countries along one or more dimensions is either based on the observation of different financial reporting patterns (discursive comparative research) or on statistical techniques (e.g. factor analysis) (*Samuels/Piper* (1985), p. 31). *Wallace/Gernon* subdivide 'Nation as unit of analysis' studies further into typology (also classification) studies (**descriptive studies**) and contingency theory studies (**explanatory studies**).

Descriptive studies on accounting typologies and classifications seek to divide countries into groups with similar accounting or non-accounting characteristics. For example, *Hatfield* (1966) discusses differences between the accounting practices in the USA, United Kingdom, France, and Germany and concludes with a classification into US, UK, and Continental European accounting practice (*Hatfield* (1966), p. 169).[54] In another pioneer work, *Mueller* (1967) suggests classifications of accounting systems into four patterns of development[55] and stresses that these four types are a product of social, economic, legal, and other individual environments (*Mueller* (1967), p. 1). In most of the succeeding studies, classifications are developed by using statistical techniques such as factor or cluster analysis (*Da Costa et al.* (1978); *Frank* (1979)). The necessary data are mainly obtained from large polycentric studies conducted by multinational accounting and audit firms (e.g. survey data from *Price Waterhouse* (1973, 1976) and *Fitzgerald et al.* (1979)).

Nobes criticizes prior studies on accounting classification in a paper from 1983 for the inappropriate data used[56] and for not testing a particular hypothetical classification (*Nobes* (1983), p. 3). He points out that sensible classification cannot be theory-free and that statistical techniques should be used to test, but not to generate, hypotheses (*Nobes* (1992), p. 55). His hypothetical classification of financial reporting measurement practices in developed Western countries (*Nobes* (1983)), which has later been supported by *Doupnik/Salter* (1993), can be regarded as one of the first **explanatory studies** in the field of accounting classification research. The determinants that have yet been identified to explain national accounting patterns vary from economic, political, and civil indicators (*Belkaoui* (1983)) to variables such as the strength of equity markets and the degree of cultural dominance (*Nobes* (1998)).[57]

> *"Classification is fundamental to understanding and analyzing **why** and **how** national accounting systems differ. We can also analyze whether these systems are converging or diverging."*
>
> (*Choi/Meek* (2011), p. 30)

Hence, classification studies and contingency theory studies can be regarded as highly relevant for the accomplishment of this study because they refine polycentric and SACC studies and provide valuable insight into the state of international harmonization of na-

---

[54] This tripartite classification was later criticized for overemphasizing the differences between US and UK accounting practice and adjusted into a dyadic classification (Anglo-Saxon and Continental European). Cf. *Nobes* (1992), p. 39.

[55] The four defined patterns of development are: accounting within a macroeconomic framework, the microeconomic approach, accounting as an independent discipline, and uniform accounting. Cf. for more details *Choi/Mueller* (1978), p. 37ff.

[56] Four types of problems with the survey data from *Price Waterhouse* (1973) were expressed: straightforward mistakes, misleading answers, swamping of important questions with trivial ones, and exaggeration of the differences between the USA and the UK because of the familiarity of these countries. Cf. *Nobes* (1983), p. 2.

[57] Cf. *Nobes/Parker* (2012), p. 76, for a taxonomy of accounting classifications.

tional accounting systems. Their conclusions are particularly useful for assessing the advances and impediments of domestic accounting systems' convergence with Full IFRS and IFRS for SMEs in the field of private firms.

While 'nation as object', 'nation as context', and 'nation as unit of analysis' studies rather focus on the descriptive and explanatory analysis of national accounting systems and national accounting practice, **'transnational' studies** establish a connection between national and international accounting phenomena (e.g. adoption of IFRS). By referring to *Adler* (1983), *Wallace/Gernon* divide 'transnational' studies into geocentric and synergistic studies. The former generally examine the progress of international accounting harmonization and the feasibility of an international set of accounting standards. They elaborate on transnational enterprises and seek to explain international accounting harmonization by assuming cross-national universality and by neglecting cultural differences (*Wallace/Gernon* (1991), p. 245). In comparison, synergistic studies try to reveal the strategies, which apply when people and organizations from different countries collaborate to develop global financial reporting standards and focus on patterns of universality such as the degree of international accounting harmonization (*Wallace/Gernon* (1991), p. 236, 246).

Having provided a first overview on different research streams in the area of international comparative financial accounting research, the following section focuses on various aspects of transnational studies, which are relevant for the research questions raised in this study. In particular, the section presents an overview on contemporary international accounting harmonization (IAH) research from the viewpoint of *Baker/Barbu* (2007).

1.5.2 International accounting harmonization research

Being a subset of international accounting research and financial accounting research, international accounting harmonization (IAH) research *"investigates the arguments for, efforts made towards, and trends in the direction of achieving international harmonization of financial accounting standards"* (*Baker/Barbu* (2007), p. 274). IAH research hence focuses on the international harmonization of financial reporting standards (see Figure 1-7).

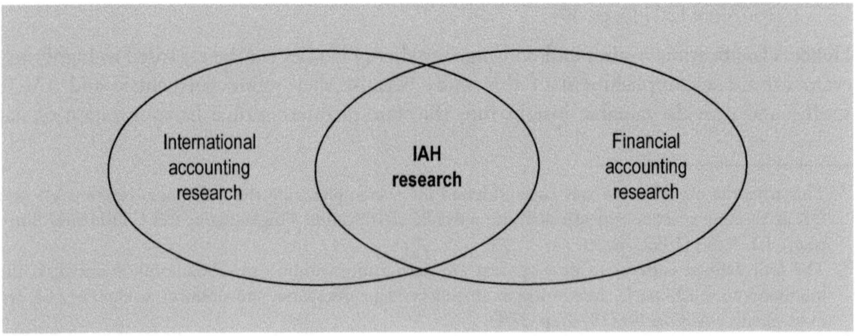

Figure 1-7: IAH research

Before the IASC was created in 1973, and the international accounting harmonization process gained further momentum due to the efforts made within the European Economic Community (EEC) from the mid-1970s onwards, IAH research had mainly been concerned with the idea of **accounting uniformity** (*Morgan* (1967)). *Wilkinson* (1965) describes accounting uniformity as a state when *"each company presents only one set of accounts for all investors, of whatever nationality"* (*Wilkinson* (1965), p. 11). In the 1960s and 1970s, comparative accounting studies primarily aimed at identifying differences in financial accounting practices between countries (e.g. *Hatfield* (1966); *Mueller* (1967); *Fitzgerald et al.* (1979)), which had to be aligned before accounting uniformity could be achieved.

As there are a number of impediments to achieving international accounting harmonization or even accounting uniformity (*Hauworth* (1973), p. 24), several authors have reflected on the necessary steps to be taken in the **international accounting harmonization process** and on the question whether this process could ever be accomplished. *Fitzgerald* summarizes the early attempts of international accounting harmonization by the IASC, OECD, United Nations, and the EEC in a paper from 1981 and warns the four institutions about overlapping activities (*Fitzgerald* (1981)). Pessimistic voices argued until the early 1990s that consistent worldwide accounting standards would remain *"an elusive goal"* (*Goeltz* (1991), p. 85).

When the IASC developed to the world's most important financial reporting standard-setter during the 1980s, two new themes have gradually become more relevant within the field of IAH research: (1) the **degree of international accounting harmonization** and (2) **complete implementation of IFRS** (*Baker/Barbu* (2007), p. 285). As this study elaborates on both topics, these two areas of IAH research are of particular relevance for this study.

Being pioneers of the first-mentioned IAH research stream, *Evans/Taylor* (1982) examine a sample of five countries (France, Japan, United Kingdom, USA, and West Germany) and test for the degree of national accounting practice's compliance with IAS. They conclude that the IASC had very little impact on the accounting practices of the countries surveyed (*Evans/Taylor* (1982), p. 126). Five years later, *Doupnik* (1987) uses data from *Price Waterhouse* (1976) and compares them to his own survey data, collected for the same 46 countries in 1983. Although the results indicate that differences in national financial reporting practices decreased, and compliance with IASC standards improved over the period of 1975 to 1983, substantial differences in accounting practice persist among the 46 countries in the survey (*Doupnik* (1987), p. 64). In 1988, *van der Tas* is the first who develops three different indices[58] to quantify the **degree of harmony of national financial reporting practice** with IAS (i.e. *de facto* harmonization) by using a sample of three countries (the Netherlands, United Kingdom, and the USA). After testing one of his indices on a sample of nine European countries over a ten-year period from 1978 to 1988, he states that harmony can still be regarded as low and that harmony gradually increased only in consolidated financial statements (*van der Tas* (1992), p. 92). *Tay/Parker* (1990) call for further research on international accounting harmonization (*Tay/Parker* (1990), p. 76,

58 Cf. for a summary of indices used to quantify the extent of de facto accounting harmonization *Roberts et al.* (2008), p. 291ff.

85) and emphasize the importance of a clear differentiation between the measurement of *de jure* (formal) and *de facto* (material) accounting harmonization.[59]

Other researchers such as *Nair/Frank* (1981), *McKinnon/Janell* (1984), and *Doupnik/Taylor* (1985) were the first that focused on measuring the **degree of harmony between national financial reporting systems** and IAS (i.e. *de jure* harmonization).[60] In 1988, the *IASC* published the first major survey on the compliance of 54 national financial reporting systems with IAS (*International Accounting Standards Committee* (1988)). *Purvis et al.* (1991) analyze the IASC data and derive two conformity indices, which display the percentage of cross-national compliance with 25 IAS (*Purvis et al.* (1991), p. 27). Among others,[61] *Rahman et al.* (1996) introduce a methodology for the empirical measurement of formal accounting harmony between countries. In an exploratory study, the authors identify similarities and differences between Australian and New Zealand measurement and disclosure requirements for listed companies by applying a multiple discriminant analysis (*Rahman et al.* (1996)). In a more recent study, *Garrido et al.* (2002) show that the IASC significantly reduced the number of accounting options in IAS & IFRS during the four different stages of its development (particularly since the publication of the Conceptual Framework in 1989 and the Comparability Project in 1990), and conclude that the IASC made great progress in regard to the level of *de jure* harmony achieved through the accounting standards it has issued and revised (*Garrido et al.* (2002), p. 14).

Since European publicly traded companies have been required to prepare consolidated financial statements under EU-IFRS from 2005 (2007) onwards, Full IFRS are adopted 'as a whole' in more and more countries worldwide. As a consequence, most IAH research that had previously dealt with the degree of harmony between national financial reporting systems and IFRS (*de jure* harmony), gradually shifted to analyzing **complete implementation of IFRS** (e.g. *Deloitte Touche Tohmatsu* (2014c)). Since 2009, IAH research also covers the worldwide adoption of **IFRS for SMEs** (e.g. *IFRS Foundation* (2014g)). IAH research dealing with the degree of *de facto* accounting harmony remains valid until today, as differences in national financial reporting practices survive under IFRS (*Chen et al.* (2002); *Ali et al.* (2009); *Nobes* (2013); *Voets* (2013)).

The following section further narrows down the field of research to those studies that are particularly relevant for this study and presents a comprehensive review and discussion of prior research.

---

59 Cf. for the public dialogue of *van der Tas* and *Tay/Parker* on the differentiation between the measurement of harmonization of accounting practice and accounting rules *Tay/Parker* (1992) and *Tay/Parker* (1992).

60 Apart from other points of criticism (e.g. limitations in data quality), some studies (e.g. *Doupnik/Taylor* (1985)) were disapproved by other researchers for mixing up accounting practice with accounting rules and presenting misleading results (*Nobes* (1987)).

61 Cf. *Saudagaran/Meek* (1997), p. 140ff., and *Ali* (2005), p. 13ff., for different measures of accounting harmonization and *Ali* (2005), p. 30ff., for a literature review on studies measuring compliance with IAS/IFRS.

1.6 Prior research

1.6.1 Overview

The previous section presented a summary of studies stemming from the field of international comparative financial accounting research (ICFAR) and international accounting harmonization research (IAHR). Contributions from both research fields are relevant for the conceptual grounding and the realization of this study. In particular, prior studies on the degree of international accounting harmonization and complete implementation of IFRS are of high relevance for this study. In order to concentrate on those research areas that are most relevant for answering the specific research questions of this study, **two research topics are excluded** from the following review of prior research:

- ICFAR on the harmonization of *accounting practice* (*de facto* harmonization) and
- IAHR *unrelated to Full IFRS* or *IFRS for SMEs adoption.*

As this study does neither intend to provide any empirical evidence on the firm level variation in national accounting practices under IFRS nor on the differences between national accounting systems other than regarding their degrees of convergence with either Full IFRS or IFRS for SMEs, the subsequent analysis of prior research merely focuses on normative-conceptual and empirical ICFAR and IAHR dealing with *de jure* accounting harmonization associated with Full IFRS or IFRS for SMEs adoption. The study's research focus is summarized in Figure 1-8.

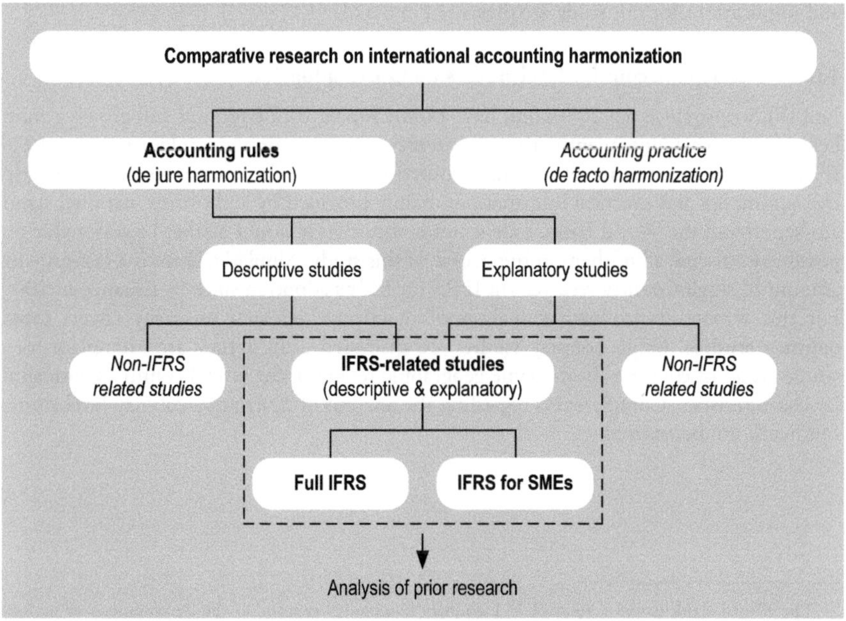

Figure 1-8: Research focus

Following the structure of this study, the review of prior research is first divided into the analysis of descriptive and explanatory country level studies. On a second level, the relevant studies are differentiated into studies focusing on either Full IFRS or IFRS for SMEs adoption. The four subareas of prior research are hence reviewed consecutively as displayed in Table 1-8.

	Descriptive country level studies (1.6.2)	Explanatory country level studies (1.6.3)
Full IFRS adoption	(1)	(3)
IFRS for SMEs adoption	(2)	(4)

Table 1-8: Review of prior research

Besides the above given structure of the review process, prior studies are further differentiated according to additional characteristics such as scope of research (single-country vs. cross-country study), research object (accounting rules for listed vs. private firms) and research design (cross-sectional vs. time series analysis). Having presented all four subareas of prior research, the studies' main limitations are discussed and research gaps are pointed out. Thereafter, the specific research opportunities available for this study are identified and implications for this study are presented in detail.

1.6.2 Descriptive country level studies on GAAP adoption

Full IFRS exist since the 1970s and have been adopted by a large and still growing number of countries. Consequently, there is extensive literature on the implementation of Full IFRS from the perspective of various jurisdictions (i.e. single-country research). Descriptive summaries and practical information, mainly provided by audit firms, national standard-setters and the World Bank,[62] are so numerous that it would neither be reasonable nor possible to discuss all of them in the course of this study. Similarly, there is a fast-growing amount of single-country research on IFRS for SMEs adoption since its issuance in 2009. For this reason, the following analysis of descriptive research primarily covers **cross-country studies**. Single-country studies are discussed only if they are exemplary for a whole group of countries in the same geographic region or for several countries with similar characteristics. Completeness regarding the analysis of descriptive country level studies can hence not be ensured.

---

62 The World Bank issued a total of 111 country-by-country reports on the development of national accounting and auditing systems and the implementation of Full IFRS and IFRS for SMEs. Cf. *World Bank* (2014).

1.6.2.1 Full IFRS

During the past 40 years of Full IFRS adoption, two main branches of descriptive country level research have evolved. The first deals with national accounting systems' degree of compliance (also: conformity) with Full IFRS. Most of this research stems from the 1980s and has disappeared almost completely since the early 2000s. The second branch of descriptive country level research on Full IFRS adoption has evolved from the early 2000s onwards and concentrates on the implementation of Full IFRS as a whole (i.e. on the substitution or complementation of Local GAAP by Full IFRS).

1.6.2.1.1 National GAAP's compliance with Full IFRS

In the early 1980s, several researchers made use of three *Price Waterhouse* surveys (1973, 1975, 1979), which are three of the first large-scale **nation-by-nation descriptions** of financial reporting rules and practices in tabular form. The *PW* survey data are compiled from information provided by various offices across the globe and the different accounting practices covered by the surveys are classified into six (1973) to eight (1979) categories ranging from 'required' to 'not permitted'.[63] *Nair/Frank* (1981) compare the national accounting practices provided by *Price Waterhouse* to the provisions in IAS 1 to IAS 10 in a sample of 37 countries and trace back a movement towards harmonization between 1973 and 1979. As the United States had already incorporated most of the accounting practices that were required under IAS into national GAAP by 1975, *Nair/Frank* come to the conclusion that other countries are moving toward the position of the US and that the US enjoys a position of leadership in international accounting (*Nair/Frank* (1981), p. 74).

McKinnon/Janell (1984) examine the **role of the IASC** by comparing the degree of acceptance of three IASC standards (depreciation, equity method, and foreign currency translation) between 33 IASC member countries and 31 other countries. Although the authors find that practices prescribed under the three chosen IAS are required significantly more often in IASC-member countries than in other countries, they point out the persistence of important accounting deviations from IAS for certain IASC members (e.g. Japan). *McKinnon/Janell* conclude that the IASC has not met its goal to change existing standards or to set new standards due to national differences and the lack of enforcement powers (*McKinnon/Janell* (1984), p. 33).

For a sample of 16 Western European countries, *Doupnik/Taylor* (1985) measure and compare the **average levels of compliance** of national accounting standards with the first eight IASC standards in 1979 and in 1983. The authors take the *Price Waterhouse* survey to calculate the values for the first measurement date (1979) and use handpicked data to assess the values for 1983. They find that, although Europe registers the lowest level of compliance with the eight chosen IASC standards among five broadly-defined geographic areas (i.e. Africa, Asia & Australia, Europe, Latin America, and North America), Europe shows the greatest percentage increase in mean level of compliance with IASC standards between 1979 and 1983. In fact, compliance scores increase for all Western European

[63] The *Price Waterhouse* surveys include a mixture of accounting rules and accounting practice (*Meek/Saudagaran* (1990), p. 147).

countries except for Austria, France, Germany, and Switzerland. In general, the English-speaking countries, France, and the Netherlands are measured to be in highest conformity and the German-speaking and Southern European countries are in least conformity (*Doupnik/Taylor* (1985), p. 33).

Although these **three comparative studies** provide important insights into the early process of *de jure* harmonization towards IAS in the late 1970s and early 1980s, they have severe **limitations**. First, the *Price Waterhouse* data have been criticized for being unsuitable for both classification purposes and for the measurement of the degree of *de jure* harmonization of national accounting systems as it does not clearly differentiate between accounting rules and practices (*Nobes* (1981), p. 268). It remains ambiguous whether a high compliance score, as measured by *Doupnik/Taylor* (1985), represents a high degree of conformity between IAS and national accounting rules or whether national accounting practices are in general accordance with IAS. Moreover, the data contain some straightforward mistakes, which make the analysis less reliable (*Nobes* (1987), p. 78).[64] Another problem results from the incompleteness of the selected accounting topics and the resulting evaluation bias. As it is impossible to include all accounting prescriptions regarding recognition, measurement, and disclosures of an entire national accounting system, professional judgement is required to select the most important and representative provisions of a specific accounting system and evaluate on the difference in relevance between certain recognition, measurement and disclosure rules.

In 1988, the *IASC* published its first own survey on the level of compliance of 54 national financial reporting systems with IAS (*International Accounting Standards Committee* (1988)). The survey is based on the responses to a questionnaire on the **use and application of IAS** in different IASC member countries. The results show that in the majority of countries, national requirements conform to 23 out of 25 IAS. Furthermore, the financial statements of listed (unlisted) companies conform to all or most IAS in 26 (18) of the 64 countries (*International Accounting Standards Committee* (1988), p. 3). In most IASC member countries, IAS had not been adopted as a national requirement and responses such as *"national rules conform in all material respects with IAS"* imply a high level of discretion. The results should therefore be interpreted with caution.

Purvis et al. (1991) analyze the IASC survey data (1988) and derive two **conformity indices** that display a relatively high percentage (about 80%) of cross-national compliance with 25 IAS (*Purvis et al.* (1991), p. 27). The authors come to the conclusion that the level of conformity with IAS is much higher regarding the early standards, which address more fundamental issues, than with those standards issued more recently. Hence they cluster the 25 IAS into three different types of standards: (1) standards issued early in the IASC's life and with which conformity was easily achieved; (2) more recent standards that require additional procedures for some countries to achieve conformity, and (3) standards, which have not been adopted by the majority of the IASC's member countries (*Purvis et al.* (1991), p. 28). Compared to the IASC summary of the survey, *Purvis et al.'s* findings

[64] For example, the full compliance of France in 1979 is unrealistic and the apparent fall in French compliance from 1979 to 1983 rather results from a change in response than from a change in reality. Cf. *Nobes* (1987), p. 78.

are more critical and reveal some descent within the group of IAS regarding the level of compliance by national accounting standards.

Larson/Kenny (1999) examine whether the national accounting standards of 33 (21)[65] countries are in **compliance with IAS by the early 1990s.** By using data from *Coopers/Lybrand* (1991, 1993) and *Price Waterhouse* (1995), the authors compare national accounting rules to IAS in 26 to 28 different accounting areas and find that the accounting standards of about half of the examined countries, consisting of the United States, United Kingdom, former colonies of the United Kingdom (e.g. Australia and Canada), and the Netherlands, are in general compliance with IAS by 1993 (*Larson/Kenny* (1999), p. 6). Countries from Continental Europe, Asia, and South America seem to comply with IAS to a medium extent (i.e. in more than half of the 26 accounting areas) whereas Switzerland and China are the two countries in the sample that least comply with IAS (i.e. in less than a third of the 26 accounting areas).

While compliance is high regarding basic accounting concepts and the accounting for investments, receivables, and equity, deviations from IAS largely occur in the field of related party transactions and segment reporting (*Larson/Kenny* (1999), p. 7). Although the cross-country findings show that the majority of countries is moving toward harmonization with IAS, the study reveals that the **average level of compliance with IAS decreased in 1995** due to the elimination of several accounting options in the course of the IASC's 'Comparability Project' (*Larson/Kenny* (1999), p. 9).

In the early 2000s, the world's largest seven audit firms[66] conducted a survey of national accounting standards benchmarked against IAS in 53 (62) countries (2000, 2001). On a country-by-country level, the two studies display in which areas national rules differ from IAS due to the absence of specific rules on recognition, measurement, or disclosure. Furthermore, the inconsistencies between national rules and IAS are summarized. The two years of GAAP comparison show that **much progress has been made toward the convergence of accounting standards** in many countries. However, there are approximately 30 countries with major differences but with no indication of proposed changes. Among other accounting topics, the lack of convergence is most obvious for the recognition and measurement of financial assets and the accounting for business combinations (*Andersen et al.* (2001), p. 5).

In a summary of the results from *Andersen et al.'s* (2001) survey, *Street* (2002) adds that for many countries, **convergence with IAS will be a monumental task** that requires a joint effort by the government, stock market regulators, financial statement users, standard-setters and the accounting profession (*Street* (2002), p. 89). The results of the two studies show that it is much more difficult to quantify the overall degree of compliance with IAS than to describe the major deviations country-by-country.

[65] National accounting standards of 33 countries are examined in the years 1991 and 1993. The analysis of the 1995 data only contains 21 countries.

[66] These were Andersen, BDO, Deloitte Touche Tohmatsu, Ernst & Young, Grant Thornton, KPMG and PricewaterhouseCoopers. Cf. *Andersen et al.* (2001).

Besides the few global surveys of the IASC and global audit firms such as *Price Waterhouse*, *Andersen*, or *KPMG*, several academic researchers and practitioners have analyzed the progress towards international accounting harmonization from the perspective of a specific jurisdiction, a geographic region, or an economic area. For example, *Agami/Monsen's* survey of four Scandinavian countries' Local GAAP's level of **compliance with the EU Directives and IAS** by 1995 show that the selected countries (Denmark, Finland, Norway, and Sweden) have achieved a high degree of accounting standards harmonization among each other. For example, their accounting standards for consolidation are identical (*Agami/Monsen* (1995), p. 199). Moreover, the four countries' accounting standards are assumed to be 'consistent with IAS' with some exceptions.

Manzano/Conesa (2005) conduct a conceptual analysis of the efforts made towards national accounting standards' **convergence with Full IFRS in Latin America** (Argentina, Brazil, Chile, and Mexico). According to their judgmental assessment, Latin America has made good progress in converging national accounting standards with Full IFRS. However, significant differences remain, especially regarding the accounting for intangibles, research and development costs, and business combinations (*Manzano/Conesa* (2005), p. 116).[67]

Ampofo/Sellani (2005) are two of several accounting researchers who examine the similarities and **differences between US GAAP and Full IFRS**.[68] The authors state the exact content of Full IFRS may not be the same as in US GAAP, but in many ways the approach and degree of detail are similar (e.g. in the areas of conceptual framework, related party transactions, contingencies, and provisions). They further conclude that differences between US GAAP and Full IFRS *"are not necessarily a bad thing"* as they reflect the diversity of society and the differences in political, economic, social, cultural, technological, legal, and business environments (*Ampofo/Sellani* (2005), p. 228). All in all, *Ampofo/ Sellani* summarize their findings by saying that US GAAP and Full IFRS are more similar than dissimilar and the movement toward harmonization is bringing both GAAPs closer together.

All in all, conclusions derived in international comparative accounting studies such as *Agami/Monsen* (1995), *Manzano/Conesa* (2005), and *Ampofo/Sellani* (2005) should be interpreted with caution as they are based on a limited number of accounting topics. Whether compliance with IFRS is regarded as high or low thus largely depends on the personal judgement of the authors. Furthermore, the process of de jure harmonization underlies rapid changes, which make evaluations of National GAAP's compliance levels with IFRS become outdated very quickly.

A summary of the above reviewed studies on the degree of National GAAP's compliance with Full IFRS is provided in Table 1-9.

---

[67] Cf. for *single-country* studies on the process and the state of convergence of local accounting standards with Full IFRS *Haller/Eierle* (2004b) on Germany, *Fontes et al.* (2005) on Portugal, *Chand/Patel* (2008), on countries from the South Pacific region (e.g. Australia & New Zealand), and *Qu/Zhang* (2010) on China.

[68] Cf. for similar studies e.g. *Street et al.* (2000) and *Pacter* (2002).

Reference	Methodology	Key results
Nair/Frank (1981)	Analysis of survey data provided by PWI (1973, 1975, 1979) regarding the level of compliance of accounting standards (practices) with IAS in 37 countries (1975-1978).	The period of the IASC's existence has coincided with a growing harmonization of accounting standards. The accounting practices in the United States seem to serve as a model for this harmonization process.
McKinnon/Janell (1984)	Analysis of survey data provided by PWI (1979) regarding the degree of acceptance of 3 IASC standards in 64 countries (1978).	The IASC has not met its goal to change existing standards or to set new standards due to national differences and the lack of enforcement powers.
Doupnik/Taylor (1985)	Comparison of survey data provided by PWI (1979) with handpicked data (1983) regarding the level of compliance of accounting standards (practices) with IASC in 16 Western European countries (1979-1983).	Europe registers the lowest level of compliance with IASC standards among five broadly-defined geographic areas. However, the European level of compliance with IASC standards increased significantly between 1979 and 1983. Therefore, resistance to conforming to IASC standards might have decreased during that period.
IASC (1988)	Survey of IASC Member Bodies on the level of compliance of national accounting standards with 25 IAS in 54 countries (1988).	In the majority of countries, national requirements or practice conform to 23 out of 25 IAS. The financial statements of listed (unlisted) companies conform to all or most IAS in 26 (18) countries.
Purvis et al. (1991)	Analysis of IASC survey data (1988) regarding the level of compliance of national accounting standards with 25 IAS in 54 countries (1988).	The level of conformity with IAS is higher regarding the early standards, which address more fundamental issues than with those standards issued more recently.
Agami/Monsen (1995)	Survey of national accounting standards' level of compliance with IAS in 4 Nordic countries (1995).	Denmark, Finland, Norway, and Sweden have achieved a high degree of accounting standards harmonization among each other. Their accounting standards are largely consistent with IAS.
Larson/Kenny (1999)	Survey of accounting standards' level of compliance with IAS in 33 (21) countries (1991, 1993, 1995).	Due to the elimination of accounting options in the 'Comparability Project' of the IASC, the average level of compliance decreased after the 1995 changes.
Andersen et al. (2000, 2001)	Survey of national accounting standards benchmarked against IAS in 53 (62) countries (2000, 2001).	Despite the progress in harmonization, a lack of convergence is still obvious (e.g. regarding the recognition and measurement of financial assets and the accounting for business combinations).
Street (2002)	Summary of the results from Andersen et al.'s (2001) survey of accounting standards benchmarked against IAS in 62 countries (2001).	Convergence with IAS is a monumental task that requires a joint effort by the government, stock market regulators, financial statement users, standard-setters, and the accounting profession.
Manzano/Conesa (2005)	Conceptual analysis of the efforts made towards national accounting standards' convergence with Full IFRS in 4 Latin American countries (1992-2005).	Argentina, Brazil, Chile and Mexico have made good progress in converging Local GAAP with Full IFRS. However, significant differences remain (e.g. regarding the accounting for intangibles, research and development costs and business combinations).
Ampofo/Sellani (2005)	Examination of the differences between US GAAP and Full IFRS (2005).	The content of Full IFRS may not be the same as US GAAP but the approach and degree of detail are similar. Harmonization is bringing both GAAPs closer together.

Table 1-9: Descriptive cross-country studies on National GAAP's compliance with Full IFRS

1.6.2.1.2 Full IFRS implementation as a whole

Since the early 2000s, research on the degree of national GAAP's compliance with Full IFRS has become fairly scarce. Apparently, the **researchers' focus has changed** towards the implementation of Full IFRS as a whole. In a follow-up study of *Andersen et al.'s* (2001) survey of national accounting standards benchmarked against Full IFRS, *BDO et al.* (2003) analyze the convergence plans of 59 countries in the field of listed companies' financial reporting. They find that only two countries (Cyprus and Kenya) had already adopted Full IFRS as their mandatory standard by 2002, but that 54 (92%) of the sampled countries either intend to adopt or intend to converge with Full IFRS in the field of listed firms. Only Iceland, Japan, and Saudi Arabia had not yet expressed an intention to converge with Full IFRS. More than half of the respondents to *BDO et al.'s* survey considered **replacing national GAAP with Full IFRS** (supplemented only for issues not addressed in Full IFRS) as the most favorable approach to convergence (*BDO et al.* (2003), p. 7ff.). The study reveals that after IAS had been acknowledged by IOSCO in 2000, and the IASC had been further professionalized and restructured into the IASB the year after, the majority of countries intended to **adopt Full IFRS** at least in the field of listed firms.

Disregarding this fact, the **type and scope of Full IFRS adoption varies** significantly from one country to another. This is shown by a series of eight case studies conducted by the *United Nations* in 2008.[69] While mandatory Full IFRS adoption is restricted to the consolidated financial statements of publicly traded companies in Germany, Full IFRS have been adopted for the largest possible group of domestic companies in many other countries (e.g. India, Jamaica and Pakistan). Furthermore, the case studies point out that several different factors exist that contribute to the introduction of Full IFRS within a jurisdiction (*United Nations* (2008), p. 1).

In a commentary under the title *"Has Australia (or Any Other Jurisdiction) 'Adopted' IFRS?"*, *Zeff/Nobes* (2010) discuss several ways of Full IFRS implementation in eight different jurisdictions[70] and criticize the frequent and inconsiderate **use of the word 'adopt'** in cases when Full IFRS are not implemented word for word or if the standards are not made applicable immediately after they have been issued by the IASB. The authors' recommendation is that national regulators should rather 'adopt' Full IFRS in the pure sense by adopting the IASB's process than to use alternative implementation strategies (such as endorsement or convergence), which provide opportunities for political interference that bring delays in the availability of the IASB's output and can lead to confusion about which accounting rules are being used (*Zeff/Nobes* (2010), p. 183).

Due to the coherent decision of the countries of the European Union and the European Economic Area in 2002 to mandatorily adopt Full IFRS in the consolidated accounts of companies whose securities are traded in a regulated market from 2005 (2007) onwards, much research was conducted on the process, the scope of application, and on the **implications of Full IFRS adoption within Europe**. *Street/Larson* (2004) evaluate the results

[69] The report covers the implementation of Full IFRS in Brazil, Germany, India, Jamaica, Kenya, Pakistan, South Africa, and Turkey. Cf. *United Nations* (2008).

[70] The jurisdictions include Australia, Canada, China, European Union, Israel, South Africa, Switzerland, and Venezuela.

from *BDO et al.'s* (2003) survey for 15 EU countries and find that, despite the mandatory adoption of Full IFRS in the consolidated accounts of publicly traded companies, most EU member states do not plan to converge their national GAAPs with Full IFRS and continue to require or allow national GAAP in the individual accounts of resident (unlisted) companies. The authors are concerned that this development could lead to the emergence of a **'two standard' system in the European Union** (*Street/Larson* (2004), p. 1). *Sellhorn/Gornik-Tomaszewski* come to a similar conclusion when analyzing the status of implementation of the IAS Regulation in the 28 countries of the European Economic Area by 2006. While several countries in the EEA require Full IFRS in the individual financial statements of publicly traded companies, most countries still permit Local GAAP in the financial statements of non-publicly traded firms (*Sellhorn/Gornik-Tomaszewski* (2006), p. 195). By 2014, European non-publicly traded firms have been obliged or permitted to use Full IFRS in their individual financial statements in only 19 of 28 EU countries.

Procházka (2012) tries to quantify the scope of Full IFRS adoption in 27 European countries by developing an **'IFRS Adoption Index'** and finds that patterns of *de jure* harmonization differ substantially between the countries of the European Union. He thereby defines eight areas of Full IFRS adoption ranging from the consolidated accounts of listed companies to separate financial statements of a non-consolidated unlisted company and tax accounts. By assigning points to those EU countries, where Full IFRS are required or permitted in the predefined areas, he ends up with a total score of Full IFRS adoption (*Procházka* (2012), p. 377). This straightforward attempt to quantify the scope of *de jure* harmonization in the European Union reveals once again the difficulty in finding objective measures of IFRS adoption other than 'yes' or 'no'. Both metric and ordinal measures suffer from limitations regarding their ambiguous composition and evaluation of the input data (e.g. areas of application).

A summary of the above presented descriptive studies on worldwide Full IFRS adoption is provided in Table 1-10.

The **most up-to-date information** on worldwide Full IFRS adoptions is provided by large audit firms such as *PricewaterhouseCoopers* and *Deloitte*. In an annual survey, *PricewaterhouseCoopers* presents a tabular summary of the financial reporting rules for listed and statutory filings and an outlook on future IFRS conversions in 147 jurisdictions. According to the *PwC* survey in 2013, Full IFRS (incl. modifications)[71] are either permitted or required for listed filings in 117 of the 147 jurisdictions (80%). Regarding statutory filings, Full IFRS (incl. modifications)[72] are permitted or required in 118 jurisdictions (80%). Full IFRS conversion plans exist in 39 jurisdictions (*PricewaterhouseCoopers* (2013)).

[71] For example, regardless of the carve-out of the European Union regarding the application of IAS 39, EU-IFRS are still counted as Full IFRS. If all modified versions of Full IFRS are excluded from the group of adopters, Full IFRS (as issued by the IASB) are either permitted or required for *listed* filings in 60 of the 147 jurisdictions (41%).

[72] If all modified versions of Full IFRS are excluded from the group of adopters, Full IFRS (as issued by the IASB) are either permitted or required for *statutory* filings in 65 of the 147 jurisdictions (44%).

Reference	Methodology	Key results
BDO et al. (2003)	Follow-up of Andersen et al.'s (2001) survey of national accounting standards for listed firms benchmarked against Full IFRS in 59 countries (2002).	In the field of listed companies, 56 (95%) of the sampled countries either have adopted, intend to adopt, or intend to converge with Full IFRS.
Street/Larson (2004)	Evaluation of the results from BDO et al.'s (2003) survey of 59 countries' accounting convergence plans with Full IFRS in the field of listed firms for 15 EU countries (2002).	Most EU members do not plan to converge national GAAP with Full IFRS and continue to require or allow national GAAP for individual accounts. This leads to the emergence of a 'two standard' system in the European Union.
Sellhorn/Gornik-Tomaszewski (2006)	Analysis of the status of implementation of the IAS Regulation in the 28 countries of the European Economic Area (2006).	While several countries in the EEA require Full IFRS in the individual financial statements of publicly traded firms, most countries only permit Full IFRS in the individual and consolidated statements of non-publicly traded firms.
United Nations (2008)	Case studies on Full IFRS adoption in eight countries (1973-2010).	The extent of application of Full IFRS varies from one country to another, especially regarding the adoption by listed and non-listed companies.
Zeff/Nobes (2010)	Conceptual analysis of different methods of Full IFRS implementation in eight jurisdictions (2002-2010).	The word 'adopt' is ambiguous as it refers to several different methods of Full IFRS implementation by jurisdictions.
Procházka (2012)	Analysis of the scope of Full IFRS application in 27 European countries (2011).	The patterns of de jure harmonization differ substantially between the countries of the European Union.

Table 1-10: Descriptive cross-country studies on Full IFRS adoption

The **most comprehensive database** on worldwide Full IFRS adoptions is provided by *Deloitte* on the iasplus.com website. In 2003, *Deloitte* began to track the process of Full IFRS adoptions by publishing a yearly booklet called 'IFRSs in your pocket'. The booklets contained a summary of Full IFRS adoptions by listed firms in 95 (in 2003) to 109 (in 2012) jurisdictions (*Deloitte Touche Tohmatsu* (2003-2012)). Today, the iasplus.com website has superseded the yearly booklet and provides the timeliest information on Full IFRS adoptions by listed and unlisted firms in 173 jurisdictions (*Deloitte Touche Tohmatsu* (2014c)).

According to **iasplus.com** (as of July 2014), 128 jurisdictions permit or require Full IFRS for domestic listed companies by 2014. Furthermore, in 106 jurisdictions, Full IFRS are permitted or required for domestic unlisted companies. Although the website is updated on a regular basis, it is not free of mistakes. It seems that the **primary focus is on listed companies**, as the corresponding information is presented in great detail,[73] whereas information on the use of Full IFRS by domestic unlisted companies is only supplemented

[73] The information is displayed in five different columns representing the following five categories of Full IFRS adoption: (1) IFRSs not permitted, (2) IFRSs permitted, (3) IFRSs required for some, (4) IFRSs required for all, and (5) Audit report states compliance with IFRS. Cf. *Deloitte Touche Tohmatsu* (2014c).

within a single column. In addition, the iasplus.com website does rarely provide information on the scope of Full IFRS adoptions.

Since 2013, the *IFRS Foundation* offers its own **open source database** on the use of Full IFRS in individual jurisdictions on the **ifrs.org** website. The Foundation uses responses to a survey provided by standard-setters and other relevant bodies to draft 130 jurisdiction profiles (as of July 2014) that include country-by-country information on Full IFRS adoptions by listed and unlisted firms. Regulators and international audit firms are invited to review the drafts and their comments are reflected in the profiles (*IFRS Foundation* (2014g)). According to ifrs.org (2014), 122 of the 130 jurisdictions have made a public commitment to IFRSs as the single set of high quality global accounting standards. 105 jurisdictions (81%) require Full IFRS for all or most domestic publicly accountable entities (listed companies and financial institutions) in their capital markets. Furthermore, around 60% of these 105 jurisdictions also require Full IFRS for some domestic companies, whose securities are not publicly traded, generally financial institutions, and large unlisted companies (*IFRS Foundation* (2014g)).

Apart from the information given on Full IFRS adoptions, the jurisdiction profiles also provide an overview of the endorsement process and the degree of modification to the IASB standards. According to the *IFRS Foundation* (2014), the 122 jurisdictions only made very few **modifications to Full IFRS** and the few that were made are generally regarded as temporary steps in the jurisdiction's plans to adopt Full IFRS as a whole (*Pacter* (2014), p. 9).

The *IFRS Foundation's* **jurisdiction profiles** are the most comprehensive and detailed database on the use of Full IFRS worldwide. Furthermore, the given information has been verified by several local accounting experts such as national standard-setters and audit firms that provide the data with the highest possible reliability. The main objective of the database is to give the most recent information on the current Full IFRS adoption status of a large number of jurisdictions. However, unlike in this study, historic information on the past convergence process is provided in rare circumstances only.

A summary of the above presented databases, which provide cross-country information on the process and the scope of worldwide Full IFRS adoption, is provided in Table 1-11.

Reference	Methodology	Key results
IFRS Adoption Research Group (2011)	Summary of country-by-country information on Full IFRS adoptions by listed firms in 240 jurisdictions (1981-2011).	Between 1981 and 2011, 31 jurisdictions have adopted Full IFRS for domestic listed companies.
Deloitte (2003-2012)	Summary of Full IFRS adoptions by listed firms in 95 (2003) to 109 (2012) jurisdictions in tabular form (2003-2012).	The worldwide use of Full IFRS increased significantly between 2003 and 2012. Full IFRS are either permitted or required for domestic listed companies in 49 jurisdictions (2003) and in 87 jurisdictions (2012).
PwC (2009-2013)	Survey of PwC member firms on rules for listed and statutory filings and IFRS conversion plans in 108 (2009) to 147 (2013) jurisdictions in tabular form (2009-2013).	Full IFRS (incl. modifications) are either permitted or required for listed filings in 117 jurisdictions (2013). Full IFRS (incl. modifications) are either permitted or required for statutory filings in 118 jurisdictions (2013). Full IFRS conversion plans exist in 39 jurisdictions (2013).
Deloitte (2014)	Summary of Full IFRS adoptions by listed and unlisted firms in 173 jurisdictions in tabular form (2014).	By 2014, 128 jurisdictions permit or require Full IFRS for domestic listed companies. Furthermore, in 106 jurisdictions, Full IFRS is also permitted or required for domestic unlisted companies.
IFRS Foundation (2014)	Jurisdiction profiles summarizing information on Full IFRS adoption by listed and unlisted firms in 130 jurisdictions (2014).	122 of the 130 jurisdictions have made a public commitment to Full IFRS as the single set of high quality global accounting standards. 105 jurisdictions (81% of the profiles) require Full IFRS for all or most domestic publicly accountable entities (listed companies and financial institutions) in their capital markets.

Table 1-11: Cross-country databases on Full IFRS adoption

1.6.2.2 IFRS for SMEs

Due to the recent issue date of the IFRS for SMEs in 2009, the time frame for gradual convergence of National GAAPs with IFRS for SMEs is significantly shorter than in the case of Full IFRS. Consequently, partial convergence with IFRS for SMEs has yet been observed in rare circumstances only. One example of partial convergence with IFRS for SMEs is the United Kingdom and the Republic of Ireland. In 2010, the UK Accounting Standards Board agreed on a complete replacement of the UK accounting standards by the IFRS for SMEs (*Boyle* (2010), p. 58). However, due to the **IFRS for SMEs' non-compliance with EU law** and the criticism received by UK preparers and users, the new UK GAAP (FRS 102) differs from the IFRS for SMEs in several respects. Among other deviations, the revaluation of tangible and intangible fixed assets, although forbidden under IFRS for SMEs, has been reintroduced in the standard as an accounting option (*Institute of Chartered Accountants in England and Wales* (2013), p. 3).[74]

To a large extent, the sources of information regarding IFRS for SMEs adoption are the same as for Full IFRS adoption. However, cross-country research on the characteristics of IFRS for SMEs adoption is still scarce. Instead, there are only a few databases, which provide information on worldwide IFRS for SMEs adoption (see Table 1-12).

[74] Cf. section 1.3.2.4 for more details on the development of FRS 102.

Reference	Methodology	Key results
IFRS Foundation (2011)	Summary of IFRS for SMEs adoption by unlisted firms in nine geographic regions (2011).	73 countries have adopted IFRS for SMEs or announced to do so.
IFRS Foundation (2012)	Summary of IFRS for SMEs adoption by unlisted firms in eight geographic regions (2012).	Over 80 countries have adopted IFRS for SMEs or announced to do so.
PwC (2009-2013)	Survey of PwC member firms on rules for statutory filings and IFRS for SMEs conversion plans in 108 (2009) to 147 (2013) jurisdictions in tabular form (2009-2013).	IFRS for SMEs (incl. modifications) is either permitted or required for statutory filings in 57 jurisdictions (2013). IFRS for SMEs conversion plans exist in 18 jurisdictions (2013).
Deloitte (2014)	Summary of IFRS for SMEs adoption by unlisted firms in seven jurisdictions in tabular form (2014).	By 2014, IFRS for SMEs is permitted or required for domestic unlisted companies in Antigua and Barbuda, Bahamas, Barbados, Guyana, Panama, Sierra Leone, and South Africa.
IFRS Foundation (2014)	Jurisdiction profiles summarizing information on IFRS for SMEs adoption by unlisted firms in 130 jurisdictions (2014).	63 of the 130 jurisdictions require or permit IFRS for SMEs for domestic unlisted firms. It is also currently under consideration in a further 16 jurisdictions.

Table 1-12: Cross-country databases on IFRS for SMEs adoption

Contrary to the comprehensive and detailed database on Full IFRS adoption, especially in the field of listed companies, *Deloitte's* iasplus.com website does only contain **limited information on IFRS for SMEs adoption**. In fact, the website merely confirms IFRS for SMEs adoption for seven jurisdictions[75] (*Deloitte Touche Tohmatsu* (2014c)). Additional information is provided on the basis of individual jurisdiction updates, yet not for all countries within one table (*Deloitte Touche Tohmatsu* (2014b)). The yearly surveys of *PwC* member firms also include a country-by-country summary of financial reporting rules for statutory filings in 147 jurisdictions. According to this, IFRS for SMEs (incl. modifications)[76] is either permitted or required for statutory filings in 57 jurisdictions (39%). IFRS for SMEs conversion plans exist in 18 jurisdictions (*PricewaterhouseCoopers* (2013)).

Apart from the adoption updates provided by large audit firms, the *IFRS Foundation* reports regularly on IFRS for SMEs adoptions. In the **IFRS for SMEs Update** (Issue 2011-7), the *IFRS Foundation* declared that 73 countries have adopted IFRS for SMEs or announced to do so (*IFRS Foundation* (2011)). In 2012, the assumed number of IFRS for SMEs adopting countries rose to more than 80 countries (*IFRS Foundation* (2012a), p. 1). These early numbers on current and future IFRS for SMEs adopters contain several mistakes. For example, Canada considered but rejected adoption of IFRS for SMEs because

[75] According to iasplus.com, IFRS for SMEs is permitted or required for domestic unlisted companies in Antigua and Barbuda, Bahamas, Barbados, Guyana, Panama, Sierra Leone, and South Africa by 2014.

[76] If all modified versions of IFRS for SMEs are excluded from the group of adopters, IFRS for SMEs (as issued by the IASB) is either permitted or required for *statutory* filings in 49 of the 147 jurisdictions (33%).

constituents in the private enterprise sector preferred made-in-Canada standards tailored to their needs (*IFRS Foundation* (2014d), p. 6).

In 2013, the *IFRS Foundation* combined the data from prior IFRS for SMEs updates with the 130 jurisdiction profiles that also contain country-by-country information on the use of Full IFRS. According to ifrs.org (2014), 63 of the 130 sampled jurisdictions require or permit IFRS for SMEs for domestic unlisted firms. Furthermore, the standard is under consideration in a further 16 jurisdictions (*IFRS Foundation* (2014g)). Given these verified numbers, the IFRS Foundation has slightly **overestimated the use of IFRS for SMEs** during the first five years after its issuance. The Foundation's jurisdiction profiles provide reliable up-to-date information on the scope of application and deviations from IFRS for SMEs. The profiles hence represent the most important source of information on the worldwide use of IFRS for SMEs. However, the jurisdiction profiles neither contain historic information on the country-specific convergence process towards IFRS for SMEs adoption starting in 2009 or earlier, nor do they provide detailed information on the modifications made to the IFRS for SMEs on country level.

Having reviewed a selected series of descriptive research on Full IFRS and IFRS for SMEs adoption, the following section presents a review of prior studies that focus on the determinants of Full IFRS and IFRS for SMEs adoption.

1.6.3 Explanatory country level studies on GAAP adoption

The question *why* countries adopt IFRS or at least converge their national accounting systems with IASB standards has been discussed by accounting experts since the early 1970s. Hence, the following analysis of prior research cannot include all studies, which have been conducted on the drivers and impediments of Full IFRS and IFRS for SMEs adoption by countries worldwide. It rather contains the most relevant literature to this particular study (esp. theory-based, archival, and cross-country studies).

1.6.3.1 Full IFRS

The review of prior research on the determinants of Full IFRS adoption by countries is divided into **four different research fields**: (1) economic factors, (2) political factors, and (3) network effects, as well as (4) national culture. The allocation of studies to one of these four research areas is not always clear, as most conceptual studies discuss more than one reason for or against Full IFRS adoption. The same holds true for the majority of archival studies. Nevertheless, the reviewed studies are classified into one of the four given areas according to their main research focus. Within each of the four research fields, the primary focus of the analysis will be on prior archival cross-country studies, as they are of higher relevance to this study due to the similar research design. Hence, archival studies will be discussed in more detail than conceptual analyses and normative policy recommendations.

1.6.3.1.1 Economic factors

According to *Hauworth* (1973), the need for worldwide accounting standards exists on two levels. First, there is an interest of multinational companies to report on each of their segments on a comparable basis for internal information purposes. Second, users of financial statements need worldwide accounting standards to be assured that the financial statements of all companies regardless of their country of origin will be comparable and reflect economic facts in the same way (*Hauworth* (1973), p. 23). Regardless of this need for international accounting harmonization, *Hauworth* lists the following eight impediments of the development of worldwide accounting standards:

> *(1) "the diversity of views that exist regarding the* ***purpose*** *of financial statements,*
>
> *(2) differences in the extent to which the* ***accounting profession*** *has developed in various countries,*
>
> *(3) the influence of* ***tax laws*** *on financial reporting,*
>
> *(4) the requirements of* ***company laws****,*
>
> *(5) differences among countries in* ***basic economic facts*** *affecting financial reporting,*
>
> *(6) differences among countries in practices recommended by the accounting profession,*
>
> *(7) failure of professional pronouncements to accord with economic facts, and*
>
> *(8) lack of an agency to enforce worldwide accounting standards."*
>
> (*Hauworth* (1973), p. 24)

Although *Hauworth* (1973) does not discuss the reasons for and against Full IFRS adoption in particular, he already raises several relevant subject areas that were later studied in detail by other accounting researchers. For example, when analyzing the *IASC's* (1988) survey on the level of compliance of national accounting standards with 25 IAS in 54 countries, *Purvis et al.* (1991) find that countries with **weak or newly established accounting professions** tend to adopt IAS without modifications whereas countries with a strong tradition of accounting or powerful accounting institutions typically issue standards independently of the IASC. The authors conclude that the greater the degree of dependence on the IASC, the greater a country's conformity with IAS (*Purvis et al.* (1991), p. 28ff.).

BDO et al. (2003) analyze 59 countries' plans to promote and achieve convergence with Full IFRS in the field of listed firms. Their results show that there is tension between the capital markets orientation of Full IFRS and the **tax-driven nature** of some national accounting regimes. Furthermore, the complicated nature of particular standards is seen as one of the main obstacles to Full IFRS adoption.

The above findings are reaffirmed by *Larson/Street* (2004), who evaluate *BDO et al.'s* (2003) survey for 17 EU countries. Apart from problems arising from the complicated nature of particular IFRS (e.g. IAS 39, accounting for financial instruments) and the tax-orientation of many European accounting systems, they find that **underdeveloped national capital markets**, insufficient guidance on first-time application of Full IFRS, and limited experience with certain types of transactions (e.g. pensions) are seen as other important barriers to Full IFRS adoption (*Larson/Street* (2004), p. 89).

By analyzing the differences between the implementation of the IAS Regulation in 28 countries of the European Economic Area, *Sellhorn/Gornik-Tomaszewski* (2006) add to these findings that national rules for **capital maintenance and profit distribution** impede Full IFRS adoption in the individual financial statements of European companies. For example, individual financial statements prepared under German GAAP are primarily aimed at determining 'distributable profit' in a conservative and prudent way in order to protect creditors from excessive distributions. As financial statements prepared under Full IFRS are intended to provide decision-useful information to a wide range of users, there is an obvious contradiction in purposes between these two accounting systems (*Sellhorn/Gornik-Tomaszewski* (2006), p. 203). Full IFRS adoption in the individual financial statements of German companies is hence likely to result in unfavorable consequences and is associated with high economic burdens.

Following the idea of *Hauworth* (1973) that differences among countries in basic economic factors affect financial reporting, *Hegarty et al.* (2004) conclude that Full IFRS are not appropriate for use by all reporting entities and recommend that separate standards should apply to entities other than public interest entities, especially in less developed countries (*Hegarty et al.* (2004), p. 7). In the summary report on the 'Lessons Learned' from the World Bank's Accounting and Auditing ROSC Program,[77] *Hegarty et al.* (2004) provide an insight into their experiences with Full IFRS adoption in 38 countries. They state that the use of Full IFRS as the single set of accounting requirements has frequently led to unintended negative consequences. In particular, the **lack of human and financial resources** is a significant impediment to de facto implementation of Full IFRS (*Hegarty et al.* (2004), p. ii).

The recommendations of *Hegarty et al.* (2004) are supported by a study on the implementation of Full IFRS in Nigeria. *Okaro/Tauringana's* (2012) survey of 50 accounting professionals on Full IFRS adoption in Nigeria reveals a lack of training on Full IFRS at tertiary institutions and the insufficient capacity of Nigerian regulators to drive the transition process. These two lacking resources are seen as the main reasons for the delayed and uncompleted transition from SAS (local Nigerian GAAP) to Full IFRS in the field of listed firms (*Okaro/Tauringana* (2012), p. 155).

Hail et al. (2010) analyze the economic factors related to the *potential* adoption of Full IFRS by the United States. The authors say that Full IFRS adoption in the United States involves a trade-off between the short-term **costs of transitioning** to a new accounting system, the modest comparability benefits and the recurring cost savings of US multinational companies (*Hail et al.* (2010a), p. 386ff.). According to this, every country's decision to substitute Full IFRS for its national accounting system is determined by the level of transition and subsequent costs and the long-term benefits of the system change. *Hail et al.'s* vague conclusions regarding future Full IFRS adoption by the United States illustrate how difficult it is to quantify reliably the costs and potential benefits of Full IFRS adoption on country level.

[77] The objectives of the World Bank's Accounting and Auditing ROSC Program are to assess the comparability of national accounting and auditing standards with Full IFRS and International Standards on Auditing (ISA) and assist countries in developing and implementing an action plan for improving their financial reporting regimes. Cf. *World Bank* (2004e), p. 2.

In a commentary, *Selling* (2013) presents ten reasons why the United States should not adopt Full IFRS for domestic listed companies. Among others, *Selling* claims that US GAAP is superior to Full IFRS and that the SEC's financial reporting purposes significantly differ from those of other national regulators. Taken the ten reasons together, **Full IFRS would be unsuitable for the US financial reporting landscape** (*Selling* (2013), p. 156). Although the recommendations of *Selling* merely represent a personal remark on the potential adoption of Full IFRS in the United States, they show that a perceived high quality of Local GAAP and a high level of appreciation for local standards can be important sources of opposition to Full IFRS adoption.

Contrary to the view of *Hail et al.* (2010) that countries encounter a **cost-benefit trade-off** when deciding on the implementation of a new accounting system such as Full IFRS, *Ball* (2001) claims that countries adopt Full IFRS because it is costless to do so. By referring to the signaling model of *Spence* (1973), *Ball* assumes that the adopting countries are able to signal high-quality financial reporting although little changes in accounting practice (*Ball* (2001), p. 167). However, if Full IFRS adoption was costless and always led to positive outcomes, it is surprising why Full IFRS have yet not been adopted by all countries worldwide. One argument against *Ball's* thesis is that a country's announcement to adopt Full IFRS in the near future raises expectations on the national standard-setter and other national accounting institutions. If these expectations are not satisfied, it is unlikely that the country is able to signal high-quality financial reporting and benefits from Full IFRS adoption.

A summary of the above reviewed studies on the economic determinants of Full IFRS adoption is presented in Table 1-13.

Compared to the above presented studies that largely consist of conceptual analyses and normative policy recommendations, theory-based, archival, cross-country studies are rather scarce. In one of the first archival macro-level studies on Full IFRS adoption conducted by *Hope et al.* (2006), two theoretical hypotheses are empirically tested within a sample of 38 countries. The authors predict that countries with relatively **weak investor-protection mechanisms** (measured as mandatory disclosure requirements of securities laws and level of anti-director rights) are more likely to adopt Full IFRS as they seek to improve their investor protection by 'bonding' to a high-quality reporting system (*Hope et al.* (2006), p. 2). By drawing on a cost/benefit framework, *Hope et al.* predict a positive association between the **access level of a country's capital markets** and the adoption of Full IFRS. In their view, a country already committed to opening up its capital market is more likely to adopt Full IFRS to increase access and attract additional investors (*Hope et al.* (2006), p. 2). Using a logistic regression model with the depending variable taking the value 1 if a country has adopted Full IFRS as of December 31, 2004, and 0 otherwise, *Hope et al.* find evidence that is consistent with their hypotheses. In their study, Full IFRS adoption refers to the use of Full IFRS as the primary GAAP in the consolidated financial statements of listed companies for investor reporting. The corresponding data are obtained from *Deloitte's* iasplus.com website (2004).

Reference	Methodology	Key results
Hauworth (1973)	Conceptual analysis of the problems in the development of worldwide accounting standards (1973).	The diversity in national accounting purposes, the influence of national tax and company law, and cross-country differences in basic economic factors and in the development of the accounting profession impede the international harmonization of accounting standards.
Purvis et al. (1991)	Statistical analysis of IASC survey data (1988) regarding the level of compliance of national accounting standards with 25 IAS in 54 countries (1988).	Countries with weak or newly established accounting professions tend to adopt IAS without modifications whereas countries with a strong tradition of accounting or powerful accounting institutions typically issue standards independently of the IASC.
Ball (2001)	Conceptual analysis of the reasons and the potential gains of IAS adoption by countries (2001).	Countries adopt IAS because it is costless to do so. They hereby signal high-quality financial reporting despite little changes in accounting practice.
BDO et al. (2003)	Follow-up of Andersen et al.'s (2001) survey of national accounting standards for listed firms benchmarked against Full IFRS in 59 countries (2002).	The complicated nature of particular standards and the tax-driven nature of the national accounting regime are the two main obstacles to Full IFRS adoption.
Larson/Street (2004)	Evaluation of the results from BDO et al.'s (2003) survey of 59 countries' accounting convergence plans with Full IFRS in the field of listed firms for 17 EU countries (2002).	Underdeveloped national capital markets, insufficient guidance on first-time application of Full IFRS and limited experience with certain types of transactions (e.g. pensions) are barriers to Full IFRS convergence in the European Union.
Hegarty et al. (2004)	Conceptual evaluation of the Lessons Learned from the World Bank's Accounting and Auditing ROSC Program in 38 countries (2001-2004).	Full IFRS are not appropriate for use by all reporting entities and separate standards should apply to entities other than public interest entities. The use of Full IFRS as the single set of standards has frequently led to unintended negative consequences.
Sellhorn/Gornik-Tomaszewski (2006)	Analysis of the status of implementation of the IAS Regulation in the 28 countries of the European Economic Area (2006).	National rules for capital maintenance, profit distribution and taxation impede the implementation of Full IFRS in the individual financial statements of companies.
Hail et al. (2010a)	Economic analysis of the potential adoption of Full IFRS by the United States (2010).	Full IFRS adoption in the United States involves a trade-off between the short-term costs of transitioning to a new system, the modest comparability benefits and the recurring cost savings of US multinational companies' reporting.
Okaro/Tauringana (2012)	Survey of 50 accounting professionals on Full IFRS adoption by listed firms in Nigeria (2010-2012).	The lack of training on IFRS at tertiary institutions and the insufficient capacity of Nigerian regulators to drive the transition process are the main reasons for the delayed and uncompleted transition from SAS (national GAAP) to IFRS.
Selling (2013)	Conceptual analysis of the problems of Full IFRS adoption by the United States (2013).	The United States should not adopt Full IFRS because of many different reasons. For example, US GAAP is superior to Full IFRS. In case of IFRS adoption, the US would suffer from a loss of sovereignty over its ability to set accounting standards.

Table 1-13: Selected studies on economic determinants of Full IFRS adoption

Zeghal/Mhedhbi (2006) conduct an archival study on the determinants of Full IFRS adoption in 64 developing countries. They select various environmental factors, which they say have 'a very strategic importance' in the adoption decision. By using a matched sample design, 32 Full IFRS 'adopters' are compared to the same number of 'non-adopters'. The similarity of the countries is based on the average GDP during the study period (1991-2000) (*Zeghal/Mhedhbi* (2006), p. 379). The adoption variable takes the value 1 if a country has adopted Full IFRS 'with or without modification', and 0 if it has not. The degree of modification that is still accepted for the group of adopters is not specified though. The results of the logistic regression show that developing countries with the **highest literacy rates**, that have capital markets and that have an Anglo-American culture are most likely to 'adopt' Full IFRS in the field of listed companies. The authors justify the positive association between the level of education and Full IFRS adoption by pointing out that Full IFRS adoption requires a high level of education to be able to understand, interpret, and then make use of the standards, and that a low education level can be a real barrier to Full IFRS adoption (*Zeghal/Mhedhbi* (2006), p. 377). When interpreting *Zeghal/Mhedhbi's* findings, it is crucial to consider that the sample consists of developing countries only and that the results might change if other countries are included in the sample.

Ding et al. (2007) use survey data on the differences between domestic accounting standards and Full IFRS from *Andersen et al.* (2001) to quantify for 30 countries the degree of *absence* and *divergence* of domestic accounting systems compared to Full IFRS. Absence is defined as the extent to which certain accounting issues are missing in Local GAAP but are covered in Full IFRS. The divergence score is built upon the number of differences between Local GAAP and Full IFRS. *Ding et al.* test empirically to which extent economic and legal factors determine the absence of Local GAAP and its divergence from Full IFRS. The results of the regression models show that *absence* (i.e. 'no Local GAAP') is constrained by the **importance of the equity market** and the **diversification of ownership**. According to the authors' view, the higher needs of information users in higher developed capital markets with diversified ownership make the country's financial reporting standards more sophisticated (*Ding et al.* (2007), p. 15). The stepwise regression models reveal that *divergence* (i.e. 'Local GAAP differs from Full IFRS') is also constrained by the importance of equity markets and that *divergence* is positively associated with the **level of economic development** and the **importance of the accounting profession**. The authors justify their findings by concluding that developed countries with a strong accounting profession tend to be more confident of their own accounting standards and more reluctant to adopt Full IFRS without modification (*Ding et al.* (2007), p. 16). By introducing a score for *absence* and *divergence* of Local GAAP compared to Full IFRS, *Ding et al.* create a new measure of international accounting differences on country level. The reliability of this measure is debatable as it is based on survey questions and hence relies upon subjective responses.

Following the general idea that accounting is a social system that exists within the context of larger social systems, *Archambault/Archambault* (2003) model corporate disclosure as a function of economic and national political systems. In 2009, *Archambault/Archambault* conduct an archival study on the determinants of Full IFRS adoption in 120 countries. They hereby seek to determine whether economic and political systems (and national culture) influence the national policy regarding the use of Full IFRS (*Archambault/Archambault* (2009), p. 40). The adoption group consists of countries, which have permitted or required the use of Full IFRS for some or all domestic listed companies by 2004. The corresponding data are derived from *Deloitte's* iasplus.com website.

Among other hypotheses, *Archambault/Archambault* predict that countries with high literacy rates are more likely to adopt Full IFRS and that low economic development and **net import activity** positively influence countries' decision to adopt Full IFRS. In the authors' view, Full IFRS adoption may help importing companies that buy goods on credit to obtain more favorable credit terms because their financial statements can be understood more easily than if domestic standards were used (*Archambault/Archambault* (2009), p. 42). The applied regression models show results that are consistent with this hypothesis. However, when including data on post-2004 Full IFRS adoptions, the results regarding the impact of economic development and net import activity are not significant at the 5% level anymore (*Archambault/Archambault* (2009), p. 49). This is mainly due to the inclusion of Full IFRS adoptions in the European Union in 2005. EU countries are rather highly developed and do generally not have trade deficits.

The main findings of the above reviewed archival studies on the economic determinants of Full IFRS adoption are summarized in Table 1-14.

Reference	Methodology	Key results
Hope et al. (2006)	Archival macro-level study on the determinants of Full IFRS adoption by listed firms in 38 countries (2004).	Countries with weaker investor protection mechanisms and countries that are perceived to provide better access to their domestic capital markets are more likely to adopt Full IFRS.
Zeghal/Mhedhbi (2006)	Archival macro-level study on the determinants of Full IFRS adoption by listed firms in 64 developing countries (1991-2000).	Developing countries with the highest literacy rates, that have capital markets and that have an Anglo-American culture, are the most likely to adopt Full IFRS.
Ding et al. (2007)	Archival macro-level study on the determinants and implications of the absence and divergence of national accounting standards compared to IAS in 30 countries based on survey data provided by Andersen et al. (2001).	Absence of Local GAAP (compared with Full IFRS) is constrained by the importance of the equity market and is positively associated with ownership concentration, while divergence of Local GAAP from Full IFRS is positively associated with the level of economic development and the importance of the accounting profession, but is constrained by the importance of equity markets.
Archambault/ Archambault (2009)	Archival macro-level study on the determinants of Full IFRS adoption by listed firms in 120 countries (2004).	Literacy rates and net import activity positively influence the decision to allow Full IFRS. Less economically developed countries are more likely to allow Full IFRS.

Table 1-14: Archival studies on economic determinants of Full IFRS adoption

All in all, prior research has shown that a **variety of economic factors** has determined Full IFRS adoption on country level. In particular, prior studies assume that different accounting purposes (e.g. contracting), a high perceived quality of local accounting systems as well as the development of a strong local accounting profession rather impede Full IFRS adoption. Furthermore, prior archival studies reveal that capital market characteristics such as the degree of investor protection determine the probability of Full IFRS adoption in the field of listed companies.

1.6.3.1.2 Political factors

Conceptual and empirical accounting research shows that political factors can complement or even override the economic determinants of Full IFRS adoption. In particular, this is due to the political interference in standard-setting and due to internal and external pressures.

In a theoretical analysis of the driving forces of the standard-setting process in Australia, especially regarding IAS adoption between 1997 and 2000, *Brown/Tarca* (2001) state that, although strong pressure exists for the internationalization of Australian accounting standards, political forces, and the personalities of **key players** are obstacles to IAS adoption in Australia (*Brown/Tarca* (2001), p. 290). The authors regret the political forces at work in standard-setting and predict that standard-setters will always be subject to political interference and not left to go about their own business in an undisturbed manner (*Brown/Tarca* (2001), p. 291).

Xiao et al. (2004) analyze the process of international accounting harmonization in China from 1949 to 2004 and find that **strong political influence**, together with a weak equity market and the tradition of relying on a uniform accounting system (UAS), has led to the coexistence of a UAS and IAS-type accounting standards in China. Although the Chinese government has been put under external pressure to develop accounting standards in harmony with Full IFRS, strong state-ownership, accounting traditions, and cultural factors have impeded the Chinese transition towards full implementation of Full IFRS (*Xiao et al.* (2004), p. 193).

Chand/White (2007) identify **multinational enterprises** and **large international audit firms** ('Big Four') as the main promoters of Full IFRS adoption in Fiji. The authors state that although Full IFRS cannot be meaningfully applied in the context of Fiji's economy and society, the lobbying of multinational enterprises and large international audit firms makes the local regulator move towards Full IFRS adoption (*Chand/White* (2007), p. 608). According to *Chand/White*, this leads to a transfer of economic resources in their favor. In particular, Full IFRS adoption in Fiji is in the interest of the Big Four, as they can keep their overall operating costs down and secure a competitive advantage over smaller operations (*Chand/White* (2007), p. 614).

In the second part of *Hail et al.'s* (2010) analysis of the implications of Full IFRS adoption by the United States, the authors focus on the political factors related to the possible US adoption of Full IFRS and discuss several scenarios for the evolution of US accounting standards. They conclude that the main political benefit from Full IFRS adoption by the United States is the signal to be willing to cooperate internationally. On the contrary, political costs evolve from seizing legislative power to a supranational institution, which might obtain a monopoly status in accounting standard-setting. *Hail et al.'s* analysis reveals that the **loss of legislative sovereignty** is one of the most important reasons why powerful jurisdictions like the United States hesitate to adopt Full IFRS unless they find a way to control or dominate the work of the IASB. This is why the governance structure of the IASB is of central interest to various US constituents (*Hail et al.* (2010b), p. 584).

Ramanna (2013) analyzes in four field studies (Canada, China, India, and the United States) the **political dynamics** regarding various countries' **Full IFRS harmonization strategies.** The author hereby describes unique elements of domestic political economies that are shaping IFRS policies. For example, while Full IFRS adoption in Canada can be explained by the country's cultural ties to Britain and France, in China, unique economic pressures on local exporters have influenced China's MOF to converge national standards with Full IFRS although the standards are not well-suited to China's emerging market conditions and pose compliance complexity for China's state-owned enterprises (*Ramanna* (2013), p. 28). From the four field studies, *Ramanna* inductively develops a framework for analyzing how international politics shape countries' harmonization strategies in the field of financial reporting. The framework consists of a 2x2 matrix, which reflects four different national strategies regarding Full IFRS adoption.

According to that, a country's harmonization strategy is dependent on its **cultural distance to the IASB** (x-axis) and its **potential political power** (y-axis) (*Ramanna* (2013), p. 29). The more political power a jurisdiction has, the more is the jurisdiction able to either set the direction of Full IFRS (in case of low cultural distance to the IASB; e.g. European Union) or to diverge from it (e.g. China, as its cultural distance to the IASB is high). In comparison, less powerful countries do rather align their rules with Full IFRS (e.g. Canada, whose cultural distance to the IASB is low) or form regional alliances to develop carve-outs (e.g. India, a country with high cultural distance to the IASB) (*Ramanna* (2013), p. 30). The study provides a valuable overview on the different IFRS harmonization paths jurisdictions may follow and sheds light on the possible implications of differences in political forces between powerful and less powerful countries on the adoption of Full IFRS.

In a series of eight case studies, the *United Nations* (2008) discuss various factors that have contributed to the introduction of Full IFRS in Brazil, Germany, India, Jamaica, Kenya, Pakistan, South Africa, and Turkey. For example, while Full IFRS adoption in Germany was mainly driven by the economic needs of domestic listed companies that strived for access to the global financial markets, the cases of Kenya, Pakistan, South Africa, and Turkey rather show the national desire of less developed countries to **raise local standards to international best practice** without allocating large resources to the development of local accounting standards (*United Nations* (2008), p. 1). Moreover, in most of the latter cases (and also in Jamaica) international and regional development banks have played an influential role in the implementation of Full IFRS by providing resources to developing countries and economies in transition. The case studies indicate that substantial financial support is needed to achieve the goal of Full IFRS adoption (*United Nations* (2008), p. 14).

In a conceptual paper *Singh/Newberry* (2008) discuss the appropriateness of Full IFRS adoption by developing countries. They state that corporate governance requirements imposed internationally as part of the New International Financial Architecture (NIFA) include compliance with Full IFRS. In accordance with *Soederberg* (2002), *Singh/Newberry* criticize that the International Monetary Fund (IMF) and the World Bank would use their considerable **international surveillance powers** to encourage developing countries to adopt Full IFRS (*Singh/Newberry* (2008), p. 484). In particular, the World Bank, as one of the largest users of financial statements worldwide, has become a 'major force' in efforts to impose Full IFRS on developing countries (*Singh/Newberry* (2008), p. 491). For example, in the case of Ghana, the World Bank recommended that Ghana should adopt Full IFRS without modification after it had studied the local accounting system and prepared a Report on Observance of Standards and Codes (ROSC) in 2004 (*Gyasi* (2010), p. 63).

In another conceptual paper *Rodrigues/Craig* (2007) discuss the global phenomenon of international accounting harmonization by using Hegelian dialectic. Following *Hegel's* theory of dialectic, in which contradiction is regarded as the root of all change (*Hegel/Wallace* (1975)), the authors state that convergence of accounting standards is a dialectical process of thesis, antithesis, and synthesis. *Rodrigues/Craig* discuss a series of theses and antitheses regarding international accounting harmonization by drawing on neoliberalism, free culture theory, and environmental determinism theory, and present a synthesis of their analysis, according to which (1) companies should keep applying local standards but should be required to reconcile their domestic financial statements with Full IFRS, (2) more efforts should be made regarding **regional harmonization** with the IASB serving as a guiding mechanism or clearing house (see also *Craig/Diga* (1996)), and (3) a clear differentiation should be made between the financial reporting rules of listed and unlisted companies (*Rodrigues/Craig* (2007), p. 750).

Chua/Taylor (2008) analyze the factors influencing worldwide Full IFRS adoption since the 1970s and state that widespread diffusion of Full IFRS can only partially be explained as an economically rational phenomenon. Instead, **political pressures and social considerations** have played a key role in the development and diffusion of Full IFRS (*Chua/Taylor* (2008), p. 462). The authors assume that the desire by the Anglo-American accounting and audit industry to retain control over the international accounting standard-setting process has been one important reason for the success of the IASB. Second, *Chua/Taylor* state that financial scandals and regional economic crises such as in Asia in 1997/1998 have boosted Full IFRS adoption at certain points in time (*Chua/Taylor* (2008), p. 469). Eventually, *Chua/Taylor* draw on the **institutional theory of isomorphism** to assume that, due to the adoption decision by powerful first movers, Full IFRS has become a field norm that others follow because adoption confers social legitimacy (*Chua/Taylor* (2008), p. 470). The authors thereby provide suggestions for future research, which are addressed in this study.[78]

A summary of the above reviewed studies on the political determinants of Full IFRS adoption is displayed in Table 1-15.

[78] The *institutional theory of isomorphism* represents one of two pillars of the theoretical foundation of this study. The *economic theory of networks* represents the second pillar.

Reference	Methodology	Key results
Brown/Tarca (2001)	Theoretical analysis of the driving forces of the standard-setting process in Australia, especially regarding IAS adoption (1997-2000).	Political forces and the personalities of key players were obstacles to IAS adoption in Australia. Pressure still exists for the internationalization of Australian accounting standards.
Xiao et al. (2004)	Conceptual review of factors influencing national accounting regulation and international accounting harmonization in China (1949-2004).	Strong political influence together with a weak equity market and the tradition of relying on a uniform accounting system (UAS) has led to the coexistence of a UAS and IAS-type accounting standards in China.
Chand/White (2007)	Critical comment on the driving forces of Full IFRS adoption in Fiji (1983-2006)	The influence of multinational enterprises and international audit firms on Full IFRS adoption in Fiji has led to a transfer of economic resources in their favor. Public interests are ignored.
Rodrigues/Craig (2007)	Theoretical analysis of the reasons for and against international accounting harmonization (1970s-2006).	Companies should be required to reconcile Local GAAP financial statements with Full IFRS. More regional harmonization efforts are needed and a clear differentiation between the financial reporting of listed and unlisted companies instead of global convergence with Full IFRS.
Chua/Taylor (2008)	Conceptual analysis of the factors influencing Full IFRS diffusion (1970-2008).	Widespread diffusion of Full IFRS can only be partially explained as an economically rational phenomenon. Political pressures and social considerations have played a key role in the development and diffusion of Full IFRS.
Singh/Newberry (2008)	Conceptual analysis of the determinants and the appropriateness of Full IFRS adoption by developing countries (1970-2008).	The IMF and World Bank use their considerable international surveillance powers to ensure developing countries comply with 'New International Financial Architecture' (NIFA) and thus adopt Full IFRS.
United Nations (2008)	Case studies on Full IFRS adoption in eight countries (1973-2010).	The factors contributing to the introduction of Full IFRS vary across countries. Observable drivers for Full IFRS implementation are the desire to raise national standards to international best practice and the influence and financial support by the World Bank and by national central banks.
Hail et al. (2010b)	Political analysis of the potential adoption of Full IFRS by the United States (2010).	The political benefits of Full IFRS adoption by the United States result from the signal to be willing to cooperate internationally. Political costs evolve from seizing legislative power to a supranational institution, which might obtain a monopoly status in accounting standard-setting.
Ramanna (2013)	Field studies on Full IFRS adoption in 3+1 countries (1970-2012).	Cultural distance and the potential power to shape political decisions at the IASB influence countries' IFRS harmonization strategies.

Table 1-15: Selected studies on political determinants of Full IFRS adoption

There are two archival cross-country studies that deal with the political determinants of Full IFRS adoption. *Judge et al.* (2010) conduct empirical research on the influence of institutional pressures on countries to adopt Full IFRS in the consolidated financial statements of publicly-listed domestic companies. For a total sample of 132 countries, data on the dependent variable are obtained from *Deloitte's* iasplus.com website as of August 2008. By referring to the institutional theory of isomorphism of *DiMaggio/Powell* (1983), *Judge et al.* test three hypotheses for the effect of three typical **isomorphic pressures** (i.e. coercive, mimetic, and normative pressures) on countries' decision to implement Full IFRS in their regulatory accounting framework. The authors predict that the selected proxies for the three isomorphic pressures (foreign aid, import penetration, and the level of education) have a positive influence on Full IFRS adoption (*Judge et al.* (2010), p. 163). In the applied regression models the results are consistent with the three hypotheses showing that the process of Full IFRS adoption is driven by social legitimization pressures (*Judge et al.* (2010), p. 168). Although the links between mimetic pressures and import penetration and the one between normative pressures and level of education are debatable and raise doubts about the testability of the applied theory, the study proves that isomorphic pressures (esp. coercive pressures represented by the **transfer of financial aid**) are at work when countries make their decision on the use of Full IFRS in the field of listed companies.

In the second archival macro-level study that covers political determinants of Full IFRS adoption, *Johnson* (2011) analyzes internal political forces affecting the Full IFRS adoption decision of 57 countries in the area of listed companies. *Johnson* finds that political systems with more political actors capable of blocking change (i.e. **'veto players'**) and with more influential **lobbying activity** are associated with delayed adoption of Full IFRS. By using a Hazard function, the dependent variable is constructed as the time period until Full IFRS adoption ranging from one (year 2002) to five (year 2007). As the IASB did not start operations before 2001, the year 2002 is chosen as the first possible year of Full IFRS adoption (*Johnson* (2011), p. 14). Following the literature on political economics, the underlying assumption of the applied duration analysis is that changes in accounting standards alter the distribution of power between groups and thereby potentially alter the payoffs to transacting parties (*Johnson* (2011), p. 2). According to that, the author predicts that countries with majoritarian systems (few veto players) will adopt Full IFRS more quickly than countries with consensus systems (many veto players). Furthermore, the author hypothesizes that the effect of veto players will be heightened (muted) in countries where lobbying efforts are more (less) effective (*Johnson* (2011), p. 5). The corresponding data regarding Full IFRS adoption during the years 2002-2007 are obtained from *Deloitte's* iasplus.com website.

Although the results in the regression models are consistent with *Johnson's* hypothesis, the study has certain limitations. The proxy used for measuring 'lobbying effectiveness' is the mean country-level response (ranging from 1-7) to a question of the World Economic Forum's annual Executive Opinion Survey, which was repeated annually in the years 2003 to 2007. For countries that adopted Full IFRS in 2002, the answer stems from a time after the adoption date and can hence not serve as a determinant of the Full IFRS adoption decision in the duration analysis. The variable should have been 'lagged' by at least two years like all the other independent variables in *Johnson's* study (*Johnson* (2011), p. 14).

The key results of the two presented archival cross-country studies on the political determinants of Full IFRS adoption are summarized in Table 1-16.

Reference	Methodology	Key results
Judge et al. (2010)	Archival macro-level study on the determinants of Full IFRS adoption in the consolidated accounts of listed firms in 132 countries (2008).	Isomorphic pressures (i.e. coercive, mimetic, and normative pressures) are predictive of Full IFRS adoption. The process of Full IFRS adoption is driven more by social legitimization pressures than it is by economic logic.
Johnson (2011)	Archival macro-level study on the determinants of Full IFRS adoption by listed firms in 57 countries (2002-2007).	Political systems with more political actors capable of blocking change (i.e. 'veto players') are associated with delayed adoption of Full IFRS. The effect of veto players is greater when lobbying efforts have a stronger relation with political outcomes.

Table 1-16: Archival studies on political determinants of Full IFRS adoption

In conclusion, prior research has revealed that economic factors are not the only drivers of the IFRS adoption process. On the contrary, the probability of Full IFRS adoption has also been influenced by the power of key political players and by various external pressures. For example, prior studies assume that supranational institutions such as the IMF and the World Bank as well as multinational corporations and audit firms have played an important role in many countries' decision process to adopt Full IFRS.

1.6.3.1.3 Network effects

Ramanna/Sletten (2009) combine economic, political, and cultural explanations for Full IFRS adoption in the field of listed firms by applying the **economic theory of networks** (*Ramanna/Sletten* (2009), p. 5). Network theory suggests that there are generally two factors to consider in adopting a network-dependent product: (1) the intrinsic value of the product (direct benefits), and (2) the value of the product's network (indirect benefits) (*Katz/Shapiro* (1985)). In literature, the direct benefits stemming from a network-dependent product are referred to as the **autarky value**, and the network-related benefits are called **synchronization value** (*Liebowitz/Margolis* (1994)).

Ramanna and Sletten's underlying assumption is that countries only adopt Full IFRS if the sum of the autarky value and the synchronization value stemming from Full IFRS adoption is higher than the total value of maintaining Local GAAP. Assuming that Local GAAP cannot have any synchronization value as it is only applied within one country, the equation can be rewritten in a way that countries will only adopt Full IFRS if the sum of the *net* autarky value (i.e. the difference between the autarky value of Full IFRS and Local GAAP) and the synchronization value of Full IFRS adoption is greater than zero (*Ramanna/Sletten* (2009), p. 7).

Ramanna/Sletten then subdivide the *net* autarky value of Full IFRS in **net economic benefits** and **net political benefits** and rename the synchronization value into **network benefits**. The authors end up with a cost-/benefit analysis regarding Full IFRS adoption by considering three different types of benefits. To test their influence on Full IFRS adoption by countries *Ramanna/Sletten* use a Hazard function, in which Full IFRS adoption is modeled as a 'failure event', i.e. the dependent variable is constructed as the time period until Full IFRS adoption. The study period starts in the first possible year of Full IFRS adoption (2002) and ends in 2007 (*Ramanna/Sletten* (2009), p. 22). The corresponding data are obtained for 102 non-European Union countries from *Deloitte's* iasplus.com website as of July 2008. The countries of the European Union (and from the European Economic Area) are excluded from the sample as their decision to adopt Full IFRS was closely tied to the establishment of the IASB itself. Furthermore, all EU member states (and countries from the EEA) jointly adopted Full IFRS in the consolidated financial statements of publicly traded companies between 2005 and 2007, thus making an analysis of their individual adoption decisions infeasible (*Ramanna/Sletten* (2009), p. 1). To increase the reliability of the iasplus data, the information has partly been verified by managing partners of big-4 audit firms and complemented by web searches of newswire archives and World Bank country reports (*Ramanna/Sletten* (2009), p. 13).

The most important finding of *Ramanna/Sletten* (2009) is that a country is more likely to adopt Full IFRS if **countries within its geographic region are Full IFRS adopters**. In addition, the authors find that more powerful countries (measured by GDP) are less likely to adopt Full IFRS and the likelihood of Full IFRS adoption at first increases and then decreases in the quality of countries' domestic governance institutions (*Ramanna/Sletten* (2009), p. 25). The findings regarding the network benefits of Full IFRS adoption suggest that (1) countries internalize the network effects of Full IFRS in their adoption decision, and that (2) as the network benefits from Full IFRS adoption get large, countries may adopt Full IFRS even if little or no net economic or net political benefits exist (*Ramanna/Sletten* (2009), p. 28). However, the study cannot provide any empirical evidence of cultural differences between the adopters' and the non-adopters' group.

Ramanna/Sletten (2009) is the **first study that addresses network effects** in the context of Full IFRS adoption and sheds light on the indirect benefits stemming from a wide diffusion of Full IFRS in countries' geographic neighborhood. Due to its great explanatory power, the hereby applied *economic theory of networks* is selected as one of two pillars of this study's theoretical foundation.[79] One important limitation of *Ramanna/Sletten* (2009) and many other archival studies on Full IFRS adoption lies in the fact that the iasplus.com data, notwithstanding their reliability, do not say to which degree Full IFRS have been modified before being adopted locally. This raises doubts about the precision and completeness of the Full IFRS adoption variable (*Ramanna/Sletten* (2009), p. 30).

In a subsequent study *Ramanna/Sletten* (2013) further evaluate the influence of network effects on countries' decision to adopt Full IFRS for domestic listed companies. Deviating from their prior hypothesis that a country is more likely to adopt Full IFRS if countries within its geographic region are Full IFRS adopters, *Ramanna/Sletten* hypothesize in this second paper that a country's decision to adopt Full IFRS is also related to the magnitude of its **economic relations with other countries that have adopted Full IFRS** (*Ramanna/Sletten* (2013), p. 2). They hereby refer to this magnitude as the IFRS *network value*, which is captured by a three-year lagged country-year variable representing the proportion of dyadic trade with Full IFRS adopting countries weighted with national GDP (*Ramanna/Sletten* (2013), p. 16). The time period between the decision to adopt Full IFRS and the date of its implementation is estimated to be two years on average (*Ramanna/Sletten*

[79] The *institutional theory of isomorphism* is chosen as the second pillar.

(2013), p. 10). To avoid any compounding affects between dependent and independent variables, the independent variables are lagged by one year more (three years) than the dependent variable is (two years).

The dependent variable is constructed as an ordinal measure of **Full IFRS adoption** including the following **three categories**: (1) non-adopters; (2) countries requiring Full IFRS for all listed companies (i.e. full adopters), and (3) all remaining countries with convergence projects, countries that allow voluntary Full IFRS adoption and countries that require Full IFRS for some listed companies only (i.e. partial adopters) (*Ramanna/Sletten* (2013), p. 12). The necessary data are obtained for 89 jurisdictions (representing 117 countries)[80] and the years 2003-2008 from *Deloitte's* iasplus website, *Pricewaterhouse-Coopers'* surveys on Full IFRS adoption by country and the World Bank's country Reports on the Observance of Standards and Codes (ROSC).

By using ordinary least squares (OLS) regressions, *Ramanna/Sletten* show that a country's Full IFRS adoption status, as measured by the ordinal dependent variable, is an increasing function of the **perceived value of its Full IFRS network**. The derived implication is that worldwide diffusion of Full IFRS is a self-reinforcing process, which might eventually lead to a situation, in which innovations that are superior to Full IFRS may not be implemented anymore (*Ramanna/Sletten* (2013), p. 7). The study of *Ramanna/Sletten* (2013) reveals that **network effects matter more to countries with smaller GDPs**. The authors explain this finding by arguing that larger countries, due to the size of their markets, are likely to attract foreign capital and maintain international trade even if they continue using domestic standards (*Ramanna/Sletten* (2013), p. 5).

The key findings of the two archival studies of *Ramanna/Sletten* are summarized in Table 1-17.

Reference	Methodology	Key results
Ramanna/Sletten (2009)	Archival macro-level study on the determinants of Full IFRS adoption by listed firms in 102 non-European Union countries (2002-2007).	More powerful countries are less likely to adopt Full IFRS. In addition, a country is more likely to adopt Full IFRS if countries within its geographic region are Full IFRS adopters. The likelihood of Full IFRS adoption at first increases and then decreases in the quality of countries' domestic governance institutions.
Ramanna/Sletten (2013)	Archival macro-level study on the determinants of Full IFRS adoption by listed firms in 89 jurisdictions (117 countries) countries (2003-2008).	The degree of Full IFRS harmonization in a country is an increasing function of the perceived value of its IFRS network. Network effects matter more to countries with smaller GDPs.

Table 1-17: Archival studies on network effects and Full IFRS adoption

All in all, the research of *Ramanna/Sletten* has set the stage for future studies on network effects and international accounting harmonization. As *Ramanna/Sletten* have only fo-

80 The 27 member countries of the European Union and Norway and Iceland (members of the EEA) are treated as one observation due to their joint decision to require Full IFRS in the consolidated financial statements of publicly traded firms from 2005-2007 onwards. Cf. *Ramanna/Sletten* (2013), p. 12.

cused on the role of network effects in the field of Full IFRS adoption by listed companies so far, this study takes the opportunity to transfer and adapt their research design to Full IFRS and IFRS for SMEs adoption in the field of private firms.

1.6.3.1.4 National culture

This study follows a culture-free approach to describe and explain countries' process towards international accounting harmonization in the field of private firms. However, selected studies on the cultural determinants of Full IFRS adoption are also discussed in this review of prior research to illustrate the various ways by which national culture determines the shape of accounting systems as well as to point out the conceptual difficulties in developing a coherent and measurable construct of 'national culture'.

Kikuya (2001) analyzes in a conceptual single-country study the history of international accounting harmonization from 1949 to 2001 and its impact on accounting in Japan. Although being a founding member of the IASC, Japan has always had a strong local accounting tradition and national accounting standards that have not fully converged with Full IFRS. According to *Kikuya*, Japanese accounting practices have originally been quite different from standards modelled on British-American accounting standards. The author concludes that **local accounting conventions and customs** stemming from the specific cultural, economic and social environments have hindered international harmonization of Japanese accounting standards (*Kikuya* (2001), p. 367).

As Full IFRS are closely linked to the Anglo-American accounting tradition rooted in the United Kingdom and the United States, cultural barriers to international accounting harmonization especially exist in the countries of the Middle East. In a survey of 120 accounting professionals on Full IFRS adoption by listed firms in Saudi Arabia, *Alkhtani* (2012) finds that cultural factors such as **religion**, **language**, **national pride**, and **accounting illiteracy** may impede developing countries to adopt Full IFRS (*Alkhtani* (2012), p. 20). For example, Islamic law (*Sharia*) forbids the charging or payment of interests, which gives rise to specific accounting needs of Islamic states. While local accounting standards generally comply with Islamic law, this is not necessarily the case for Western accounting standards such as Full IFRS. For the case of Saudi Arabia, *Alkhtani* concludes that the influence of religion (Islam) on accounting regulation is limited. However, the lack of English language knowledge still represents a difficulty for Full IFRS implementation (*Alkhtani* (2012), p. 20).

Reference	Methodology	Key results
Kikuya (2001)	Conceptual review of international accounting harmonization and its impact on Japan (1949-2001).	Although Japan made its best endeavors to adopt IAS, accounting conventions and customs, cultural, economic, and social environments have hindered international harmonization of Japanese accounting standards.
Alkhtani (2012)	Survey of 120 accounting professionals on Full IFRS adoption by listed firms in Saudi Arabia (2012).	Several cultural factors such as religion, language, national pride, and accounting illiteracy may influence developing countries' decision to adopt Full IFRS.

Table 1-18: Selected studies on cultural determinants of Full IFRS adoption

A brief summary of the key findings of the two above reviewed studies on cultural determinants of Full IFRS adoption is presented in Table 1-18.

In an archival study *Ding et al.* (2005) present empirical evidence of **national culture** being an important determinant of the *absence* (no accounting rules) and *divergence* (different accounting rules) of national accounting standards compared to Full IFRS. Based on survey data from 52 countries, provided by *Andersen et al.* (2001), the authors find that national culture matters more than legal origin in explaining divergences from Full IFRS. *Ding et al.* measure national culture by the four dimensions of *Hofstede* (1980) (power distance, individualism, masculinity, and uncertainty avoidance) as well as by two (hierarchy and autonomy) of the seven value types (conservatism, intellectual and affective autonomy, hierarchy, mastery, egalitarian commitment, and harmony) of *Schwartz* (1994). The findings suggest that technical and political dimensions of the Full IFRS adoption debate, although essential, are not the only ones involved (*Ding et al.* (2005), p. 325). One **limitation** of the study other than the subjective measurement of *absence* and *divergence* lies in the application of the *Hofstede* model, which has been criticized for not being able of measuring national culture (*Baskerville* (2003)). *Ding et al.* respond to this limitation by adding a model using the value types of *Schwartz*, which also generate robust results (*Ding et al.* (2005), p. 343).

Clements et al. (2010) seek to empirically test whether the four different dimensions of national culture provided by *Hofstede* (1980) have influenced the Full IFRS adoption decision of 61 countries in the field of listed companies. Contrary to *Ding et al.* (2005), the authors are **unable to document any cultural influences**. Instead, they find that larger countries are less likely to adopt Full IFRS. In conformity with most other archival macro-level studies on the determinants of Full IFRS adoption, the dependent variable describing Full IFRS adoption is dichotomous and takes the value 1 if a country is in the adopter group, and 0 if it is not. Data are obtained from *Deloitte's* iasplus.com website as of September 2009 and countries are classified as Full IFRS adopters only if Full IFRS is 'required for all' domestic listed companies. Countries, in which the use of Full IFRS is 'not permitted', are hence classified as non-adopters. All remaining countries, where Full IFRS is 'required for some' or only 'permitted' for listed companies, are excluded from the sample as no clear distinction between adoption or non-adoption can be made (*Clements et al.* (2010), p. 120). Although *Clements et al.* admit that the empirical measures of national culture based on *Hofstede* might not adequately reflect cultural diversity across countries, they interpret their findings in a way that there is no association between national culture and the Full IFRS adoption decision (*Clements et al.* (2010), p. 124).

The key results of the two above presented archival studies on cultural determinants of Full IFRS adoption are summarized in Table 1-19.

Reference	Methodology	Key results
Ding et al. (2005)	Archival macro-level study on the determinants and implications of the 'absence' and 'divergence' of national accounting standards compared to IAS in 52 countries based on survey data provided by Andersen et al. (2001).	National culture matters more than legal origin in explaining divergences from IAS and complements the technical and/or political dimensions of the IAS adoption debate.
Clements et al. (2010)	Archival macro-level study on the determinants of Full IFRS adoption by listed firms in 61 countries (2009).	Larger countries are less likely to adopt Full IFRS. Cultural diversity is not associated with the likelihood of Full IFRS adoption.

Table 1-19: Archival studies on cultural determinants of Full IFRS adoption

In conclusion, **national culture is not considered in this study**, because most prior research has been unable to document any cultural influences on Full IFRS adoption (*Ramanna/Sletten* (2009); *Clements et al.* (2010)). Moreover, culturally grounded studies bear problems regarding the operationalization of national culture, data collection, and interpretation (*Tayeb* (1994)). In particular, the two dominating models by *Hofstede* (1980) and *Gray* (1988) have been criticized for their methodological inadequacies (*Baskerville* (2003); *Heidhues/Patel* (2011)).

1.6.3.2 IFRS for SMEs

Contrary to the extensive conceptual and empirical research that has been conducted on the determinants of Full IFRS adoption, mainly in the field of listed companies, **cross-country research** on the determinants of IFRS for SMEs adoption is **almost non-existent.**

Grant Thornton stated in September 2009:

> *"IFRS for SMEs will be particularly welcome in those countries that currently require full IFRS to be used for all entities, listed and unlisted, due to the reduced complexity of the Standard compared to full IFRS."*
>
> (*Grant Thornton* (2009), p. 6)

The proof of this and similar predictions regarding the adoption of IFRS for SMEs has yet been to come. From a European background *Masca* (2012) analyzes the diverse answers that were given in response to the *European Commission* (2010) questionnaire on the *potential* adoption of IFRS for SMEs in the European Union. *Masca* suggests that the opinions of national institutions regarding the future implementation of IFRS for SMEs within a legal EU framework and the perceived benefits resulting from an increase in European SMEs' financial statements' comparability are influenced by the **accounting culture of the geographic area** in which they operate in (*Masca* (2012), p. 574). For example, the majority of countries that have a common accounting culture (such as France, Germany, Austria, Belgium, and Italy) reject the adoption of IFRS for SMEs (*Masca* (2012), p. 572). In view of the fact that the questionnaire is strongly dominated by German preparers and users and hence lacks representativeness, *Masca's* study can only provide limited and vague insight into the potential drivers of IFRS for SMEs adoption in the European Union.

Kaya/Koch (2013) is the only archival study to date that empirically tests the influence of country-specific determinants on (early) IFRS for SMEs adoption (prior to July 2011). The authors use a cost-benefit analysis to develop their hypotheses. They argue that the level of **transitional costs** is the key driver for or against IFRS for SMEs adoption in the context of private firms (*Kaya/Koch* (2013), p. 3). *Kaya/Koch* specify their rationale by selecting the following five independent variables: (1) availability of National GAAP; (2) legal origin; (3) requirement for private firms to comply with Full IFRS; (4) official language, and (5) governance quality.

According to *Kaya/Koch* (2013), the mandatory linkage between tax law, capital maintenance rules, and National GAAP can make the adoption of IFRS for SMEs particularly burdensome as it would either lead to the **duplication of reporting requirements** for domestic companies or to high costs resulting from a change in tax and company law (*Kaya/Koch* (2013), p. 11). The authors hypothesize that countries are more likely to adopt IFRS for SMEs if they do not have any national GAAP for private firms. Second, *Kaya/Koch* suggest that IFRS for SMEs adoption is more likely for countries that have a common law tradition because *"domestic standards of common-law countries are closer in the spirit of the IFRS-framework than the national GAAP of code law countries"* (*Kaya/Koch* (2013), p. 15). Consistent with the idea of differences in transitional costs, the authors also predict that countries that already require private firms to prepare annual accounts under Full IFRS and countries whose official or native language is English are more likely to adopt IFRS for SMEs.

While *Kaya/Koch* apply binary variables for all of the four above stated constructs, they use the average score of the six World Bank's Worldwide Governance Indicators (WGI) that were collected by *Kaufmann et al.* (2010) to measure governance quality. They assume that countries with lower governance quality will be more likely to adopt IFRS for SMEs because national institutions face lower opportunity and switching costs (*Kaya/Koch* (2013), p. 18). The dependent variable is constructed as an **ordinal measure of IFRS for SMEs adoption** that takes the value 0 for non-adopters, the value 1 for partial adopters (i.e. countries allowing voluntary IFRS for SMEs adoption), and the value 2 for full adopters (i.e. countries requiring IFRS for SMEs for all private firms). The corresponding data are handpicked from various sources[81] for 135 jurisdictions as of July 2011.

By using multinomial and logistic regression, *Kaya/Koch* find that countries without **Local GAAP** and with a low **governance quality** are more likely to adopt IFRS for SMEs. Furthermore, countries that already adopt Full IFRS for private firms are more likely to adopt IFRS for SMEs. These findings are consistent with the applied theory of transitional costs and remain robust when testing for other determinants of IFRS for SMEs adoption (e.g.

---

81 Information is obtained from the *IASB's* website, IFRS for SMEs update newsletters, *Deloitte's* iasplus website, *PricewaterhouseCoopers*, *Ernst&Young*, the *IFRS Adoption Research Group*, the *Financial Standards Foundation*, the *International Federation of Accountants* (IFAC), the World Bank's country Reports on the Observance of Standards and Codes (ROSC), and websites of national standard-setters. Cf. *Kaya/Koch* (2013), p. 19.

level of development and import penetration). Nevertheless, the results should be interpreted with caution as the study has certain limitations.

First, data on *early* IFRS for SMEs adoption decisions (prior to July 2011) are likely to contain mistakes as several countries reversed, postponed, or changed their adoption decision in the following years. For example, Canada considered adoption of IFRS for SMEs but withdrew from it (*IFRS Foundation* (2014d), p. 6). In fact, the IFRS Foundation slightly overestimated the use of IFRS for SMEs during the first five years after its issuance. Another **caveat to the study's findings** is the selection and definition of some of the independent variables. As far as the variable 'National GAAP' is concerned, the reliability and completeness of *Naeg et al.'s* (2009) list of 30 jurisdictions without National GAAP is debatable. The question whether, and if yes, which type of National GAAP has existed in a certain country at a certain time, can only be answered by accounting experts of the respective jurisdiction. The data should hence be verified by auditors or national standard-setters before being used. Moreover, the indicator variable, which is announced to capture *mandatory* Full IFRS adoption in the field of private firms, takes the value of one already in case of *voluntary* adoption.

In conclusion, *Kaya/Koch* (2013) provide some insights into countries' cost-/benefit trade-off between the adoption of IFRS for SMEs and the maintenance of National GAAP. However, due to the limited theory base, the study cannot explain why countries adopt IFRS for SMEs even if transitional costs are high. The key findings of the two above presented studies dealing with (potential) determinants of IFRS for SMEs adoption are summarized in Table 1-20.

Reference	Methodology	Key results
Masca (2012)	Analysis of the answers to the EU Commission's questionnaire on the potential adoption of the IFRS for SMEs in the 27 member countries of the European Union (2010).	The opinions of national institutions regarding the potential adoption of IFRS for SMEs in the EU are influenced by the accounting culture of the geographic area in which they operate.
Kaya/Koch (2013)	Archival macro-level study on the determinants of IFRS for SMEs adoption by private firms in 135 countries (2009-2011).	The likelihood of IFRS for SMEs adoption increases if transitional costs are relatively low. In particular, countries without Local GAAP and with poor governance quality are more likely to adopt IFRS for SMEs. Moreover, countries that already adopt Full IFRS for private firms are more likely to adopt IFRS for SMEs.

Table 1-20: Studies on determinants of IFRS for SMEs adoption

In summary, the discussion of prior explanatory country level studies has revealed that the probability of Full IFRS and IFRS for SMEs adoption by countries is mainly determined by **economic and political factors** as well as by **network effects**. The strength of each determinant is assumed to vary between countries and it depends on the specific firm context, in which the IASB standards are implemented.

Having reviewed a large sample of relevant prior research on the characteristics and determinants of Full IFRS and IFRS for SMEs adoption on country level, the following section presents a summary of the main limitations of prior research in each of the four predefined research areas. Furthermore, the section identifies evident research gaps and reveals concrete research opportunities available for this study.

1.6.4 Limitations and implications for this study

The analysis of descriptive and explanatory research shows that studies on Full IFRS adoption are by far more numerous than studies on IFRS for SMEs adoption.[82] Second, research on Full IFRS adoption is relatively scarce in the field of private firms compared to the context of listed companies.[83]

Regarding the descriptive research on Full IFRS and IFRS for SMEs adoption, it is evident that recent studies have focused on providing an overview on the number of Full IFRS and IFRS for SMEs adopting countries worldwide (*IFRS Foundation* (2014g)). While this information is well documented and verified by several different sources, little is known about the **continued existence of domestic accounting systems**. The growing number of Full IFRS and IFRS for SMEs adopting countries, as reported by Big-4 audit firms and by the IFRS Foundation, suggests that domestic accounting systems have vanished completely due to their replacement by Full IFRS or IFRS for SMEs. But this is not the case for countries, in which Full IFRS and IFRS for SMEs only complement domestic accounting standards in certain limited areas (e.g. in the consolidated financial statements of listed corporations).

For example, *Street/Larson's* (2004) survey of 15 EU countries reveals that **most EU member states continue to require or allow national GAAP** in the individual accounts of domestic unlisted companies (*Street/Larson* (2004), p. 1). Reports on worldwide Full IFRS and IFRS for SMEs adoption hence largely ignore the remaining importance of domestic accounting systems. In addition, most prior studies remain silent about the deviations and carve-outs that are being made by national regulators in the course of Full IFRS and IFRS for SMEs adoption (e.g. *Deloitte Touche Tohmatsu* (2014c).

The second main limitation of prior descriptive research on Full IFRS and IFRS for SMEs adoption is that *cross-country research* rarely focuses on **local accounting systems' level of convergence with IFRS** (e.g. *Andersen et al.* (2001)). Even if domestic standards are still in use besides Full IFRS and IFRS for SMEs in many jurisdictions, these standards have been subject to international harmonization since several decades. For this reason, it is likely that many or even most of these domestic accounting systems have reached a considerable level of compliance with either Full IFRS or IFRS for SMEs.[84] As empirical cross-country research on the degree of *de jure* harmonization has scarcely been conducted

[82] While 22 descriptive and 31 explanatory studies are reviewed in the field of Full IFRS adoption, only five descriptive and two explanatory studies are identified in the field of IFRS for SMEs adoption.

[83] For example, none of the eight reviewed archival studies on the determinants of Full IFRS adoption focus on the context of private firms' financial reporting.

[84] For example, local accounting systems have substantially been aligned with Full IFRS in Germany *Haller/Eierle* (2004b), Portugal *Fontes et al.* (2005), the United States *Ampofo/Sellani* (2005), Latin America *Manzano/Conesa* (2005), the South Pacific region *Chand/Patel* (2008), and in China *Qu/Zhang* (2010).

since the early 2000s, little is known about this development on a global scale. Moreover, descriptive research on *de jure* harmonization of domestic accounting systems does rarely differentiate between national accounting rules for listed and private firms. In other words, due to the explicit or implicit focus on accounting rules for listed firms, the field of private firms' financial reporting has been neglected (e.g. *BDO et al.* (2003)).

In conclusion, **prior descriptive research** on Full IFRS and IFRS for SMEs adoption is **one-dimensional** in several aspects. By concentrating on the growing diffusion of Full IFRS and IFRS for SMEs across the globe, it neglects the wide range of domestic but internationalized accounting systems that exist in the field of private firms. This is problematic, as it gives the impression that domestic accounting systems have largely been replaced by IASB standards. In contrast, such domestic accounting systems are still in place in many countries and they still include (1) local standards that are entirely independent from the IASB, (2) standards that have gradually converged with Full IFRS or IFRS for SMEs, and (3) modified versions of either Full IFRS or IFRS for SMEs that generally comply with one of the two IASB standards, but deviate from them in some aspects.

The descriptive part of **this study hence addresses these limitations** of prior descriptive research by conducting *time series* and *cross-sectional analyses*, which aim at answering the following main research question:

How are accounting systems shaped in the field of private firms?

Time series analysis (2002-2014) shall provide an insight into the *process* of domestic accounting standards' gradual convergence with Full IFRS and IFRS for SMEs. Contrary to prior descriptive studies, it presents empirical evidence on the gradual substitution and complementation of private firms' local accounting systems by IASB standards. The study thereby matches each of the 110 countries' accounting system(s) to different levels of Full IFRS and IFRS for SMEs compliance and thus reveals the entire spectrum of Full IFRS and IFRS for SMEs adoption on a global scale. In summary, it reveals which countries have adopted accounting systems for private firms that are (1) entirely independent from, (2) partially comply with, or (3) are identical to Full IFRS or IFRS for SMEs.

In addition, the descriptive part of this study shall discuss the local patterns of Full IFRS and IFRS for SMEs adoption in 2014. Prior descriptive studies do rarely differentiate between the adoption of IASB standards in the individual and in the consolidated financial statements of companies and thus remain silent on the precise scope of adoption (e.g. *Deloitte Touche Tohmatsu* (2014c)). The descriptive research conducted in this study addresses this limitation by clarifying which countries *allow or require* the use of Full IFRS or IFRS for SMEs in the *individual or consolidated* financial statements of *all or some* domestic private firms in 2014. Hence, **cross-sectional analysis (2014)** shall display the *status quo* of local Full IFRS and IFRS for SMEs implementation by revealing local adoption specifics. It complements the time series analysis by providing an overview on the similarities and differences regarding the local implementation of Full IFRS and IFRS for SMEs in nine different regions of the world. Due to the large country coverage (110 jurisdictions), the descriptive research in this study provides a unique and comprehensive insight into the process and the local patterns of global Full IFRS and IFRS for SMEs adoption in the field of private firms in the last decade.

Regarding prior **explanatory research** on Full IFRS and IFRS for SMEs adoption, two main research gaps can be identified. First, there is no single archival macro-level study that examines the determinants of Full IFRS adoption in the field of private firms. Secondly, archival macro-level research on the determinants of IFRS for SMEs adoption is scarce, too.[85]

This study approaches the above identified research opportunities by conducting **three cross-sectional analyses**, which seek to answer the following main research question:

Why do countries adopt Full IFRS or IFRS for SMEs in the field of private firms?

First, this study aims at **transferring a wide range of theory-based hypotheses** about the determinants of Full IFRS adoption from the field of listed to the field of private firms. On the basis of a broad theoretical foundation, countries' Full IFRS adoption decision shall be analyzed from several different perspectives. By drawing on the *economic theory of networks* and the *institutional theory of isomorphism*, the study provides a solid theoretical foundation for analyzing the influence of net economic benefits, political pressures and network effects on Full IFRS adoption.

The second research opportunity addressed in this part of the study is to analyze the **interdependencies between Full IFRS and IFRS for SMEs adoption** in the field of private firms. The study's descriptive research on Full IFRS and IFRS for SMEs adoption reveals that since the IFRS for SMEs was issued in 2009, the new standard has had a strong impact on the financial reporting landscape in the field of private firms including those accounting systems that have already been closely aligned with Full IFRS. Although the rise of IFRS for SMEs may not directly affect countries' decision to adopt Full IFRS in the field of listed firms, it clearly has an impact on Full IFRS adoption in the context of private firms (and vice versa). Prior archival studies analyze the determinants of Full IFRS adoption only at a time when IFRS for SMEs had not yet been adopted (e.g. *Hope et al.* (2006); *Judge et al.* (2010); *Ramanna/Sletten* (2013)).

Given the above identified **limitations of prior explanatory research**, the first of the three cross-sectional analyses shall provide a basic understanding of the factors that have influenced countries' Full IFRS adoption decision in the field of private firms prior to 2009 and also reveal whether these factors differ from those that have already been identified in the field of listed companies. The corresponding cut-off date of the analysis is the last year before the IFRS for SMEs was put into place (i.e. 2008). By repeating the cross-sectional analysis with data on Full IFRS adoptions by 2014, the study shall examine how the explanatory power of the determinants of Full IFRS adoption has changed during the years 2009-2014. The results can thus be interpreted in view of the fact that a second IASB standard has become available for adoption in the field of private firms. The third cross-sectional analysis shall eventually focus on the driving factors of IFRS for SMEs

[85] *Kaya/Koch* (2013) is the only archival study that examines the determinants of IFRS for SMEs adoption.

adoption by 2014. The results shall indicate how the determinants of IFRS for SMEs adoption might differ from the determinants of Full IFRS adoption in the field of private firms.

While the first two research questions were not addressed by any archival macro-level study before, *Kaya/Koch* elaborate on the third research question in a working paper from 2013. **This study's research design sets itself apart** from *Kaya/Koch* (2013) in several aspects. Most importantly, *Kaya/Koch's* data on IFRS for SMEs adoptions are from July 2011. The authors hence concentrate on *early* IFRS for SMEs adoptions, which raises doubts about the reliability of the data. Furthermore, by drawing on a theory of transitional costs, *Kaya/Koch's* focus is on the economic determinants of IFRS for SMEs adoption only. Contrary to that, this study uses more recent data on IFRS for SMEs adoption and is based on a wider theoretical foundation covering the *economic theory of networks* and the *institutional theory of isomorphism*. This approach offers the possibility of discussing the impact of non-economic factors such as institutional pressures. Furthermore, the research design of this study differs from *Kaya/Koch* (2013) regarding the definition of the IFRS for SMEs adopters group.

While *Kaya/Koch* construct the IFRS for SMEs adoption variable as an ordinal measure that takes the value 0 for non-adopters, the value 1 for partial adopters (i.e. countries allowing voluntary IFRS for SMEs adoption), and the value 2 for full adopters (i.e. countries requiring IFRS for SMEs for all private firms), this study uses a variety of dichotomous sub-variables that take the value 0 for non-adopters and the value 1 for adopters. This **differentiation of the IFRS for SMEs adopters group** shall be applied in all three cross-sectional analyses (also in the models on Full IFRS adoption by 2008 and 2014), which opens up the possibility of identifying differences in the explanatory power of certain independent variables within one cross-sectional analysis. In addition, this approach offers more scope for interpreting the interdependencies between Full IFRS and IFRS for SMEs adoption on the basis of certain adoption specifics (e.g. mandatory adoption).

In conclusion, this study takes up a series of research opportunities in the field of descriptive and explanatory research regarding the adoption of Full IFRS and IFRS for SMEs in the field of private firms. It shall hence reduce several research gaps in the area of international accounting harmonization (IAH) research.

The following chapter elaborates on the theoretical foundation of this study. On the basis of the *economic theory of networks* and the *institutional theory of isomorphism,* the next section develops a conceptual framework, from which theory-based hypotheses are derived.

2 Theory and hypotheses development

2.1 Theoretical foundation

National accounting systems differ from each other for numerous reasons. Legal systems, taxation, and providers of finance are only three of several factors that shape the national financial reporting environment of countries and hence determine their domestic financial reporting systems (*Nobes/Parker* (2012), p. 27ff.). Yet, these country characteristics cannot per se explain why some countries adopt Full IFRS or IFRS for SMEs whereas others do not. Prior research shows that there is a **long list of possible reasons for and against IFRS adoption.** In Germany, for example, Full IFRS adoption was mainly driven by the economic needs of domestic listed companies (*United Nations* (2008), p. 1). In contrast, the national desire to raise local standards to international best practice can be regarded as one important reason why so many less developed countries have adopted Full IFRS during the last decade (*United Nations* (2008), p. 1). Countries such as Botswana or Nicaragua, which have never developed their own set of accounting standards, are also assumed to be more open to adopt Full IFRS or IFRS for SMEs than countries with a strong national accounting tradition like France (*Purvis et al.* (1991), p. 28ff.; *Kaya/Koch* (2013), p. 11). In addition, countries also appear to consider the drawbacks of different accounting systems and institutional effects before deciding on which system to adopt. For example, the unwillingness to lose control of rule-making power is regarded as the primary obstacle to Full IFRS adoption in the context of domestic listed companies in the United States (*Hail et al.* (2010b), p. 584).

This study's approach for explaining why some countries choose to adopt Full IFRS and IFRS for SMEs in the field of private firms whereas others do not can be summarized as follows:

> *"Countries adopt IASB standards because they want to or because they have to."*

In other words, the decision whether to adopt Full IFRS and IFRS for SMEs or not is determined by two factors: (1) the perceived benefits from adoption and (2) the external pressures a country is subject to. Based on this study's scientific research strategy and conceptualization outlined in chapter one, the following sections will present two scientific concepts that are later applied to describe and explain the phenomenon of Full IFRS and IFRS for SMEs adoption in the field of private firms:

- *economic theory of networks* and
- *institutional theory of isomorphism.*

2.1.1 Economic theory of networks

In an influential paper on 'network externality', *Katz/Shapiro* (1985) define the concept of networks as follows:

> *"There are many products for which the utility that a user derives from consumption of the good increases with the number of other agents consuming the good."*
>
> (*Katz/Shapiro* (1985), p. 424)

According to **network theory**, the total value of a network-dependent product is determined by the sum of its intrinsic value and the value of the product's network. While the intrinsic value (also autarky value) describes the value of the product as such, the value of the product's network (also synchronization value) arises from other agents joining the product's network. Hence, network effects can be defined as *"the circumstance[s] in which the net value of an action [...] is affected by the number of agents taking equivalent actions"* (*Liebowitz/Margolis* (1994), p. 135).

Katz/Shapiro (1985) distinguish between the following **three types of network effects**:

- direct network effects on the quality of the product,
- indirect network effects on the quality of the product, and
- indirect network effects arising for a durable product when the quality and availability of post-purchase service for the product depend on the experience and size of the service network (*Katz/Shapiro* (1985), p. 424).

Direct network effects arise in particular if the product contains communication technologies. For example, the utility derived from using a smartphone clearly depends on the number of other people also using smartphones. The possibility of making a phone call, sending e-mails, or sharing files brings about direct benefits that increase with the size of the smartphone network and can largely determine the value of the product. A growing amount and variety of software applications resulting from an increasing number of smartphone users can be considered as **indirect network effects**. Furthermore, having a smartphone that is widely used within a certain network can also create indirect network benefits in case of damage or hardware failure due to the higher quality and availability of post-purchase service. In all of these cases the utility that a given user derives from the smartphone depends on the number of other users who are in the same smartphone 'network'.[86]

Liebowitz/Margolis (1994) elaborate the concept of networks in several aspects. They add to *Katz/Shapiro* (1985) that network effects, which arise from an increasing size of the product's network, can also be negative. For example, if a smartphone network becomes overloaded, the effect of an additional subscriber will deteriorate the smartphone's network value. Products hence exhibit network effects wherever the consumer enjoys benefits or suffers costs from changes in the size of the associated network (*Liebowitz/Margolis* (1994), p. 134). Another distinction that is being made is between networks that can be owned (private goods) and networks that cannot be owned (public goods). Besides, in **'literal' networks** participants are literally connected to each other in some way. For example, telephone, gas pipeline, or cable television systems are manifested physically and require an investment of capital to build the network. On the contrary, **'metaphorical' networks**, such as the global network of English speakers, provide interrelationships in which there are no physical connections (*Liebowitz/Margolis* (1994), p. 135).

According to the economic theory of networks, a user purchases a network-dependent product only if that user's private benefits, being the sum of the intrinsic value and the

[86] Cf. *Katz/Shapiro* (1985), p. 424, on the network effects of telephones, personal computers and cars.

value from the product's network, exceed the costs of the product (*Katz/Shapiro* (1994), p. 96). It is assumed that **consumers form expectations** regarding the size of competing networks and 'internalize' these expectations into their purchase decision.[87] If consumers expect a seller of a network-dependent product to be dominant, consumers will be willing to pay more for the product and it will become dominant. Hence, the perceived benefits from the product's future network determine the buyer's current willingness to pay and the de facto dominance of the future network (*Katz/Shapiro* (1985), p. 425). As a consequence, perceived network benefits can lead to a self-reinforcing process of consumption.

Due to the relatively high importance of some products' network value, network effects may also **retard innovation.** Systems tend to get locked into obsolete standards or technologies as users stick with an established technology even if the intrinsic value of the product is shrinking (*Katz/Shapiro* (1994), p. 108). This is because new products may be incompatible with the current product's network and may thus have a low synchronization value. One example is the QWERTY keyboard, which is said to entail certain drawbacks, but which has maintained its strong market position due to wide diffusion and the related network benefits (*Liebowitz/Margolis* (1994), p. 147).

2.1.2 Institutional theory of isomorphism

A key element of institutional theory (*Meyer/Rowan* (1977); *DiMaggio/Powell* (1983); *Scott* (1987)) is the assumption that *"organizations are driven to incorporate the practices and procedures defined by prevailing rationalized concepts of organizational work and institutionalized in society"* (*Meyer/Rowan* (1977), p. 340). The process of incorporating such practices is named **isomorphism** (also convergence) and can best be described as *"the process whereby one organization [...] becomes more similar to another organization [...] by adopting (or moving closer to) the characteristics of the other organization"* (*Rodrigues/Craig* (2007), p. 742).

Institutional theorists argue that if there is homogeneity among organizations, it is not necessarily due to market competition that these organizations adhere to the same optimal form. Instead, organizations embark on a process of adaptation and convergence **to achieve social legitimacy** in the eyes of the world, state, powerful professions, or society as a whole (*Carruthers* (1995), p. 317). Organizations conform to a set of common beliefs because they are rewarded for doing so through legitimacy (*Scott* (1987), p. 498) and not by becoming more efficient (*DiMaggio/Powell* (1983), p. 147). It is assumed that organizations do not only compete for resources and customers, but also for political power (*DiMaggio/Powell* (1983), p. 150). Accordingly, isomorphism can be differentiated into two types: *competitive* and *institutional* isomorphism (*DiMaggio/Powell* (1983), p. 149). While competitive isomorphism is concerned with efficiency (i.e. cases of isomorphism, whereby the adoption of certain practices is because they are the best, cheapest, or most efficient) (*Carruthers* (1995), p. 317), institutional isomorphism describes the process, *"in*

[87] If an agent buys a network-dependent product solely because of its intrinsic value without noticing the value from its network, the network effects are not internalized in the purchase decision and are referred to as 'network externalities' (*Liebowitz/Margolis* (1994), p. 135).

which organizations tend to adopt the same practices over time in response to common institutional pressures from similar organizations or industries" (*Rodrigues/Craig* (2007), p. 742).

DiMaggio/Powell (1983) identify three types of **institutional pressures** through which institutional isomorphic changes occur: (1) coercive, (2) mimetic, and (3) normative pressures (*DiMaggio/Powell* (1983), p. 150ff.).

- **Coercive isomorphism** concerns the ways in which organizations may be subject to external pressures, either from organizations they are dependent upon, or from more general cultural expectations (*Carruthers* (1995), p. 317). For example, coercive pressures can be exerted by government regulators, parent companies, or supranational institutions. Such pressures may be felt as force, persuasion, or as invitations to join in collusion (*DiMaggio/Powell* (1983), p. 150).
- **Mimetic isomorphism** describes a standard response to uncertainty: imitation. Especially when organizational technologies are poorly understood, goals are ambiguous, or the environment creates symbolic uncertainty, organizations tend to model themselves on other organizations (*DiMaggio/Powell* (1983), p. 151). By emulating (mimic) the actions of similar organizations that are perceived to be more legitimate or successful in the institutional environment (e.g. by adopting best practice solutions), they try to enhance their own social legitimacy (*Rodrigues/Craig* (2007), p. 743).
- **Normative isomorphism** primarily stems from professionalization (*DiMaggio/Powell* (1983), p. 152). Professions exert normative pressures due to their formal education and as they provide legitimacy to the cognitive base of discipline specialists in universities. Second, professions develop networks that facilitate the rapid diffusion of new models and practices. Such mechanisms create a pool of almost interchangeable individuals who possess similar orientations and dispositions that can override variations in tradition and control that might otherwise shape organizational structure (*DiMaggio/Powell* (1983), p. 152).

According to *DiMaggio/Powell* (1983), p. 150, this typology is an analytic one and the types are not always empirically distinguishable. For example, external actors (coercive pressures) may induce an organization to conform to certain regulations by expecting the organization to perform a particular task and specifying the profession (normative pressures) that is responsible for its performance (*DiMaggio/Powell* (1983), p. 150). Professions can be subject to the same coercive and mimetic pressures as organizations (*DiMaggio/Powell* (1983), p. 152). For this reason, this study concentrates on elaborating coercive and mimetic isomorphism and **excludes normative isomorphism** from the analysis.

In the next section, the conceptual underpinnings of the *economic theory of networks* and the *institutional theory of isomorphism* are applied to this study's specific research object: Full IFRS and IFRS for SMEs adoption in the field of private firms. The following section thereby develops a conceptual framework that combines both theories and that is further refined in the course of this chapter.

2.1.3 Integration of theoretical perspectives

This study follows the argument of *Ramanna/Sletten* (2009), who hypothesize that countries adopt Full IFRS in the field of listed firms only if the sum of direct net benefits and network benefits are greater than zero (*Ramanna/Sletten* (2009), p. 7). In accordance with the economic theory of networks, *Ramanna/Sletten* (2009) consider **Full IFRS as a network-dependent product**, whose overall value is divided into (1) its intrinsic value (autarky value) and (2) the value of the Full IFRS network (synchronization value).

Countries that assess the intrinsic value of Full IFRS to be higher than the intrinsic value of alternative (local) accounting standards thus perceive a positive **net intrinsic value** (i.e. direct net benefits) from Full IFRS adoption. According to *Ramanna/Sletten* (2009), countries may either perceive such direct net benefits if they expect that Full IFRS adoption will result in a higher quality of governance than the use of local standards (*net economic benefits*), or if the political costs related to Full IFRS adoption are considered to be smaller than the political costs that result from non-adoption (*net political benefits*) (*Ramanna/Sletten* (2009), p. 9ff.). Hence, *Ramanna/Sletten* (2009) subdivide the net intrinsic value of Full IFRS adoption into net economic and net political benefits.

This study separates **net political benefits** of Full IFRS and IFRS for SMEs adoption from net economic benefits. Political determinants are discussed from an institutional perspective. Therefore, the net intrinsic value of Full IFRS and IFRS for SMEs adoption, as defined in this study, only includes **net economic benefits**. These result from the trade-off between initial and long-term benefits (e.g. higher quality of local governance institutions) and the costs arising from the transition to and the maintenance of the new set of accounting standards.

In line with *Ramanna/Sletten* (2009), it is assumed that Local GAAP does not have any synchronization value across countries as it is only applied within one jurisdiction. On the contrary, the overall value of Full IFRS and IFRS for SMEs adoption also depends on the number of other countries that adopt the IASB standards. As we know from network theory, **network effects** can largely determine the perceived quality of network-dependent products such as Full IFRS and IFRS for SMEs. The network of Full IFRS and IFRS for SMEs adopters constitutes a metaphorical network without any physical connections. In contrast to literal networks, there are no additional costs to join the network other than the opportunity costs not to join it (*Liebowitz/Margolis* (1994), p. 136). Furthermore, as metaphorical networks cannot become overloaded, negative network effects cannot occur either.

In the context of Full IFRS and IFRS for SMEs adoption by private firms, **direct network benefits** primarily arise from the increased comparability of private firms' financial statements across countries. Domestic private firms, which form part of an international group or reach for international sources of financing, may benefit from the comparability between their financial statements and those of their international partners due to lower transaction costs. These network benefits are expected to increase with the size of the Full IFRS and IFRS for SMEs network. In addition, the more countries join the Full IFRS and IFRS for SMEs network, the more sophisticated IFRS institutions become. This may give rise to **indirect network benefits** stemming from improvements in the IASB's standard setting process and from the supply of a wider range of post-implementation guidance. Furthermore, indirect network benefits may also arise from the increasing use of IFRS-based contracting (e.g. trade agreements, financial covenants, and taxation).

As network benefits are independent from the product's net intrinsic value, jurisdictions might consider the net economic benefits of Full IFRS and IFRS for SMEs adoption as low, but perceive high network benefits from adoption (or vice versa). In conclusion, countries are expected to adopt Full IFRS and IFRS for SMEs in the field of private firms if the sum of perceived net economic benefits and network benefits is greater than zero.

Regardless of the economic incentives that make countries adopt Full IFRS and IFRS for SMEs in the field of private firms, countries are also subject to **institutional pressures**. In accordance with the institutional theory of isomorphism, it is expected that once powerful first movers adopt Full IFRS and IFRS for SMEs in the field of private firms, the IASB standards can be regarded as the field norm and other countries follow suit because adoption confers social legitimacy (*Chua/Taylor* (2008), p. 470). This study focuses on external institutional pressures that are either *coercive* or *mimetic* in nature. These external pressures can either originate from the country's specific status in the international community or from the Full IFRS and IFRS for SMEs network.

Following *DiMaggio/Powell* (1983), **coercive pressures** towards Full IFRS and IFRS for SMEs adoption originate from institutions that are able to force or persuade countries to adopt IASB standards (*Judge et al.* (2010), p. 163). Apart from the persuasive power of the IFRS Foundation or other IFRS-related institutions that promote worldwide adoption of IFRS, coercive pressures can also originate from supranational financial institutions such as the International Monetary Fund and the World Bank, which make IFRS adoption a condition for the transfer of financial resources (*Singh/Newberry* (2008), p. 484). Besides, trade partners and supranational associations such as the EU, ASEAN, or USAN have the potential power to prevail on countries to adopt Full IFRS and IFRS for SMEs in the field of private firms. In general, coercive pressures are assumed to be more influential if countries depend more strongly on international norms and standards (*Judge et al.* (2010), p. 163).

Apart from coercive pressures, the strength of the Full IFRS and IFRS for SMEs network within a country's sphere of influence can also affect its decision to adopt the IASB standards due to **mimetic pressures**. Countries may want to imitate peers by adopting Full IFRS and IFRS for SMEs in the field of private firms to achieve social legitimacy. By following the same logic as applied when discussing the importance of network benefits, these mimetic pressures are expected to increase with the size of the country's Full IFRS and IFRS for SMEs network. Evidently, mimetic pressures and network benefits are hardly empirically distinguishable. For this reason, both theoretical concepts are included in the same construct: network effects. The theoretical foundation of this study is displayed in the conceptual framework (see Figure 2-1).

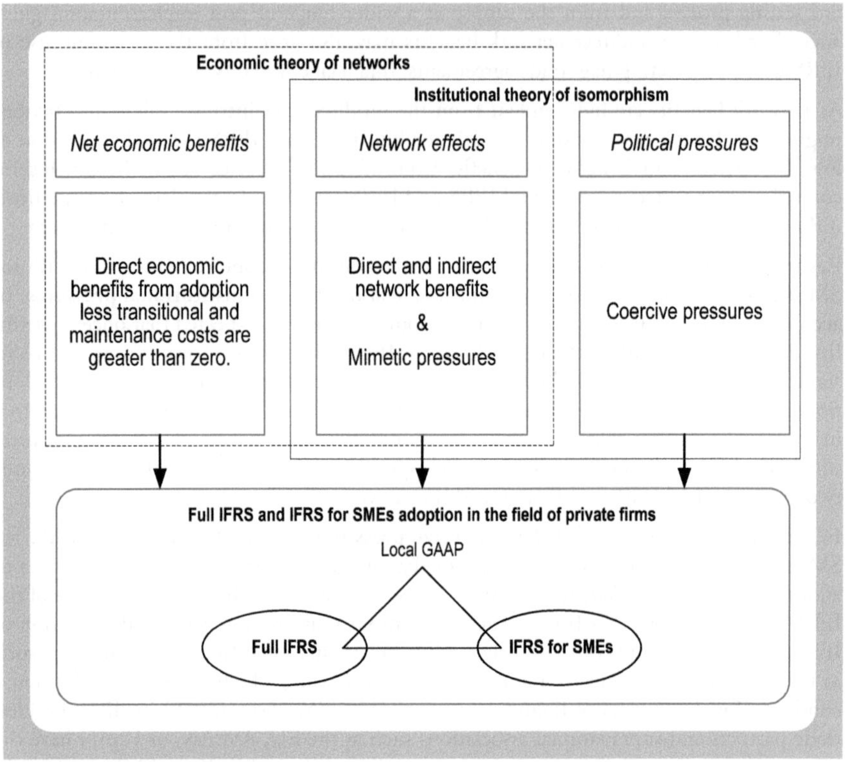

Figure 2-1: Conceptual framework

Hence, two theoretic concepts form this study's conceptual framework. Countries are expected to adopt Full IFRS and IFRS for SMEs in the field of private firms if:

- they perceive **net economic benefits** from adoption,
- **network effects** give rise to additional perceived benefits or mimetic pressures,
- **political pressures** enforce adoption.

On the basis of the conceptual framework, the following section develops theory-based hypotheses, which shall be confronted with the empirical evidence derived by this study.

2.2 Hypotheses development

On the basis of *Popper's* critical rationalism and this study's theoretical foundation, the following sections first develop **propositions** regarding the characteristics of Full IFRS and IFRS for SMEs adoption in the field of private firms and thereafter postulate **falsifiable hypotheses** regarding their determinants. The propositions and hypotheses are summarized in a refined conceptual framework at the end of this chapter.

2.2.1 Describing Full IFRS and IFRS for SMEs adoption

According to this study's conceptual framework, a country's Full IFRS and IFRS for SMEs adoption decision is assumed to be determined by its level of net economic benefits, network effects and political pressures. As these factors are expected to vary across countries, the *process*, *type*, and *scope* of Full IFRS and IFRS for SMEs adoption are also expected to vary internationally.

Prior research has shown significant **cross-country differences** in the **compliance levels** of National GAAP compared with IAS/IFRS, particularly during the 1980s and 1990s. For example, *Doupnik/Taylor* (1985) find that Europe registers the lowest level of compliance with eight chosen IASC standards among five broadly-defined geographic areas (Africa, Asia & Australia, Europe, Latin America, and North America). Within Europe, English-speaking countries, France, and the Netherlands are measured to be in highest conformity with IAS whereas German-speaking and Southern European countries are in least conformity with IAS (*Doupnik/Taylor* (1985), p. 33). *Purvis et al.* (1991) add to these findings that the level of conformity with IAS is much higher regarding the early standards, which address more fundamental issues, than with those standards issued more recently. Three years prior to the foundation of the IASB, *Larson/Kenny* (1999) showed that the accounting standards of the United States, Commonwealth countries, and the Netherlands were in general compliance with IAS by 1993 already, whereas countries from Continental Europe, Asia, and South America complied with IAS only to a medium extent. Little compliance was found for Switzerland and China (*Larson/Kenny* (1999), p. 6).

The first proposition regarding the **process** towards Full IFRS (*P1a*) and IFRS for SMEs adoption (*P1b*) is postulated as follows:

*P1a: The process towards **Full IFRS** adoption in the field of private firms varies across countries.*

*P1b: The process towards **IFRS for SMEs** adoption in the field of private firms varies across countries.*

Prior research also indicated that the adoption of IASB standards can vary across countries regarding the type and scope of adoption. In this study, voluntary and mandatory adoption are referred to as two different 'types' of adoption. In comparison, restrictions to the use of Full IFRS and IFRS for SMEs (e.g. regarding the adoption in the individual financial statements or the adoption by some private firms) are referred to as differences in the 'scope' of adoption. The *United Nations* (2008) pointed out that there are various factors that contribute to the type and scope of Full IFRS adoption within a jurisdiction (*United Nations* (2008), p. 1). For example, while in Germany mandatory Full IFRS adoption is restricted to the consolidated financial statements of publicly traded companies, Full IFRS have been adopted either mandatorily or voluntarily for the largest possible group of domestic companies in several other countries (e.g. India, Jamaica, and Pakistan). Hence, the proposition regarding the **type** of Full IFRS (*P2a*) and IFRS for SMEs adoption (*P2b*) is postulated as follows:

*P2a: The type of **Full IFRS** adoption in the field of private firms varies across countries.*

*P2b: The type of **IFRS for SMEs** adoption in the field of private firms varies across countries.*

Similarly, there is empirical evidence that countries come to different decisions with regard to the **scope** of IFRS adoption. For example, *Street/Larson* (2004) find that, despite the mandatory adoption of EU-IFRS in the consolidated financial statements of publicly traded EU companies since 2005 (2007), most member states of the European Union continue to require or allow Local GAAP in the individual accounts of domestic unlisted companies. Furthermore, they differentiate the scope of IFRS adoption on the basis of company size and legal form (*Street/Larson* (2004)). In accordance with these findings from the EU, the following proposition regarding the scope of Full IFRS (*P3a*) and IFRS for SMEs adoption (*P3b*) is postulated as follows:

*P3a: The scope of **Full IFRS** adoption in the field of private firms varies across countries.*

*P3b: The scope of **IFRS for SMEs** adoption in the field of private firms varies across countries.*

2.2.2 Explaining Full IFRS and IFRS for SMEs adoption

By drawing on the *economic theory of networks* and the *institutional theory of isomorphism*, this study's conceptual framework is based on two pillars that shall help to explain why some countries adopt Full IFRS and IFRS for SMEs in the field of private firms, whereas others do not. The following section develops five hypotheses that are grounded on the economic theory of networks and postulate that countries adopt IASB standards due to perceived net economic benefits.

2.2.2.1 Net economic benefits

Prior research on the determinants of Full IFRS adoption in the field of listed companies has shown that certain characteristics of the local capital market (e.g. degree of investor protection, economic openness, and accessibility) can give rise to net economic benefits from IFRS adoption on country level (e.g. *Hope et al.* (2006); *Zeghal/Mhedhbi* (2006)). In the field of private firms, though, these capital market-related determinants of Full IFRS adoption do not apply. As a consequence, other measures of net economic benefits have to be developed to represent the institutional context of private firms' financial reporting.

2.2.2.1.1 Perceived quality of accounting standards

Among other potential benefits, the **higher quality of IASB standards** compared to domestic or localized accounting systems is claimed to be one of the most powerful drivers for IFRS adoption in general (*Ball* (2001), p. 166). Vice versa, evidence from Australia shows that the fear of adopting inferior standards, which might lower the quality of financial reporting, can create opposition to IFRS adoption (*Picker* (2007), p. 100). Similarly,

Hail et al. (2010a) argue that direct effects of IFRS adoption on the quality of financial reporting in the USA are likely to be small as US GAAP already constitutes a set of high-quality standards and the move to IFRS would bring no significant improvement (*Hail et al.* (2010a), p. 387). Although higher-quality standards do not automatically result in higher-quality financial reporting, it is the **perceived value added** by international standards that represents one important component of the total net economic benefits countries can gain from Full IFRS and IFRS for SMEs adoption in the field of private firms.

In conclusion, **direct economic benefits** from Full IFRS and IFRS for SMEs adoption in the field of private firms are assumed to be higher in countries where the perceived quality of domestic or localized financial reporting standards is low. These include accounting standards that are entirely independent from the IASB, standards that have partially converged with Full IFRS or IFRS for SMEs, and modified versions of either Full IFRS or IFRS for SMEs. Hence, the improvement of the local financial reporting environment is expected to be a main driver for the adoption of IASB standards from an economic perspective. In conclusion, the first hypothesis regarding the economic determinants of Full IFRS (*H1a*) and IFRS for SMEs adoption (*H1b*) is postulated as follows:

H1a: *The more a country considers its accounting standards as weak, the more likely is* ***Full IFRS*** *adoption in the field of private firms.*

H1b: *The more a country considers its accounting standards as weak, the more likely is* ***IFRS for SMEs*** *adoption in the field of private firms.*

While the above stated hypothesis only relates to the direct economic benefits arising from Full IFRS and IFRS for SMEs adoption, the following sections also include the level of transitional and maintenance costs.

2.2.2.1.2 Local GAAP

Contrary to many African countries, which have never developed Local GAAP (e.g. Botswana, Tanzania), all but one current EU member state (Cyprus) once developed a set of national accounting standards that local private firms were or still are obliged to adhere to when preparing financial statements. Private firms are required by law to prepare (individual) financial statements in many civil code countries worldwide, too, as these have a legal relevance (*Kaya/Koch* (2013), p. 11). For example, financial statements of private firms are used by fiscal authorities to assess the amount of taxable profits as well as to determine income distribution (*PricewaterhouseCoopers* (2013)). In addition, financial reporting may serve further **contracting purposes** such as bank financing and management compensation (*Fülbier/Gassen* (2010), p. 4).

If countries decide to adopt IASB standards, **transitional costs** result from the necessary adaptation of legal systems (*Kaya/Koch* (2013), p. 11) as well as due to the adjustment of the contractual relationships that have priorly been based on domestic accounting standards (*Hail et al.* (2010a), p. 372). Besides the **direct economic benefits** from Full IFRS and IFRS for SMEs adoption in the field of private firms, which are assumed to be higher in countries without a history of Local GAAP, these countries are also expected to encounter lower transitional costs than those which had once tied legal and contractual consequences to financial statements prepared under Local GAAP. The inflexibility of national legal requirements might even result in duplicating financial reporting requirements, which creates additional **maintenance costs** in case of IFRS adoption (*European Commission* (2010), p. 2). In contrast, countries that never had a Local GAAP do not sacrifice the resources that would be necessary to develop their own financial reporting system. They can simply adopt IASB standards (*Kaya/Koch* (2013), p. 12).

In summary, it is not only the perceived quality of the local financial reporting system that determines the country-specific net economic benefits from Full IFRS and IFRS for SMEs adoption in the field of private firms, but also the mere existence of Local GAAP. In accordance with the theoretic foundation of this study and the evidence from prior research (*Kaya/Koch* (2013)), the second hypothesis regarding the economic determinants of Full IFRS (*H2a*) and IFRS for SMEs adoption (*H2b*) is postulated as follows:

H2a: ***Full IFRS** adoption in the field of private firms is more likely in countries that have never developed Local GAAP.*

H2b: ***IFRS for SMEs** adoption in the field of private firms is more likely in countries that have never developed Local GAAP.*

2.2.2.1.3 Local Full IFRS

From an economic perspective, the existence of Local Full IFRS may indicate that the **direct economic benefits** of complete IFRS adoption are rather small (or even negative) as such a country has already adopted a local 'best fit version' of IFRS. Due to the necessary adaptation of legal requirements and contractual relationships that have been tied to private firms' Local Full IFRS financial statements, **transitional costs** are likely to outweigh these benefits.

Prior research has shown that Full IFRS and IFRS for SMEs adoption can be **lengthy processes** that are mostly achieved in stages. For example, due to regulatory efforts by the European Commission, EU countries' recognition and measurement rules have gradually drifted towards fair value accounting and other IFRS characteristics since the early 2000s (*Sellhorn/Gornik-Tomaszewski* (2006), p. 205). Moreover, prior research revealed that legal requirements and the contracting purpose of financial reporting have impeded complete adoption of Full IFRS in the field of European private firms (*Street/Larson* (2004), p. 2). The disagreement with certain IFRS and their complicated nature represent additional barriers to IFRS convergence within the EU (*Street/Larson* (2004), p. 2). As a result, most European countries have developed local versions of Full IFRS (so-called 'Local Full IFRS') that only partially comply with IASB-IFRS.

However, from a global perspective, there is also evidence against this conjecture. If a country has already adopted a financial reporting system that is quite close to IFRS, complete adoption should be less of a problem than if there was a completely different set of local accounting standards in place. In accordance with this view, *Chand/Patel* (2008) conclude from their analysis of the convergence and harmonization of accounting standards in Fiji that a reasonably well-established set of accounting standards already prevailing in the country may be indicative of its **readiness to adopt IFRS** in full or in part. Fiji had already implemented generally accepted accounting principles based on a combination of Australian, New Zealand, and IASB standards before the country adopted Full IFRS selectively in 2002 (*Chand/Patel* (2008), p. 87). The challenges in the convergence with IFRS faced by India are another example for the potentially high level of transitional costs that can result from substantial differences between local accounting concepts and the IFRS approach (*Indapurkar et al.* (2009), p. 4).

All in all, there is **mixed evidence** regarding the effect of local versions of Full IFRS on the probability of complete IFRS adoption. However, in accordance with prior research from the EU (*Street/Larson* (2004)), this study assumes that the existence of Local Full IFRS rather impedes the adoption of IASB standards as it causes lower direct economic benefits and higher transitional costs. In conclusion, the third hypothesis regarding the economic determinants of Full IFRS (*H3a*) and IFRS for SMEs adoption (*H3b*) is postulated as follows:

H3a: ***Full IFRS*** *adoption in the field of private firms is more likely in countries without local versions of Full IFRS.*

H3b: ***IFRS for SMEs*** *adoption in the field of private firms is more likely in countries without local versions of Full IFRS.*

2.2.2.1.4 Full IFRS adoption for listed firms

IAS/IFRS were initially developed for the special purpose of the preparation of financial statements of large listed companies. Hence, the IASC's primary goal was for many years to promote the use of IAS/IFRS among listed companies worldwide and to be finally acknowledged by the IOSCO (*Nobes/Parker* (2012), p. 89). It is not surprising that countries had first made a decision about Full IFRS adoption in the context of listed companies before they balanced reasons for and against the adoption of IASB standards in the field of private firms. Due to this timing, a country's Full IFRS adoption decision in the context of listed firms is likely to determine its Full IFRS and IFRS for SMEs adoption behavior in the field of private firms.

If a country has already adopted Full IFRS in the field of listed firms, Full IFRS and IFRS for SMEs adoption in the field of private firms are likely to cause lower **transitional costs.** Ceteris paribus, this leads to a higher level of net economic benefits. This is because the local accounting infrastructure has already been adapted to the IFRS accounting system and larger companies, auditors, and financial statement users have already made some experiences with IFRS financial statements. According to *Pacter* (2014), the majority of the jurisdictions, which have yet been included in the IFRS jurisdiction profiles and that require Full IFRS for listed companies, also require Full IFRS for unlisted financial institutions or large unlisted companies (*Pacter* (2014), p. 8).

Therefore, the fourth hypothesis regarding the economic determinants of Full IFRS (*H4a*) and IFRS for SMEs adoption (*H4b*) is postulated as follows:

H4a: ***Full IFRS** adoption in the field of private firms is more likely in countries that have adopted Full IFRS in the field of listed firms.*

H4b: ***IFRS for SMEs** adoption in the field of private firms is more likely in countries that have adopted Full IFRS in the field of listed firms.*

2.2.2.1.5 Full IFRS adoption for private firms

Since the mid-2000s, Full IFRS have been increasingly criticized by international institutions such as the World Bank (*Hegarty et al.* (2004), p. 8) as well as by national standard-setters (especially from Africa and South America) for being inappropriate for small and medium-sized entities (*Kaya/Koch* (2013), p. 16). Hence, the primary objective of the IFRS for SMEs-project was to design an internationally harmonized, self-contained accounting standard of limited size but high quality, which would be tailored for the special needs and capabilities of SMEs around the world. In view of this fact, it seems likely that countries, which have already required local private firms to use Full IFRS for financial reporting purposes, perceive higher **direct economic benefits** from IFRS for SMEs adoption than other countries. Reflecting this assertion, *Grant Thornton* revealed in September 2009 that they expect the **IFRS for SMEs** will be particularly adopted in those countries that have already required Full IFRS to be used for all entities, listed and unlisted, due to the reduced complexity of the standard compared to Full IFRS (*Grant Thornton* (2009), p. 6).

In **South Africa**, for example, the potential benefits from IFRS for SMEs adoption were perceived as so high that the country already adopted the Exposure Draft, which preceded the final standard in October 2007, as a Statement of Generally Accepted Accounting Practice for SMEs (*Grant Thornton* (2009), p. 6). The reduction in costs and auditing time, the lower complexity of the standard as well as the relief from the burden of Full IFRS were seen as the major advantages of IFRS for SMEs adoption (*Stainbank* (2010), p. 66). To the contrary, some members of the Australian Accounting Standards Board (AASB) hold the opinion that IFRS for SMEs adoption would be a retrograde step for **Australia** as it has already adopted Full IFRS recognition and measurement accounting policy options (*Australian Accounting Standards Board* (2010), BC73(g)).

Equally to the assumed negative effect of Full IFRS adoption for listed firms on the transitional costs of Full IFRS and IFRS for SMEs adoption in the field of private firms (*H4a* & *H4b*), IFRS for SMEs adoption is expected to cause lower **transitional costs** if the country has previously required private firms to adopt Full IFRS due to prior adaptation to the IFRS accounting system. Besides, **maintenance costs** of IFRS for SMEs adoption are likely to be lower compared to Full IFRS adoption as the frequency of changes made to the IFRS for SMEs (only every three to five years) is significantly lower than for Full IFRS (continuous revisions). Focusing on the effect of transitional costs, *Kaya/Koch* (2013) show that Full IFRS adoption for private firms is indeed indicative for early IFRS for SMEs adoption by 2011 (*Kaya/Koch* (2013), p. 25). Therefore, the hypothesis (*H5*) is postulated as follows:

> *H5:* ***IFRS for SMEs*** *adoption in the field of private firms is more likely in countries that have previously required private firms to adopt Full IFRS.*

H5 is the single hypothesis that only addresses IFRS for SMEs adoption. It shall shed light on the interdependent effects between Full IFRS and IFRS for SMEs adoption in the field of private firms.

Having discussed the potential influence of **net economic benefits** – defined as direct economic benefits less transitional and maintenance costs – on the probability of Full IFRS and IFRS for SMEs adoption in the field of private firms, the following section will focus on the network benefits and the related mimetic pressures that may also determine the decision to adopt or not adopt the two sets of IASB standards regardless of their country-specific 'intrinsic value'.

2.2.2.2 Network effects

According to the economic theory of networks (*Katz/Shapiro* (1985), the **total value of a network-dependent product** is the sum of its intrinsic value and the value of the product's network. The latter value arises from other agents joining the product's network (*Liebowitz/Margolis* (1994), p. 135). In accordance with prior research that has already analyzed the impact of network effects on Full IFRS adoption in the field of listed companies (*Ramanna/Sletten* (2009); *Ramanna/Sletten* (2013)), this study applies a similar technique to present empirical evidence on the determining role of network effects in the context of Full IFRS and IFRS for SMEs adoption by private firms.

By defining the circle of Full IFRS and IFRS for SMEs adopting countries as two distinct networks, the perceived value of Full IFRS and IFRS for SMEs adoption is expected to increase with the number of countries that have already joined either of the two networks. As a consequence, non-adopting countries are likely to perceive greater economic benefits from adoption the more other countries have already adopted Full IFRS and IFRS for SMEs. In particular, due to the strong economic, social, and cultural relationships that generally exist between bordering countries and between countries within a specific geographic region, a country is expected to perceive the highest **network benefits** from Full IFRS and IFRS for SMEs adopters that are located within close geographic proximity.

Vice versa, existing network benefits from the adoption of other harmonized accounting systems (e.g. the EU Accounting Directives) can possibly counteract the potential network benefits of Full IFRS and IFRS for SMEs adoption. For example, the *Committee on Economic and Monetary Affairs* of the European Parliament fears that if a few EU member states decide to apply the IFRS for SMEs as issued by the IASB, this could lead to a **fragmentation of the European internal market** and might even prejudice accounting for SMEs across the entire EU (*Radwan* (2008), p. 10).

From the perspective of institutional theory, a growing Full IFRS and IFRS for SMEs adoption rate within a specific geographic region also creates **mimetic pressures** for those countries that have not yet adopted either of the two IFRS accounting systems. Countries often take their neighbors as peers and benchmark their own systems against them. Federations of countries from the same geographic region (e.g. African Union, ASEAN, or USAN) increase such desires to achieve social legitimacy and reputation (*Chua/Taylor* (2008), p. 470).

In particular, network benefits and mimetic pressures are expected to be the highest if neighboring countries have 'recently' joined the Full IFRS and IFRS for SMEs network. In this study, **'recent' adoptions** are defined as adoptions of other countries within the same geographic region that have occurred during the past two years. For example, when the European Union decided to require Full IFRS in the consolidated financial statements of publicly traded firms from 2005 (2007) onwards (*European Commission* (2002)), the Turkish Accounting Standards Board (TASB), which oversees Turkish Accounting Standards (TAS), immediately accepted harmonization with the IASB principles to receive international acceptance (*Yalkin et al.* (2008), p. 279).

While Full IFRS adoption for publicly traded companies has been the field norm for many years already, IFRS-based accounting harmonization in the field of private firms can still be regarded as an innovative step similar to the **adoption of a new technology**. According to *Baptista* (2000), regional differences in the diffusion of innovations result from the geographical clustering of innovators and early adopters of new technology and it is the geographical proximity that stimulates networking between them (*Baptista* (2000), p. 516).

In line with the empirical evidence on network benefits provided by *Ramanna/Sletten* (2009, 2013) and considering the corresponding mimetic pressures derived from institutional theory of isomorphism, the following hypothesis regarding network effects and Full IFRS (*H6a*) and IFRS for SMEs adoption (*H6b*) is postulated as follows:

*H6a: The more other countries within the same geographic region have recently adopted Full IFRS in the field of private firms, the more likely is **Full IFRS** adoption of a particular country in that geographic region.*

*H6b: The more other countries within the same geographic region have recently adopted IFRS for SMEs in the field of private firms, the more likely is **IFRS for SMEs** adoption of a particular country in that geographic region.*

Having discussed the influence of **net economic benefits** and **network effects**, the following section will complete the refinement of the conceptual framework by establishing four hypotheses on coercive isomorphic pressures and Full IFRS and IFRS for SMEs adoption.

2.2.2.3 Political pressures

State sovereignty and independence generally allow countries to choose freely any accounting system they prefer. However, if powerful institutions such as the World Bank, the International Monetary Fund, or supranational associations such as the European Union come to accept Full IFRS or IFRS for SMEs as a legitimate form of international best practice, political pressures can force jurisdictions, directly or indirectly, to embark on a process towards IFRS adoption regardless of the IASB standards' local appropriateness.

2.2.2.3.1 Economic power

Based on the institutional theory of isomorphism, smaller economies are expected to be more dependent on international norms and standards due to their higher resource dependency (*Judge et al.* (2010), p. 163). Hence, they are likely to perceive higher **coercive pressures** to adopt IASB standards than more powerful economies. In accordance with that, *Ramanna/Sletten* (2009) show for a sample of 102 non-European countries that less powerful countries were more likely to adopt Full IFRS in the field of listed companies between 2002 and 2007.

In a later paper from 2013, *Ramanna* develops a framework for analyzing how **international politics** can shape countries' **IFRS harmonization strategies** in the field of financial reporting. According to the framework, a country's harmonization strategy is mainly determined by its potential political power (*Ramanna* (2013), p. 29). The more powerful a jurisdiction is, the more is the jurisdiction able to either set the direction of the IASB (e.g. European Union) or to diverge from it (e.g. China). On the contrary, less powerful countries may only give way to the pressures they are subject to and align their rules with IFRS or try to form regional alliances to develop carve-outs (*Ramanna* (2013), p. 30). The United States, one of the most powerful economies in the world, still rejects Full IFRS adoption in the field of domestic listed companies. Contrary to smaller economies that have already ceded rule-making power to the IASB due to coercive pressures, the US are neither willing to experience any loss of sovereignty over its ability to set accounting standards (*Selling* (2013), p. 162) nor do they want to confer monopoly status to the IASB (*Hail et al.* (2010b), p. 584).

Developing countries have long been subject to **'accounting colonialism'** that has been imposed by the coercive power of international capital (*Briston* (1978)). In his influential paper from 1978, *Briston* points out that external pressures, mainly stemming from the UK accounting profession and multinational companies, have been so great that none of the studied African (Nigeria & Tanzania) and Asian countries (Indonesia & Sri Lanka) countries have been able to develop their own accounting system but adopted foreign standards instead (*Briston* (1978), p. 116). More recent evidence from Pakistan (*Ashraf/Ghani* (2005)), Fiji (*Chand/White* (2007)), and the United Arab Emirates (*Irvine* (2008)) suggests that less developed countries and emerging economies are still subject to strong external pressures that shape the choice of their accounting systems. For example, *Tyrrall et al.* (2007) analyze the relevance of IFRS to Kazakhstan and state that the weak equity market creates little demand for and supply of high quality IFRS financial statements. They conclude that IFRS adoption in Kazakhstan was enforced by an external investment need, not an accounting need, and that the development of local standards without reference to outside influences was not an option (*Tyrrall et al.* (2007), p. 99).

In accordance with institutional theory and prior research, the first hypothesis regarding the effect of coercive isomorphic pressures on Full IFRS (*H7a*) and IFRS for SMEs adoption (*H7b*) is postulated as follows:

*H7a: The lower a country's economic power, the more likely is **Full IFRS** adoption in the field of private firms.*

*H7b: The lower a country's economic power, the more likely is **IFRS for SMEs** adoption in the field of private firms.*

2.2.2.3.2 Political power

Prior research has shown that larger countries are less likely to adopt Full IFRS in the field of listed companies than smaller countries (*Clements et al.* (2010)). In line with this, *Ramanna/Sletten* (2009) argue that country size can be a **proxy for political power** since larger countries are historically more powerful as they require larger militaries to establish and maintain their territories (*Ramanna/Sletten* (2009), p. 17). From an institutional theoretical perspective, smaller countries are expected to encounter higher external pressures to adopt international standards than larger countries due to their lack of political power.

However, the effect of coercive pressures on the higher probability of IFRS adoption by countries with less political power can hardly be distinguished from economic **cost-benefit considerations**. Particularly smaller countries may find it cheaper to copy IASB standards than to maintain their own standard setting bodies (*Ball* (2001), p. 166). In line with *Ball*, *Ramanna/Sletten* (2013) show that perceived network benefits increase the degree of IFRS harmonization among countries and that smaller countries have a differentially higher response to these benefits (*Ramanna/Sletten* (2013), p. 26).

Despite the revealed **conceptual ambiguity**, this study defines the level of a country's political power as an indirect measure of external coercive pressures instead of net economic benefits from Full IFRS and IFRS for SMEs adoption. This is because the economic measures used in this study are much more geared to countries' financial reporting context than the overall concept of political power.

In line with institutional theory, the hypothesis regarding the effect of coercive isomorphic pressures on Full IFRS (*H8a*) and IFRS for SMEs adoption (*H8b*) is postulated as follows:

*H8a: The lower a country's political power, the more likely is **Full IFRS** adoption in the field of private firms.*

*H8b: The lower a country's political power, the more likely is **IFRS for SMEs** adoption in the field of private firms.*

2.2.2.3.3 Import dependency

The effect of import dependency (also import penetration) on IFRS adoption has yet been studied in the context of listed companies only. *Archambault/Archambault* (2009) conducted an archival study on the determinants of Full IFRS adoption in 120 countries by 2004 and found that **countries with net import activity are more likely to adopt Full IFRS** in the field of listed companies. They conclude that Full IFRS adoption may help importing companies that buy goods on credit to obtain more favorable credit terms because their financial statements can be understood more easily than if domestic standards were used (*Archambault/Archambault* (2009), p. 42).

Rodrigues/Craig (2007) argue that social systems often emulate the success of others and that this could influence the accounting harmonization process. In line with that, *Judge et al.* (2010) investigate the relationship between import penetration and Full IFRS adoption and explain the identified positive association by institutional theory. *Judge et al.* postulate that the more integrated the national economy is within the global marketplace, the more complete is Full IFRS adoption due to **mimetic pressures**. By assuming that multinational firms have the resources and the incentives to adopt Full IFRS, *Judge et al.* conclude that when there is extensive import penetration in an economy, the country is more likely to emulate the accounting standards of the multinational firms involved (*Judge et al.* (2010), p. 165).

While *Judge et al.* (2010) define import penetration as a mimetic pressure, this study argues that foreign trade partners (especially suppliers) rather enforce Full IFRS and IFRS for SMEs adoption by domestic private firms as they have an interest in the comparability of the financial statements of their business partners. These **coercive pressures** are expected to cumulate most in an economy with high import dependency and finally result in IFRS adoption on country level. Hence, a higher responsiveness to coercive pressures is expected for countries that are more dependent on imports. In accordance with this, the *Summary Report* (2010) of the responses received to the European Commission's consultation on the IFRS for SMEs lists expanded cross-border trade as one of several potential benefits of IFRS for SMEs adoption by EU private firms (*European Commission* (2010), p. 2).

Hence, the third hypothesis regarding the effect of coercive isomorphic pressures on Full IFRS (*H9a*) and IFRS for SMEs adoption (*H9b*) is postulated as follows:

H9a: *The more dependent a country is on imports, the more likely is **Full IFRS** adoption in the field of private firms.*

H9b: *The more dependent a country is on imports, the more likely is **IFRS for SMEs** adoption in the field of private firms.*

2.2.2.3.4 Pressures from supranational institutions

Contrary to the above defined variables, which represent country-specific characteristics that are assumed to result in a higher or lower exposure to coercive isomorphic pressures (*Oliver* (1991)), some of the external pressures can be measured directly. According to different sources, **supranational institutions** such as the International Monetary Fund and the World Bank do not only play an important role in the implementation of IFRS by providing financial resources (*United Nations* (2008), p. 14), but also use their considerable international surveillance powers to encourage countries to adopt IFRS (*Singh/Newberry* (2008), p. 484). *Gyasi* (2010) highlights from an African perspective (Ghana) that these influential financial institutions would mastermind the formulation of

IFRS and that their **influence** on countries to adopt the standards would be **highly imperative** (*Gyasi* (2010), p. 19).

In particular the **World Bank**, as one of the largest users of financial statements worldwide, has become a 'major force' in efforts to impose IFRS on developing countries (*Singh/Newberry* (2008), p. 491). In the World Bank's accounting manual, which was first published in 1995, the Bank justifies its request for IASB standards as their use would *"facilitate comparability between projects and countries, ensures consistent presentation of financial statements, and facilitates their interpretation"* (*Camfferman/Zeff* (2007), p. 442). One important instrument used by the World Bank to recommend and enforce IFRS adoption by developing countries is the World Bank's **Report on the Observance of Standards and Codes (ROSC)**. The objective is to assess the comparability of national accounting and auditing standards with Full IFRS and International Standards on Auditing (ISA) and assist countries in developing and implementing an action plan for improving their financial reporting regimes (*World Bank* (2004e), p. 2).

When analyzing the content of all existing World Bank reports,[88] it becomes clear that while the World Bank strongly recommends complete Full IFRS adoption in the field of publicly traded companies and public interest entities (and sometimes large unlisted companies), the Bank's view is that Full IFRS are generally inappropriate for the use by private firms due to their lack of accounting expertise, financial resources and due to the corresponding compliance problems (*Hegarty et al.* (2004), p. ii). The following two excerpts from ROSC prepared for Ghana (2004) and Uruguay (2006) illustrate the **direct coercive pressures** that are exerted from the World Bank on countries regarding Full IFRS and IFRS for SMEs adoption in the field of private firms:

> ***"Agree to a simplified financial reporting framework for small and medium enterprises.*** *All but the smallest enterprises may be subjected to a simplified financial reporting framework. Until finalization of the IASB project, Accounting by Small and Medium Entities and in Emerging Economies, the national accounting standard setters should agree on standards for small- and medium-size enterprises. Once the international standard is available, national standards should conform to the international standards. Reasons for any necessary derogation would need justification."*
>
> (*World Bank* (2004c), p. 18)
>
> ***"Adopt IFRS in full for financial reporting by all public interest entities and, in their simplified version, for SMEs.*** *The different rules dealing with accounting at present in the enterprise sector should ultimately give way to IFRS as the single set of standards for all enterprises in the country. This will simplify and clarify Uruguay's accounting regime. For SMEs, the IASB is currently developing a simplified version of IFRS which is expected to be released as draft in 2006 and as final in 2007 or 2008; Uruguay should adopt these SME-IFRS once they become*

88 Between 2001 and 2012, the World Bank issued a total of 111 country-by-country reports on the development of national accounting and auditing systems and the implementation of Full IFRS and IFRS for SMEs. Cf. *World Bank* (2004e).

> *available. This would allow issuers and auditors to refer to IFRS, thereby enhancing investors' confidence in applicable standards and thus in the financial statements."*
>
> (*World Bank* (2006d), p. 30)

Hence, the final hypothesis regarding the effect of coercive isomorphic pressures on Full IFRS (*H10a*) and IFRS for SMEs adoption (*H10b*) is postulated as follows:

H10a: ***Full IFRS*** *adoption in the field of private firms is* ***less likely*** *in countries, which have been subject to pressures from supranational institutions that oppose adoption.*

H10b: ***IFRS for SMEs*** *adoption in the field of private firms is* ***more likely*** *in countries, which have been subject to pressures from supranational institutions that support adoption.*

2.2.3 Refined conceptual framework

This study applies a conjunction of two basic theoretic concepts: *economic theory of networks* and *institutional theory of isomorphism* to provide a comprehensive theoretic basis for describing and explaining Full IFRS and IFRS for SMEs adoption in the field of private firms. Figure 2-2 summarizes this study's refined conceptual framework.

The framework includes three **research propositions** (*P1-P3*) that postulate potential differences regarding the process (2002-2014) and the type and scope of Full IFRS and IFRS for SMEs adoption (2014) across countries. In addition, the framework provides a list of **falsifiable hypotheses** on net economic benefits (*H1-H5*), network effects (*H6*), and political pressures (*H7-H10*), which are assumed to determine the probability of Full IFRS adoption (2008 & 2014) and IFRS for SMEs adoption (2014) in the field of private firms. The hypotheses are subject to empirical testing in chapter four. Due to the comprehensiveness of this study's explanatory approach, the refined conceptual framework does not contain any more control variables. However, alternative explanations are discussed in chapter five.

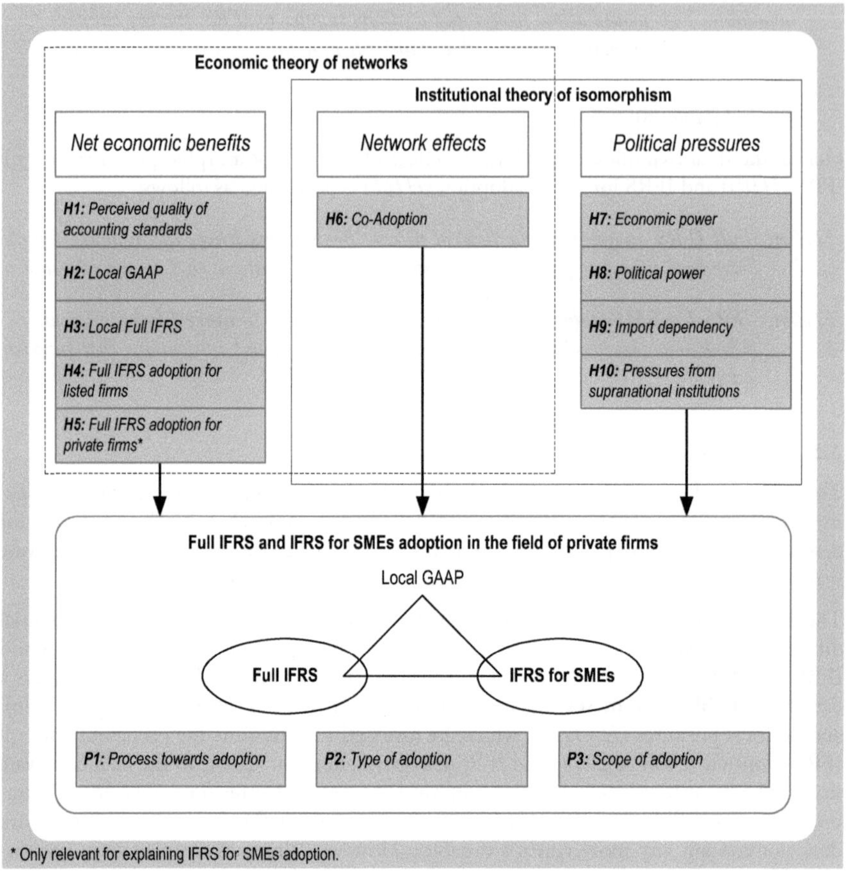

Figure 2-2: Refined conceptual framework

3 Characteristics of Full IFRS and IFRS for SMEs adoption

3.1 Research design

As explained in chapter one, this chapter presents a two-part descriptive analysis of *de jure* international accounting harmonization in the field of private firms in 110 countries. While **time series analysis** will display the process of Full IFRS and IFRS for SMEs adoption between 2002 and 2014, **cross-sectional analysis** provides insights into the status quo of local Full IFRS and IFRS for SMEs implementation in 2014. For reasons of presentation and comparability, both analyses will be conducted separately for the following nine geographic regions:

North America	European Union	Middle East
Central America & Caribbean	Southeast Europe	Asia
South America	Africa	Australia & Oceania

Before developing the conceptual foundation and presenting the empirical results of the descriptive study, the following section will briefly describe the process of data collection and the sample.

3.1.1 Data collection and sample

3.1.1.1 Sample selection procedure

Country level analyses typically result in smaller sample sizes than firm level studies, which generally reduces the power of the empirical tests. However, country level data provide the basis for macro-level analyses and thus offer unique insights into country characteristics (*Gordon et al.* (2013), p. 146).

The United Nations (UN) count 193 member states as of July 2014 (*United Nations* (2014)). For the sake of completeness, this study adds three disputed sovereign states and fourteen jurisdictions with limited sovereignty to the list of UN member states. This leads to a total of **210 countries**[89] (and jurisdictions) representing the **basic population** of this study.

To collect **primary data** on the process (2002-2014) and the status quo (2014) of Full IFRS and IFRS for SMEs adoption in as many countries as possible, *Grant Thornton* and *PricewaterhouseCoopers (PwC)* were asked to participate in the process of data collection by providing access to their international network of auditors. In May 2012, an **e-mail-based survey**[90] was sent to 109 country offices of *Grant Thornton* and in September 2012, the same survey was sent to 128 country offices of *PwC*. The survey was forwarded to the respective Head of Assurance and then distributed internally among the participating

[89] Cf. Table A-1 for a list of the 210 countries arranged on the basis of their geographic location.

[90] Cf. survey questions in Figure A-1.

managing partners. Due to the fact that both *Grant Thornton* and *PwC* have offices in the same 99 jurisdictions, the total outreach of data collection included 138 countries. From these 138 countries, 140 responses were received for **110 countries.**[91] Hence, dual data were obtained for 30 countries. The sample selection procedure is illustrated in Table 3-1.

	UN Member States		**193**
+	Disputed sovereign states claimed by other countries	+ 3	
+	Jurisdictions with limited sovereignty	+ 14	
=	**Total population**		**210**
	(thereof countries with *Grant Thornton* office)		(109)
	(thereof countries with *PwC* office)		(128)
-	Countries without *Grant Thornton* and without *PwC* office	- 72	
=	**Countries with Grant Thornton and/or PwC office**		**138**
-	Countries excluded from the sample due to non-response	- 28	
=	**Sample**		**110**
	(thereof responses received from *Grant Thornton* only)		(32)
	(thereof responses received from *PwC* only)		(48)
	(thereof responses received from *Grant Thornton* and *PwC*)		(30)

Table 3-1: Sample selection procedure

In addition to the data provided in the survey, several answers were discussed via e-mail and on the phone to verify the provided information and to improve the answers' comparability regarding their length and level of detail. In case of contradictory statements, the given answers were discussed in detail and the contradiction was resolved. To further increase the reliability of the *Grant Thornton* and *PwC* data, the information was verified by drawing on **public sources** such as the *IFRS Foundation's* jurisdiction profiles and various national standard-setters' websites. Primary data collection was completed in March 2013.

As the **study period** starts in **2002** and ends in **2014**, all responses regarding Full IFRS and IFRS for SMEs adoptions later than March 2013 are based on estimates provided by managing partners of *Grant Thornton* and *PwC*. As the time span between a country's decision to adopt IFRS and the date of its implementation is approximately two years on average (*Ramanna/Sletten* (2013), p. 10), the predicted adoptions for 2013 and 2014 can be regarded as reliable. In addition, all adoption dates have been verified by several public sources as of July 2014.[92] The study period starts in 2002 as this is the first year after the formation of the IASB (*Ramanna/Sletten* (2009), p. 14; *Johnson* (2011), p. 14). Hence, any convergence of national accounting standards with IAS prior to 2002 is excluded from the scope of this study.

---

91 Cf. Table A-2 for a list of the 110 sampled countries arranged according to their geographic location.

92 In particular, the *IFRS Foundation's* jurisdiction profiles have been used to verify the adoption data.

In addition to the primary data on the process (2002-2014) and the status quo (2014) of Full IFRS and IFRS for SMEs adoption in the 110 sampled countries, the descriptive study uses **secondary data** on the countries' Gross Domestic Product (GDP) in US $ for the years 2008 and 2014. The data were obtained from the *International Monetary Fund's* World Economic Outlook Database as of May 2014.

3.1.1.2 Characteristics of the sample

Based on the *United Nations* geoscheme and political considerations, the 110 sampled countries are allocated to **nine macro-geographic regions** (see Table 3-2).

Geographic region	Total			Sample		
	No. (countries)	GDP (in US $ bill.)	Population (in mill.)	No. (countries)	GDP (in US $ bill.)	Population (in mill.)
North America	4	18,091	353	2 (50%)	18,091 (99%)	353 (99%)
Central America & Caribbean	26	1,606	187	7 (27%)	1,475 (92%)	163 (87%)
South America	12	4,446	405	9 (75%)	4,409 (99%)	392 (97%)
European Union *(incl. EEA)* [1]	30	18,117	507	28 (93%)	18,108 (99%)	507 (99%)
Southeast Europe *(incl. others)* [2]	19	2,048	181	13 (68%)	2,023 (99%)	177 (98%)
Africa	55	2,166	1,070	19 (35%)	1,759 (81%)	649 (61%)
Middle East	14	2,627	203	10 (71%)	2,389 (91%)	175 (86%)
Asia	32	24,554	4,082	19 (59%)	24,250 (99%)	3,741 (92%)
Australia & Oceania	18	1,867	38	3 (17%)	1,843 (99%)	29 (75%)
Total	**210**	**75,522**	**7,026**	**110 (52%)**	**74,347 (98%)**	**6,186 (88%)**

[1] The European Union group includes the EU member states (27) at the cut-off date for data collection in March 2013. As Croatia joined the EU in July 2013, it is assigned to Southeast Europe. Furthermore, the EU group is supplemented by three non-EU countries that are member states of the European Economic Area (Iceland, Liechtenstein, and Norway). Cf. Table A-1. These countries generally comply with all EU requirements including the regulation of private firms' financial reporting and thus are included in the EU group. [2] The Southeast Europe group consists of Southeastern European countries plus Andorra, Isle of Man, and Switzerland. Cf. Table A-1.

Table 3-2: Characteristics of the sample

In deviation from the *United Nations Statistics Division* (2013), Central America and the Caribbean are combined into one geographic region as data are only available for seven out of 26 Central American and Caribbean (CAC) countries. Furthermore, the countries from the Middle East are not included in the Asian region but displayed as a separate geographic area due to their specific economic and cultural characteristics. To take into account the political interdependencies within the European Union and between countries of the European Economic Area, the European continent is divided into the European Union (including the European Economic Area) and Southeast Europe (including the remaining countries in Europe).

Some prior studies on Full IFRS adoption exclude the countries of the European Union and European Economic Area from their analyses (*Ramanna/Sletten* (2009), p. 1) or treat these countries as one observation only (*Ramanna/Sletten* (2013), p. 12). This is due to the EU countries' joint decision to require Full IFRS in the consolidated financial statements of publicly traded firms from 2005 (2007) onwards (*European Commission* (2002)). However, outside of the scope of publicly traded EU companies, there is significant variation in the scope of Full IFRS adoption within the European Union as each member state can decide individually to require, permit, or prohibit the use of Full IFRS in the individual and consolidated financial statements of domestic private firms (*European Commission* (2012)). Hence, **EU countries are included in the sample** since they offer significant opportunities for comparative accounting research in the field of private firms' financial reporting.

In summary, the sample consists of slightly more than half of the world's total number of countries and jurisdictions (52%). On the basis of GDP, the sample contains 98% of the global economic power. Moreover, the 110 sampled countries represent approximately 88% of the earth's total population. While the sample includes almost all EU member states (26 out of 27), countries from Africa (35%), the Caribbean (11%), and Oceania (17%) are underrepresented in the sample. Given these numbers, the **sample is biased** towards larger, densely populated, and economically more powerful countries. This is because *Grant Thornton's* and *PwC's* international network does not comprise the world's very smallest jurisdictions, which leads to the poor data availability for these countries. Hence, the empirical results of this study do not apply to all jurisdictions worldwide. Nevertheless, the sample represents a comprehensive database for the descriptive analysis of worldwide Full IFRS and IFRS for SMEs adoption in the field of private firms.

3.1.2 Conceptual foundation

To precisely describe the worldwide process of accounting systems' early or late, rapid or gradual, completed or uncompleted convergence with Full IFRS and IFRS for SMEs in the field of private firms, this study develops a detailed classification of accounting systems that is based on their degree of compliance with Full IFRS and IFRS for SMEs. The study further distinguishes between different types and scopes of adoption.

3.1.2.1 Classifying accounting systems

In view of the following statement, the *IFRS Foundation's* strategy regarding global IFRS adoption is clear:

> *"[...] the IFRS Foundation must remain committed to the long-term goal of the* ***global adoption of IFRSs as developed by the IASB****, in their entirety and without modification. Convergence may be an appropriate short-term strategy for a particular jurisdiction and may facilitate adoption over a transitional period. Convergence, however, is not a substitute for adoption. Adoption mechanisms [...] should enable and require relevant entities to state that their financial statements are in full compliance with IFRSs as issued by the IASB."*
>
> (*IFRS Foundation* (2012b), p. 11)

Hence, **partial compliance** with IFRS is only seen as an **intermediate state** within a country's long-term convergence process. The ultimate goal, however, is national accounting systems' full compliance with IFRS as issued by the IASB. *Nobes* shows in a paper from 2013 that this goal is far from being achieved. Even though the *IFRS Foundation* reports that more than 100 jurisdictions require Full IFRS for all or most domestic publicly accountable entities (*IFRS Foundation* (2014g)), *Nobes* (2013) argues that 'IASB-IFRS' are not even required for the reporting of all types of regulated entities in any of the 16 countries with the world's largest stock markets (*Nobes* (2013), p. 86).

This apparent **contradiction** can be resolved by considering the slight differences that result from national implementation of IFRS (*Nobes* (2013), p. 84ff.). Errors in translation and the addition of local disclosure requirements are only two of several reasons why some observers may refer to local versions of IFRS while others still consider these standards as IFRS. The question is to which degree accounting systems are allowed to differ from Full IFRS or IFRS for SMEs without losing its status as 'IASB-compliant'. In other words, there is a need of defining different categories of accounting systems on the basis of their degree of compliance with Full IFRS and IFRS for SMEs.

While accounting systems could only converge towards Full IFRS prior to 2009, national standard-setters nowadays face a **three-dimensional financial reporting environment** (see Figure 3-1). Since the IFRS for SMEs was issued, Local GAAP may either move towards Full IFRS or IFRS for SMEs. Hence, this study classifies accounting systems according to their degree of compliance with either Full IFRS or IFRS for SMEs. Mixed versions of Full IFRS and IFRS for SMEs are excluded from the classification as the only known example of such 'hybrid' IFRS are the Australian Accounting Standards (AAS) – Reduced Disclosure Requirements (RDR), which combine Full IFRS standards on recognition & measurement with IFRS for SMEs disclosure rules (*Australian Accounting Standards Board* (2010)). In this study, AAS-RDR are classified as a local version of IFRS for SMEs.

In conclusion, this study defines **five basic categories** of accounting systems including the three edges of the triangle illustrated in Figure 3-1 (Local GAAP, Full IFRS and IFRS for SMEs) as well as the two lateral connecting lines (Local Full IFRS and Local IFRS for SMEs).

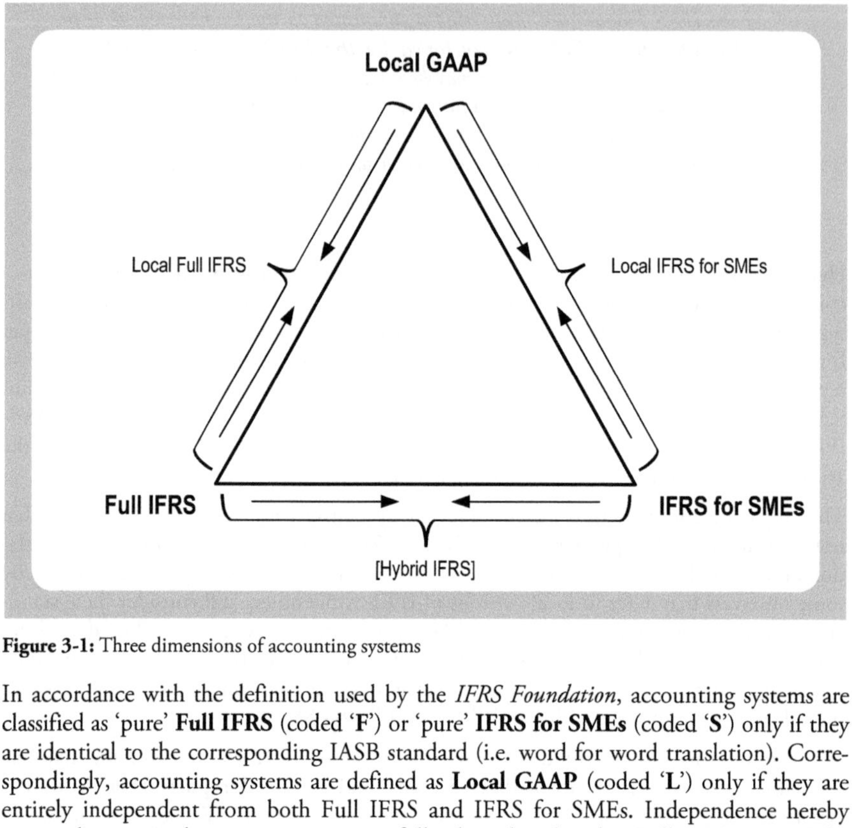

Figure 3-1: Three dimensions of accounting systems

In accordance with the definition used by the *IFRS Foundation*, accounting systems are classified as 'pure' **Full IFRS** (coded '**F**') or 'pure' **IFRS for SMEs** (coded '**S**') only if they are identical to the corresponding IASB standard (i.e. word for word translation). Correspondingly, accounting systems are defined as **Local GAAP** (coded '**L**') only if they are entirely independent from both Full IFRS and IFRS for SMEs. Independence hereby means that no single accounting topic is fully aligned with either Full IFRS or IFRS for SMEs, and neither of the two sets of IASB standards is used as a guideline for the financial reporting of domestic companies.

As shown by the two pairs of arrows that point to each other (see Figure 3-1), local versions of Full IFRS and IFRS for SMEs can result from two separate developments:

(1) **convergence** of Local GAAP with Full IFRS or IFRS for SMEs and

(2) local **modification** of Full IFRS or IFRS for SMEs.

According to *Wagenhofer* (2013), there are **several ways to converge Local GAAP with IFRS.** For example, countries such as the United States and Japan have initiated long-term convergence projects, which shall narrow the gap between the countries' Local GAAPs and Full IFRS.[93] Furthermore, China and Germany are two of several countries

[93] In 2002, the FASB and IASB signed a Memorandum of Understanding, known as the Norwalk Agreement, in which they agreed to make the two sets of standards fully compatible and to coordinate the future development of standards. In 2007, the IASB and the Accounting Standards Board of Japan

that make one-sided efforts to converge their local accounting standards with Full IFRS.[94] In comparison, keeping Local GAAP but adopting additional disclosures that may include a reconciliation of financial statements from local standards to IFRS[95] is regarded as a 'minimal form of convergence' (*Wagenhofer* (2013), p. 257).

When countries incorporate IFRS into their domestic accounting framework, they are likely to modify and **adapt IASB standards to local conditions** (*Kothari et al.* (2010), p. 65). For example, when Full IFRS was 'adopted' in Australia in 2005, the Australian Accounting Standards Board changed the designation of certain standards (e.g. from IAS 7 to AASB 107), added references, inserted departures for not-for-profit entities, and added local disclosure requirements (*Nobes/Zeff* (2008), p. 282).[96] Hence, *Zeff/Nobes* (2010) argue that Australia has not 'fully' adopted IFRS although there are countries that have achieved less convergence with IFRS than Australia (e.g. China). Comparable to the Australian modifications to Full IFRS, the EU-IFRS also differ from IASB-IFRS in one specific aspect. Over the course of the EU endorsement of IAS 39, the European parliament restricted the permission for hedge accounting in 2005, which led to more flexibility in the EU-endorsed IAS 39 than in the IASB's version (so-called IAS 39 carve-out) (*Whittington* (2005), p. 137ff.).

Regardless of whether IFRS are modified over the course of adoption or Local GAAPs are converged only partially with IFRS, the result is the same: **Local IFRS**. In both cases, the local version of IFRS differs from the original IFRS due to the omittance of certain IFRS topics, local modifications, and the persistence or addition of local financial reporting requirements (see Figure 3-2).

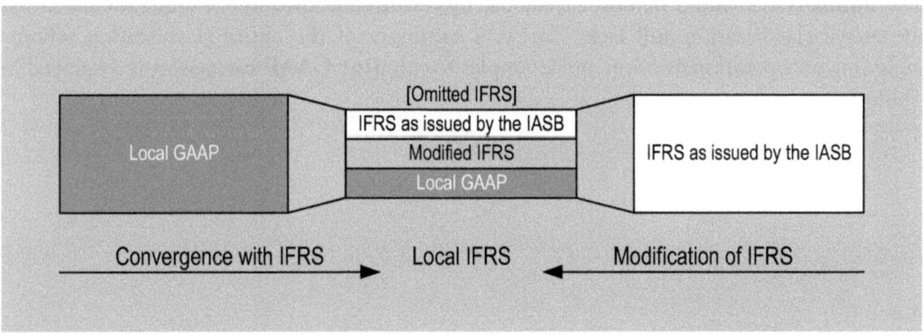

Figure 3-2: Development of Local IFRS

Besides the content-related differences between local versions of IFRS and the original IASB standards, a lengthy adoption process may also lead to temporary differences between local and international accounting standards (**time lag of adoption**). For example,

(ASBJ) signed the Tokyo Agreement, in which the two boards agreed to eliminate major differences in their standards. Cf. *Wagenhofer* (2013), p. 257.

94 China follows a continuous convergence process to reduce differences between Chinese standards and Full IFRS, while German GAAP was amended significantly in 2009. Cf. *Wagenhofer* (2013), p. 257.

95 Cf. *Adams et al.* (1993) for a study of IFRS reconciliations of Finnish corporate reports.

96 Cf. for similar actions in New Zealand *Chand/Patel* (2008), p. 88.

the Fiji Institute of Accountants adopted Full IFRS selectively in 2002 and deferred the adoption of the remaining and the new standards to a later date (*Chand/Patel* (2008), p. 87). The EU endorsement process takes at least several months. As a consequence, some parts of IFRS may have been published by the IASB but have not yet been endorsed by the European Union (*Nobes* (2006), p. 236).

In conclusion, this study generally differentiates between accounting systems that are entirely independent from Full IFRS and IFRS for SMEs ('**L**'), accounting systems that are identical to Full IFRS ('**F**') or IFRS for SMEs ('**S**') as well as accounting systems that are local versions of IFRS. Considering the content-related and temporary differences between local versions of IFRS and those that have been issued by the IASB, this study further differentiates 'Local Full IFRS' ('FL') and 'Local IFRS for SMEs' ('SL') into three sub-categories each:

- accounting systems that *comply* with Full IFRS *almost completely* ('**FL1**'),
- accounting systems that *comply* with IFRS for SMEs *almost completely* ('**SL1**'),

- accounting systems that *comply* with Full IFRS only *in part* ('**FL2**'),
- accounting systems that *comply* with IFRS for SMEs only *in part* ('**SL2**'),

- accounting systems that *comply* with Full IFRS *in almost nothing* ('**FL3**'), and
- accounting systems that *comply* with IFRS for SMEs *in almost nothing* ('**SL3**').

The numbers 1,2, and 3 hereby display the increasing modification of IASB standards. As the above classification still lacks clarity, a summary of the entire classification scheme including an operationalization and examples for all **nine GAAP categories** is displayed in Table 3-3.

Category			Code	Definition	Operationalization	Examples
Full IFRS			F	Accounting systems that are identical to Full IFRS (IFRS for SMEs) as issued by the IASB.	• Word for word translation of Full IFRS (IFRS for SMEs) • Insignificant time lag of adoption (endorsement within one year)	• Botswana (IFRS) • Hong Kong (HKFRS) • Moldova (IFRS)
IFRS for SMEs			S			• Brazil (CPC for SMEs) • Singapore (SFRS for Small Entities)
Modification: weak	Local Full IFRS / Local IFRS for SMEs	Convergence: strong	FL1	Accounting systems that comply with Full IFRS (IFRS for SMEs) almost completely.	• Very few omitted IFRS topics • Very few modifications • Very few additional local requirements • Considerable time lag of adoption (endorsement within two years)	• Australia (AAS) • EU (EU-IFRS) • Thailand (TFRS)
			SL1			• Fiji (IFRS for SMEs) • Hong Kong (HKFRS for Private Entities)
Modification: medium		Convergence: medium	FL2	Accounting systems that comply with Full IFRS (IFRS for SMEs) only in part.	• Numerous omitted IFRS topics • Numerous modifications • Numerous additional local requirements • Significant time lag of adoption (endorsement after two years)	• Argentina (ATR) • France (French GAAP) • USA (US GAAP)
			SL2			• Indonesia (SAK-ETAP) • Sweden (K3) • UK/Ireland (FRS 102)
Modification: strong		Convergence: weak	FL3	Accounting systems that comply with Full IFRS (IFRS for SMEs) in almost nothing.	• Very few accounting topics that are fully aligned with Full IFRS (IFRS for SMEs) • Full IFRS (IFRS for SMEs) may be used as a guideline	• Finland (Fin GAAP) • Germany (HGB) • India (Indian GAAP)
			SL3			• China (ASSE) • Thailand (TFRS for NPAEs)
Local GAAP			L	Accounting systems that are entirely independent from Full IFRS and IFRS for SMEs.	• No single accounting topic that is fully aligned with Full IFRS or IFRS for SMEs • Neither Full IFRS nor IFRS for SMEs is used as a guideline	• Russia (Russian accounting standards) • Switzerland (Code of Obligation)

Table 3-3: Classification of accounting systems

To further clarify the above presented classification, Table 3-4 displays five statements on the basis of which accounting systems for private firms have been classified in this study.

Accounting system	Category	Basis for conclusion
Hong Kong FRS	F	*"The HKFRS is a continuity of the Hong Kong Statements of Standard Accounting Practice (the 'Local GAAP'). In 2005, the Local GAAP was converged to IFRS word by word and renamed as HKFRS (i.e. equivalent to the IFRS). While HKFRS have been converged with IFRS, differences remain primarily in respect of transitional provisions."*
EU-IFRS	FL1	*"UK companies may only apply EU-adopted IFRS. Currently the only differences to IFRS are macro (or portfolio) hedge accounting (the IAS 39 carve-out) and in the timing of adoption of changes to the existing standards (as the EU endorsement process must be followed)."*
Swedish GAAP (K3)	SL2	*"IFRS for SMEs cannot be applied by Swedish entities. However, a new set of general advice of the Swedish Accounting Standards Board have recently been published (K3) and they are broadly based on IFRS for SMEs. K3 has to be adopted by larger entities by 2014 at the latest."*
Finnish GAAP	FL3	*"There are differences between Finnish GAAP and IFRS, and the Finnish GAAP is independent from IFRS. However, IFRS standards have had an influence on Finnish Accounting Standards. For example, in some Finnish Accounting Board's general guidance there has been referred to IFRS standards. Besides taking some IFRS methods into the Finnish GAAP, IFRS is used as a guideline when The Finnish Accounting Board solves accounting issues that are not specifically dealt with in the Finnish accounting standards."*
Russian GAAP	L	*"The non-public entities are obliged to report under the statutory rules. Despite the fact that statutory standards are said by the Government to be converged with IFRS in the future, as of now they are significantly different to IFRS. It is expected that by 2015 there should be a convergence but the date is constantly delayed."*

Table 3-4: Examples of accounting systems' classification[97]

While in the first part of the time series analysis all nine GAAP categories are used to present the entire spectrum of accounting systems in each geographic region, the study thereafter focuses on Full IFRS and IFRS for SMEs adopting countries. In doing so, Full IFRS and IFRS for SMEs are defined as accounting systems that are either identical to Full IFRS (IFRS for SMEs) as issued by the IASB ('F' and 'S') or that comply with Full IFRS (IFRS for SMEs) almost completely ('FL1' and 'SL1').

In summary, the two GAAP categories 'F' and 'FL1' are combined into one ('**FULL**') to describe Full IFRS adopting countries. Accordingly, countries are defined as IFRS for SMEs adopters ('**SME**') if they have accounting systems that are classified as 'S' or 'SL1'.

97 This information was provided by *Grant Thornton* and *PwC*. Cf. Table A-12 for a basis for conclusions regarding all classified accounting systems in this study.

3.1.2.2 Type of adoption

Countries require, permit, or prohibit the use of Full IFRS and IFRS for SMEs by domestic private firms (*Nobes* (2010), p. 222). In case of adoption, it is important to differentiate between **voluntary** and **mandatory adoption** as the related implications for a country's regulatory financial reporting environment are not the same. While mandatory adoption always involves a partial or complete substitution of prior accounting standards, voluntary adoption implies that Full IFRS or IFRS for SMEs may only complement local standards (or each other). Depending on the sequence of Full IFRS and IFRS for SMEs adoption, countries' financial reporting environments might be shaped by different patterns ranging from full **complementation** to full **substitution** of local accounting systems. For example, Switzerland has retained two domestic accounting systems (Swiss Code of Obligation and Swiss GAAP FER) although the country adopted both Full IFRS and IFRS for SMEs for voluntary use by domestic private firms. In contrast, Ghana had already aligned Local GAAP with IAS in the late 1990s and then replaced all local standards by Full IFRS (2007) and thereafter by IFRS for SMEs (2013).

In countries where domestic private firms are allowed to choose between different sets of accounting standards, the total number of accounting systems becomes larger than in countries that replace one accounting system by another. Voluntary adoption may hence add **complexity** to a local financial reporting environment. For example, in the United States voluntary Full IFRS and IFRS for SMEs adoption has contributed to the coexistence of four different accounting systems for domestic private firms. Besides the two sets of IASB standards, US private firms are allowed to prepare financial statements under US GAAP and in accordance with the Other Comprehensive Basis of Accounting (OCBOA). Despite the fact that Full IFRS and IFRS for SMEs adoption increase the international comparability of local companies' financial statements, voluntary IFRS adoption may also impair intra-national comparability.

While a worldwide move towards mandatory Full IFRS and IFRS for SMEs adoption strengthens the position of the IASB as a global standard-setter, voluntary adoption allows for **competition** among different accounting systems. Such competition may increase innovation in standard setting and reduce standard-setters' susceptibility to political pressures. However, disadvantages may arise from reduced benefits from standardization (*Wagenhofer* (2013), p. 260f.).

In conclusion, Full IFRS and IFRS for SMEs adopting countries are differentiated into two sub-groups in this study: voluntary (coded '**VOL**') and mandatory adopters (coded '**MAND**'). A country may be classified as a voluntary and a mandatory adopter if mandatory adoption is limited to certain firms or types of financial statements (i.e. limited scope of adoption).

3.1.2.3 Scope of adoption

According to *Nobes* (2013), one important caveat of academic research dealing with worldwide IFRS adoption is that various restrictions in the scope of adoption are not or insufficiently taken into account.[98] If the use of IFRS is restricted in some countries to certain types of financial statements (e.g. consolidated financial statements) or to a limited group of local companies (e.g. listed firms), and in other jurisdictions it is not, IFRS adoption cannot be regarded as the same phenomenon across countries. For example, **consolidated financial statements** are the predominant scope of Full IFRS adoption in the context of listed firms, as the consolidated accounts are considered as the primary financial information for investors (*Wagenhofer* (2013), p. 259). In the field of private firms, however, investors, debt holders, and other financial statement users may also focus on **individual financial statements**, since the majority of private firms do not have any interests in subsidiary companies and hence do not prepare consolidated financial statements.

To further specify the group of Full IFRS and IFRS for SMEs adopters regarding their scope of adoption, this study differentiates between countries that adopt the IASB standards in the individual (coded '**IND**') and in the consolidated (coded '**CONS**') financial statements of domestic private firms. For example, Germany allows Full IFRS adoption in the consolidated financial statements of private firms only, and IFRS for SMEs adoption in Macedonia is limited to the individual financial statements of private companies.[99]

In addition to the above limitations regarding the use of IFRS in the individual or consolidated financial statements, countries' adoption decision can also vary regarding the group of local entities that is permitted or required to use the IASB standards. Full IFRS and IFRS for SMEs might be made applicable for **all or only a subset of private firms.** For example, Singapore restricts the use of IFRS for SMEs to small private entities[100] and in the Republic of Fiji Full IFRS are only used by large- and medium-sized private companies.[101]

Accordingly, this study also differentiates between countries that adopt a set of IASB standards for all domestic private firms (coded '**ALL**') and those who restrict adoption to some domestic private firms (coded '**SOME**'). While jurisdictions may adopt Full IFRS and IFRS for SMEs both in the individual and in the consolidated financial statements of local companies, the adoption categories 'ALL' and 'SOME' are mutually exclusive.

As a consequence of the above listed limitations regarding the type and scope of adoption, this study first defines Full IFRS and IFRS for SMEs adopting countries in the broadest possible way (coded '**ANY**') and thereafter narrows down the group of adopters on the basis of three adoption criteria ('**MAND**', '**IND**', and '**ALL**'). According to the broadest definition applied in this study, Full IFRS (IFRS for SMEs) adopters are countries that:

---

98 Cf. section 1.6 for more details.

99 Under the requirements of Macedonian Company Law, private firms that prepare consolidated financial statements are categorized as large companies and have to comply with Full IFRS for the purpose of financial reporting. This information was provided by *Grant Thornton* and *PwC*.

100 In Singapore, private firms are classified as 'small' if they satisfy at least two of the three following criteria: (1) total annual revenue of not more than Singapore $ 10 million, (2) total gross assets of not more than Singapore $ 10 million, and (3) total number of employees of not more than 50. Cf. *Accounting Standards Council Singapore* (2011), p. 7.

101 These are entities with annual group turnover of at least Fiji $ 20 million or with assets exceeding Fiji $ 20 million. This information was provided by *Grant Thornton* and *PwC*.

> *"**permit** or **require all** or **some** domestic private firms to prepare **individual** or **consolidated** financial statements in accordance with accounting standards that are identical to or comply almost completely with Full IFRS (IFRS for SMEs) as issued by the IASB."* ('**ANY**')

Over the course of the descriptive analysis, this definition is specified by eliminating those countries from the respective adopter group that (1) merely permit but not require adoption, (2) restrict adoption to the consolidated financial statements, or (3) restrict adoption to some private firms. In conclusion, these three criteria are used to narrow down the Full IFRS and IFRS for SMEs adopter group to countries that:

> *"**require** all or some domestic private firms to prepare individual or consolidated financial statements in accordance with accounting standards that are identical to or comply almost completely with Full IFRS (IFRS for SMEs) as issued by the IASB",* ('**MAND**')
>
> *"permit or require all or some domestic private firms to prepare **individual financial statements** in accordance with accounting standards that are identical to or comply almost completely with Full IFRS (IFRS for SMEs) as issued by the IASB",* ('**IND**') and
>
> *"permit or require **all domestic private firms** to prepare individual or consolidated financial statements in accordance with accounting standards that are identical to or comply almost completely with Full IFRS (IFRS for SMEs) as issued by the IASB."* ('**ALL**')

3.2 Empirical results

The empirical results are structured in the same way for all of the nine macro-geographic regions. First, the **time series analysis** displays the process towards Full IFRS and IFRS for SMEs adoption from 2002 to 2014. After presenting some background information on the respective local financial reporting environment, the analysis reveals the distribution of different GAAP categories since 2002 and the share of each GAAP category per year. Moreover, a general view is given of the type and the scope of Full IFRS and IFRS for SMEs adoption between 2002 and 2014. In the following, the **cross-sectional analysis** provides a detailed description of the country-specific characteristics of Full IFRS and IFRS for SMEs adoption in the field of private firms in 2014. Finally, the cross-regional findings are summarized to present a global perspective on prior and current trends in international accounting harmonization in the field of private firms.

3.2.1 North America

Canada	United States

Table 3-5: Sampled countries from North America

3.2.1.1 Time series analysis

Despite the strong economic links between Canada and the United States, there are significant differences in the financial reporting requirements for private firms between the two countries. While in the US, non-listed companies do not have general legal requirements for the preparation and publication of periodic audited financial statements (*Choi/Meek* (2011), p. 87), federal and provincial statutory regulations require Canadian private firms to prepare financial statements in accordance with Canadian GAAP (*Mersereau* (2002), p. 1).[102] Regardless of this fact, both countries share a common history of gradual international accounting harmonization towards IFRS. In 1994, the US standard-setting body (FASB) added the promotion of international comparability to its mission statement, and six years later, *Street et al.* (2000) found that differences between US GAAP and IAS were already narrowing (*Street et al.* (2000), p. 60). In Canada, years of harmonization with US and IASB standards have led to Canadian accounting standards' internationalization and have also contributed to the development of a **differential reporting regime** for private firms (*Mersereau* (2002), p. 30).

In 1999, the Canadian Institute of Chartered Accountants (CICA) proposed a set of Canadian **GAAP with exclusions** from certain standards for small business enterprises (SBEs) (*Canadian Institute of Chartered Accountants* (1999)). Three years later, Canada implemented a public/non-public 'bright line' to determine which entities should be exempted from the application of certain accounting rules that do not meet their special needs (*Certified General Accountants Association of Canada*, p. 2). In the United States, the pros and cons of differential reporting had already been discussed in the late 1970s and the controversies have recently been raised by various parties.[103] By 2014, US private firms are allowed to apply the Other Comprehensive Basis of Accounting (OCBOA), which is a purely American **cash-based accounting system** that is much less burdensome than US GAAP.[104]

Due to the US and Canadian accounting systems' convergence with Full IFRS since the early 1990s, and due to the **growing importance of differential reporting regimes** in both countries, there is significant variety in the shape of applicable accounting standards for private firms in North America. Figure 3-3 displays the distribution of different GAAP categories during the years 2002-2014. It thereby reveals in how many countries from North America a specific GAAP category has been adopted each year. To ensure the comparability between the same figure from different geographic regions, the number of countries per GAAP category is displayed in percent of all countries from the respective geographic region.

---

[102] Canadian non-listed entities (excluding non-listed financial institutions) are not obliged to publish their financial statements. This information was provided by *Grant Thornton* and *PwC*.

[103] Cf. section 1.3.2.4 for current trends in differential reporting in the United States.

[104] Cf. *Ratcliffe* (2003) for more details on OCBOA.

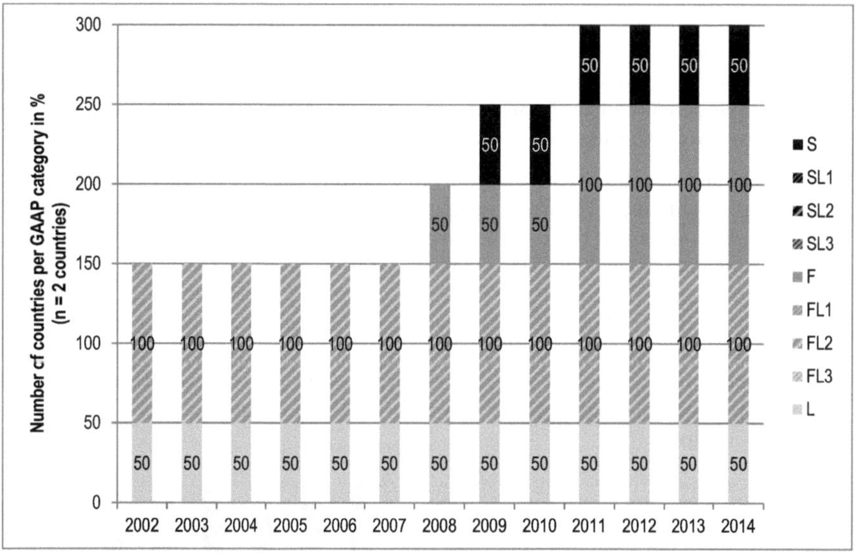

Figure 3-3: Distribution of GAAP categories in North America

In 2002, Canadian private firms were obliged to use Canadian GAAP for financial reporting purposes while US private firms were allowed to choose between US GAAP and the OCBOA. While Canadian and US GAAP had already been converged with Full IFRS in part at that time (GAAP-category 'FL2'), the OCBOA is regarded as Local GAAP (L). On average, one and a half different GAAPs existed per country (see Figure 3-3). This suddenly changed in 2008/2009, when the **AICPA governing Council accepted the IASB** as an accounting standard-setting body and provided US private firms the additional option to prepare generally accepted financial statements in conformity with either Full IFRS (F) or IFRS for SMEs (S) (*Fitzpatrick/Frank* (2009), p. 51).

At the same time, the Canadian AcSB began to reconsider its previous harmonization strategy with US GAAP and IFRS (*Accounting Standards Board of Canada* (2014)) because the Canadian standards were regarded as too complex and certain accounting topics were assumed to be of little relevance for the users of private firms' financial statements (*Maingot/Zeghal* (2006), p. 521). In 2011, the Canadian AcSB implemented a **two-tier financial reporting regime** for private firms by adopting Full IFRS (F) and issuing a set of differential financial reporting standards named 'Accounting Standards for Private Enterprises (ASPE)'[105] (FL2) that superseded prior Canadian GAAP from that year onwards.

In North America, the past decade of international accounting harmonization can be described as a continuing process of domestic accounting standards' gradual **convergence**

---

[105] ASPE are influenced by Full IFRS to a medium extent as the starting point was Canadian GAAP and to the extent that Canadian GAAP was already aligned and influenced by Full IFRS (e.g. inventories, accounting policy changes etc.). This information was provided by *Grant Thornton* and *PwC*.

with Full IFRS and these standards' **complementation** by Full IFRS and IFRS for SMEs (as issued by the IASB). Furthermore, both countries have maintained simplified financial reporting systems for domestic private firms. As compared to the year 2002, the process of GAAP complementation has **doubled the number of GAAPs** per country from one and a half to three (two in Canada, four in the US) by 2014.

Figure 3-4 illustrates the development of the four different GAAP categories' respective share in the total number of GAAP categories per year in North America between 2002 and 2014. As Canada and the United States have both adopted Full IFRS, and the USA have also adopted the IFRS for SMEs, half of 2014's total GAAPs are 'pure' IASB standards. The other half consists of two domestic accounting systems that partially comply with Full IFRS (i.e. US GAAP & ASPE) and a cash-based US accounting system that is entirely independent from the IASB standards (OCBOA). Compared to the years 2002-2007, North America's current financial reporting landscape is much **more diversified** and hence offers more financial reporting options for domestic private firms (in particular for US private firms).[106]

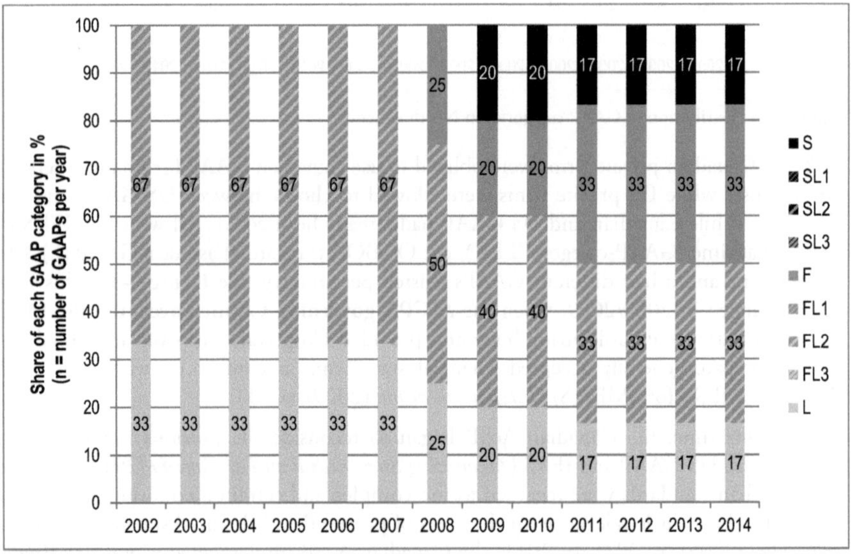

Figure 3-4: Share of each GAAP category in North America

Figure 3-5 displays the process of Full IFRS and IFRS for SMEs adoption in North America during the years 2002-2014. The GAAP categories 'F' and 'FL1' are hereby combined to represent a single Full IFRS category (coded 'FULL ANY'). Accordingly, 'S' and 'SL1' constitute the IFRS for SMEs category (coded 'SME ANY'). In addition, the group of Full IFRS and IFRS for SMEs adopting countries is further specified on the basis of three adoption specifics: (1) mandatory adoption (coded 'MAND'), (2) adoption in the indi-

[106] Cf. Table A-3 for a summary of the classification of GAAP for private firms in *North America*.

vidual financial statements (coded 'IND'), and (3) adoption for all domestic private firms (coded 'ALL').

Regarding the process of Full IFRS and IFRS for SMEs adoption in North America, Figure 3-5 reveals that neither of the two countries have mandatorily adopted Full IFRS or IFRS for SMEs. On the contrary, Canada and the United States offer domestic private firms the possibility of voluntarily adopting IASB standards. There is **no variation in the scope** of Full IFRS and IFRS for SMEs adoption in North America as the standards are applicable in the individual and consolidated financial statements of all private firms.

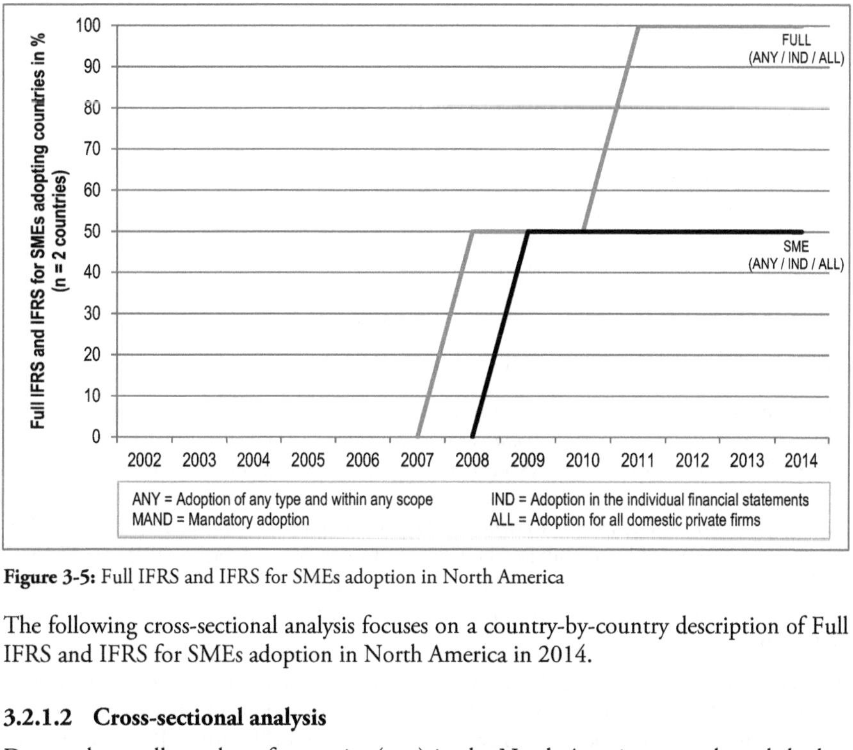

Figure 3-5: Full IFRS and IFRS for SMEs adoption in North America

The following cross-sectional analysis focuses on a country-by-country description of Full IFRS and IFRS for SMEs adoption in North America in 2014.

3.2.1.2 Cross-sectional analysis

Due to the small number of countries (two) in the North American sample and the homogeneity in both countries' adoption specifics, data on Full IFRS and IFRS for SMEs adoption in North America are summarized in two short tables. Table 3-6 displays that **both Canada and the United States have adopted Full IFRS** in the field of private firms by 2014. In both countries, domestic private firms are allowed but not required to apply Full IFRS in their individual and consolidated financial statements. Furthermore, there are no restrictions regarding the use of Full IFRS within the group of private firms (neither based on company size nor on qualitative criteria).

Full IFRS adopters (2) *(date of adoption)*	**VOL**	**MAND**	**IND**	**CONS**	**ALL**
Canada *(2011)*	Yes	No	Yes	Yes	Yes
United States *(2008)*	Yes	No	Yes	Yes	Yes
Percentage (n=2 countries)	**100%**	**0%**	**100%**	**100%**	**100%**
VOL = Voluntary adoption; MAND = Mandatory adoption; IND = Adoption in the individual financial statements; CONS = Adoption in the consolidated financial statements; ALL = Adoption for all domestic private firms.					

Table 3-6: Characteristics of Full IFRS adoption in North America

As IFRS for SMEs adoption was eventually denied by the Canadian AcSB in 2007,[107] the United States are the only jurisdiction in the North American sample that has adopted IFRS for SMEs (see Table 3-7). Identical to the country's Full IFRS adoption specifics, **all US private firms are allowed to apply the IFRS for SMEs** in their individual and consolidated financial statements.

IFRS for SMEs adopters (1) *(date of adoption)*	**VOL**	**MAND**	**IND**	**CONS**	**ALL**
United States *(2009)*	Yes	No	Yes	Yes	Yes
Percentage (n=2 countries)	**50%**	**0%**	**50%**	**50%**	**50%**
VOL = Voluntary adoption; MAND = Mandatory adoption; IND = Adoption in the individual financial statements; CONS = Adoption in the consolidated financial statements; ALL = Adoption for all domestic private firms.					

Table 3-7: Characteristics of IFRS for SMEs adoption in North America

Although the IFRS for SMEs was expected to *"find enthusiastic support among smaller US reporting entities and their professional services providers"* (*MacKenzie* (2013), p. 11), and the AICPA promoted the new IASB accounting option via an online-based wiki platform (*DeFelice* (2010), p. 30), only every second US private firm was aware of the new standard by 2011 (*American Institute of Certified Public Accountants* (2011), p. 24). As most US-American CPAs would only advise their clients to consider adopting IFRS for SMEs if Full IFRS were required for US public companies, **IFRS for SMEs has been adopted rarely** by private firms in the US so far (*American Institute of Certified Public Accountants* (2011), p. 25).

The lack of experience among the users of financial statements and the insufficient training given on Full IFRS and IFRS for SMEs by US institutions of higher education are two of many reasons for the unpopularity of Full IFRS and IFRS for SMEs in the US setting (*Fitzpatrick/Frank* (2009), p. 53). Given the non-GAAP character of OCBOA, the perceived inappropriateness of US GAAP, and the minor relevance of Full IFRS and IFRS for SMEs in the context of US private firms, more than half of the US small and medium-sized private companies **support separate national accounting standards** for private and public companies (*Deloitte Touche Tohmatsu* (2009b), p. 1).

[107] International comparability was regarded as an issue of minor importance for the vast majority of Canadian private enterprises as the external users of their financial statements (esp. bank lenders) are primarily domestic (*Accounting Standards Board of Canada* (2007), p. 72).

The **future outlook** of Full IFRS and IFRS for SMEs adoption by North American private firms thus remains **unpredictable.** While the FASB advocates modified US standards that are derived from US GAAP by the Private Company Council (PCC), the AICPA promotes a new *non-GAAP* set of accounting standards called 'Financial Reporting Framework for Small and Medium-sized Entities' (FRF for SMEs) (*Pounder* (2013), p. 16). Although US private firms have been given the option to adopt Full IFRS and IFRS for SMEs since 2008, the rigid efforts of FASB and AICPA to develop localized and differential financial reporting rules for domestic private firms raise doubts about the future relevance of Full IFRS and IFRS for SMEs to North American private firms.

3.2.2 Central America & Caribbean

Dominican Republic	Honduras	Mexico	Panama
Guatemala	Jamaica	Nicaragua	

Table 3-8: Sampled countries from Central America & Caribbean

3.2.2.1 Time series analysis

The statutory frameworks of Central American and Caribbean (CAC) countries vary significantly in terms of accounting, auditing, and reporting requirements. In response to specific business needs and the respective financial and economic environment, CAC countries have developed financial reporting requirements that differ in completeness, coherence, adaptability, and differentiation (*Fortin et al.* (2010), p. 23f.). As a general rule, the **level of transparency is low** regarding the financial reporting of private firms (*Shah et al.* (2007), p. 20). Non-publicly traded companies are generally not required to publish their financial statements in Central America and the Caribbean.[108]

In the early 2000s, several CAC countries (e.g. Guatemala, Honduras, and Panama) had their own Local GAAPs (L). These national sets of accounting rules were usually **US standards that were simplified and adapted** to national requirements (*Fortin et al.* (2010), p. 78). In contrast, countries such as Nicaragua had not developed any local accounting system (*Ampofo/Sellani* (2005), p. 221) and made foreign GAAP (mostly US GAAP) applicable for all domestic entities. As foreign GAAP is not included in the nine different GAAP categories defined in this study, Figure 3-6 displays for the seven sampled CAC countries less than one GAAP category per country on average during the years 2002-2004.

From the year 2005 onwards, nearly all **Local GAAPs have gradually been substituted by Full IFRS**. While almost 60% of the sampled CAC countries had their own local standards in 2002, Guatemala is the only country in the sample that has still maintained its Local GAAP by 2014. In fact, the Commercial Code of Guatemala requires domestic companies to prepare their financial statements according to 'GAAP', but does not define

[108] This information was provided by *Grant Thornton* and *PwC.*

them (*Shah et al.* (2007), p. 104). As a result, private companies still prepare their financial statements according to local tax rules, which are completely independent from IFRS.

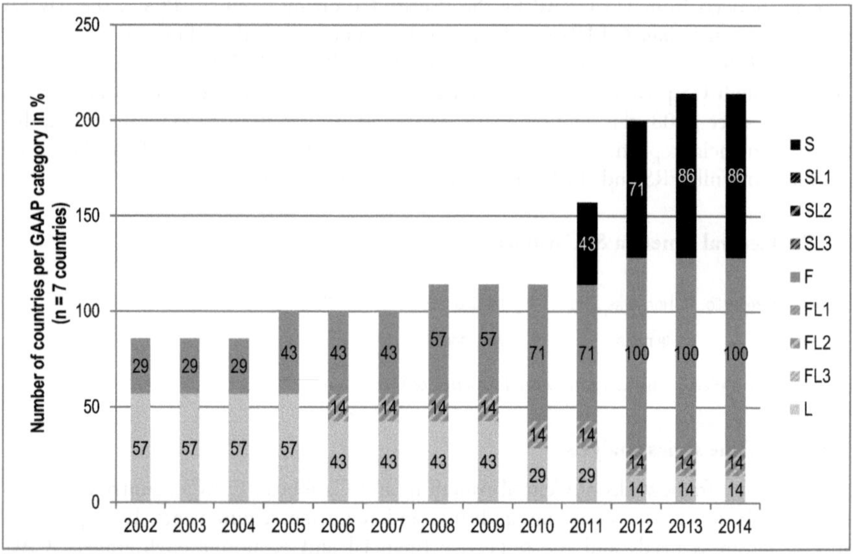

Figure 3-6: Distribution of GAAP categories in CAC countries

Full IFRS adoption in the field of private firms has gained momentum since the mid-2000s. At that time, the **World Bank** conducted a series of country studies on the comparability of national accounting and auditing standards with Full IFRS and ISAs (International Standards on Auditing) and assisted countries in developing and implementing an action plan for improving their financial reporting regimes (*World Bank* (2004e), p. 2). Since 2012, all seven sampled CAC countries have permitted or required domestic private firms to prepare their financial statements according to Full IFRS as issued by the IASB (F). In Central America and the Caribbean, the implementation of high quality financial reporting standards is regarded as an effective mechanism to **facilitate access to finance** for local enterprises (particularly SMEs), which is regarded as a major problem in CAC countries (*Fortin et al.* (2010), p. 3). Furthermore, sound accounting, auditing, and reporting practices shall enable sustainable and equitable private sector-led growth and strengthen governance and accountability in the countries of the CAC region (*Fortin et al.* (2010), p. xxi).

In 2014, **Mexico** is the only sampled CAC country that has retained a set of domestic financial reporting standards that have been converged with Full IFRS only in part (FL2). As a founding member of the IASC, Mexico is committed to convergence with IFRS. Especially in cases where no domestic standards exist, Mexico **looks to the IASB for guidance** on accounting issues (*Choi/Meek* (2011), p. 93). As a general rule, smaller CAC countries tend to adopt IFRS 'in full', whereas larger countries continue to develop their own standards which they feel are more amenable to their respective environments (*Fortin et al.* (2010), p. 78).

Since 2011, the substitution of Local GAAPs by Full IFRS has been accompanied by the **widespread adoption of IFRS for SMEs**. Within three years, six out of seven CAC countries have adopted IFRS for SMEs as issued by the IASB (S). Hence, IFRS for SMEs adoption has proceeded in a much shorter period than Full IFRS adoption. As compared to the years prior to 2011, the complementation of Full IFRS by IFRS for SMEs has almost **doubled the number of GAAPs** per country (see Figure 3-6).

Figure 3-7 displays the development of the four existing GAAP categories' respective share in the total number of GAAP categories in CAC countries per year between 2002 and 2014. At first view, the decline of the Local GAAP category becomes evident (decrease from 67% in 2002 to only 7% in 2014). The chart also reveals that Full IFRS and IFRS for SMEs make up for nearly 90% of all GAAPs in 2014. Compared to the early 2000s, Central America's and the Caribbean's current financial reporting environment has developed to a **highly internationalized field**, in which nearly all private companies use either Full IFRS or IFRS for SMEs.[109]

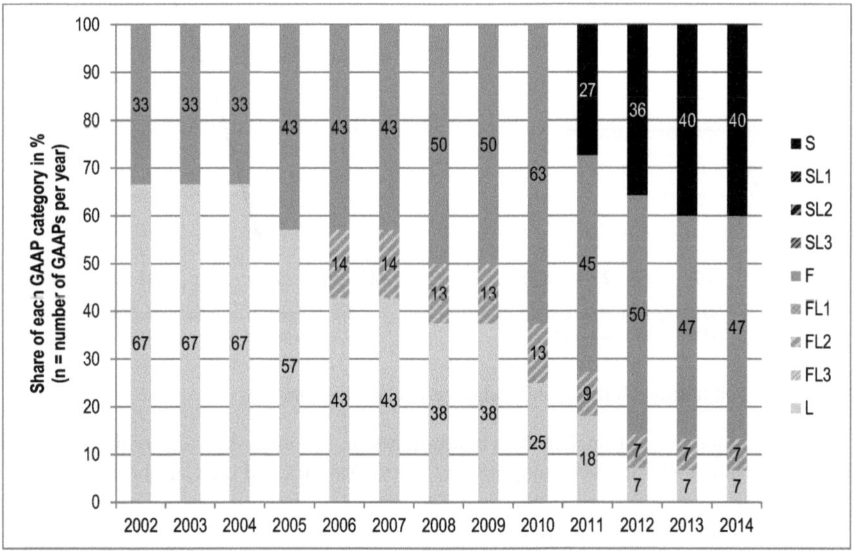

Figure 3-7: Share of each GAAP category in CAC countries

By focusing on the process of Full IFRS and IFRS for SMEs adoption in CAC countries, Figure 3-8 illustrates that none of the seven sampled countries have mandatorily adopted IFRS for SMEs. This shows that Full IFRS have not been banned or excluded from any country's financial reporting regulation. Instead, **IFRS for SMEs constitutes an addi-**

[109] Cf. Table A-4 for a summary of the classification of GAAP for private firms in *Central America and the Caribbean*.

tional accounting option for private firms. The first rising (2002-2010) and then falling (2010-2014) share of mandatory Full IFRS adopters reveals the effect of Full IFRS's complementation by IFRS for SMEs. While more than half of the Full IFRS adopting CAC countries also required domestic private firms to apply Full IFRS in the mid-2000s, widespread IFRS for SMEs adoption has turned this trend around.

Regarding the scope of Full IFRS and IFRS for SMEs adoption, there is **little variation** between CAC countries as both IASB standards are applicable in the individual and consolidated financial statements of private firms. There is only one country (the Dominican Republic) in the sample that restricts IFRS for SMEs adoption to some private companies in 2014.

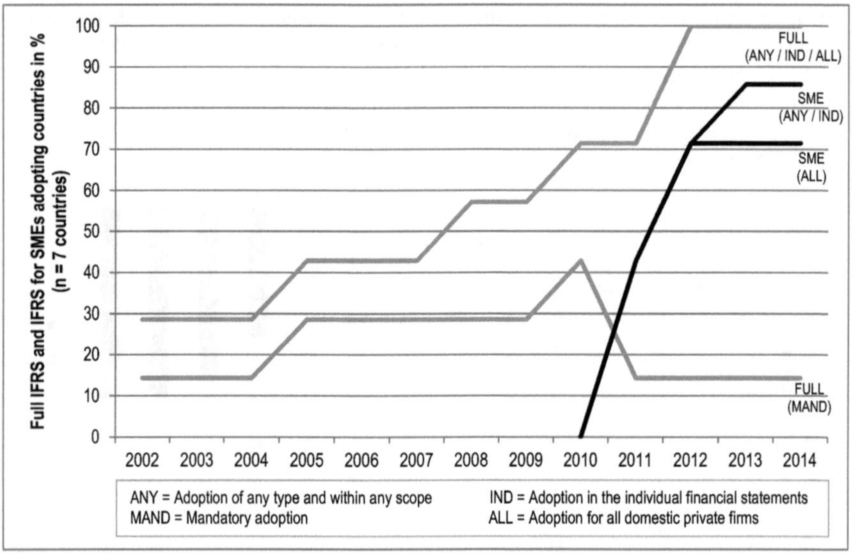

Figure 3-8: Full IFRS and IFRS for SMEs adoption in CAC countries

The following cross-sectional analysis concentrates on a country-by-country description of Full IFRS and IFRS for SMEs adoption in Central America and the Caribbean in 2014.

3.2.2.2 Cross-sectional analysis

As displayed in Table 3-9, **all seven sampled CAC countries have adopted Full IFRS** in the field of private firms by 2014. In six out of seven CAC countries, all domestic private firms are allowed but not obliged to apply Full IFRS in their individual and consolidated financial statements. The **Dominican Republic** is the only sampled country that requires larger private firms to adopt Full IFRS. Until 2010, three other countries (**Jamaica, Nicaragua,** and **Panama**) had required domestic private firms to prepare their financial statements under Full IFRS. For example, Jamaica adopted Full IFRS with effect from 1 July 2002 and made all domestic companies, including listed and private firms, comply with

Full IFRS. In addition, every Jamaican company was obliged to have its financial statements audited in accordance with ISAs (*United Nations* (2008), p. 65).

Before CAC countries started to adopt IFRS for SMEs in 2011, the widespread mandatory adoption of Full IFRS in smaller CAC countries had led to a **'paradoxical situation'**. The countries with relatively small securities markets had required Full IFRS for the broadest range of companies, including private firms. As a result, these countries struggled to equip their business communities and accounting professions with the necessary knowledge to prepare and audit Full IFRS financial statements (*Fortin et al.* (2010), p. 80). As most private firms were not capable of applying Full IFRS or did not want to spend a considerable amount of money on accountants with the necessary skills (*Fortin et al.* (2010), p. 34), **compliance with Full IFRS in practice was low** (*Shah et al.* (2007), p. 127). As a consequence, lenders and other users of financial statements had low confidence in the reliability and trustworthiness of private firms' financial statements (*Fortin et al.* (2010), p. 34).

Full IFRS adopters (7) *(date of adoption)*	**VOL**	**MAND**	**IND**	**CONS**	**ALL**
Dominican Republic *(2012)*	Yes	Yes[1]	Yes	Yes	Yes
Guatemala *(2008)*	Yes	No	Yes	Yes	Yes
Honduras *(2012)*	Yes	No	Yes	Yes	Yes
Jamaica *(2002)*	Yes	No[2]	Yes	Yes	Yes
Mexico *(2002)*	Yes	No	Yes	Yes	Yes
Nicaragua *(2005)*	Yes	No[3]	Yes	Yes	Yes
Panama *(2010)*	Yes	No[4]	Yes	Yes	Yes
Percentage (n=7 countries)	**100%**	**14%**	**100%**	**100%**	**100%**

[1] Companies with annual sales of more than Pesos 150 million; [2] Mandatory until 2010; [3] Mandatory until 2011; [4] Mandatory until 2010.

VOL = Voluntary adoption; MAND = Mandatory adoption; IND = Adoption in the individual financial statements; CONS = Adoption in the consolidated financial statements; ALL = Adoption for all domestic private firms.

Table 3-9: Characteristics of Full IFRS adoption in CAC countries

In 2008, **Honduras** enacted the Accounting and Auditing Law, which should have mandated the application of Full IFRS by all domestic entities regardless of size. However, the World Bank observed that Full IFRS were not designed for small and medium-sized entities and argued that Full IFRS should only apply to Honduran public-interest entities (*World Bank* (2007c), p. 6f.). As a result, the 2008 law did never come into effect and Honduras allowed private firms to choose between Full IFRS and IFRS for SMEs from 2012 onwards (see Table 3-10).

By 2014, **every sampled CAC country except Mexico has adopted IFRS for SMEs** in the field of private firms. In all adopting CAC countries, IFRS for SMEs is permitted but not required for the preparation of individual and consolidated financial statements. The **Dominican Republic** is the only country that restricts the use of IFRS for SMEs to companies below a certain size (annual sales not higher than Pesos 150 million).

IFRS for SMEs adopters (6) *(date of adoption)*	VOL	MAND	IND	CONS	ALL
Dominican Republic *(2013)*	Yes	No[1]	Yes	Yes	No[2]
Guatemala *(2011)*	Yes	No	Yes	Yes	Yes
Honduras *(2012)*	Yes	No	Yes	Yes	Yes
Jamaica *(2011)*	Yes	No	Yes	Yes	Yes
Nicaragua *(2012)*	Yes	No	Yes	Yes	Yes
Panama *(2011)*	Yes	No	Yes	Yes	Yes
Percentage (n=7 countries)	**86%**	**0%**	**86%**	**86%**	**71%**

[1] Mandatory adoption planned for large and medium-sized unlisted companies from July 2014 onwards; [2] All except companies with annual sales of more than Pesos 150 million.

VOL = Voluntary adoption; MAND = Mandatory adoption; IND = Adoption in the individual financial statements; CONS = Adoption in the consolidated financial statements; ALL = Adoption for all domestic private firms.

Table 3-10: Characteristics of IFRS for SMEs adoption in CAC countries

International experience shows that companies, users, accountants, and regulators need at least four years to prepare themselves adequately for the implementation of a new accounting system once it goes into effect (*Fortin et al.* (2010), p. 80). As CAC countries have not adopted IFRS for SMEs before 2011, little is known about the actual number of Central American and Caribbean private firms already applying IFRS for SMEs in their financial statements. However, large audit firms observe that a significant number of private firms is in the process of changing its accounting framework and that this is a **transition from Full IFRS to IFRS for SMEs.**[110]

3.2.3 South America

Argentina	Chile	Ecuador	Peru	Venezuela
Brazil	Colombia	Paraguay	Uruguay	

Table 3-11: Sampled countries from South America

3.2.3.1 Time series analysis

Due to their significant economic influence on the South American continent, most of the **local financial reporting frameworks** of South American countries have largely been **shaped by the United States** (*Nexia International* (1993), p. 63). For example, Chilean and Venezuelan GAAP were historically developed on the basis of US GAAP (*World Bank* (2004a), p. 17; *Financial Standards Foundation* (2009), p. 1), and the local accounting system of Brazil was initially developed under the influence of European countries (mainly Italy) and was later affected by US accounting practices (*United Nations* (2008), p. 16). Until the late 1990s, South American countries experienced a lack of accounting harmonization. Although the free trade agreement 'Mercosur' in 1991 strengthened the economic links between South American countries and made trade among the member states

[110] This information was provided by *Grant Thornton* and *PwC.*

more than triple within five years, membership in Mercosur – unlike in NAFTA – did not require a commitment to harmonize tax, accounting or other macroeconomic policies (*Garcia et al.* (2001), p. 9).

During the past decade, Argentina, Brazil, and smaller South American economies have experienced a **period of economic growth**, foreign direct investment and accelerated integration into global markets (*World Bank* (2011a), p. 21; *Organisation for Economic Cooperation and Development* (2013), p. 30). These trends have underpinned local efforts aimed at converging national accounting standards with IFRS (*United Nations* (2008), p. 15). In the field of private firms, the adoption of international accounting standards is regarded as one important vehicle to make SMEs gain easier access to credit and equity financing (*Fortin et al.* (2010), p. 3).

As Figure 3-9 illustrates, South American countries have embarked on a process of long-term and **stepwise convergence of Local GAAP with Full IFRS**. Although South American countries had already narrowed down the gap between local standards and Full IFRS by the mid-2000s (*Manzano/Conesa* (2005)), several shortcomings remained. While Argentina had only adopted 'portions' of Full IFRS (*World Bank* (2007a), p. ii), countries such as Ecuador and Uruguay did not regularly update their standards after Full IFRS adoption and hence did not sufficiently include future amendments to Full IFRS (*World Bank* (2004b), p. i; *World Bank* (2006d), p. ii). This led to a large number of South American accounting systems that complied with Full IFRS only in part (FL2). Between 2009 and 2011, two out of three South American countries provided such a local version of Full IFRS ('FL2-GAAP') to local private firms.

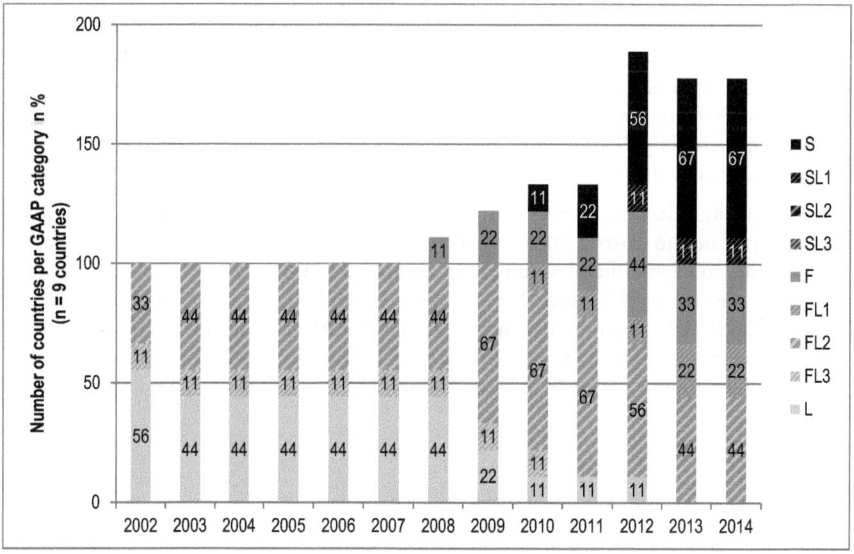

Figure 3-9: Distribution of GAAP categories in South America

During the years 2003-2007, the **World Bank** had also prepared Accounting and Auditing Reports on the Observance of Standards and Codes (ROSC) in eight out of the nine sampled South American countries.[111] Among other things, the World Bank criticized the overall quality of financial reporting (*World Bank* (2003a), p. 12) and the insufficient level of disclosure (*World Bank* (2007a), p. 32). Until today, private firms are not required to publish their financial statements in the majority of South American countries.[112] As the World Bank's general advice was to complete convergence with Full IFRS (e.g. *World Bank* (2003a), p. 1) and to adopt simplified international accounting standards for SMEs (e.g. *World Bank* (2006d), p. 30), a second major trend in South American international accounting harmonization was triggered: **parallel adoption of Full IFRS and IFRS for SMEs**. Within five years only, the percentage of Full IFRS adopting countries (GAAP category F or FL1) increased from 11% in 2008 to 55% in 2013. In the same period of time, two thirds of the South American countries also adopted IFRS for SMEs (GAAP category S or SL1). In some South American countries, the IASB standards have been modified to a negligent extent. For example, Argentina has made one modification to the IFRS for SMEs, namely that in separate company financial statements the equity method is required to account for investments in subsidiaries, associates, and joint ventures (*IFRS Foundation* (2014e), p. 5). In Brazil, there are some differences regarding the level of disclosures between the Brazilian version of Full IFRS (Comitê de Pronunciamentos Contábeis - CPCs) and the original version as issued by the IASB.[113]

By 2014, the majority of South American countries have adopted Full IFRS and IFRS for SMEs in the field of private firms. In most of these countries, Local GAAPs (L) and local versions of Full IFRS (FL2) have been replaced by Full IFRS *and* IFRS for SMEs (e.g. in Brazil, Ecuador and Peru). Chile is the only country in the South American sample that had temporarily adopted Full IFRS in the context of private firms (2009-2012) and later **substituted Full IFRS by IFRS for SMEs.** All in all, the process of parallel Full IFRS and IFRS for SMEs adoption has caused a significant increase in the total number of GAAPs in South America. By 2014, almost two different GAAPs exist for private firms in each South American country on average.

Figure 3-10 illustrates the decline of the Local GAAP category in South America, which completely ceased to exist in 2013. Furthermore, the figure shows that the FL2 category first becomes more and then less important compared to other GAAPs. This is due to the increasing number of IFRS for SMEs adopters since 2010. Three years later, IFRS for SMEs (S & SL1) has become the most common GAAP category in the field of private firms' financial reporting in South America by making up for 44% (38% + 6%) of all GAAPs. Compared to the years prior to 2008, South America's financial reporting envi-

[111] The World Bank prepared Accounting and Auditing ROSC for Argentina, Brazil, Chile, Colombia, Ecuador, Paraguay, Peru, and Uruguay.

[112] Publication of financial statements is mandatory for private firms only in Brazil, Colombia, and Uruguay. However, Colombia is the only country that provides an online-based registry for financial statements. This information was provided by *Grant Thornton* and *PwC*.

[113] This information was provided by *Grant Thornton* and *PwC*.

ronment has **recently been strongly internationalized** and builds on IFRS for SMEs adoption like no other continent in the world.[114]

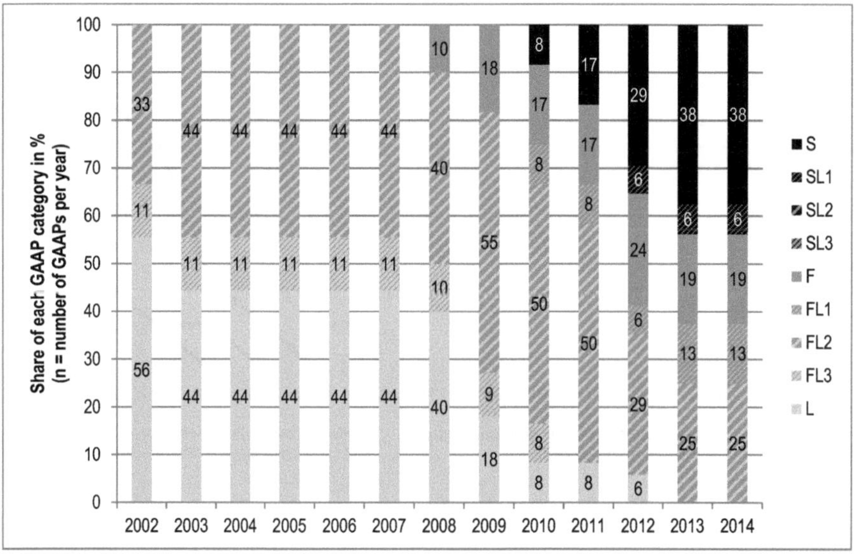

Figure 3-10: Share of each GAAP category in South America

The process of Full IFRS and IFRS for SMEs adoption in South America is illustrated in Figure 3-11. It becomes evident that Full IFRS and IFRS for SMEs have been adopted simultaneously by the majority of South American countries during five to seven years. IFRS for SMEs adoption had started in 2010 with a time lag of two years, but outpaced Full IFRS adoption in 2013. Regarding mandatory Full IFRS and IFRS for SMEs adoption, Figure 3-11 reveals that Full IFRS are still required in more South American countries than IFRS for SMEs. While every IFRS for SMEs adopting country has made the standard applicable in both individual and consolidated financial statements, there is one Full IFRS adopting country (Argentina) that has adopted Full IFRS only for the consolidated financial statements of domestic private firms. Apart from that, there is significant variation regarding the scope of Full IFRS and IFRS for SMEs adoption as in almost half of the Full IFRS adopting countries and in two out of three IFRS for SMEs adopting countries, **adoption is restricted to some domestic private companies.**

[114] Cf. Table A-5 for a summary of the classification of GAAP for private firms in *South America.*

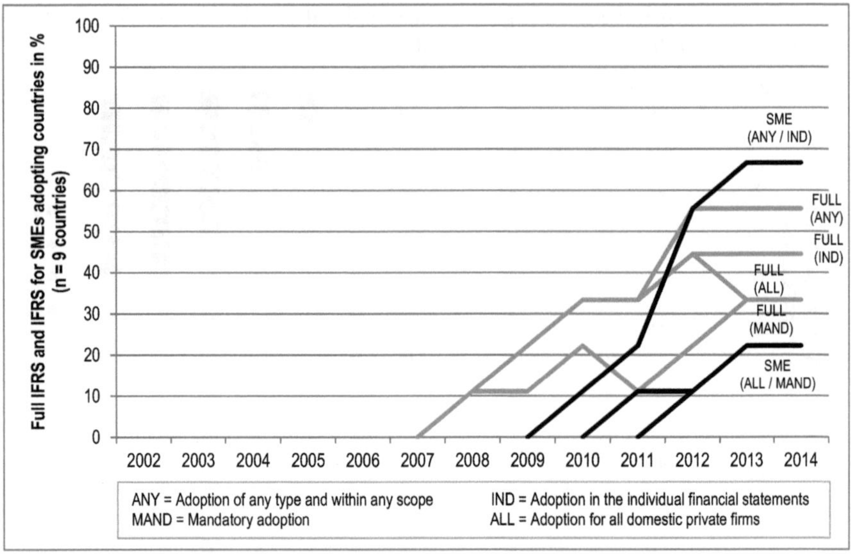

Figure 3-11: Full IFRS and IFRS for SMEs adoption in South America

The following cross-sectional analysis will describe Full IFRS and IFRS for SMEs adoption in South America in 2014 on a country-by-country basis.

3.2.3.2 Cross-sectional analysis

Five out of nine sampled South American countries have adopted Full IFRS in the field of private firms by 2014 (Argentina, Brazil, Ecuador, Peru, and Venezuela). The same five countries plus Chile have adopted the IFRS for SMEs (see Tables 3-12 and 3-13).

Full IFRS adopters (5) *(date of adoption)*	**VOL**	**MAND**	**IND**	**CONS**	**ALL**
Argentina *(2012)*	Yes	No	No	Yes	No[1]
Brazil *(2010)*	Yes	Yes[2]	Yes	Yes	Yes
Ecuador *(2012)*	Yes	Yes[3]	Yes	Yes	Yes
Peru *(2013)*	No	Yes	Yes	Yes	No[4]
Venezuela *(2008)*	Yes	No[5]	Yes	Yes	Yes
Percentage (n=9 countries)	**44%**	**33%**	**44%**	**56%**	**33%**

[1] All except companies with no relation to a listed company; [2] Companies with turnover in excess of Real 300 million and total assets in excess of Real 250 million; [3] Companies with assets in excess of US $ 4 million, gross sales of more than US $ 5 million and more than 200 employees; [4] All except companies with assets or revenue under US $ 10 million; [5] Mandatory for some in 2008-2010.

VOL = Voluntary adoption; MAND = Mandatory adoption; IND = Adoption in the individual financial statements; CONS = Adoption in the consolidated financial statements; ALL = Adoption for all domestic private firms.

Table 3-12: Characteristics of Full IFRS adoption in South America

Based on their local adoption specifics, the six adopting countries can be differentiated into **four different types of adopters**. As Tables 3-12 and 3-13 illustrate, **Argentina** and **Venezuela** have made domestic private firms decide whether they want to use Full IFRS or IFRS for SMEs in their financial statements. While Argentina adopted both IASB standards simultaneously in 2012, Venezuela had required some larger unlisted companies to adopt Full IFRS during the years 2008-2010 and withdrew this obligation when IFRS for SMEs (Ven NIF – SMEs) was adopted in 2011. From that year onwards, all Venezuelan private firms regardless of size have been permitted to use either Full IFRS or IFRS for SMEs for financial reporting purposes.

In contrast, **Brazil** and **Ecuador**, although having adopted IFRS for SMEs in 2010 (2012), still require large domestic private firms to prepare their financial statements according to Full IFRS. As described in Table 3-12 and Table 3-13, Brazilian companies with turnover in excess of Real 300 million and total assets in excess of Real 250 million and Ecuadorian companies with assets in excess of US $ 4 million, gross sales of more than US $ 5 million, and more than 200 employees are obliged to use Full IFRS. All other private companies are allowed to choose between Full IFRS and IFRS for SMEs.

IFRS for SMEs adopters (6) *(date of adoption)*	**VOL**	**MAND**	**IND**	**CONS**	**ALL**
Argentina *(2012)*	Yes	No	Yes[1]	Yes	No[2]
Brazil *(2010)*	Yes	No	Yes	Yes	No[3]
Chile *(2013)*	No	Yes	Yes	Yes	Yes
Ecuador *(2012)*	Yes	No	Yes	Yes	No[4]
Peru *(2012)*	No	Yes	Yes	Yes	No[5]
Venezuela *(2011)*	Yes	No	Yes	Yes	Yes
Percentage (n=9 countries)	**44%**	**22%**	**66%**	**66%**	**22%**

[1] Minor modification of IFRS for SMEs in the individual financial statements (application of participation method as described in section 14); [2] All except companies outside the scope of Technical Resolution No. 29; [3] All except companies with turnover in excess of Real 300 million and total assets in excess of Real 250 million; [4] All except companies with assets in excess of US $ 4 million, gross sales of more than US $ 5 million and more than 200 employees; [5] All except companies with assets or revenue above US $ 10 million.

VOL = Voluntary adoption; MAND = Mandatory adoption; IND = Adoption in the individual financial statements; CONS = Adoption in the consolidated financial statements; ALL = Adoption for all domestic private firms.

Table 3-13: Characteristics of IFRS for SMEs adoption in South America

In 2012, **Peru** introduced a clear **segmentation** of the financial reporting requirements for private firms. The country developed a size test that determines the mandatory financial reporting provisions of all Peruvian private firms. According to that, companies with assets or revenue above US $ 10 million are obliged to use Full IFRS whereas smaller companies are required to prepare financial statements under IFRS for SMEs. **Chile** represents the fourth type of adopter as it required all domestic private firms to prepare their financial statements according to the IFRS for SMEs starting on 1 January 2013 (*IFRS Foundation* (2014c), p. 5).

In summary, although several South American countries have adopted Full IFRS and IFRS for SMEs simultaneously, **significant differences** remain regarding the **two IASB standards' local implementation**. In particular, there are differences in the country-specific definition of the type of private entities that are eligible to use the IASB standards. Only two out of six South American IFRS for SMEs adopters (Chile and Venezuela) made the standard applicable for all domestic private firms. This indicates the strong differentiation of the South American financial reporting requirements on the basis of firm size and shows that the IFRS for SMEs is not regarded as a full-value alternative to Full IFRS but is viewed as 'little GAAP for small private firms'.

Similar to the situation in Central America and the Caribbean, little is known about the actual number of South American private firms already using Full IFRS or IFRS for SMEs in their financial statements. An exploratory study that investigates the level of use of the Brazilian version of IFRS for SMEs in the cities of Araguari, Uberaba, and Uberlândia in 2010/2011 finds that most local companies have not yet adopted the standard and that less than half of them know its content in full (*Prado et al.* (2011), p. 2). On country level, future IFRS for SMEs adoption is under consideration in **Uruguay**,[115] and Full IFRS and IFRS for SMEs adoption are planned in **Colombia** for 2016.[116]

3.2.4 European Union

Austria	Estonia	*Iceland*	Netherlands	Slovenia
Belgium	Finland	Ireland	*Norway*	Spain
Bulgaria	France	Italy	Poland	Sweden
Cyprus	Germany	Latvia	Portugal	United Kingdom
Czech Republic	Greece	Lithuania	Romania	
Denmark	Hungary	Luxembourg	Slovakia	

Table 3-14: Sampled countries from the European Union (incl. EEA)[117]

3.2.4.1 Time series analysis

The Treaty of Rome in 1957 not only represents the legal foundation of the constitution of the European Economic Community (EEC) in 1958 and the establishment of the European Union (EU) in 1993, but it was also the starting point for the harmonization of financial reporting on the European continent. The basic idea expressed in the Treaty of

[115] The Association of Accountants, Economists and Managers of Uruguay states that Uruguay has not yet adopted the IFRS for SMEs because of concerns that it is too complex for small and medium-sized entities. However, IFRS for SMEs adoption is under consideration by the Uruguayan government. Cf. *IFRS Foundation* (2014b), p. 4.

[116] Colombia has adopted the IFRS for SMEs for a large group of companies starting in 2016, with the date of transition being 1 January 2015. Pursuant to Law 1314/2009, the IFRS for SMEs will be required for all companies whose securities are not publicly traded other than micro sized entities and large companies whose parent or subsidiaries report under full IFRSs and major exporters or importers (who must use full IFRSs starting 2015). Micro entities may also elect to use the IFRS for SMEs. Cf. *IFRS Foundation* (2014f), p. 4.

[117] The 28 sampled countries include all 27 EU member states (as of March 2013) except Malta plus two non-EU countries that are part of the European Economic Area (Iceland & Norway).

Rome is the creation of a free internal market, in which goods, services, people, and capital can move freely from one country to another (so-called 'four freedoms'). The wish to facilitate the free movement of capital led to the **harmonization of European company law** and through that to the harmonization of European countries' accounting principles (*Burnett* (1975), p. 24).

The need for accounting harmonization within Europe is grounded on the **fundamental differences** that existed (and still exist) between the EU member states in their company law and their national accounting systems.[118] While some European countries (e.g. France, Germany) have traditionally focused on prudent measurement designed to ensure the repayment of debt out of existing assets, others (e.g. Netherlands, United Kingdom) have rather aimed at 'fair' profit reporting, which shall support economic decision making (*Alexander* (2007), p. 48). These different purposes of financial reporting are reflected in the creditor/secrecy orientation of the traditional Franco-German systems and in the investor/disclosure orientation of the Anglo-Dutch systems (*Nobes/Parker* (2012), p. 310).

Moreover, the European accounting systems differ due to divergent legal traditions (Roman code law vs. Anglo-Saxon common law) and due to differences in the influence of tax laws on accounting numbers (e.g. authoritative principle in Germany). Lastly, there are strong accounting traditions in some European countries (e.g. France, Germany, United Kingdom), whereas in other countries generally not (e.g. Bulgaria, Cyprus).

The EU attempt to harmonize national company law is based on two main instruments: **Directives** and **Regulations.** While Regulations become law throughout the EU without the need to pass through national legislatures, Directives have to be incorporated into the laws of EU member states (*Nobes/Parker* (2012), p. 310f.). European private firms' financial reporting requirements have been subject to harmonization through the 4th and 7th EU Directive (so-called 'Accounting Directives') since the late 1970s. The 4th EU Directive (1978) covered common accounting rules for the preparation of individual financial statements of certain companies with limited liability. The 7th Directive (1983) included financial reporting requirements for the preparation of consolidated financial statements. Unlike the IAS Regulation 1606/2002, which mandates all EU-resident publicly traded companies to prepare consolidated financial statements in accordance with Full IFRS, the two EU Accounting Directives have only ensured a **low degree of accounting harmonization** without being related to IASB standard setting.

In fact, the 4th Directive was regarded as a *"highly uneasy compromise involving much optionality"* (*Alexander* (2007), p. 50). Although the two Accounting Directives have been amended several times since their issuance and were finally replaced by a new single EU Accounting Directive in June 2013 (*European Commission* (2013)), there still is **no single accounting system for European private firms.** On the contrary, the new Directive still includes a number of accounting options that permit the continuing diversity of national accounting systems for private firms and does not force EU member states to fully converge their financial reporting systems with either Full IFRS or IFRS for SMEs.

---

[118] Cf. *Walton* (1995) for the particularities of national accounting systems across Europe.

Disregarding this fact, the national accounting systems of EU countries have gone through a process of **stepwise convergence with Full IFRS** since the early 2000s. As Figure 3-12 illustrates, Full IFRS (F & FL1) or Full IFRS-based accounting systems (FL2 & FL3) existed in about half of the 28 sampled EU countries by 2002. This number increased to above 80% by 2004. During the same period of time, the percentage of countries with Local GAAPs (L) dropped from 54% to 36%.

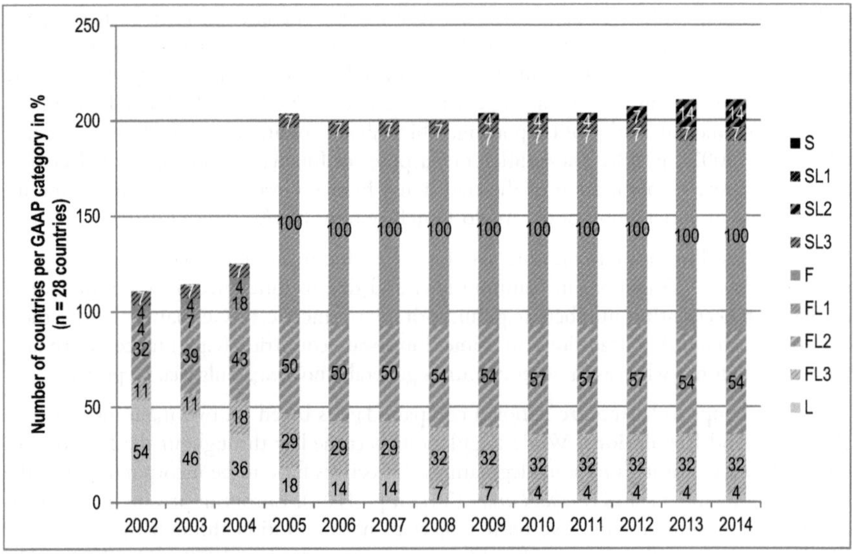

Figure 3-12: Distribution of GAAP categories in the EU (incl. EEA)

One example for a **Local GAAP's gradual convergence with Full IFRS** in the European Union is France. The French accounting regulator initiated an in-depth review of the national accounting standards in 2002 to have Local GAAP converging (at least in part) with Full IFRS. The aim of the convergence process was to modify current accounting standards and to incorporate some of the IFRS principles. France is currently following a policy of 'progressive convergence' and there are still several dichotomies between French GAAP and EU-IFRS.[119] In comparison, the German accounting reform strategy was long regarded as being *"slow, conservative and reactive, following a marginal step-by-step approach"* (*Haller/Eierle* (2004b), p. 27). In 2009, German GAAP was brought closer to Full IFRS, when the Accounting Law Modernization Act (Bilanzrechtsmodernisierungsgesetz) became effective. The law led to a closer alignment of national accounting standards and practices with Full IFRS, although a large number of differences remain (*Nobes/Parker* (2012), p. 334). Hence, **Germany prefers to have national rules** for the financial report-

[119] This information was provided by *Grant Thornton* and *PwC*.

ing of domestic private companies and considers Full IFRS *"cost-intensive and highly complex"* (*Deloitte Touche Tohmatsu* (2009a), p. 4).[120]

Although the IAS Regulation 1606/2002 did not impose Full IFRS adoption to any EU member state outside the scope of consolidated financial statements of publicly traded companies, it clearly had a great impact on the financial reporting requirements for European private firms. This is because the IAS Regulation included a **member state option**, which allows EU countries to permit or require Full IFRS also in the individual and consolidated financial statements of non-publicly traded firms (*European Commission* (2002), p. 3). As Figure 3-12 illustrates, every sampled member state of the European Union has used this option to adopt Full IFRS in the context of private firms. EU countries are classified as 'FL1-adopters', because **EU-IFRS differ slightly from IASB-IFRS** regarding the accounting of macro and portfolio hedges (so-called IAS 39 carve-out) as well as due to the timing of EU-IFRS adoption (as the EU endorsement process must be followed). For this reason, EU-IFRS are not classified as 'Full IFRS as issued by the IASB' but as a local version of Full IFRS with minor modifications.

Despite the 100% Full IFRS adoption rate, many EU member states have not fully converged their national GAAPs with Full IFRS and continue to require or allow national GAAP in the individual financial statements of domestic private companies. The continuity of national GAAPs besides Full IFRS has been described as a **'two standard' system** in the European Union (*Street/Larson* (2004), p. 1). Figure 3-12 visualizes the persistence of such GAAPs that comply with Full IFRS only in part, by displaying consistent percentages for FL2 and FL3 during the years 2005-2014. Hence, the chart reveals that Full IFRS have complemented but not substituted European national GAAPs for private firms since 2005. This has led to an increase in the total number of GAAPs by almost 100%.

Figure 3-12 does not display any IFRS for SMEs adoption (S & SL1) in the European Union. This is because **no single EU member state has yet adopted the IFRS for SMEs** (with or without minor modifications) in the field of domestic private firms. By the mid-2000s, the development of the IFRS for SMEs had already resulted in an intense debate among EU member states as to whether international accounting harmonization would be desirable in the field of European private firms. While French and German SMEs largely opposed the IFRS for SMEs, most British SMEs had no or only little difficulty in the reconciliation of their financial statements from UK GAAP to the ED-IFRS for SMEs (*Association of Chartered Certified Accountants* (2008), p. 8). In November 2009, the European Commission asked the European Financial Reporting Advisory Group (EFRAG) to prepare a review on the IFRS for SMEs regarding its compatibility with the 4th and 7th EU Directive. In their final report, EFRAG identified the following six areas in which the IFRS for SMEs was **incompatible with the two EU Accounting Directives** (*European Financial Reporting Advisory Group* (2010), p. 2f.):

120 Cf. for further studies on the process and the state of convergence of local accounting systems with Full IFRS in EU member states *Boross et al.* (1995) (Hungary), *Fontes et al.* (2005) (Portugal), *Lainez et al.* (1999) (Spain), and *Provasoli et al.* (2007) (Italy).

- prohibition to present or describe any items of income and expense as 'extraordinary items' in the statement of comprehensive income (or in the income statement, if presented) or in the notes (IFRS for SMEs Par. 5.10),[121]
- requirement to measure financial instruments within the scope of section 12 of the IFRS for SMEs (non-basic financial instruments) at fair value (IFRS for SMEs Par. 12.7 and 12.8),
- requirement to presume the useful life of goodwill to be ten years if an entity is unable to make a reliable estimate of the useful life (IFRS for SMEs Par. 19.23),[122]
- requirement to recognize any negative goodwill immediately in profit or loss (IFRS for SMEs Par. 19.24),
- requirement to present the amount receivable from equity instruments issued before the entity receives the cash or other resources, as an offset to equity and not as an asset (IFRS for SMEs Par. 22.7(a)), and
- prohibition to reverse an impairment loss recognized for goodwill (IFRS for SMEs Par. 27.28).

Given these points of incompatibility, it was up to the European Commission to decide whether and in which way the IFRS for SMEs would be incorporated into the European financial reporting framework for private firms. In summary, there were only **two scenarios** for **IFRS for SMEs adoption in the European Union** (*Kajüter/Saucke* (2012); number 494):

- The conflicting aspects in the EU Accounting Directives would be eliminated. Hence, EU member states intending to adopt IFRS for SMEs for domestic private firms could adopt the IASB standard without violating EU company law (implicit option).
- The conflicting aspects in the EU Accounting Directives would not be eliminated, but an explicit member state option would offer EU member states the possibility of adopting the IFRS for SMEs without modification (explicit option).

When the new EU Accounting Directive was issued in June 2013, neither of these two strategies was followed. The **European Commission rejects to adopt the IFRS for SMEs** at EU level for the following reasons:

> *"introducing the IFRS for SMEs would not appropriately serve the objectives of simplification and reduction of administrative burden. Moreover, considering that the IFRS for SMEs is a relatively new standard, experience with its implementation worldwide was still lacking."*
>
> (*European Commission* (2011), p. 7)[123]

---

[121] This point of incompatibility has been resolved by 2013 due to amendments to the EU Accounting Directive. Cf. *European Commission* (2013), p. 49, in comparison to *European Commission* (1978), p. 19.

[122] This point of incompatibility has been resolved by 2013 due to amendments to the IFRS for SMEs. Cf. *IFRS Foundation* (2013).

While the **lack of experience** with worldwide implementation of IFRS for SMEs can be regarded as a valid argument against adoption, it is debatable how the IASB standard can be deemed inappropriate due to its **lack of simplification.** After all, the IFRS for SMEs is the result of a process of simplification whose starting point was Full IFRS – which itself is available for adoption in the field of European private firms since 2005.

Among the EU member states, the non-adoption of IFRS for SMEs has not been approved unanimously. On the contrary, the results of a consultation on the IFRS for SMEs that was conducted between November 2009 and March 2010 rather indicate that the **majority of EU countries favor a member state option** that would allow them to opt for or against the use of IFRS for SMEs within their jurisdiction (*European Commission* (2010), p. 11). Especially Anglo-Nordic countries are open towards IFRS for SMEs adoption, whereas German-speaking countries largely oppose the implementation of IFRS for SMEs (*Quagli/Paoloni* (2012), p. 151f.).[124]

According to the Federation of European Accountants (FEE), the differences between the EU Directive and the IFRS for SMEs are of relatively minor matters, and IFRS for SMEs adoption could be of help to certain EU countries, in particular to member states with limited standard setting capabilities (*Fédération des Experts comptables Européens* (2012), p. 3). By 2014, at least **two of the six conflicting aspects of incompatibility have already been resolved** due to changes made in the new EU Accounting Directive (ban of extraordinary items) as well as due to the Comprehensive Review of the IFRS for SMEs (2012-2014), which brought the SME-accounting for goodwill closer to current EU law.[125]

As long as the European Commission is not willing to allow IFRS for SMEs adoption at EU level, the member states cannot adopt the IFRS for SMEs without modifications. Even if these modifications are restricted to the remaining four points of incompatibility, and thus do not change the IASB standard substantially, European private companies that apply such **local versions of IFRS for SMEs** will not be allowed to describe their financial statements as conforming to the IFRS for SMEs (IFRS for SMEs Par. 1.6 & 3.3).

---

[123] Cf. *Radwan* (2008), p. 9–11, for more background information on the reasons against IFRS for SMEs adoption in the European Union.

[124] In Germany, the main points of criticism concern the complexity and the conceptual inconsistency of the IFRS for SMEs. Cf. *Janssen/Gronewold* (2010). In addition, doubts have been raised on the qualification of the IASB for SME accounting standard setting. Cf. *Fülbier/Gassen* (2010), p. 6. Most importantly, German regulators fear distortions and unpredictable consequences on different contracting purposes of private firms' financial reporting (esp. taxation and dividend distribution). Cf. *Fülbier/Klein* (2013), p. 18. However, some voices call for IFRS for SMEs adoption in the consolidated financial statements of German private firms. Cf. *Kirsch/Schellhorn* (2011).

[125] According to Article 12 No. 11 of the new EU Accounting Directive, intangible assets shall be written off over the useful economic life of the intangible asset. In exceptional cases where the useful life of goodwill and development costs cannot be reliably estimated, such assets shall be written off within a maximum period set by the member state. That maximum period shall not be shorter than five years and shall not exceed 10 years. Cf. *European Commission* (2013), p. 182/34. The revised IFRS for SMEs requires that if an entity is unable to make a reliable estimate of the useful life of goodwill or another intangible asset, the useful life should not exceed 10 years. In the original version of IFRS for SMEs, the useful life was required to be fixed at 10 years (*IFRS Foundation* (2013), p. 6).

The Accounting Standards Boards of the United Kingdom and the Republic of Ireland were among the first national regulators in the EU, which made plans to adopt the IFRS for SMEs with certain modifications. In 2010, the two standard-setters agreed on a comprehensive reform of their prior financial reporting system (UK GAAP). Due to the IFRS for SMEs' non-compliance with EU law and criticism received in response to earlier drafts by UK preparers and users, the final version of the **new UK GAAP** (FRS 102), which is effective for periods beginning on or after 1 January 2015, **is based broadly on the IFRS for SMEs** but differs from the IASB standard in some significant respects (e.g. revaluation of tangible and intangible fixed assets, capitalization of borrowing costs) (*Institute of Chartered Accountants in England and Wales* (2013), p. 3). Besides the United Kingdom and the Republic of Ireland, there are a few other EU countries that have developed domestic accounting systems for private firms that are based on the IFRS for SMEs (Estonia, the Netherlands, Portugal, and Sweden). In 2014, local versions of IFRS for SMEs (SL2 & SL3) are implemented in every fifth European country (21%).

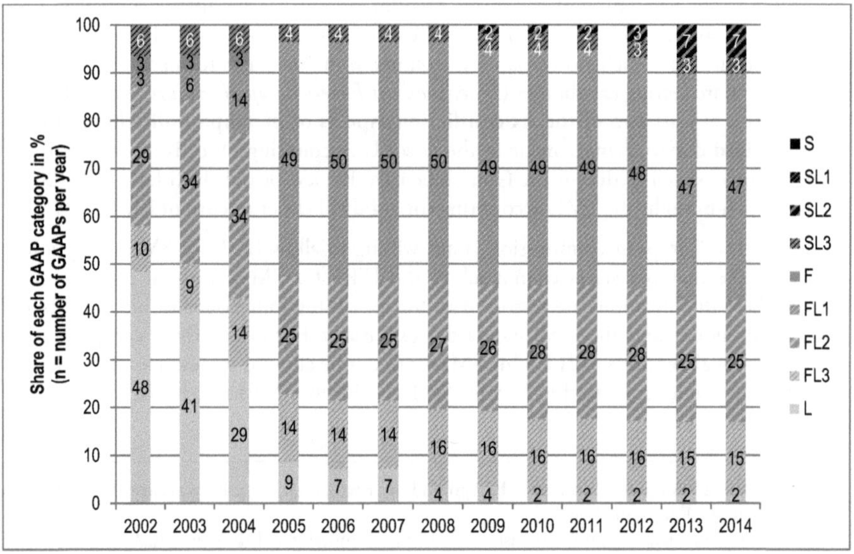

Figure 3-13: Share of each GAAP category in the EU (incl. EEA)

Figure 3-13 illustrates the **rapid decline of the Local GAAP category** (L), which was traditionally strong in the European Union prior to 2005. While in 2002 every second national GAAP in the EU was entirely independent from IFRS, the Local GAAP category has nearly disappeared since 2008. In comparison, EU-IFRS (FL1) made up for almost one half of the total number of European GAAPs for private firms by the end of the years 2000. The second half included national accounting systems that had been converged with Full IFRS only in part (FL2 & FL3). Since the IFRS for SMEs was issued in 2009, a small but increasing number of EU countries has developed local versions of IFRS for SMEs (SL2 & SL3). Compared to the early 2000s, the financial reporting environment for private firms in the European Union was **abruptly internationalized in 2005**. Furthermore, a continuous convergence process has brought the remaining local accounting systems closer to either Full IFRS or IFRS for SMEs.[126]

The process of Full IFRS adoption in the European Union is illustrated in Figure 3-14. Although the IAS Regulation 1606/2002 did not require EU countries to adopt Full IFRS in the field of private firms, every EU country opted for Full IFRS adoption in 2005. Regardless of that, there is **significant variation in the type and the scope of Full IFRS adoption** among EU countries, which is visualized by the four parallel running lines in Figure 3-14. First, only a small minority of EU countries (14%) have opted for mandatory Full IFRS adoption in the field of private firms. Secondly, while Full IFRS have unanimously been adopted in the consolidated financial statements of European companies, almost one third of the EU member states (32%) has rejected the use of Full IFRS in the individual financial statements of domestic private firms. In addition, almost every fifth EU country (18%) excludes some types of private companies from Full IFRS adoption.[127]

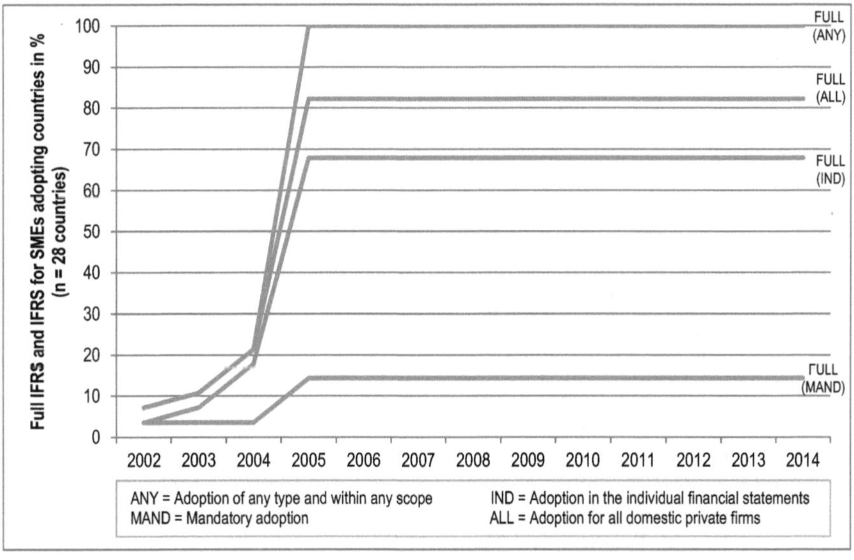

Figure 3-14: Full IFRS and IFRS for SMEs adoption in the EU (incl. EEA)

In contrast to the lacking disclosure requirements in most other geographic regions, Full IFRS financial statements of European private firms have to be made **publicly available in almost every EU member state**. In all 28 sampled countries, except in Poland, Portu-

---

[126] Cf. Table A-6 for a summary of the classification of GAAP for private firms in the *European Union* and in the *European Economic Area*.

[127] Cf. *European Commission* (2012) for more details on the implementation of Full IFRS in the field of European private firms.

gal, and Romania, domestic private firms have the obligation to send their financial statements to a national registry, which can be accessed online by interested parties.

The following cross-sectional analysis includes a country-by-country description of Full IFRS adoption in the European Union in 2014.

3.2.4.2 Cross-sectional analysis

In accordance with the empirical findings from the time series analysis, EU countries can be differentiated into the following four types of Full IFRS adopters:

- 'Voluntary for all' adopters,
- 'Mandatory' adopters,
- 'Consolidated accounts only' adopters, and
- 'Some companies only' adopters.

The largest of the four groups consists of 'Voluntary for all' Full IFRS adopters. In eleven out of the 28 sampled EU countries (almost 40%), all domestic private firms are allowed but not required to use Full IFRS for the preparation of their individual and consolidated financial statements. Especially **Scandinavian** (Denmark, Finland, and Norway) and **Eastern European countries** (Czech Republic, Estonia, Lithuania, and Slovenia) as well as countries with **Anglo-Dutch** accounting traditions (Ireland, Netherlands, and the United Kingdom) belong to the group of voluntary Full IFRS adopters in 2014.

Bulgaria, Cyprus, Greece, and Slovakia are four smaller EU member states (14%) that require Full IFRS adoption in the field of private firms. While **Cyprus** is the only EU country that mandates all domestic private firms to adopt Full IFRS, Bulgaria, Greece, and Slovakia have made Full IFRS mandatory for large companies (**Bulgaria** and **Slovakia**) or subsidiaries of listed entities (**Greece**) only.

Large Central European countries such as **France** and **Germany** limit the use of Full IFRS to the consolidated financial statements of local private firms. These countries consider Full IFRS adoption in the individual financial statements as burdensome, as it would imply an in-depth reform of fiscal, commercial, and civil law (*Evraert/Des Robert* (2007), p. 141). Among others, countries associated with the traditional Franco-German accounting system (**Austria**, **Belgium**, and **Hungary**) belong to this type of Full IFRS adopter (32% in total).

The remaining four sampled EU countries (14%) allow the use of Full IFRS in the individual and consolidated financial statements of private companies but exclude small businesses from the scope of Full IFRS adoption (**Iceland** and **Italy**) or restrict its use to subsidiaries of groups that already apply Full IFRS in their consolidated financial statements (**Poland** and **Portugal**).

The characteristics of local implementation of Full IFRS in the field of European private firms are summarized in Table 3-15.

Full IFRS adopters (28) *(date of adoption)*	**VOL**	**MAND**	**IND**	**CONS**	**ALL**
Austria *(2002)*	Yes	No	No	Yes	Yes
Belgium *(2005)*	Yes	No	No	Yes	Yes
Bulgaria *(2005)*	Yes	Yes[1]	Yes	Yes	Yes
Cyprus *(2005)*	No	Yes	Yes	Yes	Yes
Czech Republic *(2004)*	Yes	No	Yes	Yes	Yes
Denmark *(2004)*	Yes	No	Yes	Yes	Yes
Estonia *(2003)*	Yes	No	Yes	Yes	Yes
Finland *(2005)*	Yes	No	Yes	Yes	Yes
France *(2005)*	Yes	No	No	Yes	Yes
Germany *(2005)*	Yes	No	No	Yes	Yes
Greece *(2005)*	Yes	Yes[2]	Yes	Yes	Yes
Hungary *(2005)*	Yes	No	No	Yes	Yes
Iceland *(2005)*	Yes	No	Yes	Yes	No[3]
Ireland *(2005)*	Yes	No	Yes	Yes	Yes
Italy *(2005)*	Yes	No	Yes	Yes	No[4]
Latvia *(2005)*	Yes	No	No	Yes	Yes
Lithuania *(2004)*	Yes	No	Yes	Yes	Yes
Luxembourg *(2005)*	Yes	No	Yes	Yes	Yes
Netherlands *(2005)*	Yes	No	Yes	Yes	Yes
Norway *(2005)*	Yes	No	Yes	Yes	Yes
Poland *(2005)*	Yes	No	Yes	Yes	No[5]
Portugal *(2005)*	Yes	No	Yes	Yes	No[6]
Romania *(2005)*	Yes	No	No	Yes	Yes
Slovakia *(2005)*	No	Yes	Yes	Yes	No[7]
Slovenia *(2005/2006)*[8]	Yes	No	Yes	Yes	Yes
Spain *(2005)*	Yes	No	No	Yes	Yes
Sweden *(2005)*	Yes	No	No	Yes	Yes
United Kingdom *(2005)*	Yes	No	Yes	Yes	Yes
Percentage (n=28 countries)	**93%**	**14%**	**68%**	**100%**	**82%**

[1] Large companies exceeding two of the three following criteria: total assets of Leva 8 million, net revenue from sales of Leva 15 million, and 250 employees; [2] Subsidiaries of listed companies; [3] All except small entities with assets less than ISK 230 thousand, operating revenues smaller than ISK 460 thousand, or fewer than 50 employees; [4] All except small businesses as defined in Article eleven of the Fourth EU Directive (78/660/EEC); [5] All except companies that do not strive for a listing or are no subsidiaries of parent companies that use EU-IFRS; [6] All except companies that do not present audited consolidated financial statements or that are no subsidiaries of a group that presents consolidated financial statements under EU-IFRS; [7] All except companies with total assets less than € 165,970, total revenues smaller than € 165,970, or fewer than 2,000 employees; [8] EU-IFRS since 2005, Slovene Accounting Standards since 2006.

VOL = Voluntary adoption; MAND = Mandatory adoption; IND = Adoption in the individual financial statements; CONS = Adoption in the consolidated financial statements; ALL = Adoption for all domestic private firms.

Table 3-15: Characteristics of Full IFRS adoption in the EU (incl. EEA)

In contrast to unexceptional Full IFRS adoption, **none of the EU countries have adopted IFRS for SMEs** by 2014. However, certain EU countries have implemented local accounting systems for private firms that are generally based on the IFRS for SMEs but differ from the standard in several respects. In 2013, **Estonia** adopted a local version of the IFRS for SMEs by aligning Estonian standards (RTJ) with the IASB standard. There are a few minor differences between the new Estonian GAAP and IFRS for SMEs, in particular in the areas where the IFRS for SMEs is incompatible with the new EU Accounting Directive. Furthermore, disclosure requirements are slightly different to the IASB standard and there are a couple of other areas where Estonian GAAP allows policy choices that do not exist in the IFRS for SMEs (e.g. capitalization of development costs).

A similar adoption scenario was chosen by **Sweden**, where a new local accounting standard (K3 - BFNAR 2012-1) was developed by the Swedish Accounting Standards Board (BFN). K3 is broadly based on the IFRS for SMEs but has been adapted to Swedish law, national accounting practice, and local tax law (*IFRS Foundation* (2014r), p. 6). Larger non-publicly accountable Swedish entities have been required to adopt the standard from 2013 onwards.[128]

Should the European Commission introduce a member state option, which allows EU member states to adopt IFRS for SMEs without modifications, several other EU countries would probably opt for the adoption of IFRS for SMEs in their local context. For example, IFRS for SMEs adoption is subject to discussions in **Cyprus** and **Hungary**. The Latvian Ministry of Finance, which supervises accounting matters and legislation in the country, explained that it would wait until the IFRS for SME is being adopted by the EU before it might implement the standard in **Latvia.**[129]

3.2.5 Southeast Europe

Albania	Belarus	Macedonia	Serbia	Ukraine
Armenia	Croatia	Moldova	*Switzerland*	
Azerbaijan	Georgia	Montenegro	Turkey	

Table 3-16: Sampled countries from Southeast Europe (incl. Switzerland)

3.2.5.1 Time series analysis

The former local financial reporting systems of Southeastern European countries were largely dominated by the communist system of the Soviet Union. While local Eastern European companies relied on government finance and prepared financial statements primarily for taxation purposes prior to the fall of the Iron Curtain in 1989, these companies needed access to non-governmental sources of finance from the early 1990s onwards. This led to the development of accounting rules, which were either oriented towards creditor protection or followed Anglo-Saxon concepts to attract foreign investment (*Nobes/Parker* (2012), p. 316).

---

128 In Sweden, large companies are defined as companies with at least two of the following criteria fulfilled two years in a row: more than 50 employees, more than SEK 40 million (approximately € 5 million) in total assets, and SEK 80 million (approximately € 10 million) in yearly turnover. Cf. *IFRS Foundation* (2014r), p. 6.

129 This information was provided by *Grant Thornton* and *PwC*.

Although the laws and regulations in the area of financial reporting have been subject to **rapid change** since then, the overall quality of financial reporting and the general level of transparency were still regarded as low by the mid-2000s (*World Bank* (2006b), p. 2; *World Bank* (2007b), p. 2). This **lack of transparency** in Southeastern European countries has impeded the ability of domestic small and medium-sized enterprises to access credit from the financial sector (*World Bank* (2006a), p. 2). In 2014, financial statements of private firms are made publicly available in a few Southeastern European countries only (e.g. Albania, Croatia, and Macedonia).[130]

Since the beginning of the last decade, most Southeastern European countries have made strong efforts to improve the quality of domestic accounting standards for private firms. The aim to raise local standards to global best practice has resulted in two parallel developments. First, several Southeastern European countries have followed a strategy of **gradual convergence of national accounting standards with Full IFRS**. For example, economic reforms in Ukraine led to an accounting reform based on international harmonization in the late 1990s, and Armenia implemented national accounting standards based on IAS in 2000 (*Balchenko* (2001), p. 2; 4). Parallel to this process of stepwise substitution of Local GAAPs (L) by local versions of Full IFRS (FL2) during the years 2002-2008 (see Figure 3-15), several Southeastern European countries (also) **adopted Full IFRS without modifications** (F) in the context of private firms (e.g. Albania, Croatia, Georgia, Macedonia, Serbia, and Montenegro).

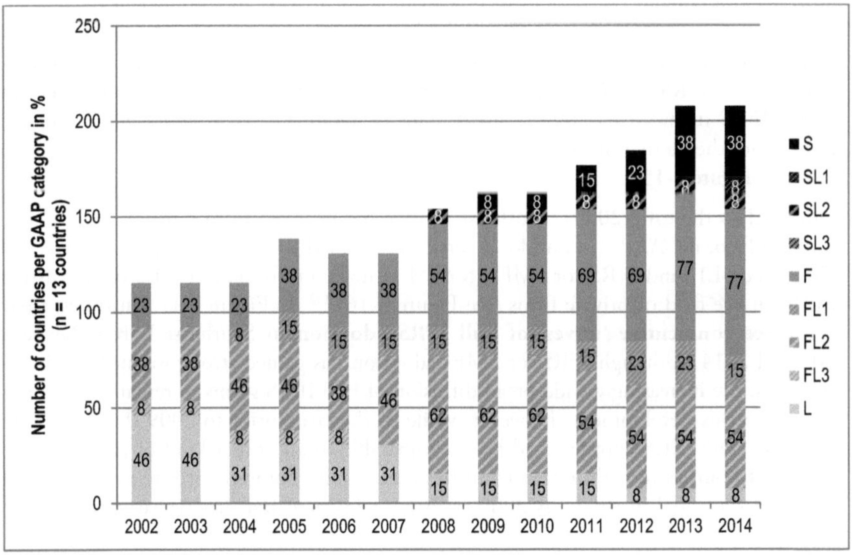

Figure 3-15: Distribution of GAAP categories in Southeast Europe

[130] This information was provided by *Grant Thornton* and *PwC*.

By the late 2000s, the **World Bank** had analyzed the quality and appropriateness of local accounting and auditing systems in almost every Southeastern European country. The World Bank's general view on Full IFRS adoption was that Full IFRS would not be well suited for SMEs as these standards would impose a high administrative burden on smaller companies (*World Bank* (2002a), p. 9) and put an unnecessary strain on scarce institutional and professional accounting resources (*World Bank* (2007e), p. ii). Moreover, the World Bank feared that SMEs were struggling with the adoption of Full IFRS and that compliance would suffer (*World Bank* (2005a), p. 2). For this reason, the World Bank recommended to Southeastern European countries to adopt Full IFRS only in the field of publicly traded companies (and large unlisted companies) and to make small and medium-sized entities subject to simplified reporting requirements that are appropriate to their size and nature (*World Bank* (2009), p. vii). In particular, it was **suggested to consider the adoption of IFRS for SMEs** as soon as the standard would be available (*World Bank* (2008a), p. v).

Unsurprisingly, IFRS for SMEs was adopted by several Southeastern European countries during the years 2009-2014. As Figure 3-15 displays, almost half of the sampled countries (46%) have adopted the IFRS for SMEs (38% S and 8% SL1) by 2014. Albania is the only country in the sample that has adopted a local version of the IFRS for SMEs (SL2).[131] Instead of replacing Full IFRS or local versions of Full IFRS, in most Southeastern European countries **IFRS for SMEs has only complemented** the existing financial reporting standards in the field of private firms, which made the number of GAAPs increase by almost 50% per country. Serbia is the only country in the Southeastern European sample where Full IFRS have been substituted by IFRS for SMEs. Despite the growing importance of IFRS for SMEs, several **national accounting systems were brought closer to Full IFRS** in the years 2009 to 2014. This development has resulted in 77% of the sampled Southeastern European countries to adopt Full IFRS as issued by the IASB in 2014 (see Figure 3-15).

Compared to the early 2000s, Southeast Europe has changed from a region with a large number of Local GAAPs (L) and local versions of Full IFRS (FL2) to a place, where Full IFRS (F & FL1) and IFRS for SMEs (S & SL1) make up for almost 70% of all existing GAAPs in the field of private firms (see Figure 3-16).[132] As Figure 3-17 illustrates, there were **three consecutive 'waves' of Full IFRS adoption** in Southeast Europe between 2002 and 2014. Although IFRS for SMEs adoption has gained strong momentum in recent years, the increasingly widespread diffusion of Full IFRS seems to remain largely unaffected by this development. However, while in the years prior to 2009 the increase in mandatory Full IFRS adopters had been comparable to any other kind of adoption, the number of Southeastern European countries that require domestic private firms to adopt Full IFRS stagnated in the years 2009 to 2012, and thereafter dropped to only 23% in

[131] Albanian national accounting standards can be regarded as accounting standards developed in general conformity with Full IFRS, but which represent a more simplified version similar to the IFRS for SMEs. This information was provided by *Grant Thornton* and *PwC*.

[132] Cf. Table A-7 for a summary of the classification of GAAP for private firms in *Southeast Europe*.

2014. This indicates the differentiation of the Southeast European financial reporting landscape due to its complementation by IFRS for SMEs.

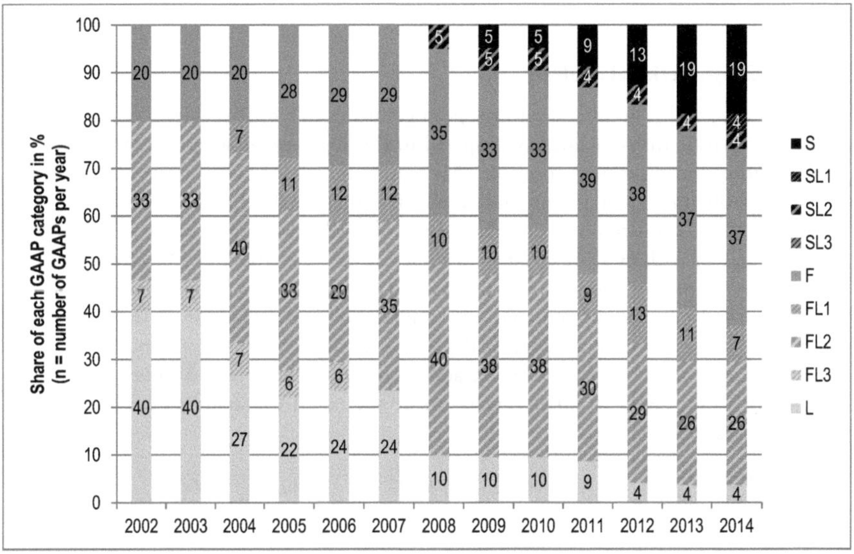

Figure 3-16: Share of each GAAP category in Southeast Europe

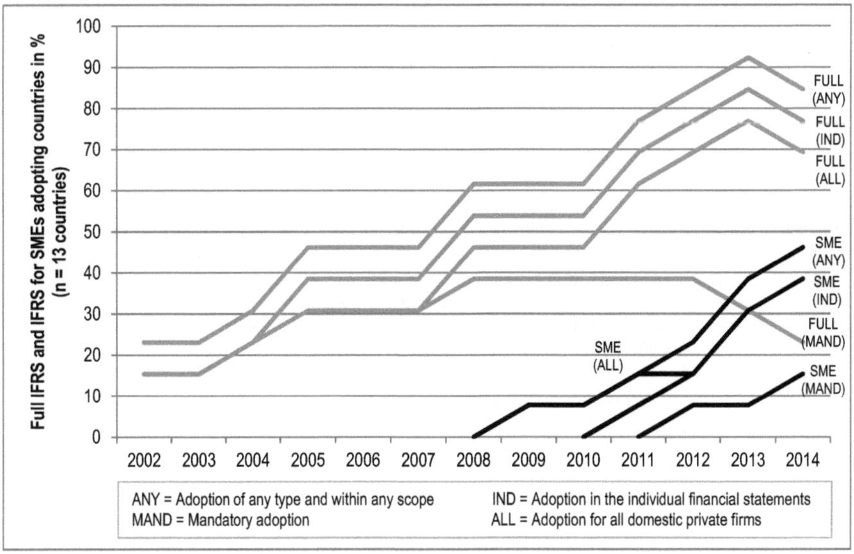

Figure 3-17: Full IFRS and IFRS for SMEs adoption in Southeast Europe

The following cross-sectional analysis reveals the characteristics of Full IFRS and IFRS for SMEs adoption in Southeast Europe (incl. Switzerland) in 2014 on a country-by-country basis.

3.2.5.2 Cross-sectional analysis

Eleven of 13 sampled Southeastern European countries (85%) have adopted Full IFRS in the field of private firms by 2014. Compared to this high overall adoption rate, the number of Southeastern European countries that require the use of Full IFRS by domestic private firms (Albania, Croatia, and Macedonia) is rather small (23%). As Table 3-17 displays, these three countries restrict mandatory Full IFRS adoption either to subsidiaries of listed companies (**Albania**) or to larger private entities (**Croatia** and **Macedonia**). Every Southeastern European country that has adopted Full IFRS after 2009 (Armenia, Moldova, Turkey, and Ukraine) permits but not requires Full IFRS adoption in the field of private firms. When **Georgia** adopted IFRS for SMEs in 2013, the country also changed from mandatory to voluntary Full IFRS adoption. On the contrary, **Serbia** replaced Full IFRS by IFRS for SMEs in 2014 and has made the new IASB standard applicable to all domestic private entities.

Full IFRS adopters (11) *(date of adoption)*	**VOL**	**MAND**	**IND**	**CONS**	**ALL**
Albania *(2008)*	Yes	Yes[1]	Yes	Yes	Yes
Armenia *(2011)*	Yes	No	Yes	Yes	Yes
Azerbaijan *(2008)*	Yes	No	Yes	Yes	Yes
Croatia *(2002)*	No	Yes[2]	Yes	Yes	No[3]
Georgia *(2002)*	Yes	No[4]	Yes	Yes	Yes
Macedonia *(2005)*	No[5]	Yes	Yes	Yes	No[6]
Moldova *(2011)*	Yes	No	Yes	Yes	Yes
Montenegro *(2005/2005)*[7]	Yes	No	Yes	Yes	Yes
Switzerland *(2002)*	Yes	No	No[8]	Yes	Yes
Turkey *(2013)*	Yes	No	Yes	Yes	Yes
Ukraine *(2012)*	Yes	No	Yes	Yes	Yes
Percentage (n=13 countries)	**69%**	**23%**	**77%**	**85%**	**69%**

[1] Subsidiaries of listed companies and companies with annual turnover in excess of Lek 1,250 million and more than 100 employees; [2] Mandatory for all until 2007; [3] All except small and medium-sized countries with turnover less than HRK 260 million, total assets less than HRK 130 million, or fewer than 250 employees; [4] Mandatory until 2012; [5] Voluntary until 2011; [6] All except small entities with annual turnover of less than € 2 million, total assets of less than € 2 million, and fewer than 50 employees and entities that do not prepare consolidated financial statements; [7] IFRS and Montenegrin GAAP (only differ in the mandatory chart of accounts); [8] Reconciliation to Swiss Code of Obligation required.

VOL = Voluntary adoption; MAND = Mandatory adoption; IND = Adoption in the individual financial statements; CONS = Adoption in the consolidated financial statements; ALL = Adoption for all domestic private firms.

Table 3-17: Characteristics of Full IFRS adoption in Southeast Europe

Contrary to all other countries in the Southeastern European sample, **Switzerland** is the only country that adopted Full IFRS in the consolidated financial statements of domestic private firms only. Similar to other German-speaking countries in the European Union (e.g. Austria) and countries with accounting systems that are related to the traditional

Franco-German creditor/secrecy orientation (e.g. Belgium and Hungary), Switzerland disapproves Full IFRS adoption in the individual financial statements of local companies and requires a reconciliation to Local GAAP (Swiss Code of Obligation) for taxation and profit distribution purposes.

Despite the **need for reconciliation**, Switzerland offers local private firms the possibility of applying three other sets of accounting standards. Besides Full IFRS, private entities can also adopt the IFRS for SMEs or a more sophisticated Swiss-made financial reporting system (Swiss GAAP FER) that is tailored to Swiss-oriented companies with demanding financial statement users (*Meyer* (2008)). Although the IASB does not allow countries to **adopt the IFRS for SMEs in the field of (small) publicly accountable entities**, in Switzerland the IFRS for SMEs is seen as a potential alternative to Full IFRS in the field of Mid and Small Caps. Small and medium-sized listed companies often withdraw from the Swiss Exchange to avoid Full IFRS adoption as they fear the burdensome and detailed disclosures (*Glanz/Pfaff* (2011), p. 28). Regardless of the potential scope of IFRS for SMEs adoption in the field of smaller listed companies in Switzerland, only a small percentage of Swiss private firms have considered IFRS for SMEs adoption so far due to the strong reputation of Swiss GAAP FER (*Stiftung für Fachempfehlungen zur Rechnungslegung/Institut für Rechnungswesen und Controlling der Universität Zürich* (2009), p. 53).

Including Switzerland, six out of thirteen sampled Southeastern European countries (46%) have adopted IFRS for SMEs by 2014. **Serbia** and **Macedonia** are the only countries that require all (Serbia) or some (Macedonia) domestic private firms to prepare financial statements under IFRS for SMEs. Macedonia restricts the use of IFRS for SMEs to the individual financial statements of smaller entities with annual turnover and total assets below € 2 million and fewer than 50 employees and hence provides a segmented financial reporting environment without accounting system choices on firm level.

IFRS for SMEs adopters (6) *(date of adoption)*	**VOI**	**MAND**	**IND**	**CONS**	**ALL**
Armenia *(2011)*	Yes	No	Yes	Yes	Yes
Georgia *(2013)*	Yes	No	Yes	Yes	Yes
Macedonia *(2012)*	No	Yes	Yes	No[1]	No[2]
Serbia *(2014)*	No	Yes	Yes	Yes	Yes
Switzerland *(2009)*	Yes	No	No[3]	Yes	Yes
Turkey *(2013)*	Yes	No	Yes	Yes	Yes
Percentage (n=13 countries)	**31%**	**15%**	**38%**	**38%**	**38%**

[1] If consolidated financial statements are issued, the company is categorized as large and has to apply Full IFRS; [2] All except entities with annual turnover of more than € 2 million, total assets of more than € 2 million, and more than 50 employees and entities that prepare consolidated financial statements; [3] Reconciliation to Swiss Code of Obligation required.

VOL = Voluntary adoption; MAND = Mandatory adoption; IND = Adoption in the individual financial statements; CONS = Adoption in the consolidated financial statements; ALL = Adoption for all domestic private firms.

Table 3-18: Characteristics of IFRS for SMEs adoption in Southeast Europe

The fact that nearly half of the sampled Southeastern European countries have already adopted IFRS for SMEs gives an impression on how the IFRS for SMEs might be adopted in the countries of the European Union if adoption was not forbidden by the European Commission. **Turkey**, which has applied for EU membership for several years, adopted IFRS for SMEs in 2013.[133] If Turkey is finally offered to become part of the EU, the country will need to modify the IFRS for SMEs to align it with EU law.

In summary, the Full IFRS adoption rate is very high in Southeast Europe and IFRS for SMEs has also been adopted by every second country in the region. Mandatory adoption is low for both IASB standards as in most countries private firms have the option to choose between two or more accounting systems. Some countries differentiate these accounting choices on the basis of specific firm characteristics such as size or group affiliation.

Future adoptions of IFRS for SMEs are under consideration in Albania, Azerbaijan, and Moldova. The National Accounting Council of **Albania** (NACA) has announced its intent to continue the implementation of the National Accounting Standards based on IFRS for SMEs and to reassess the need for adopting IFRS for SMEs in full depending on the degree of the remaining differences as well as on the decisions to be made at EU level. Albania has applied for membership in the European Union. This would require Albania to transpose the EU's Accounting Directives into Albanian law (*IFRS Foundation* (2014t), p. 4). In **Azerbaijan**, the Ministry of Finance might require smaller entities to follow IFRS for SMEs in the future, but the exact timing is still to be clarified.[134] Although the **Moldovan** government has not made any decisions yet, the government considers basing National Accounting Standards on the IFRS for SMEs.[135]

3.2.6 Africa

Algeria	Egypt	Morocco	Senegal	Uganda
Angola	Ghana	Mozambique	South Africa	Zambia
Botswana	Kenya	Namibia	Tanzania	Zimbabwe
Côte d'Ivoire	Mauritius	Nigeria	Tunisia	

Table 3-19: Sampled countries from Africa

3.2.6.1 Time series analysis

In line with several other economic and socio-political characteristics of African countries, the financial reporting environment has been strongly influenced by their history of colonization. In particular, **France** exercised power over large parts of Northwestern Africa until the middle of the 20th century. Furthermore, several Northeastern and Southern African countries were ruled by the **United Kingdom** until the countries declared their independence. These two predominant spheres of influence can still be observed through the diffusion of Anglo-Saxon and Continental European accounting concepts across the

[133] Cf. *Alp/Ustundag* (2009), p. 694f., for an overview on the SME project conducted by the Turkish Accounting Standards Board (TASB).

[134] This information was provided by *Grant Thornton* and *PwC*.

[135] This information was provided by *Grant Thornton* and *PwC*.

African continent (*Wallace* (1993), p. 125). In addition, they have contributed to different patterns of Full IFRS and IFRS for SMEs adoption by African countries in the field of private firms.

Figure 3-18 illustrates that only two out of the 19 sampled African countries (11%) still had a Local GAAP by 2002, and almost every fifth African country had not adopted any of the nine predefined GAAP categories at all. Mostly smaller, African countries never felt that developing a Local GAAP was cost-effective. Hence, several of them adopted **foreign GAAP** (e.g. French or UK GAAP) for the use by domestic private firms. As the adoption of foreign GAAP, including non-African and non-IFRS-related accounting systems, is not captured by the nine different GAAP categories defined in this study, the sum of percentages of African countries per GAAP category (as shown in Figure 3-18) is less than 100% during the years 2002-2004.

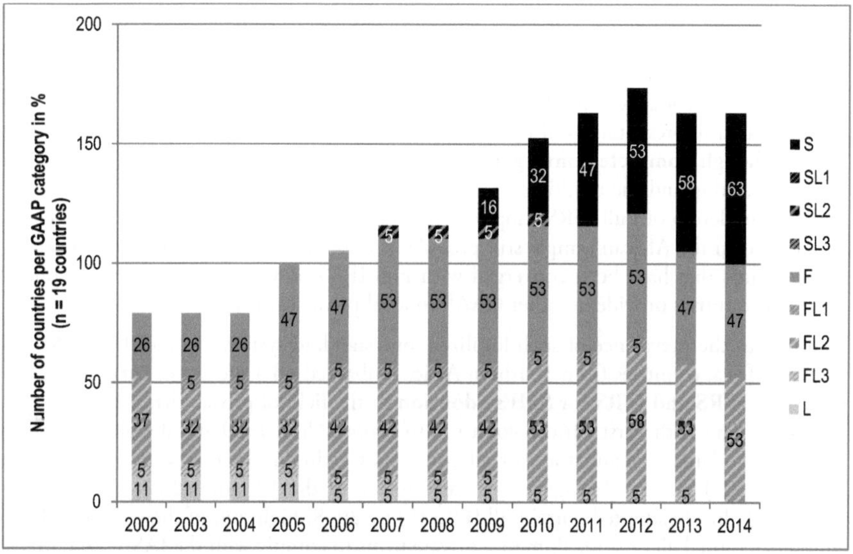

Figure 3-18: Distribution of GAAP categories in Africa

For example, Zambia and Zimbabwe (both former British colonies) used UK GAAP as the basis for the financial reporting of private firms until the early-2000s. In these countries, accounting practice has always had a **very strong British influence** just like their education system in general. For instance, in Zimbabwe school exams were run by the universities of Cambridge and Oxford until the early 1990s, and the original local university (University of Zimbabwe, previously University of Rhodesia) was initially established as a college affiliated to the University of London. Similarly, Mauritius, also being a former British colony, was greatly shaped by UK accounting principles and practices as most of the local accountants were members of the six principal accountancy institutes in the UK and Ireland in the early 1990s (*Nexia International* (1993), p. 225). In comparison, the Moroccan financial reporting system was rather influenced by French law and Continental European accounting directives (*World Bank* (2002b), p. 10).

Although empirical research suggests that African private firms have limited international structures and activities that do not result in a need for internationally comparable financial reporting information (*Aboagye-Otchere/Agbeibor* (2012)), Africa is the continent where Full IFRS and IFRS for SMEs have been adopted by jurisdictions most often. The mode of adoption can generally be differentiated into **two different patterns**: while in most **UK-dominated Southern African** countries, Full IFRS and IFRS for SMEs were early adopted as issued by the IASB (F & S), the **French speaking North and Northwestern African** countries rather opted for accounting systems, which they would harmonize gradually with IASB standards (FL2-GAAPs).

For example, Côte d'Ivoire and Senegal adopted the 'Système Comptable Ouest Africain' (**SYSCOA**) released by the 'Organisation pour l'Harmonisation en Afrique du Droit des Affaires' (OHADA) together with six other members[136] of the 'Union Economique et Monétaire Ouest Africaine' (UEMOA) in 1997. SYSCOA was tailored to be relatively close to IASC standards, but whilst IAS/IFRS kept evolving over the years, SYSCOA remained static. Representatives of the UEMOA zone plan to bring SYSCOA closer to Full IFRS, although **complete convergence is still denied**. Apparently, the concept of fair value accounting and the resulting asset and income volatility are two major impediments for the completion of Full IFRS adoption in West Africa.[137] In 2014, ten out of 19 countries (53%) in the African sample still provide local private firms with domestic accounting standards that have been converged with Full IFRS only in part (FL2). Seven out of these ten countries provide no other GAAP to local private firms.[138]

Contrary to the prevalence of such localized 'one standard systems' in North and Northwestern Africa, countries from Southern Africa embarked on a process of **early and complete Full IFRS and IFRS for SMEs adoption** in the field of private firms. For example, Kenya was one of the first African countries to adopt IAS in 1999 and declared the international standards as mandatory for all companies including local private firms (*United Nations* (2008), p. 79). As Figure 3-18 reveals, ten of the 19 sampled African countries (53%) had already adopted 'pure' Full IFRS (F) by 2008. Eight out of these ten Full IFRS adopters required all or some domestic private firms to comply with the IASB standards at that time. By doing so, Southern African countries substituted insufficient local accounting standards or foreign GAAPs by Full IFRS.

Due to the **lack of expertise and training in IFRS** and the general weakness of local financial reporting institutions, Full IFRS adoption has constituted a major challenge for African countries and, in particular, for the private sector (*Boolaky* (2010), p. 2). Struggles in language translation and the absence of good corporate governance and enforcement mechanisms have impeded the transition process in many African countries.[139] As a consequence, especially small and medium-sized private firms have had severe difficulties in

136 Togo, Bénin, Niger, Mali, Burkina Faso, and Guinea Bissau.

137 This information was provided by *Grant Thornton* and *PwC*.

138 Cf. Table A-8 for a summary of the classification of GAAP for private firms in *Africa*.

139 Cf. *Okaro/Tauringana* (2012) for the IFRS transition process in Nigeria.

applying Full IFRS, in particular regarding the issue of fair value measurement (*Mwaura/Nyaboga* (2009), p. 42). Taking the case of Kenya, empirical research showed that while both private and public firms were required to adhere to Full IFRS, public, rather than private firms, exhibited greater Full IFRS compliance (*Bova/Pereira* (2012)).

The general **lack of compliance** with Full IFRS in several African countries[140] was also found by the **World Bank**, which analyzed the state of development of local financial reporting and auditing systems and their degree of compliance with Full IFRS and International Standards on Auditing (ISAs) in all but three (Algeria, Angola, and Namibia) of the 19 sampled African countries during the early and mid-2000s. In the executive summary of the lessons learned from the World Bank's Accounting and Auditing ROSC Program *Hegarty et al.* (2004) reflect on the compliance problems and state the following:

> *"International standards are not necessarily appropriate to govern all financial reporting obligations, this being especially the case with International Accounting Standards (IAS) / International Financial Reporting Standards (IFRS).*
>
> *There is an urgent need for the International Accounting Standards Board to specify the circumstances in which the use of "full" IAS/IFRS is appropriate, and to develop different standards that would meet the needs applicable to the users of financial statements of other entities, particularly small and medium-sized enterprises (SMEs).*
>
> *Many stakeholders continue to have misunderstandings with respect to the very nature of international standards, which complicates efforts to plan, define and measure progress towards successful implementation."*
>
> (*Hegarty et al.* (2004), p. ii)

In accordance with this general view on the **inappropriateness of Full IFRS adoption in the field of private firms**, the World Bank recommended African countries such as Botswana (*World Bank* (2006c), p. 24) and Ghana (*World Bank* (2004c), p. 18) to require only listed companies and public interest entities to comply with Full IFRS and develop or adopt simplified financial reporting requirements for SMEs. As displayed by the black bars in Figure 3-18, the majority of the sampled African countries (63%) has already followed the World Bank's recommendation and adopted the IFRS for SMEs within five years after its issuance. In South Africa, the provided simplifications of recognition and measurement principles as well as the reduced disclosures prescribed by the IFRS for SMEs as compared to Full IFRS were regarded as a considerable relief from accounting burdens for SMEs (*van Wyk/Rossouw* (2009), p. 112).

In ten out of the twelve IFRS for SMEs adopting countries in the sample, the new standard has been adopted as an additional set of accounting standards, which is regarded as an alternative to Full IFRS (F) or local versions of Full IFRS (FL2). In contrast to this process of **GAAP complementation**, Ghana is the only sampled African country where the IFRS for SMEs has substituted a local version of Full IFRS completely. Due to the move

[140] Cf. *World Bank* (2001), p. 5, on non-compliance in Kenya and *World Bank* (2005b), p. 11f., on non-compliance in Tanzania.

from a one (Full IFRS) to a two (Full IFRS & IFRS for SMEs) standard system in several Southern African countries, the total number of GAAPs has increased by roughly 50% in Africa since 2009. In 2014, each African country provides approximately one and a half different GAAPs for local private firms on average.

Considering the increasing number of different GAAPs per year, Figure 3-19 shows the development of each GAAP category's respective share in the 19 sampled African countries on average. The figure reveals the fundamental changes the African financial reporting landscape was subject to during the years 2002-2014. First, it shows the increasing (2002-2008) and then decreasing (2009-2014) importance of 'pure' Full IFRS compared to other GAAPs. Secondly, it becomes evident that the **IFRS for SMEs** constitutes the **most important GAAP category in Africa** since 2013. Regardless of that, local versions of Full IFRS (FL2) still account for nearly one third of all GAAP categories on the African continent in 2014.

Compared to the years prior to 2009, Africa has turned away from comprehensive Full IFRS adoption in the field of private firms and developed to one of the **world's most ambitious IFRS for SMEs adopters.** Despite these changes, the overall level of financial reporting transparency of African private firms still has room for improvement as financial statements are made publicly available in only four sampled African countries (Algeria, Ghana, Mauritius, and Zimbabwe), none of which provide online access to registered financial statements.[141]

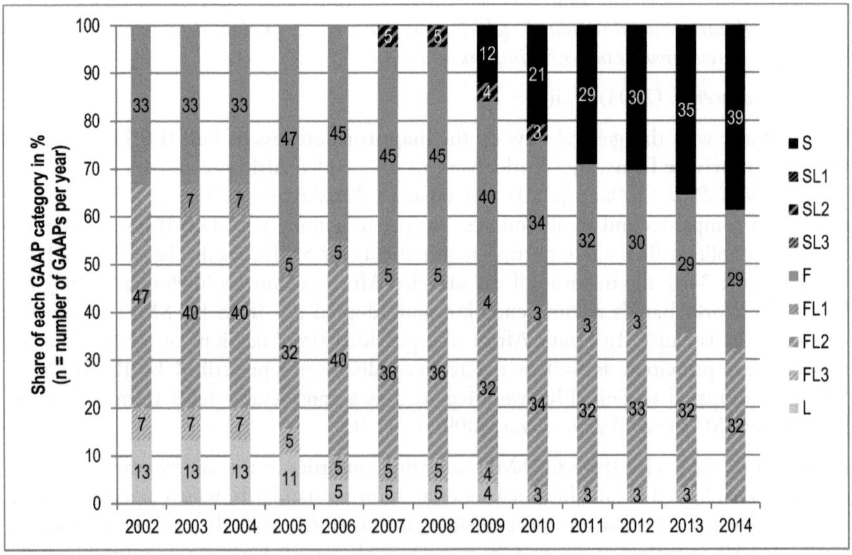

Figure 3-19: Share of each GAAP category in Africa

[141] This information was provided by *Grant Thornton* and *PwC.*

Figure 3-20 focuses on the process and the general characteristics of Full IFRS and IFRS for SMEs adoption in Africa during the years 2002-2014. First, it illustrates that until the year 2004, all sampled Full IFRS adopting countries (six out of 19) mandatorily adopted the IASB standards in the individual financial statements of all domestic private firms. Only after that year African countries began to **differentiate the type and scope of Full IFRS adoption.** In particular, mandatory Full IFRS adoption has dropped to only about 20% by 2014 while Full IFRS adoption in general has stagnated in Africa since 2007. The slight drop of Full IFRS adopters from 2012 to 2013 also points to substitution effects resulting from increasing IFRS for SMEs adoption.

Over 60% of the sampled African countries have already adopted the IFRS for SMEs in the field of private firms and have made the new standard applicable in the individual financial statements without any exception. However, almost half of the IFRS for SMEs adopting countries (5 out of 12) have restricted the use of the IFRS for SMEs to some private firms by introducing certain thresholds. Due to the **complementary status of the IFRS for SMEs** in most African countries, only three jurisdictions (16%) have required local private firms to adopt the IFRS for SMEs by 2014.

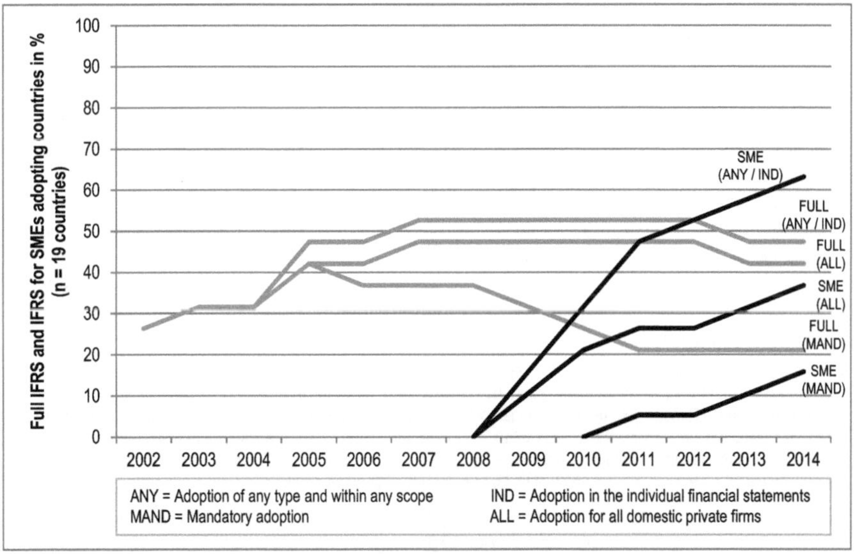

Figure 3-20: Full IFRS and IFRS for SMEs adoption in Africa

The following cross-sectional analysis concentrates on a country-by-country description of Full IFRS and IFRS for SMEs adoption in Africa in 2014.

3.2.6.2 Cross-sectional analysis

As the time series analysis revealed, the number of African mandatory Full IFRS adopters has decreased by half in the field of private firms since 2005. **Botswana, Mauritius, Tan-**

zania, and **Zambia** are four sampled African countries that had required all local private firms to use Full IFRS until the years 2005-2011. By 2014, all of these four countries have **restricted the mandatory use of Full IFRS** to public interest entities and large private companies and thus differentiated the financial reporting requirements for local private firms on the basis of qualitative criteria and firm size. For example, Botswana requires public interest entities and companies with turnover in excess of Pula 10 million and total assets in excess of Pula 5 million to use Full IFRS in their financial statements. All other private firms have the option to either adopt Full IFRS or IFRS for SMEs.

As Table 3-20 shows, **Kenya**, **Namibia**, **South Africa**, **Uganda**, and **Zimbabwe** have made Full IFRS **optional for all** domestic private firms regardless of legal form or firm size. Contrary to countries such as Botswana, these jurisdictions provide every single private firm with the option to choose between Full IFRS and IFRS for SMEs in their individual and consolidated financial statements.

In summary, nine out of the 19 sampled African countries (47%) have adopted Full IFRS in the field of private firms by 2014, and all of them provide all or some local entities with the option to use the IFRS for SMEs as an alternative set of accounting standards.

Full IFRS adopters (9) *(date of adoption)*	**VOL**	**MAND**	**IND**	**CONS**	**ALL**
Botswana *(2002)*	Yes	Yes[1,2]	Yes	Yes	Yes
Kenya *(2002)*	Yes	No[3]	Yes	Yes	Yes
Mauritius *(2002)*	Yes	Yes[4,5]	Yes	Yes	Yes
Namibia *(2005)*	Yes	No	Yes	Yes	Yes
South Africa *(2005)*	Yes	No	Yes	Yes	Yes
Tanzania *(2005)*	Yes	Yes[6,7]	Yes	Yes	Yes
Uganda *(2002)*	Yes	No[8]	Yes	Yes	Yes
Zambia *(2005)*	Yes	Yes[9,10]	Yes	Yes	No[11]
Zimbabwe *(2002)*	Yes	No[12]	Yes	Yes	Yes
Percentage (n=19 countries)	**47%**	**21%**	**47%**	**47%**	**42%**

[1] Mandatory for all until 2008; [2] Public interest entities, companies with turnover in excess of Pula 10 million and total assets in excess of Pula 5 million; [3] Mandatory until 2008; [4] Mandatory for all until 2011; [5] Companies with turnover in excess of Mauritius Rupees 200 million; [6] Mandatory for all until 2009; [7] Entities that have essential public responsibility or provide essential public service and entities with 100 or more employees or with capital investment in non-current assets above TShs. 800 million; [8] Mandatory until 2009; [9] Mandatory for all until 2010; [10] Public interest entities; [11] All except small entities with turnover of less than Kwacha 20 billion; [12] Mandatory until 2010.

VOL = Voluntary adoption; MAND = Mandatory adoption; IND = Adoption in the individual financial statements; CONS = Adoption in the consolidated financial statements; ALL = Adoption for all domestic private firms.

Table 3-20: Characteristics of Full IFRS adoption in Africa

The first of the two above described groups of Full IFRS adopters can be labeled **'mandatory for some'** Full IFRS adopters. Accordingly, this group constitutes the **'voluntary for some'** IFRS for SMEs adopters. Botswana, Mauritius, Tanzania, and Zambia offer only smaller domestic private firms the option to adopt the IFRS for SMEs instead of Full IFRS. For example, Tanzania allows IFRS for SMEs adoption by all private firms except entities that have essential public responsibility or provide essential public service and entities with 100 or more employees or with capital investment in non-current assets above

TShs. 800 million (Table 3-21). In comparison, Kenya, Namibia, South Africa, Uganda, and Zimbabwe are **'voluntary for all'** Full IFRS and IFRS for SMEs adopters.

Contrary to the above listed African countries that have adopted a two standard system based on Full IFRS and IFRS for SMEs, Ghana, Nigeria, and Mozambique have adopted the IFRS for SMEs, but not Full IFRS (anymore). While **Ghana** replaced the mandatory use of Full IFRS into a mandatory use of IFRS for SMEs by all domestic private firms in 2013, **Nigeria** substituted its local version of Full IFRS by the IFRS for SMEs and has made the standard obligatory for all domestic private firms except for micro entities from 2014 onwards (*IFRS Foundation* (2014m), p. 5). Ghana and Nigeria are the only sampled African **'mandatory for all'** IFRS for SMEs adopters as **Mozambique** requires only smaller private firms (i.e. companies with turnover below Metical 500,000) to adopt the IFRS for SMEs and mandates all other entities to follow a local version of Full IFRS.

In summary, twelve out of the 19 sampled African countries (63%) have adopted IFRS for SMEs by 2014. While three jurisdictions require the use of the IFRS for SMEs by all or some domestic private firms, the great majority of countries allow local private firms to choose between the IFRS for SMEs and Full IFRS. Regardless of the differences in the type of adoption and certain restrictions regarding the eligible entities, the IFRS for SMEs is applicable both in the individual and consolidated financial statements in all adopting countries.

IFRS for SMEs adopters (12) *(date of adoption)*	**VOL**	**MAND**	**IND**	**CONS**	**ALL**
Botswana *(2009)*	Yes	No	Yes	Yes	No[1]
Ghana *(2013)*	No	Yes	Yes	Yes	Yes
Kenya *(2009)*	Yes	No	Yes	Yes	Yes
Mauritius *(2012)*	Yes	No	Yes	Yes	No[2]
Mozambique *(2011)*	No	Yes	Yes	Yes	No[3]
Namibia *(2010)*	Yes	No	Yes	Yes	Yes
Nigeria *(2014)*	No	Yes	Yes	Yes	Yes
South Africa *(2009)*	Yes	No	Yes	Yes	Yes
Tanzania *(2010)*	Yes	No	Yes	Yes	No[4]
Uganda *(2010)*	Yes	No	Yes	Yes	Yes
Zambia *(2011)*	Yes	No	Yes	Yes	No[5]
Zimbabwe *(2011)*	Yes	No	Yes	Yes	Yes
Percentage (n=19 countries)	**47%**	**16%**	**63%**	**63%**	**37%**

[1] All except public interest entities, companies with turnover in excess of Pula 10 million and total assets in excess of Pula 5 million; [2] All except companies with turnover in excess of Mauritius Rupees 200 million or less than Mauritius Rupees 50 million; [3] All except companies with turnover in excess of Metical 500,000; [4] All except entities that have essential public responsibility or provide essential public service and entities with 100 or more employees or with capital investment in non-current assets above TShs. 800 million; [5] All except public interest entities and small entities with turnover of less than Kwacha 20 billion.

VOL = Voluntary adoption; MAND = Mandatory adoption; IND = Adoption in the individual financial statements; CONS = Adoption in the consolidated financial statements; ALL = Adoption for all domestic private firms.

Table 3-21: Characteristics of IFRS for SMEs adoption in Africa

As Full IFRS and IFRS for SMEs have already been adopted by most Southern African countries in the field of private firms, plans for future adoptions are limited to the North and Northwestern African region. In **Tunisia**, for instance, the official reporting basis is Tunisian GAAP (for listed and non-listed companies). The Tunisian accounting principles and their conceptual framework are similar to those of Full IFRS. The standards are basically inspired by Full IFRS, however, not by the current version but by IAS applicable in 1995. The adoption of Full IFRS in Tunisia has been discussed over the last years and transition was planned for 2014. As Tunisia is currently in a period of political transition, there is uncertainty about when convergence will be realized.[142]

Moreover, IFRS for SMEs adoption is under consideration in **Egypt** and **Morocco**. The Egyptian Society of Accountants and Auditors has recently developed an exposure draft of a proposed Egyptian Accounting Standard for SMEs. The exposure draft is based on the IFRS for SMEs but is expected to propose several differences, including modifications in the areas of leases and distribution of profits to employees. However, the effective date for implementation has not yet been fixed.[143]

3.2.7 Middle East

Bahrain	Iraq	Jordan	Lebanon	Saudi Arabia
Iran	Israel	Kuwait	Oman	United Arab Emirates

Table 3-22: Sampled countries from the Middle East

3.2.7.1 Time series analysis

Countries from the Middle East are known for their economic diversity. While some countries are among the world's resource-richest (e.g. Kuwait, Saudi Arabia), others are particularly resource-scarce (e.g. Jordan, Lebanon). Furthermore, Middle Eastern countries differ strongly from Western countries in terms of culture, religion, and business customs (*Abd El Razik* (2009), p. 1). Despite these differences, the financial reporting and accounting practices in Middle Eastern countries have been influenced by **Anglo-American accounting concepts**. In Iran, for example, financial reporting has been shaped by Anglo-American practices since the late 1970s (*Mashayekhi/Mashayekh* (2008), p. 79). Financial reporting in Jordan was influenced by the educational background of accountants, who received their accounting education in the United States or in the United Kingdom (*Al-Akra et al.* (2009), p. 168). One reason for the strong Anglo-American influence on financial reporting in the Middle East is the absence of national accounting standards in the majority of Middle Eastern countries. For example, there was never a Local GAAP in Oman and the United Arab Emirates (*Abd El Razik* (2009), p. 1). In Saudi Arabia, local accounting standards were criticized for their insufficiency, ambiguity, and overall weakness by accountants, auditors, and academics in the 1990s (*Al-Hussaini et al.* (2008), p. 54).

---

[142] This information was provided by *Grant Thornton* and *PwC*.

[143] This information was provided by *Grant Thornton* and *PwC*.

Figure 3-21 reveals that there was only one jurisdiction among the ten sampled Middle Eastern countries (Saudi Arabia) that still had its own Local GAAP by 2002, whereas the majority of countries (60%) had already adopted **'pure' Full IFRS** (F) in the field of private firms at that time. The remaining four sampled countries provided accounting standards that had at least been partially converged with Full IFRS (FL2) by 2002. Among others, Iran has employed Full IFRS as the basis for developing national accounting standards, but some differences still remain (*Mashayekhi/Mashayekh* (2008), p. 66). The financial reporting for private firms in the Middle East had been **strongly internationalized** even before the IASB became operational in 2002. For this reason, there had been only a few changes in the Middle Eastern financial reporting landscape until the IFRS for SMEs was issued in 2009.

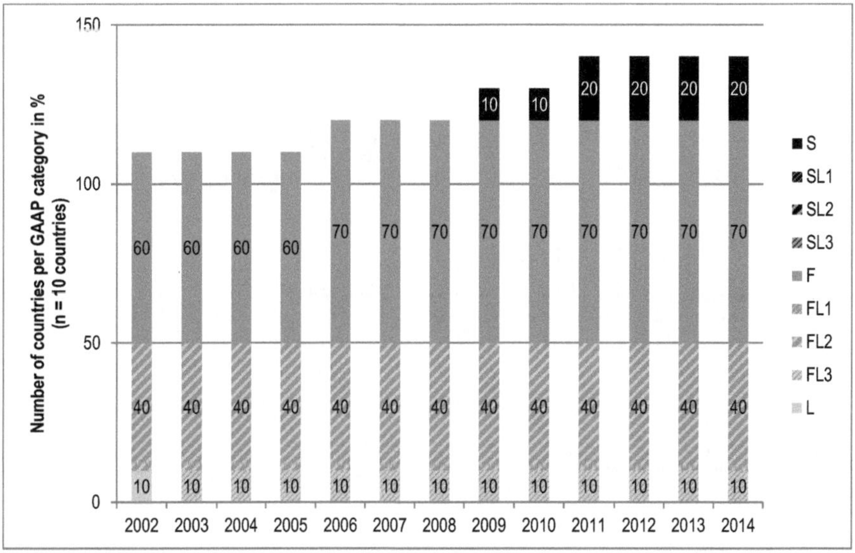

Figure 3-21: Distribution of GAAP categories in the Middle East

By 2014, two sampled Middle Eastern countries (Israel, Lebanon) have adopted the IFRS for SMEs and several others (e.g. Bahrain, United Arab Emirates) are close to adoption. It is expected that IFRS for SMEs adoption will largely be a **process of complementation** rather than substitution in most Middle Eastern countries. For example, Lebanon and Israel adopted the IFRS for SMEs as an additional accounting option for private firms in 2009 (2011), so that local private entities can choose between Full IFRS and IFRS for SMEs.

Compliance with Full IFRS was priorly regarded as an actual **challenge** in the Middle Eastern region (*Irvine* (2008), p. 137; *Abd El Razik* (2009), p. 4). Hence, particularly smaller and less developed countries such as Lebanon were given the advice to relax the financial reporting regulations for private firms by introducing a simplified reporting framework more adapted to their size (*World Bank* (2003b), p. 12). Due to the issuance of the IFRS for SMEs, several Middle Eastern countries (e.g. Jordan and Oman) are expected to change their financial reporting system from a one to a **two standard system** based on Full IFRS and IFRS for SMEs in the following years (*IFRS Foundation* (2014l), p. 4; *IFRS Foundation* (2014n), p. 4). This development will lead to a significant increase in the total number of legitimate GAAPs per country.

Although most of the Middle Eastern countries in the sample have adopted Full IFRS in the field of private firms by 2014, the overall quality of financial reporting and the general level of transparency vary significantly. While Saudi Arabia can be regarded as a country with traditionally strong accounting institutions (*Nexia International* (1993), p. 295), Jordan was criticized by the World Bank for the **lack of enforcement mechanisms** and the poor quality of corporate financial reporting (*World Bank* (2004d), p. 13). In 2014, financial statements of private firms are made publicly available in only one sampled Middle Eastern country (Bahrain). However, the financial statements are not uploaded to an online-registry.[144]

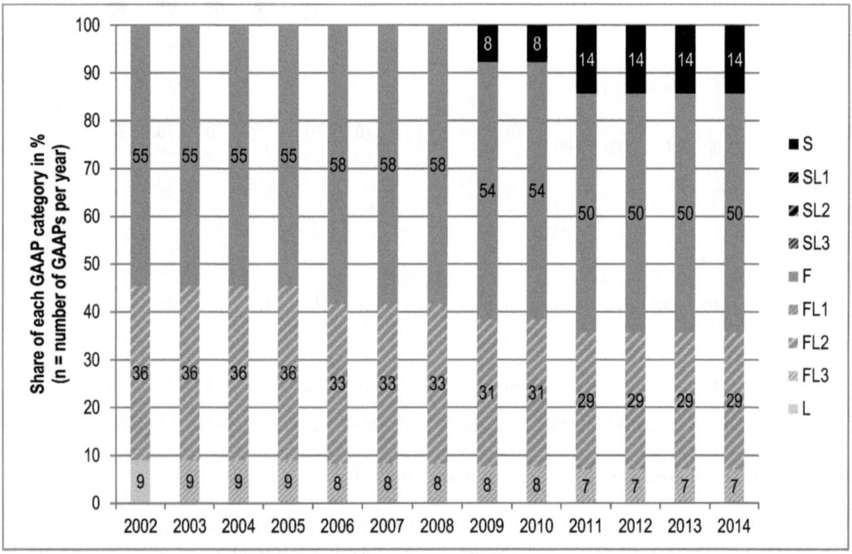

Figure 3-22: Share of each GAAP category in the Middle East

Figure 3-22 shows the development of the five existing GAAP categories' respective share in the total number of GAAP categories in the countries from the Middle East between 2002 and 2014. Although the **proportions have not changed significantly** over the years, the figure shows the high percentages of 'pure' IASB standards (F & S), which have not been modified by any national standard-setter. Due to the growing adoption of IFRS for SMEs, the total share of 'pure' IASB standards rose from 55% in 2002 to 64% in 2014 (50% Full IFRS and 14% IFRS for SMEs). Compared to the early 2000s, the coun-

[144] This information was provided by *Grant Thornton* and *PwC*.

tries from the Middle East have developed their standards further towards 'pure' versions of Full IFRS and IFRS for SMEs and this process is likely to continue in the future.[145]

As Figure 3-23 illustrates, **little variation** can be observed **in the type and scope** of Full IFRS and IFRS for SMEs adoption in the Middle East since 2002. All of the seven (two) sampled Full IFRS (IFRS for SMEs) adopters have adopted the IASB standards also in the individual financial statements and for all domestic private firms, regardless of legal form or firm size. The number of mandatory Full IFRS adopters fell slightly, from six to five, in the year the IFRS for SMEs was issued (2009). Due to the complementary status of the IFRS for SMEs, no sampled country has yet decided to require domestic private firms to adopt the IFRS for SMEs.

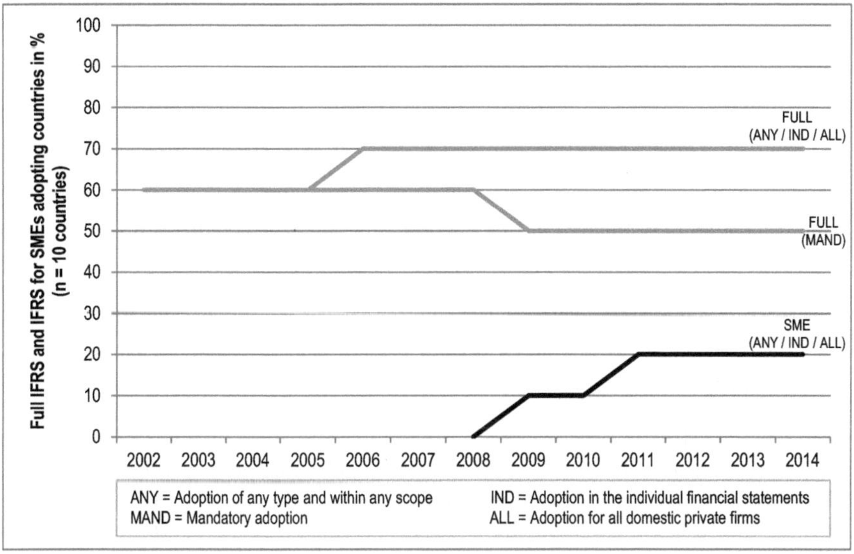

Figure 3-23: Full IFRS and IFRS for SMEs adoption in the Middle East

The following cross-sectional analysis will describe Full IFRS and IFRS for SMEs adoption in the Middle East in 2014 on a country-by-country basis.

3.2.7.2 Cross-sectional analysis

The seven Full IFRS adopters from the Middle Eastern sample can be divided into two separate groups. First, **Bahrain**, **Jordan**, **Kuwait**, and **Oman** still provide only one financial reporting system for all local private firms and hence prefer a one standard system based on mandatory Full IFRS adoption (see Table 3-23). All of these four countries did never develop their own national accounting standards and have looked after IASC and IASB standards since 2002 or earlier (e.g. *Al-Akra et al.* (2009), p. 180).

[145] Cf. Table A-9 for a summary of the classification of GAAP for private firms in the countries from the *Middle East*.

Full IFRS adopters (7) *(date of adoption)*	VOL	MAND	IND	CONS	ALL
Bahrain *(2002)*	No	Yes	Yes	Yes	Yes
Israel *(2006)*	Yes	No	Yes	Yes	Yes
Jordan *(2002)*	No	Yes	Yes	Yes	Yes
Kuwait *(2002)*	No	Yes	Yes	Yes	Yes
Lebanon *(2002)*	Yes	No[1]	Yes	Yes	Yes
Oman *(2002)*	No	Yes	Yes	Yes	Yes
United Arab Emirates *(2002)*	Yes	Yes[2]	Yes	Yes	Yes
Percentage (n=10 countries)	**30%**	**50%**	**70%**	**70%**	**70%**
[1] Mandatory until 2008; [2] Regulated service entities.					
VOL = Voluntary adoption; MAND = Mandatory adoption; IND = Adoption in the individual financial statements; CONS = Adoption in the consolidated financial statements; ALL = Adoption for all domestic private firms.					

Table 3-23: Characteristics of Full IFRS adoption in the Middle East

In comparison, **Israel**, **Lebanon,** and the **United Arab Emirates** offer all or some domestic private firms the option to choose between Full IFRS and one or two other sets of accounting standards (IFRS for SMEs or local versions of Full IFRS). Lebanon switched from mandatory to voluntary Full IFRS adoption in 2009 and adopted IFRS for SMEs in the same year. Although the group of mandatory Full IFRS adopters is still slightly larger than the group of voluntary Full IFRS adopters, it is likely to shrink further if more countries decide to adopt IFRS for SMEs as their second set of accounting standards.

As Table 3-24 reveals, **Israel** and **Lebanon** are the only two sampled Middle Eastern countries that have already adopted the IFRS for SMEs. Both countries made the IASB standard applicable in the individual and consolidated financial statements of all domestic private firms and allow entities to choose from two or three, respectively, different sets of accounting standards (Full IFRS, IFRS for SMEs, and a local version of Full IFRS). The Israel Accounting Standards Board intends to reconsider the adoption of IFRS for SMEs after its first revision following the comprehensive review in 2014 (*IFRS Foundation* (2014h), p. 5).

IFRS for SMEs adopters (2) *(date of adoption)*	VOL	MAND	IND	CONS	ALL
Israel *(2011)*	Yes	No	Yes	Yes	Yes
Lebanon *(2009)*	Yes	No	Yes	Yes	Yes
Percentage (n=10 countries)	**20%**	**0%**	**20%**	**20%**	**20%**
VOL = Voluntary adoption; MAND = Mandatory adoption; IND = Adoption in the individual financial statements; CONS = Adoption in the consolidated financial statements; ALL = Adoption for all domestic private firms.					

Table 3-24: Characteristics of IFRS for SMEs adoption in the Middle East

In summary, the Full IFRS adoption rate is traditionally high in the Middle East, and IFRS for SMEs adoption is on the rise. Almost all Middle Eastern countries that have not yet adopted the IFRS for SMEs consider adopting the standard in the future. For example, IFRS for SMEs adoption is close to realization in **Bahrain**, **Iraq,** and the **United Ar-**

ab Emirates.[146] Among other countries, future IFRS for SMEs adoption is discussed in **Oman** (*IFRS Foundation* (2014n), p. 4). Since all private firms in Oman, other than micro entities, follow Full IFRS for statutory filings, managers and auditors of SMEs are under strong pressure to meet the filing criterion. IFRS for SMEs adoption could reduce the time spent for the preparation of financial statements. Accounting firms have already begun to provide IFRS for SMEs training programs in conjunction with the Chamber of Commerce, Ministry of Finance, Central Bank of Oman and the Capital Market Authority (*IFRS Foundation* (2014n), p. 4).

In **Saudi Arabia**, private firms are currently obliged to use accounting standards issued by the Saudi Organization for Certified Accountants (SOCPA). Under SOCPA's 'IFRS convergence plan' non-publicly accountable entities would be required to report under a modified version of the IFRS for SMEs (*IFRS Foundation* (2014j), p. 5).

3.2.8 Asia

Brunei	Indonesia	Malaysia	Russia	Thailand
China	Japan	Mongolia	Singapore	Uzbekistan
Hong Kong	Kazakhstan	Pakistan	Sri Lanka	Vietnam
India	Korea	Philippines	Taiwan	

Table 3-25: Sampled countries from Asia

3.2.8.1 Time series analysis

Company law, and through that the financial reporting regulation of private firms, have been **subject to various foreign influences** in a considerable number of Asian countries since the beginning of the 19th century. In particular, each country's former colonial links have shaped its regulatory environment for many years. In Northwest and Central Asia, local accounting systems mainly derived from the Soviet plan/chart-based system used to exercise central control over enterprises' assets and operations. For example, the Soviet macro-economic, rules-based government model can be considered to be the historic basis for the local accounting systems in Kazakhstan (*Tyrrall et al.* (2007), p. 87), and in Chinese accounting history financial reporting regulation was referred to as 'in tandem with Russia' from 1949 to 1957 (*Zhang/Lu* (2007), p. 198).

Apart from the **Soviet influence** on accounting systems in Northwest and Central Asia, particularly Southern and Southeastern Asian countries, many of them former British colonies, derived their corporate laws and accounting concepts from the **United Kingdom**. For example, Brunei, Malaysia, and Singapore once adopted a Companies Act modelled on the UK Companies Act 1948 and the Australian Uniform Companies Act 1961 (*Craig/Diga* (1996), p. 245) and thus derived their accounting standards from common law sources (*Ball et al.* (2003), p. 235). The same holds true for the Indian subcontinent with the former provinces of British India (*Ashraf/Ghani* (2005), p. 181). Besides these

[146] This information was provided by *Grant Thornton* and *PwC*.

two main spheres of foreign influences, the Asian countries' local accounting systems have also been shaped by US and Dutch (Indonesia),[147] French (Vietnam)[148], and German (Thailand)[149] accounting concepts as well as by the Islam (Malaysia)[150].

In conclusion, Asian countries' local accounting systems have **long-standing traditions** and have been shaped by each country's **colonial history** and regulatory preferences. Due to this heterogeneity and the fairly low level of economic integration, regional accounting harmonization was not seen as the preferred course of action in most parts of Asia (*Saudagaran/Diga* (2003), p. 259f.). Instead, several Asian countries have embarked on a process towards international accounting harmonization by gradually replacing prior accounting systems by IASC/IASB standards. For instance, *Gray* already suggested in 1984 that the Thai accounting standards would reflect significant IASC influences (*Gray et al.* (1984)).

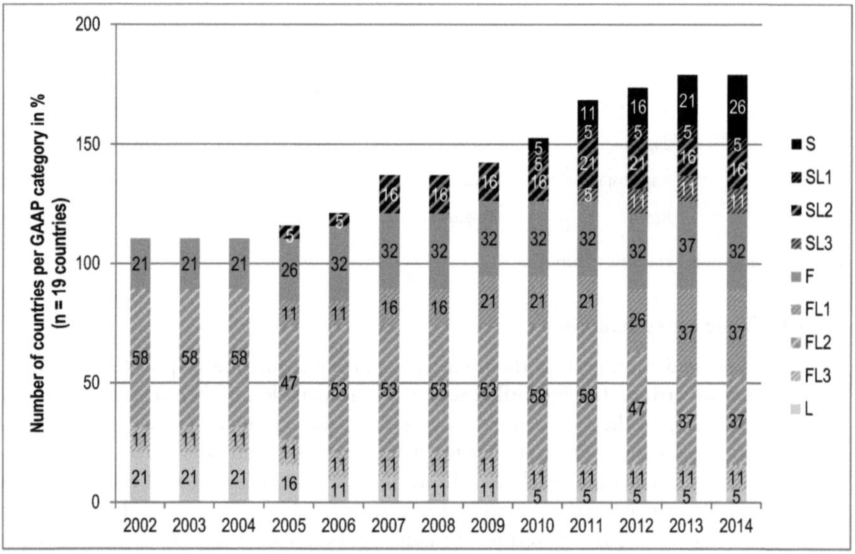

Figure 3-24: Distribution of GAAP categories in Asia

Analyzing the process towards Full IFRS and IFRS for SMEs adoption in the field of Asian private firms since 2002, Figure 3-24 illustrates that the number of Asian countries

[147] Cf. *Briston* (1978), p. 111, for the Dutch influence and *Ibarra/Suez-Sales* (2011), p. 49, for the US influence on the Indonesian accounting system.

[148] Vietnamese Accountancy was also influenced by the Soviet Union and the US. Cf. *Sarikas et al.* (2009), p. 184ff.

[149] The past Thai accounting system can be characterized as a mixed-country approach building on the British notion of 'true accounts' and elements of Japanese and German code law. Cf. *Craig/Diga* (1996), p. 245.

[150] Cf. *Nasir/Zainol* (2007), p. 269ff., for Malaysia's approach to the globalization of Sharia-compliant accounting standards.

that have Local GAAPs (L) or local versions of Full IFRS (FL2 & FL3) decreased from 2002 to 2014. While 58% of the sampled countries provided accounting systems, which were partly converged with Full IFRS (FL2) by the early 2000s, only 37% of the sampled Asian countries still have such local versions of Full IFRS in 2014. This is because almost half of the 19 sampled Asian countries have adopted Full IFRS either completely (F) or with minor modifications (FL1) from the year 2005 onwards (69% in total by 2014).

For example, Korean IFRS (K-IFRS), which are available for use by local private firms since 2009, are identical to Full IFRS except for some timing differences and certain requirements specific to Korea (*Standard & Poor's* (2011), p. 2). K-IFRS have replaced local Korean GAAP that had been influenced by IAS/IFRS since 2001.[151] Other examples of **stepwise Full IFRS adoption** in the field of private firms are Indonesia and Thailand, which had local versions of Full IFRS (FL2) until 2011/2012 and thereafter adopted Full IFRS with minor modifications (FL1).

More often than in other geographic regions, Asian countries introduced early simplified, **differential accounting standards for private firms**. In accordance with the recommendations made by the World Bank in the mid-2000s,[152] some Asian countries had even **modelled local standards on the IFRS for SMEs** before the IASB standard was issued in 2009. For example, Pakistan introduced the Accounting Financial Reporting Standards (AFRS) for Medium-Sized Entities (MSEs) and Small-Sized Entities (SSEs) in 2006 (*Dossa* (2013), p. 745). Both standards were materially influenced by the IFRS for SMEs project. One year earlier, Hong Kong had already adopted a simplified accounting standard, the Small and Medium-sized Entity Financial Reporting Framework and Financial Reporting Standard (SME-FRF&FRS) for smaller, non-publicly accountable entities (*Financial Standards Foundation* (2010), p. 2), in which it was referred to the respective draft version of the IFRS for SMEs.[153] After the IFRS for SMEs was published in 2009, China, Indonesia, and Thailand also considered the new IASB standard when developing simplified accounting standards for local private firms. For example, China used the IFRS for SMEs as a reference when developing the Chinese Accounting Standard for Small Entities (*IFRS Foundation* (2014s), p. 4).

Besides the adoption of local versions of the IFRS for SMEs (SL2 & SL3), six out of the 19 Asian countries (31%) have already adopted IFRS for SMEs completely (S) or with minor modifications (SL1) by 2014. Figure 3-24 shows that **complementary IFRS for SMEs adoption** has largely contributed to the increase in the number of GAAPs per country. In 2014, Asian private firms are provided with almost two different GAAPs on average.

Irrespective of the growing number of Asian Full IFRS and IFRS for SMEs adopters, more than half of the sampled Asian countries (53%) still provide either Local GAAP or

---

[151] This information was provided by *Grant Thornton* and *PwC*.

[152] Cf. *World Bank* (2007d), p. 24, for the corresponding recommendations to the Republic of Kazakhstan and *World Bank* (2008b), p. 24, for the case of Thailand. In 2011, the World Bank also held a workshop in Astana, Kazakhstan, to present the main features of the IFRS for SMEs. Cf. *World Bank* (2011b), p. 1.

[153] This information was provided by *Grant Thornton* and *PwC*.

local versions of Full IFRS (FL2 & FL3) to domestic private firms. Especially larger and more powerful jurisdictions (i.e. India, Japan, and Russia) seem to be among the most hesitant IFRS adopters on the Asian continent. Although the differences between the Indian accounting standards and Full IFRS have been narrowing (*Narayanaswamy* (2007), p. 255), Indian GAAP still deviates from Full IFRS fundamentally. The **main challenges** and issues concerning **IFRS convergence** in India are legal problems (*United Nations* (2008), p. 51), high costs of practical implementation and the reluctance to adopt the fair value approach (*Indapurkar et al.* (2009), p. 4).

In comparison, local accounting conventions (*Kikuya* (2001), p. 367) and the specific 'keiretsu' business model[154] are two possible reasons for the **delayed and uncompleted international harmonization** of Japanese accounting standards. Although the IASB and the Accounting Standards Board of Japan (ASBJ) signed the Tokyo Agreement in 2007 and agreed to eliminate major differences in their standards (*Wagenhofer* (2013), p. 257), the convergence process has slowed down since 2011 (*Japanese Institute of Certified Public Accountants* (2014)). In Russia, Full IFRS are mandatory for the consolidated financial statements of most publicly traded companies and financial institutions since 2012 (*IFRS Foundation* (2014o), p. 2). Regardless of that, Russian private firms are still required to prepare financial statements according to Russian GAAP, which is entirely independent from IASB influence. Accounting reforms in Russia have been described as *"slow"* (*Balchenko* (2001), p. 3) and *"haphazard"* (*Gethin* (2008), p. 25), which makes it difficult to anticipate any future steps of convergence towards IFRS.

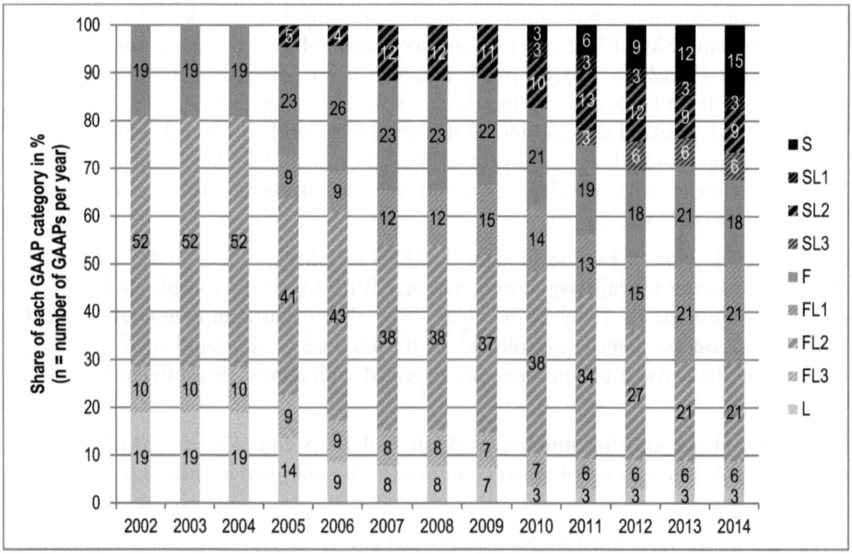

Figure 3-25: Share of each GAAP category in Asia

[154] The Japanese business system is unique, dominated by intertwining main banks with large industrial conglomerates (so-called *keiretsu*). Cf. *Koga/Rimmel* (2007), p. 218.

Figure 3-25 shows the development of each GAAP category's respective share in the 19 sampled Asian countries on average. By considering the total number of GAAPs per year, the figure shows the **gradual and steady shift** from local and localized accounting systems **towards Full IFRS and IFRS for SMEs adoption** in the field of private firms. In particular, local versions of Full IFRS (FL2) have been brought closer to the original IASB version (F) and do only include minor modifications (FL1) by now. Full IFRS (F & FL1) constitute almost 40% of all GAAPs in Asia in 2014 and more than 30% of all GAAPs are related to the IFRS for SMEs. Compared to the early 2000s, Asian countries have largely narrowed down the differences between their Local GAAPs for private firms and Full IFRS and IFRS for SMEs, but still retain certain deviations from the IASB standards.[155]

As Figure 3-26 illustrates, there were **two periods of accelerated Full IFRS adoption** in Asia: the first between 2004 and 2007 and the second during the years 2012 and 2013. On the contrary, mandatory Full IFRS adoption has stagnated since 2007. In comparison, a constantly growing number of Asian countries have adopted the IFRS for SMEs since 2010. The minor drop in the number of Full IFRS adopters from 2013 to 2014 might indicate first substitution effects resulting from widespread IFRS for SMEs adoption. In all Full IFRS and IFRS for SMEs adopting countries, the scope of adoption includes individual financial statements, however, only some of them adopt the IASB standards for all domestic private firms. This pattern points to the increasing differentiation of the Asian financial reporting regulation based on firm size.

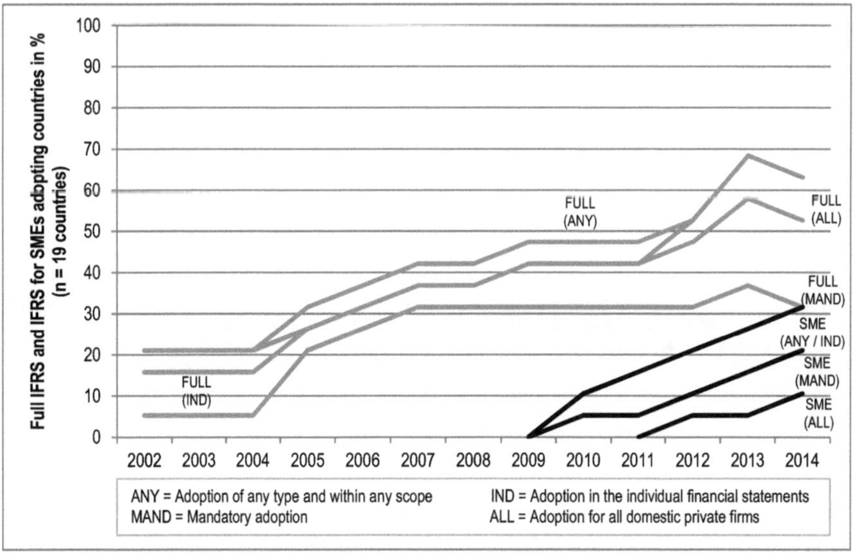

Figure 3-26: Full IFRS and IFRS for SMEs adoption in Asia

[155] Cf. Table A-10 for a summary of the classification of GAAP for private firms in *Asia*.

In Asia, the development towards Full IFRS and IFRS for SMEs adoption has been **more heterogeneous than in other regions**. Similarly, there are many differences between the national requirements regarding the publication of private firms' financial statements. In eleven out of the 19 sampled countries, all or at least some private firms' financial statements are made publicly available.[156] However, in only five of these eleven countries (Japan, Korea, Malaysia, Russia, and Singapore) the registered financial statements can be accessed online.[157]

The following cross-sectional analysis provides a country-by-country description of Full IFRS and IFRS for SMEs adoption in Asia in 2014.

3.2.8.2 Cross-sectional analysis

Twelve out of 19 sampled Asian countries (63%) have adopted Full IFRS in the field of private firms by 2014.

Full IFRS adopters (12) *(date of adoption)*	**VOL**	**MAND**	**IND**	**CONS**	**ALL**
Brunei *(2002)*	Yes	No	Yes	Yes	Yes
China *(2007)*	Yes	Yes[1]	Yes	Yes	Yes
Hong Kong *(2005)*	Yes	Yes[2]	Yes	Yes	Yes
Indonesia *(2012)*	Yes	No	Yes	Yes	Yes
Kazakhstan *(2006)*	Yes	Yes[3]	Yes	Yes	Yes
Korea *(2009)*	Yes	No	Yes	Yes	Yes
Malaysia *(2012)*	Yes	No	Yes	Yes	Yes
Pakistan *(2013)*	No	Yes	Yes	Yes	No[4]
Philippines *(2005)*	No	Yes	Yes	Yes	No[5]
Singapore *(2002/2005)*[6]	Yes	Yes[7,8]	Yes	Yes	Yes
Taiwan *(2013)*	Yes	No	Yes	Yes	Yes
Thailand *(2013)*	Yes	No	Yes	Yes	Yes
Percentage (n=19 countries)	**53%**	**32%**	**63%**	**63%**	**53%**

[1] Medium-sized and large companies; [2] Companies incorporated under Hong Kong Companies Ordinance unless they satisfy the criteria for using HKFRS for Private Entities (Hong Kong version of IFRS for SMEs) or SME-FRF&SME-FRS (locally developed standards for small entities); [3] Subsoil users and large business entities; [4] All except medium-sized entities (MSEs) and small-sized entities (SSEs) with turnover of less than Pakistan Rupees 1 billion, fewer than 750 employees, and total borrowings of less than Pakistan Rupees 500 million (i.e. only economically significant entities - ESEs); [5] All except entities with (consolidated) total assets of less than Pesos 350 million or (consolidated) total liabilities of less than Pesos 250 million (i.e. only economically significant entities); [6] IFRS since 2002, Singapore Financial Reporting Standards since 2005; [7] SFRS mandatory for all until 2010; [8] SFRS mandatory for companies that satisfy at least two of the three following criteria: total annual revenue of more than Singapore $ 10 million, total gross assets of more than Singapore $ 10 million, and total number of employees more than 50.

VOL = Voluntary adoption; MAND = Mandatory adoption; IND = Adoption in the individual financial statements; CONS = Adoption in the consolidated financial statements; ALL = Adoption for all domestic private firms.

Table 3-26: Characteristics of Full IFRS adoption in Asia

---

[156] Financial statements of all domestic private companies are generally made publicly available in India, Philippines, Russia, Singapore, Sri Lanka, and Thailand. The publication of financial statements is restricted to some private firms in Indonesia, Japan, Korea, Malaysia, and Pakistan.

[157] This information was provided by *Grant Thornton* and *PwC*.

As can be seen in Table 3-26, all of these twelve jurisdictions have adopted Full IFRS both in the individual and consolidated financial statements of domestic private firms. While most Southeast Asian Full IFRS adopters (**Brunei**, **Indonesia**, **Korea**, **Malaysia**, **Taiwan**, and **Thailand**) have made the use of Full IFRS voluntary for all local private firms, Full IFRS adopters from Central and South Asia rather require certain larger domestic private firms to use Full IFRS in their financial statements. For example, **China**, **Hong Kong**, and **Singapore** have made the use of Full IFRS mandatory for larger private firms and provide all other private companies with the option to choose between Full IFRS and other legitimate GAAPs (local versions of Full IFRS and IFRS for SMEs). In **Kazakhstan**, large business entities and subsoil users are obliged to prepare their financial statements according to Full IFRS while all other private firms are allowed to use national accounting standards that are based on the IFRS for SMEs. **Pakistan** and the **Philippines** are the only two countries in the Asian sample that restrict the use of Full IFRS to larger private companies, which are regarded as 'significant' for the national economy.

All other, non-economically significant, private entities in **Pakistan** and the **Philippines** are required to prepare their financial statements according to the IFRS for SMEs. Pakistan and the Philippines are two out of six IFRS for SMEs adopting countries in the Asian sample that have adopted the IFRS for SMEs in both the individual and consolidated financial statements of local private firms (see Table 3-27). While these two countries strictly divide domestic private firms into Full IFRS and IFRS for SMEs adopters and, therefore, do not provide any accounting system choices on firm level (segmentation of financial reporting requirements), **Hong Kong** and **Singapore** make smaller private firms choose between Full IFRS and IFRS for SMEs. In comparison, **Mongolia** and **Sri Lanka** have made IFRS for SMEs the only legitimate accounting system for all local private firms since 2014 and 2012, respectively.

IFRS for SMEs adopters (6) *(date of adoption)*	**VOL**	**MAND**	**IND**	**CONS**	**ALL**
Hong Kong *(2010)*	Yes	No	Yes	Yes	No[1]
Mongolia *(2014)*	No	Yes	Yes	Yes	Yes
Pakistan *(2013)*	No	Yes	Yes	Yes	No[2]
Philippines *(2010)*	No	Yes	Yes	Yes	No[3]
Singapore *(2011)*	Yes	No	Yes	Yes	No[4]
Sri Lanka *(2012)*	No	Yes	Yes	Yes	Yes
Percentage (n=19 countries)	**11%**	**21%**	**32%**	**32%**	**11%**

[1] All except companies with total annual revenue of more than Hong Kong $ 50 million, total assets of more than Hong Kong $ 50 million, and more than 50 employees; [2] All except economically significant entities (ESEs) with turnover of more than Pakistan Rupees 1 billion, more than 750 employees, and total borrowings of more than Pakistan Rupees 500 million; [3] All except economically significant entities with (consolidated) total assets of more than Pesos 350 million or (consolidated) total liabilities of more than Pesos 250 million and entities with total assets (liabilities) of less than Pesos 3 million; [4] All except companies that satisfy at least two of the three following criteria: total annual revenue of more than Singapore $ 10 million, total gross assets of more than Singapore $ 10 million, and total number of employees more than 50.

VOL = Voluntary adoption; MAND = Mandatory adoption; IND = Adoption in the individual financial statements; CONS = Adoption in the consolidated financial statements; ALL = Adoption for all domestic private firms.

Table 3-27: Characteristics of IFRS for SMEs adoption in Asia

In summary, Full IFRS (63%) is still twice as 'popular' as the IFRS for SMEs (32%) among Asian countries in 2014. Both the relatively large number of mandatory IFRS for SMEs adopters as well as the numerous limitations regarding the scope of IFRS for SMEs adoption for larger private companies indicate the strong segmentation and differentiation of the financial reporting requirements for Asian private firms. Although IFRS for SMEs adoption is on the rise in Asia, the new IASB standard is rather viewed as 'little GAAP for small firms' than as a full-value alternative to Full IFRS.

Future IFRS convergence plans exist, among others, in **India**. In a move towards convergence with Full IFRS, the Institute of Chartered Accountants of India (ICAI) started a process of developing a complete set of accounting standards that are converged with Full IFRS in 2007. The standards are known as Indian Accounting Standards (Ind AS) and should have been implemented since April 2011 (*IFRS Foundation* (2014u), p. 1). Although a series of Ind AS are already 'in force' in 2014, many modifications to Full IFRS remain and the implementation date has been postponed several times. Once enacted, Ind AS will be required to be followed by all listed and large private firms in India (*IFRS Foundation* (2014u), p. 1).

IFRS for SMEs adoption is under way in **Malaysia**. On 14 February 2014, the Malaysian Accounting Standards Board (MASB) issued a new set of accounting standards for local private entities, the Malaysian Private Entities Reporting Standard (MPERS). MPERS takes effect for financial statements with annual periods beginning on or after 1 January 2016. The MPERS is a word-for-word translation of the IFRS for SMEs except for some terminology changes and deviating requirements on income tax and property development activities (*IFRS Foundation* (2014p), p. 4). Furthermore, a study is in progress on the future adoption of IFRS for SMEs in **Thailand** (*IFRS Foundation* (2014q), p. 6). Besides, IFRS for SMEs adoption is discussed in **Kazakhstan** and **Russia** (*IFRS Foundation* (2014o), p. 5).

3.2.9 Australia & Oceania

Australia	Fiji	New Zealand

Table 3-28: Sampled countries from Australia & Oceania

3.2.9.1 Time series analysis

As members of the Commonwealth (Australia and New Zealand) or former colonies of the British Empire (Fiji), the three sampled countries from Oceania have traditionally tended to follow accounting principles adopted in the **United Kingdom** (*Nexia International* (1993), p. 31; 261). In New Zealand, for example, the Companies Act of 1955 included to a considerable extent accounting requirements of the UK Companies Act (*Nexia International* (1993), p. 261). Early accounting practices in smaller South Pacific Island nations such as Fiji were mostly imposed by the British colonial power and have subsequently been reinforced by the **trade relationships with Commonwealth countries** (*Chand/White* (2007), p. 612). Due to the fact that either UK standards were followed or the UK standards were modified slightly and have gradually been converged with IASC and IASB standards since the early 1970s, the three sampled Oceanic countries (Australia, New Zealand and Fiji) are considered as jurisdictions without Local GAAPs.[158]

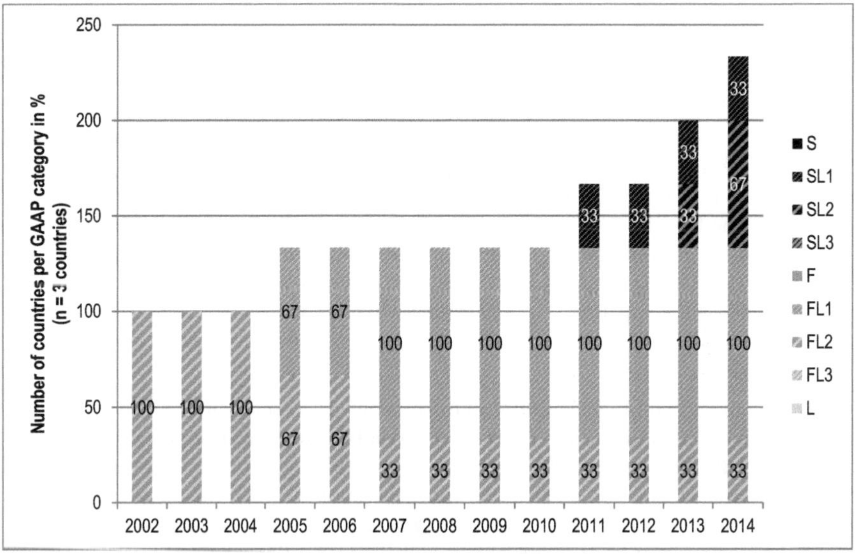

Figure 3-27: Distribution of GAAP categories in Australia and Oceania

In accordance with this view, Figure 3-27 shows that all three sampled countries had adopted **local versions of Full IFRS** (FL2) in the field of private firms by 2002. In Fiji, the Accounting and Auditing Standards Committee (AASC) had established the Fiji Accounting Standards (FAS) in 1971 and continued setting these standards until the late 1990s based on IAS/IFRS and the Australian and New Zealand accounting standards (*IFRS Adoption Research Group* (2014)). As many of the FAS were outdated, the Fiji Institute of Accountants (FIA) adopted Full IFRS selectively in 2002 and deferred the adoption of the remaining and new IFRSs to a later date (*Chand/Patel* (2008), p. 87). In comparison, the Australian Accounting Standards Board (AASB) also followed a gradual and selective IFRS harmonization strategy over several years. When the AASB considered certain provisions in IAS or IFRS appropriate and of sufficient quality, it included them in the Australian standards. However, where it considered that the existing AAS were superior to the international standards, it retained the Australian ones (*Picker* (2007), p. 99).

As one of the first countries in the South Pacific region, **New Zealand** developed a **differential reporting system** for local private firms in the early 2000s. In spite of having two different sets of accounting standards (one for listed and one for unlisted companies), legitimate New Zealand private firms (i.e. entities without public accountability) were provided with reporting concessions that were based on the Framework for Differential Reporting (DIFF) being issued in 1994 (*Samujh* (2007), p. 8). In comparison, financial re-

[158] Cf. Table A-11 for a summary of the classification of GAAP for private firms in *Australia & Oceania*.

porting requirements for Australian private companies were the same as for all 'reporting entities'[159] until 2010. In that year, the AASB released *AASB 1053 Application of Tiers of Australian Accounting Standards* to implement 'Stage 1' of its revised differential reporting regime (*Deloitte Touche Tohmatsu* (2014a), p. 1).

In response to the common decision of the European Union to adopt Full IFRS in the consolidated financial statements of publicly traded companies from 2005 onwards, Australia and New Zealand took the same step and voted for **Full IFRS adoption** from 2005 onwards.[160] While New Zealand kept its old accounting standards ('Old NZ GAAP'),[161] Australia replaced the prior standards completely by Full IFRS. It is important to note that unlike the European Union, Australia adopted Full IFRS for all domestic companies including all Australian reporting entities: private, public, listed, unlisted, corporate, and non-corporate. As a consequence, particularly smaller non-listed reporting entities, which were generally not competing in global capital markets and incurred relatively high compliance costs, called for deferral of Full IFRS adoption or even for complete relief (*Picker* (2007), p. 102).

Since Fiji adopted Full IFRS in 2007, all three sampled Oceanic countries have completely (Australia and Fiji) or partially (New Zealand) **substituted local versions of Full IFRS** (FL2) **by Full IFRS** in the field of private firms. Although none of the three Oceanic countries actually adopted Full IFRS 'as issued by the IASB' (F), the modifications were only of minor relevance (FL1). As **Australia's major concern** was that the **quality of financial reporting would decrease** due to Full IFRS adoption, the AASB decided to remove certain accounting policy options[162] from the IASB standards and to include additional mandatory disclosures without losing the conformity with Full IFRS. Similarly, there are some minor differences between NZ IFRS and Full IFRS due to different wording, fewer policy options, and additional disclosures.

Because of the **lacking differentiation of financial reporting requirements** and the large economic implications of Full IFRS adoption in the field of private firms, the IFRS for SMEs project was regarded as very important in the South Pacific region since the mid-2000s (*Institute of Chartered Accountants of New Zealand* (2004), p. 2). In 2011, Fiji was among the first Oceanic countries that adopted the IFRS for SMEs with minor modifications (SL1) as an alternative set of accounting standards in the field of local private firms.

[159] According to the Australian reporting entity concept reporting entities are *"entit[ies] in respect of which it is reasonable to expect the existence of users who rely on the entity's general purpose financial statement for information that will be useful to them for making and evaluating decisions about the allocation of resources. A reporting entity can be a single entity or a group comprising a parent and all of its subsidiaries."* (*Australian Accounting Standards Board* (2012), p. 55). Reporting requirements hence differ between reporting entities that prepare general purpose financial statements and non-reporting entities that prepare special purpose financial statements.

[160] In New Zealand, Full IFRS was adopted in 2007, but early adoption was allowed from 2005 onwards. Cf. *Cordery/Baskerville* (2006), p. 19.

[161] Cf. *Grant Thornton* (2011), p. 10, for an overview of the legitimate entities (mainly non-large companies) that are still allowed to follow 'Old NZ GAAP'.

[162] For example, the AASB initially prohibited the 'corridor approach' option in IAS 19 Employee Benefits. Cf. *Picker* (2007), p. 102.

Differences to the original IFRS for SMEs are mainly in relation to disclosures and policy notes. Although IFRS for SMEs adoption was regarded as desirable by several stakeholders in Australia and New Zealand,[163] both countries have taken different steps towards international accounting harmonization.

By 2014, Australia and New Zealand have developed similar concepts of differential reporting requirements in the field of private firms, which rely on a **one standard system** (Full IFRS) but include **reduced disclosure requirements** (RDR) for certain legitimate private firms. This concept's particularity is that the RDR are essentially the same as the mandatory disclosures in the IFRS for SMEs (*Australian Accounting Standards Board* (2010), p. 6; *IFRS Foundation* (2014i), p. 6). In conclusion, this second tier of Australian and New Zealand financial reporting provisions is defined as a local version of the IFRS for SMEs (SL2). By introducing a two-tier financial reporting system, the AASB's primary goal was to reduce the burden of financial reporting for those non-publicly accountable entities, which had previously been required to apply Full IFRS in the preparation of general purpose financial statements (*Australian Accounting Standards Board* (2010), BC19). As Figure 3-27 reveals, the **complementary adoption** of both the **IFRS for SMEs** as well as **IFRS for SMEs-based accounting standards** has led to an increase in the average number of GAAPs per country from one in 2002 to nearly two and a half in 2014.

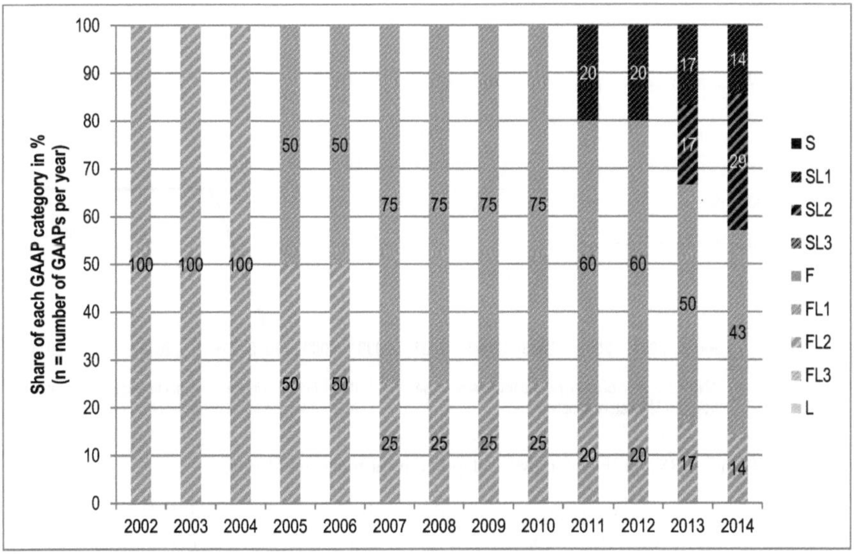

Figure 3-28: Share of each GAAP category in Australia and Oceania

Compared to the early 2000s, when each of the three sampled Oceanic countries provided one localized set of IASB standards to domestic private firms, the financial reporting land-

[163] Cf. *Australian Government's Department of Finance and Administration* (2004) for Australia and *Walker* (2004) for New Zealand.

scape has become much **more diversified** today due to the adoption of Full IFRS and IFRS for SMEs and the introduction of differential reporting requirements that are based on both sets of IASB standards (see Figure 3-28). In 2014, only large private companies are required to publish their financial statements in Australia and New Zealand. Fiji does not prescribe any local private firms to make their financial statements publicly available.[164]

Figure 3-29 illustrates the process of Full IFRS and IFRS for SMEs adoption in the South Pacific region and thereby displays the **type and scope of adoption** in Australia, New Zealand, and Fiji since 2002. The figure reveals that all three sampled Oceanic countries have also adopted Full IFRS in the individual financial statements since 2005 or 2007, respectively, and that one of the three countries has mandatorily adopted IFRS for SMEs for some domestic private firms since 2011. In comparison, two out of the three jurisdictions have required at least some private firms to prepare their individual financial statements under Full IFRS since 2007.

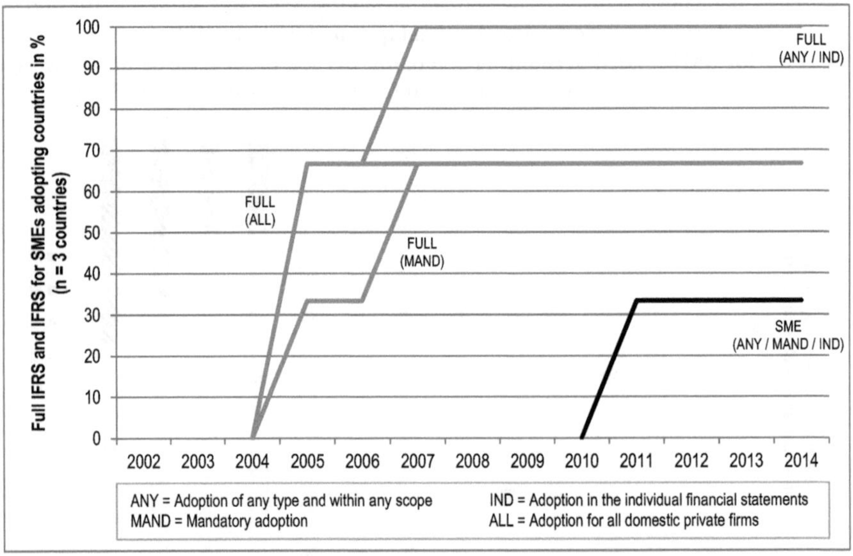

Figure 3-29: Full IFRS and IFRS for SMEs adoption in Australia and Oceania

The following cross-sectional analysis reveals the characteristics of Full IFRS and IFRS for SMEs adoption in Australia & Oceania in 2014 on a country-by-country basis.

3.2.9.2 Cross-sectional analysis

As the time series analysis has shown, Australia, New Zealand, and Fiji have all adopted Full IFRS in the individual and consolidated financial statements of local private firms by

164 This information was provided by *Grant Thornton* and *PwC*.

2014. While **Australia** has made the use of the IASB standards voluntary for all domestic private entities, **New Zealand** requires subsidiaries and branches of overseas companies to prepare their financial statements in accordance with Full IFRS. All other New Zealand private entities can choose to adopt the IASB standards on a voluntary basis. **Fiji** is the only jurisdiction from the Oceanic sample that restricts the use of Full IFRS to large private companies. Table 3-29 reveals that these are private entities with turnover of more than Fiji $ 20 million and with assets above Fiji $ 20 million.

Full IFRS adopters (3) *(date of adoption)*	**VOL**	**MAND**	**IND**	**CONS**	**ALL**
Australia *(2005)*	Yes	No	Yes	Yes	Yes
Fiji *(2007)*	No	Yes[1]	Yes	Yes	No[2]
New Zealand *(2005)*	Yes	Yes[3]	Yes	Yes	Yes
Percentage (n=3 countries)	**67%**	**67%**	**100%**	**100%**	**67%**

[1] Mandatory for all until 2010; [2] All except entities with annual group turnover of less than Fiji $ 20 million or with assets of less than Fiji $ 20 million; [3] Overseas companies that have subsidiaries and branches carrying on business in New Zealand.

VOL = Voluntary adoption; MAND = Mandatory adoption; IND = Adoption in the individual financial statements; CONS = Adoption in the consolidated financial statements; ALL = Adoption for all domestic private firms.

Table 3-29: Characteristics of Full IFRS adoption in Australia and Oceania

While Australia and New Zealand have still not adopted the IFRS for SMEs, Fiji requires the use of the IASB standard by all private entities except for those that have to prepare their financial statements under Full IFRS. Fiji hence divides its financial reporting framework for private firms into two different segments: mandatory Full IFRS adopters and mandatory IFRS for SMEs adopters (see Table 3-30).

IFRS for SMEs adopters (1) *(date of adoption)*	**VOL**	**MAND**	**IND**	**CONS**	**ALL**
Fiji *(2011)*	No	Yes	Yes	Yes	No[1]
Percentage (n=3 countries)	**0%**	**33%**	**33%**	**33%**	**0%**

[1] All except entities with annual group turnover of more than Fiji $ 20 million and with assets of more than Fiji $ 20 million.

VOL = Voluntary adoption; MAND = Mandatory adoption; IND = Adoption in the individual financial statements; CONS = Adoption in the consolidated financial statements; ALL = Adoption for all domestic private firms.

Table 3-30: Characteristics of IFRS for SMEs adoption in Australia and Oceania

In **Australia**, the **opinions on future IFRS for SMEs adoption are mixed**. While many constituents of the AASB support the reduction in disclosure requirements, they have concerns about introducing recognition and measurement principles that differ from those included in Full IFRS (*Australian Accounting Standards Board* (2010), BC67). As the AASB had already raised major concerns that Full IFRS adoption could possibly harm the high quality of financial reporting in Australia, it is not surprising that the adoption of the IFRS for SMEs has been seen, so far, even more as a 'retrograde step' (*Australian Accounting Standards Board* (2010), BC73(g)). Although the AASB continues to monitor the IFRS for SMEs for potential adoption in Australia (*IFRS Foundation* (2014k), p. 5), it has determined that the IFRS for SMEs is still not suitable as a second tier of financial reporting requirements in the Australian context (*Meade* (2012), p. 3).

3.3 Discussion

The subsequent discussion of the above presented empirical results is divided into the two analyses that have priorly been carried out separately for each of the nine macro-geographic regions: the **time series** and **cross-sectional analysis**. First, the findings from the time series analyses are aggregated to a global perspective on the process towards Full IFRS and IFRS for SMEs adoption in the field of private firms since 2002. In the following, general trends of Full IFRS and IFRS for SMEs adoption are identified and it is discussed in how far these trends differ across countries and continents. The second section summarizes the empirical evidence that was drawn from the cross-sectional analyses and displays the degree of worldwide variation in the type and scope of Full IFRS and IFRS for SMEs adoption in the field of private firms in 2014.[165]

3.3.1 Time series analysis

The region-specific analysis of the process towards Full IFRS and IFRS for SMEs adoption in the field of private firms has shown that each jurisdiction has its own **historical and institutional background** that affects, among other factors, the development and shape of today's financial reporting regulation for local private firms. While countries from the European Union and North America generally have a long history of Local GAAP and strong accounting traditions (e.g. Germany and the United Kingdom), African countries and countries from the Middle East hardly ever developed their own accounting rules but rather adopted foreign GAAP or IAS/IFRS for local financial reporting purposes. In Africa, the Middle East and other parts of the world (e.g. Asia and Oceania), Anglo-Saxon accounting concepts have spread widely due to the age of colonization, international trade and the continuing existence of the British Commonwealth.

In 2002, the year the IASB started operations, only one third (35%) of all countries worldwide (38 of the 110 sampled countries) still provided domestic private firms with accounting rules that were entirely independent from IASB standards (L). The majority of countries had already converged their Local GAAPs with Full IFRS to a small (7%) or medium (40%) extent or had already adopted Full IFRS with or without minor modifications (20%). While this state of **early convergence with IFRS** could have been expected in the field of listed companies, it is a surprising observation in the field of private firms. It confirms the view that although IAS and IFRS have initially been designed for the accounting of large listed multinationals, the standards had already had a strong impact on the development of domestic financial reporting rules for private firms by the early 2000s. In 2002, each jurisdiction roughly provided one single accounting system to all domestic private firms, which was frequently based on Full IFRS, however, rarely free of local modifications (see Figure 3-30).

[165] In addition, data on Full IFRS adoptions by 2008 are used as reference points.

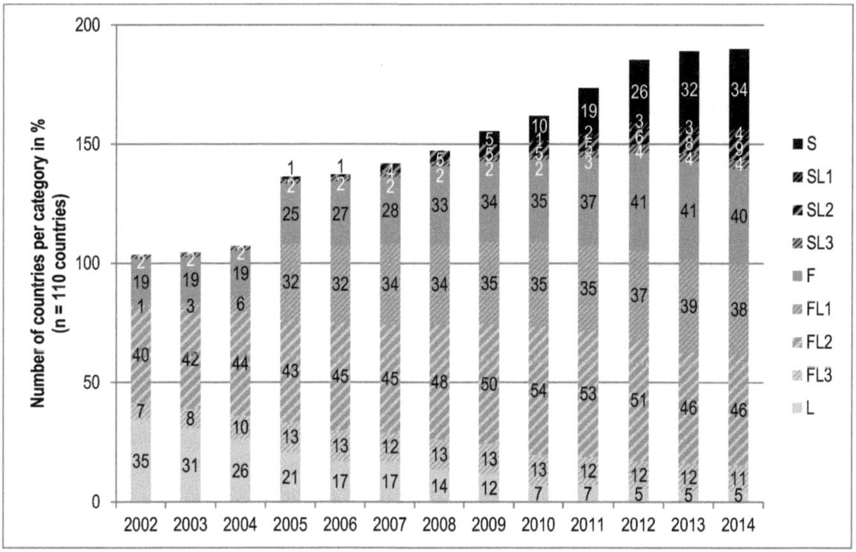

Figure 3-30: Worldwide distribution of GAAP categories

During the last decade, the remaining **Local GAAPs gradually ceased to exist**. Until 2014, the percentage of countries with Local GAAPs has decreased to only 5%. This development has mainly been caused by two different trends in global financial reporting: (1) gradual convergence of local accounting systems with Full IFRS and (2) Full IFRS and IFRS for SMEs adoption. Despite the fact that 'full adoption' of IASB standards has become more and more common during the past decade, Figure 3-30 reveals that in 2014, **local versions of Full IFRS** (FL2) still represent the largest category of GAAPs in the field of private firms. Such FL2-GAAPs are implemented in almost every second country worldwide (46%). In particular, more than half of the EU countries (54%) provide those local versions of Full IFRS (FL2) to domestic private firms, and approximately one out of three EU countries (32%) have adopted accounting standards that comply with Full IFRS only in a few areas (FL3). Similarly, local versions of Full IFRS also persist in North America and in more than half of the sampled Southeastern European, North, and Northwest African countries.

Ever since 2005, the year in which all EU countries adopted Full IFRS also in the field of private firms, Full IFRS have become the predominant accounting system worldwide. By 2014, almost 80% of all sampled countries have adopted Full IFRS either word for word (40%) or with minor modifications (38%). In all geographic regions except for North America and the European Union, Full IFRS adoption has gone along with **GAAP substitution**. For example, countries from Southern Africa and the Middle East substituted foreign GAAP (mainly UK and US GAAP) by Full IFRS already in the early 2000s.[166]

[166] Most countries from the Middle East had already adopted IAS in the field of private firms during the 1990s.

Similarly, several countries from Central America and the Caribbean were among the earliest Full IFRS adopters in the field of private firms when adopting the standards in the early and mid-2000s. In comparison, South American countries did not replace their Local GAAPs and local versions of Full IFRS by 'pure' IASB standards until 2008. While the EU countries, Australia, and New Zealand jointly adopted Full IFRS almost at the same time (2005-2007), Full IFRS adoption has gradually spread over Asia and Southeast Europe over the past ten years.

Cross-national differences in the characteristics of Full IFRS adoption also exist regarding the **minor modifications** that have been made by jurisdictions over the course of adoption. While all sampled Central American and Caribbean countries and the large majority of Southeast European, Southern African, and Middle Eastern Full IFRS adopters have implemented Full IFRS word for word (F), EU-IFRS and Australian IFRS – although being defined as Full IFRS in this study (FL1) – are two out of several local versions of Full IFRS that deviate slightly from the original IASB version. These minor deviations, which do not generally lead to non-compliance with Full IFRS, mainly result from lagged adoption or endorsement (e.g. European Union) and from the addition of local requirements (mainly disclosures, e.g. in Australia and New Zealand).

It is important to note that there is **no global consensus** on when a national regulator refers to a local version of IFRS as **'IFRS'**. On the one hand, both financial statement preparers and users have to be aware of the fact that several country-specific deviations from IFRS may exist although the standards are still labeled 'IFRS'. Vice versa, certain jurisdictions would not say that they have 'adopted' IFRS although their domestic accounting standards have been converged substantially with IASB standards. For this reason, this study differentiates local versions of IFRS from 'pure' IFRS in great detail and thus provides a new insight into the **degree of Full IFRS and IFRS for SMEs adoptions** in the field of private firms worldwide.

Besides the process of Local GAAP's substitution by Full IFRS, the time series analysis also demonstrates a global trend of **GAAP complementation**. For example, Canada, the United States, and several EU countries have adopted Full IFRS only as an additional accounting system for domestic private firms. Until 2014, Full IFRS have therefore complemented but not replaced Local GAAPs and local versions of Full IFRS in the field of private firms. As a consequence, these local versions of Full IFRS are still in place besides IASB standards. This finding is relevant for the IASB as it raises doubts about the de facto adoption of Full IFRS in the field of private firms. Even though US and EU private firms are allowed to use Full IFRS for financial reporting purposes since 2008 and 2005, respectively, little is known about the actual number of Full IFRS adopting private companies.

As long as US resident listed firms are not permitted to report under Full IFRS, the adoption rate among US private firms is likely to remain insignificant (*American Institute of Certified Public Accountants* (2011)). In comparison, empirical evidence from Europe shows that a considerable number of German non-publicly traded, parent companies (18%) use the option to prepare consolidated financial statements according to EU-IFRS

(*Eierle/Haller* (2010), p. 9).[167] The worldwide empirical evidence on GAAP complementation that is provided in this study adds to prior research that has already predicted the emergence of a **'two standard system'** in the European Union (*Street/Larson* (2004)). While in the European context the two standard systems are the result of the coexistence of EU-IFRS and local versions of Full IFRS, this study reveals a global trend towards two standard systems that result from parallel Full IFRS and IFRS for SMEs adoption.

Except for North and Northwest Africa as well as some parts of the Middle East, where local versions of Full IFRS still remain the only accounting system in place, in almost all regions worldwide the **total number of GAAPs per country has almost doubled** in the field of private firms since 2002 (see Figure 3-30). To a large extent, this is due to the complementary adoption of the IFRS for SMEs. Many countries from Africa, Central America, and the Caribbean rapidly adopted the new IASB standard after its issuance in July 2009. A few years later, the IFRS for SMEs has also become quite popular in South America, Southeast Europe, and large parts of Asia. By 2014, almost 40% of all sampled jurisdictions have adopted 'pure' IFRS for SMEs (34%) or IFRS for SMEs with minor modifications (4%). In all but a few cases (e.g. Chile, Ghana, Nigeria), IFRS for SMEs adoption has been a process of GAAP complementation and not substitution. While in 2005 the first global increase in the number of GAAPs per country was largely driven by the complementary adoption of Full IFRS in the European Union, the subsequent increase has clearly been related to worldwide IFRS for SMEs adoption.

Some jurisdictions have not adopted the IFRS for SMEs but have taken the standard as a benchmark when developing their own differential accounting standards for domestic private firms. For example, Asian countries (e.g. Hong Kong, Indonesia), Australia, New Zealand, as well as a few members of the European Union (e.g. Estonia, Sweden, United Kingdom) have based or plan to base domestic accounting standards on the IFRS for SMEs. By 2014, more than every tenth country worldwide (13%) has developed such **local versions of IFRS for SMEs**.

The trends of stepwise GAAP convergence with Full IFRS and complementary adoption of Full IFRS and IFRS for SMEs in the field of private firms are also reflected in the development of each GAAP category's respective share in the 110 sampled countries on average. Hence, Figure 3-31 reveals the fundamental changes the global financial reporting landscape was subject to during the years 2002-2014.

First, Figure 3-31 illustrates the **vanishing share of Local GAAPs** that has decreased from one third (33%) in 2002 to almost nothing in 2014 (2%). Secondly, local versions of Full IFRS (FL2) still have the highest share of all single GAAP categories worldwide in 2014 (24%) although their share has decreased by 15 percentage points since 2002. In accounting terms, the FL2-GAAP category can be described as an 'item in transit'. On the one hand, its share has increased during the past decade due to the gradual convergence of Local GAAPs with Full IFRS. On the other hand, this increase was overcompensated by

---

167 The disproportionally stratified random sampling included 4,000 German non-publicly traded companies with a turnover of more than € 10 mill. In total, 322 surveys were completed (8.1%). 248 of these 322 companies prepared consolidated financial statements. Among these 248 entities, there were 45 companies that used EU-IFRS. Cf. *Eierle/Haller* (2010), p. 4f.

the completion of Full IFRS convergence processes, which has led to its substitution by Full IFRS and IFRS for SMEs.

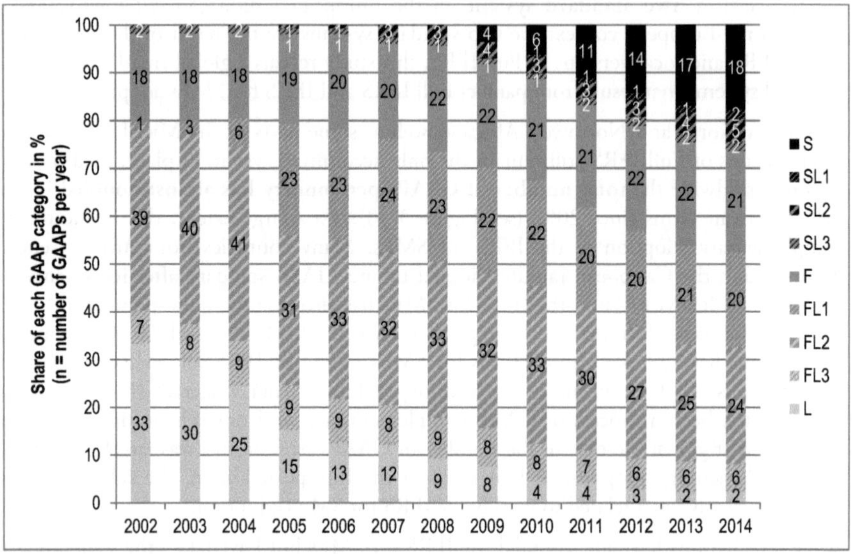

Figure 3-31: Worldwide share of each GAAP category

Although **more and more countries have adopted Full IFRS 'as issued by the IASB'**, the share of the F-GAAPs remains stable at about 20% during all years. This is because the FL1-category, representing Full IFRS with minor modifications (since 2005 mainly EU-IFRS), makes up for another 20% of all GAAPs. In summary, the two Full IFRS categories combine more than 40% of all applicable GAAPs worldwide. The complementary adoption of the IFRS for SMEs has further increased the total number of GAAPs per country and thus reduced the shares of all other GAAPs. In 2014, one out of five GAAPs (20%) is IFRS for SMEs (including S & SL1) and another 7% of all GAAPs worldwide are at least IFRS for SMEs-related (sum of SL2 & SL3).

Compared to the early 2000s, domestic accounting systems in the field of private firms have become **significantly more international**, either through stepwise convergence with Full IFRS or due to Full IFRS and IFRS for SMEs adoption. In 2014, almost 60% of all accounting systems worldwide are 'IFRS', either with (22%) or without (39%) minor modifications. The remaining 40% of GAAPs combine local accounting systems that have been converged with Full IFRS (30%) or IFRS for SMEs (7%) to a differing extent.

These findings contribute to prior empirical research that has already detected cross-national variation in the degree of domestic accounting standards' level of compliance with Full IFRS in the 1980s and 1990s (e.g. *Doupnik* (1987); *Purvis et al.* (1991); *Larson/Kenny* (1999)). More importantly, this research reveals that although the gap between Local GAAPs and Full IFRS has been narrowed down during the past decade and a large number of countries has either adopted Full IFRS or IFRS for SMEs in the field of private firms, many local versions of Full IFRS still **lack compliance with Full IFRS**. In summary, almost half of the sampled countries (46%) still provide such local versions of Full IFRS (FL2) to domestic private firms in 2014. These results are in accordance with *Andersen et al.* (2001), who benchmarked national accounting systems against IAS in 62 countries by 2001 and stated that there would still be approximately 30 countries with major differences from IAS but with no indication of proposed changes. It seems that these countries have meanwhile adopted Full IFRS and/or IFRS for SMEs as an additional accounting system in the field of private firms, however, have not yet abandoned their national accounting systems.

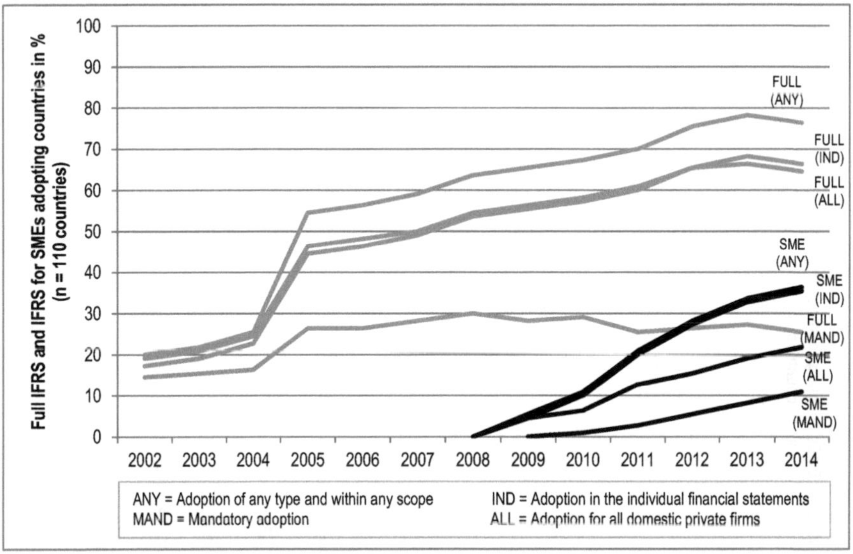

Figure 3-32: Worldwide Full IFRS and IFRS for SMEs adoption

By combining the GAAP categories F & FL1 to 'FULL' as well as S & SL1 to 'SME', Figure 3-32 illustrates the process and the characteristics of Full IFRS and IFRS for SMEs adoption in the 110 sampled countries during the years 2002-2014. It allows for a differentiation between Full IFRS and IFRS for SMEs adopters on the basis of the type and scope of adoption. First, Figure 3-32 reveals that more than three out of four countries (76%) have adopted Full IFRS in the field of private firms by 2014.

In 2005, the number of Full IFRS adopting countries suddenly doubled due to **Full IFRS adoption in the European Union**. The year 2005 also represents the point in time when jurisdictions began to restrict the use of Full IFRS either to the consolidated financial statements or to certain types of private firms. Hence, the number of countries that have adopted Full IFRS also in the individual financial statements (66%) and for all domestic private firms (65%) is considerably smaller than the overall number of Full IFRS adopters by 2014.

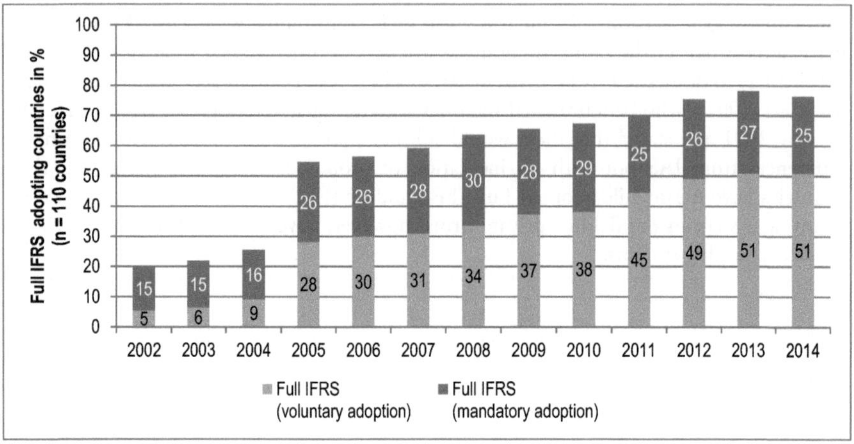

Figure 3-33: Worldwide voluntary and mandatory Full IFRS adoption

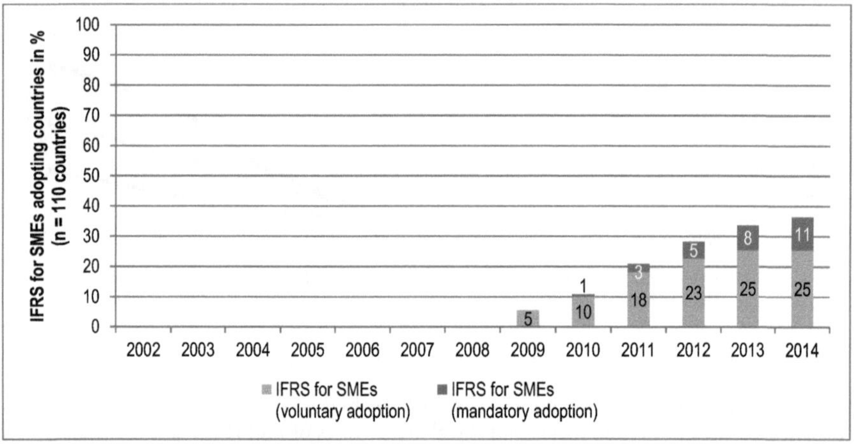

Figure 3-34: Worldwide voluntary and mandatory IFRS for SMEs adoption

In contrast to the increasing number of Full IFRS adopters, the significantly smaller and unaltered number of **mandatory Full IFRS adopters** amounts to approximately 25% since 2005. While three out of four countries, which adopted Full IFRS prior to 2005, required all or some domestic private firms to use Full IFRS for financial reporting purposes, two out of three Full IFRS adopters allow domestic private firms to choose between two or more sets of accounting standards in 2014 (see Figure 3-33).

This change has mainly been caused by voluntary Full IFRS adoption in the European Union and increasing IFRS for SMEs adoption. While 36% of all sampled countries worldwide have adopted IFRS for SMEs by 2014, less than one third (11%) have required local private firms to use the new IASB standard (see Figure 3-34). All other countries still allow private firms to use Full IFRS or local accounting systems for financial reporting purposes.

While almost every seventh Full IFRS adopting country (13%) has limited the use of Full IFRS to the consolidated financial statements of private firms by 2014, Switzerland is the only IFRS for SMEs adopter that does not allow domestic private firms to prepare individual financial statements according to the IFRS for SMEs. Vice versa, more than every third IFRS for SMEs adopting country (39%) has **restricted the use of IFRS for SMEs to smaller entities**, whereas Full IFRS adoption has been limited to larger private companies or to economically significant entities in some cases (e.g. Macedonia, Philippines, and Zambia).

These findings are in accordance with the observation that parallel adoption of Full IFRS and IFRS for SMEs has led to an increasing differentiation of local financial reporting regulation for private firms. In the majority of countries, which have adopted Full IFRS and IFRS for SMEs, all domestic private firms are allowed to prepare their financial statements according to Full IFRS but the use of IFRS for SMEs is restricted to smaller entities that meet certain size criteria (**differentiation**). In comparison, only a few countries (e.g. Peru, Pakistan) require domestic private firms to adopt either of the two sets of standards (**segmentation**). In some countries (e.g. Macedonia) the preparation of consolidated financial statements makes parent companies being categorized as large and thus results in an obligation to use Full IFRS.

In accordance with the research propositions *P1a* & *P1b*, the empirical evidence presented in the time series analysis (2002-2014) indicates **significant variation in the process towards Full IFRS and IFRS for SMEs adoption** across countries. Compared to the rapid and complete adoption of Full IFRS in the field of listed companies, the 'road to' Full IFRS and IFRS for SMEs adoption in the field of private firms has been full of bends and junctions. It remains to be seen in how far the IFRS for SMEs will further gain in importance so that the 'smaller brother' (IFRS for SMEs) might eventually rule out the 'bigger brother' (Full IFRS) in the private firms' financial reporting arena. Until today, there is only little evidence that supports this prediction.

3.3.2 Cross-sectional analysis

While the time series analysis has focused on the global process towards Full IFRS and IFRS for SMEs adoption since 2002, the cross-sectional analysis reveals cross-regional variation in the type and scope of Full IFRS and IFRS for SMEs adoption in 2014. For example, Figure 3-35 illustrates that the overall Full IFRS (76%) and IFRS for SMEs (36%) **adoption rates vary significantly between different geographic regions.**[168] Data from 2008 serves as a reference point for 'early' Full IFRS adoptions at a time IFRS for SMEs did not yet exist. Besides, the time period between 2002 and 2008 almost exactly corresponds to the time that has passed since the issuance of the IFRS for SMEs in 2009.

[168] Full IFRS and IFRS for SMEs adoption rates are displayed for seven macro-geographic regions. The EU and Southeast Europe as well as Asia and the Middle East are pooled into one region each.

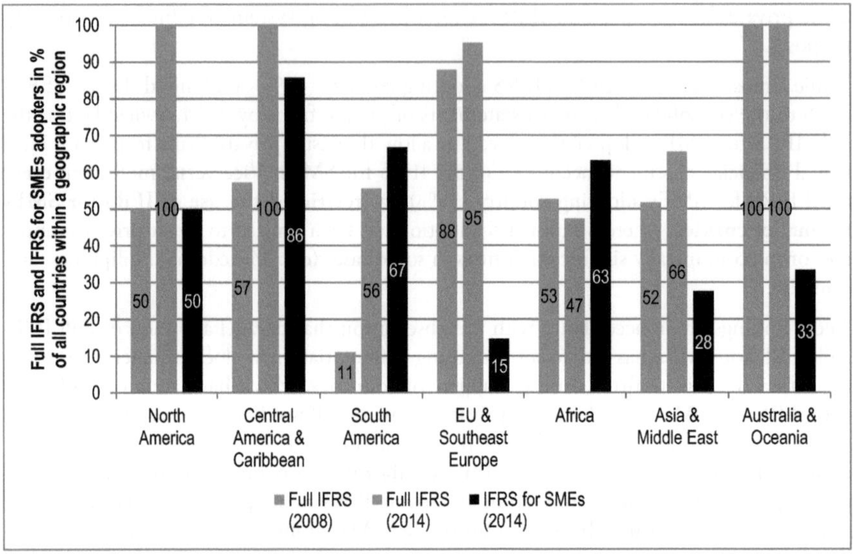

Figure 3-35: Full IFRS and IFRS for SMEs adoption per region

Figure 3-35 shows 100% Full IFRS adoption rates for North America, Central America & Caribbean as well as for Australia & Oceania in 2014. Moreover, Full IFRS have been adopted by almost all European countries (95%). On the contrary, only every second country from South America (56%) and Africa (47%) and not more than two out of three countries from Asia & Middle East (66%) have so far adopted Full IFRS in the field of domestic private firms. In comparison, **the distribution of IFRS for SMEs adopters** is quite the **opposite from the distribution of Full IFRS adopters.**

Apart from the highest IFRS for SMEs adoption rate, which is 86% for Central America & Caribbean, the IFRS for SMEs has been most frequently adopted in South America (67%) and Africa (63%), where it is applicable for private firms in more countries than Full IFRS by 2014. The lowest IFRS for SMEs adoption rate by far has Europe (15%), which is due to the **non-adoption of the IFRS for SMEs in the European Union.** Comparing the IFRS for SMEs adoption rates from 2014 to those of Full IFRS by 2008, IFRS for SMEs adoption has spread much faster than Full IFRS adoption in South America, Africa, and CAC countries, whereas IFRS for SMEs adoption still lags behind Full IFRS adoption in Europe, Asia, and Oceania.

When narrowing down the group of Full IFRS and IFRS for SMEs adopters to countries that have required all or some domestic private firms to prepare their financial statements in accordance with one of the two IASB standards, the worldwide adoption rates change considerably (see Figure 3-36).

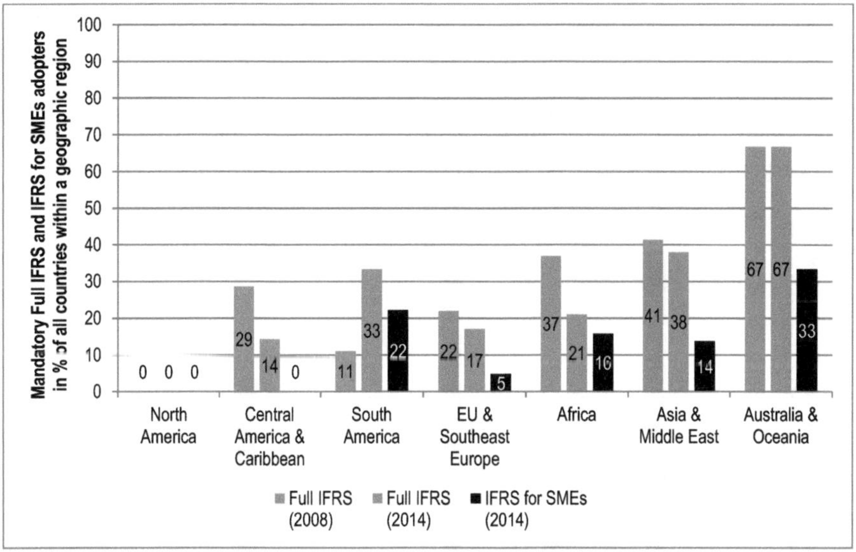

Figure 3-36: Mandatory Full IFRS and IFRS for SMEs adoption per region

As the **level of mandatory Full IFRS and IFRS for SMEs adoption** lies by far below the overall adoption rates, Figure 3-36 gives the impression that IASB standards have not been 'adopted' very often. The only relatively high Full IFRS and IFRS for SMEs adoption rates are now measured for Australia & Oceania although this is only due to the small sample of three countries. No country from North America (0%) and barely any country from the EU and Southeast Europe (5%) and Central America & Caribbean (14%) has mandatorily adopted Full IFRS by 2014. The number of mandatory Full IFRS adopters has even decreased in most regions since 2008, in particular in Central America & Caribbean (from 29% to 14%) and Africa (from 37% to 21%). While in North America and the European Union the low number of mandatory Full IFRS adopters can be explained by the persistence of national accounting systems, the drop of mandatory Full IFRS adopters in Central America & Caribbean and Africa has been caused by the widespread adoption of IFRS for SMEs since 2009.

When measuring the share of Full IFRS and IFRS for SMEs adopters not on the basis of the total number of countries within a geographic region but on the basis of their Gross Domestic Products (GDP), the **relative economic power of Full IFRS and IFRS for SMEs adopting countries** is revealed.

Figure 3-37 illustrates that (except for South America) Full IFRS adoption rates measured in GDP are almost the same as those measured on the basis of the number of Full IFRS adopting countries (comparing to Figure 3-35). This implies that Full IFRS have generally been adopted by countries with larger and smaller GDPs alike in the field of private firms. To the contrary, the percentages that represent IFRS for SMEs adopters have mostly become smaller, particularly in Central America & Caribbean (from 86% to 13%), Asia

& Middle East (from 28% to 5%) as well as in Australia & Oceania (from 33% to 0%).[169] This observation indicates that in these geographic regions the **IFRS for SMEs has rather been adopted by countries with smaller GDPs.** By contrast, the IFRS for SMEs has also been adopted by larger economies in Africa (e.g. South Africa) and South America (e.g. Brazil), as the GDP-based adoption rates are similar or even higher than those reported on the basis of the total number of countries (comparing to Figure 3-35).

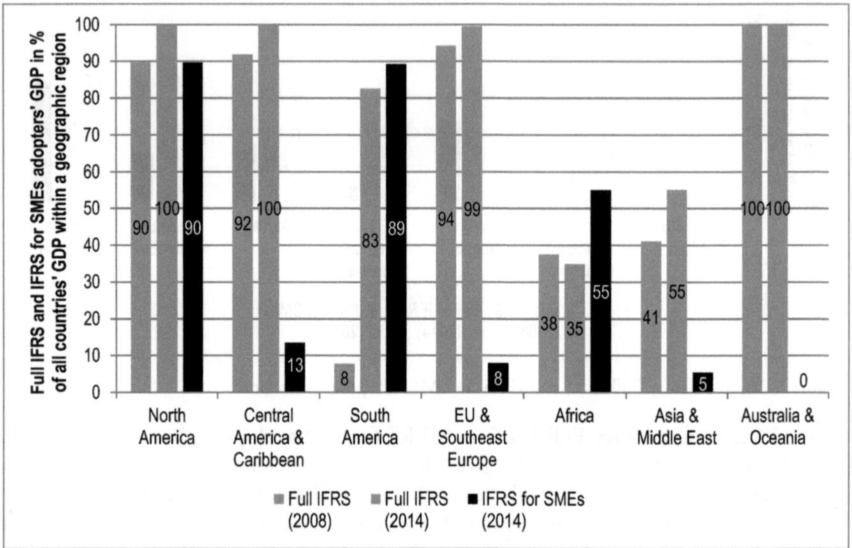

Figure 3-37: Full IFRS and IFRS for SMEs adoption (in GDP) per region

When measuring the share of mandatory Full IFRS and IFRS for SMEs adopters on the basis of their GDPs within a geographic region, the adoption rates shrink to insignificant numbers almost everywhere. Figure 3-38 emphasizes that **the world's largest economies** have so far **rarely adopted Full IFRS or IFRS for SMEs for mandatory use** in the field of private firms. The only exceptions are Brazil (South America) and China (Asia), which have required certain larger private firms to comply with Full IFRS. As far as IFRS for SMEs adoption is concerned, Chile, Peru (both South America), Nigeria (Africa), and the Philippines (Asia) are the only larger economies that have so far adopted IFRS for SMEs for mandatory use by local private firms.

[169] The GDP of Fiji is insignificant compared to the GDPs of Australia and New Zealand.

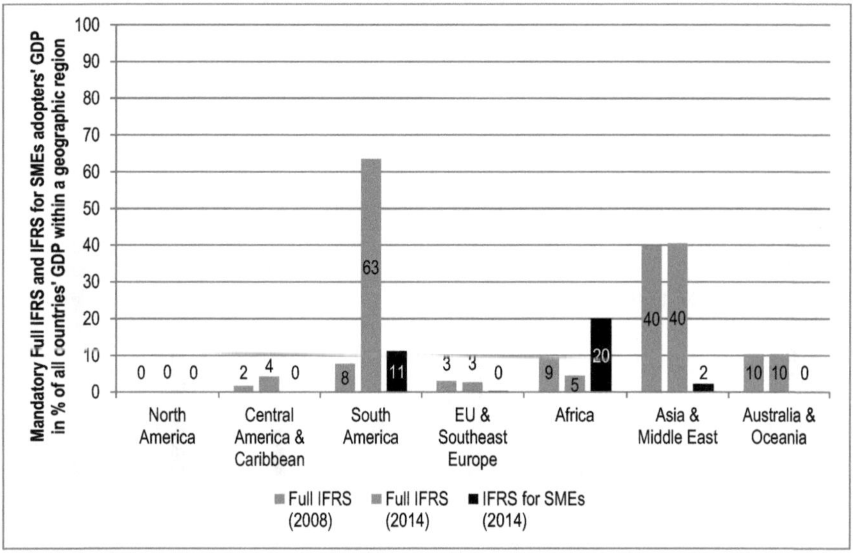

Figure 3-38: Mandatory Full IFRS and IFRS for SMEs adoption (in GDP) per region

In summary, the level of Full IFRS and IFRS for SMEs adoption in the field of private firms strongly depends on how 'adoption' is defined. While most countries have implemented the two sets of IASB standards only for voluntary use, mandatory adoption is still rare. This observation holds true for both Full IFRS and IFRS for SMEs and all geographic regions worldwide except for the South Pacific region and the Middle East. In these regions, at least half of the jurisdictions have required certain types of domestic private firms to prepare their financial statements according to Full IFRS.[170] In conclusion, the **extent of worldwide Full IFRS and IFRS for SMEs adoption** in the field of private firms is **high and low at the same time**. This leaves room for different interpretations, also regarding the overall success of the IASB in promoting their standards in the field of private firms.

The empirical evidence provided in this study is in accordance with the research propositions *P2a* & *P2b* that assume significant **variation in the type of Full IFRS and IFRS for SMEs adoption** in the field of private firms across countries. This study is the first to depict and describe in detail the cross-regional variation in the type of Full IFRS and IFRS for SMEs adoption in the field of private firms on a global scale. While the focus of the existing 'IFRS adoption summaries', such as those from Big4 audit firms (e.g. *PricewaterhouseCoopers* (2013); *Deloitte Touche Tohmatsu* (2014c)), has yet been on displaying characteristics of Full IFRS adoption in the field of listed companies, this study extends this field of descriptive research to the area of private firms and IFRS for SMEs adoption. Be-

[170] Cf. Table A-15 for all Full IFRS and IFRS for SMEs adoption rates referring to adoption of any type and within any scope (ANY) and mandatory adoption (MAND) in the nine identified geographic regions by 2008 and 2014.

sides, it does not merely summarize certain features of Full IFRS and IFRS for SMEs adoption country-by-country (*IFRS Foundation* (2014g)), but identifies transnational patterns.

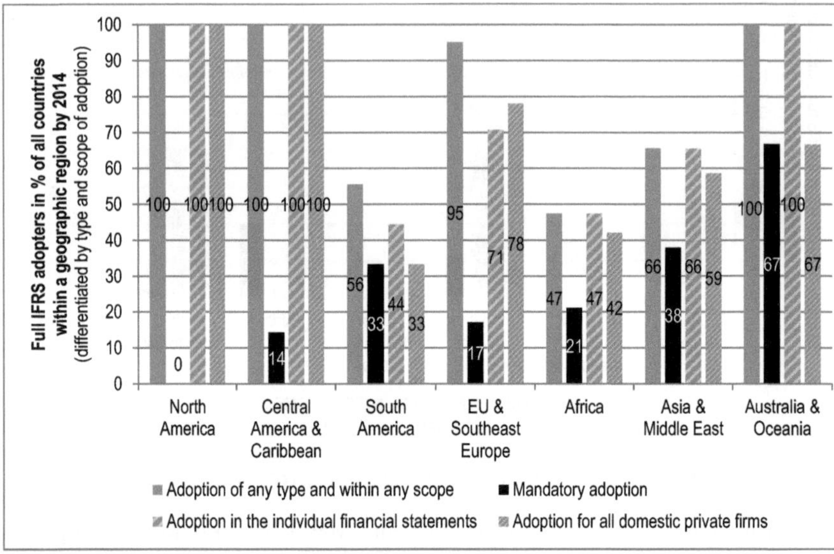

Figure 3-39: Types and scopes of Full IFRS adoption per region

As displayed in Figures 3-39 and 3-40, this research also reveals cross-regional variation in the scope of Full IFRS and IFRS for SMEs adoption in 2014. In the two figures, countries are only defined as Full IFRS and IFRS for SMEs adopters if they have adopted the IASB standards also in the individual financial statements and for all domestic private firms. Hence, the group of adopters is specified further on the basis of the scope of adoption.

Compared to the overall Full IFRS adoption rates, Figure 3-39 shows that the share of countries that have adopted Full IFRS also in the individual financial statements of domestic private firms by 2014 is significantly smaller in the European Union & Southeast Europe (71% instead of 95%). More precisely, the **restriction of Full IFRS adoption to the consolidated financial statements** of domestic private firms is a **Central European phenomenon**. With the exception of Argentina, which requires local companies to make certain modifications to Full IFRS if the standards are applied in the individual financial statements, Central European countries (e.g. France and Germany) are the only Full IFRS adopters worldwide that exclude individual financial statements from the scope of Full IFRS adoption. As far as the IFRS for SMEs is concerned, Switzerland is the only country worldwide that has adopted the IFRS for SMEs only in the consolidated financial statements of local private firms.

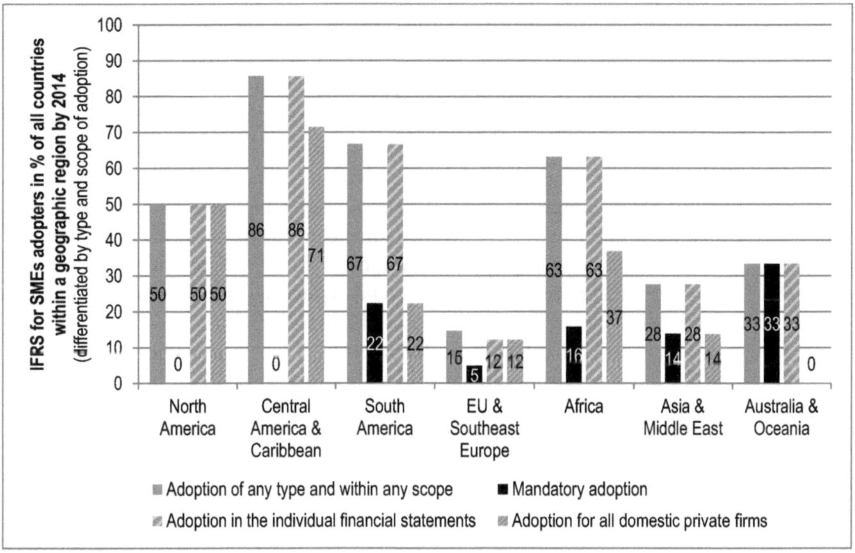

Figure 3-40: Types and scopes of IFRS for SMEs adoption per region

Much more common than limitations related to the individual financial statements of private companies are restrictions that are based on certain firm characteristics (e.g. size or affiliation to a group). In five (six) of the seven illustrated geographic regions, countries have restricted the use of Full IFRS (IFRS for SMEs) to certain priorly defined private companies. In the large majority of cases, the **differentiation** (or segmentation) of the local financial reporting regime is **based on size criteria.**

As Figure 3-39 displays, only one third (33%) of the sampled South American countries has adopted Full IFRS for all domestic private firms by 2014, whereas the overall adoption rate is 56%. This is due to the fact that Argentina and Peru have excluded smaller private firms (Peru) and private companies that are no subsidiaries of listed companies (Argentina) from Full IFRS adoption. Similarly, some countries from the European Union (e.g. Italy, Portugal), Southeast Europe (Croatia, Macedonia), Africa (Zambia), Asia (Pakistan, Philippines), and Oceania (Fiji) do **not allow smaller private firms to use Full IFRS** for financial reporting purposes. Vice versa, there are several IFRS for SMEs adopters in almost all geographic regions worldwide that have **restricted the use of IFRS for SMEs to small and medium-sized private companies** (see Figure 3-40). This development is most prevalent in South America, Africa, and Asia, where one half (Africa) to two thirds (South America, Asia) of the IFRS for SMEs adopters have limited the scope of adoption to smaller private firms.[171] Limitations in the scope of Full IFRS and IFRS for SMEs adoption can also go along with the persistence of localized accounting systems that

[171] Cf. Table A-16 for the Full IFRS and IFRS for SMEs adoption rates referring to adoption in the individual financial statements (IND) and adoption for all domestic private firms (ALL) in the nine geographic regions by 2008 and 2014.

are tailored for the special needs of small businesses and which remain despite worldwide IFRS for SMEs adoption (e.g. SME-FRF & SME-FRS in Hong Kong).

In accordance with the research propositions *P3a* & *P3b*, there is significant **variation in the scope of Full IFRS and IFRS for SMEs adoption** in the field of private firms across countries. While Central Europe is the only region where Full IFRS adoption is restricted to the consolidated financial statements of private firms, limitations in the scope of Full IFRS and IFRS for SMEs adoption based on size criteria can be observed worldwide except for North America and the Middle East. Gradual convergence towards Full IFRS, the persistence of localized accounting systems and IFRS for SMEs adoption have made **countries increasingly differentiate their financial reporting regulation** in the field of private firms. Either they clearly define mandatory financial reporting provisions (i.e. Full IFRS, IFRS for SMEs, or local IFRS) for different types of local companies or they introduce differential financial reporting standards (mostly based on IFRS for SMEs) for smaller private firms only and make Full IFRS applicable on a voluntary basis for all local companies. In view of these findings, this study contributes to prior research that has revealed differences in the scope of Full IFRS adoption by private firms in the European Union (*Street/Larson* (2004); *Sellhorn/Gornik-Tomaszewski* (2006)) and expands these findings by IFRS for SMEs adoption in a large global sample.

In January 2014, *Paul Pacter*, former member of the IASB and current director of the *IFRS Foundation's* study of IFRS use around the world, summarized the state of IFRS adoption in a CPA Journal article and highlighted **several questions**:

> *"Adoption of IFRS is not black or white (yes or no) – it is shades of gray. For example, is IFRS for listed companies only or unlisted as well? Is it only for some unlisted companies, such as financial institutions? Is it required or permitted? Is it for consolidated financial statements only or also for separate company statements? Is it for domestic listed companies only or foreign listed companies as well? Are IFRSs written into law? Is there some sort of endorsement process and, if so, is that done on a timely basis? Did the jurisdiction add any disclosures or other requirements? Did it make any modifications to IFRSs? Did it change the effective dates? Does the process for translating IFRSs from the original English ensure a faithful translation?"*
>
> (*Pacter* (2014), p. 6)

In line with *Pacter's* expectations, the descriptive research part in this study presents quite a bit of cross-regional variation regarding the *process* towards Full IFRS and IFRS for SMEs adoption as well as the *type* and *scope* of their adoption. Hence, it may provide some answers to the above questions, in particular regarding the shape of international accounting harmonization in the field of private firms.

Having discussed the empirical evidence on the worldwide characteristics of Full IFRS and IFRS for SMEs adoption in the field of private firms, the following chapter presents empirical evidence on the determining role of **net economic benefits**, **network effects**, and **political pressures** on countries' decisions to adopt either of the two sets of IASB standards in the field of private firms by 2008 and by 2014.

4 Determinants of Full IFRS and IFRS for SMEs adoption

4.1 Research design

This chapter comprises the following **three sub-studies**:

(1) determinants of Full IFRS adoption by 2008,

(2) determinants of Full IFRS adoption by 2014, and

(3) determinants of IFRS for SMEs adoption by 2014.

As the three sub-studies are based on the same sample of **110 countries** as the descriptive analysis in chapter three, primary data were obtained through the same e-mail-based survey sent to managing partners of *Grant Thornton* and *PwC*.[172] In addition, secondary data were obtained from the *World Economic Forum*, *Deloitte*, the *United Nations Statistics Division*, the *International Monetary Fund*, and the *World Bank*.

Before presenting the empirical results, the following two sections present the methodological approach that is applied to (1) describe the group of Full IFRS and IFRS for SMEs adopting and non-adopting countries by 2008 and by 2014 and to (2) empirically test the hypotheses, which have been derived from the *economic theory of networks* and the *institutional theory of isomorphism*, via multivariate logistic regression.

4.1.1 Descriptive analysis

In each of the three sub-studies, the sample is divided into two different groups of countries: **IFRS adopters** and **non-adopters**. Hence, the objective of the descriptive analysis is to identify differences between these two groups of countries in the **central tendency** of the collected data. To reveal these differences, the arithmetic mean is computed for all variables and for each of the adopter and non-adopter groups. In the following, the mean of the non-adopter group is deducted from the mean of the adopter group to illustrate mean differences. Besides, more descriptive statistics, including the median, the 25th and 75th percentile as well as the standard deviation, are provided to describe the data (see Tables A-17, A-18 and A-19). In summary, the descriptive analysis allows for a detailed description of every single explanatory variable (e.g. perceived quality of accounting standards) for each of the two groups. Furthermore, statistical inferences are applied to test whether the prevailing mean differences are likely to prevail for the underlying population.

For the metric variables, **parametric tests** (i.e. unpaired t-test) are conducted to examine differences between the parameters of central tendency and dispersion of the adopter and non-adopter group. Parametric tests such as the t-test generally require the variables to be normally distributed in the population (*Leonhart* (2013), p. 203). According to the central limit theorem, a variable is assumed to be normally distributed if the sample size exceeds roughly 30 observations (*Auer/Rottmann* (2012), p. 364).[173] As this is not the case

[172] Cf. section 3.1.1 for the sample selection procedure and the characteristics of the sample.

[173] The normality of the tested variables will not be tested separately if the number of observations available for the test exceeds 30 observations (i.e. countries per group).

for all of the twelve models, **non-parametric tests** (i.e. Wilcoxon Mann-Whitney rank-sum test) are performed instead to provide robust evidence on group differences.[174] Non-parametric tests base their inference statistics on ranked variables or the direction with which a variable varies from a certain value. Hence, non-parametric tests do not rely on an assumption about the distribution of the tested variable in the population under consideration (*Leonhart* (2013), p. 229).

Both parametric and non-parametric tests generally require the populations to have homogeneous variances with respect to the analyzed variable (homoscedasticity) (*Leonhart* (2013), p. 211ff.; *Kasuya* (2001), p. 1247). If a Levene test (*Levene* (1960)) detects **heteroscedasticity**, t-tests will be transformed into more robust parametric Welch tests (*Leonhart* (2013), p. 229). Accordingly, the non-parametric Wilcoxon Mann-Whitney rank-sum tests are substituted by Fligner-Policello rank order tests in case of heteroscedasticity (as suggested by *Siegel/Castellan* (1988), p. 137). Regarding the indicator variables (also categorical or nominally scaled variables), comparisons between the adopter and non-adopter groups are based on a Chi^2 distribution test, or, if fewer than five observations are present for each category in the Chi^2 table, they are based on the Fisher's exact test. For both parametric and non-parametric tests, the symbols *, **, and *** are applied to indicate whether an alternative hypothesis can be falsified at a **significance level** of 10 % (marginally significant), 5 % (significant), and 1 % (highly significant).

To provide further evidence on the differences between the characteristics of the Full IFRS and IFRS for SMEs adopter and non-adopter groups and with a view to the subsequent explanatory analysis, **bivariate correlations** between the independent and the dependent variable are investigated. Furthermore, the analysis includes bivariate correlations between the independent variables to test for **multicollinearity**. Correlations measure the strength and the direction between two constructs (*Auer/Rottmann* (2012), p. 92). There are two alternatives to express the correlation between two variables. While *Pearson's* correlation coefficients reveal linear interdependencies, *Spearman*'s rank correlation coefficients show monotonic interdependencies only. Both coefficients vary between minus one (negative association) and plus one (positive interdependency). The higher the absolute value of the coefficients, the stronger is the correlation. A value higher than 0.5 (0.8) indicates a medium (strong) correlation, whereas a value between 0.2 and 0.5 is regarded as a weak correlation (*Auer/Rottmann* (2012), p. 92ff.). Whether the correlation between the respective variables is statistically significant is assessed by interference statistics that indicate significance at the 10%, 5%, and 1% level.

As *Spearman's* rank coefficients illustrate how well an arbitrary monotonic function can describe a relationship between two variables without making any assumptions about the frequency distribution of the variables and without requiring the variables to be measured on metric scales (*Hauke/Kossowski* (2011)), the coefficients by *Spearman* will be applied in this study.

---

[174] Non-parametric tests are conducted for Models 5, 6, 10, and 12 as the number of (non-)adopting countries is below 30.

Although the above parameters provide a first insight into the mean differences between explanatory variables of the adopter and non-adopter groups as well as into the corresponding correlations between the dependent and independent variables, they cannot be used for hypotheses testing. For this reason, this study also applies multivariate logistic regression. The logistic regression model and the definition of the included variables are presented in the following section.

4.1.2 Explanatory analysis

4.1.2.1 Logistic regression model

Full IFRS and IFRS for SMEs adoption are indicator variables that take the value 1 if a country is considered an adopter and 0 if otherwise. Hence, multiple logistic regression (*UCLA Statistical Consulting Group* (2014c)) is applied to test whether the predefined independent variables are associated with an increase or decrease of the probability of Full IFRS and IFRS for SMEs adoption in the field of private firms. The chance that a country adopts Full IFRS (or IFRS for SMEs) can be described by the **odds ratio.** As Formula 4-1 displays, 'adoption odds' are calculated by the fraction of two probabilities: the probability of adoption and non-adoption (*Cohen* (2003), p. 492ff.).

$$Odds(Adopt = 1) = \frac{P(Adopt = 1)}{1 - P(Adopt = 1)}$$

Formula 4-1: Odds ratio

where:

P *is probability and*

Adopt *is any dependent variable measuring adoption.*

An odds ratio, which is greater (smaller) than one, reflects the factor by which an increase in the analyzed independent variable increases (decreases) the likelihood of Full IFRS (IFRS for SMEs) adoption. An odds ratio of one indicates the absence of any association between the two variables. For reasons of presentation and comparability, odds can be transformed into **logits,** which are the natural logarithms of odds. While odds lie between 0 and +∞, logits reach out from -∞ to +∞. Hence, they can express the direction of the relationship between an independent variable and the likelihood of Full IFRS (IFRS for SMEs) adoption. A positive logit means that there is a positive association, whereas a negative logit indicates a negative association (*Cohen* (2003), p. 492ff.). Formula 4-2 illustrates the corresponding logistic regression equation.

$$L_i = \beta_0 + \beta_1 x_{1i} + \beta_2 x_{2i} \ldots + \beta_k x_{ki}$$

Formula 4-2: Logistic regression equation

where:

L	*is the logarithmized estimated odds-ratio (logit),*
i	*indicates the number of observations (i=1,2,...N),*
x	*is any independent variable (n=k),*
β_0	*indicates the constant and*
$\beta_1 - \beta_k$	*are the regression coefficients.*

The logistic regression model (logit-model) assumes that the independent variables $x_1 - x_k$ have an influence on the logarithmized chance to have the value 1 as dependent variable. The objective of the logistic regression analysis is to estimate the unknown regression coefficients $\beta_1 - \beta_k$. The **maximum-likelihood-principle** is used to estimate the regression coefficients in a way that the proportions that have been observed become most probable (*Kohler/Kreuter* (2012), p. 334).

The overall **fit of the logistic regression models** can be evaluated by several different test statistics (*Lemeshow/Hosmer* (1982)). First, the overall percentage of correctly classified cases (**count R^2**, also 'area under the ROC curve') is calculated. This percentage can only be interpreted in relation to the overall proportion of adopters and non-adopters. Given that 70% of the sampled countries are in the adopter group (and 30% in the non-adopter group), a count R^2 of 70% would merely state that the model fits exactly as well as if all countries were estimated to be adopters. Hence, it would have no additional explanatory value.

Besides the count R^2, this study also determines the **McFadden's pseudo R^2**. As logistic regressions do not have an equivalent to the R^2 that is found in OLS (Ordinary Least Squares) regressions, there are a wide variety of pseudo-R-square statistics (*Cohen* (2003), p. 502). As these statistics do not mean exactly the same what R^2 means in OLS regressions (i.e. the proportion of variance explained by the predictors), pseudo-R-square statistics should be interpreted with caution (*UCLA Statistical Consulting Group* (2014b)).

The log likelihood ratio test (also **LR Chi² test**) is an omnibus test to see if the model as a whole is statistically significant (*UCLA Statistical Consulting Group* (2014a)). It provides additional evidence on the overall fit of the logistic regression model by testing its additional explanatory power compared to the null model (i.e. the constant only). More precisely, LR Chi² measures the difference between the deviance of the null model and the full model. The greater this difference, the more explanatory power the independent variables have as a whole. The number of degrees of freedom equals the number of independent variables, and the difference between the two models is statistically significant if the LR value is greater than the tabulated Chi² value (*Backhaus* (2011), p. 268f.). In accordance with all other test statistics, the symbols *, **, and *** indicate whether the overall model is significant at the 10%, 5%, and 1% level.

Multicollinearity describes the phenomenon that independent variables are linear functions of one another. High levels of multicollinearity can bias the estimations of linear regressions due to redundant information (*Backhaus* (2011), p. 93f.). Hence, the regression analysis is validated by variance inflation factors (**VIF**) to test for multicollinearity. A

VIF of one indicates that there is no multicollinearity at all between a particular variable and all other independent variables in the regression model (*Chatterjee/Hadi A. S.* (2012), p. 250.). A high level of multicollinearity is given if a variable's VIF is greater than ten (*Hair* (2010), p. 204). The VIF values obtained for the independent variables in this study are all below three and suggest that multicollinearity is not causing problems in estimation.

Furthermore, this study focuses on the analysis of potential **specification errors**. Misspecification may result from the omittance of relevant independent variables or from the fact that the logit function is not a linear combination of the predictors (*UCLA Statistical Consulting Group* (2014a)). Different test statistics are applied to detect a specification error in any of the logistic regression models. As all corresponding p-values are insignificant at the 10% level, the regression models are generally expected to include all relevant variables and a misspecification of the link function can be denied.

Autocorrelation can occur in time series analyses if the observations are not independent from each other. In this study, the assumption that one country's decision to adopt Full IFRS or IFRS for SMEs is independent from another country's adoption decision is denied a priori. In fact, the autocorrelation issue is explicitly addressed by the inclusion of network effects that are expected to influence the probability of Full IFRS and IFRS for SMEs adoption due to network benefits and mimetic pressures.

Moreover, the issue of **endogeneity** (e.g. reversed causalities) can generally be neglected in this study due to the specific research design of the logistic regression models. As the following section will show, the independent variables lag two to four years behind the adoption dates thus making reversed causalities rather unlikely.

4.1.2.2 Variables

4.1.2.2.1 Dependent variables

Based on the empirical evidence derived from the descriptive analysis of the characteristics of Full IFRS and IFRS for SMEs adoption between 2002 and 2014 (chapter three), this study defines **twelve models** measuring Full IFRS and IFRS for SMEs adoption. In accordance with the conceptual foundation laid out in chapter three, **Full IFRS** and **IFRS for SMEs** are defined as accounting systems that are either identical to Full IFRS (IFRS for SMEs) as issued by the IASB (i.e. GAAP categories 'F' and 'S') or that comply almost completely with Full IFRS (IFRS for SMEs) (i.e. GAAP categories 'FL1' and 'SL1'). The explanatory analysis is structured along the following two dimensions: (1) timing of the cut-off date and (2) differentiation of the adoption variable.

To provide an insight into the determinants of Full IFRS adoption in the field of private firms prior to the existence of the IFRS for SMEs, the first cut-off date is fixed at the end of the year **2008**. Models 1-4 thus divide the 110 sampled countries into Full IFRS adopters and non-adopters by means of their adoption behavior between 2002 and 2008. In addition, this study provides empirical evidence on the determinants of Full IFRS and IFRS for SMEs adoption by **2014**. While Models 5-8 focus on Full IFRS adoptions between 2002 and 2014, Models 9-12 include IFRS for SMEs adoptions between 2009 and 2014.

As described above, Full IFRS and IFRS for SMEs adoption are indicator variables that take the value 1 if a country is considered an adopter and 0 if otherwise. However, the **indicator variable is differentiated further** on the basis of the type and scope of adoption. In accordance with the conceptual foundation laid out in chapter three, the following four definitions are applied to develop four different models per set of IASB standards:

- adoption of any type and within any scope (**ANY**),[175]
- mandatory adoption (**MAND**),
- adoption in the individual financial statements (**IND**), and
- adoption for all private firms (**ALL**).

Considering the two cut-off-dates (2008 and 2014), this differentiation results in eight Full IFRS adoption models (4x 2008 and 4x 2014) and in another four IFRS for SMEs adoption models in 2014. The proportion of Full IFRS and IFRS for SMEs adopters is displayed for all of the twelve above defined models in Figure 4-1.

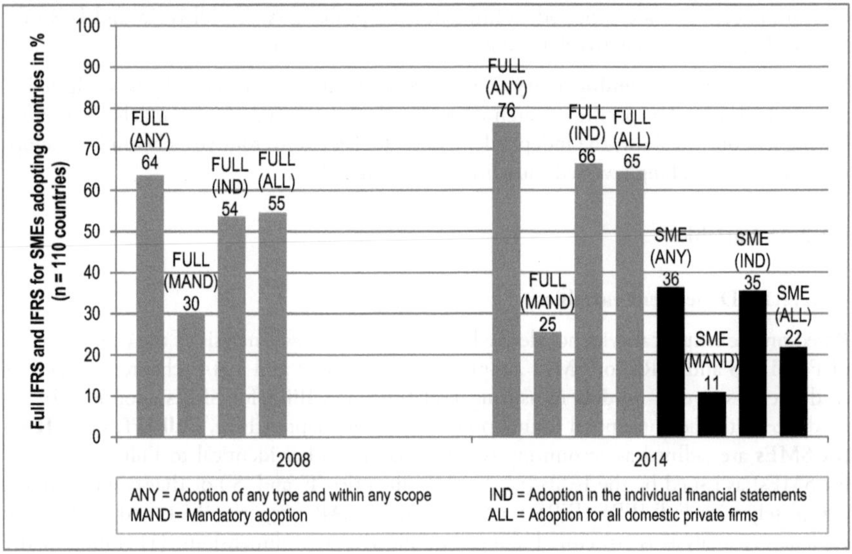

Figure 4-1: Dependent variables

175 This means that countries adopt Full IFRS (IFRS for SMEs) either *voluntarily* or *mandatorily* in the *individual* or *consolidated* financial statements of *all* or *some* private firms.

4.1.2.2.2 Independent variables

As described in chapter two, the *economic theory of networks* and the *institutional theory of isomorphism* are applied to derive falsifiable hypotheses on the economic and institutional determinants of Full IFRS and IFRS for SMEs adoption in the field of private firms. In the course of the explanatory analysis, ten hypotheses will either be rejected or not rejected through empirical testing.

As this study seeks to explain which economic and institutional factors have influenced countries' IFRS adoption *decision*, the **decision date** has to be distinguished from the **date of adoption**. *Ramanna/Sletten* (2013) calculate the mean distance between the Full IFRS adoption decision and the corresponding implementation date of 89 jurisdictions between 2001 and 2008 and find that the distance is two years on average (*Ramanna/Sletten* (2013), p. 10). In accordance with these findings, the independent variables included in the explanatory analysis are lagged by two years. Hence, the independent variables included in Models 1-12 are based on country data from 2000 to 2012 (see Figure 4-2). Correspondingly, data from Full IFRS and IFRS for SMEs non-adopters are from 2006 (Models 1-4) or from 2012 (Models 5-12) as their decision dates are assumed to be two years prior to the respective cut-off dates (2008 and 2014).

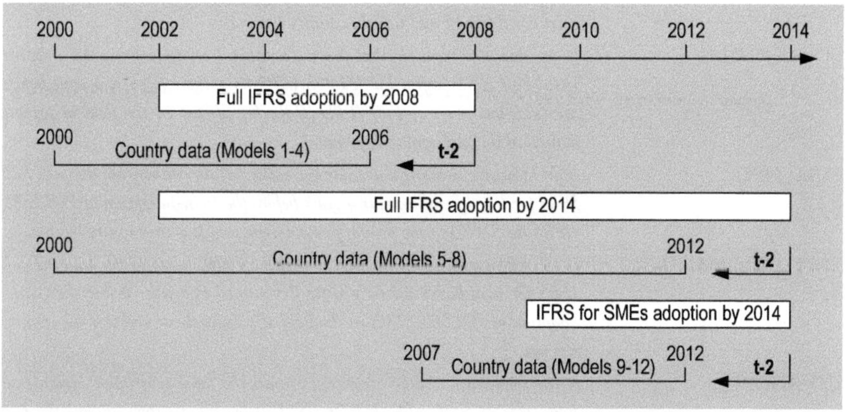

Figure 4-2: Lagged independent variables

All in all, the explanatory analyses of Full IFRS adoption by 2008 (Models 1-4) and by 2014 (Models 5-8) include nine independent variables, whereas the four Models (9-12) on IFRS for SMEs adoption by 2014 include ten. Due to the comprehensiveness of this study's explanatory approach, the applied models do not contain any further control variables. However, alternative explanations are discussed in chapter five. The logistic regression equations are displayed by Formula 4-3 and Formula 4-4.

$$Logit(Adopt)_t = \beta_0 + \beta_1 ACC\_QUAL_{i,t-4} + \beta_2 LOCAL\_GAAP_i + \beta_3 LOCAL\_FULL_{i,t-2} + \beta_4 FULL\_LIST_{i,t-2} + \beta_5 CO\_ADOPT_{i,t-2} + \beta_6 EC\_POW_{i,t-2} + \beta_7 POL\_POW_{i,t-2} + \beta_8 IMPORT_{i,t-2} + \beta_9 PRESSURE_{i,t-2} + \varepsilon_i$$

Formula 4-3: Logistic regression (Models 1-8)

$$Logit(Adopt)_t = \beta_0 + \beta_1 ACC\_QUAL_{i,t-4} + \beta_2 LOCAL\_GAAP_i + \beta_3 LOCAL\_FULL_{i,t-2} + \beta_4 FULL\_LIST_{i,t-2} + \beta_5 FULL\_PRIV\_MAND_{i,t-2} + \beta_5 CO\_ADOPT_{i,t-2} + \beta_6 EC\_POW_{i,t-2} + \beta_7 POL\_POW_{i,t-2} + \beta_8 IMPORT_{i,t-2} + \beta_9 PRESSURE_{i,t-2} + \varepsilon_i$$

Formula 4-4: Logistic regression (Models 9-12)

where, for country *i*:

$ACC\_QUAL_{i,t-4}$	*is a variable that ranges between 0 and 7 and represents a country's perceived quality of accounting standards* <u>*four years*</u>[176] *before the (non-)adoption of Full IFRS (IFRS for SMEs) in the field of private firms,*
$LOCAL\_GAAP_i$	*is an indicator variable that takes the value 1 if the country has ever developed Local GAAP and 0 if the country has not,*
$LOCAL\_FULL_{i,t-2}$	*is an indicator variable that takes the value 1 if the country has adopted Local Full IFRS (defined as 'FL2-GAAP') for private firms two years before the (non-)adoption of Full IFRS (IFRS for SMEs) in the field of private firms and 0 if the country has not,*
$FULL\_LIST_{i,t-2}$	*is an indicator variable that takes the value 1 if the country has adopted Full IFRS for listed firms until two years before the (non-)adoption of Full IFRS (IFRS for SMEs) in the field of private firms and 0 if the country has not,*
$FULL\_PRIV\_MAND_{i,t-2}$	*is an indicator variable that takes the value 1 if the country has adopted Full IFRS for mandatory use by private firms until two years before the (non-)adoption of IFRS for SMEs in the field of private firms and 0 if the country has not,*
$CO\_ADOPT_{i,t-2}$	*is the percentage of other countries within the same geographic region that have adopted Full IFRS (IFRS for SMEs) for private firms during the past two years before the country's (non-)adoption of Full IFRS (IFRS for SMEs) in the field of private firms,*
$EC\_POW_{i,t-2}$	*is a variable that ranges between 0 and 1 and represents the in sample percentage rank of the country's GDP two years before the (non-)adoption of Full IFRS (IFRS for SMEs) in the field of private firms,*
$POL\_POW_{i,t-2}$	*is the natural logarithm of the country's land area two years before the (non-)adoption of Full IFRS (IFRS for SMEs) in the field of private firms,*

[176] As the ACC_QUAL-variable is based on the answers in a survey, it can be expected that the given answers internalize well-known future changes in the regulation of local financial reporting (such as the adoption of Full IFRS or IFRS for SMEs). Hence, these anticipation effects shall be eliminated by an additional lag of two years.

$IMPORT_{i,t-2}$	*is the difference between the country's imports and exports in percent of its GDP two years before the (non-)adoption of Full IFRS (IFRS for SMEs) in the field of private firms,*
$PRESSURE_{i,t-2}$	*is an indicator variable that takes the value 1 if the World Bank has prepared an Accounting and Auditing Report on the Observance of Standards and Codes (ROSC) for the country until two years before the (non-)adoption of Full IFRS (IFRS for SMEs) in the field of private firms and 0 if it has not,*
ε_i	*is the confounding factor.*

Data on the perceived quality of accounting standards (**ACC_QUAL**) were derived from the annual **Global Competitiveness Report**, published by the World Economic Forum since 2002.[177] In the Global Competitiveness Report, the World Economic Forum analyses the various factors underpinning national competitiveness *"to stimulate discussion among all stakeholders about the best strategies and policies to help countries to overcome the obstacles to improved competitiveness"* (*World Economic Forum* (2014), p. 4). Since 2005, the report includes the Global Competitiveness Index, which is a comprehensive tool that measures the micro- and macroeconomic foundations of national competitiveness. The World Economic Forum defines twelve pillars of competitiveness, of which the first one covers the quality of public and private institutions. From this pillar, this study retrieves the item on the 'strength of auditing and reporting standards' (*World Economic Forum* (2014), p. 49) to measure the perceived net economic benefits of Full IFRS and IFRS for SMEs adoption in the field of private firms.

The country scores are derived from the annual **Executive Opinion Survey**, which builds on information on a broad range of factors that are critical for a country's competitiveness and for which data sources are scarce or nonexistent (*World Economic Forum* (2014), p. 83). The 2013/2014 report is based on over 13,000 surveys that were retained for 148 countries. This adds up to approximately 90 respondents per country on average. With the assistance of 160 partner institutes worldwide (academic institutes, business organizations, and national competitiveness councils), business executives from small and medium-sized as well as large companies from various sectors have been asked the following question each year since 2002:

> *"In your country, how strong are financial auditing and reporting standards? [1 = extremely weak; 7 = extremely strong]"*
>
> (*World Economic Forum* (2014), p. 427)

Although this question does also refer to a country's auditing standards and can therefore not provide a clear and unaffected indication on the perceived quality of accounting

177 The Global Competitiveness and Benchmarking Network of the World Economic Forum has published reports measuring country competitiveness since 1979. At that time, the report covered only 16 European countries.

standards, it is the best proxy available and best reflects a country's level of direct economic benefits from Full IFRS and IFRS for SME adoption over time (2002-2014).[178]

While data on the variables **LOCAL_GAAP**, **LOCAL_FULL**, and **FULL_PRIV_MAND** were obtained through the e-mail-based survey sent to managing partners of *Grant Thornton* and *PwC*, data on Full IFRS adoption in the field of listed firms (**FULL_LIST**) were obtained from the *Deloitte* 'IFRSs in your pocket' booklets. The booklets contain a summary of Full IFRS adoptions by listed firms in up to 109 jurisdictions (*Deloitte Touche Tohmatsu* (2003-2012)). In addition, more recent and comprehensive data were obtained from *Deloitte's* iasplus.com website as of May 2014.[179]

In distinction from the geographic clustering applied in chapter three (nine geographic regions), the **CO_ADOPT**-variable is based on a more detailed geoscheme that includes the following 16 macro geographic regions: North America, Central America, Caribbean, South America, European Union, Southeast Europe, Northern, Western, Eastern, and Southern Africa, Middle East, Central, South, East, and Southeast Asia, as well as Australia & Oceania. The geoscheme was derived from the *United Nations Statistics Division's* composition of macro geographical regions and geographical sub-regions (*United Nations Statistics Division* (2013)).

Furthermore, data on GDP (**EC_POW**), land area (**POL_POW**), exports and imports (**IMPORT**) were obtained from the *International Monetary Fund's* World Economic Outlook Database as of May 2014. In addition, data on the World Bank Reports on the Observance of Standards and Codes (**PRESSURE**) were obtained from the *World Bank's* website also as of May 2014.

4.2 Empirical results

The empirical results are presented separately in the following **three sections**:

(1) Full IFRS adoption by 2008,

(2) Full IFRS adoption by 2014, and

(3) IFRS for SMEs adoption by 2014.

Each section first provides an overview on the differences between the Full IFRS (IFRS for SMEs) adopter and non-adopter groups. In the following, bivariate evidence is given on the independent variables' association with Full IFRS (IFRS for SMEs) adoption and multicollinearity issues are addressed in the correlation analysis. Thirdly, the hypotheses are tested via multivariate logistic regression. After the empirical results have been checked for robustness, the most important findings are summarized and their implications are discussed in the final section of chapter four.

---

[178] No data were available for Belarus, Fiji, Iraq, and Uzbekistan. In these cases, country scores are estimated on the basis of the mean score of the three nearest countries within its geographic region.

[179] No data were available for Angola. It is assumed that Angola has adopted Full IFRS in the field of listed companies since 2002 as this is the case for all of the other eight sampled Southern African countries except for Mozambique and Tanzania, which did not adopt Full IFRS until 2008 (2005).

4.2.1 Full IFRS adoption by 2008

4.2.1.1 Descriptive statistics

Table 4-1 presents the mean values of the nine independent variables for the adopter and non-adopter groups in Models 1-4.

Variables	Statistics	Model 1 (ANY)			Model 2 (MAND)			Model 3 (IND)			Model 4 (ALL)		
Groups (countries)		Adopt (70)	Non-Adopt (40)	Total (110)	Adopt (33)	Non-Adopt (77)	Total (110)	Adopt (59)	Non-Adopt (51)	Total (110)	Adopt (60)	Non-Adopt (50)	Total (110)
ACC_QUAL	mean	4.99	4.24	4.72	4.63	4.76	4.72	4.91	4.50	4.72	5.01	4.33	4.70
	mean diff.	0.75***			-0.14			0.41***			0.68***		
	t-value	(4.4546)			(0.8024)			(2.3931)			(4.1867)		
LOCAL_GAAP	mean	0.69	0.83	0.74	0.45	0.86	0.74	0.64	0.84	0.74	0.68	0.80	0.74
	mean diff.	-0.14			-0.41***			-0.20**			-0.12		
	Pearson Chi²	(2.5438)			(19.287)			(5.5839)			(1.9122)		
LOCAL_FULL	mean	0.37	0.60	0.45	0.33	0.55	0.48	0.39	0.55	0.46	0.35	0.58	0.45
	mean diff.	-0.23**			-0.22**			-0.16*			-0.23**		
	Pearson Chi²	(5.3638)			(4.1631)			(2.7875)			(5.8190)		
FULL_LIST	mean	0.63	0.38	0.54	0.79	0.60	0.65	0.63	0.51	0.57	0.68	0.48	0.59
	mean diff.	0.25***			0.19*			0.12			0.20**		
	Pearson Chi²	(6.5816)			(3.7065)			(1.5384)			(4.6645)		
CO_ADOPT	mean	0.42	0.12	0.31	0.20	0.03	0.08	0.30	0.10	0.20	0.33	0.10	0.23
	mean diff.	0.30***			0.17***			0.20***			0.23***		
	t-value	(6.4144)			(4.6282)			(5.6686)			(5.7262)		
EC_POW	mean	0.46	0.57	0.50	0.34	0.57	0.50	0.42	0.60	0.50	0.47	0.54	0.50
	mean diff.	-0.11**			-0.23***			-0.18***			-0.07*		
	t-value	(1.9691)			(4.1256)			(3.3538)			(1.3219)		
POL_POW	mean	11.55	13.16	12.14	11.29	12.50	12.14	11.50	12.87	12.14	11.55	12.84	12.13
	mean diff.	-1.61***			-1.21***			-1.37***			-1.29***		
	t-value	(4.3323)			(2.9869)			(3.8565)			(3.5406)		
IMPORT	mean	-0.01	-0.04	-0.02	-0.01	-0.02	-0.01	-0.01	-0.02	-0.02	-0.02	-0.02	-0.02
	mean diff.	0.03*			0.01			0.01			0.00		
	t-value	(1.4824)			(0.4061)			(0.7807)			(0.0150)		
PRESSURE	mean	0.24	0.63	0.38	0.24	0.49	0.42	0.24	0.57	0.39	0.20	0.62	0.39
	mean diff.	-0.39***			-0.25**			-0.33***			-0.42***		
	Pearson Chi²	(15.749)			(5.9854)			(12.613)			(20.206)		

The table displays the mean values, mean differences, and the corresponding test statistics in parentheses for the independent variables in Model 1 (Full IFRS adoption of any type and within any scope by 2008), Model 2 (Mandatory Full IFRS adoption by 2008), Model 3 (Full IFRS adoption in the individual financial statements by 2008), and Model 4 (Full IFRS adoption for all domestic private firms by 2008).

If heteroscedasticity is detected for any metric variable (Levene test shows $p < 5\%$), t-tests are transformed into Welch tests (t-test with unequal variances).

*, **, and *** indicate significance at the 10%, 5%, and 1% level (one-tailed if applicable).

Table 4-1: Mean comparisons (Models 1-4)

The proportion of adopters to non-adopters varies between 70 to 40 in Model 1 (Full IFRS adoption of any type and within any scope) and 33 to 77 in Model 2 (Mandatory Full IFRS adoption). By using different test statistics, the table shows that Full IFRS adopting countries significantly differ from non-adopters in all of the four models and in almost every variable.

For example, **Local GAAP** existed significantly more often in countries that have not adopted Full IFRS in the field of private firms by 2008. The highest negative mean difference can be found in Model 2 (mandatory adoption): while 86% of the non-adopters had once applied Local GAAP in their jurisdiction, Local GAAP had once existed in fewer than half (45%) of the countries, which had adopted Full IFRS for mandatory use until 2008. Besides, local versions of Full IFRS (**LOCAL_FULL**) have existed significantly less often in Full IFRS adopting countries (two years prior to adoption) than in non-adopting countries. As discussed earlier, the independent variables are two-year lagged values to account for the time lapse between the Full IFRS adoption decision and their implementation. In case of ACC_QUAL, though, the time lag is four years to avoid anticipation effects.

Furthermore, Full IFRS adopters in the field of private firms have priorly adopted Full IFRS in the field of listed firms significantly more often than non-adopters. For example, the share of **FULL_LIST** is 25% higher in the adopter group than in the non-adopter group in Model 1.

In comparison, Table 4-1 provides mixed results regarding the different level of the perceived quality of accounting standards (**ACC_QUAL**) in the adopter and non-adopter groups. In all models except for the one dealing with mandatory adoption, Full IFRS adopting countries have perceived the quality of their accounting standards significantly higher (four years prior to adoption)[180] than non-adopters.

Figure 4-3 compares the boxplot diagrams of **ACC_QUAL** between the non-adopter and the adopter group of Model 1. While more than half of the Full IFRS adopters gave their country's accounting standards a grade higher than 5 (on a scale from 1 to 7), four years prior to adoption, the median of ACC_QUAL in the non-adopter group is only 4.06 and the poorest estimates are below 2.5.[181] Contrary to this, mandatory Full IFRS adopters (Model 2) gave their country's accounting standards a slightly lower grade (4.63) than the group of non-adopters (4.76).

[180] As described above, the corresponding estimates on ACC_QUAL are four-year lagged values to account for the time lapse between the Full IFRS adoption decision and implementation as well as to avoid anticipation effects. This implies that the self-assessment of a country's accounting standards is independent from any future Full IFRS adoption decision. As no data on ACC_QUAL are available for the years 1998-2000, the variable is lagged by only one year for the Full IFRS adopters in 2002. As a consequence, anticipation effects cannot be ruled out completely.

[181] Cf. Table A-17 for more descriptive statistics including the median, the 25th and 75th percentile as well as the standard deviation of all independent variables in Models 1-4.

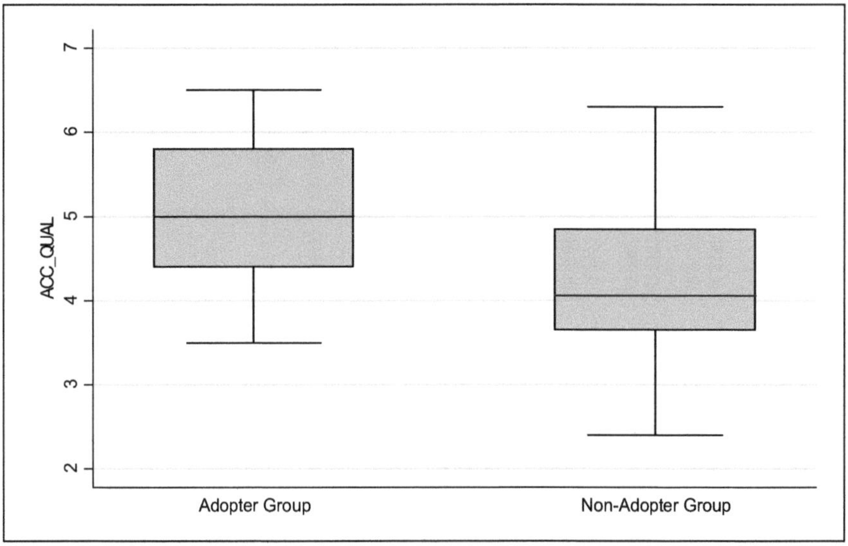

Figure 4-3: ACC_QUAL boxplot diagram (Model 1)

CO_ADOPT measures for each of the sampled countries the percentage of *other countries* from the same geographic region, which have (also) adopted Full IFRS in the field of private firms during the past two years. Table 4-1 shows that in all of the four models, the percentage of co-adopters is significantly higher among Full IFRS adopters than among non-adopters. Taking Model 1 as an example, an average Full IFRS adopter has encountered 42% of co-adoption in its geographic region, whereas an average non-adopter has only seen 12% of its neighboring countries adopting Full IFRS during the past two years.

Regarding the remaining independent variables, Table 4-1 illustrates that Full IFRS adopting countries tend to be significantly smaller (**POL_POW**) and rather have less powerful economies (**EC_POW**) than non-adopting countries. Furthermore, the World Bank has prepared a Report on the Observance and Codes (**PRESSURE**) in about six out of ten non-adopting countries by 2006, whereas the percentage of ROSC in the adopter groups does not exceed 24%. With the exception of Model 1, there is no significant difference between the adopters' and non-adopters' average import dependency (**IMPORT**).

4.2.1.2 Correlation analysis

Table 4-2 provides the Spearman's rank correlation coefficients for Model 1 (Full IFRS adoption of any type and within any scope by 2008) in the bottom left corner and for Model 2 (Mandatory Full IFRS adoption by 2008) in the top right corner.[182]

[182] Cf. Table A-20 for the Spearman's rank correlation coefficients of Model 3 (Full IFRS adoption in the individual financial statements by 2008) and Model 4 (Full IFRS adoption for all domestic private firms by 2008), which are not substantially different from those reported in Table 4-2.

MAND / ANY	ADOPT (FULL)	ACC_QUAL	LOCAL_GAAP	LOCAL_FULL	FULL_LIST	CO_ADOPT	EC_POW	POL_POW	IMPORT	PRESSURE
ADOPT (FULL)		**-0.0794 (0.4096)**	**-0.4187*** (0.0000)**	**-0.1945** (0.0417)**	**0.1836* (0.0549)**	**0.4667*** (0.0000)**	**-0.3689*** (0.0001)**	**-0.2352** (0.0134)**	**0.1071 (0.2652)**	**-0.2333** (0.0142)**
ACC_QUAL	**0.3809*** (0.0000)**		-0.0039 (0.9677)	0.0605 (0.5302)	0.0883 (0.3592)	-0.1300 (0.1759)	0.2298** (0.0157)	-0.1583* (0.0986)	-0.1383 (0.1495)	-0.3134*** (0.0009)
LOCAL_GAAP	**-0.1521 (0.1128)**	0.0091 (0.9248)		0.2053** (0.0314)	-0.0442 (0.6467)	-0.2425** (0.0107)	0.3857*** (0.0000)	0.0549 (0.5689)	-0.0250 (0.7953)	0.0890 (0.3553)
LOCAL_FULL	**-0.2208** (0.0204)**	0.0273 (0.7768)	0.1733* (0.0702)		-0.2943*** (0.0018)	-0.1109 (0.2489)	0.1785* (0.0621)	0.0547 (0.5702)	-0.0329 (0.7326)	0.1784* (0.0622)
FULL_LIST	**0.2446** (0.0100)**	-0.1270 (0.1862)	-0.1012 (0.2929)	-0.3595*** (0.0001)		0.0146 (0.8800)	-0.1746* (0.0681)	-0.2228** (0.0193)	0.1571 (0.1011)	-0.2368** (0.0128)
CO_ADOPT	**0.3954*** (0.0000)**	0.3636*** (0.0001)	0.0263 (0.7851)	-0.0692 (0.4723)	0.0770 (0.4241)		-0.1475 (0.1242)	-0.0834 (0.3862)	-0.0817 (0.3962)	-0.0163 (0.8660)
EC_POW	**-0.1875** (0.0498)**	0.2707*** (0.0042)	0.3824*** (0.0000)	0.2171** (0.0227)	-0.3034*** (0.0013)	0.0214 (0.8247)		0.4773*** (0.0000)	-0.3160*** (0.0008)	-0.0694 (0.4715)
POL_POW	**-0.4095*** (0.0000)**	-0.1768* (0.0646)	0.0549 (0.5689)	0.0805 (0.4032)	-0.2162** (0.0233)	-0.2026** (0.0338)	0.4744*** (0.0000)		-0.1829* (0.0558)	0.0726 (0.4513)
IMPORT	**0.2149** (0.0242)**	-0.2035** (0.0329)	-0.0627 (0.5152)	-0.0615 (0.5232)	0.0657 (0.4950)	0.0657 (0.4955)	-0.3263*** (0.0005)	-0.1981** (0.0381)		0.2798*** (0.0031)
PRESSURE	**-0.3784*** (0.0000)**	-0.3592*** (0.0001)	0.0880 (0.3605)	0.1845* (0.0537)	-0.1324 (0.1681)	-0.1401 (0.1443)	-0.0466 (0.6291)	0.1090 (0.2569)	0.1892** (0.0478)	

The table displays Spearman's rank correlation coefficients with the corresponding p-values in parentheses for Model 1 (Full IFRS adoption of any type and within any scope by 2008) in the bottom left corner and for Model 2 (Mandatory Full IFRS adoption by 2008) in the top right corner. *, **, and *** indicate significance at the 10%, 5%, and 1% level.

Table 4-2: Correlation analysis (Model 1 and Model 2)

Many of the correlation coefficients between the independent variables and the adoption dummy are significant at the 5% or 1% level, which confirms the priorly reported differences between the adopter and the non-adopter groups. Hence, the correlation coefficients provide a first indication on the independent variables' potential influence on the probability of Full IFRS adoption in the field of private firms by 2008.

Regarding Model 1, the strongest correlations exist between the Full IFRS adoption variable and **CO_ADOPT** (0.40), **POL_POW** (-0.41), and **PRESSURE** (-0.38). Similar results can be found for the mandatory adoption model (Model 2): CO_ADOPT (0.47), POL_POW (-0.24), and PRESSURE (-0.23). In addition, there is a weak negative association between the mandatory adoption dummy and **EC_POW** (-0.37) as well as with **LOCAL_GAAP** (-0.42). **FULL_LIST** and **IMPORT** are positively associated with Full IFRS adoption in the field of private firms and the correlation is significant at the 5% level (Model 1). In accordance with the mixed results on **ACC_QUAL**, Table 4-2 reports a highly significant positive association (0.38) between Full IFRS adoption by 2008 (Model 1) and the perceived quality of accounting standards. In contrast, the association between these two variables is negative (-0.08) but not significant in Model 2 (mandatory adoption).

Although **multicollinearity** is relatively low in all of the four models (maximum VIF = 2.12), there are some independent variables in the data set, which show weak but significant correlations with others.

In particular, **EC_POW** is positively associated with the following four variables: ACC_QUAL (0.27), LOCAL_GAAP (0.38), LOCAL_FULL (0.22), and POL_POW (0.47). In addition, EC_POW is negatively associated with FULL_LIST (-0.30) and IMPORT (-0.33). This means that countries with large economies tend to be larger in size and rather have an export surplus. Furthermore, Local GAAP and local versions of Full IFRS can be found more often in countries with larger economies, whereas Full IFRS adoption in the field of listed firms is more common in smaller economies. All of these correlations (stemming from Model 1) are significant at the 1% level and indicate that EC_POW can be explained in large by other independent variables. This implies that some explanatory power of EC_POW might be absorbed by other independent variables in the multivariate regression, which can lead to insignificant regression coefficients of EC_POW.

Besides, there is a weak negative association (-0.36) between **ACC_QUAL** and **PRESSURE** (Model 1). As expected, the World Bank has prepared ROSC significantly more often in countries that perceive their accounting standards as rather weak. In addition, there is a weak negative association (-0.36) between **LOCAL_FULL** and **FULL_LIST**. This implies that countries with local versions of Full IFRS might be less likely to adopt Full IFRS in the field of listed firms. Similarly, a negative association can be found between LOCAL_FULL and Full IFRS adoption in the field of private firms (-0.22 in Model 1 and -0.19 in Model 2).

In the following section it is estimated via multivariate logistic regression whether the above reported bivariate correlations between the independent variables and the Full IFRS adoption dummy have the potential to **explain the probability of Full IFRS adoption** in the field of private firms by 2008.

4.2.1.3 Multivariate logistic regression

Table 4-3 provides the results of the multivariate logistic regressions conducted for Models 1-4. The values from the log likelihood ratio test (LR Chi^2 test) indicate that all of the four models are significant as a whole at the 1% level. Across all models, almost 90 out of the 110 sampled countries have been correctly classified, which corresponds to a count R^2 of above 80%.

Variables	Expect. sign	Model 1 (ANY)	Model 2 (MAND)	Model 3 (IND)	Model 4 (ALL)
ACC_QUAL	(-)	0.82 (1.97)	-0.80 ** (-2.05)	0.20 (0.59)	0.54 (1.51)
LOCAL_GAAP	(-)	-0.72 (-1.01)	-1.71 *** (-2.34)	-0.71 (-1.09)	-0.56 (-0.83)
LOCAL_FULL	(-)	-0.80 (-1.27)	0.51 (0.74)	-0.32 (-0.56)	-1.08 ** (-1.79)
FULL_LIST	(+)	0.82 * (1.31)	0.43 (0.60)	-0.01 (-0.02)	0.42 (0.69)
CO_ADOPT	(+)	3.73 *** (2.80)	10.23 *** (3.28)	5.53 *** (3.55)	5.36 *** (3.42)
EC_POW	(-)	-0.72 (-0.50)	-0.98 (-0.77)	-1.79 * (-1.38)	-0.76 (-0.60)
POL_POW	(-)	-0.35 ** (-1.78)	-0.45 *** (-2.41)	-0.24 * (-1.47)	-0.25 * (-1.48)
IMPORT	(+)	4.79 * (1.57)	3.19 (1.18)	3.46 * (1.29)	0.60 (0.21)
PRESSURE	(-)	-1.62 *** (-2.53)	-1.90 *** (-2.53)	-1.67 *** (-2.76)	-1.83 *** (-3.09)
Constant		1.99 (0.62)	9.18 (2.64)	3.56 (1.21)	1.55 (0.54)
n, thereof: - Adopter (in %) - Non-Adopter (in %)		110 70 (64%) 40 (36%)	110 33 (30%) 77 (70%)	110 59 (54%) 51 (46%)	110 60 (55%) 50 (45%)
Count R^2 (correctly classified)		83.64 %	84.55 %	80.91 %	80.00 %
McFadden's R^2		46.29 %	42.43 %	36.54 %	41.71 %
LR Chi^2 (9)		66.76 ***	57.03 ***	55.51 ***	63.22 ***
Maximum VIF		2.08	2.01	2.12	2.02

The table displays the results of the multivariate logistic regressions (coefficients and z-values in parentheses) conducted for Model 1 (Full IFRS adoption of any type and within any scope by 2008), Model 2 (Mandatory Full IFRS adoption by 2008), Model 3 (Full IFRS adoption in the individual financial statements by 2008), and Model 4 (Full IFRS adoption for all domestic private firms by 2008).

*, **, and *** indicate significance at the 10%, 5%, and 1% level (one-tailed).

Table 4-3: Multivariate logistic regressions (Models 1-4)

When focusing on the **ACC_QUAL**-variable, Table 4-3 displays positive coefficients of ACC_QUAL in Models 1, 3 and 4, but a significant negative coefficient of ACC_QUAL in Model 2. According to the economic theory of networks, it can be expected that all coefficients are negative because a low perceived quality of accounting standards is assumed to promote Full IFRS adoption due to the potentially high direct economic benefits resulting from adoption. However, the empirical results only correspond to the theoretic expectations in case of mandatory adoption.

A possible explanation for this finding is that the level of direct economic benefits varies significantly according to the **type of adoption.** While voluntary adoption implies the complementation of one set of accounting standards by another, mandatory adoption always results in a (partial) substitution of priorly used accounting standards. Hence, direct economic benefits are expected to be lower in case of voluntary adoption (included in Model 1) than in case of mandatory adoption (Model 2). In conclusion, *H1a* is **rejected** regarding all types of Full IFRS adoption other than mandatory adoption.

One question still remains: *"why have rather those countries adopted Full IFRS for voluntary use by domestic private firms until 2008, which priorly perceived the highest quality of accounting standards?"* If adoption does not require the abandonment of local standards, it is quasi costless and rather corresponds to pro forma adoption. Hence, high quality countries might have felt little concerns about Full IFRS adoption, although the real economic benefits might have been low. For low quality countries, however, complementary Full IFRS adoption was not an option as this would have not improved the low quality of local financial reporting. As a consequence, **voluntary Full IFRS adoption** might have been **less favorable for low quality countries** than for high quality countries.

As expected, prior existence of **Local GAAP** lowers the probability of Full IFRS adoption due to the high level of transitional costs. The four coefficients of the LOCAL_GAAP-variable are all negative, although only the one from Model 2 (mandatory adoption) is significant at the 1% level. This means that whether a jurisdiction once had Local GAAP or not, is rather irrelevant for the probability of Full IFRS adoption in general, but it is not for the probability of mandatory adoption. In fact, prior existence of Local GAAP has had a considerable negative impact on the probability of mandatory Full IFRS adoption in the field of private firms by 2008. In accordance with the mixed results regarding ACC_QUAL, these findings provide further evidence that the type of Full IFRS adoption determines the level of transitional costs, which is again influenced by the existence of Local GAAP. In conclusion, *H2a* is **rejected** regarding all types of Full IFRS adoption other than mandatory adoption.

According to *H3a*, countries with local versions of Full IFRS are expected to rather not adopt Full IFRS in the field of private firms as they have already developed their 'best fit version' of IFRS that leaves little room for improvement. In Models 1, 3, and 4, the coefficients of **LOCAL_FULL** are negative, whereby only the one from Model 4 (adoption for *all* domestic private firms) is significant at the 5% level. The LOCAL_FULL-coefficient is positive but insignificant in Model 2 (mandatory adoption). These findings indicate that local versions of Full IFRS go hand in hand with a differentiation of the local financial reporting regime. Although the existence of LOCAL_FULL does not impede countries to adopt Full IFRS in general, it potentially narrows down the scope of IFRS implementation. In other words, countries with local versions of Full IFRS are less likely to adopt Full IFRS for all domestic private firms. Instead, Full IFRS adoption might be limited to some private firms only. In summary, *H3a* is generally **rejected**, but not regarding Full IFRS adoption for *all* domestic private firms (Model 4).

As expected, Full IFRS adoption in the field of listed firms (**FULL_LIST**) increases the probability of Full IFRS adoption in the field of private firms (Model 1). However, the effect is significant at the 10% level only and diminishes in Models 2-4. Hence, *H4a* is **not rejected** regarding Full IFRS adoption of any type and within any scope (Model 1), but **rejected** for the three other models.

In summary, **net economic benefits** have played an important role in countries' decision-making regarding the adoption of Full IFRS in the field of private firms by 2008. However, as the level of net economic benefits depends on the type and scope of adoption, their explanatory power varies systematically across the four presented adoption models.

In comparison, network effects strongly determine the probability of Full IFRS adoption regardless of the type and scope of adoption. The four coefficients of **CO_ADOPT** are all positive and significant at the 1% level. This means that *recent* Full IFRS adoptions in a country's geographic proximity have significantly increased the probability of Full IFRS adoption in the field of private firms by 2008 due to perceived network benefits and mimetic pressures. While *Ramanna/Sletten (2009, 2013)* provide empirical evidence on the determining role of network effects in the context of Full IFRS adoption by listed companies, these findings reveal similar mechanisms in the field of private firms. In conclusion, *H6a* is **not rejected.**

Furthermore, the empirical results provide evidence on the determining power of various political pressures. As expected, economic power (**EC_POW**) and political power (**POL_POW**) decrease the probability of Full IFRS adoption because smaller and weaker countries are more susceptible to external coercive pressures than larger countries as well as strong economies. Hence, the results are in line with *Ramanna/Sletten (2009, 2013)* and *Clements et al.* (2010), who find the same determining effects regarding Full IFRS adoptions in the context of listed firms. While the coefficients of POL_POW are negative and significant at the 10%, 5%, or 1% level across all models (*H8a* is **not rejected**), the negative impact of EC_POW is significant at the 10% level only in Model 3 (adoption in the individual financial statements). Hence, *H7a* is generally **rejected**, but not regarding Full IFRS adoption in the individual financial statements (Model 3).

In addition, Table 4-3 illustrates that countries that highly depend on imports have been more likely to adopt Full IFRS in the field of private firms by 2008 because they have been subject to higher coercive pressures evolving from external suppliers and other trade partners. Hence, this study extends the existing empirical evidence that has been provided by *Archambault/Archambault* (2009) and *Judge et al.* (2010)) on institutional pressures and Full IFRS adoption in the field of listed firms to the field of private companies. The positive coefficients of **IMPORT** are significant at the 10% level in Models 1 and 3. Hence, *H9a* is **not rejected** regarding these two models. However, due to the lack of significance, *H9a* is **rejected** regarding Models 2 and 4.

Apart from the three variables above (EC_POW, POL_POW and IMPORT), which rather measure the level of susceptibility to external pressures than coercive pressures themselves, the empirical results show that direct coercive pressures have been exerted on countries by the World Bank. Once the World Bank has prepared a Report on the Observance of Standards and Codes (**PRESSURE**), the probability of future Full IFRS adoption in the field of private firms is significantly smaller than if no report has been prepared. This is in line with the results from the content analysis of ROSC, according to which the Bank's opinion is that Full IFRS are generally inappropriate for the use by private firms due to their lack of accounting expertise, financial resources and due to the corresponding compliance problems (*Hegarty et al.* (2004), p. ii). As all of the four PRESSURE-coefficients are negative and significant at the 1% level, *H10a* is **not rejected**. This study supports the view of *Chua/Taylor* (2008), according to which political pressures and social considerations have played a key role in the development and diffusion of Full IFRS until 2008 (*Chua/Taylor* (2008), p. 462).

All in all, the results from Models 1-4 show that **network effects** and **political pressures** have played the strongest determining role regarding Full IFRS adoption in the field of private firms by 2008. In comparison, cost-/benefit considerations have also been a driver for and against Full IFRS adoption, although their impact depends on the type and scope of adoption.

4.2.2 Full IFRS adoption by 2014

4.2.2.1 Descriptive statistics

Table 4-4 presents the mean values of the nine independent variables for the adopter and non-adopter groups in Models 5-8. The proportion of adopters to non-adopters varies between 84 to 26 in Model 5 (Full IFRS adoption of any type and within any scope) and 28 to 82 in Model 6 (Mandatory Full IFRS adoption). As the number of Full IFRS non-adopters in Model 5 and the number of Full IFRS adopters in Model 6 are below 30, non-parametric tests (Wilcoxon Mann-Whitney rank-sum test and Fligner-Policello rank order test) are applied to provide more robust results.

The test statistics show that most of the inter group differences, which have been detected in Models 1-4 (Full IFRS adoption by 2008), still prevail in Models 5-8 (Full IFRS adoption by 2014). For example, Table 4-4 provides the same mixed results regarding the level of the perceived quality of accounting standards (**ACC_QUAL**) in the adopter and non-adopter group. This means that in all models except for the one dealing with mandatory adoption (Model 6), Full IFRS adopters have perceived the quality of their accounting standards significantly higher (four years prior to adoption) than non-adopting countries.

The mean values of **LOCAL_GAAP** and **LOCAL_FULL** are still significantly smaller in the adopter groups than in the non-adopter groups. Taking Model 7 (Full IFRS adoption in the individual financial statements) as an example, the mean values of both variables are smaller by almost 20 percentage points in the adopter group. This means that (1) Local GAAP had once existed in significantly fewer Full IFRS adopting countries than in non-adopting countries and (2) local versions of Full IFRS have been significantly less common in Full IFRS adopting countries two years prior to adoption than in non-adopting countries.

Variables	Statistics	Model 5 (ANY)			Model 6 (MAND)			Model 7 (IND)			Model 8 (ALL)		
Groups (countries)		Adopt (84)	Non-Adopt (26)	Total (110)	Adopt (28)	Non-Adopt (82)	Total (110)	Adopt (73)	Non-Adopt (37)	Total (110)	Adopt (71)	Non-Adopt (39)	Total (110)
ACC_QUAL	mean	4.92	4.31	4.78	4.69	4.79	4.77	4.86	4.59	4.77	4.96	4.41	4.76
	mean diff.	0.61***			-0.10			0.27*			0.55***		
	t-value	Wilcoxon			Wilcoxon			(1.6435)			(3.7641)		
LOCAL_GAAP	mean	0.71	0.81	0.74	0.46	0.83	0.74	0.67	0.86	0.74	0.72	0.77	0.74
	mean diff.	-0.10			-0.37***			-0.19**			-0.05		
	Pearson Chi²	(0.8923)			(14.323)			(4.7423)			(0.3362)		
LOCAL_FULL	mean	0.45	0.69	0.51	0.50	0.57	0.55	0.48	0.65	0.54	0.42	0.69	0.52
	mean diff.	-0.24**			-0.07			-0.17*			-0.27***		
	Pearson Chi²	(4.5732)			(0.4524)			(2.8267)			(7.3377)		
FULL_LIST	mean	0.58	0.62	0.59	0.64	0.77	0.74	0.58	0.73	0.63	0.63	0.69	0.65
	mean diff.	-0.04			-0.13			-0.15			-0.06		
	Pearson Chi²	(0.0844)			(1.6917)			(2.5033)			(0.3811)		
CO_ADOPT	mean	0.37	0.05	0.30	0.15	0.00	0.04	0.27	0.04	0.19	0.31	0.00	0.20
	mean diff.	0.32***			0.15***			0.23***			0.31***		
	t-value	Fligner-Policello			Fligner-Policello			(6.3537)			(7.5642)		
EC_POW	mean	0.50	0.52	0.51	0.42	0.53	0.50	0.47	0.57	0.50	0.50	0.51	0.51
	mean diff.	-0.02			-0.11*			-0.10**			-0.01		
	t-value	Wilcoxon			Wilcoxon			(1.7996)			(0.0790)		
POL_POW	mean	11.78	13.27	12.14	11.44	12.37	12.14	11.73	12.94	12.14	11.71	12.91	12.14
	mean diff.	-1.49***			-0.93*			-1.21***			-1.20***		
	t-value	Fligner-Policello			Fligner-Policello			(3.6126)			(3.4877)		
IMPORT	mean	0.00	0.01	0.00	-0.02	0.01	0.00	0.00	0.00	0.00	-0.01	0.02	0.00
	mean diff.	-0.01			-0.03			0.00			-0.03*		
	t-value	Wilcoxon			Wilcoxon			(0.3279)			(1.3279)		
PRESSURE	mean	0.38	0.69	0.45	0.43	0.57	0.54	0.38	0.59	0.45	0.34	0.69	0.46
	mean diff.	-0.31***			-0.14			-0.21**			-0.35***		
	Pearson Chi²	(7.7631)			(1.7550)			(4.4106)			(12.705)		

The table displays the mean values, mean differences, and the corresponding test statistics in parentheses for the independent variables in Model 5 (Full IFRS adoption of any type and within any scope by 2014), Model 6 (Mandatory Full IFRS adoption by 2014), Model 7 (Full IFRS adoption in the individual financial statements by 2014), and Model 8 (Full IFRS adoption for all domestic private firms by 2014).

If heteroscedasticity is detected for any metric variable (Levene test shows p < 5%), t-tests are transformed into Welch tests (t-test with unequal variances). More robust non-parametric tests (Wilcoxon Mann-Whitney rank-sum test for metric variables with equal variances and Fligner-Policello rank order test for metric variables with unequal variances) are conducted for Models 5 and 6 as the number of Full IFRS (non-)adopting countries is below 30.

*, **, and *** indicate significance at the 10%, 5%, and 1% level (one-tailed if applicable).

Table 4-4: Mean comparisons (Models 5-8)

In contrast to the positive mean differences detected for **FULL_LIST** in Models 1-4 (Full IFRS adoption by 2008), Models 5-8 (Full IFRS adoption by 2014) display that Full IFRS adoption in the field of listed firms has become less common in the adopter groups (two years prior to adoption) than in the non-adopter groups. These results suggest that the positive association between Full IFRS adoption in the field of listed and private firms has been detached during the years 2009-2014. Whether this assumption holds true and to which extent the IFRS for SMEs has triggered this development, will be verified in the following sections via multivariate logistic regression.

The significant positive mean differences of the **CO_ADOPT**-variable, which have already been detected in Models 1-4, prevail in Models 5-8. In all of the four models, the positive mean difference in the percentage of co-adopters is significant at the 1% level. Figure 4-4 compares the boxplot diagrams of CO_ADOPT between the non-adopter and the adopter group of Model 5 (adoption of any type and within any scope).

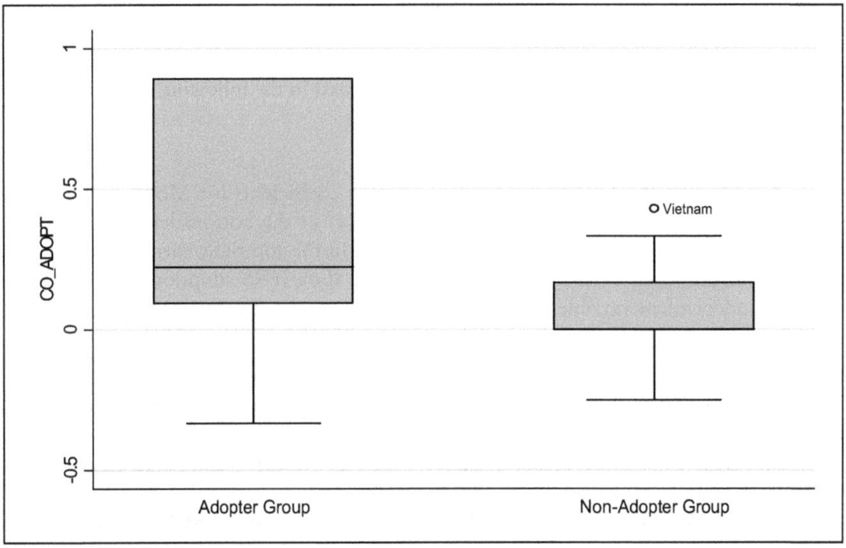

Figure 4-4: CO_ADOPT boxplot diagram (Model 5)

While more than half of the Full IFRS adopting countries have experienced co-adoption of more than 22% in their geographic proximity (i.e. more than 22% of the countries within the same geographic region have also adopted Full IFRS in the field of private firms during the past two years), only one out of four non-adopters have encountered a co-adoption rate of above 17%. One statistical outlier is **Vietnam**, which has not adopted Full IFRS in the field of private firms by 2014 (i.e. non-adopter) although three out of seven sampled countries from Southeast Asia had recently adopted the IASB standards (Indonesia & Malaysia in 2012 and Thailand in 2013). In contrast, **Pakistan** adopted Full IFRS in 2013 (i.e. adopter) although Sri Lanka, one of three sampled neighboring countries from South Asia, had refrained from Full IFRS only one year earlier. This explains the negative co-adoption rate of -33% in the adopter group.

Two out of the four independent variables that represent political pressures (**EC_POW** and **IMPORT**) show less significant or adverse mean differences in Models 5-8 compared to Models 1-4. Since a number of countries with large economies (e.g. Brazil and Canada) and high export rates (e.g. South Korea) have adopted Full IFRS in the field of private firms during the years 2009-2014, the significant negative mean difference in economic power has become insignificant (Models 5 and 8). At the same time, the positive mean difference in import dependency has turned negative in Models 5, 6, and 8. On the other hand, the variables **POL_POW** and **PRESSURE** still show negative mean differences that remain significant at the 5% or 1% level except for Model 6 (mandatory adoption). This implies that Full IFRS adopters are – on average – still significantly smaller than non-adopters by 2014 and the World Bank ROSC program seems to retain its determining role regarding Full IFRS adoption in the field of private firms.

In summary, most of the inter group differences between Full IFRS adopters and non-adopters have remained the same since 2008. However, the descriptive statistics of Models 5-8 provide a first insight into the changes that occurred during the years 2009-2014. The implications of these changes will be further investigated in the following section.

4.2.2.2 Correlation analysis

Table 4-5 provides the Spearman's rank correlation coefficients for Model 5 (Full IFRS adoption of any type and within any scope by 2014) in the bottom left corner and for Model 6 (Mandatory Full IFRS adoption by 2014) in the top right corner.[183] Compared to the correlation coefficients provided by Table 4-2 (Full IFRS adoption by 2008), there are fewer independent variables that are significantly associated with the adoption dummy by 2014.

In particular, **EC_POW** and **IMPORT** are not associated with Full IFRS adoption anymore. **FULL_LIST** was positively correlated with Full IFRS adoption in the field of private firms by 2008, but it is not any longer by 2014. In contrast, the correlation coefficients of FULL_LIST have turned negative (-0.03 in Model 5 and -0.12 in Model 6). Apart from that, weak correlations prevail between the categorical Full IFRS adoption variable and **CO_ADOPT** (0.43), **POL_POW** (-0.35), and **PRESSURE** (-0.27) (all coefficients from Model 5). Furthermore, there still is a weak negative association between the mandatory adoption dummy (Model 6) and **LOCAL_GAAP** (-0.36). In accordance with the mixed results provided on **ACC_QUAL** in Models 1-4, Table 4-5 displays a highly significant positive association (0.29) between Full IFRS adoption by 2014 (Model 5) and the perceived quality of accounting standards four years prior to adoption. In contrast, the association between these two variables is negative (-0.05) but not significant in Model 6 (mandatory adoption).

Compared to Models 1-4, there are mainly the same **multicollinearity** issues in Models 5-8. In particular, weak positive correlations exist between **EC_POW** and ACC_QUAL (0.25), LOCAL_GAAP (0.38), LOCAL_FULL (0.23), and POL_POW (0.49). Besides, EC_POW remains negatively associated with FULL_LIST (-0.28) and IMPORT (-0.38). All of these correlations (related to Model 1) are significant at the 1% level and indicate that EC_POW can be explained in large by other independent variables from Models 5-8.

---

183 Cf. Table A-21 for the Spearman's rank correlation coefficients of Model 7 (Full IFRS adoption in the individual financial statements by 2014) and Model 8 (Full IFRS adoption for all domestic private firms by 2014), which are not substantially different from those reported in Table 4-5.

ANY \ MAND	ADOPT (FULL)	ACC_ QUAL	LOCAL_ GAAP	LOCAL_ FULL	FULL_ LIST	CO_ ADOPT	EC_POW	POL_ POW	IMPORT	PRES- SURE
ADOPT (FULL)		**-0.0503 (0.6019)**	**-0.3608*** (0.0001)**	**-0.0641 (0.5057)**	**-0.1240 (0.1968)**	**0.4848*** (0.0000)**	**-0.1571 (0.1012)**	**-0.1643* (0.0863)**	**-0.1032 (0.2834)**	**-0.1263 (0.1885)**
ACC_QUAL	**0.2936*** (0.0019)**		-0.0136 (0.8875)	-0.1123 (0.2427)	0.2307** (0.0153)	0.1135 (0.2377)	0.1570 (0.1015)	-0.2248** (0.0182)	-0.2707*** (0.0042)	-0.4082*** (0.0000)
LOCAL_GAAP	**-0.0901 (0.3494)**	0.0231 (0.8109)		0.2525*** (0.0078)	0.0166 (0.8633)	-0.2878*** (0.0023)	0.3918*** (0.0000)	0.0549 (0.5689)	-0.1270 (0.1860)	0.0643 (0.5044)
LOCAL_FULL	**-0.2039** (0.0326)**	-0.0676 (0.4829)	0.1966** (0.0395)		-0.2457*** (0.0097)	-0.1258 (0.1904)	0.2284** (0.0164)	0.1385 (0.1489)	-0.1777* (0.0633)	0.0103 (0.9146)
FULL_LIST	**-0.0277 (0.7740)**	-0.0882 (0.3593)	-0.1621* (0.0906)	-0.3732*** (0.0001)		-0.0878 (0.3616)	-0.0390 (0.3550)	-0.1420 (0.1390)	0.0867 (0.3675)	-0.1012 (0.2929)
CO_ADOPT	**0.4291*** (0.0000)**	0.3622*** (0.0001)	0.0141 (0.8834)	-0.2270** (0.0171)	-0.0100 (0.9172)		-0.0759 (0.4305)	0.0472 (0.6246)	-0.1659* (0.0832)	-0.1331 (0.1658)
EC_POW	**-0.0246 (0.7987)**	0.2527*** (0.0077)	0.3815*** (0.0000)	0.2257** (0.0178)	-0.2757*** (0.0035)	-0.0001 (0.9988)		0.5047*** (0.0000)	-0.4090*** (0.0000)	-0.2222** (0.0196)
POL_POW	**-0.3497*** (0.0002)**	-0.1697* (0.0763)	0.0549 (0.5689)	0.1919** (0.0447)	-0.1517 (0.1137)	-0.2081** (0.0292)	0.4916*** (0.0000)		-0.0435 (0.6520)	0.0439 (0.6487)
IMPORT	**-0.0660 (0.4930)**	-0.3095*** (0.0010)	-0.0023 (0.9812)	-0.0722 (0.4538)	0.1313 (0.1715)	0.0213 (0.8253)	-0.3754*** (0.0001)	-0.1234 (0.1991)		0.5055*** (0.0000)
PRESSURE	**-0.2657*** (0.0050)**	-0.4038*** (0.0000)	0.0904 (0.3476)	0.2390** (0.0119)	-0.0574 (0.5515)	-0.1304 (0.1746)	-0.0828 (0.3898)	0.1305 (0.1741)	0.3536*** (0.0002)	

The table displays Spearman's rank correlation coefficients with the corresponding p-values in parentheses for Model 5 (Full IFRS adoption of any type and within any scope by 2014) in the bottom left corner and for Model 6 (Mandatory Full IFRS adoption by 2014) in the top right corner. *, **, and *** indicate significance at the 10%, 5%, and 1% level.

Table 4-5: Correlation analysis (Model 5 and Model 6)

In addition, there are weak associations between **ACC_QUAL** and **IMPORT** (-0.31), **ACC_QUAL** and **PRESSURE** (-0.40), and between **IMPORT** and **PRESSURE** (0.35). Hence, countries that perceive their accounting standards as rather weak are generally more dependent on imports and come into view of the World Bank more often.

More importantly, Model 6 still displays a weak negative association (-0.25) between **LOCAL_FULL** and **FULL_LIST**. This implies that countries with local versions of Full IFRS are still less likely to adopt Full IFRS in the field of listed firms. This is important because the association between FULL_LIST and Full IFRS adoption in the field of private firms has turned from positive (0.18) to negative (-0.12) between 2008 and 2014. The expected negative influence of LOCAL_FULL (-0.19 by 2008) on the probability of (mandatory) Full IFRS adoption in the field of private firms (-0.06 by 2014) could thus have been moderated by the adverse effect of FULL_LIST.

4.2.2.3 Multivariate logistic regression

Table 4-6 provides the results of the multivariate logistic regressions conducted for Models 5-8. The values from the log likelihood ratio test (LR Chi^2 test) indicate that all of the four models are significant as a whole at the 1% level. However, as the proportions between adopters and non-adopters are more unequal than in Models 1-4 (e.g. 76% adoption rate in Model 5), the models have less power to predict the probability of Full IFRS adoption by 2014. As a consequence, the count R^2 of Models 5 (88%) and 6 (80%) are only slightly higher than the respective (non-)adoption rate (76% and 75%). The maximum VIFs remain below three in all models indicating that multicollinearity is of minor relevance for the multivariate regression results.

Beginning with the group of independent variables representing net economic benefits of Full IFRS adoption, the **ACC_QUAL**-variable still provides mixed results. Table 4-6 displays insignificant coefficients of ACC_QUAL in Models 1, 3, and 4, but a significant negative coefficient of ACC_QUAL in Model 2, which is in line with the empirical results of Models 1-4 (Full IFRS adoption by 2008). In conclusion, these more recent findings provide the same evidence on the varying level of direct economic benefits depending on the **type of adoption** as Models 1-4. While voluntary adoption only leads to the complementation of one set of accounting standards by another, mandatory adoption equals substitution. Hence, the level of direct economic benefits from Full IFRS adoption is expected to be higher in case of mandatory adoption (Model 6) than in case of voluntary adoption (included in Model 5). In accordance with the findings from Models 1-4, *H1a* is **rejected** regarding all types of Full IFRS adoption other than mandatory adoption.

As already detected in Models 1-4 (Full IFRS adoption by 2008), prior existence of Local GAAP has lowered the probability of Full IFRS adoption by 2014. All of the four coefficients of **LOCAL_GAAP** are negative, although only the one from Model 6 (mandatory adoption) is significant at the 1% level. These findings also indicate that the type of Full IFRS adoption determines the level of transitional costs, which is itself dependent on variables such as ACC_QUAL and LOCAL_GAAP. In conclusion, *H2a* is **rejected** regarding all types of Full IFRS adoption other than mandatory adoption.

Variables	Expect. sign	Model 5 (ANY)	Model 6 (MAND)	Model 7 (IND)	Model 8 (ALL)
ACC_QUAL	(-)	0.23 (0.57)	-0.88 ** (-2.01)	-0.20 (-0.53)	0.13 (0.33)
LOCAL_GAAP	(-)	-0.93 (-1.24)	-1.53 *** (-2.37)	-0.87 (-1.21)	-0.28 (-0.39)
LOCAL_FULL	(-)	-0.47 (-0.76)	0.18 (0.30)	-0.08 (-0.15)	-0.55 (-0.92)
FULL_LIST	(+)	-0.76 (-1.21)	-0.73 (-1.22)	-1.47 (-2.40)	-1.10 (-1.70)
CO_ADOPT	(+)	4.56 *** (2.51)	5.25 *** (2.75)	7.94 *** (3.33)	10.65 *** (3.29)
EC_POW	(-)	2.14 (1.37)	1.20 (0.94)	-0.09 (-0.06)	0.83 (0.60)
POL_POW	(-)	-0.62 *** (-2.54)	-0.41 ** (-2.27)	-0.38 ** (-2.01)	-0.38 ** (-1.93)
IMPORT	(+)	1.93 (0.52)	1.83 (0.63)	1.55 (0.42)	1.60 (0.44)
PRESSURE	(-)	-1.22 ** (-1.80)	-0.73 (-1.14)	-1.19 ** (-1.91)	-1.63 *** (-2.48)
Constant		8.25 (2.23)	8.96 (2.50)	7.69 (2.38)	5.32 (1.61)
n, thereof: - Adopter (in %) - Non-Adopter (in %)		110 84 (76%) 26 (24%)	110 28 (25%) 82 (75%)	110 73 (66%) 37 (34%)	110 71 (65%) 39 (35%)
Count R^2 (correctly classified)		88.18 %	80.00 %	82.73 %	87.27 %
McFadden's R^2		34.44 %	26.31 %	33.77 %	43.47 %
LR Chi^2 (9)		41.43 ***	32.84 ***	47.45 ***	62.18 ***
Maximum VIF		2.15	2.14	2.14	2.16

The table displays the results of the multivariate logistic regressions (coefficients and z-values in parentheses) conducted for Model 5 (Full IFRS adoption of any type and within any scope by 2014), Model 6 (Mandatory Full IFRS adoption by 2014), Model 7 (Full IFRS adoption in the individual financial statements by 2014), and Model 8 (Full IFRS adoption for all domestic private firms by 2014).

*, **, and *** indicate significance at the 10%, 5%, and 1% level (one-tailed).

Table 4-6: Multivariate logistic regressions (Models 5-8)

The negative coefficients of **LOCAL_FULL** in Models 1-4 have shown that local versions of Full IFRS go hand in hand with a differentiation of the local financial reporting regime and potentially narrow down the scope of IFRS implementation. The results from Models 5-8 support this view, although the coefficients are less significant. This means that by 2014, there is no significant empirical evidence that countries with local versions of Full IFRS are less likely to adopt Full IFRS in the field of private firms. A possible explanation is that a significant part of the more recent Full IFRS adopters had already converged their local accounting principles with IASB standards before Full IFRS was adopted in full (e.g. in Indonesia and Turkey). In conclusion, the EU-based perspective, according to which the existence of LOCAL_FULL rather indicates that the **direct economic benefits** of complete Full IFRS adoption may be small (*Street/Larson* (2004)), does not hold true from a global point of view. Hence, *H3a* is **rejected** for Models 5-8.

While the positive coefficient of **FULL_LIST** is significant at the 10 % level in Model 1 and thus indicates that Full IFRS adoption in the field of listed firms has increased the probability of Full IFRS adoption in the field of private firms by 2008, only six years later, all coefficients of FULL_LIST have turned negative and two of them (Models 7 and 8) are even significant at the 5% (10%) level (two-tailed). This means that by 2014, Full IFRS adoption in the field of listed firms does not increase the probability of Full IFRS adoption in the field of private firms anymore. To the contrary, it has a negative effect. Evidently, the widespread adoption of the IFRS for SMEs has delinked the synchronized harmonization of national financial reporting standards in the field of listed and private firms. While countries have priorly adopted Full IFRS both for listed and private firms, many of them now opt for the IFRS for SMEs in the field of private companies. The empirical results from Models 9-12 (IFRS for SMEs adoption by 2014) will provide further evidence regarding this development. In conclusion, *H4a* is **rejected.**

In summary, the influence of **net economic benefits** on the probability of Full IFRS adoption by 2014 can only be demonstrated for the ACC_QUAL- and LOCAL_GAAP-variable and only in case of mandatory adoption. The explanatory power of net economic benefits thus decreased during the years 2009-2014.

In comparison, network effects still strongly determine the probability of Full IFRS adoption by 2014. The four coefficients of **CO_ADOPT** are all positive and significant at the 1% level. This means that *recent* Full IFRS adoptions in a country's geographic proximity have significantly increased the probability of Full IFRS adoption in the field of private firms by 2014 due to the perceived network benefits and mimetic pressures. *H6a* is **not rejected**. Compared to earlier findings from *Ramanna/Sletten* (2009, 2013), this study provides more recent evidence on the determining role of network effects and is the first study that focuses on the context of private firms.

As displayed in Models 1-4, political pressures have had a strong influence on the probability of Full IFRS adoption in the field of private firms by 2008. The empirical results from Models 5-8 confirm these earlier findings only in part. As expected, **POL_POW** and **PRESSURE** still have negative coefficients across all four models and they are significant at the 5% or 1% level. This implies that a large country size and World Bank 'surveillance' are two of the most important impediments for Full IFRS adoption by 2014. While smaller countries are expected to be more susceptible to external coercive pressures than larger countries, the World Bank advises jurisdictions against Full IFRS adoption as it generally disapproves the use of Full IFRS by private firms due to their lack of accounting expertise, financial resources and due to the corresponding compliance problems (*Hegarty et al.* (2004), p. ii). In summary, *H8a* and *H10a* are **not rejected**.

In contrast, *H7a* and *H9a* are **rejected** as **EC_POW** and **IMPORT** do not have any significant explanatory power by 2014 anymore. While all of the four IMPORT-coefficients are still positive and thus indicate that high import countries might still be more likely to adopt Full IFRS in the field of private firms, the negative coefficients of EC_POW have turned positive in three out of the four models (Models 5, 6, and 8). As discussed earlier, this might be due to the increasing number of Full IFRS adopting countries with large economies (e.g. Brazil, Canada, South Korea) during the years 2009-2014.

In conclusion, the results from the multivariate regression models show that **network effects** play the strongest determining role regarding Full IFRS adoption in the field of private firms by 2008 and by 2014. Furthermore, **political pressures** mainly resulting from country size and the World Bank ROSC program have strongly shaped the decision of countries regarding the international harmonization of their accounting standards. Finally, the analysis has shown that **net economic benefits** also influence the probability of Full IFRS adoption in the field of private firms, but only in case the IASB standards are implemented for mandatory use.

4.2.3 IFRS for SMEs adoption by 2014

Having analyzed the influence of net economic benefits, network effects and political pressures on the probability of Full IFRS adoption in the field of private firms by 2008 and 2014, the following sections will focus on the determinants of IFRS for SMEs adoption by 2014. The descriptive and explanatory analyses hereby include one additional, two-year lagged independent variable: **FULL_PRIV_MAND** (mandatory Full IFRS adoption in the field of private firms). This section thus focuses in particular on the interdependencies between Full IFRS and IFRS for SMEs adoption in the field of private firms by 2014.

4.2.3.1 Descriptive statistics

Table 4-7 presents the mean values of the ten independent variables for the adopter and non-adopter groups in Models 9-12. The proportion of adopters to non-adopters varies between 40 to 70 in Model 9 (IFRS for SMEs adoption of any type and within any scope) and 12 to 98 in Model 10 (Mandatory IFRS for SMEs adoption). In accordance with the statistical tests applied in Models 5 and 6, non-parametric tests (Wilcoxon Mann-Whitney rank-sum test and Fligner-Policello rank order test) are conducted for Models 10 and 12, as the number of IFRS for SMEs adopters is below 30.

The inter group differences correspond by and large to those that have already been detected in Models 1-4 (Full IFRS adoption by 2008) and in Models 5-8 (Full IFRS adoption by 2014). For example, the mean values of **LOCAL_GAAP** and **LOCAL_FULL** are significantly smaller in the adopter groups than in the non-adopter groups. This proves that Local GAAP had once existed significantly less often in IFRS for SMEs adopting countries than in non-adopting countries. Furthermore, local versions of Full IFRS have been implemented significantly less often by adopters (two years prior to adoption) than by non-adopters.

In contrast to the mixed results provided by Models 1-4 and Models 5-8 regarding the level of the perceived quality of accounting standards (**ACC_QUAL**), the mean differences displayed by Table 4-7 are negative across all models. This implies that IFRS for SMEs adopting countries have, on average, perceived the quality of their accounting standards (four years prior to adoption) lower than non-adopting countries. In accordance with the Full IFRS models, the highest negative mean difference is measured for Model 10 (mandatory adoption).

Variables	Statistics	Model 9 (ANY)			Model 10 (MAND)			Model 11 (IND)			Model 12 (ALL)		
Groups (countries)		Adopt (40)	Non-Adopt (70)	Total (110)	Adopt (12)	Non-Adopt (98)	Total (110)	Adopt (39)	Non-Adopt (71)	Total (110)	Adopt (24)	Non-Adopt (86)	Total (110)
ACC_QUAL	mean	4.73	4.88	4.83	4.45	4.87	4.82	4.71	4.89	4.83	4.74	4.85	4.83
	mean diff.	-0.15			-0.42*			-0.18			-0.11		
	t-value	(0.9326)			Wilcoxon			(1.1893)			Wilcoxon		
LOCAL_ GAAP	mean	0.60	0.81	0.74	0.50	0.77	0.74	0.59	0.82	0.74	0.67	0.76	0.74
	mean diff.	-0.21**			-0.27**			-0.23*			-0.09		
	Pearson Chi^2	(6.0208)			(3.8762)			(6.6910)			(0.7681)		
LOCAL_ FULL	mean	0.35	0.63	0.53	0.50	0.52	0.52	0.33	0.63	0.53	0.38	0.57	0.53
	mean diff.	-0.28***			-0.02			-0.30***			-0.19*		
	Pearson Chi^2	(7.9249)			(0.0178)			(9.1177)			(2.8556)		
FULL_LIST	mean	0.85	0.74	0.78	0.92	0.80	0.81	0.85	0.75	0.78	0.96	0.77	0.81
	mean diff.	0.11			0.12			0.10			0.19**		
	Pearson Chi^2	(1.7130)			Fisher's exact			(1.4661)			Fisher's exact		
FULL_PRIV _MAND	mean	0.48	0.20	0.30	0.42	0.24	0.26	0.49	0.20	0.30	0.42	0.30	0.33
	mean diff.	0.28***			0.18			0.29***			0.12		
	Pearson Chi^2	(9.1667)			(1.6248)			(10.081)			(1.1142)		
CO_ADOPT	mean	0.24	0.09	0.14	0.06	0.06	0.06	0.24	0.09	0.14	0.14	0.06	0.08
	mean diff.	0.15***			0.00			0.15***			0.08*		
	t-value	(3.6133)			Wilcoxon			(3.5893)			Fligner-Policello		
EC_POW	mean	0.40	0.55	0.50	0.40	0.51	0.50	0.39	0.55	0.50	0.39	0.53	0.50
	mean diff.	-0.15***			-0.11			-0.16***			-0.14**		
	t-value	(2.6899)			Wilcoxon			(2.8352)			Wilcoxon		
POL_POW	mean	12.04	12.19	12.14	12.50	12.09	12.14	12.07	12.17	12.14	12.17	12.13	12.14
	mean diff.	-0.15			0.41			-0.10			0.04		
	t-value	(0.3988)			Wilcoxon			(0.2487)			Wilcoxon		
IMPORT	mean	0.04	-0.02	0.00	0.05	0.00	0.01	0.04	-0.02	0.00	0.06	-0.01	0.00
	mean diff.	0.06***			0.05			0.06***			0.07***		
	t-value	(2.7764)			Wilcoxon			(2.9929)			Wilcoxon		
PRESSURE	mean	0.78	0.49	0.59	0.92	0.55	0.59	0.79	0.48	0.59	0.75	0.55	0.59
	mean diff.	0.29***			0.37**			0.31***			0.20*		
	Pearson Chi^2	(8.8121)			Fisher's exact			(10.398)			(3.2141)		

The table displays the mean values, mean differences, and the corresponding test statistics in parentheses for the independent variables in Model 9 (IFRS for SMEs adoption of any type and within any scope by 2014), Model 10 (Mandatory IFRS for SMEs adoption by 2014), Model 11 (IFRS for SMEs adoption in the individual financial statements by 2014), and Model 12 (IFRS for SMEs adoption for all domestic private firms by 2014).

If heteroscedasticity is detected for any metric variable (Levene test shows $p < 5\%$), t-tests are transformed into Welch tests (t-test with unequal variances). More robust non-parametric tests (Wilcoxon Mann-Whitney rank-sum test for metric variables with equal variances and Fligner-Policello rank order test for metric variables with unequal variances) are conducted for Models 10 and 12 as the number of IFRS for SMEs adopting countries is below 30. Regarding the indicator variables, Pearson's Chi^2-tests are replaced by Fisher's exact tests if a number in the Chi^2-table is below 5.

*, **, and *** indicate significance at the 10%, 5%, and 1% level (one-tailed if applicable).

Table 4-7: Mean comparisons (Models 9-12)

Full IFRS adoption in the field of listed firms (**FULL_LIST**) is more common in IFRS for SMEs adopting countries (two years prior to adoption) than in non-adopting countries. These findings are in line with the positive mean differences detected for FULL_LIST in Models 1-4 (Full IFRS adoption by 2008). However, they contradict the results of Models 5-8 (Full IFRS adoption by 2014), which have illustrated that Full IFRS adoption in the field of listed firms has become less common in countries that adopt Full IFRS in the field of private firms by 2014. In conclusion, the positive association between Full IFRS adoption in the field of listed and private firms, which existed until 2008, has been transformed into a positive association between Full IFRS adoption in the field of listed firms and IFRS for SMEs adoption in the field of private firms by 2014.

The above described change from Full IFRS to IFRS for SMEs adoption becomes most evident when considering the positive mean differences of the **FULL_PRIV_MAND**-variable. While only 20 to 30% of the non-adopting countries have required domestic private firms to use Full IFRS for financial reporting purposes by 2012 (two years prior to 2014), the corresponding Full IFRS adoption rate is almost twice as high (42-49%) in the group of IFRS for SMEs adopters. Hence, *Grant Thornton* was right when they stated in September 2009 that they expect the IFRS for SMEs would become particularly welcome in those countries that have already required Full IFRS to be used for all entities, listed and unlisted, due to the reduced complexity of the standard compared to Full IFRS (*Grant Thornton* (2009), p. 6).

Co-adoption remains significantly more common in the adopter than in the non-adopter groups. The significant positive mean differences of the **CO_ADOPT**-variable, which have already been detected in Models 1-4 and in Models 5-8, generally prevail in Models 9-12. Only Model 10 (mandatory adoption) does not show any mean difference at all, which could be due to the small number of IFRS for SMEs adopters (12) in the model. In all other models, the positive mean differences are significant at the 1% or 10% level.

While the negative mean difference of **EC_POW** and the positive mean difference of **IMPORT** have been less significant in Models 5-8 compared to Models 1-4, they remain significant in Models 9-12. Except for Model 10 (mandatory adoption), IFRS for SMEs adopting countries are, on average, significantly smaller than non-adopting countries and they have significantly higher import rates. While an average IFRS for SMEs non-adopter has an export surplus of 1-2% of its GDP per year, IFRS for SMEs adopters rather have import surpluses of 4-6% on average. Figure 4-5 compares the boxplot diagrams of IMPORT between the non-adopter and the adopter group of Model 12 (IFRS for SMEs adoption for all domestic private firms). While three out of four IFRS for SMEs adopters have a trade deficit, more than half of the non-adopting countries have a positive trade balance. In addition, the most export driven countries in the sample (Singapore, Saudi Arabia, Kuwait, and Brunei) have not adopted the IFRS for SMEs for all domestic private firms by 2014. Another statistical outlier is **Montenegro**, which has not adopted the IFRS for SMEs although its trade deficit amounts to 20%.

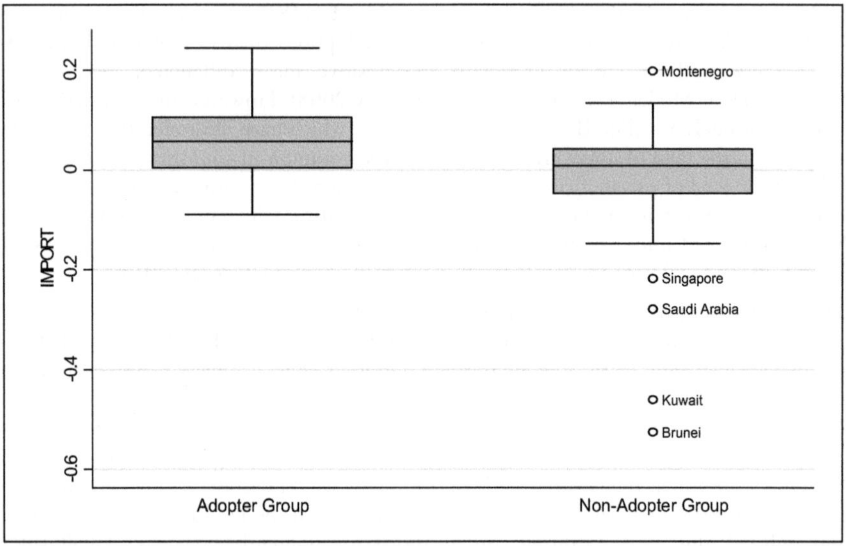

Figure 4-5: IMPORT boxplot diagram (Model 12)

Contrary to the expectations, the sampled IFRS for SMEs adopters are not significantly smaller than non-adopters. Although the **POL_POW**-variable shows negative mean differences for Models 9 and 11,[184] they are not significant at the 10% level. A possible explanation is that the sample is biased towards larger countries. The IFRS for SMEs has been adopted, in particular, by many small (island) jurisdictions (e.g. Aruba, Cayman Islands, and Curacao), which are not included in the sample due to the lack of data.

As expected, the **PRESSURE**-variable shows **positive** mean differences that are significant at the 10%, 5%, or 1% level. This means that the World Bank has prepared a Report on the Observance of Standards and Codes (ROSC) significantly more often in IFRS for SMEs adopting countries than elsewhere. In particular, eleven out of the twelve mandatory IFRS for SMEs adopters (92%) have been subject to World Bank 'surveillance' two years prior to adoption. While the World Bank ROSC are expected to have a negative impact on the probability of Full IFRS adoption in the field of private firms, they are expected to increase the probability of IFRS for SMEs adoption, since the Bank has strongly recommended the application of the new standard during the last decade. For example, the World Bank advised Ghana in 2004 and Uruguay in 2005 to adopt the IFRS for SMEs as soon as it becomes available (*World Bank* (2004c), p. 18; *World Bank* (2006d), p. 30).

In summary, most of the inter group differences between IFRS for SMEs adopters and non-adopters are similar to those between Full IFRS adopters and non-adopters. How-

[184] The positive mean differences in Models 10 and 12 can be neglected due to the small number of IFRS for SMEs adopting countries in the respective model.

ever, the descriptive statistics of Models 9-12 have revealed certain differences regarding the effect of net economic benefits (esp. FULL_LIST) as well as regarding the impact of political pressures (esp. PRESSURE).

4.2.3.2 Correlation analysis

Table 4-8 provides the Spearman's rank correlation coefficients for Model 9 (IFRS for SMEs adoption of any type and within any scope by 2014) in the bottom left corner and for Model 10 (Mandatory IFRS for SMEs adoption by 2014) in the top right corner.[185]

Compared to the many significant correlations in Model 9, there are much fewer independent variables (only ACC_QUAL and PRESSURE) that are significantly associated with the adoption dummy in Model 10. As discussed earlier, this is due to the unequal proportion between adopters (12) and non-adopters (98) in the mandatory adoption model, which makes it harder to detect correlations. When focusing on Model 9, Table 4-8 shows significant correlation coefficients between IFRS for SMEs adoption and all of the independent variables except ACC_QUAL, FULL_LIST, and POL_POW.

In contrast to the results provided by Models 5-8 (Full IFRS adoption by 2014), the correlation coefficient of **ACC_QUAL** has turned negative and the coefficient of **FULL_LIST** is positive in Models 9-12. This indicates that, unlike in the case of Full IFRS adoption for private firms, a low perceived quality of accounting standards as well as Full IFRS adoption in the field of listed firms might increase the probability of IFRS for SMEs adoption by 2014.

As expected, **LOCAL_GAAP** (-0.23) and **LOCAL_FULL** (-0.27) are negatively associated with IFRS for SMEs adoption and the coefficients are significant at the 1% or 5% level. Compared to the findings from Models 5-8 (Full IFRS adoption by 2014), the correlations are stronger and they also prevail in the models other than mandatory adoption. In addition, the newly introduced variable **FULL_PRIV_MAND** has a positive association (0.29) with IFRS for SMEs adoption that is significant at the 1% level. All in all, the coefficients of the 'net economic benefits'-variables are expected to carry more determining power regarding the probability of IFRS for SMEs adoption than in case of Full IFRS adoption by 2014.

Apart from that, Table 4-8 reports a weak correlation between the categorical IFRS for SMEs adoption variable and **CO_ADOPT** (0.40). Together with the earlier findings from Models 1-4 and Models 5-8, this supports the view that co-adoption determines the probability of international accounting harmonization regardless of which set of IASB standards is adopted.

[185] Cf. Table A-22 for the Spearman's rank correlation coefficients of Model 11 (IFRS for SMEs adoption in the individual financial statements by 2014) and Model 12 (IFRS for SMEs adoption for all domestic private firms by 2014), which are not substantially different from the coefficients of Model 9.

Table 4-8: Correlation analysis (Model 9 and Model 10)

MAND / ANY	ADOPT (SME)	ACC_QUAL	LOCAL_GAAP	LOCAL_FULL	FULL_LIST	FULL_PRIV_MAND	CO_ADOPT	EC_POW	POL_POW	IMPORT	PRES-SURE
ADOPT (SME)		-0.1745* (0.0683)	-0.1877 (0.0496)	-0.0127 (0.8950)	0.0958 (0.3196)	0.1215 (0.2059)	0.0398 (0.6794)	-0.1171 (0.2231)	0.0716 (0.4571)	0.1194 (0.2141)	0.2318** (0.0148)
ACC_QUAL	-0.1161 (0.2273)		-0.0029 (0.9758)	-0.1011 (0.2931)	0.2794*** (0.0031)	0.0120 (0.9008)	-0.3278*** (0.0005)	0.1828* (0.0559)	-0.2389** (0.0120)	-0.2268** (0.0172)	-0.4312*** (0.0000)
LOCAL_GAAP	-0.2340** (0.0139)	0.0003 (0.9973)		0.1663* (0.0825)	-0.0282 (0.7703)	-0.3444*** (0.0002)	0.1331 (0.1657)	0.3905*** (0.0000)	0.0549 (0.5689)	-0.1927** (0.0437)	-0.0362 (0.7070)
LOCAL_FULL	-0.2684*** (0.0046)	-0.1199 (0.2123)	0.2187** (0.0217)		-0.2369** (0.0127)	-0.2902*** (0.0021)	0.1561 (0.1034)	0.2117** (0.0264)	0.1607* (0.0935)	-0.2260** (0.0176)	0.0118 (0.9028)
FULL_LIST	0.1248 (0.1940)	0.2246** (0.0183)	-0.0663 (0.4913)	-0.2357** (0.0132)		0.2382** (0.0122)	-0.2510*** (0.0082)	-0.1133 (0.2387)	-0.1854* (0.0525)	0.0965 (0.3158)	-0.0278 (0.7731)
FULL_PRIV_MAND	0.2887*** (0.0022)	0.0034 (0.9716)	-0.4187*** (0.0000)	-0.4132*** (0.0000)	0.2498*** (0.0085)		-0.0149 (0.8770)	-0.2450*** (0.0099)	-0.2076** (0.0295)	0.0302 (0.7540)	0.0782 (0.4167)
CO_ADOPT	0.3991*** (0.0000)	-0.3900*** (0.0000)	-0.1309 (0.1728)	-0.0010 (0.9921)	-0.0989 (0.3040)	0.0253 (0.7929)		0.1130 (0.2398)	0.0853 (0.3758)	0.0334 (0.7291)	0.2969*** (0.0016)
EC_POW	-0.2488*** (0.0088)	0.2113** (0.0267)	0.3892*** (0.0000)	0.2099** (0.0277)	-0.1542 (0.1076)	-0.3764*** (0.0001)	-0.2449*** (0.0099)		0.5037*** (0.0000)	-0.4391*** (0.0000)	-0.2821*** (0.0028)
POL_POW	0.0048 (0.9606)	-0.2098** (0.0278)	0.0549 (0.5689)	0.1244 (0.1952)	-0.1851* (0.0529)	-0.2352** (0.0134)	0.1210 (0.2078)	0.5050*** (0.0000)		-0.0468 (0.6271)	0.0923 (0.3376)
IMPORT	0.2601*** (0.0061)	-0.2726*** (0.0040)	-0.1296 (0.1771)	-0.1193 (0.2145)	0.0582 (0.5457)	0.1109 (0.2488)	0.2971*** (0.0016)	-0.3536*** (0.0002)	-0.0364 (0.7062)		0.4586*** (0.0000)
PRESSURE	0.2830*** (0.0027)	-0.4306*** (0.0000)	-0.0362 (0.7070)	0.0269 (0.7800)	-0.0814 (0.3979)	0.1009 (0.2944)	0.4963*** (0.0000)	-0.2833*** (0.0027)	0.0923 (0.3376)	0.4516*** (0.0000)	

The table displays Spearman's rank correlation coefficients with the corresponding p-values in parentheses for Model 9 (IFRS for SMEs adoption of any type and within any scope by 2014) in the bottom left corner and for Model 10 (Mandatory IFRS for SMEs adoption by 2014) in the top right corner. *, **, and *** indicate significance at the 10%, 5%, and 1% level.

In deviation from the correlation analysis conducted for Models 5-8, the variables **EC_POW** (-0.25), **IMPORT** (0.26), and **PRESSURE** (0.28) are significantly associated with IFRS for SMEs adoption by 2014. Hence, these findings indicate that IFRS for SMEs adopting countries have rather small economies and depend more on imports than non-adopting countries. Moreover, the results suggest that the probability of IFRS for SMEs adoption might increase if the country has been subject to the World Bank ROSC program.

Compared to Models 1-4 and Models 5-8, there are basically the same **multicollinearity** issues in Models 9-12. Additional multicollinearity only results from the introduction of the **FULL_PRIV_MAND**-variable, which equals an integration of Model 6 into Models 9-12.[186]

4.2.3.3 Multivariate logistic regression

Table 4-9 provides the results of the multivariate logistic regressions conducted for Models 9-12. The values from the log likelihood ratio test (LR Chi^2 test) indicate that Models 9, 11, and 12 are significant as a whole at the 1% (5%) level. In contrast, the LR Chi^2 test of Model 10 is insignificant, which is due to the fact that the proportion between adopters (12) and non-adopters (98) in Model 10 is too unequal for a sample of only 110 countries (small treatment group). For this reason, the model has not enough power to predict the probability of IFRS for SMEs adoption by 2014. Accordingly, the count R^2 of Model 10 (90%) is only 1% higher than the model's non-adoption rate (89%). The maximum VIFs remain below three in all of the four models indicating that multicollinearity is negligible.

Contrary to the negative correlation coefficients reported for **ACC_QUAL** and IFRS for SMEs adoption in Table 4-8 (Models 9 and 10) and in Table A-22 (Models 11 and 12), the regression coefficients of ACC_QUAL turn positive in Models 9, 11, and 12, whereas the regression coefficient is negative in Model 10 (mandatory adoption). Similar to the regression results of Models 1-4 and Models 5-8, the ACC_QUAL-variable still provides **mixed results** in Models 9-12. One reason, why the regression coefficients are not negative and significant in the IFRS for SMEs models, might be that the ACC_QUAL-variable has been influenced by Full IFRS adoptions prior to 2005-2010 (i.e. four years prior to 2009-2014). The ACC_QUAL-score of countries with poor accounting standards is likely to have improved after Full IFRS adoption had been made public. As the IFRS for SMEs has been adopted by many countries that had priorly adopted Full IFRS in the field of private firms, the ACC_QUAL scores will have internalized these related improvements and retain only little power to operationalize net economic benefits stemming from IFRS for SMEs adoption. In conclusion, *H1b* must be **rejected**.

186 However, the country values of the FULL_PRIV_MAND-variable in Models 9-12 differ from the values of the dependent variable in Model 6 due to other time references. While Model 6 draws on adoption data from 2014, the timing of the FULL_PRIV_MAND-variable in Models 9-12 depends on the corresponding IFRS for SMEs adoption date, as it is a two-year lagged variable.

Variables	Expect. sign	Model 9 (ANY)	Model 10 (MAND)	Model 11 (IND)	Model 12 (ALL)
ACC_QUAL	(-)	0.16 (0.41)	-0.66 (-1.11)	0.06 (0.16)	0.23 (0.51)
LOCAL_GAAP	(-)	-0.54 (-0.90)	-1.17 * (-1.52)	-0.61 (-1.00)	-0.07 (-0.10)
LOCAL_FULL	(-)	-0.79 * (-1.50)	0.46 (0.56)	-0.95 ** (-1.78)	-0.39 (-0.63)
FULL_LIST	(+)	0.48 (0.76)	1.32 (1.07)	0.38 (0.60)	2.39 ** (1.98)
FULL_PRIV_MAND	(+)	0.83 * (1.38)	0.39 (0.52)	0.87 * (1.42)	-0.33 (-0.46)
CO_ADOPT	(+)	3.43 ** (2.30)	-0.73 (-0.20)	3.18 ** (2.14)	4.09 ** (1.90)
EC_POW	(-)	0.24 (0.20)	0.25 (0.14)	0.17 (0.13)	-1.20 (-0.89)
POL_POW	(-)	-0.02 (-0.13)	0.07 (0.30)	0.01 (0.03)	0.15 (0.18)
IMPORT	(+)	3.25 (1.13)	2.00 (0.38)	3.66 (1.21)	7.58 ** (1.70)
PRESSURE	(+)	0.68 (1.10)	1.69 * (1.40)	0.81 (1.28)	0.03 (0.04)
Constant		-2.02 (-0.68)	-2.13 (-0.46)	-1.75 (-0.57)	-6.03 (-1.61)
n, thereof: - Adopter (in %) - Non-Adopter (in %)		110 40 (36%) 70 (64%)	110 12 (11%) 98 (89%)	110 39 (35%) 71 (65%)	110 24 (22%) 86 (78%)
Count R^2 (correctly classified)		76.36 %	90.00 %	77.27 %	81.82 %
McFadden's R^2		22.07 %	18.62 %	24.53 %	20.03 %
LR Chi^2 (10)		31.82 ***	14.12	35.09 ***	23.12 **
Maximum VIF		2.26	2.24	2.25	2.19

The table displays the results of the multivariate logistic regressions (coefficients and z-values in parentheses) conducted for Model 9 (IFRS for SMEs adoption of any type and within any scope by 2014), Model 10 (Mandatory IFRS for SMEs adoption by 2014), Model 11 (IFRS for SMEs adoption in the individual financial statements by 2014), and Model 12 (IFRS for SMEs adoption for all domestic private firms by 2014).

*, **, and *** indicate significance at the 10%, 5%, and 1% level (one-tailed).

Table 4-9: Multivariate logistic regressions (Models 9-12)

In conformity with the findings from Models 1-4 (Full IFRS adoption by 2008) and Models 5-8 (Full IFRS adoption by 2014), prior existence of Local GAAP has lowered the probability of IFRS for SMEs adoption by 2014. All of the four **LOCAL_GAAP**-coefficients are negative, although only the one from Model 10 (mandatory adoption) is significant at the 10% level. All in all, the findings from Models 1-12 indicate that the type of Full IFRS and IFRS for SMEs adoption clearly determines the level of transitional costs. Only if transitional costs are high (i.e. in case of mandatory adoption), prior existence of Local GAAP reduces the probability of Full IFRS and IFRS for SMEs adoption. These findings add to the empirical evidence provided by *Kaya/Koch* (2013), who find that prior existence of Local GAAP has reduced the probability of early IFRS for SMEs adoption by 2011. In conclusion, *H2b* is **rejected** regarding all types of IFRS for SMEs adoption other than mandatory adoption.

In contrast to Models 5-8 (Full IFRS adoption by 2014), Models 9-12 show that local versions of Full IFRS (LOCAL_FULL) and prior adoption of Full IFRS in the field of listed firms (FULL_LIST) determine the probability of IFRS for SMEs adoption by 2014. The **LOCAL_FULL**-coefficients are negative and significant at the 10% (5%) level in Models 9 and 11. Hence, these findings suggest that the implementation of local versions of Full IFRS is more of an impediment to IFRS for SMEs adoption than to Full IFRS adoption. Considering that many European countries have adopted EU-IFRS on top of a local version of Full IFRS (*Street/Larson* (2004); *Sellhorn/Gornik-Tomaszewski* (2006)), but not the IFRS for SMEs, makes these findings seem reasonable at least from a European point of view. In conclusion, *H3b* is **not rejected** regarding Models 9 and 11.[187]

The positive regression coefficients of **FULL_LIST** in Models 9-12 indicate that Full IFRS adoption in the field of listed firms has increased the probability of IFRS for SMEs adoption by 2014. However, the effect is significant at the 5% level in Model 12 only (adoption for all domestic private firms). Hence, *H4b* is **rejected** regarding all types of IFRS for SMEs adoption other than adoption for all domestic private firms (Model 12). Considering the findings from Models 1-4 (Full IFRS adoption by 2008) and Models 5-8 (Full IFRS adoption by 2014), the multivariate regression results show that Full IFRS adoption in the field of listed firms does not increase the probability of Full IFRS adoption in the field of private firms anymore. Instead, it seems to make IFRS for SMEs adoption more likely. In summary, this study provides comprehensive evidence that the growing success of the IFRS for SMEs has terminated the synchronized, Full IFRS-based harmonization of national financial reporting standards in the field of listed and private firms.

In line with *Grant Thornton's* prediction that the IFRS for SMEs would become most accepted in those countries that have already required Full IFRS to be used for all entities, listed and unlisted, (*Grant Thornton* (2009), p. 6), the coefficients of **FULL_PRIV_MAND** are positive and significant at the 10% level in Models 9 and 11. These findings thus add to the evidence provided by *Kaya/Koch* (2013), who find that prior adoption of Full IFRS has increased the probability of early IFRS for SMEs adoption by 2011. In conclusion, *H5* is **not rejected** regarding Models 9 and 11.[188]

While the influence of **net economic benefits** on the probability of Full IFRS adoption seems to have decreased between 2008 and 2014, the results from Models 9-12 demonstrate that cost-benefit-considerations have played an important role in the context of IFRS for SMEs adoption by 2014. In particular, the characteristics of a country's prior accounting system (i.e. LOCAL_GAAP, LOCAL_FULL, FULL_LIST, and FULL_

[187] The adverse direction of the LOCAL_FULL-coefficient in Model 10 and the non-significant negative coefficient in Model 12 can be traced back to the small treatment groups.

[188] The non-significant positive coefficient of FULL_PRIV_MAND in Model 10 and its adverse direction in Model 12 can be traced back to the small treatment groups.

PRIV_MAND) have had a significant impact on the level of perceived net economic benefits resulting from IFRS for SMEs adoption.

In comparison, network effects have strongly determined the probability of both Full IFRS and IFRS for SMEs adoption between 2002 and 2014. The coefficients of **CO_ADOPT** are positive and significant at the 5% level in Models 9, 10, and 12. Only Model 10 shows an adverse effect, which can be traced back to the small treatment group. In conclusion, *H6b* is **not rejected**. All in all, the results show that *recent* adoptions in a country's geographic proximity have significantly increased the probability of Full IFRS and IFRS for SMEs adoption in the field of private firms. This is because network benefits and mimetic pressures are expected to be the highest if neighboring countries have recently joined the Full IFRS and IFRS for SMEs network. These findings add to prior studies that have already demonstrated the impact of network effects on Full IFRS adoptions in the field of listed companies (*Ramanna/Sletten* (2009); *Ramanna/Sletten* (2013)).

Regarding the political pressures, Models 9-12 provide no empirical evidence on the determinant role of economic power (**EC_POW**) and political power (**POL_POW**). Hence, *H7b* and *H8b* must be **rejected**. Again, it is likely that the lack of empirical evidence is due to the fact that the sample does not include the smallest jurisdictions that have adopted the IFRS for SMEs by 2014 (e.g. Belize, Dominica, or Samoa). Future research could strive after integrating these jurisdictions into the analysis to find empirical evidence on the role of economic and political power in the context of IFRS for SMEs adoption.

While Models 1-4 and Models 5-8 reveal that political power (POL_POW) is a significant impediment to Full IFRS adoption in the field of private firms, Models 9-12 rather demonstrate that import dependency increases the probability of IFRS for SMEs adoption by 2014. As expected, the coefficients of **IMPORT** are positive across all four models. However, only the coefficient in Model 12 (adoption for all domestic private firms) is significant at the 5% level. For these reasons, *H9b* must be **rejected** regarding all types of IFRS for SMEs adoption other than adoption for all domestic private firms (Model 12).

Although the correlation analysis has illustrated that the preparation of a World Bank ROSC is positively associated with IFRS for SMEs adoption, the regression coefficients of **PRESSURE** in Models 9-12 are not significant at the 10% level except in Model 10 (mandatory adoption). As the results of Model 10 have to be interpreted with great caution due to the small treatment group, the multivariate regression results provide only little evidence on the coercive pressures exerted by the World Bank in the context of IFRS for SMEs adoption. In contrast to *H10a* (Full IFRS adoption), *H10b* is **rejected**.

A possible explanation for the **lack of empirical evidence regarding the World Bank's influence** on IFRS for SMEs adoption is that, unlike the Bank's strong disapproval of Full IFRS adoption in the field of private firms, its recommendation to adopt a set of simplified accounting standards for SMEs has not always been related to the IFRS for SMEs-project (e.g. *World Bank* (2012), p. 39). In some of the reports (e.g. Thailand (2008)), the World Bank rather advised countries to develop national accounting standards that are modified versions of Full IFRS or IFRS for SMEs:

> *"**Develop simplified financial reporting requirements for small and medium enterprises (SME).** It is commonly acknowledged that financial reporting requirements for small and medium enterprises should be commensurate with their smaller size, simpler transactions, and narrower range of stakeholders. From this perspective, arrangements should be made for development of a simplified set of accounting standards based on international good practices and more appropriate to small and medium enterprises in Thailand. In this regard, collaborative arrangements should be developed with the members of regional bodies of professional accountants. Efforts should be made to contribute to the development and dissemination of regional guidelines on simplified financial reporting requirements for SMEs. Consideration should be given to local/regional adaptation of the IASB's SME Accounting Standards."*
>
> (*World Bank* (2008b), p. 24)

In conclusion, the results from the multivariate regression models (1-12) demonstrate that **network effects** have consistently determined the probability of Full IFRS and IFRS for SMEs adoption between 2002 and 2014. In comparison, the influence of **net economic benefits** and **political pressures** varies over time, it differs between Full IFRS and IFRS for SMEs adoption and it depends on the type and scope of adoption. In how far these findings prevail if the countries from the European Union are eliminated from the sample, will be discussed in the following section.

4.2.4 Robustness tests

The results of the empirical analysis may depend on the definition and time reference of the independent variables as well as on the composition of the sample. To increase the confidence in the robustness of the presented results, alternative measures for CO ADOPT, EC_POW, POL_POW, and IMPORT are applied to test for the sensitivity of the twelve provided models.

Regarding the **CO_ADOPT**-variable, geographic proximity is additionally measured by a second geoscheme, which defines geographic regions in a broader way. While the study's principal geoscheme includes 16 different geographic regions worldwide, the geoscheme used for robustness testing consists of eight regions only.[189] Regardless of which of the two geoschemes is chosen for the analysis, the regression coefficients of the CO_ADOPT-variable in Models 1-12 remain unaltered regarding direction and significance. Besides, the empirical results of the **EC_POW**- and **IMPORT**-variable do not change materially if Gross Domestic Product is measured based on purchasing-power-parity (PPP) instead of US $. The same holds true for the **POL_POW**-variable if measured by a country's total population instead of land area.

[189] These geographic regions are North America, Central America, Caribbean, South America, Europe, Africa, Asia, and Australia & Oceania.

One key specification of the twelve models is the two-year time lag of the independent variables.[190] To prove the robustness of the empirical results to changes in the time reference of the independent variables, each of the twelve models is computed again with one- and with three-year lagged variables. In all scenarios the empirical results do not change materially. If the **ACC_QUAL**-variable is lagged fewer than four years, the models still provide the same mixed results. However, the coefficients are less significant.

The descriptive analysis of the characteristics of Full IFRS and IFRS for SMEs adoption between 2002 and 2014 (chapter three) has shown that the process of Full IFRS and IFRS for SMEs adoption in the **European Union** has been widely different from other parts in the world. While all EU member states (including the two sampled countries from the EEA) have commonly adopted Full IFRS in the field of private firms from 2005 onwards, none of the 28 sampled EU countries has adopted the IFRS for SMEs without modification by 2014. For this reason, the group of EU countries is expected to have a considerable impact on the results of the twelve regression models. In particular, the European Union is likely to be a significant source of network effects (as suggested by *Ramanna/Sletten* (2013), p. 32). To test for the EU's specific influence on the results of the explanatory analysis, the twelve regression models are calculated again by excluding the 28 EU countries from the sample.

Table 4-10 provides the corresponding results of the multivariate logistic regressions conducted for Models 1-4 (Non-EU countries only). The values from the log likelihood ratio test (LR Chi^2 test) indicate that all of the four models are still significant as a whole at the 1% level and the count R^2 remains at about 80%. Most importantly, Table 4-10 reveals that, without including the 28 EU countries in the sample, the coefficients of **CO_ADOPT** are not significant anymore except in Model 2 (mandatory adoption). This implies that the European Union has truly been a significant source of network effects in the context of Full IFRS adoption by 2008 and that network effects have played only a minor role outside of the European Union at that time.

Besides, the coefficients of other independent variables such as **POL_POW** and **IMPORT** lose their significance in Models 1, 3, and 4. This is due to the fact that many of the excluded EU countries, which have adopted Full IFRS by 2008, are rather small in size and depend heavily on imports (e.g. Latvia, Hungary, and Greece). On the other hand, Table 4-10 shows a significant negative effect of **LOCAL_GAAP** in Model 1, which supports the view that prior existence of Local GAAP has significantly impeded Full IFRS adoption by 2008, in particular outside of the European Union.

190 The independent variables are two-year lagged values, as discussed earlier, to account for the time lapse between the Full IFRS and IFRS for SMEs adoption decision and their date of implementation. In case of ACC_QUAL, though, the time lag is four years to avoid anticipation effects.

Variables	Expect. sign	Model 1 (ANY)	Model 2 (MAND)	Model 3 (IND)	Model 4 (ALL)
ACC_QUAL	(-)	1.02 (2.20)	**-0.35** **(-0.75)**	0.69 (1.64)	0.77 (1.81)
LOCAL_GAAP	(-)	**-1.12** * **(-1.54)**	-1.28 * (-1.60)	-0.87 (-1.28)	-0.67 (-0.95)
LOCAL_FULL	(-)	-0.58 (-0.91)	0.25 (0.33)	-0.55 (-0.89)	-0.96 * (-1.44)
FULL_LIST	(+)	0.98 * (1.47)	0.77 (1.01)	0.53 (0.86)	0.69 (1.02)
CO_ADOPT	(+)	**-0.21** **(-0.09)**	7.92 *** (2.55)	**0.78** **(0.37)**	**1.31** **(0.61)**
EC_POW	(-)	-1.74 (-1.06)	-1.14 (-0.76)	**-1.90** **(-1.22)**	-1.08 (-0.70)
POL_POW	(-)	**-0.20** **(-0.98)**	-0.37 ** (-1.94)	**-0.13** **(-0.73)**	**-0.14** **(-0.78)**
IMPORT	(+)	**3.54** **(1.15)**	3.20 (1.11)	**3.47** **(1.23)**	1.99 (0.70)
PRESSURE	(-)	-1.74 *** (-2.63)	-2.01 *** (-2.46)	-1.75 *** (-2.72)	-2.16 *** (-3.32)
Constant		0.25 (0.08)	6.15 (1.64)	0.75 (0.24)	-0.18 (-0.06)
n, thereof: - Adopter (in %) - Non-Adopter (in %)		82 42 (51%) 40 (49%)	82 29 (35%) 53 (65%)	82 40 (49%) 42 (51%)	82 37 (45%) 45 (55%)
Count R^2 (correctly classified)		79.27 %	84.15 %	75.61 %	80.49 %
McFadden's R^2		37.83 %	43.91 %	32.71 %	35.75 %
LR Chi^2 (9)		42.99 ***	46.79 ***	37.16 ***	40.35 ***
Maximum VIF		2.13	2.24	2.45	2.31

The table displays the results of the multivariate logistic regressions (coefficients and z-values in parentheses) conducted for Model 1 (Full IFRS adoption of any type and within any scope by 2008), Model 2 (Mandatory Full IFRS adoption by 2008), Model 3 (Full IFRS adoption in the individual financial statements by 2008), and Model 4 (Full IFRS adoption for all domestic private firms by 2008).

*, **, and *** indicate significance at the 10%, 5%, and 1% level (one-tailed).

Table 4-10: Multivariate logistic regressions (Models 1-4; non-EU)

In contrast to the high sensitivity of Models 1-4 (Full IFRS adoption by 2008), the results of Models 5-8 (Full IFRS adoption by 2014) are more robust to the exclusion of the European Union. For example, Table 4-11 displays that the coefficients of **CO_ADOPT** remain positive and significant at the 5% or 1% level across all models. In conclusion, network effects have also had a significant impact on the probability of Full IFRS adoption outside of the European Union, although not prior to 2009. Besides, the non-EU results of Models 5-8 provide further evidence on the negative impact of Local GAAP. As reported in Model 1, the coefficient of **LOCAL_GAAP** is negative and significant also in Model 5. Hence, prior existence of Local GAAP in countries outside of the European Union keeps impeding Full IFRS adoption in the field of private firms by 2014.

Variables	Expect. sign	Model 5 (ANY)	Model 6 (MAND)	Model 7 (IND)	Model 8 (ALL)
ACC_QUAL	(-)	0.18 (0.44)	**-0.53** **(-1.15)**	0.12 (0.28)	0.03 (0.07)
LOCAL_GAAP	(-)	**-0.99 *** **(-1.35)**	-1.23 ** (-1.81)	-0.80 (-1.11)	-0.19 (-0.26)
LOCAL_FULL	(-)	-0.47 (-0.74)	0.15 (0.22)	-0.52 (-0.81)	-0.42 (-0.64)
FULL_LIST	(+)	-0.80 (-1.29)	-0.40 (-0.64)	-1.00 (-1.61)	-0.89 (-1.37)
CO_ADOPT	(+)	4.21 ** (2.12)	4.25 ** (2.33)	4.93 ** (2.07)	9.31 *** (2.97)
EC_POW	(-)	1.94 (1.24)	1.10 (0.78)	1.00 (0.68)	1.27 (0.81)
POL_POW	(-)	-0.55 ** (-2.26)	-0.33 ** (-1.81)	-0.44 ** (-2.05)	-0.41 ** (-1.96)
IMPORT	(+)	1.49 (0.40)	0.92 (0.30)	2.02 (0.56)	2.24 (0.63)
PRESSURE	(-)	-1.09 * (-1.59)	-0.90 (-1.27)	-1.09 * (-1.62)	-1.73 *** (-2.43)
Constant		7.57 (2.08)	6.21 (1.69)	6.81 (1.98)	5.91 (1.73)
n, thereof: - Adopter (in %) - Non-Adopter (in %)		82 56 (68%) 26 (32%)	82 24 (29%) 58 (71%)	82 54 (66%) 28 (34%)	82 48 (59%) 34 (41%)
Count R^2 (correctly classified)		82.93 %	76.83 %	80.49 %	85.37 %
McFadden's R^2		24.79 %	23.60 %	25.07 %	34.83 %
LR Chi^2 (9)		25.40 ***	23.39 ***	26.40 ***	38.76 ***
Maximum VIF		2.47	2.38	2.44	2.40

The table displays the results of the multivariate logistic regressions (coefficients and z-values in parentheses) conducted for Model 5 (Full IFRS adoption of any type and within any scope by 2014), Model 6 (Mandatory Full IFRS adoption by 2014), Model 7 (Full IFRS adoption in the individual financial statements by 2014), and Model 8 (Full IFRS adoption for all domestic private firms by 2014).

*, **, and *** indicate significance at the 10%, 5%, and 1% level (one-tailed).

Table 4-11: Multivariate logistic regressions (Models 5-8; non-EU)

As the IFRS for SMEs has not yet been adopted by any of the 28 EU countries, the empirical results of Models 9-12 are likely to change if the European Union is excluded from the sample. As expected, some of the independent variables gain in importance, whereas others are less significant. Similar to the non-EU results of **CO_ADOPT** in Models 1-4 (Full IFRS adoption by 2008), Table 4-12 shows that the coefficients of CO_ADOPT lose their significance in Models 9-12 when omitting the EU.

Despite the lack of empirical evidence regarding network effects outside of the European Union by 2014, it can be expected that **network effects will become stronger** with every new country that joins the IFRS for SMEs network. The case of Full IFRS adoption

(Models 1-8) has shown that network effects become larger over time as the related network benefits and mimetic pressures are self-reinforcing.

Variables	**Expect. sign**	**Model 9** (ANY)	**Model 10** (MAND)	**Model 11** (IND)	**Model 12** (ALL)
ACC_QUAL	(-)	0.29 (0.72)	-0.55 (-0.92)	0.20 (0.48)	0.33 (0.71)
LOCAL_GAAP	(-)	-0.06 (-0.10)	**-0.83** **(-1.06)**	-0.16 (-0.25)	0.60 (0.75)
LOCAL_FULL	(-)	-0.93 * (-1.55)	0.78 (0.92)	-1.04 ** (-1.75)	-0.51 (-0.70)
FULL_LIST	(+)	**1.01 *** **(1.62)**	1.48 (1.24)	**0.86 *** **(1.38)**	2.65 ** (2.31)
FULL_PRIV_MAND	(+)	**0.20** **(0.29)**	0.42 (0.53)	**0.32** **(0.45)**	-0.02 (-1.01)
CO_ADOPT	(+)	**1.72** **(1.15)**	-2.07 (-0.53)	**1.56** **(1.06)**	**1.97** **(0.95)**
EC_POW	(-)	0.16 (0.12)	0.37 (0.20)	0.11 (0.08)	-1.34 (-0.87)
POL_POW	(-)	-0.12 (-0.78)	0.01 (0.03)	-0.09 (-0.58)	0.04 (0.23)
IMPORT	(+)	**4.89 *** **(1.63)**	2.29 (0.44)	**5.19 **** **(1.66)**	8.38 ** (1.85)
PRESSURE	(+)	0.29 (0.40)	**1.54** **(1.23)**	0.44 (0.60)	-0.63 (-0.77)
Constant		-0.77 (-0.24)	-1.95 (-0.43)	-0.63 (-0.20)	-4.38 (-1.10)
n, thereof: - Adopter (in %) - Non-Adopter (in %)		82 40 (49%) 42 (51%)	82 12 (15%) 70 (85%)	82 39 (48%) 43 (52%)	82 24 (29%) 58 (71%)
Count R^2 (correctly classified)		70.73 %	86.59 %	74.39 %	78.05 %
McFadden's R^2		19.90 %	15.19 %	21.19 %	23.29 %
LR Chi^2 (10)		22.61 **	10.37	24.05 ***	23.09 **
Maximum VIF		2.44	2.41	2.43	2.34

The table displays the results of the multivariate logistic regressions (coefficients and z-values in parentheses) conducted for Model 9 (IFRS for SMEs adoption of any type and within any scope by 2014), Model 10 (Mandatory IFRS for SMEs adoption by 2014), Model 11 (IFRS for SMEs adoption in the individual financial statements by 2014), and Model 12 (IFRS for SMEs adoption for all domestic private firms by 2014).

*, **, and *** indicate significance at the 10%, 5%, and 1% level (one-tailed).

Table 4-12: Multivariate logistic regressions (Models 9-12; non-EU)

Table 4-12 also illustrates that, outside of the European Union, Full IFRS adoption in the field of listed companies (**FULL_LIST**) has significantly increased the probability of IFRS for SMEs adoption by 2014. These results are weaker in the total sample because all of the 28 sampled EU countries have adopted Full IFRS in the field of listed firms, but not the IFRS for SMEs (yet). The coefficients of FULL_LIST are positive and significant at the 10% or 5% level in Models 9, 11, and 12.

Similarly, the coefficients of **IMPORT** become significant in Models 9 and 11 when excluding the EU. This means that import-driven countries are significantly more likely to adopt the IFRS for SMEs by 2014, in particular outside of the European Union. However, it is also the import-driven EU countries from Eastern Europe that are expected to be among the first IFRS for SMEs adopters as soon as adoption is permitted by the European Commission.

In summary, the robustness tests show that the empirical results derived from the twelve multivariate regression models are robust to alternative measures and varying time references of the independent variables. However, **some results are mainly driven by the European Union** and thus change if the 28 EU countries are excluded from the sample. The following section will summarize the most important findings and thereafter discuss their implications for the IASB, national standard-setters and for other stakeholders in the international accounting harmonization process.

4.3 Discussion

The objective of the above analysis was to explain why some countries adopt Full IFRS and IFRS for SMEs in the field of private firms, whereas others do not. Summed up in one sentence, the answer would still be: *"Countries adopt IASB standards because they want to or because they have to."* Although this study is not able to provide an equally universal but more specific answer to the given research question, it demonstrates that the reasons why countries voluntarily adopt Full IFRS and IFRS for SMEs in the field of private firms and the reasons why they are forced to adopt these standards are numerous and diverse.

During the years 2002-2008 **political pressures** had the strongest influence on the probability of Full IFRS adoption in the field of private firms. On the one hand, especially smaller countries adopted Full IFRS not only in the field of listed companies but also for domestic private firms as they were more susceptible to external coercive pressures than larger countries. On the other hand, the **World Bank** ROSC program exerted direct coercive pressures on countries not to adopt Full IFRS beyond the context of publicly traded companies and financial institutions. If the World Bank prepared a Report on the Observance of Standards and Codes, the probability of future Full IFRS adoption in the field of private firms was lowered by about 30 percentage points on average.

Apart from that, the decision of the **European Union** to adopt Full IFRS in the consolidated financial statements of publicly traded companies from 2005 onwards had also a pulling effect on Full IFRS adoption in the field of private firms. Although the EU member states were free to decide whether they want to expand the scope of Full IFRS adoption to private firms or not, all of them voted for adoption in one way or another. This homogeneous behavior can be explained most notably by the **network benefits** and **mimetic pressures** that evolved within the EU in the aftermath of the IAS-Regulation.

In comparison, cost-/benefit considerations were another driver for and against Full IFRS adoption, although their impact was limited to the case of **mandatory adoption**. As the level of perceived **net economic benefits** depends on the type and scope of adoption, their explanatory power in this study's regression models varies systematically. While voluntary adoption implies the complementation of one set of accounting standards by another, mandatory adoption always results in a (partial) substitution of priorly used accounting standards. Hence, **transitional costs** are expected to be significantly higher in case of mandatory adoption than in case of voluntary adoption. The empirical evidence presented in this study indicates that only if transitional costs are high (i.e. in case of mandatory adoption), net economic benefits are important enough to determine the probability of Full IFRS adoption by 2008. For example, countries may perceive net economic benefits from mandatory Full IFRS adoption due to a low quality of the existent accounting standards or, in contrast, they rather expect net economic losses if local versions of Full IFRS have already been adopted or if they have a history of Local GAAP.

During the years 2009-2014, most of the prior political pressures remained unchanged. In particular, the **World Bank** still disapproved Full IFRS adoption in the field of private firms and thus continued to exert coercive pressures on countries not to adopt Full IFRS. Furthermore, due to the increasing number of Full IFRS adopting countries worldwide, network effects became a significant driver for Full IFRS adoption also outside of the European Union. This means that *recent* Full IFRS adoptions in geographic proximity have significantly increased the probability of Full IFRS adoption in the field of private firms by 2014. The case of Full IFRS adoption shows that network effects become larger over time as the related **network benefits** and **mimetic pressures** are **self-reinforcing**. In comparison, the influence of net economic benefits on the probability of Full IFRS adoption has decreased between 2008 and 2014 as their influence can only be demonstrated for one out of four variables (Local GAAP) and only in case of mandatory adoption.

Besides, the empirical results reveal that Full IFRS adoption in the field of listed firms significantly increased the probability of Full IFRS adoption in the field of private firms by 2008, but not by 2014 anymore. Instead, it now seems to make IFRS for SMEs adoption more likely (at least outside of the European Union). In conclusion, the empirical evidence indicates the **end of synchronized, Full IFRS-based accounting harmonization** in the field of listed and private firms. While several countries adopted Full IFRS both for listed and private firms until 2008, many of them now opt for the IFRS for SMEs in the field of private companies. In particular, IFRS for SMEs adoption is more likely in countries outside of the EU that have required Full IFRS to be used for all entities (listed and unlisted) due to the reduced complexity of the standard compared to Full IFRS. Contrary to the diminishing importance of **net economic benefits** in the context of Full IFRS adoption between 2008 and 2014, the empirical results show that cost-benefit-considerations have played a more important role in the context of IFRS for SMEs adoption. For example, the implementation of local versions of Full IFRS has been more of an impediment to IFRS for SMEs adoption than to Full IFRS adoption.

Furthermore, import dependency is identified as an important driver for IFRS for SMEs adoption by 2014. This is explained by the **coercive pressures** that originate from foreign trade partners (especially suppliers), which have an interest in the comparability of the financial statements of their business partners, and that cumulate most in an economy with high import dependency. On the contrary, significant network effects cannot (yet) be observed on a global scale (apart from the negative network effects within the EU) but they are likely to become stronger with every new country that joins the IFRS for SMEs network. The results of the hypothesis testing are summarized in Figures 4-6 and 4-7.

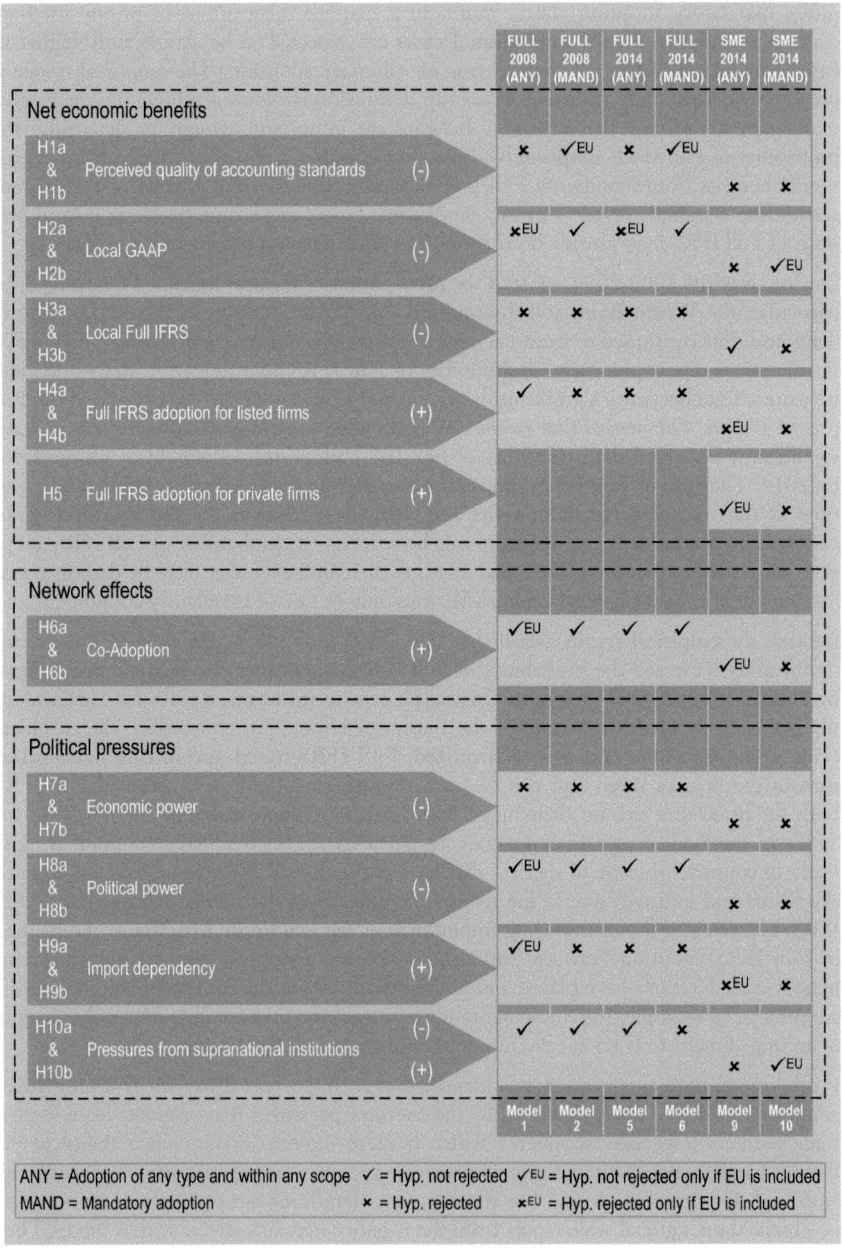

Figure 4-6: Results of the hypothesis testing (ANY & MAND)

Hypothesis		Sign	FULL 2008 (IND)	FULL 2008 (ALL)	FULL 2014 (IND)	FULL 2014 (ALL)	SME 2014 (IND)	SME 2014 (ALL)
Net economic benefits								
H1a & H1b	Perceived quality of accounting standards	(-)	×	×	×	×	×	×
H2a & H2b	Local GAAP	(-)	×	×	×	×	×	×
H3a & H3b	Local Full IFRS	(-)	×	✓	×	×	✓	×
H4a & H4b	Full IFRS adoption for listed firms	(+)	×	×	×	×	×EU	✓
H5	Full IFRS adoption for private firms	(+)					✓EU	×
Network effects								
H6a & H6b	Co-Adoption	(+)	✓EU	✓EU	✓	✓	✓EU	✓EU
Political pressures								
H7a & H7b	Economic power	(-)	✓EU	×	×	×	×	×
H8a & H8b	Political power	(-)	✓EU	✓EU	✓	✓	×	×
H9a & H9b	Import dependency	(+)	✓EU	×	×	×	×EU	✓
H10a & H10b	Pressures from supranational institutions	(-) / (+)	✓	✓	✓	✓	×	×
			Model 3	Model 4	Model 7	Model 8	Model 11	Model 12

IND = Adoption in the individual fin. statements; ALL = Adoption for all domestic private firms; ✓ = Hyp. not rejected; × = Hyp. rejected; ✓EU = Hyp. not rejected only if EU is included; ×EU = Hyp. rejected only if EU is included

Figure 4-7: Results of the hypothesis testing (IND & ALL)

All in all, the empirical results provided on the determinants of Full IFRS and IFRS for SMEs adoption in the field of private firms do not give a coherent picture, but they rather resemble to a mosaic of different determinants and trends. As expected, there are various motivations and pressures that make countries adopt IFRS (*United Nations* (2008)). This study is one of the first (besides *Kaya/Koch* (2013)) that lays the **focus on the context of private firms** and thus adds to prior research (e.g. *Hope et al.* (2006); *Judge et al.* (2010); *Ramanna/Sletten* (2013)) that has yet analyzed the determinants of Full IFRS adoption in the field of listed companies. By and large, the revealed determinants are the same as in prior studies. However, apart from transferring well-known theoretic concepts (*economic theory of networks* and *institutional theory of isomorphism*) from the field of listed to the field of private firms, this study demonstrates **changes in the explanatory power of theoretic concepts over time** and relates these changes to the issuance and diffusion of the IFRS for SMEs.

For example, the empirical results clearly demonstrate since the IFRS for SMEs was issued in 2009, **cost-/benefit considerations** have played a more important role in the context of IFRS for SMEs adoption than in the case of Full IFRS adoption. Regardless of that, the empirical evidence suggests that the principal benefits and pressures of international accounting harmonization originate from network effects. These effects evolve with a certain time lag and become stronger if a certain 'network relevant threshold' of adopters is passed. In the case of Full IFRS adoption, network benefits and mimetic pressures have pushed many countries towards adoption although net economic benefits have been negligible or negative. In contrast, the IFRS for SMEs is likely to bring considerable net economic benefits compared to local standards and to Full IFRS. For this reason, it can be expected that the **IFRS for SMEs might become more diffused than Full IFRS** in the field of private firms.

In particular, network effects, as opposed to net economic benefits and political pressures, will determine the way by which the **European Union** will proceed in the context of international accounting harmonization for private firms. As soon as the IFRS for SMEs network has reached a certain scope, it is unlikely that the EU will resist the network benefits and mimetic pressures that result from worldwide IFRS for SMEs adoption in the long run. While the IASB can rely on the IFRS for SMEs' improved cost-/benefit package and on the self-reinforcing power of network effects, national standard-setters, especially those from the EU, still have to realize the **power of network effects**. It appears that some European standard-setters focus more on the analysis of the potential net economic benefits and losses resulting from adoption than on the network-related implications. However, if they want to keep an active role in the international accounting harmonization process, national standard-setters have to consider and internalize network effects into their adoption decision.

Preparers and users of private firms' financial statements will need to **improve their knowledge** in Full IFRS and IFRS for SMEs and auditors are expected to **build new capacities** to cope with the increasing number of Full IFRS and IFRS for SMEs financial statements. After all, the success of the international accounting harmonization process will not depend on the adoption decisions made on country level, but on effective Full IFRS and IFRS for SMEs implementation in financial reporting practice.

5 Conclusions

5.1 Main findings and implications

This study has analyzed the process of international accounting harmonization in the field of private firms in 110 countries between 2002 and 2014. In particular, it has aimed at answering the following two main research questions:

(1) How are accounting systems shaped in the field of private firms?

(2) Why do countries adopt Full IFRS or IFRS for SMEs in the field of private firms?

The first sub-study includes a **time series analysis** (2002-2014) and a **cross-sectional analysis** (2014). While the former presents the process towards Full IFRS and IFRS for SMEs adoption between 2002 and 2014, the latter provides a detailed description of the country-specific characteristics of Full IFRS and IFRS for SMEs adoption in the field of private firms in 2014.

First, the results from the time series analysis make aware of the fact that by 2002, the year the IASB started operations, only one third of the 110 sampled countries worldwide still provided domestic private firms with accounting standards that were entirely independent from those issued by the IASB. Instead, every second country had already converged their Local GAAP with Full IFRS to a small or medium extent and the remaining 20% had already adopted Full IFRS with or without minor modifications. This state of **early convergence with IFRS** is a surprising observation in the field of private firms as IAS and IFRS have initially been designed for the accounting of large listed multinationals only. The time series analysis clearly indicates though that IAS and IFRS already had a strong impact on domestic financial reporting systems for private firms by the early 2000s. Furthermore, this study shows that most of the remaining **Local GAAPs have ultimately ceased to exist** by 2014.

During the years 2002-2014, the following two major trends in international accounting harmonization can be observed in the context of private firms' financial reporting:

(1) gradual convergence of local accounting systems with Full IFRS and

(2) Full IFRS and IFRS for SMEs adoption.

While convergence implies that one accounting system is gradually replaced by another, Full IFRS and IFRS for SMEs adoption in the field of private firms have often led to **GAAP complementation**. As a consequence, local versions of Full IFRS are still in use in almost every second country worldwide. In particular, more than half of the EU countries provide such **local versions of Full IFRS** to European private firms. If such 'localized' standards are still in place besides Full IFRS and IFRS for SMEs, there can be doubts about the de facto adoption of Full IFRS and IFRS for SMEs in the field of private firms because little is known about the actual number of Full IFRS and IFRS for SMEs adopting private companies worldwide.

As the number of GAAPs per country has roughly doubled due to GAAP complementation since 2002, the process of international accounting harmonization has also led to **more intra-national GAAP diversity**. The evidence on worldwide GAAP complementation thus adds to prior research that has already predicted the emergence of a **'two standard system'** in the European Union (*Street/Larson* (2004)). While in the European context two standard systems have resulted from the coexistence of 'Local Full IFRS' and EU-IFRS, the parallel adoption of Full IFRS and IFRS for SMEs has led to the emergence of a two standard system in many countries outside of the European Union.

In addition, this study raises awareness of the **ambiguous meaning** of the terms **'adopt'** (*Zeff/Nobes* (2010)) and **'IFRS'** (*Nobes* (2013)). As there is no global consensus on when a national regulator is allowed to label its domestic accounting system 'IFRS', both financial statement preparers and users have to be aware of the fact that several country-specific deviations from IFRS may exist although the standards are named 'IFRS'. Vice versa, some jurisdictions would not confirm that they have 'adopted' IFRS although their domestic accounting standards equal IFRS in almost every aspect. Modifications to IFRS combined with ambiguous IFRS definitions represent a major challenge to financial statement users worldwide. It seems that diversity between Local GAAPs has been superseded by a new **diversity 'within IFRS'**. For this reason, this study differentiates local versions of IFRS from 'pure' Full IFRS and IFRS for SMEs in great detail and thus provides a new insight into the degree of Full IFRS and IFRS for SMEs adoption in the field of private firms worldwide.

Compared to the early 2000s, domestic accounting systems in the field of private firms have become **significantly more international**, either through stepwise convergence with Full IFRS or due to Full IFRS and IFRS for SMEs adoption. In 2014, about 60% of all accounting systems worldwide are Full IFRS or IFRS for SMEs (either with or without minor modifications). The remaining 40% of GAAPs are local accounting systems that have been converged with Full IFRS or IFRS for SMEs to a varying extent. These findings contribute to prior empirical research that has already detected cross-national variation in the degree of domestic accounting standards' level of compliance with Full IFRS in the 1980s and 1990s (e.g. *Doupnik* (1987); *Purvis et al.* (1991); *Larson/Kenny* (1999)). More importantly, this research reveals that although the gap between Local GAAPs and Full IFRS has been narrowed down during the past decade and a large number of countries has either adopted Full IFRS or IFRS for SMEs in the field of private firms, many local versions of Full IFRS still **lack compliance with Full IFRS**.

The year 2005, when the number of Full IFRS adopting countries suddenly doubled due to Full IFRS adoption in the European Union, represents the point in time when jurisdictions began to **restrict the use of Full IFRS** either to the consolidated financial statements or to certain types of domestic private firms. For this reason, the percentage of countries that have adopted Full IFRS in the individual financial statements and for all domestic private firms is considerably smaller than the overall percentage of Full IFRS adopters by 2014. Moreover, this study demonstrates that while most countries, which had adopted Full IFRS prior to 2005, required all or some domestic private firms to use Full IFRS for financial reporting purposes. On the contrary, the large majority of today's

Full IFRS adopting countries allow domestic private firms to choose between two or more sets of accounting standards.

These findings are in accordance with the observation that parallel adoption of Full IFRS and IFRS for SMEs has led to an **increasing differentiation** of local financial reporting regulation for private firms. In the majority of Full IFRS and IFRS for SMEs adopting countries, all domestic private firms are allowed to use Full IFRS, whereas IFRS for SMEs adoption is often restricted to smaller entities that satisfy certain size criteria (**differentiation**). In comparison, only a few countries (e.g. Peru, Pakistan) require domestic private firms to adopt either of the two IASB standards (**segmentation**).

All in all, the empirical evidence presented in the time series analysis (2002-2014) shows **significant variation in the process towards Full IFRS and IFRS for SMEs adoption** worldwide. It is the first study that provides global empirical evidence on the process towards Full IFRS and IFRS for SMEs adoption and on the persistence of localized accounting systems in the field of private firms after 2002. Due to the long observation period, the time series analysis provides a comprehensive overview on the process of worldwide international accounting harmonization during the last decade in the field of private firms. In conclusion, the findings may help the IASB and national standard-setters to better understand regional patterns of accounting harmonization and predict future developments.

While the time series analysis has focused on the global process towards Full IFRS and IFRS for SMEs adoption since 2002, the cross-sectional analysis reveals cross-regional variation in the type and scope of Full IFRS and IFRS for SMEs adoption in 2014. 76% (36%) of the 110 sampled countries have adopted Full IFRS (IFRS for SMEs) in the field of private firms by 2014 and the worldwide **distribution of IFRS for SMEs adopters** is quite the **opposite from the distribution of Full IFRS adopters.** While Full IFRS have been adopted by almost every country in North America, Central America & Caribbean, Australia & Oceania, and Europe, only every second country from South America and Africa and not more than two out of three countries from Asia & the Middle East have so far adopted Full IFRS in the field of private firms. Vice versa, the IFRS for SMEs has been adopted most frequently (besides Central America & Caribbean) in South America and Africa (above 60%), whereas Europe has the lowest IFRS for SMEs adoption rate (15%), which is due to the **non-adoption of the IFRS for SMEs in the European Union.**

Due to the persistence of 'localized' accounting systems (esp. in North America and the European Union) and parallel adoption of Full IFRS and IFRS for SMEs, **mandatory adoption is rare.** In fact, the number of mandatory Full IFRS adopters has decreased in most regions since 2008, in particular in CAC countries and Africa. If the **GDP** of Full IFRS and IFRS for SMEs adopting countries is considered, the results indicate that the IFRS for SMEs has been adopted more often by countries with smaller economies, in particular in Central America & Caribbean (Honduras, Jamaica), Asia & Middle East (Sri Lanka, Lebanon), and in Australia & Oceania (Fiji). By contrast, the IFRS for SMEs has also been adopted by larger economies in Africa (South Africa) and South America (Brazil). **The world's largest economies** have so far **rarely adopted Full IFRS or IFRS for SMEs for mandatory use** in the field of private firms. The only exceptions are Brazil

(South America) and China (Asia), which require larger private firms to comply with Full IFRS (with minor modifications), and Chile and Peru (both South America), Nigeria (Africa), and the Philippines (Asia), which have so far adopted the IFRS for SMEs for mandatory use by domestic private firms.

In conclusion, the extent of worldwide Full IFRS and IFRS for SMEs adoption is high and low at the same time as it depends on how 'adoption' is defined. This study is the first to depict and describe in detail the cross-regional **variation in the type of Full IFRS and IFRS for SMEs adoption** in the field of private firms on a global scale. While the focus of the existing 'IFRS adoption summaries', such as those from Big4 audit firms (e.g. *PricewaterhouseCoopers* (2013); *Deloitte Touche Tohmatsu* (2014c)), has so far been on summarizing Full IFRS adoptions in the field of listed companies, this study extends this field of descriptive research to the area of private firms and IFRS for SMEs adoption.

In addition, the cross-sectional analysis reveals cross-regional variation in the scope of Full IFRS and IFRS for SMEs adoption in 2014. For example, fewer European countries have adopted Full IFRS also in the individual financial statements of domestic private firms. More precisely, the **restriction of Full IFRS adoption to the consolidated financial statements** of domestic private firms is a **Central European phenomenon** (e.g. France and Germany). As far as IFRS for SMEs adoption is concerned, Switzerland is the only country worldwide that has adopted the IFRS for SMEs only in the consolidated financial statements of local private firms.

More common than that are restrictions of the scope of Full IFRS and IFRS for SMEs adoption that are based on firm characteristics. In the majority of cases, the **differentiation** (or segmentation) of national financial reporting regimes is **based on size criteria**. For example, there are several countries from each continent (e.g. Peru, Italy, Zambia, and Pakistan) that do not allow smaller private firms to use Full IFRS for financial reporting purposes. Vice versa, there are various IFRS for SMEs adopting countries in almost all geographic regions worldwide that have restricted the use of the IFRS for SMEs to small and medium-sized private companies. In conclusion, the increased differentiation of national financial reporting requirements on the basis of firm size indicates that the **IFRS for SMEs** is not regarded as a full-value alternative to Full IFRS yet. Instead, it is rather viewed as **'little GAAP for small private firms'**. In some cases, limitations in the scope of Full IFRS and IFRS for SMEs adoption go along with the persistence of localized accounting systems that are tailored for the special needs of small businesses (e.g. SME-FRF & SME-FRS in Hong Kong). In view of these findings, this study adds to prior research that has already revealed differences in the scope of Full IFRS adoption by private firms in the European Union (*Street/Larson* (2004); *Sellhorn/Gornik-Tomaszewski* (2006)) by focusing on Full IFRS and IFRS for SMEs adoption in a large Non-European sample.

Finally, the second sub-study identifies net economic benefits, network effects, and political pressures as important determinants of Full IFRS and IFRS for SMEs adoption in the field of private firms by 2008 and by 2014. While **political pressures** resulting from country size and the World Bank ROSC program have mainly determined the probability of Full IFRS adoption in the field of private firms by 2008, **network effects** have become larger outside of the European Union since 2009 and have determined the probability of

Full IFRS adoption by 2014 to a large extent. Meanwhile, the issuance of the IFRS for SMEs has influenced the determining role of **net economic benefits** in the context of Full IFRS adoption.

In particular, Full IFRS adoption in the field of listed firms significantly increased the probability of Full IFRS adoption in the field of private firms by 2008, but not by 2014 anymore. Instead, it now seems to make IFRS for SMEs adoption more likely (at least outside of the European Union). Hence, the empirical evidence indicates that the period of **synchronized, Full IFRS-based accounting harmonization** in the field of listed and private firms **has come to an end**. Besides, the results show that IFRS for SMEs adoption is more likely in countries outside of the EU that have required Full IFRS to be used for all entities (listed and unlisted) due to the reduced complexity of the standard compared to Full IFRS. In addition, the implementation of local versions of Full IFRS has been more of an impediment to IFRS for SMEs adoption than to Full IFRS adoption. All in all, the empirical results suggest that cost-benefit-considerations have played a more important role in the context of IFRS for SMEs adoption than in the context of Full IFRS adoption. In addition, the findings suggest that only if transitional costs are high (i.e. in case of mandatory adoption), net economic benefits are important enough to determine the probability of Full IFRS adoption in the field of private firms.

Although the influence of network effects on the probability of IFRS for SMEs adoption has still been negligible by 2014, they are likely to become stronger with every new country that joins the IFRS for SMEs network. In the case of Full IFRS adoption, network benefits and mimetic pressures have pushed many countries towards adoption although net economic benefits have been small or even negative. In conclusion, the **IFRS for SMEs is expected** to become even **more diffused than Full IFRS** in the field of private firms as it can bring considerable net economic benefits compared to the adoption of local standards or Full IFRS.

The second sub-study **adds to prior research** in three major aspects: first, the study focuses on financial reporting regulation in the field of private firms in 110 countries at two different points in time (2008 & 2014). Hence, it is able to derive statements on the main drivers of international accounting harmonization before and after private firms' financial reporting landscape was changed dramatically due to the issuance of the IFRS for SMEs in 2009. Second, it integrates two theoretic concepts (*economic theory of networks* and *institutional theory of isomorphism*) into one comprehensive conceptual framework to provide a broad foundation for testing hypotheses regarding the determinants of Full IFRS and IFRS for SMEs adoption. Third, it differentiates Full IFRS and IFRS for SMEs adoption on the basis of the type and scope of adoption and thus provides a more detailed view on the relative explanatory power of the various determinants than prior studies.

For these multiple reasons, the second sub-study contributes to the scarce empirical, cross-country research that has so far provided evidence on the determinants of Full IFRS (and IFRS for SMEs) adoption on country level (e.g. *Hope et al.* (2006); *Judge et al.* (2010); *Ramanna/Sletten* (2013) and *Kaya/Koch* (2013)). In particular, it is the first study that focuses on Full IFRS adoption in the field of private firms after 2009 and thus provides an insight into the **interdependencies between Full IFRS and IFRS for SMEs adoption**.

In summary, the study's descriptive and explanatory results provide the IASB and national standard-setters new insights into the characteristics and determinants of international accounting harmonization in the field of private firms. They may thereby help to explain why Full IFRS and IFRS for SMEs adoption have so far been perceived as desirable in many parts of the world, whereas some jurisdictions still oppose the IASB standards.

5.2 Limitations

This study is subject to methodological limitations that may impair the **generalizability** (external validity) of the above presented results. First, data collection was limited to the international network of *Grant Thornton* and *PricewaterhouseCoopers*. As these two international audit firms have fewer or no offices in the very smallest jurisdictions (e.g. Gambia, Dominica, and Tuvalu), **data availability** is poor for these jurisdictions. For these reasons, the sample of 110 countries is biased towards larger, densely populated, and economically more powerful countries. The implications of this study may thus not be transferred to the world's smallest jurisdictions. Nevertheless, the sample still represents a comprehensive database for a global analysis of international accounting harmonization in the field of private firms.

All data on the process towards Full IFRS and IFRS for SMEs adoption between 2002 and 2014 were obtained from an e-mail-based survey sent to managing partners of the two above stated international audit firms. Although the given information was verified by drawing on various public sources such as *IFRS Foundation* (2014g), *PricewaterhouseCoopers* (2013), and national standard-setters' websites (if available), errors cannot be ruled out completely. Due to the dynamics in national standard setting, countries might also have adjusted, postponed, or reversed their Full IFRS and IFRS for SMEs adoption decision without notice, which might impair the **reliability** of the results. However, even in case of single errors or outdated information, the general view on the global trends in international accounting harmonization remains unaffected.

The first sub-study presents a **classification** of accounting systems based on their degree of compliance with Full IFRS and IFRS for SMEs. Although the applied methodology is made comprehensible and comparable by the use of definitions and examples, the classification itself remains ambiguous to some extent. It shall therefore be regarded as a first attempt only to capture the three-dimensional structure of accounting standard setting in the field of private firms that has evolved since the issuance of the IFRS for SMEs in 2009.

The second sub-study draws on the *economic theory of networks* and the *institutional theory of isomorphism* to determine the probability of Full IFRS and IFRS for SMEs adoption in the field of private firms by 2008 and by 2014. It thereby defines three groups of determinants, namely *net economic benefits*, *network effects*, and *political pressures*. Although the test statistics indicate that the applied models are significant as a whole and the count R^2 amounts to above 80% on average, this study's conceptual framework is not able to explain all reasons for and against Full IFRS and IFRS for SMEs adoption on country level. Undoubtedly, there are **alternative explanations** that are not included in this study (e.g. the influence of **culture**). While the characteristics of a country's **capital market** seem to be less relevant in the financial reporting context of private firms, there might also be an influence of a country's **legal tradition** (common law vs. code law) on the probability of Full IFRS and IFRS for SMEs adoption. In particular, *Kaya/Koch* (2013) suggest that IFRS for SMEs adoption is more likely for countries that have a common law tradition because their domestic standards would be *"closer in the spirit of the IFRS-framework than the national GAAP of code law countries"* (*Kaya/Koch* (2013), p. 15). However, the distinction between common law and code law countries is problematic since the common/code law groups are not homogeneous and thus hide important differences within each category (*Raffournier* (2013), p. 291). In addition, recent trends make the common/code law distinction even less persuasive as most countries' legal systems have been strongly internationalized (*Siems* (2008), p. 9). As legal systems have changed substantially over time, it remains unclear whether to refer to a country's legal tradition or to its current state of development.

Besides, (normative) **pressures** arising from institutions **inside a country** might also determine the probability of Full IFRS and IFRS for SMEs adoption in the field of private firms. For example, IFRS for SMEs adoption has been strongly opposed by various professional associations in Germany during the IFRS for SMEs' due process.[191] Due to the lack of data and the difficulty in measuring internal pressures consistently on a global scale, this study has focused on external coercive pressures only.

As discussed in chapter four, data on the perceived quality of accounting standards (ACC_QUAL) were derived from the *World Economic Forum's* annual Global Competitiveness Report and build on the answers to a question in the annual Executive Opinion Survey. As this question does also refer to a country's auditing standards, the proxy can be regarded as problematic due to the possible lack of **internal validity**. The study might therefore not provide a clear and entirely unaffected indication on the direct economic benefits from Full IFRS and IFRS for SME adoption resulting from the perceived quality of accounting standards.

Based on the empirical evidence provided in this study, the following section presents opportunities for future research and a brief outlook on future developments in international accounting harmonization, especially in the field of private firms.

5.3 Perspectives

During the past decade, international accounting research has more and more shifted from the analysis of national accounting systems (de jure harmonization) to the analysis of national accounting practice under IFRS (de facto harmonization). This is not surprising considering that *"more than 100 jurisdictions have now adopted IFRS"* (*Pacter* (2014), p. 6). Self-evidently, the analysis of different national accounting systems would come to naught if IFRS were the only accounting system in place. While this statement may hold true for Full IFRS adoption in the field of listed companies, this study clearly tells a different story about international accounting harmonization in the field of private firms. In contrast to

[191] Cf. among others *Verband der Elektrizitätswirtschaft* (2004), *Bundessteuerberaterkammer* (2004), and *Genossenschaftsverband Bayern* (2007).

the mandatory adoption of Full IFRS and the related process of GAAP substitution in the context of listed firms, the past decade was rather characterized as a period of voluntary Full IFRS and IFRS for SMEs adoption and GAAP complementation in the field of private firms. In particular, the persistence of localized accounting systems as well as the issuance of a second set of IASB standards – the IFRS for SMEs – have contributed to a **new diversity of national accounting systems** for private firms. For this reason, there are still large opportunities for future research in the field of de jure harmonization related to Full IFRS and IFRS for SMEs.

This study has classified accounting systems on the basis of their degree of compliance with Full IFRS and IFRS for SMEs. Future research could develop **new classifications** by measuring the degree of IFRS compliance in more detail. For example, future research could precisely identify the accounting areas, in which jurisdictions have modified, extended, or omitted IASB standards in the course of adoption or convergence. In particular, this research could not only include the minor modifications that are observable today in local versions of IFRS such as EU-IFRS or Australian-IFRS, but it could focus on the large number of national accounting systems that have been subject to convergence with IFRS to a varying extent during the past three or four decades. Simply put: *"what must happen that French GAAP, German GAAP, or US GAAP become (a local version of) IFRS?"* **Modifications to IFRS** might be rare (*Pacter* (2014), p. 9) if the definition of IFRS is narrow. However, if all existing accounting systems worldwide are defined as being related to IFRS in some way or another, the analysis of modifications to IFRS becomes a promising new field of international accounting research, especially in the field of private firms.

One limitation of this study is that the very smallest jurisdictions are not included in the sample. Future research could aim at integrating these jurisdictions into the analysis to provide further empirical evidence on the characteristics and determinants of international accounting harmonization in the field of private firms. The **IFRS jurisdiction profiles** on IFRS.org already cover 130 countries including many smaller jurisdictions. This new open source data base offers great opportunities for future research, especially regarding the process of international accounting harmonization over time.

The results of this study suggest that the principal benefits and pressures of international accounting harmonization originate from network effects. Future research could aim at defining and measuring different types of **network effects** (e.g. those that result from cross-border trade, investment, or other transnational linkages) and evaluate their specific impact on the probability of Full IFRS and IFRS for SMEs adoption in the field of private firms. In particular, network effects are expected to become more relevant in the context of IFRS for SMEs adoption if worldwide adoption gains further momentum. Aside from the network effects that arise from an increasing diffusion of Full IFRS and IFRS for SMEs on country-level, it can be expected that any future steps towards *de jure* accounting harmonization in the field of private firms will be strongly influenced by those network effects that arise from *de facto* harmonization in financial reporting practice. Today, only little is known about the actual number of private companies using Full IFRS or IFRS for SMEs for financial reporting purposes. Hence, future research could aim at collecting data on the share of Full IFRS and IFRS for SMEs adopting private firms per country and thereby derive new measures for global network effects.

All in all, this study has shed light on the fact that the issuance of the **IFRS for SMEs** in 2009 has truly mixed up the bipolar financial accounting landscape between Local GAAP and Full IFRS by adding a **third dimension to international GAAP choice**. Even if modifications to the two existing sets of IFRS were negligible, the IFRS for SMEs has still led to a new, irrevocable diversity of accounting systems in the field of private firms. Although the IFRS for SMEs might be more suitable for private firms than Full IFRS and might thus provide more net economic benefits than its 'bigger brother', the spread of IFRS for SMEs around the world challenges a key objective of the IASB: *"to increase the comparability of financial statements"*.

National standard-setters like the UK Accounting Standards Board as well as professional bodies such as the AICPA seem to be more willing to modify the IFRS for SMEs according to their individual needs than they have dared to change Full IFRS. Hence, international **comparability of private firms' financial statements is at risk** despite the great progress that has been made during the past decade. No matter what happens, financial statement users have to be aware of this new diversity of accounting systems and should not fall for 'pseudo comparability' under the name of IFRS.

Finally, one question remains: *"how will the European Union respond to the spread of IFRS for SMEs around the world?"* In 2002, the EU became the world's most important promoter of Full IFRS as it mandatorily adopted the IASB standards in the field of publicly traded companies. According to *Hans Hoogervorst*, Chairman of the IASB, the reason for this decision was simple: *"they could not have a single financial market with 20 different accounting languages."* (*Hoogervorst* (2014), p. 3). On the contrary, the European Union, now consisting of 28 members, still accepts the persistence of various national accounting languages in the field of private firms by 2014. Although these different accounting systems still serve national purposes such as being the basis for taxation and profit distribution, it is unlikely that the present state of European accounting harmonization will be sufficient in the long run as the **need for international comparability will not spare European private firms** and intra-European comparability has already been impaired due to the coexistence of EU-IFRS and local versions of IFRS.

If the European Union continues to oppose IFRS for SMEs adoption within its borders, it implicitly supports that more and more national versions of the IFRS for SMEs will be established following the example set by the United Kingdom (FRS 102). However, this cannot be the **future of international accounting harmonization** in the field of private firms (neither in the European Union nor anywhere else) given the tremendous efforts that have been made to develop and diffuse two sets of high quality and globally comparable financial reporting standards: Full IFRS and IFRS for SMEs. To quote *Ian Mackintosh*, Vice-Chairman of the IASB, as saying:

> *"Now is not the time to turn back the clock, and thereby put at risk the hard-fought gains of the last decade."*
>
> (*Mackintosh* (2014), p. 7)

Appendix

Figure A-1: Survey questions

Has Full IFRS been adopted for <u>non-listed companies</u> in your country?

If yes, please answer the following questions on <u>Full IFRS adoption</u> to your best knowledge:

Questions		Full IFRS adoption
(a)	From which financial year on have Full IFRS been adopted for non-listed companies in your country?	
(b)	Which types of non-listed companies adopt Full IFRS voluntarily or mandatorily?	
(c)	Which other GAAP (if any) is applicable for non-listed companies?	
(d)	Does the adoption of Full IFRS encompass individual and group financial statements?	
(e)	Do the adopted Full IFRS deviate from the original version of the IASB? If yes, please describe the differences briefly.	
(f)	Prior to IFRS adoption, had there ever been a Local GAAP in your country that was entirely independent from IFRS or might this Local GAAP had been influenced by other foreign GAAP (i.e. US GAAP)?	

1 – Full IFRS

Has a <u>country-specific version</u> of Full IFRS been adopted for non-listed companies in your country?

If yes, please answer the following questions on <u>Full IFRS adoption "as adopted locally"</u> to your best knowledge:

Questions		**Full IFRS adoption "as adopted locally"***
(a)	From which year has Local GAAP for non-listed companies been (materially) influenced by or (partly) converged with IFRS in your country?	
(b)	Which types of non-listed companies adopt Full IFRS "as adopted locally" voluntarily or mandatorily?	
(c)	Which other GAAP (if any) is applicable for non-listed companies?	
(d)	Does the adoption of Full IFRS "as adopted locally" encompass individual and group financial statements?	
(e)	In which way does Full IFRS "as adopted locally" deviate from the original version of the IASB?	
(f)	Prior to Local IFRS adoption, had there ever been a Local GAAP in your country that was entirely independent from IFRS or might this Local GAAP had been influenced by other foreign GAAP (i.e. US GAAP)?	

**** Full IFRS "as adopted locally" is defined as a Local GAAP that has been (materially) influenced by or (partly) converged with IFRS during previous years.***

Has IFRS for SMEs been adopted for non-listed companies in your country?

If yes, please answer the following questions on IFRS for SMEs adoption to your best knowledge:

Questions		IFRS for SMEs adoption
(a)	From which financial year on have IFRS for SMEs been adopted for non-listed companies in your country?	
(b)	Which types of non-listed companies adopt IFRS for SMEs voluntarily or mandatorily?	
(c)	Which other GAAP (if any) is applicable for non-listed companies?	
(d)	Does the adoption of IFRS for SMEs encompass individual and group financial statements?	
(e)	Do the adopted IFRS for SMEs deviate from the original version of the IASB? If yes, please describe the differences briefly.	
(f)	Prior to IFRS for SMEs adoption, had there ever been a Local GAAP in your country that was entirely independent from IFRS or might this Local GAAP had been influenced by other foreign GAAP (i.e. US GAAP)?	

Has a <u>country-specific version</u> of IFRS for SMEs been adopted for non-listed companies in your country?

If yes, please answer the following questions on <u>IFRS for SMEs adoption "as adopted locally"</u> to your best knowledge:

Questions		**IFRS for SMEs adoption "as adopted locally"***
(a)	From which year has Local GAAP for non-listed companies been (materially) influenced by or (partly) converged with IFRS for SMEs in your country?	
(b)	Which types of non-listed companies adopt IFRS for SMEs "as adopted locally" voluntarily or mandatorily?	
(c)	Which other GAAP (if any) is applicable for non-listed companies?	
(d)	Does the adoption of IFRS for SMEs "as adopted locally" encompass individual and group financial statements?	
(e)	In which way does IFRS for SMEs "as adopted locally" deviate from the original version of the IASB?	
(f)	Prior to Local IFRS for SMEs adoption, had there ever been a Local GAAP in your country that was entirely independent from IFRS or might this Local GAAP had been influenced by other foreign GAAP (i.e. US GAAP)?	

**** IFRS for SMEs "as adopted locally" is defined as a Local GAAP that has been (materially) influenced by or (partly) converged with IFRS for SMEs during previous years.***

Table A-1: Countries and jurisdictions worldwide

North America
Bermuda, Canada, Greenland, United States
Central America & Caribbean
Antigua and Barbuda, Aruba, Bahamas, Barbados, Belize, Cayman Islands, Costa Rica, Cuba, Curacao, Dominica, Dominican Republic, El Salvador, Grenada, Guadeloupe, Guatemala, Haiti, Honduras, Jamaica, Mexico, Montserrat, Nicaragua, Panama, Saint Kitts and Nevis, Saint Lucia, Saint Vincent and the Grenadines, Trinidad and Tobago
South America
Argentina, Bolivia, Brazil, Chile, Colombia, Ecuador, Guyana, Paraguay, Peru, Suriname, Uruguay, Venezuela
European Union *(incl. European Economic Area)*
Austria, Belgium, Bulgaria, Cyprus, Czech Republic, Denmark, Estonia, Finland, France, Germany, Greece, Hungary, *Iceland*, Ireland, Italy, Latvia, *Liechtenstein*, Lithuania, Luxembourg, Malta, Netherlands, *Norway*, Poland, Portugal, Romania, Slovakia, Slovenia, Spain, Sweden, United Kingdom
Southeast Europe *(incl. others)*
Albania, *Andorra*, Armenia, Azerbaijan, Belarus, Bosnia and Herzegovina, Croatia, Georgia, *Isle of Man*, Kosovo, Macedonia, Moldova, Monaco, Montenegro, San Marino, Serbia, *Switzerland*, Turkey, Ukraine
Africa
Algeria, Angola, Benin, Botswana, Burkina Faso, Burundi, Cameroon, Cape Verde, Central African Republic, Chad, Comoros, Democratic Republic Congo, Republic Congo, Côte d'Ivoire, Djibouti, Egypt, Equatorial Guinea, Eritrea, Ethiopia, Gabon, Gambia, Ghana, Guinea, Guinea Conakry, Guinea-Bissau, Kenya, Lesotho, Liberia, Libya, Madagascar, Malawi, Mali, Mauritania, Mauritius, Morocco, Mozambique, Namibia, Niger, Nigeria, Rwanda, Sao Tomé and Principe, Senegal, Seychelles, Sierra Leone, Somalia, South Africa, South Sudan, Sudan, Swaziland, Tanzania, Togo, Tunisia, Uganda, Zambia, Zimbabwe
Middle East
Bahrain, Iran, Iraq, Israel, Jordan, Kuwait, Lebanon, Oman, Palestine, Qatar, Saudi Arabia, Syria, United Arab Emirates, Yemen
Asia
Afghanistan, Bangladesh, Bhutan, Brunei, Cambodia, China, Hong Kong, India, Indonesia, Japan, Kazakhstan, North Korea, Korea, Kyrgyzstan, Laos, Macao, Malaysia, Maldives, Mongolia, Myanmar, Nepal, Pakistan, Philippines, Russia, Singapore, Sri Lanka, Taiwan, Tajikistan, Thailand, Turkmenistan, Uzbekistan, Vietnam
Australia & Oceania
Australia, Fiji, French Polynesia, Guam, Kiribati, Marshall Islands, Micronesia, Nauru, New Caledonia, New Zealand, Palau, Papua New Guinea, Samoa, Solomon Islands, Timor-Leste, Tonga, Tuvalu, Vanuatu

Table A-2: Countries and jurisdictions in the sample

North America				
Canada	United States			
Central America & Caribbean				
Dominican Republic	Honduras	Mexico	Panama	
Guatemala	Jamaica	Nicaragua		
South America				
Argentina	Chile	Ecuador	Peru	Venezuela
Brazil	Colombia	Paraguay	Uruguay	
European Union *(incl. European Economic Area)*				
Austria	Estonia	*Iceland*	Netherlands	Slovenia
Belgium	Finland	Ireland	*Norway*	Spain
Bulgaria	France	Italy	Poland	Sweden
Cyprus	Germany	Latvia	Portugal	United Kingdom
Czech Republic	Greece	Lithuania	Romania	
Denmark	Hungary	Luxembourg	Slovakia	
Southeast Europe *(incl. others)*				
Albania	Belarus	Macedonia	Serbia	Ukraine
Armenia	Croatia	Moldova	*Switzerland*	
Azerbaijan	Georgia	Montenegro	Turkey	
Africa				
Algeria	Egypt	Morocco	Senegal	Uganda
Angola	Ghana	Mozambique	South Africa	Zambia
Botswana	Kenya	Namibia	Tanzania	Zimbabwe
Côte d'Ivoire	Mauritius	Nigeria	Tunisia	
Middle East				
Bahrain	Iraq	Jordan	Lebanon	Saudi Arabia
Iran	Israel	Kuwait	Oman	United Arab Emirates
Asia				
Brunei	Indonesia	Malaysia	Russia	Thailand
China	Japan	Mongolia	Singapore	Uzbekistan
Hong Kong	Kazakhstan	Pakistan	Sri Lanka	Vietnam
India	Korea	Philippines	Taiwan	
Australia & Oceania				
Australia	Fiji	New Zealand		

Table A-3: Accounting systems for private firms in North America

North America	L	FL3	FL2	FL1	F	SL3	SL2	SL1	S
Canada	*(prior to 2002)*		**ASPE** **(since 2011)** *(priorly CGAAP)*		**IFRS** **(since 2011)**				
United States	**OCBOA** **(prior to 2002)**	*(prior to 2002)* Planned (US GAAP with modifications)	**US GAAP** **(since 2002)**		**IFRS** **(since 2008)**				**IFRS for SMEs** **(since 2009)**

Table A-4: Accounting systems for private firms in Central America & Caribbean

Central America & Caribbean	L	FL3	FL2	FL1	F	SL3	SL2	SL1	S
Dominican Republic					**IFRS (since 2012)**				**IFRS for SMEs (since 2013)**
Guatemala	**Guatemala GAAP (prior to 2002)**				**IFRS (since 2008)**				**IFRS for SMEs (since 2011)**
Honduras	*(until 2011)*				**IFRS (since 2012)**				**IFRS for SMEs (since 2012)**
Jamaica			*(prior to 2002)*		**IFRS (since 2002)**				**IFRS for SMEs (since 2011)**
Mexico	*(until 2005)*		**MFRS (since 2006)**		**IFRS (since 2002)**				
Nicaragua					**IFRS (since 2005)**				**IFRS for SMEs (since 2012)**
Panama	*(until 2009)*				**IFRS (since 2010)**				**IFRS for SMEs (since 2011)**

Table A-5: Accounting systems for private firms in South America

South America	L	FL3	FL2	FL1	F	SL3	SL2	SL1	S
Argentina	*(until 2002)*		**Argentine Technical Resolutions (since 2003)**		**IFRS (since 2012)**			**IFRS for SMEs (individual accounts) (since 2012)**	**IFRS for SMEs (consolidated accounts) (since 2012)**
Brazil	*(until 2009)*			**CPC (since 2010)**					**CPC for SMEs (since 2010)**
Chile	*(until 2012)*				*(2009-2012)*				**IFRS for SMEs (since 2013)**
Colombia	*(prior to 2002)*		**Colombian GAAP (prior to 2002)**		Planned				Planned
Ecuador	*(prior to 2002)*		*(until 2011)*		**IFRS (since 2012)**				**IFRS for SMEs (since 2012)**
Paraguay	*(until 2008)*		**Paraguayan GAAP (since 2009)**						
Peru	*(until 2008)*		*(2009-2012)*	**Peruvian IFRS (since 2013)**					**IFRS for SMEs (since 2012)**
Uruguay	*(prior to 2002)*		**Uruguayan GAAP (prior to 2002)**						Planned
Venezuela	*(prior to 2002)*	*(until 2010)*			**Ven NIF (since 2008)**				**Ven NIF – SMEs (since 2011)**

Table A-6: Accounting systems for private firms in the European Union

European Union *(incl. EEA)*	L	FL3	FL2	FL1	F	SL3	SL2	SL1	S
Austria	*(until 2007)*	**UGB (since 2008)**		**EU-IFRS (since 2002)**					
Belgium	*(prior to 2002)*	**Belgian GAAP (prior to 2002)**		**EU-IFRS (since 2005)**					
Bulgaria	*(until 2002)*		**NFRSSME (since 2003)**	**EU-IFRS (since 2005)**					
Cyprus				**EU-IFRS (since 2005)**	*(until 2004)*				Planned
Czech Republic	*(prior to 2002)*	**Czech GAAP (prior to 2002)**		**EU-IFRS (since 2004)**					
Denmark	*(prior to 2002)*		**Årsregns-kabsloven (prior to 2002)**	**EU-IFRS (since 2004)**					
Estonia	*(prior to 2002)*		*(until 2012)*	**EU-IFRS (since 2003)**			**RTJ (since 2013)**		
Finland	*(until 2004)*	**Finnish Acc. Standards (since 2005)**		**EU-IFRS (since 2005)**					
France	*(prior to 2002)*		**French GAAP (since 2002)**	**EU-IFRS (since 2005)**					
Germany	*(until 2003)*	**HGB (since 2004)**		**EU-IFRS (since 2005)**					

European Union *(incl. EEA)* **(continued)**	**L**	**FL3**	**FL2**	**FL1**	**F**	**SL3**	**SL2**	**SL1**	**S**
Greece	*(until 2004)*	**Greek GAAP (since 2005)**		**EU-IFRS (since 2005)**					
Hungary	*(until 2003)*	**Hungarian Acc. Standards (since 2004)**		**EU-IFRS (since 2005)**					Planned
Iceland	*(until 2005)*		**ISGAAP (since 2006)**	**EU-IFRS (since 2005)**					
Ireland	*(prior to 2002)*		**Irish GAAP (prior to 2002)**	**EU-IFRS (since 2005)**		**FRSSE (prior to 2002)**	Planned (FRS 102)		
Italy	*(until 2004)*	**Italian GAAP (since 2005)**		**EU-IFRS (since 2005)**					
Latvia	*(prior to 2002)*		**Latvian GAAP (prior to 2002)**	**EU-IFRS (since 2005)**					Planned
Lithuania	*(until 2003)*		**Lithuanian Business Acc. Standards (since 2004)**	**EU-IFRS (since 2004)**					
Luxembourg	*(until 2009)*	**Luxembourg GAAP (since 2010)**		**EU-IFRS (since 2005)**					
Netherlands	*(until 2004)*		**Dutch Commercial Code (since 2005)**	**EU-IFRS (since 2005)**			**Modified IFRS for SMEs (since 2009)**		
Norway	*(prior to 2002)*		**Norwegian GAAP (prior to 2002)**	**EU-IFRS (since 2005)**					Planned

European Union *(incl. EEA)* **(continued)**	L	FL3	FL2	FL1	F	SL3	SL2	SL1	S
Poland	*(prior to 2002)*		**Polish GAAP (since 2002)**	**EU-IFRS (since 2005)**					
Portugal	*(prior to 2002)*	*(until 2009)*	**SNC (since 2010)**	**EU-IFRS (since 2005)**			**GAAP for SMEs (since 2012)**		
Romania	*(until 2004)*		**Romanian GAAP (since 2005)**	**EU-IFRS (since 2005)**					
Slovakia	*(until 2002)*		**Slovak GAAP (since 2003)**	**EU-IFRS (since 2005)**					
Slovenia	*(prior to 2002)*		*(until 2005)*	**EU-IFRS & Slovenian Acc. Standards (since 2005/2006)**					
Spain	*(until 2007)*		**Spanish GAAP (since 2008)**	**EU-IFRS (since 2005)**					
Sweden	**Swedish GAAP (other than K3) (prior to 2002)**			**EU-IFRS (since 2005)**			**K3 (since 2013)**		
United Kingdom	*(prior to 2002)*		**UK GAAP (prior to 2002)**	**EU-IFRS (since 2005)**		**FRSSE (prior to 2002)**	Planned (FRS 102)		

Table A-7: Accounting systems for private firms in Southeast Europe

Southeast Europe	L	FL3	FL2	FL1	F	SL3	SL2	SL1	S
Albania	*(until 2007)*				**IFRS (since 2008)**		**National Acc. Standards (since 2008)**		Planned
Armenia	*(until 2000)*		*(until 2010)*		**IFRS (since 2011)**				**IFRS for SMEs (since 2011)**
Azerbaijan	*(until 2007)*		**NASCO (since 2008)**		**IFRS (since 2008)**				Planned
Belarus	*(until 2011)*		**Belarusian Rep. Standards (since 2012)**						
Croatia			**Croatian Acc. Standards for SMEs (since 2008)**	*EU-IFRS (since 2013)*	**IFRS (since 2002)**				
Georgia	*(prior to 2002)*				**IFRS (since 2002)**				**IFRS for SMEs (since 2013)**
Macedonia	*(prior to 2002)*		*(until 2011)*		**IFRS (since 2005)**				**IFRS for SMEs (since 2012)**
Moldova			**National Acc. Standards (prior to 2002)**		**IFRS (since 2011)**			Planned	
Montenegro	*(until 2003)*		*(2004-2005)*	**Montenegrin GAAP (since 2005)**	**IFRS (since 2005)**				
Serbia	*(until 2003)*			*(2004-2013)*				**IFRS for SMEs (since 2014)**	

Southeast Europe (continued)	L	FL3	FL2	FL1	F	SL3	SL2	SL1	S
Switzerland	Swiss Code of Obligation (prior to 2002)	*(until 2006)*	Swiss GAAP FER (since 2007)		IFRS (since 2002)				IFRS for SMEs (since 2009)
Turkey	*(prior to 2002)*		Turkish Uniform Chart of Accounts (prior to 2002)		TAS / TFRS (since 2013)				TFRS for SMEs (since 2013)
Ukraine			Ukraine GAAP (prior to 2002)	IFRS (since 2012)					

Table A-8: Accounting systems for private firms in Africa

Africa	L	FL3	FL2	FL1	F	SL3	SL2	SL1	S
Algeria	*(until 2009)*		**(New) Financial Acc. System (since 2010)**						
Angola	*(until 2001)*		**PGC (since 2002)**						
Botswana					**IFRS (since 2002)**				**IFRS for SMEs (since 2009)**
Côte d'Ivoire	*(prior to 2002)*		**SYSCOA / OHADA (prior to 2002)**	Planned					
Egypt	*(until 2005)*		**Egyptian Acc. Standards (since 2006)**						Planned
Ghana	*(prior to 2002)*		*(until 2012)*		*(2007-2012)*				**IFRS for SMEs (since 2013)**
Kenya					**IFRS (since 2002)**				**IFRS for SMEs (since 2009)**
Mauritius			*(prior to 2002)*		**IFRS (since 2002)**				**IFRS for SMEs (since 2012)**
Morocco	*(prior to 2002)*	*(until 2013)*	**Moroccan GAAP (since 2014)**						Planned
Mozambique			**Mozambican IFRS (since 2010)**						**IFRS for SMEs (since 2011)**

Africa (continued)	L	FL3	FL2	FL1	F	SL3	SL2	SL1	S
Namibia			**NAC001 (since 2006)**		**IFRS (since 2005)**				**IFRS for SMEs (since 2010)**
Nigeria			*(until 2013)*						**IFRS for SMEs (since 2014)**
Senegal	*(prior to 2002)*		**SYSCOA / OHADA (prior to 2002)**	Planned					
South Africa	*(prior to 2002)*		*(until 2002)*	*(2003-2012)*	**IFRS (since 2005)**		*(2007-2010)*		**IFRS for SMEs (since 2009)**
Tanzania					**IFRS (since 2005)**				**IFRS for SMEs (since 2010)**
Tunisia	*(prior to 2002)*		**Tunisian GAAP (prior to 2002)**		Planned				
Uganda	*(prior to 2002)*				**IFRS (since 2002)**				**IFRS for SMEs (since 2010)**
Zambia			**ZFRS (since 2012)**		**IFRS (since 2005)**				**IFRS for SMEs (since 2011)**
Zimbabwe					**IFRS (since 2002)**				**IFRS for SMEs (since 2011)**

Table A-9: Accounting systems for private firms in the Middle East

Middle East	L	FL3	FL2	FL1	F	SL3	SL2	SL1	S
Bahrain					IFRS (since 2002)				Planned
Iran			Iranian Acc. Standards (prior to 2002)						Planned
Iraq	*(prior to 2002)*		Iraqi GAAP (prior to 2002)						Planned
Israel	*(prior to 2002)*		Israeli GAAP (prior to 2002)		IFRS (since 2006)				IFRS for SMEs (since 2011)
Jordan					IFRS (since 2002)				Planned
Kuwait					IFRS (since 2002)				Planned
Lebanon	*(prior to 2002)*				IFRS (since 2002)				IFRS for SMEs (since 2009)
Oman					IFRS (since 2002)				Planned
Saudi Arabia	*(until 2002)*	Acc. Standards by SOCPA (since 2003)			Planned			Planned	
United Arab Emirates			GAAP (prior to 2002)		IFRS (since 2002)				Planned

Table A-10: Accounting systems for private firms in Asia

Asia	L	FL3	FL2	FL1	F	SL3	SL2	SL1	S
Brunei		GAAP (prior to 2002)			IFRS (since 2002)				
China	*(prior to 2002)*		Acc. System for Business Enterprises (prior to 2002)	Chinese Acc. Standards (since 2007)	Planned	Acc. Standards for Small Enterprises (since 2012)			
Hong Kong	*(prior to 2002)*		*(until 2004)*		HKFRS (since 2005)		SME-FRF & SME-FRS (since 2005)	HKFRS for Private Entities (since 2010)	
India	*(prior to 2002)*	Indian GAAP (prior to 2002)			Planned				
Indonesia	*(prior to 2002)*		*(until 2011)*	SAK (since 2012)			SAK-ETAP (since 2011)		
Japan	*(until 2004)*		Japanese GAAP (since 2005)						
Kazakhstan	*(prior to 2002)*		*(until 2006)*		IFRS (since 2006)		National Standards on Fin. Statements (since 2007)		Planned
Korea	*(prior to 2002)*		K-GAAP (prior to 2002)	K-IFRS (since 2009)					
Malaysia	*(until 2009)*		PERs (since 2010)		MFRS (since 2012)			Planned	
Mongolia					*(until 2013)*				IFRS for SMEs (since 2014)

Asia (continued)	L	FL3	FL2	FL1	F	SL3	SL2	SL1	S
Pakistan			*(2007-2012)*		**IFRS (since 2013)**		*(2007-2012)*		**IFRS for SMEs (since 2013)**
Philippines	*(prior to 2002)*		*(until 2004)*	**PFRS (since 2005)**					**PFRS for SMEs (since 2010)**
Russia	**Russian Accounting Standards (prior to 2002)**		Planned						Planned
Singapore	*(prior to 2002)*		*(2002-2004)*	**SFRS (since 2005)**	**IFRS (since 2002)**				**SFRS for Small Entities (since 2011)**
Sri Lanka			*(until 2011)*		*(until 2011)*				**SLFRS for SMEs (since 2012)**
Taiwan	*(until 2005)*		**Taiwanese GAAP (since 2006)**	**IFRS (since 2013)**					
Thailand	*(prior to 2002)*		*(until 2012)*	**TFRS (since 2013)**		**TFRS for NPAEs (since 2011)**			Planned
Uzbekistan	*(prior to 2002)*		**National Acc. Standards (prior to 2002)**						
Vietnam	*(prior to 2002)*		**Vietnamese Acc. Standards (prior to 2002)**						

Table A-11: Accounting systems for private firms in Australia & Oceania

Australia and Oceania	L	FL3	FL2	FL1	F	SL3	SL2	SL1	S
Australia			*(until 2004)*	**AAS (Tier 1) (since 2005)**			**AAS – RDR (Tier 2) (since 2013)**		Planned
Fiji			*(until 2006)*	**IFRS (since 2007)**				**IFRS for SMEs (since 2011)**	
New Zealand			**(Old) NZ GAAP (prior to 2002)**	**NZ IFRS (since 2005)**			**NZ IFRS RDR (Tier 2) (since 2014)**		

Table A-12: Classification of accounting systems (basis for conclusions)[192]

Code	Countries
F	***All others:*** *"Full IFRS as issued by the IASB."* ***Azerbaijan (IFRS):*** *"IFRS as published by the IASB is translated to IFRS as adopted locally. There could be differences in the timing of approval. Currently all IFRS up to IFRS 7 have been approved. The adopted Full IFRS is basically a translation of the IFRS published by IASB with certain minor modifications, thus no significant deviations. The only differences, if any, may arise due to lag between timing of the amendments made by IASB and its translation by the relevant authorities."* ***Botswana (IFRS):*** *"Adopted as it is."* ***Dominican Republic (IFRS):*** *"Version of IFRS or IFRS for SMEs as published by the IASB six months after translated into Spanish."* ***Hong Kong (HKFRS):*** *"The HKFRS is a continuity of the Hong Kong Statements of Standard Accounting Practice (the "Local GAAP"). In 2005, the Local GAAP was converged to IFRS word by word and renamed as HKFRS (i.e. equivalent to then IFRS). The changes from Local GAAP to HKFRS were a change in accounting policies by applying some transitional provisions. The change to HKFRS using transitional provisions might not be the same as a conversion to IFRS adopting IFRS 1 in 2005. Dual compliance with both IFRS and HKFRS might not be achieved because of such transitional differences. While HKFRS have been converged with IFRS, differences remain primarily in respect of transitional provisions."* ***Moldova (IFRS):*** *"The adopted IFRS are the original version of IASB, translated into Romanian. Differences can arise due to timing differences of translations."*
S	***All others:*** *"IFRS for SMEs as issued by the IASB."* ***Brazil (CPC for SMEs):*** *"There is a CPC for SMEs which is essentially a translation of the IFRS for SMEs, but which can only be applied by entities which meet certain size criteria (based on revenue or assets)."* ***Dominican Republic (IFRS for SMEs):*** *"Version of IFRS or IFRS for SMEs as published by the IASB six months after translated into Spanish."* ***Jamaica (IFRS for SMEs):*** *"Same as IASB."* ***Macedonia (IFRS for SMEs):*** *"No deviation is allowed."* ***Singapore (SFRS for Small Entities):*** *"They are word for word the same, bar the title of the standard. Basically the name and difference in scope (only small entities / size criteria) and cross-reference to SFRS. No deviations from the original version of IFRS for SMEs."*
FL1	***Australia (AAS / A-IFRS (Tier 1)):*** *"Word for word with some minor edits for local regulatory references i.e. Corporations Act etc. Non-listed companies can always apply Full IFRS as issued by the IASB. However, to be fully compliant with our financial reporting legislation some additional disclosures must be made. The reason for this is that our standard-setter believes some additional disclosures over and above what is required by Full IFRS are needed (AASB 1054)."* ***Brazil (CPC):*** *"Statutory financial statements must be prepared in accordance with CPCs. There are very few other differences between CPCs and IFRS. There is a CPC for SMEs which is a translation of the IFRS for SMEs, but which can only be applied by entities which meet certain size criteria (based on revenue or assets). Brazil follows exactly the same procedures issued by the IASB for Consolidated Accounts. When it comes to individual financials there are some disclosures differences. They are very rare to be seen in practice."* ***China (CAS):*** *"The China standard-setter issued Chinese Accounting Standards in 2006 (effective from Janu-*

[192] This information was provided by *Grant Thornton* and *PwC*. In addition, the data were verified by different public sources including ifrs.org, adoptifrs.org, and national standard-setters' websites.

ary 1, 2007) and, in many ways, these standards are converged with IFRS. While there are still some differences between CAS and IFRS, the Ministry of Finance has a plan to further converge CAS with IFRS in the near future. CAS has converged to IFRS, except for the reversal of long-term asset impairment."

European Union / European Economic Area (EU-IFRS): *(Netherlands) "Although we may face carve-outs as a result of the EU endorsement process. So far we only had very few carve-outs so in practice we apply IFRS as issued by the IASB. Nevertheless we sometimes face timing issues due to delay in the EU endorsement. As a result an IFRS may be effective date on, for example, 1 January 2013, whereas it could only be applied in the EU as per 1 January 2014."*

(United Kingdom) "UK companies may only apply EU-adopted IFRS. Currently the only differences to IFRS are macro (or portfolio) hedge accounting (the IAS 39 carve-out) and in the timing of adoption of changes to the existing standards (as the EU endorsement process must be followed). IFRS as adopted by the EU is applied. IFRS as adopted by the EU differs from IASB IFRS due to certain past IAS 39 differences or where the EU adopts / approves new standards and amendments to standards at a date that differs from that reflected in the IASB IFRS."

Fiji (IFRS): *"The differences are mainly in relation to disclosures and policy notes."*

Indonesia (SAK): *"The Indonesian GAAP (thereafter called "SAK") is aligned with IFRS using gradual approach, not big bang approach like in Europe. SAK is actually translated from IFRS as issued by IASB as of 1 January 2009. By 2012, SAK is equivalent with IFRS as issued by IASB as of 1 January 2009. As mentioned above, SAK effective in 2012 is equivalent to IFRS as issued by IASB as of 1 January 2009. In 2009, Indonesian Institute of Accountants planned to fully converge the Indonesian GAAP with IFRS by 2012. So Indonesia has been amending its Local GAAP to conform to IFRS. While the whole intent is to have a Full convergence, certain differences are expected to remain by 2012 mainly because IFRS 1 is not adopted and earlier versions of the financial instruments standards may be used."*

FL1 ***Korea (K-IFRS):*** *"Korean IFRS is a translated version of IFRS issued by IASB with a couple of additional disclosure requirements which are not included in the original version. IFRS as published by the IASB and translated to Korean language word-for-word."*

Montenegro (Montenegrin GAAP): *"All companies have to adopt IFRS or Montenegrin GAAP as reporting framework. The only difference between two frameworks is mandatory Chart of Accounts for Montenegrin GAAP."*

New Zealand (NZ IFRS): *"The NZ version of IFRS eliminated certain recognition and measurement options and required additional disclosures. For example listed companies could only account for investment properties at fair value; they could not be accounted for at cost. IFRS as adopted locally. All requirements of IFRS as published by the IASB are retained, but also some additional requirements in New Zealand Equivalents to IFRS (NZ IFRS) (mainly in relation to public benefit entities). Differential reporting allows reduced measurement and disclosure requirements for those entities which meet the conditions (as detailed above). There are a number of differences between NZ-IFRSs and IFRSs."*

Peru (IFRS as approved by the Peruvian Accounting Setter): *"According to the Peruvian General Corporate Law, private entities' financial statements must be prepared according with IFRS as approved by the Peruvian Accounting Setter. Currently all IFRS up to IFRS 8 have been approved. There are differences in the timing of approval. There are also differences resulting from application of legal and tax requirements rather than Full IFRS. The following main differences, among others, are observed: the useful lives of fixed assets and restatement of financial statements by inflation during the period between 1998 and 2004 period in which the Peruvian economy did not qualify as hyperinflationary. Statutory financial statements of non-listed entities need not be filed before any governmental agency (although they are the base for determining taxes and shareholders distributions)."*

Philippines (PFRS): *"The following are the major difference/exemptions between locally adopted IFRS (or PFRS) and IFRS for the preparation of the 2011 financial statements: On initial adoption of PFRS, an entity can opt to defer the recognition of the transitional liability under PAS 19 for a period of up to five years. For pre-need companies, the accounting standards for pre-need plans and pre-need uniform chart of accounts as approved by the SEC are considered as the financial reporting framework. For Philippine financial reporting purposes, IFRIC 15 is only effective for annual periods beginning on or after January 1, 2012. The FRSC decided to require mandatory application of the Interpretation in 2012 to allow entities, engaged in real estate business, time to prepare for the implementation of the Interpretation. Entities are allowed to apply the percentage of completion method from the sales of property under pre-completion contracts in accordance with*

FL1	*Philippine Interpretation Committee (PIC) Q&A No. 2006-01 until the affectivity of IFRIC 15. The SEC, however, in its July 28, 2011 meeting, decided to further defer the mandatory adoption of IFRIC 15 while the revised Revenue standard is still being deliberated on by the IASB. Under Philippine Accounting Standards (PAS) 27, other financial reporting standards that are converged or virtually converged with IFRS are deemed acceptable in applying the provisions of PAS 27.10d on the exemption from the preparation of consolidated financial statements (PIC Q&A 2006-02)."* ***Singapore (SFRS):*** *"Since 2002, Singapore has embarked on a strategy of closely modeling Singapore FRS ("SFRS) after the IFRS. However, we still have specific differences and hence not fully aligned. Singapore FRS has been adopted locally for more than 10 years. Singapore FRS is not 100% compliant with Full IFRS, maybe around 99%. The SFRSs issued are largely aligned to the IFRS, except for certain modifications, certain transitional provisions, and differences in the timing of adoption. IFRS 9 has not been adopted in Singapore. IFRS 10, 11 and 12 has an effective date that is one year later in Singapore. Under a local amendment, no deferred tax is provided on foreign income not yet remitted to Singapore under certain circumstances. Certain transitional exemptions are allowed for non-regular revaluations of PPE if the revaluation model is applied. IFRIC 15 as adopted in Singapore as INT-FRS 115 allows the percentage of completion method. For exemptions from consolidation, one of the conditions differ from IAS 27/IFRS 10 (no necessity for parent to prepare IFRS accounts)."* ***Slovenia (Slovenian Accounting Standards):*** *"According to Slovenian Companies Act, Slovenian Accounting Standards shall not be in contradiction with IFRS as adopted in EU. According to Companies Act Slovenian Accounting Standards shall transpose the content of European Community Directives 76/660/EEC and 83/349/EEC and the amendments and additions thereto and shall not be in contradiction with IFRS."* ***Taiwan (IFRS):*** *Only time-lag: "Non-listed companies in Taiwan will adopt 2010 version of IFRS in 2013."* ***Thailand (TFRS):*** *"Thai GAAP is mostly converged with IFRS (currently updated to conform with all international standards effective January 1, 2009). IFRS will be converged with Local GAAP in phases. Some standards will be adopted as TAS in 2011 and some in 2013. Full convergence is expected by January 1, 2013. Other expected changes: As previously noted Thai GAAP is very close to IFRS and is expected to continue to converge with IFRS. Timing will likely be one or two years behind due to translation. We have adopted the convergence approach and have substantially applied IFRS since 2011 (based on BV 2009 blue book) except the industry specific standards being IFRS 4, IAS 41 and those financial instruments standards. We are currently in the process of updating Thai financial reporting standards for the amendments and changes to reflect the BV 2012 with the aim of adoption for 2015. Note that BV 2012 are those standards required for annual reporting periods beginning on 1 January 2012."* ***Ukraine (IFRS):*** *"Non-listed companies were permitted to adopt IFRS version 2009 from September 2012 by adoption of changes in Ukraine legislation (Law: About financial accounting). After these changes Ukraine non-listed companies were permitted to switch from Ukraine GAAP to IFRS."*
SL1	***Argentina (IFRS for SMEs):*** *"IFRSs for SMEs is to be adopted as issued by the IASB. The only exception is: Individual financial statements of companies that have to prepare consolidated financial statements, will apply the participation method (proportional equity value) as described in section 14, paragraph 14.8 of IFRS for SMEs to register investments in controlled companies and companies where significant influence is held (not controlled nor jointly controlled), with the same adjustments incorporated in the consolidated financial statements by application of consolidation standards as defined in sections 9 and 15 of IFRS for SMEs."* ***Fiji (IFRS for SMEs):*** *"The differences are mainly in relation to disclosures and policy notes."* ***Hong Kong (HKFRS for Private Entities):*** *"Based on IFRS for SMEs with the following amendments to suit Hong Kong's circumstances: a) to replace the recognition and measurement principles contained in Section 29 with those contained in the extant version of IAS 12 (2004 version) while retaining the relevant disclosures contained in the IFRS for SMEs; and b) the measurement of deferred tax liabilities associated with an investment property measured at fair value is capped at the amount of tax that would be payable on its sale to an unrelated market participant at fair value at the end of the reporting period."* ***Serbia (IFRS for SMEs):*** *"There is high probability that Accounting Law will include prescribed Chart of Accounts. This should be the main difference between Full IFRS and Local GAAP."*

FL2	***Algeria (New Financial Accounting System):*** *"The Algerian Financial Accounting Systems has been adopted from the 2005 version of the IFRS. All the changes made by the IASB since then are not reflected in Local GAAPs."* ***Angola (PGC):*** *"The accounting standards are based on old IAS with some exceptions and suspensions. The actual accounting standards were issued by the Finance Ministry in 2002 (Angola Accounting Plan)."* ***Argentina (Argentine Technical Resolutions):*** *"Influenced and converged towards IFRS in 2003, adopting similar valuation criteria. The standards are as issued by the IASB. The only difference is: The stand-alone (individual) financial statements prepared by entities obliged to present consolidated financial statements abide by the IFRS on a comprehensive basis, subject to the only exception discussed in this section. In the stand-alone (individual) financial statements prepared by entities obliged to present consolidated financial statements, equity investments in investees (controlled companies), in entities under joint control and in associates (entities in which significant influence is exerted but are neither controlled nor under joint control) shall be accounted for by application of the equity method described in IAS 28 "Investments in Associates". When it comes to investments in investees and in entities under joint control, it is the same adjustments made to the consolidated financial statements by virtue of the consolidation-related standards under IAS 27 and IAS 31, respectively that shall apply. The accounting criterion prescribed by this Technical Resolution for the preparation of financial statements and for measuring the investments mentioned in the preceding paragraph differs from the criterion mandated by IAS 27, paragraph 38 which requires such investments to be booked at cost or at fair value."* ***Azerbaijan (NASCO):*** *"Those non-listed companies that are classified as PIEs would apply Full IFRS. Whereas, other non-listed companies are required to apply National Accounting Standards for Commercial Organizations ("NASCO"). NASCO is basically a set of standards almost based on IFRS with certain modifications for the local specifics."* ***Belarus (Belarusian reporting standards):*** *"Since 2012 ministry of finance take steps for getting closer of Local GAAP to IFRS. But they have made only first steps. During the period of 1998 – 2008, the state developed a program to align Belarusian Accounting Principles with IFRS (i.e. some principles may be converged rather than fully adopted); because this required adoption of new laws and regulations, this program largely affected the timing of transitioning to IFRS."* ***Bulgaria (NFRSSME):*** *"Include almost all accounting standards equivalent to endorsed IFRS, but require much less disclosure (IAS 12, 16, 17, 27, 28, 31, 33, 36, 39 and 41). Bulgarian GAAP is influenced by IFRS (in 2003) but they are not converged with IFRS."* ***Canada (ASPE):*** *"Influenced by IFRS to low or medium low extent. The only changes they made that was strongly influenced by IFRS were the business combinations standard was aligned to IFRS 3 and the ARO standard was made closer to the concepts of IAS 37 (but not identical). Of course their starting point was CGAAP and to the extent that CGAAP was aligned and influenced by IFRS this is brought forward (e.g. inventory standard, accounting policy changes etc.). Now they are looking at the first wave of changes to ASPE and developments in IFRS certainly have more of an influence on what those changes will be. The process is to consider what IFRS changes are and whether they would benefit ASPE - so for example, there have been some revisions to Employee benefits based on revised IAS 19, and they are talking about some changes to align with parts of IFRS 10/IFRS 11 (although by no means a copy and paste of those standards). So on a go forward basis, I would suggest that IFRS influences ASPE to a medium extent, as it is certainly watched and considered."* ***China (Accounting System for Business Enterprises):*** *"Accounting System for Business Enterprises" was issued in 2000, and effective from Jan 1 2001. "Accounting Standards for Business Enterprises" was issued from 1992 to 2001. Both of them are influenced by IFRS at that time."* ***Colombia (Colombian GAAP):*** *"Colombia's GAAP is established by Decree No. 2649 in 1993. They are based on International Accounting Standards, which are currently the IFRSs and the U.S. GAAP."* ***Côte d'Ivoire (SYSCOA / OHADA):*** *"The SYSCOHADA was designed to be close to IAS/IFRS. Unfortunately, as the IAS/IFRS evolved and improved over the years, the SYSCOHADA which was later on adopted by French speaking countries of the CEMAC zone (Cameroon, Gabon, Congo Brazzaville, Equatorial Guinea, Chad and Central Afrique) remained static. IFRS has an influence on SYSCOA/OHADA, even if this influence is minimal. SYSCOA/OHADA designed, partly, in the context of a search for convergence with the technical solutions adopted by IASB. Below are some examples (inspiration from IAS 17, 23, 20). An asset acquired by*

FL2	*lease is recorded by the lessee provided that its value exceeds 5% of total gross assets; Borrowing costs are included in the cost of the asset if the loan is directly related to the transaction of purchase (or production) of the asset and borrowing costs are significant; the cycle of the production (or acquisition) is long (more than six months). Allowances legal career end are recorded. But it should be noted that unlike IAS 19, the evaluation method is not specifically defined by SYSCOA/OHADA. Investment grants are recognized in accordance with IAS 20. However, the method of deducting the grant from the value of the property financed is not admitted by SYSCOA/OHADA. There are very large differences between IFRS and these two accounting standards: Advertising costs can be activated (or capitalized). Expenditure of research and development can be, by choice, recognized as an expense or asset subject to meeting the criteria set (individual projects, with good chances of success and the cost can be individualized).The creation of a provision does not always require the existence of an obligation. The concept of a financial asset (or financial liabilities) does not exist in SYSCOA / OHADA. Deferred taxes are not recorded for individual accounts. Discounting receivables or payables is not allowed. The assets are valued at historical cost, except for revaluation decided by a competent authority. The concept of investment property does not exist SYSCOA / OHADA. The long-term contracts are recognized using three methods: progress, completion, partial benefit. Goodwill acquired in a business combination is depreciable. The unrealized exchange losses are not recognized, whereas unrealized gains are recorded."* ***Croatia (Croatian GAAP):*** *"At present the financial reporting requirements for Small and Medium-sized Enterprises (SMEs) are still the same as in 2002 and will only change once the FRC has issued the accounting standards for SMEs, based on IFRS and the EU Accounting Directives. The financial reporting framework in Croatia is not up-to-date and not complete and lacks alignment with the set of IFRS endorsed by the European Commission."* ***Denmark (Årsregnskabsloven):*** *"Generally, it (Årsregnskabsloven) complies with the then current International Accounting Standards. Hence, differences have arisen on the subsequent IFRS developments such as: Amortization of goodwill and intangible assets with an indefinite life is required. The maximum amortization period is 20 years. Fair value step up on obtaining and losing control over a subsidiary is not possible. Adjustments to contingent consideration are treated as an adjustment to the purchase price. Simplified purchase price allocation provisions. No requirement to recognize share based payment expense arising from equity settled arrangements."* ***Egypt (EAS):*** *"We have translated the IFRS 2005 version to be the base for Egyptian Accounting Standards. There are still some differences from the 2005 version especially in lease accounting. We did not update this translation since then. The EAS can't be considered as the same accounting framework as IFRS, we still have differences. The lease accounting for example is totally different. Also, we did not apply any revised IFRS as we have already our translated old IFRS version. The Local GAAP was materially influenced by IFRS starting from July, 2006. As the Egyptian GAAP was a translation of the IFRS 2005 version with some differences especially in leases standards. Before 2006, the Egyptian GAAP was far from IFRS. Egyptian Accounting Standards (EAS) are an Arabic version of IAS with some minor differences."* ***France (French GAAP):*** *"The French accounting regulator had at that time initiated an in-depth review of the French accounting standards in order to have Local GAAP converging (at least in part) with IFRS. The first steps of this convergence have been: 2002: Provisions (IAS 37). 2003 / 2005: Components (IAS 16 / IAS 37). 2005: Depreciations. 2005: Assets. The aim of this convergence has been to modify current accounting standards and to incorporate some of the IFRS principles. France is currently following a policy of 'progressive convergence' and there are still several dichotomies between French GAAP and the EU adopted IFRS."* ***Iceland (ISGAAP):*** *"The concepts are the same and ISGAAP uses much, but not all, of the recognition and measurement rules of IFRS. Text and therefore clarifications in the ISGAAP is little compared to IFRS. ISGAAP identifies IFRS as a generally accepted accounting principle that can be consulted when ISGAAP for further clarification. The requirements for disclosures are little compared to IFRS. Although the ISGAAP has many similarities to older versions of IFRS and identifies IFRS as a generally accepted accounting principle that can be consulted when ISGAAP has no answer, then ISGAAP is a quite simple standard and can never be considered a country - specific version of Full IFRS."* ***Iran (Iranian Accounting Standards):*** *"We use Iranian Standards, in use since 2001 which are mostly commensurate with IFRS but not quite the same. Basically, less complicated and based on local regulations. Standards were introduced gradually and project is not complete yet; they are now being modified while additional standards are being drafted. Due to limitations of the Iranian Commercial Code, Civil law, etc., some areas of IFRS were either not-applicable or not-useable. That is why they are "Iranianizing" the IFRS somehow."*

FL2

Iraq (Iraqi GAAP): *"Iraqi GAAP comprises only 14 standards which have remained unchanged since 1999 and which contain some elements of old IAS and some Iraq specific requirements. There were certainly more than 14 extant standards in 1999 and therefore a number of IAS have never been adopted. As Iraqi GAAP has not been updated, all recent Standards are not applicable and many differences exist."*

Ireland ("Old" Irish GAAP): *"UK/Irish GAAP although internationally influenced to some degree, it was essentially homegrown until recent years. However the nature of UK/Irish GAAP has changed significantly in recent years with increased influence from international standard-setters. The last conventional UK accounting standard was FRS 19 on deferred tax, which was published in December 2000. But the majority of standards since then are almost exact copies of IFRSs. Hence the role of the UK Accounting Standards Board has changed fundamentally from one of developing and improving UK GAAP to one of implementing IFRS into UK GAAP. This development is part of the convergence project which dates back to 2001."*

Israel (Israeli GAAP): *"Commencing 2001, the Israeli Accounting Standards Board has issued approximately 20 IFRS based standards dealing with various accounting issues (the "IFRS Based Standards"). The IFRS Based Standards are an integral part of the Israeli GAAP. It should be mentioned that, some of the IFRS Based Standards are based on old or not updated versions of the related IFRS standards."*

Japan (Japanese GAAP (for small and medium sized companies)): *"Japanese GAAP has been converted with Tokyo Agreement which settles a milestone related to the convergence to IFRS between IASB and ASBJ in 2007. Japan is now in the process of converging national GAAP with IFRS. In 2005, the Accounting Standard Board of Japan (ASBJ) launched a joint project with IASB aiming at achieving convergence between Japanese GAAP and IFRS. In August 2007, the ASBJ and the IASB jointly announced an agreement (known as the Tokyo Agreement) to accelerate convergence between Japanese GAAP and IFRS, a process that was started in March 2005."*

Korea (K-GAAP): *"Local Korean GAAP has been influenced by the IFRS from 2001. Korean government established Korea Accounting Institute (KAI) in 1999 according to an agreement with IBRD. KAI, as an independent and private institute, has established 28 accounting standards from 2001 to 2007 in line with the IFRS. Accounting professionals appraise that these standards accepted IFRS almost 90% in substance."*

Latvia (Latvian GAAP): *"Local GAAP is close to IFRS. Local GAAP is continuously updated. IFRS is much more specific and detailed compared to Local GAAP."*

Lithuania (Lithuanian business accounting standards): *"The Lithuanian Business accounting standards were first written based on IFRS. Still, some differences exist."*

Malaysia (PERs): *"Private Entity Reporting Standards (PERs) – based on International Accounting Standards (IAS)."*

Mexico (MFRS): *"The CINIF is in the process of converging all Mexican FRS by 2012 for all private entities. The main GAAP applicable to Mexican entities is Mexican Financial Reporting Standards (MFRS). MFRS have been in convergence process for the last seven year. All major differences are explained, with in each one of standards issued. In Mexico we have an independent standard-setter (CINIF) which issues financial standards for all none listed companies. This independent standard-setter began a process six years ago in order that the Mexican financial standards converge with IFRS. At present, Mexican standards with a few exceptions, comply with IFRS; however, as independent standard-setter this institution (CINIF) has the right to adopt or not new regulations issue by FASB (endorsement). Local GAAP applicable to Mexican non-listed entities is Mexican Financial Reporting Standards (MFRS). Local standard boards have been reviewing and modifying local standards with the aim of converging with IFRS since 2006. Nevertheless, local standard board has decided to maintain certain differences in recognition, measurement and disclosure rules in several standards."*

Moldova (NAS): *"The National Accounting Standards (Moldovan GAAP) has been developed in 1997. It was based on the 1994 IAS edition, with changes and adaptations to local conditions. In some cases, those changes were significant (for example, there is no requirement to consolidate groups; or the revaluation of PPE is recycled through PL and other cases). Also, not all the IAS standards existing in 1997 were adopted. Since then, no changes to developed standards were made; apart from adopting some new standards that were missing (for example, NAS 19 – a short copy of IAS 19 has been adopted in 2008). However, no IFRS developed after 2000 has been adopted, and no SIC, nor IFRIC. As such, there are some very important IAS/IFRSs, whose equivalent does not exist in Moldovan GAAP."*

	Morocco (Moroccan GAAP): *"Local GAAP for non-listed companies has not been (largely) influenced by Full IFRS. Conversion project underway (Scheduled in 2014)."*
	Mozambique (IFRS): *"IFRS as adopted locally except for FLs and VLIs. The Mozambican version of IFRS is based on IFRS as published at November 2008 by the IASB. Certain standards have been omitted. There is a provision to regularly update this, but the detail has not been determined yet. IFRS 2, 4 and IAS 26, 29 not in use."*
	Namibia (NAC001): *"NAC001 (since October 2006), some deviations from IFRS (fewer disclosures)."*
	Netherlands (Dutch Commercial Code): *"The Dutch Commercial Code has been influenced by IFRS as from 2005. In the past most IFRS standards were incorporated in the Dutch Commercial Code. As from 2008 the Dutch Accounting Standard-setter is more critical towards IFRS, and as from that date not all changes in IFRS are incorporated in the Dutch Commercial Code. Furthermore for some topics an alternative accounting policy has been developed by the Dutch Accounting Standard-setter, which is typically Dutch, for example pension accounting (based on IAS 37) and cost price hedge accounting."*
	New Zealand ("Old" NZ GAAP): *"We refer to it as "old NZ GAAP" and this reflected the accounting standards that were in place in New Zealand prior to the adoption of IFRS. "Old NZ GAAP" consists of two types of accounting standards: Financial Reporting Standards (FRS) and Statements of Standard Accounting Practice (SSAPs). In summary "old NZ GAAP" has been influenced by standards issued by the IASB's predecessor, the IASC, not the IASB. IFRS 3 and IFRS 10 are almost exact copies of "old NZ GAAP"."*
	Norway (Norwegian GAAP incl. three "sub-GAAPs"): *"Local GAAP, including three "sub-GAAPs": Simplifications for small companies, Adjustments for not-for-profit entities, Adaptations to Full IFRS ("simplified IFRS"). Simplified IFRS: Less complex disclosures, Some exemptions from measurement rules, Presentation in accordance with the Norwegian Law of Accounting."*
FL2	***Paraguay (Paraguayan GAAP issued by Council of Public Accountants):*** *"Paraguayan GAAP issued by Council of Public Accountants of Paraguay is not mandatory, however is accepted in order to be use by non-listed companies. These standards were prepared in order to converge with IFRS, so there are few differences between them. The main difference is the partial adjustment for inflation in PPE that is accepted by PY GAAP. Although the World Bank's website showed a report on Paraguay's compliance with standards and codes, it does not specify if any type of companies officially adopted IFRS."*
	Poland (Polish GAAP): *"Local GAAP is materially converged with IFRS. Some of its parts were directly based on IFRS regulations, nevertheless some differences still exist. Polish Accounting Act and other regulations were materially amended in 2001 (effective for financial year 2002)."*
	Portugal (SNC): *"A new Local GAAP (SNC) for non-listed companies was adopted since 2010 and it is an adoption of IFRS. Non-listed companies should, as a general principle, comply with SNC (based on IFRS and in force since January 1st 2010). Nevertheless, they can elect to comply with EU- IFRS if some conditions are met."*
	Romania (Romanian GAAP): *"Romanian Accounting Standards, based on IFRS. The Romanian GAAP is in the form of a Ministry of Finance Order, which regulates the accounting treatment for all financial statement items from all aspects – recognition, measurement, de-recognition and disclosures. This Order in its current edit is made according to 4th and 7th EU directive (as it is stated in this Order), and does not mention IFRS. We would not say that it is EU-IFRS because of the following: 1) Ministry of Finance does not endorse standards, but changes the Order every year to implement major changes in IFRSs. 2) There are departures from IFRS in several areas (for example, revaluation of PPE can be made according to fiscal rules; deferred tax balances are allowed not to be calculated, etc.). In general, it is a very light version of accounting rules. As an example, the whole document (describing accounting for all assets, liabilities, income and expense) has only 190 pages. 3) Moreover, the disclosures made in statutory financial statements are very limited compared to those disclosures made under IFRS. And in IFRS philosophy, disclosures are a crucial part of financial statements to be defined as IFRS compliant."*
	Senegal (SYSCOA / OHADA): *see* ***Côte d'Ivoire.***
	Slovakia (Slovak GAAP): *"Local Slovak GAAP, amended in order to bring up local accounting standards to European standards and effective since 2003, has been influenced largely by and is similar to IFRS."*
	Spain (Spanish GAAP): *"All Spanish companies adopted a revised Spanish GAAP from January 1, 2008 which was a partial convergence with IFRS. All companies must apply Spanish GAAP in their standalone*

financial statements, which is essentially IFRS based but presents some differences in accounting and disclosure requirements."

Switzerland (Swiss GAAP FER): *"Swiss GAAP FER gibt es bereits seit 1984. Im 2007 wurde der neue modulare Aufbau eingeführt. Swiss GAAP FER orientiert sich u.a. auch an Entwicklungen im internationalen Umfeld der Rechnungslegung, ist aber in erster Linie ein national ausgerichteter Standard. Somit hält sich der indirekte Einfluss von IFRS/IFRS for SME auf Swiss GAAP FER in Grenzen. Da Swiss GAAP FER – wie auch IFRS – den Anspruch erhebt, ein den tatsächlichen Verhältnissen entsprechendes Bild der Vermögens- und Ertragslage einer Organisation darzustellen bestehen bei Bewertungsthemen teilweise Übereinstimmungen. Allerdings gibt es viele Unterschiede: Bspw. sind im IFRS mehr Fair Value Ansätze als bei Swiss GAAP FER vorhanden. Ferner kennt Swiss GAAP FER kein OCI. Schließlich geht IFRS in den Offenlegungspflichten bedeutend weiter als Swiss GAAP FER."*

Taiwan (Taiwanese GAAP): *"In Taiwan, The GAAP amendment is approaching to the IFRS for years. Of course, there are not 100% at the same but there are pretty similar with IFRS. I have listed some of the amended ROC GAAP which are similar with IFRS: Financial instrument 2006.1.1, Non-current assets held for sale and discontinued operations 2007.1.1, Intangible assets 2007.1.1, Impairment 2007.1.1, Share-based payment 2008.1.1, Inventory 2008.1.1, Operating segments 2011.1.1."*

Tunisia (Tunisian GAAP): *"In Tunisia, the official reporting basis is Tunisian GAAP (for listed and non-listed companies). The Tunisian accounting principles and mainly the conceptual framework is similar to the IFRS conceptual framework. Accordingly, in the absence of a Tunisian accounting standard dealing with a matter, the IFRS standard could be applied in Tunisia. This is the case for example for IAS 12, IAS 19, IAS 32, IAS 39, IFRS 7, and IFRS 9 etc. which are not dealt with by Tunisian accounting standard. Tunisian GAAP is basically inspired from IFRS, but the IAS which were in application in 1995. Indeed, the major accounting principles as required by the Tunisian accounting standards are similar to IFRS except for some standards which are corresponding for their major part to an old version of IFRS."*

FL2 ***Turkey (Turkish Uniform Chart of Accounts):*** *"Turkish Uniform Chart of Accounts was promulgated around some thirty years ago and has been continued with continual revisions; majority of the principles laid therein happen to reflect sound accounting practice which probably took into account the IAS principles then in existence and therefore happen to be in line with IFRS to a large extent; there has been no attempt to converge with IFRS; the Turkish UCA will be subjected to revision and brought more into line with TFRS/IFRS. The Turkish UCA will continue to exist especially for the companies which come under the limits listed above. Probably more than 95% of companies will continue with the Uniform Chart of Accounts. Even the companies which fall within the audit thresholds above may continue to keep their records on basis of the UCA and convert their financial statements to TFRS/IFRS through out of book adjustments. All Turkish companies will apply the UCA and the accounting principles therein promulgated by the Ministry of Finance until the limits explained above are known. The accounting principles in the Turkish UCA are to a large extent in line with IFRS."*

Ukraine (Ukraine GAAP): *"Ukraine GAAP were created by Ukraine government from 1999 year by switching from Soviet Union GAAP to Ukraine GAAP. The principles and some accounting standards in Ukraine GAAP sometimes equal to IFRS, but also differences exist (disclosures, some treatments and principles). Ukraine government does not raise question about convergence Ukraine GAAP and IFRS, but simply adopt IFRS to listed companies (for non-listed voluntary use) and that's all. It deviates. The major but not all differences are: presentation, first time adoption, version of IFRS (in Ukraine adopted edition of 2009 year)."*

United Arab Emirates (UAE GAAP): *"Local GAAP in UAE are not written as a formal accounting framework, therefore many local companies adopt the accounting policies which suit their business/operational requirements. In most of the cases these accounting policies are complaint to IFRS but in some cases differ. And because this Local GAAP framework is not written anywhere for reference, these local companies decide what they want and adopt as accounting policy and the same has been accepted by the regulators. This issue has been in discussion at different forums and until the regulators adopt IFRS for the entire local and free zone unlisted companies, these companies will continue following the existing practice. Based on above I can confirm that Local GAAP still do exist and not all unlisted companies are producing their financial statements as per IFRS/UKGAAP/US GAAP etc."*

United Kingdom ("old" UK GAAP): *"UK/Irish GAAP although internationally influenced to some degree, it was essentially homegrown until recent years. However the nature of UK/Irish GAAP has changed significantly in recent years with increased influence from international standard-setters. The last conventional UK accounting standard was FRS 19 on deferred tax, which was published in December 2000. But the majority of standards since then are almost exact copies of IFRSs. Hence the role of the UK Accounting Standards Board* has changed fundamentally from one of developing and improving UK GAAP to one of implementing IFRS into UK GAAP. This development is part of the convergence project which dates back to 2001."

United States (US GAAP): *"The IASB and the US Financial Accounting Standards Board (FASB) have been working together since 2002 to achieve convergence of IFRSs and US generally accepted accounting principles (GAAP). A common set of high quality global standards remains a priority of both the IASB and the FASB. In September 2002 the IASB and the FASB agreed to work together, in consultation with other national and regional bodies, to remove the differences between international standards and US GAAP. This decision was embodied in a Memorandum of Understanding (MoU) between the boards known as the Norwalk Agreement. The boards' commitment was further strengthened in 2006 when the IASB and FASB set specific milestones to be reached by 2008 (A roadmap for convergence 2006 - 2008). In the light of the progress achieved by the boards and other factors, the US Securities and Exchange Commission (SEC) removed in 2007 the requirement for non-US companies registered in the United States to reconcile their financial reports with US GAAP if their accounts complied with IFRSs as issued by the IASB. At the same time, the SEC also published a proposed roadmap on adoption of IFRSs for domestic US companies. In 2008 the two boards issued an update to the MoU, which identified a series of priorities and milestones, emphasizing the goal of joint projects to produce common, principle-based standards. The Group of 20 Leaders (G20) called for standard-setters to re-double their efforts to complete convergence in global accounting standards. Following this request, in November 2009 the IASB and the FASB published a progress report describing an intensification of their work programme, including the hosting of monthly joint board meetings and to provide quarterly updates on their progress on convergence projects. In April 2012 the IASB and FASB published a joint progress report in which they describe the progress made on financial instruments, including a joint expected loss impairment ('provisioning') approach and a more converged approach to classification and measurement."*

Uruguay (Uruguayan GAAP): *"1991: Local GAAP first based on first IAS (Local accounting standards based on the principles of the first IAS (IAS 1 to IAS 18)). Change for FY 2009: We have not adopted Full IFRS for non-listed companies. Our local accounting standards are based on Full IFRS in force at July 2002 and certain local rules regarding the presentation of financial statements and consolidated and separate financial statements. The sentence "Full IFRS as adopted locally" could be used, but please note that the IFRS version adopted in Uruguay corresponds to 2007. In July 2007, a national decree was approved which established that IFRS in force at July 2007 will be mandatory for fiscal years beginning on or after January 1, 2009. A national uniform chart of financial statements (i.e., a presentation/disclosure accounting standard related to financial statements) remains in force. Additionally, national solutions were in force for fiscal years beginning on or after January 1, 2009. (1) Inflation adjustment is mandatory. (2) Separate financial statements should be always filed jointly consolidated financial statements and the equity method is required. In April 2012 a national decree revoked the mandatory application of the inflation adjustment. Uruguayan GAAP which consist of IFRS in force as of July 2007. Time to time, Government issues a decree updating the standards in force."*

FL2

Uzbekistan (NAS): *"Uzbekistan has not fully adopted IFRS. However, it is trying to converge to an extent with IFRS. In 1998, there has been an accounting reform in Uzbekistan for the development of a series of the first National Accounting Standards that were based upon IAS. Some of these standards were first drafted in 1997, but a few of them were approved in 1998 by the Ministry of Finance. At present, there are 21 standards effective in Uzbekistan. Each standard is based on the relevant international standard, but there are differences between respective local and international standards. In essence, Uzbekistan is in the first stage of the adoption process of IFRS. National Accounting Standards are based upon International Accounting Standards (IASs). Nineteen NASs were drafted towards the end of 1997 and, by the end of 1998, 16. Uzbekistan follows NASs designed on the basis of the Accounting Law 1996. NASs are part of the regulated system for accounting in Uzbekistan and have been developed based on IASs. Uzbekistan has developed a differential reporting regime for small and medium enterprises – it is ahead of the International Accounting Standards Committee (IASC) in this area. At present, 18 NASs have been developed and approved as follows."*

Vietnam (VAS): *"VAS were based on original version of IFRS and not any amendment or revision made subsequently as per the amendment or revision of IFRS. Vietnamese GAAP or Vietnamese Accounting Standards (VAS) are all BASED on IFRS, with certain amendments taken into account legal requirements in Vietnam. The first VAS was issued on 31 December 2001. As at today, there Are only 26 Vietnamese Accounting Standards issued. Those IFRS standards are considered complex have not been issued by the Ministry of Finance yet such as Share-based payment, Non-current Assets Held for Sale and Discontinued Operations, Exploration for Evaluation of Mineral Resources, Financial Instruments, Accounting for Government Grants and Disclosure of Government Assistance,...etc. In addition to that, VAS does not have accounting interpretations equivalent to any to any of the SIC Interpretations or IFRIC Interpretations. The Vietnam*

FL2	*Ministry of Finance ("MoF") issued a standard Vietnamese Accounting System Chart of Accounts in Decision 1141 (dated 1 November 1995). This was amended by various Circulars since. Decision 15/2006 (dated 20 March 2006) contains an updated Chart of Accounts and replaces Decision 1141. The first Vietnamese Accounting Standards were issued on 31 December 2001. As at 1 January 2011, there are 26 Vietnamese Accounting Standards issued. These are based on IFRS, with certain amendments, as highlighted in this document. This document is applicable for entities required to prepare financial statements in accordance with Vietnamese Accounting Standards, Decision 15/2006 and applicable regulations. It does not cover accounting requirements for financial institutions or small and medium-sized entities. IFRS standards in this document refer to the official pronouncement of IFRS standards as at 1 January 2011. IFRS standards which have been issued or amended after 1 January 2011 are not discussed in this publication. VAS does not have accounting interpretations equivalent to any of the SIC Interpretations or IFRIC Interpretations that are in effect as at the date of this publication. Accordingly, this document does not discuss the differences between VAS and SIC Interpretation or IFRIC Interpretations."* ***Zambia (Zambian Financial Reporting Standards):*** *"There are many major differences between Zambian Financial Reporting Standards and Full IFRS / IFRS for SMEs."*
SL2	***Albania (National Accounting Standards):*** *"National Accounting Standards - these are accounting standards developed in conformity with IFRS, but which are a more simplified version (similar to IFRS for SMEs)."* ***Australia (AAS – RDR (Tier 2)):*** *"IFRS Recognition & measurement with IFRS for SMEs disclosure (RDR – Reduced Disclosure Regime) (in fact: 'hybrid' IFRS)."* ***Estonia (RTJ):*** *"Direct adoption of IFRS for SMEs is not possible because it has not been endorsed by the EU. However, Estonia has chosen to adopt IFRS for SMEs indirectly by aligning the Estonian GAAP standards with IFRS for SMEs requirements. New Estonian GAAP standards that are based on IFRS for SMEs become effective from 1.01.2013. There will be a few minor differences between the new Estonian GAAP and IFRS for SMEs – e.g. in the areas where SME IFRS is incompatible with the EU Accounting Directives, and a couple of other areas where Estonian GAAP allows policy choice, one of the choices being equivalent to policy under SME IFRS. Also, the disclosure requirements are slightly different. While RTJ is based on IFRS for SME, they are not identical. In certain topics RTJ allows alternative methods, where not all the alternatives are in line with IFRS for SME."* ***Hong Kong (SME-FRF&SME-FRS):*** *"The background for issuing SME-FRF&SME-FRS locally is to provide a set of financial standards to smaller entities because at that time, IASB has not yet formally approved the IFRS for SMEs. Therefore when IFRS for SMEs have been issued, we adopt a local version – HKFRS for Private Entities. But instead of withdrawing SME-FRF&SME-FRS, they keep 2 sets of standards for smaller entities. SME-FRF&SME-FRS have made reference to IFRS for SMEs (draft) but not exactly the same."* ***Indonesia (SAK ETAP):*** *"In 2009, Dewan Standar Akuntansi Keuangan (DSAK; Indonesian Financial Accounting Standards Board) published Financial Accounting Standard – Entities that do not have Public Accountability (Standar Akuntansi Keuangan – Entitas Tanpa Akuntabilitas Publik or SAK-ETAP). SAK-ETAP effective by 2011 is derived from the IFRS for Small and Medium-sized Entities (IFRS for SMEs). However they made significant modifications in this standard which resulted in some major differences with IFRS for SMEs. As mentioned above, DSAK made significant modifications in SAK-ETAP which resulted in some major differences with IFRS for SMEs. SAK ETAP is not the same with IFRS's for SME. SAK ETAP is mix of some standards. SAK ETAP was prepared from some sources: 1. Indonesian old PSAK and some modification on it. 2. IFRS.s for SME. 3. Other sources. In IFRS for SMEs deferred tax accounting is applied, while in SAK ETAP no deferred tax accounting is applied."* ***Ireland (FRS 102):*** *"Although FRS 102 is based on IFRS for SMEs, it was drafted for use by UK Companies and so was influenced by current UK GAAP as well as needing to comply with UK company Law. Some of the key changes made were: Compliance with EU Directives (resolving the 6 items identified by EFRAG in their 2010 letter. Not to gold-plate the EU requirements for use of EU-adopted IFRS (FRS 102's scope encompasses all companies that are not mandatorily required to use EU IFRS). To re-introduce certain options available in current UK GAAP that were removed from the IFRS for SMEs (as a result of constituent feedback). To carry over relevant parts of UK GAAP not addressed by the IFRS for SME. To keep the format and presentation requirements of UK Company Law for the primary statements. The principle applied by the FRC when considering amendments to the IFRS for SMEs were: changes should be made to permit accounting treatments that exist in FRSs at the transition date that align with EU-adopted IFRS; changes should be consistent with EU-adopted IFRS unless a non-IFRS-based solution clearly better meets the objective of providing*

SL2	*high-quality understandable financial reporting proportionate to the size and complexity of the entity and the users' information needs. In these cases elements of an IFRS-based solution may nevertheless be retained; use should be made, where possible, of existing exemptions in company law to avoid gold-plating; and changes should be made to provide clarification, by reference to EU-adopted IFRS that will avoid unnecessary diversity in practice."* ***Kazakhstan (National Standards on Financial Statements):*** *"Currently non-public interest SMEs are required to use National Standards, which are primarily based on the IFRS for SMEs February 2007 Exposure Draft. Local Kazakh GAAP (for non-listed companies) has been materially influenced by or (partly) converged with IFRS starting from 2007. Before that Kazakhstan had KAS (Kazakhstan Accounting Standards), which were based on old version of IAS. Statement is correct. National Standard on financial statements was based on IFRS for SMEs February 2007 Exposure Draft."* ***Netherlands (IFRS for SMEs modified to comply with the EU-Directives (Dutch Commercial Code)):*** *"There were no changes in Dutch law. IFRS for SMEs is acceptable because we contemplate this standard as an alternative for the current Dutch accounting standards. In fact this is a further interpretation of the Dutch civil code. The code gives the main rules (principles based, many options) whereas the SME Standard includes the details, also re. the disclosures. The only issue we may have is a conflict between the SME Standard and the Dutch civil code."* ***New Zealand (NZ IFRS RDR):*** *"These are the most likely/significant changes: Deferred tax will not be required, companies will be able to adopt the Income Taxes Payable method. No requirement to prepare a statement of cash flows. Investment properties can be revalued or accounted for at cost (currently IFRS for SMEs prohibits revaluation). Property, plant and equipment can be revalued or accounted for at cost (currently IFRS for SMEs prohibits revaluation). Goodwill only impaired when indicators of impairment – so does not have to be dome annually if no impairment. The straight line 10 year basis of amortization in IFRS for SMEs will not be followed. You will note with the exception of cash flows, all of these differences are changes that are now being contemplated by the IASB in the next iteration of IFRS for SMEs."* ***Portugal (Local GAAP for SMEs):*** *"Portugal has developed a Local GAAP based on IFRS for SME's. It will be adopted for the first time in 2012."* ***Sweden (K3):*** *"IFRS for SMEs cannot be applied by Swedish entities. However, a new set of general advice of the Swedish Accounting Standards Board have recently been published (K3) and they are broadly based on IFRS for SMEs. K3 has to be adopted by larger entities by 2014 at the latest."* ***United Kingdom (FRS 102):*** *"Although FRS 102 is based on IFRS for SMEs, it was drafted for use by UK Companies and so was influenced by current UK GAAP as well as needing to comply with UK company Law. Some of the key changes made were: Compliance with EU Directives (resolving the 6 items identified by EFRAG in their 2010 letter. Not to gold-plate the EU requirements for use of EU-adopted IFRS (FRS 102's scope encompasses all companies that are not mandatorily required to use EU IFRS). To re-introduce certain options available in current UK GAAP that were removed from the IFRS for SMEs (as a result of constituent feedback). To carry over relevant parts of UK GAAP not addressed by the IFRS for SME. To keep the format and presentation requirements of UK Company Law for the primary statements. The principle applied by the FRC when considering amendments to the IFRS for SMEs were: changes should be made to permit accounting treatments that exist in FRSs at the transition date that align with EU-adopted IFRS; changes should be consistent with EU-adopted IFRS unless a non-IFRS-based solution clearly better meets the objective of providing high-quality understandable financial reporting proportionate to the size and complexity of the entity and the users' information needs. In these cases elements of an IFRS-based solution may nevertheless be retained; use should be made, where possible, of existing exemptions in company law to avoid gold-plating; and changes should be made to provide clarification, by reference to EU-adopted IFRS that will avoid unnecessary diversity in practice."*
FL3	***Austria (UGB):*** *"In our opinion the Austrian Commercial Code (UGB) is not 'IFRS as adopted locally'. UGB is a set of independent accounting rules based upon firm foundations. It differs in many aspects from the relevant IFRS rules. Certain limited changes made in the last few years have allowed some IFRS rules to find their way into the UGB. Examples of these include IAS 19 methodologies (NB: The changes to IAS 19 will necessitate changes to the relevant UGB paragraphs), share-based payments and taking over certain disclosure requirements from IFRS (e.g. fair value disclosures and risk disclosures of financial instruments)."*

FL3

Belgium (BGAAP): *"BGAAP has not converged with IFRS yet. For a number of accounting issues that are further examined by the Belgian Commission for Accounting Standards, which has only an advisory role, inspiration is sought in IFRS."*

Brunei (GAAP): *"There's influence but no convergence in the past. The target is to be IFRS compliant by 1.1.2014 for institutions with public accountability. I would say the IFRS influence is very insignificant. The financial reporting process is simply based on generally accepted accounting standards."*

Czech Republic (Czech GAAP): *"Although there have been some changes in the past towards IFRS principles, I would not see CZ GAAP as "IFRS as adopted locally". Although the main principles are often similar, the main difference between the GAAPs is lack of comprehensive guidance in CZ GAAP. It creates higher level of uncertainty for preparers and users of Czech accounts as well as lower level of comparability. In detailed guidance there are many differences and another huge area of inconsistency between the two GAAPs is disclosure requirements. CZ GAAP disclosure requirements are very limited. Czech GAAP has only been influenced by / partly converged with IFRS in very limited areas. The process is very slow though and only some principles here and there are adopted, not guidance similarly comprehensive as IFRS guidance. One principle difference is that under the CZ GAAP all leases (including financial leases) are accounted for as operating leases. Area where CZ accounting is relatively close to IFRS is accounting for financial instruments for banks. Other (manufacturers, trading companies, etc.) apply different rules for accounting for financial instruments."*

Finland (Finnish Accounting Standards): *"The Finnish GAAP is not as closely linked to IFRS as is, to my understanding, e.g. the Estonian GAAP. Here are some of the differences (but not all): All leases are handled as operating leases. All pensions handled as defined contribution plans. No discounting of future tax flows. Intangible assets, including goodwill, are amortized on a straight-line basis. No specific rules for impairment testing. Tax depreciation is booked also in financial statements. Percentage of completion method is optional. Booking deferred taxes is optional. Hedge accounting is optional. Differences in valuing financial assets. Presentation rules also differ. There are differences between Finnish GAAP and IFRS and the Finnish GAAP is independent from IFRS. However IFRS standards have had an influence on Finnish Accounting Standards. For example in some Finnish Accounting Board's general guidance (e.g. in the general guidance on depreciations according to the plan) there has been referred to IFRS standards. Besides taking some IFRS methods into the Finnish GAAP, IFRS is used as a guideline when The Finnish Accounting Board solves accounting issues that are not specifically dealt with in the Finnish accounting standards."*

Germany (HGB): *"In November 2007, the German Parliament passed the German Accounting Law Modernization Act which seeks a closer alignment of national accounting standards and practices with IFRS. Nevertheless, in April 2009 through the Act to Modernize Accounting Law, Germany stuck to preferring national laws for small-medium sized companies and considered IFRS "cost-intensive and highly complex"."*

Greece (Greek GAAP): *"To a very large extent, Greek GAAP has not been influenced by IFRS. The only area here IFRS has contributed to Greek GAAP is in the area of impairment testing (for non-financial assets) where aspects with respect to the valuation approach that can be applied have been influenced by IFRS. This has been since 2005 when IFRS was first implemented in Greece."*

Hungary (HAS): *"HAS have been significantly different from IFRS ever since its inception. While the stated intention of the Government is to align HAS with IFRS, this has not been the case in previous years. This is primarily due to the fact that most IFRS changes since 2005 have not been incorporated into HAS and also because most of the recent changes were due to specific local issues, which do not necessarily created convergence with IFRS. The most significant impact on HAS from IFRS relates to the introduction of the 'fair value option' in 2004 which allows for similar accounting for financial instruments as current IAS39. This however was due to a specific EU requirement. The main difference is that HAS is significantly focused on the legal form of transactions. In fact it was modeled from HGB in the 80's."*

India (Indian GAAP): *"There are some similarities with regard to standards like impairment, inventories, leases etc. but fundamental differences exists on financial instruments, business combinations, income taxes, consolidation, revenue recognition, share based payments etc. It is also not necessary that Ind GAAP would follow IFRS in the absence of an equivalent standard under Ind GAAP. So the differences are far too many. I would beg to disagree that Ind GAAP in its present state and form is IFRS as adopted locally. This is primarily because there are fundamental differences between the present Ind GAAP and IFRS. India did announce a policy of converging/adopting IFRS beginning annual periods 1 April 2011, however that plan has been shelved and no new date has been announced by the government. Therefore, it may not be appropriate to say that the present Ind GAAP is IFRS as adopted locally. The differences between Ind GAAP and IFRS are too*

FL3	*many."* ***Italy (Italian GAAP as issues by the Local Standard-setter (OIC)):*** *"Local GAAP has not been influenced significantly by ifrs. The Local Italian GAAP has been influenced by IFRS starting from fiscal year beginning the first January 2005 on the basis of a law published in February 2004."* ***Luxembourg (Luxembourg GAAP):*** *"There is no plan of convergence between Lux GAAP and IFRS as adopted by the EU. Companies can use one or the other and I do not expect that this will change in the future. The only change that took place in 2010 is the transposition of the EU directive on Fair value measurement. Companies that use Lux GAAP can use the fair value measurement model as defined by IFRS for financial instruments. This is the only convergence that took place so far and there in no other expected in the future. Outside this the convergence project, IFRS or any other comprehensive GAAP's are used in practice as a benchmark when the accounting law is silent on an accounting treatment in Lux GAAP."* ***Saudi Arabia (Accounting Standards issued by SOCPA):*** *"Differences exist for e.g. in method of inventory valuation, revaluation of fixed assets and fair valuation of investment property (not allowed under Local GAAP), etc. Also for mixed companies i.e. with Saudi and foreign ownership income tax and zakat is charged to equity accounts of respective shareholders. Further, IFRS to be used for guidance purposes on accounting matters or issues not dealt under the local standards so long it does not contradicts the measurement and recognition principles outlined in other local standards."*
SL3	***China (Accounting Standards for Small Enterprises):*** *"Accounting Standards for Small Enterprises (issued in 2012) is different with IFRS for SMEs, and is independent with IFRS influence."* ***Ireland (FRSSE):*** *"Predecessor and role model of IFRS for SMEs."* ***Thailand (TFRS for NPAEs):*** *"There is another set of accounting standards called as 'Thai Financial Reporting Standards for NPAEs' which is a local standard (only 258 pages). IFRS/IFRS for NPAEs did not influence TFRS for NPAEs. TFRS for NPAEs was adopted in 2011 – 2 years after the IFRS for SMEs was published. I would not confirm that TFRS for NPAEs was – at least partially – inspired/influenced by IFRS for SMEs in format and/or content because it is developed locally based on the old version of Thai GAAP but not IFRS for SME."* ***United Kingdom (FRSSE):*** *"Predecessor and role model of IFRS for SMEs."*
L	***Guatemala (Guatemala GAAP):*** *"Local GAAP has not been materially influenced by or (partly) converged with IFRS. Local GAAP are mainly based on tax requirements existing since the 80's."* ***Russia (Russian accounting standards):*** *"The non-public entities are obliged to report under the statutory rules. Despite the fact that statutory standards are said by the Government to be converged with IFRS in the future, as of now they are significantly different to IFRS. It is expected that by 2015 there should be a convergence but the date is constantly delayed."* ***Sweden (Swedish GAAP (other than K3)):*** *"The Local GAAP has not been influenced by IFRS at all but will be when the shift is made for K3 (non-listed companies larger than 50 employees etc.) which will take place 2014. Before that only listed companies had to follow RR which is a close translation of the old IAS rules."* ***Switzerland (Code of Obligation):*** *"Independent from IFRS."* ***United States (OCBOA – statutory basis):*** *"Locally designed 'OCBOA' – Other comprehensive bases of accounting / statutory basis (not including cash, tax, regulatory and contractual basis of accounting)."*

Table A-13: Characteristics of worldwide Full IFRS adoption in 2014

Full IFRS adopters (84) *(date of adoption)*	VOL	MAND	IND	CONS	ALL
Albania *(2008)*	Yes	Yes[1]	Yes	Yes	Yes
Argentina *(2012)*	Yes	No	No	Yes	No[2]
Armenia *(2011)*	Yes	No	Yes	Yes	Yes
Australia *(2005)*	Yes	No	Yes	Yes	Yes
Austria *(2002)*	Yes	No	No	Yes	Yes
Azerbaijan *(2008)*	Yes	No	Yes	Yes	Yes
Bahrain *(2002)*	No	Yes	Yes	Yes	Yes
Belgium *(2005)*	Yes	No	No	Yes	Yes
Botswana *(2002)*	Yes	Yes[3,4]	Yes	Yes	Yes
Brazil *(2010)*	Yes	Yes[5]	Yes	Yes	Yes
Brunei *(2002)*	Yes	No	Yes	Yes	Yes
Bulgaria *(2005)*	Yes	Yes[6]	Yes	Yes	Yes
Canada *(2011)*	Yes	No	Yes	Yes	Yes
China *(2007)*	Yes	Yes[7]	Yes	Yes	Yes
Croatia *(2002)*	No	Yes[8]	Yes	Yes	No[9]
Cyprus *(2005)*	No	Yes	Yes	Yes	Yes
Czech Republic *(2004)*	Yes	No	Yes	Yes	Yes
Denmark *(2004)*	Yes	No	Yes	Yes	Yes
Dominican Republic *(2012)*	Yes	Yes[10]	Yes	Yes	Yes
Ecuador *(2012)*	Yes	Yes[11]	Yes	Yes	Yes
Estonia *(2003)*	Yes	No	Yes	Yes	Yes
Fiji *(2007)*	No	Yes[12]	Yes	Yes	No[13]
Finland *(2005)*	Yes	No	Yes	Yes	Yes
France *(2005)*	Yes	No	No	Yes	Yes
Georgia *(2002)*	Yes	No[14]	Yes	Yes	Yes
Germany *(2005)*	Yes	No	No	Yes	Yes
Greece *(2005)*	Yes	Yes[15]	Yes	Yes	Yes
Guatemala *(2008)*	Yes	No	Yes	Yes	Yes
Honduras *(2012)*	Yes	No	Yes	Yes	Yes

[1] Subsidiaries of listed companies and companies with annual turnover in excess of Lek 1,250 million and more than 100 employees; [2] All except companies with no relation to a listed company; [3] Mandatory for all until 2008; [4] Public interest entities, companies with turnover in excess of Pula 10 million and total assets in excess of Pula 5 million; [5] Companies with turnover in excess of Real 300 million and total assets in excess of Real 250 million; [6] Large companies exceeding two of the three following criteria: total assets of Leva 8 million, net revenue from sales of Leva 15 million and 250 employees; [7] Medium-sized and large companies; [8] Mandatory for all until 2007; [9] All except small and medium-sized countries with turnover less than HRK 260 million, total assets less than HRK 130 million or fewer than 250 employees; [10] Companies with annual sales of more than Pesos 150 million; [11] Companies with assets in excess of US $ 4 million, gross sales of more than US $ 5 million and more than 200 employees; [12] Mandatory for all until 2010; [13] All except entities with annual group turnover of less than Fiji $ 20 million or with assets of less than Fiji $ 20 million; [14] Mandatory until 2012; [15] Subsidiaries of listed companies.

VOL = Voluntary adoption; MAND = Mandatory adoption; IND = Adoption in the individual financial statements; CONS = Adoption in the consolidated financial statements; ALL = Adoption for all domestic private firms.

Continued

Full IFRS adopters (84) *(date of adoption)*	**VOL**	**MAND**	**IND**	**CONS**	**ALL**
Hong Kong *(2005)*	Yes	Yes[16]	Yes	Yes	Yes
Hungary *(2005)*	Yes	No	No	Yes	Yes
Iceland *(2005)*	Yes	No	Yes	Yes	No[17]
Indonesia *(2012)*	Yes	No	Yes	Yes	Yes
Ireland *(2005)*	Yes	No	Yes	Yes	Yes
Israel *(2006)*	Yes	No	Yes	Yes	Yes
Italy *(2005)*	Yes	No	Yes	Yes	No[18]
Jamaica *(2002)*	Yes	No[19]	Yes	Yes	Yes
Jordan *(2002)*	No	Yes	Yes	Yes	Yes
Kazakhstan *(2006)*	Yes	Yes[20]	Yes	Yes	Yes
Kenya *(2002)*	Yes	No[21]	Yes	Yes	Yes
Korea *(2009)*	Yes	No	Yes	Yes	Yes
Kuwait *(2002)*	No	Yes	Yes	Yes	Yes
Latvia *(2005)*	Yes	No	No	Yes	Yes
Lebanon *(2002)*	Yes	No[22]	Yes	Yes	Yes
Lithuania *(2004)*	Yes	No	Yes	Yes	Yes
Luxembourg *(2005)*	Yes	No	Yes	Yes	Yes
Macedonia *(2005)*	No[23]	Yes	Yes	Yes	No[24]
Malaysia *(2012)*	Yes	No	Yes	Yes	Yes
Mauritius *(2002)*	Yes	Yes[25,26]	Yes	Yes	Yes
Mexico *(2002)*	Yes	No	Yes	Yes	Yes
Moldova *(2011)*	Yes	No	Yes	Yes	Yes
Montenegro *(2005/2005)*[27]	Yes	No	Yes	Yes	Yes
Namibia *(2005)*	Yes	No	Yes	Yes	Yes
Netherlands *(2005)*	Yes	No	Yes	Yes	Yes
New Zealand *(2005)*	Yes	Yes[28]	Yes	Yes	Yes
Nicaragua *(2005)*	Yes	No[29]	Yes	Yes	Yes
Norway *(2005)*	Yes	No	Yes	Yes	Yes
Oman *(2002)*	No	Yes	Yes	Yes	Yes
Pakistan *(2013)*	No	Yes	Yes	Yes	No[30]

[16] Companies incorporated under Hong Kong Companies Ordinance unless they satisfy the criteria for using HKFRS for Private Entities (Hong Kong version of IFRS for SMEs) or SME-FRF&SME-FRS (locally developed standards for small entities); [17] All except small entities with assets less than ISK 230 thousand, operating revenues smaller than ISK 460 thousand or fewer than 50 employees; [18] All except small businesses as defined in Article eleven of the Fourth EU Directive (78/660/EEC); [19] Mandatory until 2010; [20] Subsoil users, and large business entities; [21] Mandatory until 2008; [22] Mandatory until 2008; [23] Voluntary until 2011; [24] All except small entities with annual turnover of less than € 2 million, total assets of less than € 2 million and fewer than 50 employees and entities that do not prepare consolidated financial statements; [25] Mandatory for all until 2011; [26] Companies with turnover in excess of Mauritius Rupees 200 million; [27] IFRS and Montenegrin GAAP (only differ in the mandatory chart of accounts); [28] Overseas companies that have subsidiaries and branches carrying on business in New Zealand; [29] Mandatory until 2011; [30] All except medium-sized entities (MSEs) and small-sized entities (SSEs) with turnover of less than Pakistan Rupees 1 billion, fewer than 750 employees and total borrowings of less than Pakistan Rupees 500 million (i.e. only economically significant entities (ESEs)).

VOL = Voluntary adoption; MAND = Mandatory adoption; IND = Adoption in the individual financial statements; CONS = Adoption in the consolidated financial statements; ALL = Adoption for all domestic private firms.

Continued

Full IFRS adopters (84) *(date of adoption)*	**VOL**	**MAND**	**IND**	**CONS**	**ALL**
Panama *(2010)*	Yes	No[31]	Yes	Yes	Yes
Peru *(2013)*	No	Yes	Yes	Yes	No[32]
Philippines *(2005)*	No	Yes	Yes	Yes	No[33]
Poland *(2005)*	Yes	No	Yes	Yes	No[34]
Portugal *(2005)*	Yes	No	Yes	Yes	No[35]
Romania *(2005)*	Yes	No	No	Yes	Yes
Singapore *(2002/2005)*[36]	Yes	Yes[37,38]	Yes	Yes	Yes
Slovakia *(2005)*	No	Yes	Yes	Yes	No[39]
Slovenia *(2005/2006)*[40]	Yes	No	Yes	Yes	Yes
South Africa *(2005)*	Yes	No	Yes	Yes	Yes
Spain *(2005)*	Yes	No	No	Yes	Yes
Sweden *(2005)*	Yes	No	No	Yes	Yes
Switzerland *(2002)*	Yes	No	No[41]	Yes	Yes
Taiwan *(2013)*	Yes	No	Yes	Yes	Yes
Tanzania *(2005)*	Yes	Yes[42,43]	Yes	Yes	Yes
Thailand *(2013)*	Yes	No	Yes	Yes	Yes
Turkey *(2013)*	Yes	No	Yes	Yes	Yes
Uganda *(2002)*	Yes	No[44]	Yes	Yes	Yes
Ukraine *(2012)*	Yes	No	Yes	Yes	Yes
United Arab Emirates *(2002)*	Yes	Yes[45]	Yes	Yes	Yes
United Kingdom *(2005)*	Yes	No	Yes	Yes	Yes
United States *(2008)*	Yes	No	Yes	Yes	Yes
Venezuela *(2008)*	Yes	No[46]	Yes	Yes	Yes
Zambia *(2005)*	Yes	Yes[47,48]	Yes	Yes	No[49]
Zimbabwe *(2002)*	Yes	No[50]	Yes	Yes	Yes
Percentage (n=110 countries)	**65%**	**25%**	**66%**	**76%**	**65%**

[31] Mandatory until 2010; [32] All except companies with assets or revenue under US $ 10 million; [33] All except entities with (consolidated) total assets of less than Pesos 350 million or (consolidated) total liabilities of less than Pesos 250 million (i.e. only economically significant entities); [34] All except companies that do not strive for a listing or are no subsidiaries of parent companies that use EU-IFRS; [35] All except companies that do not present audited consolidated financial statements or that are no subsidiaries of a group that presents consolidated financial statements under EU-IFRS; [36] IFRS since 2002, Singapore Financial Reporting Standards since 2005; [37] SFRS mandatory for all until 2010; [38] SFRS mandatory for companies that satisfy at least two of the three following criteria: total annual revenue of more than Singapore $ 10 million, total gross assets of more than Singapore $ 10 million and total number of employees more than 50; [39] All except companies with total assets less than € 165,970, total revenues smaller than € 165,970 or fewer than 2,000 employees; [40] EU-IFRS since 2005, Slovene Accounting Standards since 2006; [41] Reconciliation to Swiss Code of Obligation required; [42] Mandatory for all until 2009; [43] Entities that have essential public responsibility or provide essential public service and entities with 100 or more employees or with capital investment in non-current assets above TShs. 800 million; [44] Mandatory until 2009; [45] Regulated service entities; [46] Mandatory for some in 2008-2010; [47] Mandatory for all until 2010; [48] Public interest entities; [49] All except small entities with turnover of less than Kwacha 20 billion; [50] Mandatory until 2010.

VOL = Voluntary adoption; MAND = Mandatory adoption; IND = Adoption in the individual financial statements; CONS = Adoption in the consolidated financial statements; ALL = Adoption for all domestic private firms.

Table A-14: Characteristics of worldwide IFRS for SMEs adoption in 2014

IFRS for SMEs adopters (40) *(date of adoption)*	VOL	MAND	IND	CONS	ALL
Argentina *(2012)*	Yes	No	Yes[1]	Yes	No[2]
Armenia *(2011)*	Yes	No	Yes	Yes	Yes
Botswana *(2009)*	Yes	No	Yes	Yes	No[3]
Brazil *(2010)*	Yes	No	Yes	Yes	No[4]
Chile *(2013)*	No	Yes	Yes	Yes	Yes
Dominican Republic *(2013)*	Yes	No[5]	Yes	Yes	No[6]
Ecuador *(2012)*	Yes	No	Yes	Yes	No[7]
Fiji *(2011)*	No	Yes	Yes	Yes	No[8]
Georgia *(2013)*	Yes	No	Yes	Yes	Yes
Ghana *(2013)*	No	Yes	Yes	Yes	Yes
Guatemala *(2011)*	Yes	No	Yes	Yes	Yes
Honduras *(2012)*	Yes	No	Yes	Yes	Yes
Hong Kong *(2010)*	Yes	No	Yes	Yes	No[9]
Israel *(2011)*	Yes	No	Yes	Yes	Yes
Jamaica *(2011)*	Yes	No	Yes	Yes	Yes
Kenya *(2009)*	Yes	No	Yes	Yes	Yes
Lebanon *(2009)*	Yes	No	Yes	Yes	Yes
Macedonia *(2012)*	No	Yes	Yes	No[10]	No[11]
Mauritius *(2012)*	Yes	No	Yes	Yes	No[12]
Mongolia *(2014)*	No	Yes	Yes	Yes	Yes
Mozambique *(2011)*	No	Yes	Yes	Yes	No[13]
Namibia *(2010)*	Yes	No	Yes	Yes	Yes
Nicaragua *(2012)*	Yes	No	Yes	Yes	Yes
Nigeria *(2014)*	No	Yes	Yes	Yes	Yes
Pakistan *(2013)*	No	Yes	Yes	Yes	No[14]
Panama *(2011)*	Yes	No	Yes	Yes	Yes
Peru *(2012)*	No	Yes	Yes	Yes	No[15]

[1] Minor modification of IFRS for SMEs in the individual financial statements (application of participation method as described in section 14); [2] All except companies outside the scope of Technical Resolution No. 29; [3] All except public interest entities, companies with turnover in excess of Pula 10 million and total assets in excess of Pula 5 million; [4] All except companies with turnover in excess of Real 300 million and total assets in excess of Real 250 million; [5] Mandatory adoption planned for large and medium-sized unlisted companies from July 2014 onwards; [6] All except companies with annual sales of more than Pesos 150 million; [7] All except companies with assets in excess of US $ 4 million, gross sales of more than US $ 5 million and more than 200 employees; [8] All except entities with annual group turnover of more than Fiji $ 20 million and with assets of more than Fiji $ 20 million; [9] All except companies with total annual revenue of more than Hong Kong $ 50 million, total assets of more than Hong Kong $ 50 million and more than 50 employees; [10] If consolidated financial statements are issued, the company is categorized as large and has to apply Full IFRS; [11] All except entities with annual turnover of more than € 2 million, total assets of more than € 2 million and more than 50 employees and entities that prepare consolidated financial statements; [12] All except companies with turnover in excess of Mauritius Rupees 200 million or less than Mauritius Rupees 50 million; [13] All except companies with turnover in excess of Metical 500,000; [14] All except economically significant entities (ESEs) with turnover of more than Pakistan Rupees 1 billion, more than 750 employees and total borrowings of more than Pakistan Rupees 500 million; [15] All except companies with assets or revenue above US $ 10 million.

VOL = Voluntary adoption; MAND = Mandatory adoption; IND = Adoption in the individual financial statements; CONS = Adoption in the consolidated financial statements; ALL = Adoption for all domestic private firms.

Continued

IFRS for SMEs adopters (40) *(date of adoption)*	**VOL**	**MAND**	**IND**	**CONS**	**ALL**
Philippines *(2010)*	No	Yes	Yes	Yes	No[16]
Serbia *(2014)*	No	Yes	Yes	Yes	Yes
Singapore *(2011)*	Yes	No	Yes	Yes	No[17]
South Africa *(2009)*	Yes	No	Yes	Yes	Yes
Sri Lanka *(2012)*	No	Yes	Yes	Yes	Yes
Switzerland *(2009)*	Yes	No	No[18]	Yes	Yes
Tanzania *(2010)*	Yes	No	Yes	Yes	No[19]
Turkey *(2013)*	Yes	No	Yes	Yes	Yes
Uganda *(2010)*	Yes	No	Yes	Yes	Yes
United States *(2009)*	Yes	No	Yes	Yes	Yes
Venezuela *(2011)*	Yes	No	Yes	Yes	Yes
Zambia *(2011)*	Yes	No	Yes	Yes	No[20]
Zimbabwe *(2011)*	Yes	No	Yes	Yes	Yes
Percentage (n=110 countries)	**25%**	**11%**	**35%**	**35%**	**22%**

[16] All except economically significant entities with (consolidated) total assets of more than Pesos 350 million or (consolidated) total liabilities of more than Pesos 250 million and entities with total assets (liabilities) of less than Pesos 3 million; [17] All except companies that satisfy at least two of the three following criteria: total annual revenue of more than Singapore $ 10 million, total gross assets more than Singapore $ 10 million and total number of employees more than 50; [18] Reconciliation to Swiss Code of Obligation required; [19] All except entities that have essential public responsibility or provide essential public service and entities with 100 or more employees or with capital investment in non-current assets above TShs. 800 million; [20] All except public interest entities and small entities with turnover of less than Kwacha 20 billion.

VOL = Voluntary adoption; MAND = Mandatory adoption; IND = Adoption in the individual financial statements; CONS = Adoption in the consolidated financial statements; ALL = Adoption for all domestic private firms.

Table A-15: Type of Full IFRS and IFRS for SMEs adoption per region

	Adoption (ANY)			Adoption (MAND)		
	Full IFRS		IFRS for SMEs	Full IFRS		IFRS for SMEs
	2008	2014	2014	2008	2014	2014
North America	50%	100%	50%	0%	0%	0%
Central America & Caribbean	57%	100%	86%	29%	14%	0%
South America	11%	56%	67%	11%	33%	22%
European Union	100%	100%	0%	14%	14%	0%
Southeast Europe	62%	85%	46%	38%	23%	15%
Africa	53%	47%	63%	37%	21%	16%
Middle East	70%	70%	20%	60%	50%	0%
Asia	42%	63%	32%	32%	32%	21%
Australia & Oceania	100%	100%	33%	67%	67%	33%
World	**64%**	**76%**	**36%**	**30%**	**25%**	**11%**

ANY = Adoption of any type and within any scope; MAND = Mandatory adoption.

Table A-16: Scope of Full IFRS and IFRS for SMEs adoption per region

	Adoption (IND)			Adoption (ALL)		
	Full IFRS		IFRS for SMEs	Full IFRS		IFRS for SMEs
	2008	2014	2014	2008	2014	2014
North America	50%	100%	50%	50%	100%	50%
Central America & Caribbean	57%	100%	86%	57%	100%	71%
South America	11%	44%	67%	11%	33%	22%
European Union	68%	68%	0%	82%	82%	0%
Southeast Europe	54%	77%	38%	46%	69%	38%
Africa	53%	47%	63%	47%	42%	37%
Middle East	70%	70%	20%	70%	70%	20%
Asia	37%	63%	32%	37%	53%	11%
Australia & Oceania	100%	100%	33%	67%	67%	0%
World	**54%**	**66%**	**35%**	**55%**	**65%**	**22%**

IND = Adoption in the individual financial statements; ALL = Adoption for all domestic private firms.

Table A-17: Descriptive statistics (Models 1-4)

Variables	Statistics	Model 1 (ANY)			Model 2 (MAND)			Model 3 (IND)			Model 4 (ALL)		
Groups (countries)		Adopt (70)	Non-Adopt (40)	Total (110)	Adopt (33)	Non-Adopt (77)	Total (110)	Adopt (59)	Non-Adopt (51)	Total (110)	Adopt (60)	Non-Adopt (50)	Total (110)
ACC_QUAL	mean	4.99	4.24	4.72	4.63	4.76	4.72	4.91	4.50	4.72	5.01	4.33	4.70
	std. dev.	0.85	0.84	0.91	0.74	1.00	0.93	0.85	0.94	0.91	0.89	0.82	0.92
	25%	4.40	3.65	3.90	3.90	3.90	3.90	4.30	3.70	3.90	4.25	3.70	3.90
	median	5.00	4.06	4.70	4.60	4.80	4.71	4.80	4.60	4.70	5.15	4.25	4.70
	75%	5.80	4.85	5.40	5.20	5.70	5.60	5.70	5.20	5.40	5.80	4.93	5.40
LOCAL_ GAAP	mean	0.69	0.83	0.74	0.45	0.86	0.74	0.64	0.84	0.74	0.68	0.80	0.74
	std. dev.	0.47	0.39	0.44	0.51	0.35	0.44	0.48	0.37	0.44	0.47	0.40	0.44
	25%	0.00	1.00	0.00	0.00	1.00	0.00	0.00	1.00	0.00	0.00	1.00	0.00
	median	1.00	1.00	1.00	0.00	1.00	1.00	1.00	1.00	1.00	1.00	1.00	1.00
	75%	1.00	1.00	1.00	1.00	1.00	1.00	1.00	1.00	1.00	1.00	1.00	1.00
LOCAL_ FULL	mean	0.37	0.60	0.45	0.33	0.55	0.48	0.39	0.55	0.46	0.35	0.58	0.45
	std. dev.	0.49	0.50	0.50	0.48	0.50	0.50	0.49	0.50	0.50	0.48	0.50	0.50
	25%	0.00	0.00	0.00	0.00	0.00	0.00	0.00	0.00	0.00	0.00	0.00	0.00
	median	0.00	1.00	0.00	0.00	1.00	0.00	0.00	1.00	0.00	0.00	1.00	0.00
	75%	1.00	1.00	1.00	1.00	1.00	1.00	1.00	1.00	1.00	1.00	1.00	1.00
FULL_LIST	mean	0.63	0.38	0.54	0.79	0.60	0.65	0.63	0.51	0.57	0.68	0.48	0.59
	std. dev.	0.49	0.49	0.50	0.42	0.49	0.48	0.49	0.50	0.50	0.47	0.50	0.49
	25%	0.00	0.00	0.00	1.00	0.00	0.00	0.00	0.00	0.00	0.00	0.00	0.00
	median	1.00	0.00	1.00	1.00	1.00	1.00	1.00	1.00	1.00	1.00	0.00	1.00
	75%	1.00	1.00	1.00	1.00	1.00	1.00	1.00	1.00	1.00	1.00	1.00	1.00
CO_ADOPT	mean	0.42	0.12	0.31	0.20	0.03	0.08	0.30	0.10	0.20	0.33	0.10	0.23
	std. dev.	0.36	0.11	0.33	0.19	0.08	0.15	0.24	0.11	0.22	0.29	0.11	0.25
	25%	0.08	0.00	0.04	0.00	0.00	0.00	0.08	0.00	0.00	0.07	0.00	0.00
	median	0.33	0.11	0.17	0.14	0.00	0.00	0.22	0.10	0.14	0.22	0.11	0.15
	75%	0.89	0.17	0.50	0.33	0.08	0.11	0.61	0.15	0.33	0.71	0.15	0.33
EC_POW	mean	0.46	0.57	0.50	0.34	0.57	0.50	0.42	0.60	0.50	0.47	0.54	0.50
	std. dev.	0.29	0.28	0.29	0.24	0.28	0.29	0.29	0.27	0.29	0.28	0.30	0.29
	25%	0.19	0.37	0.25	0.13	0.34	0.25	0.17	0.39	0.25	0.21	0.26	0.25
	median	0.45	0.60	0.50	0.31	0.61	0.50	0.37	0.65	0.50	0.46	0.58	0.50
	75%	0.70	0.82	0.76	0.48	0.82	0.75	0.64	0.83	0.75	0.70	0.81	0.76
POL_POW	mean	11.55	13.16	12.14	11.29	12.50	12.14	11.50	12.87	12.14	11.55	12.84	12.13
	std. dev.	2.04	1.50	2.01	2.34	1.75	2.01	2.18	1.52	2.01	2.16	1.57	2.01
	25%	10.43	12.19	11.04	9.81	11.25	11.04	10.14	11.63	11.04	10.37	11.63	11.04
	median	11.41	13.08	12.37	11.39	12.63	12.37	11.42	12.92	12.37	11.40	12.85	12.37
	75%	12.76	14.05	13.52	12.87	13.58	13.52	12.64	13.81	13.52	12.90	13.81	13.52
IMPORT	mean	-0.01	-0.04	-0.02	-0.01	-0.02	-0.01	-0.01	-0.02	-0.02	-0.02	-0.02	-0.02
	std. dev.	0.11	0.10	0.10	0.12	0.12	0.12	0.11	0.10	0.11	0.11	0.11	0.11
	25%	-0.05	-0.06	-0.05	-0.06	-0.05	-0.06	-0.06	-0.06	-0.06	-0.06	-0.04	-0.05
	median	0.02	-0.01	0.01	0.02	0.00	0.01	0.02	-0.01	0.00	0.01	0.00	0.00
	75%	0.05	0.02	0.05	0.06	0.04	0.05	0.05	0.04	0.05	0.05	0.04	0.05
PRESSURE	mean	0.24	0.63	0.38	0.24	0.49	0.42	0.24	0.57	0.39	0.20	0.62	0.39
	std. dev.	0.43	0.49	0.49	0.44	0.50	0.50	0.43	0.50	0.49	0.40	0.49	0.49
	25%	0.00	0.00	0.00	0.00	0.00	0.00	0.00	0.00	0.00	0.00	0.00	0.00
	median	0.00	1.00	0.00	0.00	0.00	0.00	0.00	1.00	0.00	0.00	1.00	0.00
	75%	0.00	1.00	1.00	0.00	1.00	1.00	0.00	1.00	1.00	0.00	1.00	1.00

The table displays the descriptive statistics for the independent variables in Model 1 (Full IFRS adoption of any type and within any scope by 2008), Model 2 (Mandatory Full IFRS adoption by 2008), Model 3 (Full IFRS adoption in the individual financial statements by 2008) and Model 4 (Full IFRS adoption for all domestic private firms by 2008).

Table A-18: Descriptive statistics (Models 5-8)

Variables	Statistics	Model 5 (ANY)			Model 6 (MAND)			Model 7 (IND)			Model 8 (ALL)		
Groups (countries)		Adopt (84)	Non-Adopt (26)	Total (110)	Adopt (28)	Non-Adopt (82)	Total (110)	Adopt (73)	Non-Adopt (37)	Total (110)	Adopt (71)	Non-Adopt (39)	Total (110)
ACC_QUAL	mean	4.92	4.31	4.78	4.69	4.79	4.77	4.86	4.59	4.77	4.96	4.41	4.76
	std. dev.	0.84	0.71	0.85	0.70	0.77	0.75	0.83	0.82	0.83	0.88	0.64	0.84
	25%	4.30	3.85	4.00	4.30	4.15	4.16	4.30	3.87	4.04	4.10	3.87	3.97
	median	4.83	4.12	4.70	4.65	4.70	4.70	4.73	4.65	4.70	5.10	4.63	4.70
	75%	5.70	4.71	5.40	5.25	5.40	5.40	5.46	5.36	5.40	5.80	4.82	5.40
LOCAL_ GAAP	mean	0.71	0.81	0.74	0.46	0.83	0.74	0.67	0.86	0.74	0.72	0.77	0.74
	std. dev.	0.45	0.40	0.44	0.51	0.38	0.44	0.47	0.35	0.44	0.45	0.43	0.44
	25%	0.00	1.00	0.00	0.00	1.00	0.00	0.00	1.00	0.00	0.00	1.00	0.00
	median	1.00	1.00	1.00	0.00	1.00	1.00	1.00	1.00	1.00	1.00	1.00	1.00
	75%	1.00	1.00	1.00	1.00	1.00	1.00	1.00	1.00	1.00	1.00	1.00	1.00
LOCAL_ FULL	mean	0.45	0.69	0.51	0.50	0.57	0.55	0.48	0.65	0.54	0.42	0.69	0.52
	std. dev.	0.50	0.47	0.50	0.51	0.50	0.50	0.50	0.48	0.50	0.50	0.47	0.50
	25%	0.00	0.00	0.00	0.00	0.00	0.00	0.00	0.00	0.00	0.00	0.00	0.00
	median	0.00	1.00	1.00	0.50	1.00	1.00	0.00	1.00	1.00	0.00	1.00	1.00
	75%	1.00	1.00	1.00	1.00	1.00	1.00	1.00	1.00	1.00	1.00	1.00	1.00
FULL_LIST	mean	0.58	0.62	0.59	0.64	0.77	0.74	0.58	0.73	0.63	0.63	0.69	0.65
	std. dev.	0.50	0.50	0.49	0.49	0.42	0.44	0.50	0.45	0.49	0.49	0.47	0.48
	25%	0.00	0.00	0.00	0.00	1.00	0.00	0.00	0.00	0.00	0.00	0.00	0.00
	median	1.00	1.00	1.00	1.00	1.00	1.00	1.00	1.00	1.00	1.00	1.00	1.00
	75%	1.00	1.00	1.00	1.00	1.00	1.00	1.00	1.00	1.00	1.00	1.00	1.00
CO_ADOPT	mean	0.37	0.05	0.30	0.15	0.00	0.04	0.27	0.04	0.19	0.31	0.00	0.20
	std. dev.	0.35	0.17	0.34	0.22	0.12	0.17	0.23	0.14	0.23	0.27	0.15	0.28
	25%	0.09	0.00	0.00	0.00	0.00	0.00	0.08	0.00	0.00	0.08	0.00	0.00
	median	0.22	0.00	0.18	0.09	0.00	0.00	0.20	0.00	0.13	0.22	0.00	0.08
	75%	0.89	0.17	0.50	0.22	0.00	0.07	0.50	0.11	0.33	0.50	0.00	0.33
EC_POW	mean	0.50	0.52	0.51	0.42	0.53	0.50	0.47	0.57	0.50	0.50	0.51	0.51
	std. dev.	0.30	0.27	0.29	0.26	0.30	0.29	0.30	0.26	0.29	0.30	0.29	0.29
	25%	0.22	0.34	0.25	0.17	0.27	0.25	0.19	0.40	0.24	0.22	0.27	0.25
	median	0.52	0.47	0.50	0.44	0.54	0.50	0.47	0.60	0.50	0.51	0.48	0.50
	75%	0.77	0.75	0.76	0.61	0.80	0.75	0.71	0.77	0.75	0.77	0.76	0.76
POL_POW	mean	11.78	13.27	12.14	11.44	12.37	12.14	11.73	12.94	12.14	11.71	12.91	12.14
	std. dev.	2.08	1.22	2.01	2.58	1.73	2.01	2.17	1.35	2.01	2.17	1.42	2.01
	25%	10.54	12.34	11.04	9.98	11.22	11.04	10.43	12.17	11.04	10.43	12.07	11.04
	median	11.59	13.00	12.37	11.49	12.61	12.37	11.58	12.92	12.37	11.58	12.89	12.37
	75%	13.18	14.04	13.52	13.38	13.55	13.52	13.25	13.81	13.52	13.14	13.92	13.52
IMPORT	mean	0.00	0.01	0.00	-0.02	0.01	0.00	0.00	0.00	0.00	-0.01	0.02	0.00
	std. dev.	0.10	0.10	0.10	0.11	0.10	0.11	0.11	0.09	0.10	0.11	0.08	0.10
	25%	-0.03	-0.05	-0.03	-0.08	-0.03	-0.03	-0.03	-0.05	-0.05	-0.06	-0.01	-0.03
	median	0.01	0.03	0.02	0.01	0.02	0.02	0.02	0.02	0.02	0.01	0.03	0.02
	75%	0.06	0.07	0.06	0.05	0.06	0.06	0.05	0.04	0.05	0.05	0.06	0.05
PRESSURE	mean	0.38	0.69	0.45	0.43	0.57	0.54	0.38	0.59	0.45	0.34	0.69	0.46
	std. dev.	0.49	0.47	0.50	0.50	0.50	0.50	0.49	0.50	0.50	0.48	0.47	0.50
	25%	0.00	0.00	0.00	0.00	0.00	0.00	0.00	0.00	0.00	0.00	0.00	0.00
	median	0.00	1.00	0.00	0.00	1.00	1.00	0.00	1.00	0.00	0.00	1.00	0.00
	75%	1.00	1.00	1.00	1.00	1.00	1.00	1.00	1.00	1.00	1.00	1.00	1.00

The table displays the descriptive statistics for the independent variables in Model 5 (Full IFRS adoption of any type and within any scope by 2014), Model 6 (Mandatory Full IFRS adoption by 2014), Model 7 (Full IFRS adoption in the individual financial statements by 2014) and Model 8 (Full IFRS adoption for all domestic private firms by 2014).

Table A-19: Descriptive statistics (Models 9-12)

Variables	Statistics	Model 9 (ANY)			Model 10 (MAND)			Model 11 (IND)			Model 12 (ALL)		
Groups (countries)		Adopt (40)	Non-Adopt (70)	Total (110)	Adopt (12)	Non-Adopt (98)	Total (110)	Adopt (39)	Non-Adopt (71)	Total (110)	Adopt (24)	Non-Adopt (86)	Total (110)
ACC_QUAL	mean	4.73	4.88	4.83	4.45	4.87	4.82	4.71	4.89	4.83	4.74	4.85	4.83
	std. dev.	0.84	0.75	0.78	0.66	0.74	0.74	0.83	0.75	0.78	0.90	0.74	0.77
	25%	3.99	4.32	4.19	3.85	4.30	4.26	3.93	4.32	4.19	3.90	4.28	4.23
	median	4.63	4.82	4.74	4.51	4.77	4.74	4.60	4.82	4.74	4.59	4.77	4.73
	75%	5.30	5.44	5.40	4.89	5.44	5.40	5.29	5.54	5.40	5.35	5.40	5.40
LOCAL_GAAP	mean	0.60	0.81	0.74	0.50	0.77	0.74	0.59	0.82	0.74	0.67	0.76	0.74
	std. dev.	0.50	0.39	0.44	0.52	0.43	0.44	0.50	0.39	0.44	0.48	0.43	0.44
	25%	0.00	1.00	0.00	0.00	1.00	0.00	0.00	1.00	0.00	0.00	1.00	0.00
	median	1.00	1.00	1.00	0.50	1.00	1.00	1.00	1.00	1.00	1.00	1.00	1.00
	75%	1.00	1.00	1.00	1.00	1.00	1.00	1.00	1.00	1.00	1.00	1.00	1.00
LOCAL_FULL	mean	0.35	0.63	0.53	0.50	0.52	0.52	0.33	0.63	0.53	0.38	0.57	0.53
	std. dev.	0.48	0.49	0.50	0.52	0.50	0.50	0.48	0.49	0.50	0.49	0.50	0.50
	25%	0.00	0.00	0.00	0.00	0.00	0.00	0.00	0.00	0.00	0.00	0.00	0.00
	median	0.00	1.00	1.00	0.50	1.00	1.00	0.00	1.00	1.00	0.00	1.00	1.00
	75%	1.00	1.00	1.00	1.00	1.00	1.00	1.00	1.00	1.00	1.00	1.00	1.00
FULL_LIST	mean	0.85	0.74	0.78	0.92	0.80	0.81	0.85	0.75	0.78	0.96	0.77	0.81
	std. dev.	0.36	0.44	0.41	0.29	0.41	0.39	0.37	0.44	0.41	0.20	0.42	0.39
	25%	1.00	0.00	1.00	1.00	1.00	1.00	1.00	0.00	1.00	1.00	1.00	1.00
	median	1.00	1.00	1.00	1.00	1.00	1.00	1.00	1.00	1.00	1.00	1.00	1.00
	75%	1.00	1.00	1.00	1.00	1.00	1.00	1.00	1.00	1.00	1.00	1.00	1.00
FULL_PRIV_MAND	mean	0.48	0.20	0.30	0.42	0.24	0.26	0.49	0.20	0.30	0.42	0.30	0.33
	std. dev.	0.51	0.40	0.46	0.51	0.43	0.44	0.51	0.40	0.46	0.50	0.46	0.47
	25%	0.00	0.00	0.00	0.00	0.00	0.00	0.00	0.00	0.00	0.00	0.00	0.00
	median	0.00	0.00	0.00	0.00	0.00	0.00	0.00	0.00	0.00	0.00	0.00	0.00
	75%	1.00	0.00	1.00	1.00	0.00	1.00	1.00	0.00	1.00	1.00	1.00	1.00
CO_ADOPT	mean	0.24	0.09	0.14	0.06	0.06	0.06	0.24	0.09	0.14	0.14	0.06	0.08
	std. dev.	0.23	0.17	0.20	0.11	0.12	0.12	0.23	0.17	0.20	0.18	0.12	0.14
	25%	0.00	0.00	0.00	0.00	0.00	0.00	0.00	0.00	0.00	0.00	0.00	0.00
	median	0.20	0.00	0.00	0.00	0.00	0.00	0.20	0.00	0.00	0.11	0.00	0.00
	75%	0.44	0.17	0.31	0.09	0.15	0.15	0.44	0.17	0.31	0.20	0.11	0.15
EC_POW	mean	0.40	0.55	0.50	0.40	0.51	0.50	0.39	0.55	0.50	0.39	0.53	0.50
	std. dev.	0.29	0.28	0.29	0.28	0.29	0.29	0.29	0.28	0.29	0.29	0.29	0.29
	25%	0.13	0.35	0.24	0.11	0.26	0.25	0.12	0.35	0.24	0.15	0.28	0.24
	median	0.34	0.55	0.50	0.38	0.51	0.50	0.34	0.55	0.50	0.33	0.54	0.50
	75%	0.66	0.81	0.75	0.66	0.78	0.75	0.65	0.81	0.75	0.65	0.79	0.75
POL_POW	mean	12.04	12.19	12.14	12.50	12.09	12.14	12.07	12.17	12.14	12.17	12.13	12.14
	std. dev.	2.22	1.89	2.01	1.55	2.06	2.01	2.24	1.89	2.01	1.71	2.09	2.01
	25%	10.69	11.05	11.04	11.21	10.93	11.04	10.79	11.04	11.04	11.10	10.93	11.04
	median	12.38	12.37	12.37	13.06	12.28	12.37	12.42	12.35	12.37	11.95	12.45	12.37
	75%	13.60	13.12	13.52	13.65	13.25	13.52	13.62	13.12	13.52	13.59	13.27	13.52
IMPORT	mean	0.04	-0.02	0.00	0.05	0.00	0.01	0.04	-0.02	0.00	0.06	-0.01	0.00
	std. dev.	0.09	0.11	0.11	0.08	0.11	0.11	0.09	0.11	0.11	0.09	0.11	0.11
	25%	-0.01	-0.06	-0.04	0.01	-0.03	-0.03	-0.01	-0.07	-0.04	0.00	-0.05	-0.03
	median	0.03	0.00	0.02	0.02	0.02	0.02	0.03	0.00	0.02	0.06	0.01	0.02
	75%	0.09	0.04	0.06	0.09	0.06	0.06	0.10	0.04	0.06	0.10	0.04	0.06
PRESSURE	mean	0.78	0.49	0.59	0.92	0.55	0.59	0.79	0.48	0.59	0.75	0.55	0.59
	std. dev.	0.42	0.50	0.49	0.29	0.50	0.49	0.41	0.50	0.49	0.44	0.50	0.49
	25%	1.00	0.00	0.00	1.00	0.00	0.00	1.00	0.00	0.00	0.50	0.00	0.00
	median	1.00	0.00	1.00	1.00	1.00	1.00	1.00	0.00	1.00	1.00	1.00	1.00
	75%	1.00	1.00	1.00	1.00	1.00	1.00	1.00	1.00	1.00	1.00	1.00	1.00

The table displays the descriptive statistics for the independent variables in Model 9 (IFRS for SMEs adoption of any type and within any scope by 2014), Model 10 (Mandatory IFRS for SMEs adoption by 2014), Model 11 (IFRS for SMEs adoption in the individual financial statements by 2014) and Model 12 (IFRS for SMEs adoption for all domestic private firms by 2014).

Table A-20: Correlation analysis (Model 3 and Model 4)

IND \ ALL	ADOPT (FULL)	ACC_ QUAL	LOCAL_ GAAP	LOCAL_ FULL	FULL_ LIST	CO_ ADOPT	EC_POW	POL_ POW	IMPORT	PRES- SURE
ADOPT (FULL)		**0.3616*** (0.0001)**	**-0.1318 (0.1697)**	**-0.2300** (0.0156)**	**0.2059** (0.0309)**	**0.3916*** (0.0000)**	**-0.1274 (0.1848)**	**-0.3220*** (0.0006)**	**0.0563 (0.5587)**	**-0.4286*** (0.0000)**
ACC_QUAL	**0.2054** (0.0313)**		0.0202 (0.8344)	0.0806 (0.4028)	-0.1101 (0.2521)	0.3095*** (0.0010)	0.2530*** (0.0077)	-0.1794* (0.0608)	-0.1863* (0.0514)	-0.3385*** (0.0003)
LOCAL_GAAP	**-0.2253** (0.0180)**	0.0075 (0.9382)		0.1733* (0.0702)	-0.0362 (0.7070)	0.0026 (0.9781)	0.3814*** (0.0000)	0.0549 (0.5689)	-0.0497 (0.6061)	0.0565 (0.5576)
LOCAL_FULL	**-0.1592* (0.0967)**	0.0204 (0.8325)	0.1839* (0.0544)		-0.3545*** (0.0001)	-0.0357 (0.7115)	0.1791* (0.0612)	0.0707 (0.4628)	-0.0207 (0.8300)	0.1293 (0.1784)
FULL_LIST	**0.1183 (0.2185)**	-0.0573 (0.5518)	-0.0997 (0.2999)	-0.3394*** (0.0003)		0.0710 (0.4609)	-0.2717*** (0.0041)	-0.2437** (0.0103)	0.1226 (0.2021)	-0.0913 (0.3429)
CO_ADOPT	**0.3986*** (0.0000)**	0.2037** (0.0328)	-0.1110 (0.2482)	0.0275 (0.7753)	-0.0709 (0.4620)		0.0582 (0.5462)	-0.1345 (0.1612)	-0.1132 (0.2389)	-0.1097 (0.2537)
EC_POW	**-0.3086*** (0.0010)**	0.2683*** (0.0046)	0.3831*** (0.0000)	0.2254** (0.0179)	-0.2431** (0.0105)	-0.1343 (0.1619)		0.4749*** (0.0000)	-0.3081*** (0.0011)	-0.0742 (0.4409)
POL_POW	**-0.3442*** (0.0002)**	-0.1758* (0.0662)	0.0549 (0.5689)	0.0801 (0.4056)	-0.1982** (0.0379)	-0.1749* (0.0677)	0.4773*** (0.0000)		-0.2135** (0.0251)	0.1241 (0.1965)
IMPORT	**0.1599* (0.0952)**	-0.2096** (0.0280)	-0.0504 (0.6013)	-0.0296 (0.7591)	0.0790 (0.4120)	-0.0228 (0.8133)	-0.3098*** (0.0010)	-0.1857* (0.0521)		0.1963** (0.0399)
PRESSURE	**-0.3386*** (0.0003)**	-0.3464*** (0.0002)	0.0565 (0.5576)	0.2265** (0.0173)	-0.1743* (0.0686)	-0.1458 (0.1287)	-0.0478 (0.6198)	0.0936 (0.3308)	0.2145** (0.0245)	

The table displays Spearman's rank correlation coefficients with the corresponding p-values in parentheses for Model 3 (Full IFRS adoption in the individual financial statements by 2008) in the bottom left corner and for Model 4 (Full IFRS adoption for all domestic private firms by 2008) in the top right corner. *, **, and *** indicate significance at the 10%, 5%, and 1% level.

Table A-21: Correlation analysis (Model 7 and Model 8)

IND \ ALL	ADOPT (FULL)	ACC_ QUAL	LOCAL_ GAAP	LOCAL_ FULL	FULL_ LIST	CO_ ADOPT	EC_POW	POL_ POW	IMPORT	PRES- SURE
ADOPT (FULL)		**0.2969*** (0.0016)**	**-0.0553 (0.5662)**	**-0.2583*** (0.0064)**	**-0.0589 (0.5414)**	**0.6141*** (0.0000)**	**-0.0051 (0.9579)**	**-0.3025*** (0.0013)**	**-0.1005 (0.2960)**	**-0.3399*** (0.0003)**
ACC_QUAL	**0.1439 (0.1335)**		0.0146 (0.8795)	-0.0244 (0.8006)	-0.0810 (0.4002)	0.3293*** (0.0004)	0.2580*** (0.0065)	-0.1818* (0.0574)	-0.3184*** (0.0007)	-0.3667*** (0.0001)
LOCAL_GAAP	**-0.2076** (0.0295)**	0.0166 (0.8636)		0.1663* (0.0825)	-0.1310 (0.1727)	-0.0063 (0.9477)	0.3802*** (0.0000)	0.0549 (0.5689)	0.0296 (0.7591)	0.0598 (0.5348)
LOCAL_FULL	**-0.1603* (0.0943)**	-0.0583 (0.5453)	0.2298** (0.0157)		-0.3179*** (0.0007)	-0.2725*** (0.0040)	0.2163** (0.0232)	0.2203** (0.0207)	-0.0753 (0.4340)	0.2033** (0.0331)
FULL_LIST	**-0.1509 (0.1157)**	-0.0497 (0.6058)	-0.1199 (0.2123)	-0.3397*** (0.0003)		0.0046 (0.9618)	-0.2776*** (0.0033)	-0.1830* (0.0556)	0.1758* (0.0662)	-0.0530 (0.5826)
CO_ADOPT	**0.4908*** (0.0000)**	0.2443** (0.0101)	-0.1419 (0.1391)	-0.2047** (0.0319)	-0.0727 (0.4504)		0.0173 (0.8577)	-0.2209** (0.0204)	-0.1040 (0.2797)	-0.1643* (0.0863)
EC_POW	**-0.1685* (0.0785)**	0.2340** (0.0139)	0.3789*** (0.0000)	0.2713*** (0.0041)	-0.1993** (0.0369)	-0.1287 (0.1802)		0.4977*** (0.0000)	-0.3350*** (0.0003)	-0.1042 (0.2786)
POL_POW	**-0.3051*** (0.0012)**	-0.1775* (0.0636)	0.0549 (0.5689)	0.1846* (0.0536)	-0.0909 (0.3450)	-0.1982** (0.0380)	0.4968*** (0.0000)		-0.1169 (0.2238)	0.1444 (0.1323)
IMPORT	**0.0142 (0.8826)**	-0.3250*** (0.0005)	-0.0166 (0.8636)	-0.0669 (0.4875)	0.0773 (0.4223)	0.0448 (0.6422)	-0.3673*** (0.0001)	-0.1027 (0.2859)		0.3680*** (0.0001)
PRESSURE	**-0.2002** (0.0360)**	-0.4003*** (0.0000)	0.0904 (0.3476)	0.2263** (0.0174)	-0.0892 (0.3538)	-0.0894 (0.3529)	-0.0808 (0.4015)	0.1305 (0.1741)	0.3260*** (0.0005)	

The table displays Spearman's rank correlation coefficients with the corresponding p-values in parentheses for Model 7 (Full IFRS adoption in the individual financial statements by 2014) in the bottom left corner and for Model 8 (Full IFRS adoption for all domestic private firms by 2014) in the top right corner. *, **, and *** indicate significance at the 10%, 5%, and 1% level.

Table A-22: Correlation analysis (Model 11 and Model 12)

IND \ ALL	ADOPT (SME)	ACC_QUAL	LOCAL_GAAP	LOCAL_FULL	FULL_LIST	FULL_PRIV_MAND	CO_ADOPT	EC_POW	POL_POW	IMPORT	PRES-SURE
ADOPT (SME)		**-0.0957 (0.3202)**	**-0.0836 (0.3854)**	**-0.1611* (0.0927)**	**0.2006** (0.0356)**	**0.1006 (0.2955)**	**0.2312** (0.0151)**	**-0.2059** (0.0309)**	**-0.0049 (0.9599)**	**0.2773*** (0.0034)**	**0.1709* (0.0742)**
ACC_QUAL	**-0.1421 (0.1385)**		0.0153 (0.8742)	-0.0992 (0.3025)	0.2218** (0.0199)	-0.0531 (0.5818)	-0.3749*** (0.0001)	0.2050** (0.0317)	-0.2332** (0.0142)	-0.2305** (0.0154)	-0.4359*** (0.0000)
LOCAL_GAAP	**-0.2466*** (0.0094)**	-0.0023 (0.9812)		0.1360 (0.1566)	-0.0282 (0.7703)	-0.4181*** (0.0000)	0.0570 (0.5539)	0.3873*** (0.0000)	0.0549 (0.5689)	-0.1784* (0.0623)	-0.0362 (0.7070)
LOCAL_FULL	**-0.2879*** (0.0023)**	-0.1250 (0.1932)	0.2187** (0.0217)		-0.2283** (0.0165)	-0.4650*** (0.0000)	0.0685 (0.4773)	0.1884** (0.0487)	0.1795* (0.0606)	-0.1514 (0.1144)	0.0269 (0.7800)
FULL_LIST	**0.1154 (0.2297)**	0.2246** (0.0183)	-0.0663 (0.4913)	-0.2357** (0.0132)		0.2402** (0.0115)	-0.1027 (0.2855)	-0.1111 (0.2479)	-0.1650* (0.0850)	0.0492 (0.6100)	-0.0748 (0.4371)
FULL_PRIV_MAND	**0.3027*** (0.0013)**	0.0053 (0.9561)	-0.4187*** (0.0000)	-0.4132*** (0.0000)	0.2498*** (0.0085)		-0.0229 (0.8127)	-0.3444*** (0.0002)	-0.2160** (0.0234)	0.1904** (0.0464)	0.1469 (0.1257)
CO_ADOPT	**0.3877*** (0.0000)**	-0.3570*** (0.0001)	-0.1284 (0.1812)	0.0048 (0.9605)	-0.0962 (0.3174)	0.0201 (0.8348)		-0.1086 (0.2588)	0.0194 (0.8402)	0.2204** (0.0207)	0.4000*** (0.0000)
EC_POW	**-0.2618*** (0.0057)**	0.2100** (0.0277)	0.3892*** (0.0000)	0.2099** (0.0277)	-0.1542 (0.1076)	-0.3764*** (0.0001)	-0.2201** (0.0209)		0.5054*** (0.0000)	-0.3838*** (0.0000)	-0.2818*** (0.0029)
POL_POW	**0.0248 (0.7967)**	-0.2083** (0.0290)	0.0549 (0.5689)	0.1244 (0.1952)	-0.1851* (0.0529)	-0.2352** (0.0134)	0.1165 (0.2256)	0.5050*** (0.0000)		-0.0256 (0.7903)	0.0923 (0.3376)
IMPORT	**0.2858*** (0.0025)**	-0.2710*** (0.0042)	-0.1303 (0.1749)	-0.1193 (0.2145)	0.0568 (0.5553)	0.1115 (0.2461)	0.2579*** (0.0065)	-0.3541*** (0.0001)	-0.0340 (0.7245)		0.4766*** (0.0000)
PRESSURE	**0.3075*** (0.0011)**	-0.4295*** (0.0000)	-0.0362 (0.7070)	0.0269 (0.7800)	-0.0814 (0.3979)	0.1009 (0.2944)	0.4399*** (0.0000)	-0.2833*** (0.0027)	0.0923 (0.3376)	0.4522*** (0.0000)	

The table displays Spearman's rank correlation coefficients with the corresponding p-values in parentheses for Model 11 (IFRS for SMEs adoption in the individual financial statements by 2014) in the bottom left corner and for Model 12 (IFRS for SMEs adoption for all domestic private firms by 2014) in the top right corner. *, **, and *** indicate significance at the 10%, 5%, and 1% level.

References

A

Abd El Razik, A. (2009): Challenges of International Financial Reporting Standards (IFRS) in the Islamic Accounting World – Case of Middle Eastern Countries, in: Scientific Bulletin - Economic Sciences, 8 (14), p. 1–4.

Abdel-Khalik, A. R./Collins, W. A. (1983): Financial reporting by private companies – Analysis and diagnosis, Stamford, Conn (1983).

Aboagye-Otchere, F./Agbeibor, J. (2012): The International Financial Reporting Standard for Small and Medium-sized Entities (IFRS for SMEs): Suitability for small businesses in Ghana, in: Journal of Financial Reporting and Accounting, 10 (2), p. 190–214.

Accounting Standards Board of Canada (2006): Accounting Standards in Canada: New Directions – Accounting Standards Board Strategic Plan, available at: www.frascanada.ca, last revised 01/09/2014.

Accounting Standards Board of Canada (2007): Financial Reporting by Private Enterprises (Discussion Paper), available at: www.frascanada.ca, last revised 01/09/2014.

Accounting Standards Board of Canada (2014): Strategic Planning – Accounting Standards for Private Enterprises, available at: www.frascanada.ca, last revised 01/09/2014.

Accounting Standards Council Singapore (2011): Singapore Financial Reporting Standard for Small Entities, available at: www.asc.gov.sg, last revised 01/09/2014.

Adams, C. A./Weetman, P./Gray, S. J. (1993): Reconciling national with international accounting standards – Lessons from a study of Finnish corporate reports, in: European Accounting Review, 2 (3), p. 471–494.

Adler, N. J. (1983): A typology of management studies involving culture, in: Journal of International Business Studies, 14 (2), p. 29–47.

Agami, A./Monsen, N. (1995): An Appraisal of Efforts by the Nordic Countries Toward Accounting Standards Harmonization, in: Journal of International Accounting, Auditing and Taxation, 4 (2), p. 185–203.

Akerlof, G. A. (1970): The Market for 'Lemons': Quality Uncertainty and the Market Mechanism, in: The Quarterly Journal of Economics, 84 (3), p. 488–500.

Al-Akra, M./Jahangir Ali, M./Marashdeh, O. (2009): Development of accounting regulation in Jordan, in: The International Journal of Accounting, 44 (2), p. 163–186.

Albert, H. (2000): Kritischer Rationalismus – Vier Kapitel zur Kritik illusionären Denkens, Tübingen (2000).

Alexander, D. (2007): Globalisation of Accounting Standards: A UK Perspective, in: Godfrey, J. M./Chalmers, K. (eds.): Globalisation of accounting standards, Cheltenham, UK, Northampton, MA, USA (2007), p. 46–63.

Al-Hussaini, A./Al-Shammari, B./Al-Sultan, W. (2008): Development of Enforcement Mechanisms following Adoption of International Accounting Standards in the Gulf Co-Operation Council Member States, in: International Journal of Business Strategy, 8 (3), p. 50–71.

Ali, M. J. (2005): A Synthesis of Empirical Research on International Accounting Harmonization and Compliance with International Financial Reporting Standards, in: Journal of Accounting Literature, 24 (1), p. 1–52.

Ali, M. J./Ahmed, K./Eddie, I. A. (2009): The Adoption of International Financial Reporting Standards (IFRS) in Emerging Economies – The Case for South Asia, in: Tsamenyi, M./Uddin, S. (eds.): Accounting in emerging economies, Bingley, UK (2009), p. 1–30.

Alkhtani, S. (2012): The Relevance of IFRSs to Less Developed Economies – A Cultural Perspective Using Saudi Arabia as a Case Study, available at: http://dc607.4shared.com, last revised 01/09/2014.

Alp, A./Ustundag, S. (2009): Financial reporting transformation: the experience of Turkey, in: Critical Perspectives on Accounting, 20 (5), p. 680–699.

American Accounting Association Committee on Accounting in Developing Countries (1976): Report 1973-1975, in: Accounting Review, 51 (4 Supplement), p. 198–212.

American Accounting Association Committee on International Accounting Operations and Education 1976-1978 (1978): Accounting Education and the Third World, Sarasota (1978).

American Accounting Association's Financial Accounting Standards Committee (2006): Financial Accounting and Reporting Standards for Private Entities, in: Accounting Horizons, 20 (2), p. 179–194.

American Institute of Certified Public Accountants (1983): Report of the Special Committee on Accounting Standards Overload (1983).

American Institute of Certified Public Accountants (2005): Private Company Financial Reporting Task Force Report, available at: www.incpas.org, last revised 01/09/2014.

American Institute of Certified Public Accountants (2011): IFRS Readiness Tracking Survey – October 2011, available at: www.aicpa.org, last revised 01/09/2014.

American Institute of Certified Public Accountants (2013): FRF for SMEs Frequently Asked Questions, available at: www.aicpa.org, last revised 01/09/2014.

Ampofo, A. A./Sellani, R. J. (2005): Examining the differences between United States Generally Accepted Accounting Principles (U.S. GAAP) and International Accounting Standards (IAS): implications for the harmonization of accounting standards, in: Accounting Forum, 29 (2), p. 219–231.

Andersen/BDO/Deloitte Touche Tohmatsu/Ernst & Young/Grant Thornton/KPMG /PricewaterhouseCoopers (2001): GAAP 2001 – A Survey of National Accounting Rules Benchmarked against International Accounting Standards, available at: www.iasplus.com, last revised 01/09/2014.

Archambault, J. J./Archambault, M. E. (2003): A multinational test of determinants of corporate disclosure, in: The International Journal of Accounting, 38 (2), p. 173–194.

Archambault, J. J./Archambault, M. E. (2009): An analysis of social factors influencing the adoption of International Financial Reporting Standards, in: J. Global Business Advancement, 2 (1/2), p. 38–53.

ASCG/Haller, A./Löffelmann, J. V. (2008): Financial Reporting from the Perspective of Banks as a major User Group of Financial Statements – Empirical Results and Implications for the further Development of an International Financial Reporting Standard for Private Entities, available at: www.drsc.de, last revised 01/09/2014.

Ashraf, J./Ghani, W. I. (2005): Accounting development in Pakistan, in: The International Journal of Accounting, 40 (2), p. 175–201.

Association of Chartered Certified Accountants (2008): International Financial Reporting Standard for Small and Medium Sized Entities – Review of field testing results carried out by ACCA in UK in early 2008, available at: www.accaglobal.com, last revised 01/09/2014.

Auer, B./Rottmann, H. (2012): Statistik und Ökonometrie für Wirtschaftswissenschaftler, 2nd. ed., Wiesbaden (2012).

Australian Accounting Standards Board (2010): AASB 1053 – Application of Tiers of Australian Accounting Standards - June 2010, available at: www.comlaw.gov.au, last revised 01/09/2014.

Australian Accounting Standards Board (2012): Glossary of Defined Terms, available at: www.aasb.gov.au, last revised 01/09/2014.

Australian Government's Department of Finance and Administration (2004): Submission on the IASB Discussion Paper (CL 40) – Preliminary Views on Accounting Standards for Small and Medium-Sized Entities, available at: www.ifrs.org, last revised 01/09/2014.

B

Backhaus, K. (2011): Multivariate Analysemethoden – Eine anwendungsorientierte Einführung, 13th. ed., Berlin (2011).

Baker, C. R./Barbu, E. M. (2007): Trends in research on international accounting harmonization, in: The International Journal of Accounting, 42 (3), p. 272–304.

Balchenko, S. (2001): The Eurasian landscape: IAS Gap Analysis – 2nd Meeting of the Eurasian Corporate Governance Roundtable, available at: www.oecd.org, last revised 01/09/2014.

Ball, R. (2001): Infrastructure Requirements for an Economically Efficient System of Public Financial Reporting and Disclosure, in: Brookings-Wharton Papers on Financial Services, 2001 (1), p. 127–169.

Ball, R. (2006): International Financial Reporting Standards (IFRS): pros and cons for investors, in: Accounting and Business Research, 36 (Special Issue: International Accounting Policy Forum), p. 5–27.

Ball, R./Robin, A./Wu, J. S. (2003): Incentives versus standards: properties of accounting income in four East Asian countries, in: Journal of Accounting and Economics, 36 (1-3), p. 235–270.

Baptista, R. (2000): Do innovations diffuse faster within geographical clusters?, in: International Journal of Industrial Organization, 18 (3), p. 515–535.

Bartel, R. (1990): Charakteristik, Methodik und wissenschaftsmethodische Probleme der Wirtschaftswissenschaften, in: Wirtschaftswissenschaftliches Studium, 19 (2), p. 54–59.

Barth, M./Landsman, W./Lang, M. (2008): International Accounting Standards and Accounting Quality, in: Journal of Accounting Research, 46 (3), p. 467–498.

Baskerville, R. F. (2003): Hofstede never studied culture, in: Accounting, Organizations and Society, 28 (1), p. 1–14.

Basu, S. (1997): The conservatism principle and the asymmetric timeliness of earnings, in: Journal of Accounting and Economics, 24 (1), p. 3–37.

BDO/Deloitte Touche Tohmatsu/Ernst and Young/Grant Thornton/KPMG/PricewaterhouseCoopers (2003): GAAP Convergence 2002 – A survey of national efforts to promote and achieve convergence with international financial reporting standards. Researched by D. L. Street, available at: www.iasplus.com, last revised 01/09/2014.

Belkaoui, A. (1983): Economic, Political, and Civil Indicators and Reporting and Disclosure Adequacy: Empirical Investigation, in: Journal of Accounting and Public Policy, 2 (3), p. 207–219.

Benston, G. J./Bromwich, M./Litan, R. E./Wagenhofer, A. (2006): Worldwide financial reporting – The development and future of accounting standards, New York (2006).

Blue-Ribbon Panel on Standard Setting for Private Companies (2011): Report to the Board of Trustees of the Financial Accounting Foundation, available at: www.accountingfoundation.org, last revised 01/09/2014.

Bollen, L. (1996): Financial Reporting Regulation for Small and Medium Sized Private Firms, available at: www.personeel.unimaas.nl, last revised 01/09/2014.

Bolton, J. E. (1971): Small firms – Report of the Committee of Inquiry on Small Firms, London (1971).

Boolaky, P. K. (2010): IFRS in Small Island Economies: Problems and Challenges to the Private and Public-Sector Enterprises: Using Data from Mauritius, in: SSRN Electronic Journal .

Boross, Z./Clarkson, H./Fraser, M./Weetman, P. (1995): Pressures and conflicts in moving towards harmonization of accounting practice: the Hungarian experience, in: European Accounting Review, 4 (4), p. 713–737.

Bova, F./Pereira, R. (2012): The Determinants and Consequences of Heterogeneous IFRS Compliance Levels Following Mandatory IFRS Adoption: Evidence from a Developing Country, in: Journal of International Accounting Research, 11 (1), p. 83–111.

Boyle, J. (2010): Waiting for the starting signal, in: CA Magazine, 14 (1), p. 58–59.

Briston, R. J. (1978): The Evolution of Accounting in Developing Countries, in: The International Journal of Accounting, 14 (1), p. 105–120.

Brown, P./Tarca, A. (2001): Politics, Processes and the Future of Australian Accounting Standards, in: Abacus, 37 (3), p. 267–296.

Bundessteuerberaterkammer (2004): Preliminary Views on Accounting Standards for Small and Medium-sized Entities – Discussion Paper IFRS for SMEs (CL 56), available at: www.ifrs.org, last revised 01/09/2014.

Burnett, R. A. (1975): The Harmonization of Accounting Principles in the Member Countries of the European Economic Community, in: The International Journal of Accounting, 11 (1), p. 23–30.

Busse von Colbe, W. (1964): Die Planung der Betriebsgröße, Wiesbaden (1964).

C

Camfferman, K./Zeff, S. A. (2007): Financial reporting and global capital markets – A history of the International Accounting Standards Committee, 1973-2000, Oxford, New York (2007).

Campbell, J. E. (1984): An application of protocol analysis to the 'Little GAAP' controversy, in: Accounting, Organizations and Society, 9 (3-4), p. 329–342.

Canadian Institute of Chartered Accountants (1999): Financial reporting by small business enterprises, Toronto (1999).

Carnegie, G. D./Napier, C. J. (2002): Exploring comparative international accounting history, in: Accounting, Auditing & Accountability Journal, 15 (5), p. 689–718.

Carruthers, B. G. (1995): Accounting, ambiguity, and the new institutionalism, in: Accounting, Organizations and Society, 20 (4), p. 313–328.

Carsberg, B. V./Page, M./Sindall, A./Waring, I. (1985): Small company financial reporting, Englewood Cliffs, London (1985).

Certified General Accountants Association of Canada : CL 84 – Discussion Paper 'Preliminary Views on Accounting Standards for Small and Medium Sized Entities', available at: www.ifrs.org, last revised 01/09/2014.

Chand, P./Patel, C. (2008): Convergence and harmonization of accounting standards in the South Pacific region, in: Advances in Accounting, 24 (1), p. 83–92.

Chand, P./White, M. (2007): A critique of the influence of globalization and convergence of accounting standards in Fiji, in: Critical Perspectives on Accounting, 18 (5), p. 605–622.

Chatterjee, S./Hadi A. S. (2012): Regression analysis by example, 5th. ed., Hoboken, N.J (2012).

Chen, S./Sun, Z./Wang, Y. (2002): Evidence from China on Whether Harmonized Accounting Standards Harmonize Accounting Practices, in: Accounting Horizons, 16 (3), p. 183–197.

Choi, F. D. S./Bavishi, V. B. (1982): Financial Accounting Standards: A Multinational Synthesis and Policy Framework, in: The International Journal of Accounting, 18 (1), p. 159–183.

Choi, F. D. S./Meek, G. K. (2011): International accounting, 7th. ed., Upper Saddle River, N.J (2011).

Choi, F. D. S./Mueller, G. G. (1978): An introduction to multinational accounting, Englewood Cliffs, N.J (1978).

Chua, W. F./Taylor, S. L. (2008): The rise and rise of IFRS: An examination of IFRS diffusion, in: Journal of Accounting and Public Policy, 27 (6), p. 462–473.

Clements, C. E./Neill, J. D./Stovall, O. S. (2010): Cultural Diversity, Country Size, and the IFRS Adoption Decision, in: The Journal of Applied Business Research, 26 (2), p. 115–126.

CNA Interpreta s.r.l. (2011): Study on Accounting requirements for SMEs – Final Report, available at: www.peprobe.com, last revised 01/09/2014.

Coase, R. H. (1937): The Nature of the Firm, in: Economica, 4 (16), p. 386–405.

Cohen, J. (2003): Applied multiple regression/correlation analysis for the behavioral sciences, 3rd. ed., Mahwah, N.J (2003).

Cole, V./Breesch, D./Branson, J. (2009): Are Users of Financial Statements of Publicly and Non-Publicly Traded Companies Different or Not? An Empirical Study, available at: papers.ssrn.com, last revised 01/09/2014.

Collis, J. (2008): Directors' Views on Accounting and Auditing Requirements for SMEs, available at: www.bis.gov.uk, last revised 01/09/2014.

Collis, J./Jarvis, R. (2000): How owner-managers use accounts – A report, London (2000).

Consultative Committee of Accountancy Bodies (1994): Exemptions from Standards on Grounds of Size or Public Interest – Consultative Document, London (1994).

Cordery, C. J./Baskerville, R. F. (2006): Small GAAP: A Large Jump for the IASB, available at: papers.ssrn.com, last revised 01/09/2014.

Craig, R. J./Diga, J. G. (1996): Financial reporting regulation in ASEAN: Features and prospects, in: The International Journal of Accounting, 31 (2), p. 239–259.

Curran, J./Blackburn, R. A. (1994): Small firms and local economic networks – The death of the local economy?, London (1994).

Curran, J./Blackburn, R. A. (2001): Researching the small enterprise, London, Thousand Oaks, Calif (2001).

D

Da Costa, R. C./Bourgeois, J. C./Lawson, W. M. (1978): A classification of international financial accounting practices, in: International Journal of Accounting, 13 (Spring), p. 73–85.

Daske, H./Hail, L./Leuz, C./Verdi, R. (2008): Mandatory IFRS Reporting around the World: Early Evidence on the Economic Consequences, in: Journal of Accounting Research, 46 (5), p. 1085–1142.

DeFelice, A. (2010): IFRS for SMEs - U.S. GAAP – Comparison Tool Available Online, in: Journal of Accountancy, 209 (April), p. 30.

Deloitte Touche Tohmatsu (2003-2012): IFRSs in your pocket, available at: www.iasplus.com, last revised 01/09/2014.

Deloitte Touche Tohmatsu (2009a): IAS Plus Jurisdictional Updates: Germany, available at: www.adoptifrs.org, last revised 01/09/2014.

Deloitte Touche Tohmatsu (2009b): IFRS survey 2009 for private companies, available at: www.deloitte.com, last revised 01/09/2014.

Deloitte Touche Tohmatsu (2014a): Differential reporting and SMEs – The reporting entity is dead, long live the reporting entity, available at: www.deloitte.com, last revised 01/09/2014.

Deloitte Touche Tohmatsu (2014b): Jurisdictions, available at: www.iasplus.com, last revised 01/09/2014.

Deloitte Touche Tohmatsu (2014c): Use of IFRS by jurisdiction, available at: www.iasplus.com, last revised 01/09/2014.

Deutsches Bundesministerium der Justiz und für Verbraucherschutz (2014): Entwurf eines Gesetzes zur Umsetzung der Richtlinie 2013/34/EU des Europäischen Parlaments und des Rates vom 26. Juni 2013 über den Jahresabschluss, den konsolidierten Abschluss und damit verbundene Berichte von Unternehmen bestimmter Rechtsformen und zur Änderung der Richtlinie 2006/43/EG des Europäischen Parlaments und des Rates und zur Aufhebung der Richtlinien 78/660/EWG und 83/349/EWG des Rates – Bilanzrichtlinie-Umsetzungsgesetz – BilRUG, available at: www.bmjv.de, last revised 01/09/2014.

DiMaggio, P. J./Powell, W. W. (1983): The Iron Cage Revisited – Institutional Isomorphism and Collective Rationality in Organizational Fields, in: American Sociological Review, 48 (2), p. 147–160.

Ding, Y./Hope, O.-K./Jeanjean, T./Stolowy, H. (2007): Differences between domestic accounting standards and IAS: Measurement, determinants and implications, in: Journal of Accounting and Public Policy, 26 (1), p. 1–38.

Ding, Y./Jeanjean, T./Stolowy, H. (2005): Why do national GAAP differ from IAS? The role of culture, in: The International Journal of Accounting, 40 (4), p. 325–350.

Dossa, M. A. (2013): AFRs for MSEs in Pakistan (2006) challenged by IFRS for SMEs (2009), in: Pakistan Business Review, 15 (January), p. 744–764.

Doupnik, T. S. (1987): Evidence of International Harmonization of Financial Reporting, in: The International Journal of Accounting, 23 (1), p. 47–68.

Doupnik, T. S./Salter, S. B. (1993): An Empirical Test of a Judgmental International Classification of Financial Reporting Practices, in: Journal of International Business Studies, 24 (1), p. 41–60.

Doupnik, T. S./Taylor, M. E. (1985): An Empirical Investigation of the Observance of IASC Standards in Western Europe, in: Management International Review, 25 (1), p. 27–33.

E

Eierle, B. (2004): Die Entwicklung der Differenzierung der Unternehmensberichterstattung in Deutschland und Großbritannien – Ansatzpunkte für die Diskussion der zukünftigen Gestaltung der Abschlusserstellung nicht kapitalmarktorientierter Unternehmen in Deutschland, Frankfurt am Main (2004).

Eierle, B. (2005): Differential reporting in Germany – A historical analysis, in: Accounting, Business & Financial History, 15 (3), p. 279–315.

Eierle, B./Haller, A. (2010): IFRS for SMEs – Ergebnisse einer Befragung von nicht kapitalmarktorientierten Unternehmen in Deutschland, available at: www.drsc.de, last revised 01/09/2014.

Epstein, B. J./Mirza, A. A. (2001): Wiley IAS 2001 – Interpretation and application of International Accounting Standards 2001, New York, Chichester (2001).

European Commission (1978): Fourth Council Directive 78/660/EEC of 25 July 1978 based on Article 54 (3) (g) of the Treaty on the annual accounts of certain types of companies, in: Official Journal of the European Communities (L 222), p. 11–31.

European Commission (2002): Regulation (EC) No 1606/2002 of the European Parliament and of the Council of 19 July 2002 on the application of international accounting standards, in: Official Journal of the European Communities (L 243), p. 1–4.

European Commission (2003): Commission Recommendation of 6 May 2003 concerning the definition of micro, small and medium-sized enterprises (2003/361/EC), available at: www.eur-lex.europa.eu, last revised 01/09/2014.

European Commission (2005): The new SME definition – User guide and model declaration, available at: www.ec.europa.eu, last revised 01/09/2014.

European Commission (2010): Summary Report of the Responses Received to the Commission's Consultation on the International Financial Reporting Standard for Small and Medium-sized Entities, available at: www.ec.europa.eu, last revised 01/09/2014.

European Commission (2011): Proposal for a Directive of the European Parliament and of the Council on the annual financial statements, consolidated financial statements and related reports of certain types of undertakings – COM(2011) 684 final, available at: www.ec.europa.eu, last revised 01/09/2014.

European Commission (2012): Implementation of the IAS Regulation (1606/2002) in the EU and EEA, available at: www.ec.europa.eu, last revised 01/09/2014.

European Commission (2013): Directive 2013/34/EU of the European Parliament and of the Council of 26 June 2013 on the annual financial statements, consolidated financial statements and related reports of certain types of undertakings, amending Directive 2006/43/EC of the European Parliament and of the Council and repealing Council Directives 78/660/EEC and 83/349/EEC, in: Official Journal of the European Union, 56 (L 182), p. 19–76.

European Financial Reporting Advisory Group (2010): Advice on compatibility of the IFRS for SMEs and the EU Accounting Directives, available at: www.efrag.org, last revised 01/09/2014.

Evans, L./Gebhardt, G./Hoogendoorn, M./Marton, J./Di Pietra, R. (2005): Problems and Opportunities of an International Financial Reporting Standard for Small and Medium-sized Entities. The EAA FRSC's Comment on the IASB's Discussion Paper, in: Accounting in Europe, 2 (1), p. 23–45.

Evans, T. G./Taylor, M. E. (1982): 'Bottom Line' Compliance with the IASC: A Comparative Analysis, in: The International Journal of Accounting, 18 (1), p. 115–128.

Evraert, S./Des Robert, J.-F. (2007): French Accounting Revolution: Implementing IFRS in French Companies, in: Godfrey, J. M./Chalmers, K. (eds.): Globalisation of accounting standards, Cheltenham, UK, Northampton, MA, USA (2007), p. 130–143.

F

Fama, E. F./Jensen, M. C. (1983a): Agency Problems and Residual Claims, in: Journal of Law & Economics, 26 (June 83), p. 327–350.

Fama, E. F./Jensen, M. C. (1983b): Separation of Ownership and Control, in: Journal of Law & Economics, 26 (June 83), p. 301–326.

Fearnley, S./Hines, T. (2007): How IFRS has destabilised financial reporting for UK non-listed entities, in: Journal of Financial Regulation and Compliance, 15 (4), p. 394–408.

Fédération des Experts comptables Européens (2012): Policy Statement on main issues of the accountancy profession on the EC Proposals for the recast of the 4th and 7th Accounting Directives, available at: www.fee.be, last revised 01/09/2014.

Financial Accounting Standards Board/International Accounting Standards Board (2002): Norwalk Agreement, available at: www.ifrs.org, last revised 01/09/2014.

Financial Reporting Council (2013): Financial Reporting Standard for Smaller Entities (effective January 2015) – FRSSE, available at: www.frc.org.uk, last revised 01/09/2014.

Financial Standards Foundation (2009): Venezuela – Standard Report, available at: www.adoptifrs.org, last revised 01/09/2014.

Financial Standards Foundation (2010): Hong Kong SAR, available at: www.adoptifrs.org, last revised 01/09/2014.

Fitzgerald, R. D. (1981): International Harmonization of Accounting and Reporting, in: The International Journal of Accounting, 17 (1), p. 21–32.

Fitzgerald, R. D./Stickler, A. D./Watts, T. R. (1979): International survey of accounting principles and reporting practices, Multilingual ed., London (1979).

Fitzpatrick, M./Frank, F. (2009): IFRS for SMEs – The Next Standard for U.S. Private Companies?, in: Journal of Accountancy, 208 (December), p. 50–54.

Fontes, A./Rodrigues, L. L./Craig, R. (2005): Measuring convergence of National Accounting Standards with International Financial Reporting Standards, in: Accounting Forum, 29 (4), p. 415–436.

Fortin, H./Barros, A. C./Cutler, K. (2010): Accounting for growth in Latin America and the Caribbean – Improving corporate financial reporting to support regional economic development, Washington, D.C (2010).

Frank, U. (2003): Einige Gründe für die Wiederbelebung der Wissenschaftstheorie, in: Die Betriebswirtschaft, 63 (3), p. 278–292.

Frank, U. (2007): Wissenschaftstheorie, in: Köhler, R./Küpper, H.-U./Pfingsten, A. (eds.): Handwörterbuch der Betriebswirtschaft, 6th edn., Stuttgart (2007), Col. 2010-2017.

Frank, W. G. (1979): An Empirical Analysis of International Accounting Principles, in: Journal of Accounting Research, 17 (2), p. 593–605.

Freedman, D./Pisani, R./Purves, R. (1998): Statistics, 3rd. ed., New York (1998).

Fritz, S./Lämmle, C. (2003): The International Harmonisation Process of Accounting Standards, available at: liu.diva-portal.org, last revised 01/09/2014.

Fülbier, R. U. (2004): Wissenschaftstheorie und Betriebswirtschaftslehre, in: Wirtschaftswissenschaftliches Studium, 33 (5), p. 266–271.

Fülbier, R. U./Gassen, J. (2010): IFRS for European Small and Medium-Sized Entities? – A Theoretical and Empirical Analysis, available at: www.dgrv.de, last revised 01/09/2014.

Fülbier, R. U./Klein, M. (2013): Financial Accounting and Reporting in Germany – A Case Study on German Accounting Tradition and Experiences with the IFRS Adoption, available at: papers.ssrn.com, last revised 01/09/2014.

G

Gantzel, K. J. (1962): Wesen und Begriff der mittelständischen Unternehmung, Köln (1962).

Garcia, N./Porporato, M. M./Arnoletto, J. L. (2001): Argentina – Individual Accounts, in: Ordelheide, D./KPMG (eds.): Transnational accounting, 2nd edn., Hampshire [England], New York (2001), p. 1–76.

Garrido, P./León, Á./Zorio, A. (2002): Measurement of formal harmonization progress – The IASC experience, in: The International Journal of Accounting, 37 (1), p. 1–26.

Gassen, J./Sellhorn, T. (2006): Applying IFRS in Germany – Determinants and Consequences, in: Betriebswirtschaftliche Forschung und Praxis, 58 (4), p. 365–386.

Genossenschaftsverband Bayern (2007): Official statement against the application of IAS/IFRS for SMEs – Exposure Draft IFRS for SMEs (CL 3), available at: www.ifrs.org, last revised 01/09/2014.

Gernon, H. M./Meek, G. K./Mueller, G. G. (2001): Accounting – An international perspective, 5th. ed., Boston (2001).

Gethin, H. (2008): Russia's road to IFRS, in: World Congress of Accountants (special edition), p. 25–27.

Gjesdal, F. (1981): Accounting for Stewardship, in: Journal of Accounting Research, 19 (1), p. 208–231.

Glanz, S./Pfaff, D. (2011): Perspektiven des 'IFRS für KMU' in der Schweiz, in: Mathis, A./Nobs, R. (eds.): Treuhand und Revision: Jahrbuch 2011, Zürich (2011), p. 9–35.

Göbel, S./Kornmeier, B. (2007): Adressaten und deren Anforderungen an die externe Berichterstattung nicht kapitalmarktorientierter Unternehmen – Ergebnisse ausgewählter Studien, in: Kapitalmarktorientierte Rechnungslegung, 7 (10), p. 519–532.

Godfrey, J. M. (2006): Accounting theory, 6th. ed., Milton, Qld (2006).

Godfrey, J. M./Chalmers, K. (eds.) (2007): Globalisation of accounting standards, Cheltenham, UK, Northampton, MA, USA (2007).

Godfrey-Smith, P. (2003): Theory and reality – An introduction to the philosophy of science, Chicago (2003).

Goeltz, R. K. (1991): International Accounting Harmonization: The Impossible (and Unnecessary?) Dream, in: Accounting Horizons, 5 (1), p. 85–88.

Gordon, E. A./Greiner, A./Kohlbeck, M. J./Lin, S./Skaife, H. (2013): Challenges and Opportunities in Cross-Country Accounting Research, in: Accounting Horizons, 27 (1), p. 141–154.

Grant Thornton (2009): IFRS News Special Edition (September 2009), available at: www.grantthornton.com, last revised 01/09/2014.

Grant Thornton (2011): Financial Reporting Adviser October 2011 Issue 2 – Proposed changes to New Zealand's financial reporting framework, available at: www.grantthornton.co.nz, last revised 01/09/2014.

Gray, S. J. (1983): International Accounting – A Review of Academic Research in the United Kingdom, in: The International Journal of Accounting, 19 (1), p. 15–43.

Gray, S. J. (1988): Towards a theory of cultural influence on the development of accounting systems internationally, in: Abacus, 24 (1), p. 1–15.

Gray, S. J./Campbell, L. G./Shaw, J. C. (1984): International financial reporting – A comparative international survey of accounting requirements and practices in 30 countries, [Byfleet] (1984).

Grochla, E. (1978): Einführung in die Organisationstheorie, Stuttgart (1978).

Gyasi, A. K. (2010): Adoption of International Financial Reporting Standards in Developing Countries – The Case of Ghana, available at: www.theseus.fi, last revised 01/09/2014.

H

Hail, L./Leuz, C./Wysocki, P. (2010a): Global Accounting Convergence and the Potential Adoption of IFRS by the U.S. (Part I): Conceptual Underpinnings and Economic Analysis, in: Accounting Horizons, 24 (3), p. 355–394.

Hail, L./Leuz, C./Wysocki, P. (2010b): Global Accounting Convergence and the Potential Adoption of IFRS by the U.S. (Part II): Political Factors and Future Scenarios for U.S. Accounting Standards, in: Accounting Horizons, 24 (4), p. 567–588.

Hair, J. N. (2010): Multivariate data analysis, 7th. ed., Upper Saddle River, N.J (2010).

Haller, A. (2003): IFRS für alle Unternehmen – ein realisierbares Szenario in der Europäischen Union?, in: Kapitalmarktorientierte Rechnungslegung, 3 (10), p. 413–424.

Haller, A./Eierle, B. (2004a): Accounting standards for Small and Medium-sized Entities – erste Weichenstellungen durch das IASB, in: Betriebs-Berater, 59 (34), p. 1838–1845.

Haller, A./Eierle, B. (2004b): The Adaptation of German Accounting Rules to IFRS – A Legislative Balancing Act, in: Accounting in Europe, 1 (1), p. 27–50.

Hatfield, H. R. (1966): Some Variations in Accounting Practice in England, France, Germany and the United States, in: Journal of Accounting Research, 4 (2), p. 169–182.

Hauke, J./Kossowski, T. (2011): Comparison of Values of Pearson's and Spearman's Correlation Coefficients on the Same Sets of Data, in: Quaestiones Geographicae, 30 (2), p. 87–93.

Hauworth, W. P. (1973): Problems in the development of worldwide accounting standards, in: The International Journal of Accounting, 9 (1), p. 23–34.

Hegarty, J./Gielen, F./Barros, A. (2004): Implementation of International Accounting and Auditing Standards – Lessons Learned from the World Bank's Accounting and Auditing ROSC Program, available at: www.worldbank.org, last revised 01/09/2014.

Hegel, G. W. F./Wallace, W. (1975): Hegel's Logic – Being part one of the Encyclopaedia of the philosophical sciences (1830), 3rd. ed., Oxford (1975).

Heidhues, E./Patel, C. (2011): A critique of Gray's framework on accounting values using Germany as a case study, in: Critical Perspectives on Accounting, 22 (3), p. 273–287.

Henry, E./Holzmann, O. J. (2012): Costly compliance with US GAAP: The private-company dilemma, in: Journal of Corporate Accounting & Finance, 23 (3), p. 87–91.

Hill, R. C./Griffiths, W. E./Lim, G. C. (2008): Principles of econometrics, 3rd. ed., Hoboken, NJ (2008).

Hoarau, C. (1995): International accounting harmonization – American hegemony or mutual recognition with benchmarks?, in: European Accounting Review, 4 (2), p. 217–233.

Hofstede, G. H. (1980): Culture's consequences – International differences in work related values, Beverly Hills (1980).

Hong Kong Institute of Certified Public Accountants (2006): Setting Hong Kong Financial Reporting Standards – Information Paper, available at: app1.hkicpa.org.hk, last revised 01/09/2014.

Hong Kong Institute of Certified Public Accountants (2010a): Hong Kong Financial Reporting Standard for Private Entities – Statement of Intent, available at: www.hkicpa.org.hk, last revised 01/09/2014.

Hong Kong Institute of Certified Public Accountants (2010b): Simplified Financial Reporting – HKFRS for Private Entities, in: TechWatch, 10 (91).

Hoogervorst, H. (2014): Charting progress towards global accounting standards, available at: www.ifrs.org, last revised 01/09/2014.

Hoogervorst, H./Teitler-Feinberg, E. (2012): We must speak the same acccounting language! – Interview with Hans Hoogervorst, Chairman of IASB, in: Zeitschrift für Internationale Rechnungslegung, 7 (9), p. 321–322.

Hope, O.-K./Jin, J./Kang, T. (2006): Empirical Evidence on Jurisdictions that Adopt IFRS, in: Journal of International Accounting Research, 5 (2), p. 1–20.

I

Ibarra, V./Suez-Sales, M. G. (2011): A Comparison of the International Financial Reporting Standards (IFRS) and Generally Accepted Accounting Principles (GAAP) for Small and Medium-sized Entities (SMEs) and Compliances of Some Asian Countries to IFRS, in: Journal of International Business Research, 10 (3), p. 35–62.

IFRS Adoption Research Group (2014): IFRS – International Financial Reporting Standards, available at: www.adoptifrs.org, last revised 01/09/2014.

IFRS Foundation (2010): The Conceptual Framework for Financial Reporting, available at: eifrs.ifrs.org, last revised 01/09/2014.

IFRS Foundation (2011): IFRS for SMEs Update 2011-7, available at: www.ifrs.org, last revised 01/09/2014.

IFRS Foundation (2012a): IFRS for SMEs Fact Sheet, available at: www.ifrs.org, last revised 01/09/2014.

IFRS Foundation (2012b): IFRSs as the global standards – Setting a strategy for the Foundation's second decade, London (2012).

IFRS Foundation (2013): Snapshot: Comprehensive review of the IFRS for SMEs, available at: www.ifrs.org, last revised 01/09/2014.

IFRS Foundation (2014a): About the IFRS Foundation and the IASB, available at: www.ifrs.org, last revised 01/09/2014.

IFRS Foundation (2014b): IFRS application around the world – Jurisdiction profile: Uruguay, available at: www.ifrs.org, last revised 01/09/2014.

IFRS Foundation (2014c): IFRS application around the world – Jurisdiction profile: Chile, available at: www.ifrs.org, last revised 01/09/2014.

IFRS Foundation (2014d): IFRS application around the world – Jurisdiction profile: Canada, available at: www.ifrs.org, last revised 01/09/2014.

IFRS Foundation (2014e): IFRS application around the world – Jurisdiction profile: Argentina, available at: www.ifrs.org, last revised 01/09/2014.

IFRS Foundation (2014f): IFRS application around the world – Jurisdiction profile: Colombia, available at: www.ifrs.org, last revised 01/09/2014.

IFRS Foundation (2014g): IFRS application around the world – Jurisdiction profiles, available at: www.ifrs.org, last revised 01/09/2014.

IFRS Foundation (2014h): IFRS application around the world – Jurisdiction profile: Israel, available at: www.ifrs.org, last revised 01/09/2014.

IFRS Foundation (2014i): IFRS application around the world – Jurisdiction profile: New Zealand, available at: www.ifrs.org, last revised 01/09/2014.

IFRS Foundation (2014j): IFRS application around the world – Jurisdiction profile: Saudi Arabia, available at: www.ifrs.org, last revised 01/09/2014.

IFRS Foundation (2014k): IFRS application around the world – Jurisdiction profile: Australia, available at: www.ifrs.org, last revised 01/09/2014.

IFRS Foundation (2014l): IFRS application around the world – Jurisdiction profile: Jordan, available at: www.ifrs.org, last revised 01/09/2014.

IFRS Foundation (2014m): IFRS application around the world – Jurisdiction profile: Nigeria, available at: www.ifrs.org, last revised 01/09/2014.

IFRS Foundation (2014n): IFRS application around the world – Jurisdiction profile: Oman, available at: www.ifrs.org, last revised 01/09/2014.

IFRS Foundation (2014o): IFRS application around the world – Jurisdiction profile: Russia, available at: www.ifrs.org, last revised 01/09/2014.

IFRS Foundation (2014p): IFRS application around the world – Jurisdiction profile: Malaysia, available at: www.ifrs.org, last revised 01/09/2014.

IFRS Foundation (2014q): IFRS application around the world – Jurisdiction profile: Thailand, available at: www.ifrs.org, last revised 01/09/2014.

IFRS Foundation (2014r): IFRS application around the world – Jurisdiction profile: Sweden, available at: www.ifrs.org, last revised 01/09/2014.

IFRS Foundation (2014s): IFRS application around the world – Jurisdiction profile: China, available at: www.ifrs.org, last revised 01/09/2014.

IFRS Foundation (2014t): IFRS application around the world – Jurisdiction profile: Albania, available at: www.ifrs.org, last revised 01/09/2014.

IFRS Foundation (2014u): IFRS application around the world – Jurisdiction profile: India, available at: www.ifrs.org, last revised 01/09/2014.

Ijiri, Y. (1975): Theory of Accounting Measurement, Sarasota (1975).

Indapurkar, K./Chakraborty, A./Pathak, R. (2009): Convergence with IFRS: Hopes and Challenges, available at: www.indianmba.com, last revised 01/09/2014.

Institut für Mittelstandsforschung (2014): KMU-Definition des IfM Bonn, available at: www.ifm-bonn.org, last revised 01/09/2014.

Institute of Chartered Accountants in England and Wales (2013): The New UK GAAP – Updated FAQ, available at: www.icaew.com, last revised 01/09/2014.

Institute of Chartered Accountants of New Zealand (2004): Submission on the IASB Discussion Paper (CL 37) – Preliminary Views on Accounting Standards for Small and Medium-Sized Entities, available at: www.ifrs.org, last revised 01/09/2014.

International Accounting Standards Board (2012): Q&A 2012/02 – IFRS for SMEs Section 3 - Jurisdiction requires fallback to full IFRSs, available at: go.ifrs.org, last revised 01/09/2014.

International Accounting Standards Board (2013): Exposure Draft ED/2013/09 – Proposed amendments to the International Financial Reporting Standard for Small and Medium-sized Entities (IFRS for SMEs), London (2013).

International Accounting Standards Committee (1988): Survey of the Use and Application of International Accounting Standards, London (1988).

Irvine, H. (2008): The global institutionalization of financial reporting: The case of the United Arab Emirates, in: Accounting Forum, 32 (2), p. 125–142.

J

Jaafar, A./McLeay, S. (2007): Country Effects and Sector Effects on the Harmonization of Accounting Policy Choice, in: Abacus, 43 (2), p. 156–189.

Janssen, J./Gronewold, U. (2010): IFRS for Small and Medium-sized Entities – Konzeptionelle Schwächen des neuen Standards und ihre Implikationen, in: Kapitalmarktorientierte Rechnungslegung, 10 (2), p. 75–80.

Japanese Institute of Certified Public Accountants (2014): Accounting Standards, available at: www.hp.jicpa.or.jp, last revised 01/09/2014.

Jarvis, R. (1996): Users and uses of unlisted companies' financial statements – A literature review (1996).

Jarvis, R. (2003): A question of definition, in: Accountancy, 132 (November), p. 80.

Jarvis, R./Collis, J. (2003): International Financial Reporting Standards and Differential Reporting, available at: eprints.kingston.ac.uk, last revised 01/09/2014.

Jensen, M. C./Meckling, W. H. (1976): Theory of the Firm: Managerial Behavior, Agency Costs and Ownership Structure, in: Journal of Financial Economics, 3 (4), p. 305–360.

Johnson, D. C. (2011): Political Systems, Lobbying, and the Adoption of International Financial Reporting Standards, available at: papers.ssrn.com, last revised 01/09/2014.

Judge, W./Li, S./Pinsker, R. (2010): National Adoption of International Accounting Standards: An Institutional Perspective, in: Corporate Governance: An International Review, 18 (3), p. 161–174.

K

Kajüter, P./Barth, D./Dickmann, T. (2007): Rechnungslegung nach IFRS im deutschen Mittelstand? – Der Standardentwurf "IFRS für kleine und mittelgroße Unternehmen" im Licht empirischer Befunde, in: Der Betrieb, 60 (35), p. 1877–1884.

Kajüter, P./Saucke, M. (2012): IFRS for SMEs – IFRS für kleine und mittelgroße Unternehmen (International Financial Reporting Standard for Small and Medium-sized Entities), in: Hennrichs, J./Kleindiek, D./Watrin, C. (eds.): Münchener Kommentar zum Bilanzrecht. Band 1 IFRS, München (2012).

Kajüter, P./Schoberth, J./Zapp, P./Lübbig, M. (2008): IFRS im Mittelstand – Eine Beurteilung des ED IFRS for SMEs aus Sicht von sechs europäischen Ländern, in: Kapi talmarktorientierte Rechnungslegung, 8 (10), p. 589–601.

Kaminski, V. (2008): Der Mittelstand im Fokus der International Financial Reporting Standards – Internationalisierung - Rechnungslegung - Handlungsempfehlungen, Hamburg (2008).

Kamnikar, J. A./Kamnikar, E. G./Burrowes, A. (2012): One Size Does Not Fit All – A look at private company financial reporting in the U.S. and tiered GAAP alternatives being considered abroad, in: Journal of Accountancy, 213 (January), p. 46–49.

Kasuya, E. (2001): Mann–Whitney U test when variances are unequal, in: Animal Behaviour, 61 (6), p. 1247–1249.

Katz, M. L./Shapiro, C. (1985): Network Externalities, Competition, and Compatibility, in: The American Economic Review, 75 (3), p. 424–440.

Katz, M. L./Shapiro, C. (1994): Systems Competition and Network Effects, in: Journal of Economic Perspectives, 8 (2), p. 93–115.

Kaufmann, D./Kray, A./Mastrucci, M. (2010): The Worldwide Governance Indicators – Methodology and Analytical Issues, available at: info.worldbank.org, last revised 01/09/2014.

Kaya, D./Koch, M. (2013): Why Do Countries Adopt International Financial Reporting Standards for Small and Medium-sized Entities (IFRS for SMEs)? - Early Empirical Evidence, available at: www.eufin2013.com, last revised 01/09/2014.

Keasey, K./Watson, R. (1993): Small firm management – Ownership, finance, and performance, Oxford, UK, Cambridge, Mass., USA (1993).

Kikuya, M. (2001): International harmonization of Japanese accounting standards, in: Accounting, Business & Financial History, 11 (3), p. 349–368.

Kirsch, H.-J./Meth, D. (2007): Adressaten einer IFRS-Rechnungslegung für mittelständische Unternehmen, in: Betriebs-Berater, 62 (19), p. 7–12.

Kirsch, H.-J./Schellhorn, M. (2011): IFRS for SMEs – Deutschland ist keine Insel, in: Der Betrieb, 64 (16), M1.

Knutson, D./Wichmann, H. (1985): The Accounting Standards Overload Problem for American Small Business, in: Journal of Business Finance & Accounting, 12 (3), p. 387–397.

Koga, C./Rimmel, G. (2007): Accounting Harmonisation and Diffusion of International Accounting Standards – The Japanese Case, in: Godfrey, J. M./Chalmers, K. (eds.): Globalisation of accounting standards, Cheltenham, UK, Northampton, MA, USA (2007), p. 218–237.

Kohler, U./Kreuter, F. (2012): Datenanalyse mit Stata – Allgemeine Konzepte der Datenanalyse und ihre praktische Anwendung, 4th. ed., München, Wien (2012).

Kornmeier, M. (2007): Wissenschaftstheorie und wissenschaftliches Arbeiten – Eine Einführung für Wirtschaftswissenschaftler, Heidelberg (2007).

Kosiol, E. (1964): Betriebswirtschaftslehre und Unternehmensforschung – Eine Untersuchung ihrer Standorte und Beziehungen auf wissenschaftstheoretischer Grundlage, in: Zeitschrift für Betriebswirtschaft, 34 (5), p. 743–762.

Kothari, S. P./Ramanna, K./Skinner, D. J. (2010): Implications for GAAP from an Analysis of Positive Research in Accounting, available at: papers.ssrn.com, last revised 01/09/2014.

Kraayenhof, J. (1960): International Challenges for Accounting, in: Journal of Accountancy, 55 (January), p. 34–38.

Kvaal, E./Nobes, C. W. (2012): IFRS Policy Changes and the Continuation of National Patterns of IFRS Practice, in: European Accounting Review, 21 (2), p. 343–371.

L

Lafferty, M. M./Cairns, D./Carty, J. (1979): Financial Times survey of 100 major European companies' reports and accounts, 1979, London (1979).

Lafferty, M./Cairns, D. (1980): Financial Times world survey of annual reports – An analysis of 200 major quoted companies' annual reports and accounts covering 20 leading countries, London (1980).

Lainez, J. A./Jarne, J. I./Callao, S. (1999): The Spanish accounting system and international accounting harmonization, in: European Accounting Review, 8 (1), p. 93–113.

Larson, R. K./Kenny, S. Y. (1999): The Harmonization of International Accounting Standards: Progress in the 1990s?, in: Multinational Business Review, 7 (1), p. 1–12.

Larson, R. K./Street, D. L. (2004): Convergence with IFRS in an expanding Europe: progress and obstacles identified by large accounting firms' survey, in: Journal of International Accounting, Auditing and Taxation, 13 (2), p. 89–119.

Lemeshow, S./Hosmer, D. W. (1982): A Review of Goodness of Fit Statistics for Use in the Development of Logistic Regression Models, in: American Journal of Epidemiology, 115 (1), p. 92–106.

Leonhart, R. (2013): Lehrbuch Statistik – Einstieg und Vertiefung, 3rd. ed., Bern (2013).

Levene, H. (1960): Robust tests for equality of variances, in: Olkin, I./Ghurye, S./Hoeffding, W./Madow, W./Mann, H. (eds.): Contributions to probability and statistics: Essays in honor of Harold Hotelling, Stanford (1960), p. 278–292.

Liebowitz, S. J./Margolis, S. E. (1994): Network Externality: An Uncommon Tragedy, in: The Journal of Economic Perspectives, 8 (2), p. 133–150.

Lingnau, V. (1995): Kritischer Rationalismus und Betriebswirtschaftslehre, in: Wirtschaftswissenschaftliches Studium, 24 (3), p. 124–129.

Litjens, R./Bissessur, S./Langendijk, H./Vergoossen, R. (2012): How Do Preparers Perceive Costs and Benefits of IFRS for SMEs? Empirical Evidence from the Netherlands, in: Accounting in Europe, 9 (2), p. 227–250.

M

MacKenzie, B. (2013): Interpretation and application of International Financial Reporting Standards, Hoboken, N.J (2013).

Mackintosh, I. (2008): Accounting for SMEs: the European debate goes on, in: Accountancy, 141 (June), p. 83.

Mackintosh, I. (2014): Turning back the clock?, available at: www.ifrs.org, last revised 01/09/2014.

Maingot, M./Zeghal, D. (2006): Financial Reporting of Small Business Entities in Canada, in: Journal of Small Business Management, 44 (4), p. 513–530.

Manzano, M. P./Conesa, I. M. (2005): El Proceso de Armonización Contable en Latinoamérica – Camino Hacia las Normas Internacionales, in: R. Cont. Fin. - USP, Sao Paulo (39), p. 103–117.

Masca, E. (2012): Influence of Cultural Factors in Adoption of the IFRS for SMEs, in: Procedia Economics and Finance, 3 (1), p. 567–575.

Mashayekhi, B./Mashayekh, S. (2008): Development of accounting in Iran, in: The International Journal of Accounting, 43 (1), p. 66–86.

Mazars (2008): The IFRS for SMEs accounting standard: perceptions and expectations across Europe, available at: www.mazars.co.th, last revised 01/09/2014.

McKinnon, S. M./Janell, P. (1984): The International Accounting Standards Committee: A Performance Evaluation, in: The International Journal of Accounting, 18 (2), p. 19–34.

Meade, J. (2012): Reporting for reporting entities (published by the Institute of Chartered Accountants Australia), available at: www.charteredaccountants.com.au, last revised 01/09/2014.

Meek, G. K./Saudagaran, S. M. (1990): A Survey of Research on Financial Reporting in a Transnational Context, in: Journal of Accounting Literature, 9 (1), p. 145–182.

Mersereau, A. (2002): Differential reporting – A Change in Canadian GAAP that will be of interest to most Canadian corporations, in: CA Magazine (June-July: 30-32).

Meth, D. (2007): Die IFRS als Grundlage der Rechnungslegung mittelständischer Unternehmen – Eine Analyse der Eignung der IFRS für mittelständische Unternehmen unter Berücksichtigung des IASB-Projektes "Accounting standards für small und medium-sized entities", Lohmar, Köln (2007).

Meyer, C. (2008): Grundlagen zu Swiss GAAP FER – Massgeschneidertes Konzept für aussagekräftigen Abschluss nach True and Fair View, in: Der Schweizer Treuhänder (5), p. 289–294.

Meyer, J. W./Rowan, B. (1977): Institutionalized Organizations: Formal Structure as Myth and Ceremony, in: American Journal of Sociology, 83 (2), p. 340–363.

Morgan, R. A. (1967): The multinational enterprise and its accounting needs, in: The International Journal of Accounting, 3 (1), p. 21–28.

Mosso, D. (1981): Accounting for small business: Bridging a widening GAAP, in: Journal of Accountancy, 152 (December), p. 64–78.

Mueller, G. G. (1967): International accounting, New York (1967).

Mwaura, M. F./Nyaboga, A. B. (2009): International Financial Accounting Standards and the Continent of Africa, in: International Business & Economics Research Journal, 8 (3), p. 33–46.

N

Nair, R. D./Frank, W. G. (1981): The Harmonisation of International Accounting Standards, 1973-1979, in: The International Journal of Accounting, 17 (1), p. 61–77.

Nair, R. D./Rittenberg, L. E. (1983): Alternative accounting principles for smaller businesses: Proposals and analysis, in: Journal of commercial bank lending, 65 (April), p. 2–21.

Narayanaswamy, R. (2007): The Impact of Globalisation of Accounting Standards on India, in: Godfrey, J. M./Chalmers, K. (eds.): Globalisation of accounting standards, Cheltenham, UK, Northampton, MA, USA (2007), p. 238–260.

Nasir, N. M./Zainol, A. (2007): Globalisation of Financial Reporting: An Islamic Focus, in: Godfrey, J. M./Chalmers, K. (eds.): Globalisation of accounting standards, Cheltenham, UK, Northampton, MA, USA (2007), p. 261–274.

Nexia International (1993): The International handbook of financial reporting, 1st. ed., London, New York (1993).

Ng, D. (1978): An Information Economics Analysis of Financial Reporting and External Auditing, in: Accounting Review, 53 (4), p. 910–920.

Nobes, C. W. (1981): An Empirical Analysis of International Accounting Principles – A Comment, in: Journal of Accounting Research, 19 (1), p. 268–270.

Nobes, C. W. (1983): Judgemental International Classification of Financial Reporting Practices, in: Journal of Business Finance & Accounting, 10 (1), p. 1–19.

Nobes, C. W. (1987): An Empirical Investigation of the Observance of IASC Standards in Western Europe: A Comment, in: Management International Review, 27 (4), p. 78–79.

Nobes, C. W. (1992): International classification of financial reporting, 2nd. ed., London, New York (1992).

Nobes, C. W. (1998): Towards a General Model of the Reasons for International Differences in Financial Reporting, in: Abacus, 34 (2), p. 162–187.

Nobes, C. W. (2006): The survival of international differences under IFRS: towards a research agenda, in: Accounting and Business Research, 36 (3), p. 233–245.

Nobes, C. W. (2010): On Researching into the Use of IFRS by Private Entities in Europe, in: Accounting in Europe, 7 (2), p. 213–226.

Nobes, C. W. (2013): The continued survival of international differences under IFRS, in: Accounting and Business Research, 43 (2), p. 83–111.

Nobes, C. W./Parker, R. H. (2012): Comparative international accounting, 12th. ed., Harlow, England (2012).

Nobes, C. W./Zeff, S. A. (2008): Auditors' Affirmations of Compliance with IFRS around the World: An Exploratory Study, in: Accounting Perspectives, 7 (4), p. 279–292.

O

Okaro, S. C./Tauringana, V. (2012): From SAS to IFRS: An Investigation of Nigeria Transition Road Map Implementation Problems, in: Tauringana, V./Mangena, M. (eds.): Accounting in Africa, Bingley (2012), p. 155–176.

Oliver, C. (1991): Strategic Responses to Institutional Processes, in: Academy of Management Review, 16 (1), p. 145–179.

Ordelheide, D./KPMG (eds.) (2001): Transnational accounting, Hampshire [England], New York (2001).

Organisation for Economic Co-operation and Development (1980): Accounting practices in OECD member countries, Paris (1980).

Organisation for Economic Co-operation and Development (2013): Latin American Economic Outlook 2014, available at: www.keepeek.com, last revised 01/09/2014.

P

Pacter, P. (2002): Financial reporting: IAS/US comparison – Global GAAPs, in: Accountancy, 130 (1311), p. 97–100.

Pacter, P. (2004): Setting out the approach, in: Accountancy, 134 (August), p. 74–75.

Pacter, P. (2005): What exactly is convergence?, in: International Journal of Accounting, Auditing and Performance Evaluation, 2 (1/2), p. 67–83.

Pacter, P. (2009a): An IFRS for private entities, in: International journal of disclosure and governance, 6 (1), p. 4–20.

Pacter, P. (2009b): IFRS for most private companies goes live, in: Financial Executive, 25 (7), p. 28–30.

Pacter, P. (2012): The IFRS for SMEs is all about access to capital, in: Zeitschrift für Internationale Rechnungslegung, 7 (12), p. 463–466.

Pacter, P. (2014): Global Accounting Standards - From Vision to Reality – Assessing the State of IFRS Adoption, Jurisdiction by Jurisdiction, in: The CPA Journal, 84 (January), p. 6–10.

Page, M. J. (1984): Corporate Financial Reporting and the Small Independent Company, in: Accounting and Business Research, 14 (55), p. 271–282.

Pellens, B./Fülbier, R. U./Gassen, J./Sellhorn, T. (2011): Internationale Rechnungslegung, 8th. ed., Stuttgart (2011).

Picker, R. (2007): Too Special to Go Global? Too Small to be Special? – An Insight into Australia's Decision to Adopt IFRS and the Consequences for its own Standard Setting and Application, in: Godfrey, J. M./Chalmers, K. (eds.): Globalisation of accounting standards, Cheltenham, UK, Northampton, MA, USA (2007), p. 98–109.

Platon, T. (1974): Spätdialoge I, Artemis-Jubiläumsausgabe, Zurich (1974).

Popper, K. R./Keuth, H. (2005): Logik der Forschung, 11th. ed., Tübingen (2005).

Poser, H. (2001): Wissenschaftstheorie – Eine philosophische Einführung, Stuttgart (2001).

Pounder, B. (2013): Accounting for Goodwill: Back to the Good Old Days?, in: Strategic Finance, 95 (July), p. 15–16.

Prado, T. A. D. R./Teixeira, B. R./Bernardino, F. F. M. (2011): A Utilizacao do Pronunciamento do CPA Para AS Pequenas e Medias Empresas – um estudo nas cidades de Araguari, Uberaba e Uberlândia - MG, available at: www.ead.fea.usp.br, last revised 01/09/2014.

PricewaterhouseCoopers (2013): IFRS adoption by country, available at: www.pwc.com, last revised 01/09/2014.

Procházka, D. (2012): The IFRS Adoption Index – A Tool for the Measurement of Accounting Harmonisation, in: Advances in Finance and Accounting, 12 (1), p. 372–377.

Provasoli, A./Mazzola, P./Pozza, L. (2007): The Role of National Standard Setters in the Standards Developing Process: The Italian Experience, in: Godfrey, J. M./Chalmers, K. (eds.): Globalisation of accounting standards, Cheltenham, UK, Northampton, MA, USA (2007), p. 110–129.

Purvis, S. E. C./Gernon, H./Diamond, M. A. (1991): The IASC and Its Comparability Project: Prerequisites for Success, in: Accounting Horizons, 5 (2), p. 25–44.

Q

Quagli, A./Paoloni, P. (2012): How is the IFRS for SME accepted in the European context? An analysis of the homogeneity among European countries, users and preparers in the European commission questionnaire, in: Advances in Accounting, 28 (1), p. 147–156.

Qu, X./Zhang, G. (2010): Measuring the convergence of national accounting standards with international financial reporting standards: The application of fuzzy clustering analysis, in: The International Journal of Accounting, 45 (3), p. 334–355.

R

Radwan, A. (2008): European Parliament Session Document A6-0032/2008 – Report on International Financial Reporting Standards (IFRS) and the Governance of the International Accounting Standards Board (IASB), available at: www.europarl.europa.eu, last revised 01/09/2014.

Raffée, H. (1974): Grundprobleme der Betriebswirtschaftslehre, Göttingen (1974).

Raffée, H. (1989): Gegenstand, Methoden und Konzepte der Betriebswirtschaftslehre, in: Bitz, M. (ed.): Vahlens Kompendium der Betriebswirtschaftslehre, 2nd edn., München (1989), p. 1–46.

Raffée, H./Abel, B. (1979): Aufgaben und aktuelle Tendenzen der Wissenschaftstheorie in den Wirtschaftswissenschaften, in: Raffée, H./Abel, B. (eds.): Wissenschaftstheoretische Grundfragen der Wirtschaftswissenschaften, München (1979), p. 1–10.

Raffournier, B. (2013): The Application of IFRS Across Different Institutional Environments, in: van Mourik, C. (ed.): The Routledge companion to accounting, reporting and regulation, London (2013), p. 281–298.

Rahman, A./Perera, H./Ganeshanandam, S. (1996): Measurement of Formal Harmonisation in Accounting: An Exploratory Study, in: Accounting and Business Research, 26 (4), p. 325–339.

Ramanna, K. (2013): The International Politics of IFRS Harmonization, in: Accounting, Economics and Law, 3 (2), p. 1–46.

Ramanna, K./Sletten, E. (2009): Why do Countries Adopt International Financial Reporting Standards? – Harvard Business School Accounting & Management Unit Working Paper No. 09-102, available at: papers.ssrn.com, last revised 01/09/2014.

Ramanna, K./Sletten, E. (2013): Network Effects in Countries' Adoption of IFRS – Harvard Business School Accounting & Management Unit Working Paper No. 10-092, available at: papers.ssrn.com, last revised 01/09/2014.

Ratcliffe, T. A. (2003): OCBOA Financial Statements, in: Journal of Accountancy, 196 (October), p. 71–75.

Rees, R. (1985): The Theory of Principal and Agent – Part I, in: Bulletin of Economic Research, 37 (1), p. 3–26.

Reisloh, C. (2011): Influence of national culture on IFRS practice – An empirical study in France, Germany and the United Kingdom, Frankfurt am Main (2011).

Roberts, C. B./Gordon, P./Weetman, P. (2008): International corporate reporting – A comparative approach, 4th. ed., Harlow (2008).

Rodrigues, L. L./Craig, R. (2007): Assessing international accounting harmonization using Hegelian dialectic, isomorphism and Foucault, in: Critical Perspectives on Accounting, 18 (6), p. 739–757.

S

Samuels, J. M./Oliga, J. C. (1982): Accounting Standards in Developing Countries, in: The International Journal of Accounting, 18 (1), p. 69–88.

Samuels, J. M./Piper, A. (1985): International accounting – A survey, London (1985).

Samujh, R. H. (2007): IFRS for SMEs: A New Zealand perspective – Working Paper Series Number 96, available at: researchcommons.waikato.ac.nz, last revised 01/09/2014.

Sarikas, R. H./Hien, V. D./Djatej, A. M. (2009): International Influence on Accountancy in Vietnam, in: McGee, R. W. (ed.): Corporate Governance in Developing Economies, Boston, MA (2009), p. 181–190.

Saudagaran, S. M. (2001): International accounting – A user perspective, Cincinnati, Ohio (2001).

Saudagaran, S. M./Diga, J. G. (2003): Economic Integration and Accounting Harmonization Options in Emerging Markets – Adopting the IASC/IASB Model in Asean, in: Wallace, R. S. O./Samuels, J. M./Briston, R. J./Saudagaran, S. M. (eds.): Research in Accounting in Emerging Economies, Amsterdam, London (2003), p. 239–266.

Saudagaran, S. M./Meek, G. K. (1997): A Review of Research on the Relationship between International Capital Markets and Financial Reporting by Multinational Firms, in: Journal of Accounting Literature, 16 (1), p. 127–159.

Schiebel, A. (2007): Is There a Solid Empirical Foundation for the IASB's Draft IFRS for SMEs?, available at: papers.ssrn.com, last revised 01/09/2014.

Schnell, R./Hill, P. B./Esser, E. (2008): Methoden der empirischen Sozialforschung, 8th. ed., München (2008).

Schwartz, S. H. (1994): Beyond individualism/collectivism – New cultural dimensions of values, in: Kim, Ŭ.-c. (ed.): Individualism and collectivism. Theory, method, and applications, Thousand Oaks, Calif (1994), p. 85–119.

Scott, R. (1987): The Adolescence of Institutional Theory, in: Administrative Science Quarterly, 32 (4), p. 493–511.

Sellhorn, T./Gornik-Tomaszewski, S. (2006): Implications of the 'IAS Regulation' for Research into the International Differences in Accounting Systems, in: Accouting in Europe, 3 (1), p. 187–217.

Selling, T. I. (2013): Bumps in the Road to IFRS Adoption: Is a U-Turn Possible?, in: Accounting Horizons, 27 (1), p. 155–167.

Shah, H./Carvajal, A./Bannister, G./Chan-Lau, J./Guerra, I. (2007): Equity and Private Debt Markets in Central America, Panama, and the Dominican Republic – IMF Working Paper (WP/07/288), available at: www.imf.org, last revised 01/09/2014.

Sharp, I. (2004): Vive la différence?, in: Accountancy Magazine (August), p. 76.

Shivakumar, L. (2013): The role of financial reporting in debt contracting and in stewardship, in: Accounting and Business Research, 43 (4), p. 362–383.

Sian, S./Roberts, C. (2009): UK small owner-managed businesses: accounting and financial reporting needs, in: Journal of Small Business and Enterprise Development, 16 (2), p. 289–305.

Siegel, A. F. (2012): Practical business statistics, 6th. ed., Burlington, MA (2012).

Siegel, S./Castellan, N. J. (1988): Nonparametric statistics for the behavioral sciences, 2nd. ed., New York (1988).

Siems, M. M. (2008): What does not work in comparing securities laws: A critique on La Porta's et al's methodology, available at: papers.ssrn.com, last revised 01/09/2014.

Simon, H. A. (1976): Administrative Behavior – A study of Decision-Making Processes in Administrative Organization, 3rd. ed., New York (1976).

Singh, R. D./Newberry, S. (2008): Corporate Governance and International Financial Reporting Standards (IFRS): The Case of Developing Countries, in: Tsamenyi, M./Uddin, S. (eds.): Corporate governance in less developed and emerging economies, Bingley (2008), p. 483–518.

Soederberg, S. (2002): On the contradictions of the New International Financial Architecture: another procrustean bed for emerging economies?, in: Third World Quarterly, 23 (4), p. 607–620.

Spence, M. (1973): Job Market Signaling, in: Quarterly Journal of Economics, 87 (3), p. 355–374.

Stainbank, L. (2010): An examination of the due process in South Africa which led to the adoption of the draft International Financial Reporting Standard for Small and Medium-sized Entities, in: Meditari Accountancy Research, 18 (2), p. 57–74.

Standard & Poor's (2011): Credit FAQ: Korea Joins The IFRS Parade, available at: www.adoptifrs.org, last revised 01/09/2014.

Stiftung für Fachempfehlungen zur Rechnungslegung/Institut für Rechnungswesen und Controlling der Universität Zürich (2009): Rechnungslegung kleiner und mittelgrosser Unternehmen in der Schweiz – Eine empirische Erhebung zu Swiss GAAP FER, available at: www.zora.uzh.ch, last revised 01/09/2014.

Stilling, P./Norton, R./Hopkins, L. (1984): Financial Times World accounting survey 1984 – an analysis of major international companies annual reports and accounts, and digest of their results, London (1984).

Street, D. L. (2002): GAAP 2001 – Benchmarking national accounting standards against IAS: summary of results, in: Journal of International Accounting, Auditing and Taxation, 11 (1), p. 77–90.

Street, D. L./Larson, R. K. (2004): Large Accounting Firms' Survey Reveals Emergence of 'Two Standard' System in the European Union, in: Advances in International Accounting, 17 (1), p. 1–29.

Street, D. L./Nichols, N. B./Gray, S. J. (2000): Assessing the acceptability of international accounting standards in the US – An empirical study of the materiality of US GAAP reconciliations by non-US companies complying with IASC standards, in: The International Journal of Accounting, 35 (1), p. 27–35.

T

Tayeb, M. (1994): Organizations and National Culture: Methodology Considered, in: Organization Studies, 15 (3), p. 429–445.

Tay, J. S. W./Parker, R. H. (1990): Measuring International Harmonization and Standardization, in: Abacus, 26 (1), p. 71–88.

Tay, J. S. W./Parker, R. H. (1992): Measuring International Harmonization and Standardization – A Reply, in: Abacus, 28 (2), p. 217–220.

Tyrrall, D./Woodward, D./Rakhimbekova, A. (2007): The relevance of International Financial Reporting Standards to a developing country: Evidence from Kazakhstan, in: The International Journal of Accounting, 42 (1), p. 82–110.

U

UCLA Statistical Consulting Group (2014a): Logistic Regression Diagnostics, available at: www.ats.ucla.edu, last revised 01/09/2014.

UCLA Statistical Consulting Group (2014b): Stata Annotated Output, Logistic Regression Analysis, available at: www.ats.ucla.edu, last revised 01/09/2014.

UCLA Statistical Consulting Group (2014c): What statistical analysis should I use?, available at: www.ats.ucla.edu, last revised 01/09/2014.

UK Accounting Standards Board (2004): Comment Letter on IASB Discussion Paper: Preliminary views on accounting standards for Small and Medium Sized Entities, available at: www.ifrs.org, last revised 01/09/2014.

UK Accounting Standards Board (2010): The Future of Financial Reporting in the UK and Republic of Ireland – FRED 43 - Application of Financial Reporting Standards; FRED 44 - Financial Reporting Standard for Medium-sized Entities, available at: www.iasplus.com, last revised 01/09/2014.

UK Department of Trade & Industry (2006): Small and Medium Enterprise (SME) - Definitions, available at: webarchive.nationalarchives.gov.uk, last revised 01/09/2014.

Ulrich, P./Hill, W. (1976a): Wissenschaftstheoretische Grundlagen der Betriebswirtschaftslehre (Teil I), in: Wirtschaftswissenschaftliches Studium, 5 (7), p. 304–309.

Ulrich, P./Hill, W. (1976b): Wissenschaftstheoretische Grundlagen der Betriebswirtschaftslehre (Teil II), in: Wirtschaftswissenschaftliches Studium, 5 (8), p. 345–350.

United Nations (2008): Practical implementation of international financial reporting standards – Lessons learned: country case studies on IFRS, New York (2008).

United Nations (2014): Member States of the United Nations, available at: www.un.org, last revised 01/09/2014.

United Nations Statistics Division (2013): Composition of macro geographical (continental) regions, geographical sub-regions, and selected economic and other groupings, available at: millenniumindicators.un.org, last revised 01/09/2014.

V

van der Tas, L. G. (1988): Measuring harmonization of financial reporting practice, in: Accounting and Business Research, 18 (70), p. 157–169.

van der Tas, L. G. (1992): Evidence of EC financial reporting practice harmonization, in: European Accounting Review, 1 (1), p. 69–104.

van Wyk, H. A./Rossouw, J. (2009): IFRS for SMEs in South Africa – a giant leap for accouting, but too big for smaller entities in general, in: Meditari Accountancy Research, 17 (1), p. 99–116.

Verband der Elektrizitätswirtschaft (2004): Comments of the German Electricity Association on the IASB-Discussion Paper „Accounting Standards for Small and

Medium-sized Entities“ – Discussion Paper IFRS for SMEs (CL 34), available at: www.ifrs.org, last revised 01/09/2014.

Voets, C. (2013): Kulturelle Einflüsse auf die Anwendung des Impairment-Tests nach IAS 36 – Eine experimentelle Untersuchung in Asien und Europa, Frankfurt am Main (2013).

W

Wagenhofer, A. (2013): Global Convergence of Accounting Standards, in: van Mourik, C. (ed.): The Routledge companion to accounting, reporting and regulation, London (2013), p. 246–264.

Walker, R. B. (2004): Submission on the IASB Discussion Paper (CL 48) – Preliminary Views on Accounting Standards for Small and Medium-Sized Entities, available at: www.ifrs.org, last revised 01/09/2014.

Wallace, R. S. O. (1993): Development of Accounting Standards for Developing and newly Industrialized Countries, in: Wallace, R. S. O./Chaderton, R. (eds.): Research in Third World accounting. A research annual, London, England (1993), p. 121–165.

Wallace, R. S. O./Gernon, H. (1991): Frameworks for International Comparative Financial Accounting, in: Journal of Accounting Literature, 10 (1), p. 209–264.

Walton, P. J. (1995): European financial reporting – A history, London, San Diego (1995).

Wehrfritz, M./Haller, A./Walton, P. (2012): National influence on the application of IFRS – Interpretations and accounting estimates by German and British accountants, available at: www-wiwi-cms.uni-regensburg.de, last revised 01/09/2014.

Whittington, G. (2005): The adoption of International Accounting Standards in the European Union, in: European Accounting Review, 14 (1), p. 127–153.

Wilkinson, T. L. (1965): United States accounting as viewed by accountants of other countries, in: The International Journal of Accounting, 1 (1), p. 3–14.

Williamson, O. E. (1975): Markets and hierarchies – Analysis and antitrust implications, London (1975).

World Bank (2001): Report on the Observance of Standards and Codes (ROSC) Kenya – Accounting and Auditing, available at: www.worldbank.org, last revised 01/09/2014.

World Bank (2002a): Report on the Observance of Standards and Codes (ROSC) Croatia – Accounting and Auditing, available at: www.worldbank.org, last revised 01/09/2014.

World Bank (2002b): Report on the Observance of Standards and Codes (ROSC) Kingdom of Morocco (Morocco) – Accounting and Auditing, available at: www.worldbank.org, last revised 01/09/2014.

World Bank (2003a): Report on the Observance of Standards and Codes (ROSC) Colombia – Accounting and Auditing, available at: www.worldbank.org, last revised 01/09/2014.

World Bank (2003b): Report on the Observance of Standards and Codes (ROSC) Republic of Lebanon – Accounting and Auditing, available at: www.worldbank.org, last revised 01/09/2014.

World Bank (2004a): Report on the Observance of Standards and Codes (ROSC) Chile – Accounting and Auditing, available at: www.worldbank.org, last revised 01/09/2014.

World Bank (2004b): Report on the Observance of Standards and Codes (ROSC) Ecuador – Accounting and Auditing, available at: www.worldbank.org, last revised 01/09/2014.

World Bank (2004c): Report on the Observance of Standards and Codes (ROSC) Ghana – Accounting and Auditing, available at: www.worldbank.org, last revised 01/09/2014.

World Bank (2004d): Report on the Observance of Standards and Codes (ROSC) Hashemite Kingdom of Jordan (Jordan) – Accounting and Auditing, available at: www.worldbank.org, last revised 01/09/2014.

World Bank (2004e): The World Bank Reports on the Observance of Standards and Codes (ROSC) – Overview of the ROSC Accounting and Auditing Program, available at: www.worldbank.org, last revised 01/09/2014.

World Bank (2005a): Report on the Observance of Standards and Codes (ROSC) Serbia and Montenegro – Republic of Serbia – Accounting and Auditing, available at: www.worldbank.org, last revised 01/09/2014.

World Bank (2005b): Report on the Observance of Standards and Codes (ROSC) Tanzania – Accounting and Auditing, available at: www.worldbank.org, last revised 01/09/2014.

World Bank (2006a): Report on the Observance of Standards and Codes (ROSC) Albania – Accounting and Auditing, available at: www.worldbank.org, last revised 01/09/2014.

World Bank (2006b): Report on the Observance of Standards and Codes (ROSC) Azerbaijan Republic – Accounting and Auditing, available at: www.worldbank.org, last revised 01/09/2014.

World Bank (2006c): Report on the Observance of Standards and Codes (ROSC) Republic of Botswana – Accounting and Auditing, available at: www.worldbank.org, last revised 01/09/2014.

World Bank (2006d): Report on the Observance of Standards and Codes (ROSC) Uruguay – Accounting and Auditing, available at: www.worldbank.org, last revised 01/09/2014.

World Bank (2007a): Report on the Observance of Standards and Codes (ROSC) Argentina – Accounting and Auditing, available at: www.worldbank.org, last revised 01/09/2014.

World Bank (2007b): Report on the Observance of Standards and Codes (ROSC) Georgia – Accounting and Auditing, available at: www.worldbank.org, last revised 01/09/2014.

World Bank (2007c): Report on the Observance of Standards and Codes (ROSC) Honduras – Accounting and Auditing, available at: www.worldbank.org, last revised 01/09/2014.

World Bank (2007d): Report on the Observance of Standards and Codes (ROSC) Republic of Kazakhstan – Accounting and Auditing, available at: www.worldbank.org, last revised 01/09/2014.

World Bank (2007e): Report on the Observance of Standards and Codes (ROSC) The Republic of Montenegro – Accounting and Auditing, available at: www.worldbank.org, last revised 01/09/2014.

World Bank (2008a): Report on the Observance of Standards and Codes (ROSC) Armenia – Accounting and Auditing, available at: www.worldbank.org, last revised 01/09/2014.

World Bank (2008b): Report on the Observance of Standards and Codes (ROSC) Kingdom of Thailand – Accounting and Auditing, available at: www.worldbank.org, last revised 01/09/2014.

World Bank (2009): Report on the Observance of Standards and Codes (ROSC) Republic of Belarus – Accounting and Auditing, available at: www.worldbank.org, last revised 01/09/2014.

World Bank (2011a): Global Development Horizons 2011 – Multipolarity: The New Global Economy (2011).

World Bank (2011b): Kazakhstan: World Bank Helps Improve Quality of Financial Reporting for Small and Medium-sized Entities, available at: www.worldbank.org, last revised 01/09/2014.

World Bank (2012): Report on the Observance of Standards and Codes (ROSC) Malaysia – Accounting and Auditing, available at: www.worldbank.org, last revised 01/09/2014.

World Bank (2014): ROSC Accounting & Auditing modules, available at: www.worldbank.org, last revised 01/09/2014.

World Economic Forum (2014): The Global Competitiveness Report 2013-2014 – Full Data Edition, available at: www.weforum.org, last revised 01/09/2014.

X

Xiao, J. Z./Weetman, P./Sun, M. (2004): Political Influence and Coexistence of a Uniform Accounting System and Accounting Standards – Recent Developments in China, in: Abacus, 40 (2), p. 193–218.

Y

Yalkin, Y. K./Demir, V./Demir, L. D. (2008): International financial reporting standards (IFRS) and the development of financial reporting standards in Turkey, in: Research in Accounting Regulation, 20 (1), p. 279–294.

Z

Zeff, S. A. (2003): U.S. GAAP Confronts the IASB: Roles of the SEC and the European Commission, in: North Carolina Journal of International Law and Commercial Regulation, 28 (4), p. 879–892.

Zeff, S. A. (2013): The objectives of financial reporting: a historical survey and analysis, in: Accounting and Business Research, 43 (4), p. 262–327.

Zeff, S. A./Nobes, C. W. (2010): Commentary: Has Australia (or Any Other Jurisdiction) 'Adopted' IFRS?, in: Australian Accounting Review, 20 (2), p. 178–184.

Zeghal, D./Mhedhbi, K. (2006): An analysis of the factors affecting the adoption of international accounting standards by developing countries, in: The International Journal of Accounting, 41 (4), p. 373–386.

Zhang, W.-G./Lu, D.-M. (2007): Convergence of Chinese Accounting Standards with International Standards – Process, Achievements and Prospects, in: Godfrey, J. M./

Chalmers, K. (eds.): Globalisation of accounting standards, Cheltenham, UK, Northamp-Northampton, MA, USA (2007), p. 193–217.

Münsteraner Schriften zur Internationalen Unternehmensrechnung

Herausgegeben von Peter Kajüter

Band 1	Daniela Barth: Prognoseberichterstattung. Praxis, Determinanten und Kapitalmarktwirkungen bei deutschen börsennotierten Unternehmen. 2009.
Band 2	Tobias Dickmann: Controllingintegration nach M&A-Transaktionen. Eine empirische Analyse. 2010.
Band 3	Simon Esser: Produktorientiertes Kostenmanagement in der chemischen Industrie. Eine empirische Analyse. 2011.
Band 4	Christian Reisloh: Influence of National Culture on IFRS Practice. An Empirical Study in France, Germany and the United Kingdom. 2011.
Band 5	Matthias Moeschler: Cost Accounting in Germany and Japan. A Comparative Analysis. 2012.
Band 6	Martin Merschdorf: Der Management Approach in der IFRS-Rechnungslegung. Implikationen für Unternehmen und Investoren. 2012.
Band 7	Kristian Bachert: Fair Value Accounting. Implications for Users of Financial Statements. 2012.
Band 8	Daniel Blaesing: Nachhaltigkeitsberichterstattung in Deutschland und den USA. Berichtspraxis, Determinanten und Eigenkapitalkostenwirkungen. 2013.
Band 9	Christina Voets: Kulturelle Einflüsse auf die Anwendung des Impairment-Tests nach IAS 36. Eine experimentelle Untersuchung in Asien und Europa. 2013.
Band 10	Thomas Poplat: Foreign Investments in BRIC Countries. Empirical Evidence from Multinational Corporations. 2014.
Band 11	Moritz Schröder: Cost Accounting in Anglophone Subsidiaries. Empirical Evidence from Germany. 2014.
Band 12	Maximilian Saucke: Full IFRS and IFRS for SMEs Adoption by Private Firms. Empirical Evidence on Country Level. 2015.

www.peterlang.com